THE OXFORD
ENCYCLOPEDIA
OF
TREES
OF THE
WORLD

THE OXFORD ENCYCLOPEDIA OF TREES OF THE WORLD

Consultant Editor: Bayard Hora

PEERAGE BOOKS

Project Editor: Graham
   Bateman
Subeditor: Peter Forbes
Production: Ivor Parker
Picture Research: Polly
   Friedhoff
Design: John Fitzmaurice

First published in Great Britain in 1981
by Oxford University Press

This book was planned and produced by
Equinox (Oxford) Ltd, Oxford

This edition published in 1986 by
Peerage Books
59 Grosvenor Street
London W1

© 1980 Equinox (Oxford) Ltd

ISBN 1 85052 060 7

Printed in Hong Kong

Right Male catkins and buds of
the Goat Willow or Sallow
(*Salix caprea*).
Previous page. An ancient
Bristle-cone Pine (*Pinus
aristata*) clings to life in the
White Mountains, California.
Such specimens can be 8 000
years old.

Contributors

K.A.   K. L. Alvin PhD
Imperial College, University of London

P.K.B.   P. K. Barrett DipFor, MIBiol
Forestry Dept, University of Oxford

B.N.B.   B. N. Bowden DPhil
Chelsea College, University of London

D.B.   D. Bramwell MSc PhD
Jardin Botanico, Las Palmas de Gran Canaria

S.R.C.   S. R. Chant PhD DipAgSc DJA
Chelsea College, University of London

P.C.   P. Cox
Glendoick Gardens, Perth, Scotland

J.E.D.   J. E. Dandy MA
British Museum (Natural History)

M.C.D.   M. C. Doggett BSc
University of Reading

P.F.G.   P. F. Garthwaite OBE MA FIFor
Forestry Consultant, Gilling, York

N.H.   N. Hall BForSc
Formerly CSIRO (Division of Forestry Research), Canberra, Australia

T.H.R.H.   T. H. R. Hall PhD
Superintendent, Oxford University Parks

S.A.H.   S. A. Heathcote BSc
British Museum (Natural History)

V.H.H.   Professor V. H. Heywood PhD DSc FLS FIBiol
University of Reading

F.B.H.   F. B. Hora MA DPhil
University of Reading

C.J.H.   C. J. Humphries PhD
British Museum (Natural History)

A.C.J.   A. C. Jermy
British Museum (Natural History)

S.W.J.   S. W. Jones BSc
British Museum (Natural History)

L.A.S.J.   L. A. S. Johnson DSc
Royal Botanic Gardens, Sydney, Australia

S.L.J.   S. L. Jury PhD FLS
University of Reading

F.K.K.   F. K. Kupicha PhD
British Museum (Natural History)

J.F.L.   J. F. Levy DSc FIBiol FLS FIWSc
Imperial College, University of London

A.F.M.   Alan F. Mitchell BA, BAg(For) VMH
Forest Research Station, Farnham

S.P.M.   Professor S. P. Monseleise MSc PhD
The Hebrew University of Jerusalem, Israel

D.M.M.   Professor D. M. Moore PhD
University of Reading

B.M.   B. Morley PhD
The Botanic Garden of Adelaide Australia

R.B.P.   R. B. Pearce PhD
Forestry Dept, University of Oxford

R.A.P.   R. A. Plumtre MA MSc
University of Oxford

C.P.   C. Puddle
Bodnant Garden Nursery, Wales

I.B.K.R.   I. B. K. Richardson BSc
Royal Botanic Gardens, Kew

R.H.R.   R. H. Richens MA PhD
Commonwealth Bureau of Plant Breeding and Genetics, Cambridge

G.D.R.   G. D. Rowley BSc
University of Reading

W.W.S.   Professor W. W. Schwabe DIC PhD DSc
Wye College, University of London

M.R.S.   M. R. Speight DPhil
Forestry Dept, University of Oxford

C.A.S.   C. A. Stace PhD FLS
University of Leicester

R.W.   R. Watkins PhD
East Malling Research Station

E.V.W.   E. V. Watson PhD FLS
University of Reading

T.C.W.   T. C. Whitmore MA PhD ScD
Forestry Dept, University of Oxford

E.H.W.   E. H. Wilkinson PhD
Wye College, University of London

T.W.W.   T. W. Wright BSc (Hort)
Wye College, University of London

Acknowledgements

Unless otherwise stated all illustrations on a given page are credited to the same source.
Photographs supplied by:–

A–Z Botanical Collection 19 (b), 40, 172, 248 (bl), 266 (t). Alvin, K. L., 54 (l), 58 (b), 59 (l), 60 (b), 95 (b). Angel, Heather 57, 60 (t), 83, 87 (r), 103, 119 (b), 145 (b), 176 (l), 208 (b), 213, 241 (tr), 255 (b), 256, 267 (t). Audus, L. J. 146 (b). Bateman, J. G. 24 (t), †55, 56, 61, †69 (r), 72 (b), 79, 81 (tr), 85 (tl & br), 86, *87 (bl), *94 (b), 95 (l), *96 (l), *97 (t), 99, *100 (l, *r), *101, 104 (†t, c, *b), *105 (t), 106, 109, 110, 114 (t), 116, 117, 119 (t), 123 (t), 126, 131, *136, 140, 145 (t), †146 (t), †148, 159 (b), *160 (t), †174 (b), 176 (b), 178 (r), 182, *183 (l), 194, 206, 211, 214, 219 (cl & br), 221, *224 (r), 225, 229 (t), 231 (t), 236, 239, *240, 243 (b), 249. (*Courtesy Hilliers' Arboretum; †The National Trust) Bisgrove 118. Burbidge, B. 72 (tr). Dinwoodie, J. M. 15. Elsevier Archives (photos by C. E. Crichton) 4, 10, 12, 13 (l), 19 (tl & r), 24 (t), 25 (bl & r), 26, 37, 38, 51, 58 (t), 63, 64, 81 (b), 107, 108 (r), 115, 120, 121 (tr), 122 (t & bl), 123 (b), 124 (t & br), 125 (b), 128, 134, 137, 139, 143, 150, 174 (tl), 183 (t & cr), 185, 192, 193, 197, 200, 204 (b), 223 (b), 224 (l), 226, 229 (c & b), 231 (b), 246, 248 (t & br), 253, 260 (t), 264 (br), 267 (b), 268 (b). Forestry, Dept. of Oxford 42, 44 (t), 52. Fox, D. J. 8, 69 (l), 215 (t). Fyffes Group Ltd 249 (c & br). Gibbons, R. B. 165, 184, 228, 232, 259 (b), 262. Hall, T. 46, 47, 48, 87 (lt). Halliday, Sonia 245 (b). Harding, Robert & Associates 263. Harris, D. 65, 155, 261 (bl), 269 (bl). Harris, E. 74, 85 (tr), 91, 112, 212. Hepper, F. N. 20 (t), 34, 81 (tl), 208 (t), 219 (tl). Heywood, V. 22 (b). Hora, F. B. 178 (l). Iriarte 59 (r), 196. Janzen, D. H. 204 (t). Jermy, C. 96 (l). Jones, M. P. 174 (tr), 180. Keith-Lucas, D. M. 20 (b), 35, 58 (t), 259 (t). Lacey, W. S. 44 (b), 84 (t), 97 (b), 223 (t), 260 (b). Lawson, A. 205 (t). Leech, R. M. 269 (br). Lenthall, B. 242, 258 (t). Loveless, A. R. 14, 22 (t). Mabberley, D. 33, 105 (r), 261 (tr), 265 (t), 266 (b). Mansell Collection 13 (r). Mathew, B. 241 (b). Mathews, G. A. 161, 187 (t). Mitchell, A. 62, 92 (b), 168. Moore, D. M. 72 (tl), 130. Morley, B. 265 (b). Natural Science Photos 21 (C. J. Pruett), 28 (M. Freeman), 31 (t), 258 (b) & 269 (t, br) (P. Burton), 41, 45 (t) & 125 (t) (M. Chinery), 124 (bl) & 245 (t) (P. Ward). Oxford Scientific Films 45 (b), 215 (b). Picturepoint 191. Polunin, O. 25 (t), 241 (tl). Santamour, F. S. 121 (br). Schwabe, W. 187 (r), 188. Seddon, B. 162. Spectrum Colour Library 160 (b), 255 (t), 257. Watson, J. 264 (tl). Whitmore, T. C. 11, 32 (t), 39, 43 (t), 54 (r), 89, 264 (bl). Whitton, B. A. 268 (t). Woodell, S. R. J. 254 (tl). Zefa Picture Library 43 (b), 77, 237.

Artists:–
Allard 29; Alvin, K. 60, 278; Barnard, D. 32; Chidwick, B. 53; Davies, A. 122 (br), 144, 149, 151, 179, 233, 243 (t), 247, 250; Davis, J. 17, 132, 135, 138, 142, 152, 154, 157, 163, 167, 173, 175, 177, 205 (b), 207, 210, 220, 235, 244 (t), 251, 280; Harvey, B. 129; Jennings, R. 113, 147, 159 (t), 171, 189, 195, 199, 209, 227, 238, 252; Lovell Johns 31 (b); Macgregor, A. 23, 27, 67, 70, 73, 75, 76, 78, 80, 82, 84 (b), 88, 90, 92 (t), 94 (t), 98, 101 (t), 108 (l), 114 (b), 121 (l), 127, 141, 203, 217, 222, 230, 279, 281; Oxford Illustrators 30, 190; Roberts, C. 181, 186; Way, J. 18.

The Publishers have attempted to observe the legal requirements with respect to the rights of the suppliers of photographic materials. Nevertheless, persons who have claims are invited to apply to the Publishers.

Contents

Preface

From early times Man has used trees for his own purposes and too often taken them for granted. They are such a prominent and usually long-lived part of the natural scene that perhaps this is understandable. Over the centuries, however, the mantle of trees that covered so much of the world's surface has been gradually but persistently reduced or transformed, sometimes into a pleasing managed countryside, sometimes into a mere desert. In 1664 the great English diarist, John Evelyn, published, with the approval of the Royal Society of London, a book *Sylva or a Discourse of Forest Trees* in which one sees, perhaps for the first time, a realization that trees, then so important in the construction of ships, were indeed becoming sadly depleted and that something urgently needed to be done by way of deliberate planting to ensure enough for the future. By the time the second edition was published six years later he estimated that two million timber trees had been planted as a result of his message.

Since then the pace of destruction of our heritage has gained momentum, particularly in this century. In industrialized countries especially, trees have retreated before the advancing tide of urbanization, from which they are entirely banished or barely tolerated. Modern mechanized agriculture also too often leads to an almost tree-less landscape. In the tropics the short-sighted squandering of natural resources in the form of forest has proceeded apace. The danger signals which Evelyn heard 300 years ago are sounding far more loudly today.

However, the picture is not one of total darkness. Over the last century or so there has been an increasing awareness that trees are things of beauty and interest for their own sake, and that they are an important element in the aesthetic beauty of our natural surroundings. In addition, and most encouragingly, there is an awareness that trees are intrinsically valuable and that they can no longer be taken for granted. They need active protection and benevolence from mankind if they are to survive. Also, on the credit side, over the last few centuries an increasing variety of species has been introduced to countries where they are not normally indigenous, not only for purposes of forestry or economics but also simply with the idea of beautifying our gardens and the environment in which we live. There is no doubt that this has been instrumental in preserving for posterity some species which would otherwise have totally disappeared.

Although some excellent books have appeared dealing with trees from selected regions of the world, and some books indeed dealing with trees in general, none, so far as I am aware, has covered the field so widely and in such depth as the present work. Of course, to describe all the world's tree species in one modestly sized volume is an impossibility – the total of the world's tree species must certainly run into several tens of thousands. Furthermore, new species are still being discovered and described, especially from the tropics, and it is certain that many more are still waiting to be found. This book, however, represents a bringing together of the knowledge of many acknowledged experts in their particular field. One of the most striking features of trees is their diversity – a diversity that covers such widely different forms as conifers, broadleaves, palms and some bamboos and cacti. In order to understand trees it is necessary to appreciate their diversity of form, and this book rightly gives prominence to covering a wide range. Not only will the reader find described and illustrated a good selection of the most significant trees of the world but also much about the no less wonderful story of the diversity of their life histories and the roles played by trees in the communities of plants and animals which they do so much to compose.

All this is set out in an outstandingly attractive and authoritative way in a volume to which I am both honored and glad to be asked to write a preface. It will, I believe, help significantly to increase public awareness of the importance of trees and of the endless fascination of their life histories and variations in form.

Professor J. P. M. Brenan,
MA, BSc, FLS, VMH, FIBiol.
(Director, Royal Botanic Gardens, Kew)

Bamboos cannot be regarded as 'true' trees, but in some species the woody unbranched stems exceed the height of 'true' trees. This grove of giant bamboos is in the Botanic Garden, Rio de Janeiro, Brazil, with Royal Palms (*Roystonea regia*) in the background.

What is a Tree?

From the earliest times plants have been classified as herbs, shrubs or trees. Thus, the concept of a tree is extremely familiar, even to small children. Ordinarily our image of a tree is that of a perennial plant, capable of attaining at least 6m (21ft), with a single woody self-supporting trunk or stem which is usually unbranched for some distance above ground. In brief, there are two components: a stem supporting, somewhere aloft, a crown of branches. Shrubs have a lower stature, the supporting trunk is less well defined and branching is evident at virtually ground level. Yet the borderline between the two categories is not always clear and on occasion tall shrubs and low trees may intergrade. In any event, every tree must start life as a sapling, growing from a seed, or in the rarer instances of tree ferns, growing from a minute spore. The influence of Man should also be mentioned – many cultivars of true trees exist which only reach the stature of shrubs, while practices such as pruning will reduce a tree to the size and shape of a shrub.

Trees as isolated specimens are a common enough sight in parks, gardens and, most notably, in large arboreta where the massing of many individuals of different species in a single collection allows comparison of the form (morphology) of one species with another. In such circumstances it is easy to appreciate that each species is distinctive and often recognizable by a range of what the botanist

Opposite Two general forms of tree can be recognized in temperate regions – the spire-like 'fir' trees typical of most conifers and 'bushy-topped' trees characteristic of most broadleaves (dicotyledons) as exemplified here by the massive spreading dome on the English or Pedunculate Oak (*Quercus robur*). *Right* In warmer regions a third group – the palms – also achieves predominance with their characteristic single tall trunk bearing a mass of leaves at the apex, as in this Talipot Palm (*Corypha umbraculifera*). The inflorescence of this species is the largest known among flowering plants and after flowering the tree dies.

calls morphological characters. Indeed, from an early age most people, in part unconsciously, make use of such characters in getting to know the common kinds of tree. They include features of bark, leaves, buds and so on, in addition to the manner of branching which will give the tree its own distinctive shape.

Notwithstanding the importance of single specimen trees – often there as the result of a deliberate planting policy – trees are very closely associated, in the minds of most people, with the notion of a forest or woodland. To the botanist this embodies the science of plant sociology or of ecology – what might be called the gregariousness

of trees. The first concept of a forest is again often derived from childhood experiences, the earliest notion normally being of a habitat that is uniform in character and somewhat dark within. This simple picture in fact embodies two important botanical characteristics of so many forests in north temperate regions, namely the dominance of a single species (or sometimes of two or three) and, secondly, the canopy-forming capacity of trees massed together which so significantly reduces the amount of light available beneath them. Thus, there is in a certain sense a general form, or morphology, both of the individual tree and of the forest. Although the former chiefly concerns us in the present context, it is worth noting in passing how very different from our own are the forests in most parts of the humid tropics – see later. In northern regions it is customary to name the forest after a single species of dominant tree, as in oak (*Quercus* spp), beech (*Fagus* spp), pine (*Pinus* spp) or spruce (*Picea* spp) forests so widespread in Europe and North America. In the humid tropics, by contrast, scores of species of widely differing height, habit and type of foliage will commonly play approximately equal roles in the structure of the whole and the forest is a scene of bewildering diversity. Nothing is more characteristic of such a forest than those tall individual trees, known as emergents, which protrude above the general level of the canopy in many tropical forests.

Almost equally notable is the structural diversity of the trees themselves. One of the most astonishing must surely be the Banyan Tree (*Ficus benghalensis*), an evergreen tree widespread in India. It can reach some 26m (85ft) in height and has long horizontally spreading branches, which put down aerial roots at intervals; these on reaching the ground act as pillars to support the branches. These trees probably have the biggest crowns of any in the world and with their aerial pillar or prop roots, a single tree can make a small wood. The Banyan is sacred in India and an account of it was given as early as the 4th century BC during Alexander the Great's invasion of India at that time.

Our concern is therefore with this structural diversity, as seen in simple botanical terms. Yet, oak and beech, palm and pine, slender birch (*Betula* spp) and giant silk-cotton trees (*Bombax* and *Ceiba* spp) all share something in common – the essential botany which makes them all trees. In short, they exhibit structural diversity within a common plan.

GENERAL FORM OF TREES

To the public two general forms of tree are immediately recognizable – the spire-like 'fir' trees and the 'bushy-topped' deciduous trees. In general terms this division encompasses the conifers and broadleaves, respectively. Two other readily recognized, but less frequent, forms are the fastigiate types characterized by the Lombardy Poplar (*Populus nigra* 'Italica') and the classic palm tree form. Botanists recognize many more forms. Indeed, one has only to look at deciduous trees in winter to see the highly distinctive pattern of branching of each species. Similarly in early summer a score of different tree species will display as many subtly different shades of green in their foliage. Ultimately, all features of form and branching must be related to events in the growing shoot tips where the embryonic tissues are found. All these features follow in large measure a program laid down in the plant's heredity but modified by environmental influences. However, they are always under precise physiological control. This brings us to the point where we recognize the first great uniformity in tree construction – that is the fact that within every tree, no matter what its species or where it is growing, there lies an organized assemblage of cells and tissues. It is in terms of these cells and

tissues that the anatomist will see the tree.

Thus, to the trained eye, each species of tree has a characteristic form, or in botanical terms, gross morphology. This form is the outward expression of long-term events which, although physiological in character, must reveal themselves to the observer in anatomical terms. In brief, just as each species of tree has its own external form, so it will be found to exhibit distinctive and sometimes unique features in its internal anatomy. This fact opens up for botanists the whole immense field of the comparative study of the microscopic anatomy of wood. The general form of any species of tree is not something fixed and immutable, and even the most casual observer must have met with countless everyday examples of this. Certain features are constant enough but there is still a vast range of variation in general habit and stature to be found within the whole geographical range of a single species. Nowhere is this more evident than in the Douglas Fir (*Pseudotsuga menziesii*) as seen in different parts of its vast North American range. Or again, one may contrast what we know as Lawson's Cypress (*Chamaecyparis lawsoniana*), which in cultivation is

a highly variable but commonly quite low-growing ornamental tree, with the forest giants 6om (200ft) high found in western North America, where it is known as the Port Orford Cedar. Among coniferous evergreens, such as the pines, spruces and silver firs, much of the distinctive general form, or silhouette against the skyline, of a particular species turns upon the behavior of the so-called leading shoot, and its growth in relation to that of the side shoots. Marked dominance and extremely rapid growth of the leading shoot can give, over a period of years, the very elegant spire-like habit so characteristic of Engelmann Spruce (*Picea engelmannii*), as seen, for example, in the Rocky mountains. A much reduced dominance of the leader can result in the comparatively bushy-topped growth habit of certain European species of pine, such as the Umbrella Pine (*Pinus*

The form of individual trees within a species can vary immensely depending on the environment in which they grow. The dome shape of the solitary Scots Pine (*Pinus sylvestris*) shown *Below* is clearly quite different from that produced when members of the same species are grown closely together in forestry plantations (*Opposite Top*). For the forester the long straight bole produced in such dense stands has clear economic advantages.

the English Oak (*Quercus robur*), but a small group of species is well known to live for very much longer, for example the English Yew (*Taxus baccata*) is known to have reached 1 000 years. However, most notable are the Coast and Mountain Redwoods (*Sequoia sempervirens* and *Sequoiadendron giganteum*) of the Western United States and a few other conifers; also there are well authenticated long-lived individuals of the monocotyledonous Dragon Tree (*Dracaena draco*). In all of them a life span exceeding 2 000 years is attained, with isolated examples of Dragon Tree and Bristle-cone Pine (*Pinus aristata*) achieving life spans in excess of 4 000 years. In practice many trees have their natural life span cut short by demands of forest management which call for regular felling and wood utilization and of urban amenity forestry where declining trees have to be felled because of the danger to the public.

TRUNK AND WOOD STRUCTURE

Ask a child to draw a tree and he will start with the trunk, then add a fan or brush of branches. In short, the trunk is integral to the popular concept of a tree, yet the prominence and size of that trunk can vary enormously.

The Canary Island Dragon Tree (*Dracaena draco*) is renowned for its longevity, specimens sometimes exceeding 2 000 years. This famous specimen, pictured in an old engraving, was destroyed by a hurricane in 1868.

pinea). In the Scots Pine (*P. sylvestris*) it is possible to see the profound effect on overall habit of growing trees either in close stands, or as isolated individuals. Finally, as the latitudinal or altitudinal limits of a given species are approached, increasingly severely stunted and often malformed specimens are seen, scarcely recognizable as belonging to the same species as the trees which grow farther south or lower down on a mountain. It is easy to forget that some of these gnarled and stunted specimens may be of great antiquity – possibly hundreds of years old.

Probably it is true to say that few trees continue to live in a healthy state beyond four to five hundred years – and this includes allegedly long-lived species such as

The swollen trunk of the Baobab (*Adansonia digitata*) makes it an unmistakable tree of the African savannas. Its gigantic girth is rivalled only by that of the giant American redwoods, although its height is much less.

In the tropics, trees with massive trunks and relatively little in the way of crown (because of restricted branching) are conveniently called 'pachycaulous' (= thick-stemmed) whilst trees with relatively slender stems and a generous bushy crown from extensive branching, are known as 'leptocaulous' (= slender-stemmed). In many low-growing trees, and even in some large, mature individuals of certain coniferous trees such as the English Yew and the Old World cedars (*Cedrus* spp), a single, well-defined trunk may not always be readily recognizable, yet in normal full-grown specimens of most of our common deciduous trees, such as oaks, ashes and beeches, it is almost impossible to conceive of the tree without its trunk; and in the vast majority of conifers this is even more emphatically the case. The existence and continuing prominence of the trunk springs from the fact that in early life there exists a radially organized central axis extending from the young shoot tip down into the root. At first, as in a beech seedling in the first year of life, the line of demarcation between stem and root in this slender axis may not always be readily apparent. Yet their destinies are very different and it is the slender, already woody, stem of the sapling which is gradually transformed, over a period of years, into the trunk of the full-grown tree. Growing trees in close-set stands can inhibit survival of lateral branches so that it is common to see such stands of pine or spruce composed of trees,

perhaps thirty or forty years old, in which the trunks appear to rise unbranched to an impressive height. To some extent the absence of lateral branches will have been encouraged by early 'brashing' operations by foresters. Certainly, isolated individuals of the same species will present a very different picture. Many species of palm, including the Oil Palm of West Africa (*Elaeis guineensis*), Date Palm (*Phoenix dactylifera*) and Coconut Palm (*Cocos nucifera*) are structurally quite distinct in that the trunk is in a very strict sense an unbranched stem, surmounted only by a crown of enormous leaves. Palms, moreover, it may be remarked, grow in an entirely different manner from either hardwood or conifer (softwood) trees, and their 'wood,' though chemically similar and extremely tough, is in its arrangement and disposition in the stem quite unlike wood as we ordinarily know it from hardwoods and softwoods.

In many tropical trees the trunks are sinuous to a degree not readily matched in the trees of north temperate forests. In a mature Baobab (*Adansonia digitata*) the trunk is characteristically of immense width.

The anatomical arrangement of the cellular components of the trunk of a tree is basically similar in conifers and broadleaves, only the components themselves vary. In simple terms a number of layers can be recognized – from the outside, the outer protective bark, the sugar conducting phloem (or inner bark) and the inner solid core of wood (xylem) through the younger elements of which water is conducted. Between the phloem and wood there is a narrow band of actively dividing cells (vascular cambium) which produce secondary phloem to the outside and

secondary xylem or wood to the inside.

To look at these layers in detail we will start with the wood which makes up the bulk of the trunk and is obviously the element of commercial importance. In so-called 'hardwoods' or dicotyledonous (broadleaved) woody species the wood consists, in varying proportions, of five principal components. Most characteristic are the vessels, which are made up of many tubular cells placed end to end with a free and open passage-way between one vessel member and the next above or below it; these are the water-conducting pipelines of the plant. Secondly, a high proportion of most hardwoods commonly consists of the fibrous component. This is made up of a great number of long, narrow cells (fibers) with thick walls and tapering ends, more or less closely bound together to form a strong matrix in which the vessels are interspersed. The hardness of any particular wood will depend in considerable measure on the number of these cells and the thickness of their walls. Thirdly, most woods contain a certain proportion of living, fairly thin-walled cells (termed wood parenchyma), that are often loaded with storage starch. They run in vertical sequences among the other, thicker-walled components. This living part of the whole is physiologically linked to the so-called 'rays,' which are in effect walls consisting of a few vertically stacked layers of living (parenchymatous) cells, again commonly replete with storage starch. In a severed trunk or branch (that is, as seen in transverse section) these rays form a series of radiating lines, the broadest of which are often easily visible to the naked eye. The last of the five cellular components of wood are the tracheids. They are not often very plentiful in hardwoods, but nevertheless they make up almost the entire 'woody cylinder' (apart from the rays) in all the softwoods (coniferous woods) and in a very small number of exceedingly primitive dicotyledons. Tracheids are dual-purpose elements performing at one and the same time the conducting function of a vessel member and the strengthening role of a fiber. Parts of their longitudinal walls are very freely supplied with thin sites termed pits, and it is these which allow water transfer from cell to cell.

When young and living the walls of vessels, tracheids and fibers become impregnated with a substance called lignin. When they die this material remains so that the rigid cell shape is retained. Lignin is a generalized term given to a series of complex carbon compounds whose chem-

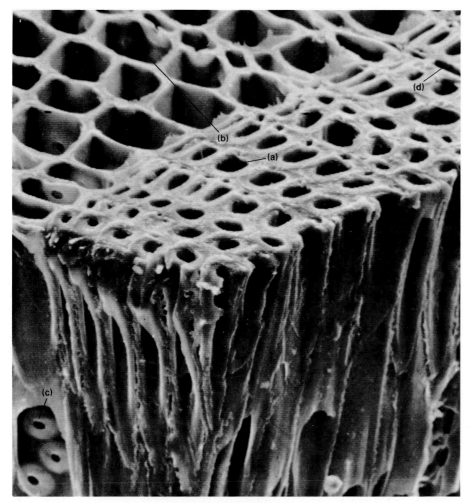

istry is imperfectly understood but it is clear there are a number of different kinds of lignin. It is interesting to note that the lignins of conifers as a group are different from those of broadleaves. The important fact for us is that these cells and their lignin confer the properties of strength and rigidity – woodiness – so that the thicker the lignified wall, the more completely are these properties conferred.

Thus we come to see the wood of a trunk or branch as composed of a vast interlocking plexus of microscopic cells, some of which are heavily lignified and dead at the functional maturity of the organ; interlaced with these are others (composing

Photographs of wood structure taken through the scanning electron microscope produce superb three-dimensional images of natural wood structure. *Left* A block of Scots Pine (*Pinus sylvestris*) magnified 500 times. (a) Tracheid of late wood; (b) tracheid of early wood; (c) bordered pit linking tracheids; (d) ray. This type of wood is known as softwood, the bulk of the tissue being the water-conducting and strengthening tracheids. *Below* A block of oak (*Quercus* sp) magnified 140 times. (a) Large vessel of early wood; (b) small vessel of late wood; (c) fibers; (d) multiseriate ray; (e) uniseriate ray; (f) vessel with tyloses (blockages). Oak is a hardwood, the bulk of the tissue comprising the structural fibers and to a lesser extent the water-conducting vessels. This form of wood is known as ring porous since the vessels of the early wood are much larger than those of the late wood. The other form of wood is known as diffuse porous where the vessels are more or less the same size in each growth ring, and are more evenly distributed across the ring.

wood parenchyma and rays) that are still alive and in varying degrees metabolically active. All these cells originate from a cylinder of delicate, meristematic (that is recurrently dividing) cells termed the vascular cambium, which forms the boundary line between wood and bark. Needless to say, this vascular cambium, being a meristematic or formative tissue, is of critical importance not only in the development of the tree, but throughout its entire life.

The question may now be asked – how do the annual growth rings arise? The answer lies in the type and size of cells produced by the vascular cambium at different times of the year. Annual rings are rendered more conspicuous in many cases on account of the first-formed vessels in spring being very much larger than those which are a component of the summer wood. English oak and ash both illustrate this feature well. Such woods are known as 'ring-porous'; in many other woods, including beech, willow, apple and others, there is no marked difference in vessel diameter between spring and summer wood. Such woods are termed 'diffuse-porous' and in them the annual rings are often less clearly defined, although in many such examples summer wood is marked by the presence of other distinctive features apart from vessel size. In a softwood such as that of Scots Pine the tracheids formed toward the end of the growth period, in summer, are of narrower bore and have much thicker walls than those formed in spring, and this fact forms the basis on which one can recognize

annual growth rings in this otherwise rather uniform wood.

In the monocotyledonous angiosperms, such as palms, there is, in general, no such annual increase in girth resulting from a cylinder of vascular cambium; in other words, there is no comparable secondary thickening. In very few cases of monocotyledonous angiosperms, however, there is a peculiar form of increase in girth quite different from that described above for the dicotyledons. A well-known example occurs in the Dragon Tree. Here cells in the general ground tissue become meristematic, that is, capable of division comparable with the cambial cells already described for dicotyledons (secondary meristem). However, instead of cutting off phloem cells toward the outside of the stem and xylem cells toward the center, both types of cells, phloem and xylem, are cut off toward the stem center in such a way that the increments replicate the pattern of the vascular bundles seen in the primary stem.

The wood anatomist, wherever possible, likes to have at his disposal thin sections cut in three planes: the transverse, the radial longitudinal (as in quarter sawn wood) – in other words parallel with a radius or diameter – and the tangential longitudinal section (as in flat sawn wood) – that is at right angles to a radius or diameter. When examined microscopically these three preparations together give him all the information needed to identify the wood. In most cases this is possible as far as the genus, sometimes even to species level. While a formidable array of charac-

Opposite Timber producing trees can be categorized into two distinct groups, the conifers (such as pines) which yield the softwoods of commerce and the broadleaves or angiosperm trees (such as oaks) which yield the hardwoods. The trunk of a tree is formed of a number of living and nonliving layers. The outermost layer is the cork which protects the tree from damage, lowers water loss and insulates against cold and heat. New layers of cork are produced by the cork cambium, these two layers collectively forming the outer bark. Below the outer bark is the phloem (bark or bast). This layer of tissue conducts essential food materials around the tree; as it dies it contributes further tissues to the outer bark. The vascular cambium is usually just one cell thick but is the life-giving zone of the trunk; by divisions it produces new phloem cells to the outside and new wood cells to the inside. The bulk of the tree comprises the true wood (or xylem). The outermost layer (sapwood) is formed of tubular cells that conduct water from the roots to the leaves; each year a new ring of sapwood (the annual rings) is added by the vascular cambium. Over a period of years the sapwood gradually loses its water-conducting function, and becomes the 'dustbin' of the plant, all the waste products of metabolism (particularly lignin) being deposited in the cells. Thus a central cylinder of heartwood is formed which acts as strength-giving backbone of the tree.

A log of wood therefore contains several types of tissue and Man must process all these if he is to make efficient use of the tree. The chipped bark is used for low-grade fuel and as a soilless compost. The wood of the tree is here shown cut for lumber, except for the outer round-sided 'slabs' which are 'chipped' and processed into chipboard. The outer portion of the wood has few knots and is usually cut into planks while the central core has more knots and is cut into thick planks or beams. Alternatively the trunk may be 'peeled' to produce plywood or processed for papermaking.

ters becomes available through this procedure, it must not be forgotten that the wood of a tree has other attributes which are readily detectable without a microscope. These include not only such features

Light micrographs of transverse sections of various types of wood (× 75) reveal that the density of the wood is clearly related to the intensity of staining and hence the thickness of the walls and the quantity of cell contents. *Left* Balsa (*Ochroma lagopus*) which is an extremely light timber (specific gravity < 0.5). The wood has very thin-walled fibers and the vessels are large and widely spaced. *Center* Boxwood (*Buxus sempervirens*) which is a dense, compact timber (specific gravity > 1.0). The fiber tracheids have a tendency to be thick-walled and the vessels are small and evenly spaced throughout the early and late wood – a characteristic of diffuse porous wood. *Right* Ebony (*Diospyros* sp) which is an extremely heavy timber (specific gravity > 1.0). The wood has very thick-walled fibers and the vessels are small, widely spaced and are frequently blocked by deposits of gum.

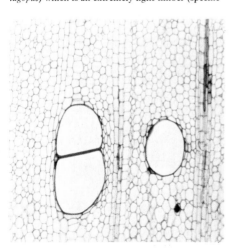

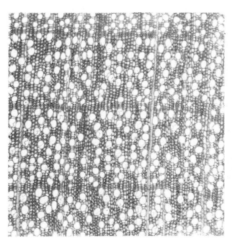

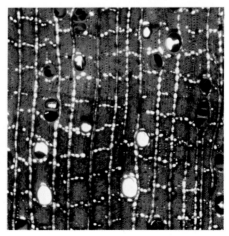

Pine (*Pinus* sp)   Oak (*Quercus* sp)

cork

cork
cambium

phloem

vascular
cambium

sapwood

heartwood

Line diagram showing the formation of various secondary tissues of the stem and root that increase the girth of these organs. In both stems and roots two types of cambia arise, which by divisions form secondary tissues: the vascular cambium produces secondary xylem (the water-conducting tissue – wood) and secondary phloem (the food-conducting tissue) while the cork cambium produces protective tissues (cork) that effectively replace the epidermis of the young organs.

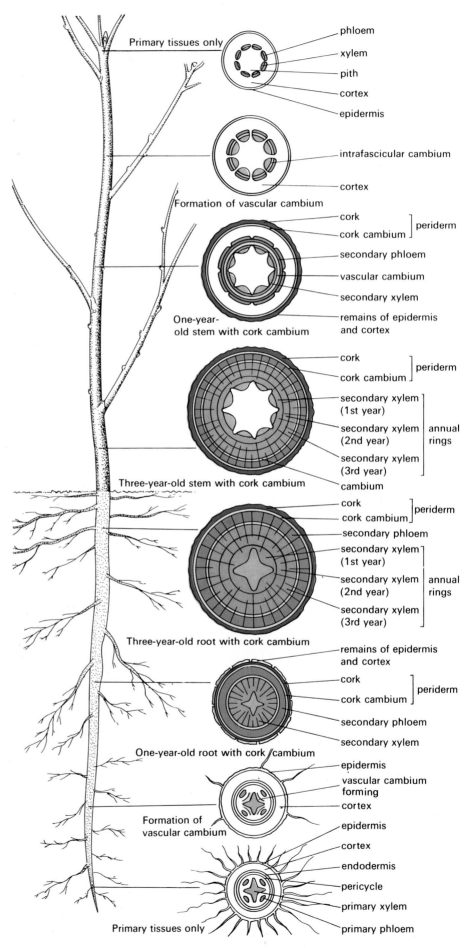

of the fine structure as will be visible under a hand lens or with the naked eye, but also such important general attributes as specific gravity and color. A consideration of color often has to take account of differences between the outer zone of living and often lighter colored sapwood and the central core of generally nonliving and darker hued heartwood. It is the heartwood which is commercially valuable. To varying degrees this is impregnated with gums, resins and other deposits which act as a natural preservative. In a limited number of woods this heartwood is a notably distinctive color, as in several species of ebony (where it is black) and the leguminous Logwood Tree (*Haematoxylon campechianum*) where it is purple in hue.

Woods vary greatly in specific gravity and this important physical character is clearly linked with the uses to which particular species are put. Teak (*Tectona grandis*) is a particularly valuable timber, being a fairly heavy close-grained wood and exceptionally resistant to decay because of the deposition of resinous materials. By contrast, American balsa wood (*Ochroma* spp) is an example of a wood valued for its exceptional lightness and the same is to some extent true of the wood of the widespread West African tree, *Triplochiton scleroxylon*. In every case the usefulness of the wood is inseparably linked to its anatomical structure as revealed by a full microscopic examination.

The importance of wood from an economic or utilitarian angle is discussed in a later chapter, as is the subject of its attack by fungi and insects. We must turn now to the bark or rind, without which the living tree would be very incomplete. Botanically, bark is defined as 'all those tissues lying external to the vascular cambium,' and as such it includes a diversity of components. In more detail bark may be divided into an 'inner bark' or 'bast' formed from the vascular cambium (already noted above) and an 'outer bark' formed largely from the cork cambium, which is discussed later. Formerly, anatomists sometimes distinguished two fractions of inner bark, namely 'hard' bast

Horizontal bands of glossy reddish–brown bark peel off to give the trunk of the Tibetan Cherry (*Prunus serrula* var *tibetica*) its distinctive appearance.

which is composed of fibers and, secondly, the 'soft' bast or living elements of the phloem. To the layman, 'bark' often means only these rough outer layers; yet the living phloem elements are indeed vital components of the tree since their function is to conduct sugars and other organic

Above The trunk of a young Sweet Chestnut (*Castanea sativa*) is smooth but as the tree ages the bark becomes more deeply fissured with an increasingly exaggerated spiral twist.

Left Commercial cork is the bark of the Cork Oak (*Quercus suber*), which can be stripped off the tree every 8–10 years for at least 100 years without destroying it. These large sections, clearly showing their origin, are in store awaiting processing.

products of metabolism from one part of the plant to another. The outer bark is protective; it is also used in tree recognition.

It is not uncommon to see trees that have been the victims of browsing animals and have had their bark more or less stripped down to the wood. If this 'ringing' of the tree is complete (that is, a complete ring of phloem is removed) death will ensue because the conduction of organic products, from the leaves down to the roots, has been fatally impeded. Phloem carries organic products about the

plant with great speed and efficiency but even now the mechanism of this process is not fully understood. The phloem of a tree, however, is predominantly of secondary origin, that is, it has been formed, like the secondary wood (or xylem), from the activity of the vascular cambium. Also, in trees, certain of the derivatives of the vascular cambium mature into fibers constituting the 'hard-bast' fraction of the inner bark, while yet others form ordinary living (parenchymatous) tissues. Thus, this secondary phloem is, like secondary xylem (or wood), a complex tissue and one that is renewed year after year. The rays, too, extend out into the phloem, often expanding there so sharply as to present a characteristic trumpet-like form in transverse section.

The papery outer bark of members of the genus *Commiphora* (myrrh) peels off easily; several of these spiny species yield myrrh resin when an incision is made in the bark.

External to this elaborately constructed inner bark, in the early life of a woody stem or branch, lies the green cortex, bounded on the outside by the original 'skin tissue' or epidermis. Such an arrangement, however, cannot accommodate any marked expansion in girth unless a mechanism exists for the epidermis and cortex to keep pace by cell division or cell expansion (or both); and this is only rather rarely the case. Normally, a special new growing zone, or secondary meristem has to arise; this is called the cork cambium or phellogen. Once formed, it can make provision for the entire protective-tissue requirement of trunk or branch and at the same time solve the girth problem. The former it does by forming seriated layers of corky tissues interrupted only by scattered 'breathing pores' termed lenticels. The girth problem is solved in various ways but often by periodic renewal of the cork cambium, in increasingly deep tissues. When a young branch or sapling trunk which is green in its first season abruptly turns brown or grayish in hue, this color change is almost invariably correlated with the appearance of the first layers of cork. Commonly, of course, the superficial cork amounts to only a thin skin but in rare cases, as in the Cork Oak (*Quercus suber*), much thicker layers are formed.

Thus, bark is functionally very important to the tree, being both the locus of conduction (translocation) of organic substances (inner bark) and the provider of the tree's outer protective skin (outer bark). Other components include nests of exceedingly hard, thick-walled cells aptly termed stone-cells. The bark in many instances is a commercial source of tannins and various crystalline deposits and in the Para Rubber Tree (*Hevea brasiliensis*) there are special vessels, the lacticifers, from which, when the bark is cut, a latex flows which is collected for conversion to (natural) rubber.

Perhaps the main interest of bark to the layman and structural botanist alike, lies in the variety and diagnostic value of its external features. Even the most casual observer can see at a glance the differences between the rugged, fissured bark of oaks, the fibrous 'stringy' bark of false acacias (*Robinia* spp), the scaly bark of planes (*Platanus* spp) with their 'jig-saw puzzle' surface pattern at some seasons of the year, and the almost papery texture of the silver-white bark clothing the upper regions of trunk and branches in several species of birch (*Betula* spp). Although most conifers have a bark that is in varying degrees scaly in texture, some are highly distinctive, such as the Mountain Redwood or Wellingtonia (*Sequoiadendron giganteum*) in which the texture is so softly spongy that it can be punched without detriment to the aggressive fist! In this tree, native to

The Pacific Madrone (*Arbutus menziesii*) from California is easily identified by its curling outer bark, which peels off to expose the smooth bright green inner bark.

western North America, the fissures and hollows in the bark have, incidentally, provided a favorite nesting site for the European Tree Creeper (*Certhia familiaris*).

Observant people of many tropical countries have, down the centuries, come to know the marks of recognition in the barks of a great many species of tree, and botanists in recent times have seen the importance of pursuing this study further on a scientific basis.

THE ROOT SYSTEM

Absorption and anchorage are the two chief functions of a root system. Examination of a tree seedling of a broadleaf such as a beech will show two deep green cotyledons (seed leaves) raised well clear of ground level. Below them the stem (hypocotylar) region passes almost imperceptibly into the crown of the young primary root or radicle which lies below ground level. Although at first a simple structure, 'programed' to grow downward into the soil (positively geotropic), it soon becomes branched, through the origin of numerous lateral roots. These arise at a deep level in the tissues of the parent root and well back from the apex. Immediately behind the apex most roots display a 'fur' of microscopically small 'root hairs' which are the principal water absorbing components of the root.

At a remarkably early stage, in most tree species, the process of secondary thickening – wood and phloem production through cambial activity – will set in. Thus, although the young root begins life with a different arrangement of vascular tissues from the stem, it will not be long before they bear a considerable resemblance to one another, at least when examined in transverse section – a central core of wood surrounded by the vascular cambium and bark. These internal similarities, at tissue level, are however overshadowed by the differences in gross morphology which are evident for all to see. Roots never bear leaves and are not a normal site of bud production. Roots, moreover, are non-green (in all typical cases) and, as already mentioned, branch in a manner peculiar to themselves. The tip of a young root, as it makes its way through the soil, is protected by a root cap which is continually renewed from behind as it gets pushed off by the root's progress through the soil. This also has no parallel in the shoot apex.

Minute anatomical details, however, concern us less than a consideration of the tree's root system seen as a whole, its general character, depth and extent of spread in the soil. These are features which vary greatly from one tree species to another. Many coniferous species, for example, are comparatively shallow rooted, hence easily storm-blown. It should be borne in mind, however, that an uprooted tree reveals only a small fraction of its total root system, the lateral spread of which may readily far exceed that of the leafy crown. When one calculates the sum of the lengths of all the multiplicity of fine branch roots that go to make up an entire root system, prodigious overall figures are revealed. The 'free space' beneath and around a tree is in a very full sense 'occupied' by its root system, and competition between root systems in a forest soil is intense and unrelenting.

The relationship between a tree's root system, the surrounding soil, and its varied microflora, is inevitably a complex one. Many factors – physical, chemical and biological – have to be taken into consideration. The study of this so-called rhizosphere is probably even now only in its infancy. Sufficient is known, however, to make it clear that the relationship between a tree's roots and soil microorganisms can be both complex and important; and to some extent the same may hold for the root systems of adjacent trees. Perhaps the best known and most fully investigated of these relationships is that between tree root and soil fungus which comes under the general heading of mycorrhiza. This relationship shows itself in the form of a mantle of fungal threads or hyphae (singular: hypha), collectively known as the mycelium, which encases many of the young rootlets and invades the intercellular space system of the root's cortex. The rootlets, stimulated by the fungal invasion to branch freely, are often conspicuous for their coralloid form. Scots Pine and European Beech (*Fagus sylvatica*) are well-known examples, but the phenomenon is very widespread in tree root systems. It seems that both fungus and host tree draw benefit, the latter especially through improved capacity for absorption of certain nutrients conferred by the presence of the mycorrhizal fungus. The roots of alders (*Alnus* spp) present another interesting association.

Here the root system has associated with it nitrogen-fixing microorganisms, the exact nature of which is not yet certain because, so far, it has not been possible to grow them in pure culture. At present there are several species referred to the genus *Frankia* and believed to be related to the filamentous bacteria sometimes known as ray fungi (actinomycetes). A similar relationship is known in some other, quite unrelated trees. Perhaps the best-known root nodules are those on roots of the members of the pea family (Leguminosae or Fabaceae) where the microorganisms involved are bacterial species belonging to the genus *Rhizobium*.

A number of distinct forms of modified roots occur in trees. Around the bases of tropical trees surface roots are often extended vertically upward as plank-like

Massive buttress roots of a tree growing in the tropical rain forest of Java. Such modified roots help support the tall, relatively slim trunks of many tropical forest trees.

triangles of wood serving as buttresses to the trunk. In other cases, for example, screw pines (*Pandanus* spp) and some mangrove species, roots arising from stems above the soil strike obliquely downward and form props or stilts; similar aerial roots occur in figs (*Ficus* spp) where they do not always reach the soil but hang below branches as aerial breathing roots. Tree roots originating underground can also assume respiratory functions as with the Swamp Cypress (*Taxodium distichum*).

LEAVES

The leaves of trees are almost infinitely diverse in size and form. Some, which are minute and scale-like, the layman might scarcely recognize as leaves at all. Examples are provided by the she-oaks (*Casuarina* spp) and some conifers. The botanist sees them as leaves, for he recognizes a more or less constant relationship between stem, leaf, and the bud or branch in its axil. Seeking out the axillary bud, he designates as compound the leaves of walnuts (*Juglans* spp), ashes (*Fraxinus* spp) and sumacs (*Rhus* spp) in all of which the leaf is composed of numerous leaflets, by contrast with such trees as oaks, elms, beeches and limes (*Tilia* spp) where the leaves are all 'simple,' though differing in shape. In short, there has arisen a considerable terminology in the descriptive morphology of leaves. The outcome is that, reading such a technical description, another botanist can form instantly in his mind a clear image of the precise shape and character of the leaf in question. Some tropical trees bear extraordinarily large leaves, for example *Anthocleista* spp, a well-known genus of forest trees in tropical West Africa in which the leaves can exceed 1m (3.3ft) in length and be proportionately broad. The same holds good in many monocotyledons; one has only to think of bananas and the related plantains, and of course the compound leaves of palms.

More interesting than purely descriptive aspects, however, is the functional view of the leaves of a tree, namely their general structural features as seen in relation to their functioning as the primary food factories of the tree. All normal leaves indeed show a remarkable compromise between the need, on the one hand, for

The aerial roots of these screw pines (*Pandanus* sp) form a system of props which help support the stem.

maximum exposure of surface to the light and for freedom of entry of the carbon dioxide essential for carbon assimilation (photosynthesis) and on the other to include adequate safeguards against excessive water loss through the process of transpiration. These considerations explain the broad expanse of leaf blade (lamina), the presence often of long leaf stalks or petioles allowing leaf blades to take up advantageous positions, the presence (most frequently on the under surface) of countless microscopic openings, the stomata and, finally, an adequate protective skin or cuticle. The venation system provides both a skeleton and conducting tissues continuous with those of the stem.

The basic anatomical plan of leaves is uniform although the variations on this plan are numerous. In all leaves the epidermis forms the outermost layer of living cells. This is normally one cell thick and is bounded on the outside by the impermeable cuticle which is interrupted only by the actual pores of the stomata (referred to above). The internal tissues or mesophyll are the powerhouse of the leaf, each cell containing numerous green chloroplasts in which photosynthesis occurs. In most leaves two types of mesophyll cell can be found. The upper or palisade mesophyll comprises columnar cells that are separated from one another by numerous narrow air channels. The lower or spongy mesophyll consists of irregularly shaped cells with large air spaces between them. Most of the chloroplasts occur in the palisade cells.

Each leaf of a tree can thus be seen as a delicately adjusted piece of machinery attuned to a functional life of immense

A number of figs (*Ficus* spp), including the Banyan, put down aerial roots which support the branches.

importance – the synthesis of organic compounds such as sugars and starch from the simple raw materials, water and carbon dioxide. In different climates very different stresses will be brought to bear on leaves. Thus, in the humid tropics there is less emphasis on the protective cuticle, whilst trees of semi-arid regions are often what are known as sclerophylls – the leaves stiff and hard in texture, limited in size and with a notably thick cuticle. Even so, astonishing diversity can prevail even in a single climatic regime, as a glance at the composition of forests in the tropics will show. There the diversity is bewildering, but even in Europe trees presenting such diversified leaf morphology as holly (*Ilex* spp), beech, ash and yew can all be components of a single wood on downland.

We still know, indeed, far too little of the individual economies of different species of tree, but one widespread aspect familiar to all is that of leaf drop. A feature of fall in north temperate lands, it is also often related to the onset of a dry season in hot countries with a markedly seasonal climate. It can be seen as a kind of economy measure, enabling a tree to shut down activity, and take a rest, in a particularly unfavorable season of any kind. Extremely widespread among dicotyledonous trees, it is rare in conifers, occurring in the larches (*Larix* spp) and swamp cypresses (*Taxodium* spp), for example. So-called evergreens always display green foliage, but they too have their times of leaf fall, though more unobtrusively. Individual leaves rarely last for more than a few seasons.

It goes without saying that leaves supply a considerable range of characters usable by taxonomic botanists. Indeed, although allowance has to be made for variation, seen for example in marked degree in mulberries (*Morus* spp), species can often be recognized by their leaves, especially if we take into account microscopic features of leaf anatomy, important among which is the hair covering or indumentum, when present. Even so, one has always to be on one's guard, for striking examples can be found of the leaves of quite unrelated plants resembling one another very closely

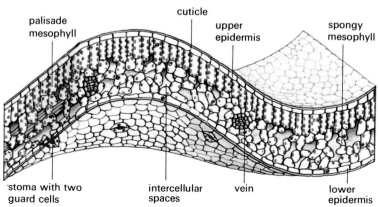

Young shoot and leaves of the European Beech (*Fagus sylvatica*) showing the main elements. Below is a stylized diagram of a cross section of a 'typical' broadleaved leaf showing the basic anatomical arrangement of the various tissues. The palisade mesophyll with its numerous chloroplasts is the main power center where photosynthetic activity occurs.

(maples (*Acer* spp) and true planes (*Platanus* spp) provide a case in point) whilst in the tropics trees of a great many quite unrelated species are alike in the possession of more or less ovate, smallish short-stalked leaves. Only in rare cases, like the fan-shaped leaves of the Maidenhair Tree (*Ginkgo biloba*) or the distinctively four-lobed leaves of the tulip trees (*Liriodendron* spp) is leaf form instantly diagnostic. Such examples are a boon to paleobotanists attempting to identify the trees of the past. The winter buds of deciduous species, like leaves, can lead to instant recognition.

Space does not permit us to make more than a passing reference to the foliage of trees as a habitat for other organisms. Clearly, they are the habitat of an almost limitless diversity of colonists and feeders, perhaps most notably in the world of the insects and the birds. However, their utilization by other organisms is always to some extent bound up with their importance as a principal primary builder of the world's organic matter. Their all-round ecological significance, therefore, needs no further stressing.

(*Juniperus* spp) and in the English Yew (*Taxus baccata*).

In conifers, the male cones (staminate flowers) in season produce myriads of tiny microspores (pollen) which in due course germinate by way of a pollen tube whence are finally released the microscopic sex cells or male gametes. At the 'receiving end' of the wind-dispersed pollen grains are the familiar female cones (ovulate flowers) that are still young and soft, with scales open. Each such female cone represents one or more so-called 'naked ovules' set among scales. Each ovule is a giant spore (megaspore) with protective 'wrappings' in the form of spore container and integuments, and concealed within it lies the female gamete – the egg cell (ovum). In due time the act of gametic union, or fertilization, takes place giving rise to a 'naked seed' (whence the term gymnosperm = naked seed). In some conifers fertilization is separated from pollination by as much as one year.

In flowering plants or angiosperms – in our context hardwood or broadleaved trees – we find more elaborately constructed and

The flowers of most insect-pollinated trees are large and colorful which assists in the attraction of pollinators. Shown here is a close up of the sex-organs of a magnolia (*Magnolia* sp) surrounded by the floral envelope which, in these primitive flowers, are not differentiated into separate petals and sepals and are hence known as tepals. At the center of the flower is a column of numerous separate female organs (carpels) which is surrounded at the base by a cluster of short-stalked stamens.

FLOWERS AND FRUITS

Flowers are often described in botanical terms as consisting of 'essential organs,' surrounded by 'floral envelopes.' The latter (petals and sepals) constitute the most conspicuous features of most flowers, including those of many trees. Numerous kinds of tree, however, including all the so-called catkin-bearing species, are without conspicuous floral envelopes, essential organs being associated only with relatively inconspicuous, scale-like structures termed bracts. The most colorful feature of many flowers is the corolla (made up of the petals) but this is not necessarily so.

Even the cones of coniferous trees constitute a type of flower, for in common with other flowers they are concerned with the transference of microspores (or pollen) to the receptive female parts. In most cases, an initially soft female cone gives rise, eventually, to an ultimately hard-scaled cone as seen in the pines. Quite different are the 'berry-like' seeds found in junipers

The typical reproductive structures of most conifers are shown here on this single shoot of an Austrian Pine (*Pinus nigra*). Each spring a cluster of small, red female cones arises at the very tip; if these are pollinated they grow during the following year to form a young fruiting cone which remains green until the eggs are actually fertilized. During the next season the cone matures to form the familiar seed-bearing brown cone. Clusters of yellow male cones are produced each spring lower down the shoot and these die soon after the pollen is dispersed.

more varied flowers, most of which show the familiar components – calyx (sepals), corolla (petals) and internal to these the pollen-producing stamens and the ovary or ovaries which contain the ovules. It is the ovary which characterizes the angiosperms, enclosing as it does, right from the beginning, the young and developing ovules and finally the seeds, so that they are at no time 'naked.' Because of this enclosing organ, a special receptive area (stigma) and conducting region (style) become essential adjuncts to the ovary. Pollen is carried by wind, water, insect or other animals to the stigma where it germinates, producing a pollen tube which grows down through the style and eventually comes into close contact with the ovule via a minute opening termed the micropyle. The pollen tube ruptures and two male gametes are discharged, one of which fuses with the egg, thus setting a seed. Again it has to be observed that pollination and fertilization are two distinct events, although the time between the two events is shorter than in conifers.

It looks as if the whole evolutionary history of flowers has been geared to pollen transference, or pollination, and the pollinating agency has profoundly modified floral form, in trees as in other flowering plants. Thus, among tree species, we can recognize on sight as wind-pollinated the bulk of catkin-bearing trees, such as hazels (*Corylus* spp), birches (*Betula* spp) and poplars (*Populus* spp), for in all of them there is an abundance of loose pollen, no nectar, and no conspicuous insect-attracting feature. Willows (*Salix* spp), with their large nectaries, constitute an exception and are insect-pollinated.

In marked contrast to the above stand those trees with large and colorful flowers – the only ones indeed which many laymen would recognize as 'flowering trees' at all. The great majority of these are adapted to a range of insect vectors of pollen, but quite numerous species, especially in the tropics, are adapted for pollination by birds. These tend to have exceptionally

Large fleshy fruits, such as these Apricots (*Prunus armeniaca*) are adapted for dispersal by mammals rather than birds, the seeds not actually being eaten since they are protected by the hard inner layer of the fruit.

Flowers of a typical wind-pollinated tree, the Common Hornbeam (*Carpinus betulus*). The male catkin (*Left*) produces large quantities of pollen grains which are carried by wind to the filamentous stigmas of the female flower (*Right*).

strongly constructed, often scarlet or multi-colored flowers. A few trees, in various parts of the world, have bat-pollinated flowers. Such flowers, which characteristically open in the evening, are often large, somber in color and capable of emitting characteristic musty odors. Examples are found in a number of families, including the Leguminosae, Myrtaceae and Cactaceae.

The expression 'flowering tree' is apt to conjure up a picture in the mind of cherries and almonds (*Prunus* spp), crab apples (*Malus* spp) and others that are grown for their blossoms in park or garden. The reality is very different, for all broadleaf trees are potentially 'flowering' at some time in their lives, otherwise reproduction could not occur, except very locally by sucker growth. The diversity of floral form cannot be encompassed in any short summary statement but will be apparent from the trees dealt with later in the book. Often in the humid tropics one meets a steady succession of flowers, of different species, throughout the year. Each must be geared to the season of availability of its principal pollinator; but too little is known as yet about the precise range of pollinators utilized by many tropical trees. In north temperate lands, where spring and summer are the seasons of flowering, bees of various kinds must surely rank as the most important group of pollinating organisms.

Flowering is but the prelude to fruit production; and just as a fruit (botanically) is a ripened or mature ovary, so a seed is a

matured fertilized ovule, carrying deep within it the embryo plant of the new generation. It is important to appreciate that if cross pollination has been achieved this new embryo will possess, in varying degree, a new genetic constitution. This is of immense significance both for the evolutionary process and for the 'improvement' of trees for use by mankind.

It is possible to look at the fruits of trees from the angle of the botanist who classifies such structures in a manner that is convenient for descriptive purposes. Thus, there are 'dry' fruits (capsules) which open (dehisce), thereby shedding their seeds; and there are 'fleshy' fruits of many kinds. Some, like Elderberry (*Sambucus nigra*) have their seeds lodged in compartments of a wholly fleshy fruit wall, whilst others, like plums and cherries, have a fruit wall (or pericarp) which is itself made up of an outer skin, a middle fleshy portion and an innermost stony layer. The seed in such a case exists as the 'kernel' within the stone. Thus, the botanist distinguishes the berry from the stone fruit or drupe. This way of looking at fruits can be rewarding, if only because it encourages us to systematize our information.

Fruit structure, however, cannot be viewed in any complete way without reference to its important ecological implications, especially in connection with seed dispersal. In this context we can contrast the dry, dehiscent capsules of willows which release their tiny seeds equipped with tufts of hairs to be dispersed by wind,

Seeds adapted for dispersal by wind are usually light and have wing-like appendages which help them float farther away from the parent tree on air currents. Shown here Winged Birch (*Betula* sp) seeds caught on a cobweb.

with the great range of drupe and berry fruits which have in every case a built-in food store that will attract a dispersal agent, most often some species of bird. Young Elder saplings lodged in unlikely places are sometimes eloquent testimony to the efficiency of a dispersal mechanism which allows the seeds to be voided in a viable state after the fleshy substance surrounding them has been digested.

Clearly, both the above mechanisms can lead readily to long-distance dispersal, an important consideration in the successful distribution of tree species in nature. It is less easy to see how this can be achieved in the case of trees where both fruit and seed are bulky, as in the horse-chestnut (*Aesculus* spp), and not obviously attractive to animal dispersal agents. Even the ingenious winged fruitlets of the various species of *Acer* (sycamores and maples) seem unlikely to carry the new plantlet far from the parent tree and the same can almost certainly be said of the explosive fruits of the tropical American Sandbox Tree (*Hura crepitans*). The light, winged fruitlets of ashes and pines, and the winged seeds which abound among the tree species of the tropical family Bignoniaceae, will surely fare better. The fruit of the Coconut Palm (*Cocos nucifera*) is exceptional among heavy fruits in that there is considerable evidence for its long-distance dispersal by ocean currents.

When the seed germinates and the new plant begins to grow, a range of controlling factors will immediately become operative. Soil reaction, available nutrients, moisture supply and temperature – all these must be right if it is to survive. Most decisive of all, perhaps, is the inevitable factor, or complex of factors, entailed by the term competition. This relates not only to pressures exerted by countless other plants in the immediate vicinity but also to the influ-

Above Left The resting buds of temperate woody plants, such as those of the Horse Chestnut (*Aesculus hippocastanum*), are surrounded by a layer of sticky scale leaves which protect the next season's embryonic leaves and flowers. *Above Center, Above Right, Right* During the spring, in response to warmer temperatures, they unfold and the leaves and flowers rapidly expand provided they have been exposed to a period of winter chilling. If maintained in warm conditions throughout the winter the buds will remain dormant.

ences exerted by various members of the animal kingdom, not least by human agency. The first mowing of a lawn in spring is often the occasion for 'elimination by decapitation' of innumerable seedlings of sycamore or maple, and sometimes of other species. Although all normal seeds carry, either free or within their cotyledons, a food reserve, it must frequently happen that this is exhausted before successful establishment has been achieved. Once established, in the face of all competitors, the young tree is free to grow.

GROWTH OF TREES

The growth of trees, our last topic in this brief botanical introduction, is a big and complex subject, and only the barest essentials can be touched upon. Whole treatises have been written on the growth of many of the economically important trees and successful growth of his introduced species must always be a primary concern of the forester. Often this entails fitting a particular exotic species into an

environment which especially suits it, as in the coastal plantings of Corsican Pine (*Pinus nigra* var *maritima*). At other times successful growth has to be coaxed from a species by appropriate treatment of an essentially unfavorable environment, as with the vast plantations of Sitka Spruce (*Picea sitchensis*) on the peat moors of Northern Europe. In natural forest communities it is probably safe to assume a strong correlation between the component species and the character of the substratum. We think of beech on the chalk, oak on heavy clays, pine and birch on nutrient-poor sands and gravels, alder along the banks of rivers or canals. Thus, the successful growth of each appears linked to a given environment; yet the ecological amplitude of most of our common native trees is certainly wider than such a generalization would indicate. Competition is still operative.

Growth will tend at all times to be closely dependent on adequate water and nutrient supplies, and temperature – the latter often a limiting factor. The seasonal character of tree growth in north temperate latitudes, although so familiar as to pass without comment, reflects this correlation with temperature, but it must not be forgotten that there are also important links with two aspects of the light factor – day length and absolute light intensity. The student of growth phenomena in trees, as in other plants, is often faced with the difficult task of elucidating the relative significance of several quite distinct factors in the environment, each of which is known to be operative in a general way. These he endeavors to study in relation to the demonstrable overall growth increment, as shown by suitable measurements, and resulting in a figure for 'net assimilation rate,' or 'productivity.' The mechanisms by which trees achieve this are clearly beyond the scope of this brief introduction. Suffice it to say that the reactivation of the cambium in spring is brought about through the production and mobilization of plant growth hormones (auxins) in the expanding buds. Meanwhile there is an upsurge of activity in the primary apical meristems in the course of which stored food is used up and energy released, sufficient to allow cell division and cell enlargement to go on apace. The reactivated vascular cambium loses no time in forming new tissues (xylem and phloem) which will facilitate rapid transport of raw materials and mobilized storage products. There is an intense level of chemical activity within the individual cells, and as this entails respiration, photosynthesis, protein-building, the fashioning of new cell walls and other processes it is easy to appreciate something of its hidden complexities.

What the eye sees as a result of all this internal activity (at cellular level) is the burgeoning of new leaves on the trees in spring. When we bear in mind that a single mature foliage leaf will commonly comprise some 15 million cells we begin to glimpse something of the unimaginable scale of cell production, each spring time, in a single forest tree. Nevertheless, this particular manifestation of growth is there for all to see. Opening buds, new leaves, elongating twigs, these cannot pass unnoticed, but not so the scarcely perceptible increments in girth and stature of the older trees. Fast-growing species of tree, for example birches, illustrate how rapidly height increases in the early years following successful establishment and how markedly it slows down later. Yet some increments will take place, however slight, in every spring for the duration of the tree's life. With few exceptions, at least in temperate regions, the increase in girth of

a tree at breast height (1.5m; 5ft) is very close to 2.5cm (1in) a year. This is for trees growing under conditions such that their crowns are not inhibited from full development by overcrowding. This figure is useful for estimating a tree's age. Thus, with a breast height girth of 2.5m (8ft) the tree will be about 100 years old.

Some exceptions to this rule are:
Wellingtonia (*Sequoiadendron giganteum*),
Coast Redwood (*Sequoia sempervirens*),
Cedar of Lebanon (*Cedrus libani*),
Douglas Fir (*Pseudotsuga menziesii*),
Southern Beeches (*Nothofagus* spp),
Turkey Oak (*Quercus cerris*),
Tulip Tree (*Liriodendron tulipifera*),
London Plane (*Platanus acerifolia*)
which increase girth at 5–7.5cm (2–3in) a year, and:
Scots Pine (*Pinus sylvestris*),
Horse Chestnut (*Aesculus hippocastanum*),
Common Lime (*Tilia × europaea*)
which increase girth at less than 2.5cm (1in) a year.

In other climates very different conditions of growth prevail. In the humid tropics two years of more or less uninterrupted growth activity can easily result in a tree many metres high. On the fringe of the great deserts of the world, notwithstanding the high temperatures, water shortage makes the trees of the specialized genera that grow there among the most slow-growing of all. In the high Arctic, temperature imposes comparably severe restrictions. On wind-exposed coastal stations both wind velocity and salt spray can play a part in restricting the height and distorting the growth of trees. Even so, for certain species at least, life itself may be retained with tenacity, in the face of all obstacles. Thus, the shock is the greater when a single virulent fungus such as *Ceratocystis ulmi* (which causes Dutch Elm Disease) can bring about the death of up to 10 million British elms in the course of a few seasons. Our knowledge of the botany of trees appears powerless to arrest this devastation. It is equally powerless to check the havoc wreaked from time to time by forest fires on the tinder-dry, oil-rich, evergreen eucalyptus forests of Australia. Our remedy must be to grow more trees.   E. V. W.

Illustration showing the natural life cycle of the Douglas Fir (*Pseudotsuga menziesii*) together with details of the management and cropping of these trees as undertaken by Man in his forests. Commercially each tree is harvested while still healthy and not allowed to deteriorate with age.

(a) Young trees 8 to 9 years old are thinned out in planted forests and frequently sold as Christmas trees.

(b) After 30 to 40 years the lower branches start to drop off; the tree can be harvested for pulping.

(c) At 50 to 60 years old the timber may be made into pulp and straight trunks are used as poles.

(d) At 100 years old the trunk can be cut for use as construction timber or "peeled" for plywood.

(e) Growth slows after 100 years, but the trunk is still used for timber. A mature tree may reach 100m (325 ft).

(f) After several centuries the tree starts to decline—the branches fall off, the bark peels and the trunk begins to rot.

(g) Even the upper branches die in the end and the rotten trunk is so weak that........

(h) it topples to the ground.

(a) (b) (c) (d) (e) (f) (g) (h)

Forests

THE FOREST ECOSYSTEM

Vegetation in which trees are important or dominant – forests and woodlands – occupies about 40 percent of the world's land surface, ranging from the tropics to high latitudes (about 70° in the Northern Hemisphere) and from sea level to about 3 800m (12 500ft) in some mountain passes. The structure of the forest, whether deciduous or evergreen, broadleaved or needleleaved, as well as the species present in it, varies considerably in response to the climate, topography, rocks, soils and past history of the different regions of the world. However, despite their diversity, forest ecosystems share certain features which make an overview possible.

When bare ground becomes available for colonization the first plants are relatively simple, often algae, mosses and lichens, which form rather simple communities. Through the action of these plants on the substrate, and the accumulation of their dead remains, a soil begins to form which permits the development of more complex communities dominated by pioneer flowering plants, usually herbs. These in their turn are succeeded by other more closed communities, increasingly rich in species and dominated by ever taller plant forms, until a stage is reached at which a relatively stable vegetation is produced. This *climax* vegetation is the most complex that can be supported under the prevailing climatic and other environmental conditions of a region. The most complex climax vegetation is usually considered to be that dominated by trees and forest ecosystems normally develop where there is a reasonably long growing season in which mean temperatures do not fall much below 10°C (50°F), a reliable supply of ground moisture and protection from drying winds during the winter when moisture cannot be absorbed from the chilled soil. Where regions are too dry, too wet, too cold or too exposed, forest gives way to ecosystems such as grassland, bogs, tundra or desert scrub, in which trees are of little or no importance.

While forest ecosystems are able to develop because of the environmental conditions prevailing in a region they are also important in modifying these conditions to provide a series of microclimates which profoundly influence the occurrence of plants and animals in forest communities. In forests the tree top canopy is often the densest part of the vegetation, reflecting or absorbing much of the sunlight, so that only 1 percent or less reaches the forest floor. Winds are also greatly reduced by tree cover; in pine forest, for example, the wind speed at ground level is less than one-quarter of that above a canopy 14m (45ft) high and there is proportionately greater reduction in taller forest. The soil, too, is modified by the dominant trees. In addition to the moisture of forest soils their chemical and physical features are affected by the leaf-litter which falls on to them. Leaf-litter supplies the humus which sustains the clay-humus complex of forest

Opposite Areas such as the tropical rain forests of the Guiana Highlands shown here have the largest standing mass (biomass) of living vegetation per unit area and also represent a natural climax vegetation (or biome) that will only alter naturally if the climate changes.

Below Forest is the climax vegetation of many regions of the world. The graph below represents the succession of vegetation types leading to climax deciduous forest and compares the biomass (amount of standing vegetation) and the net primary production of energy by that biomass. It can be seen that although the biomass of grassland is much less than that of mature forest, the net primary production differs to a much lesser extent.

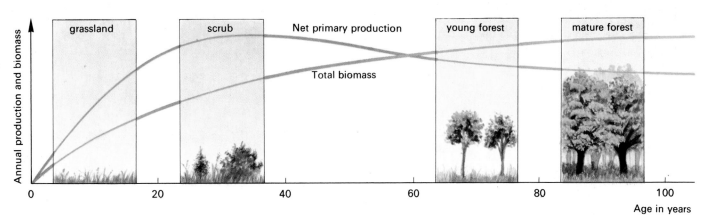

(graph) Annual production and biomass (vertical axis) — grassland, scrub, Net primary production, young forest, mature forest; Total biomass; Age in years: 0, 20, 40, 60, 80, 100

soils and contains the reserves of soluble nutrients. Leaves with abundant organic acids or very woody tissues are not easily eaten by the soil fauna and tend to decompose slowly by rotting to give a thin, leached, acid soil, as under beech, while leaves with less acid organic matter are quickly broken down to give the deeper, less acid soils, supporting abundant animal life, found under oak and holly. Such differences can be seen over quite short distances in mixed oak/beech woodland, for example. The presence of myccorhiza (fungal threads which join the tree roots to the leaf-litter) can provide the tree with nutrients derived from the saprophytic fungi thus making the tree less dependent on the soil fertility.

In forest dominated by evergreens, or in the summer phase of deciduous forest, the reduced light and wind give cool, damp conditions which fluctuate much less through the day than in more open habitats. Plants and animals unable to withstand constantly changing conditions thus find a home in these forest habitats. Forests, however, do not provide uniform

conditions, as is shown by the vertical stratification of the vegetation they contain. The canopy of the forest is made up of trees which benefit from strong light at maturity. In temperate mid-latitudes there is usually only one canopy, but in energy-rich tropical rain forests there may be two or three canopy layers, often with strongly light-demanding plants such as palms protruding above them as emergents. Beneath the canopy, shade-tolerant shrubs usually form another stratum while herb and ground layers (mosses etc) can often also be distinguished. The development of the two latter has been found to depend not only upon the available light but also upon

the amount of litter, which probably has a shading effect. It has been shown in British woods that the total mass of the herb and ground layers decreased proportionally with increasing amounts of litter and, furthermore, that certain plants, such as grasses and mosses, were more speedily eliminated than others, such as Bluebell (*Endymion non-scriptus*) and Yellow Deadnettle (*Galeobdolon luteum*).

In deciduous woodland the difference between conditions inside and outside the tree-dominated ecosystem decreases during the winter when the lack of leaves allows the increased penetration of both light and wind. Many herbaceous com-

Three food chains in typical temperate deciduous woodland with an adjacent aquatic habitat. Each chain starts with a primary producer: (1) the leaves of an oak tree; (5) planktonic algae; (9) dead oak leaves. The next level in the chains is occupied by the primary consumers which are usually herbivores: (2) Winter Moth caterpillar (*Operophtera*); (6) water flea (*Daphnia*); (9) earthworms (*Lumbricus*). In some cases, for example the food chain on the woodland floor, the dead oak leaves may be assimilated by

fungi (11) which in their turn are eaten by soil insects (12) (*Collembola*) and mites (*Acari*); these animals may also consume the dead leaves directly from the woodland floor.

The next levels (secondary and tertiary consumers) in the food chains are occupied by carnivores: (3) tit mice (*Parus*); (4) sparrow hawk (*Accipiter*); (7) predatory water fleas (*Leptodora*); (8) trout (*Salmo*); (13) predatory beetles (*Philonthus*; *Abax*); (14) shrews (*Sorex*).

munities of deciduous forests are adapted to these seasonal differences and we find in Hornbeam (*Carpinus betulus*) woodlands, for example, that the Wood Anemone (*Anemone nemorosa*), Dog's Mercury (*Mercurialis perennis*) and Celandine (*Ranunculus ficaria*) complete their flowering period and much of their leaf-production before the tree leaves expand. Other species, such as the Bluebell and Ramsons (*Allium ursinum*), probably prolong their flowering under full shade because of the food stored in their bulbs.

Because trees are relatively long-lived, opportunities for regeneration in virgin forest depend upon the death of individual trees or their destruction by winds, fire and other hazards. The seeds of many forest trees are large and rich in food reserves which enable them to germinate and survive as seedlings under the low light levels and high competition of the forest floor. Many species are able to remain as small seedlings waiting for a break to occur in the canopy; oak shoots, for example, that were aged as six years by growth rings were growing from roots as much as 31 years older. Herbivores (rabbits, rodents, insects) and fungi destroy enormous quantities of seeds and seedlings so that successful establishment only occurs in years of high seed production. When a suitable break appears in the canopy this is colonized by light-demanding plants. The tree seedlings have to compete with these initially and then, as a scrub of tree species emerges, the saplings compete with each other until, finally, one of these rises above the others to fill the gap as a mature tree.

The forest ecosystem, then, comprises a series of habitats, supporting a myriad plants and animals, dependent upon the microclimatic conditions resulting from the dominant trees, which themselves individually provide support for climbers (honeysuckles, lianes etc) and epiphytes, such as ferns, mosses and various flowering plants, and partial nutrition for parasites such as mistletoes. The forest is one of the most complex ecosystems known and its food chains are consequently long and interrelated.

Most of the nutrients in a forest are present in the bodies of the plants, animals and other organisms that make up the various communities. In virgin forest the level of nutrients is maintained relatively constant by the recycling through food chains and the importance of trees is shown by the fact that 82 percent of the total mass of land plant tissues is locked up in forests, although they cover only about 40 percent of the land area. The removal of forest interrupts this cycle and the nutrients are dissipated. In consequence, the destruction of forest by Man has not only removed the myriad habitats that depend upon tree cover but has also greatly reduced the fertility levels of many regions, which largely explains the current preoccupation with the conservation of existing forests.

D. M. M.

FORESTS OF THE WORLD

Forests are the climax vegetation over about 40 percent (4 500 million hectares or 11 115 million acres) of the world's land surface, although Man has substantially altered them or entirely removed them from vast areas – from much of Western Europe, for example. Different types of forest are found in different climates, and there are striking convergences in forest structure and general appearance between areas with the same climate in different continents where the same type of forest occurs although composed of different species. The explanation of this similarity of appearance, or epharmony as it is called, is still largely unexplained, although physiological causes such as response to

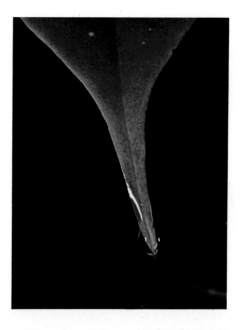

A characteristic feature of many trees in the tropical rain forests is the elongated leaf with a 'drip-tip.' It has evolved to cope with high rainfall and high humidity, supposedly providing rapid drainage and drying after rain.

water stress or mineral deficiency are clearly involved.

Tropical Rain Forests. In the tropics and subtropics evergreen tropical rain forests occupy about 1 000 million hectares (2 500 million acres) in the wettest climates. They occur in three great blocks centered on Amazonia, the Guinea-Congo region of Africa and the Malay archipelago, the latter extending from the Western Ghats of India to the wet, high islands of the Pacific. There is also an isolated small zone in east Madagascar and the Mascarenes. There are 13 major categories or formations of tropical rain forest. Three of these (lower montane, upper montane and sub-

Map showing the main areas of the world occupied by natural forest before interference by Man.

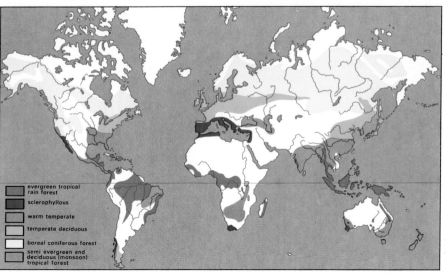

evergreen tropical rain forest
sclerophyllous
warm temperate
temperate deciduous
boreal coniferous forest
semi evergreen and deciduous (monsoon) tropical forest

and shoulders above a continuous canopy. Shrubs and herbs are rare, the undergrowth plants consisting mostly of small trees. Different tree species reach different heights at maturity, and characterize different strata in the canopy. The emergent and tallest canopy trees usually have broad, sympodial crowns, composed of numerous small rather dense subcrowns. Smaller trees commonly have crowns taller than broad, and these are frequently of monopodial construction, that is having a single main axis. Buttresses, which may reach 10m (33ft) or more up the trunk, are an important feature of many types of rain forest, and in some types stilt roots are common. Leaves are principally of meso-

Left Competition for light has resulted in the straight tall trunks of tropical rain forest trees, here seen beside a new road in Malaya. The scale can be judged from the human figure barely visible in the left foreground. *Below* Profile diagram of a climax African tropical forest showing the three layers typical of such forests. The main canopy is very dense so that the understory must cope with low light intensity and high humidity. The trees of the canopy normally have long slender trunks, much of the support coming from the association of the trees in the massed canopy, but those in the emergent layer lack this material support and often have well-developed buttress roots to help hold up the trunk.

phyll size and may have the apex extended as a prolonged drip tip. Climbers (lianes) and epiphytes are common in a great diversity of form and species. Stranglers, which start life as epiphytes but send down roots and ultimately engulf and kill the host tree, are prominent. Saprophytes and parasites occur (including in the East *Rafflesia*, which produces the largest flower in the world). The trees provide a complex framework for these other plant forms, and an intricate set of niches for animals. Both flora and fauna are exceedingly rich. For example, the rain forests of the Malay peninsula occupy an area equal to England and Wales, containing some 2 500 tree species and a total flora of about 8 000 species of vascular plants. Many botanists believe that flowering plants evolved in tropical rain forests. Today they certainly contain the greatest concentration of primitive groups. Small areas of forest in southeast Asia are richer than in Latin America. The African forests are much poorer, for example as many species of palm are found on Singapore island as on the entire continent of Africa.

Structure becomes simpler and species become fewer away from the optimum, northward and southward where tropical

alpine forest) occur at progressively higher altitudes. Beach, mangrove forest and brackish water forest are coastal. Two formations, peatswamp and freshwater swamp forest occur on inundated ground inland, three on extreme substrata (limestone, ultrabasics and nutrient-poor sands) and two on dry lowland mesic sites in continuously humid and mildly seasonal climates respectively. These last two formations include the most complex and species-rich plant communities in the world. They occur in the best conditions for plant life, with no dry or cold season to interrupt growth. The biggest trees average 30–45m (100–150ft) in height, although some reach 60m (200ft) or more. Beneath them grows a dense profusion of smaller trees. The tallest trees commonly occur as isolated emergents standing head

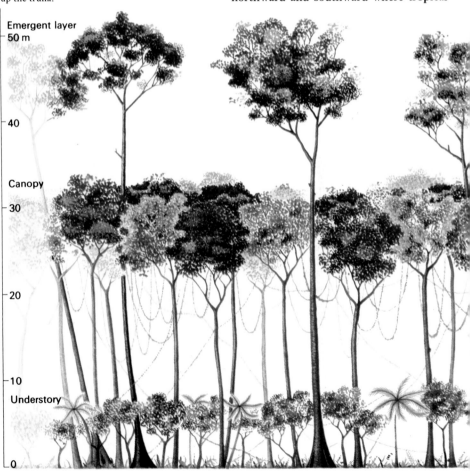

Cloud forest on the upper slopes of the Nguru mountains in Tanzania, East Africa.

forests merge into equivalent subtropical formations, for instance in Indochina and south China. There is a similar trend to simplification within the tropics to the other rain forest formations listed above. One of the most strikingly distinctive lowland rain-forest types is so-called heath forest (caatinga and campos in South America) which is, however, virtually absent from Africa. This develops on soils which even by tropical standards are impoverished, are mostly coarse, freely draining siliceous sands, and become podzozolized. Heath forest is of low stature, microphyllous and very dense, with a uniform canopy top of high albedo. Its physiognomy is an adaptation to periodic water stress and to mineral deficiency. In the eastern tropics this structure and physiognomy is also found in upper montane rain forest (cloud forest) and several species occur in both.

Upper Montane or **Cloud Forest** is rain forest which occurs above the cloud level on tropical mountains. Its lower limit is quite sharply at the cloud line. Cloud forest characteristically has a low, dense canopy of small trees with thick, gnarled crowns of tiny, leathery leaves and high reflective power. Trees and ground are thickly swathed in epiphytes, mainly filmy ferns, but including bryophytes and flowering plants. *Sphagnum* (bog moss) often occurs in open places. In very humid climates peat accumulates. The soil is waterlogged for all or much of the time. Much of the precipitation is derived by the fog (ground-level cloud) condensing on the vegetation. Cloud forest occurs as low as 600m (1970ft) in Malaysia, and at 3000–3300m (9250–10830ft) in the main cordillera of New Guinea.

On the very highest mountains subalpine forest occurs above cloud forest up to the tree line; it is of low stature with very tiny leaves of nanophyll size. Lower montane rain forest occurs between upper montane and lowland forest. It has a general resemblance to the latter and merges through a broad ecotone but differs in species composition and several structural features which taken together are diagnostic, and include lower canopy with fewer, smaller emergents, smaller buttresses and absence of big woody climbers.

Mangrove is a type of forest associated with muddy shores of a belt surrounding the equator. This belt reaches latitude 32°N, and as far south as Auckland in New Zealand and South Australia. Mangroves develop on sheltered muddy shores of deltas and estuaries exposed to the tide. They vary in width, some reaching up to several kilometres. The trees are evergreen, with the thick leathery leaves frequently associated with plants of saline soils and other physiological adaptations to live in salt water. Many species have viviparous seeds, which develop into seedlings on the parent tree and on being shed stick into the mud, when roots develop very quickly. Various types of prop and aerial root are another characteristic of these trees. Breathing roots enable the root system to respire in the anaerobic mud. The vegetation is almost entirely woody, varying from low scrub to forest 30m (100ft) high.

Mangrove swamps are one of the most unpleasant types of vegetation for the human visitor: the aerial roots make progress very difficult, and the deep mud releases unpleasant fetid gases which accumulate in the anaerobic conditions. The myriad biting insects are yet another disincentive.

There is a zonation of vegetation in mangrove swamps associated with the degree of immersion. Different species have different competitive powers according to their tolerances of salinity.

Monsoon and Savanna Forests (Dry Tropical Forests). Rain forests change with increasing length of dry season to semi-evergreen and deciduous types. Initially species composition alters although the genera and families present remain much the same and only the taller trees are deciduous. Leaf shedding and flowering become synchronized and correlated with climatic seasonality. In the strongly seasonal dry tropics, forests of much simpler structure and with fewer woody species occur and ultimately closed forest is replaced by open woodland and savanna. In all climates with a marked dry season fire is an important factor controlling structure and species composition of the vegetation. In progressively drier climates, total amount of moisture becomes more important than length of dry season. Characteristically these so-called monsoon and savanna forests form a mosaic pattern.

Closed moisture-loving, more nearly evergreen, so-called gallery forests occur along water courses. These seasonally dry tropical forests are extensive in all three continents. The flora is rich, with many fire-resistant herbs (including bulbous types) and grasses in the drier and more open types. There is a rich fauna, notably the spectacular group of ungulates in east Africa.

Sclerophyllous Forests, with winter rain, occur around the Mediterranean and in the other parts of the world with similar climate. The summers are hot and dry, the winters warm and wet due to cyclonic rain. Annual rainfall is 500–1 000mm (20–40in) but irregular, and there are prolonged periods of low relative humidity. There is no really cold season. Spring is the main growing and flowering season.

The Mediterranean basin has been the center of civilizations from ancient times and deforestation, cultivation, grazing and soil erosion have destroyed most of the original forest so that only variously degraded communities now remain. The original zonal vegetation was forest dominated by a canopy of the Holm Oak (*Quercus ilex*), 15–18m (50–60ft) tall, with shrubs and herbs beneath. Where the trees are cut about every 20 years it is replaced by a dense shrub vegetation called maquis. This is very rich in species including many geophytes, but is subject to periodic fires and becomes degraded by excessive grazing and burning to form open garigue. All the best sites are now occupied by vineyards and other agriculture. Many species are adapted to Mediterranean climatic conditions by the possession of small, leathery, evergreen leaves which minimize water loss in dry periods.

Similar vegetation occurs in central and southern California. Here evergreen forests occur to the north, but southward, with decreasing rainfall, are replaced by a scrub called chaparral which is comparable to maquis except that it is the natural zonal vegetation with lightning-induced fires as a natural controlling factor. In the Southern Hemisphere, sclerophyll forests occur in a tiny area of Chile (only relicts remain), the Cape of South Africa, where the flora is fantastically rich especially with members of the heath family (Ericaceae) and the southwest tip of Australia, where the general appearance differs due to the predominance of members of the families Epacridaceae and Proteaceae and the genus *Eucalyptus*. The area occupied by dry forest and woodlands of all kinds (Mediterranean sclerophyll type, plus the monsoon and savanna tropical and subtropical forests) is 1 400 million hectares (3 500 million acres).

Warm Temperate Evergreen Forests. There are two groups of warm temperate forests. They total 100 million hectares (247 million acres) in area. The first kind is an extension of sclerophyll forest in conditions where there is no summer drought. In California north of 36°, the coastal strip is moist from summer fogs which result from cool onshore ocean currents. Forests of the Giant Redwood (*Sequoia sempervirens*) occur. This is the tallest tree in the world, attaining 100m (330ft) and more. Farther north on the same coast there are magnificent temperate rain forests of *Tsuga heterophylla* (Western Hemlock), *Thuja plicata* (Western Red Cedar) and *Pseudotsuga menziesii* (Douglas Fir). There is a comparable forest in South America, the Valdivian forest of Chile, but none in Africa. In Australia, the Karri (*Eucalyptus diversicolor*) forest abuts the summer-dry sclerophyll forest zone. This also is a tall forest. Like the North American examples it is an important timber resource. In the Mediterranean region, this type of vegetation occurs around the Black Sea, east as far as

Fire is an important 'natural' environmental factor controlling the development of savanna forests. This dry-season bushfire in Nigeria checks the development of scrub vegetation and many nutrients bound up in the plants are released into the environment. Fire-resistant species survive.

Perhaps some of the best-known examples of warm temperate evergreen forests are those of the Sierra Redwood or Giant Sequoia (*Sequoiadendron giganteum*), seen here in the Yosemite National Park in California, United States, where the remaining forests are strictly protected.

the shores of the Caspian, and includes the species-rich Tertiary-relict Colchic forest of Transcaucasia, which lies in a region where the summers are mild and wet enough for tea cultivation to have replaced most of the zonal forest.

The main warm temperate forests are found on the eastern seaboards of the continents, exposed to monsoon or trade winds. Rainfall is plentiful, 150–300cm (60–120in), and well distributed throughout the year. In southeast Asia (Thailand, Indochina, China, Korea and southern

Japan), eastern Australia and southern Brazil there is a continuous gradation with increasing latitude from wet tropical to subtropical to warm temperate conditions. It is very difficult to distinguish zones in these evergreen forests. Characteristically penetration is difficult; they are rich in tree species including some conifers, and in epiphytes and climbers, but less so than the tropics. Plank buttresses are absent. Some trees are deciduous, giving marked seasonal differences in appearance. Mosses, liverworts and ferns are abundant on the ground and tree-trunks. Bamboos are common in some types, as are tree ferns. There are strong similarities in structure and physiognomy with montane tropical forests and at the family level also in the flora. The climate, however, has a marked annual rhythm, whereas the montane tropics have a greater diurnal than annual climatic range. General appearance varies with different regions and there is a complete change in flora from low to high latitudes. In Australia, it has been shown that tropical types extend farthest south on the best soils and moistest sites. The main temperate type is the *Nothofagus* forest of Tasmania and Victoria, whose boundaries are determined by frequency of fire. In Africa, only the Drakensburg mountains have suitably moist sites for this type of forest, and it is of limited extent. In North America it is also poorly defined because cold air masses move south as far as the Gulf of Mexico, but it is found near the coast from Louisiana, Florida and Georgia to North Carolina. The tree flora is rich including evergreen oaks (*Quercus* spp), a few palms and some climbers. Bald Cypress (*Taxodium distichum*) swamps occur in wet areas and fire-climax pine (*Pinus* spp) forests are found on dry sands. Most of the forests of New Zealand fall into this class; dominant trees include *Nothofagus*, mixed conifers, and a kauri pine (*Agathis australis*)–subtropical-broadleaved species mixture, depending on locality, soil and past history.

Temperate Deciduous Forests are perhaps the most familiar type in the world. The total area is 800 million hectares (2 000 million acres). They formerly covered most of Western Europe and are still extensive in North America. They are virtually restricted to the Northern Hemisphere (apart from an area in Patagonia, southern Chile and Tierra del Fuego). Leaf fall is an adaptation to the marked but not very prolonged cold season when water is unavailable or restricted (by contrast with the tropics where it is simply

an adaptation to drought). Annual rainfall is 70–150cm (28–60in). Evergreen broad-leaved trees cannot withstand cold or winter drought and in Western Europe Ivy (*Hedera helix*) and Holly (*Ilex aquifolium*) are both Atlantic species absent farther east where winters are more severe. *Rhododendron* and *Vaccinium* species, also evergreen, by contrast, survive winter cold below a snow covering. These forests are found on the eastern coasts of North America and Asia between the warm temperate forests and cold or arid temperate regions. In North America, they extend north to the Great Lakes and upper reaches of the Gulf of St. Lawrence, and west of the Mississippi. In Asia, they occur in northern Japan and on the adjacent part of the continent. They are also found on the western edge of Eurasia in Europe, north of the Mediterranean zone, and where the Gulf Stream causes winter rains to be replaced by evenly distributed rainfall or rain with a summer maximum, and where the cold season is relatively short. Here they range east to the Urals as a wedge between the steppes and the boreal coniferous forests. Deciduous trees occur where there are four to six months with adequate rain and this forest is absent from extreme maritime climates of the western seaboard as well as extreme continental climates.

The temperate deciduous forest zone of Western Europe is one of the most populous regions of the world because the climatic conditions also favor prosperous agriculture and grazing, and only tiny fragments of the forest remain with virtually none in virgin condition. Floristically the Western-European forests are poorer than the others due to extinction in the Pleistocene ice ages. Beeches (*Fagus* spp), oaks (*Quercus* spp), limes (*Tilia* spp) and ashes (*Fraxinus* spp), are locally dominant in the single tree layer. In wet places alders (*Alnus* spp) and willows (*Salix* spp) become common. There is a single shrub layer in which hazels (*Corylus* spp), Field Maple (*Acer campestre*) and hawthorns (*Crataegus* spp) are common, and a herb layer. There are few climbers and only cryptogamic epiphytes. The trees flower early, commonly before the leaves open, and most are wind-pollinated; this allows a long period for fruits to form and ripen before the onset of winter. In early spring before the canopy becomes leafy the forest floor herbs flower, creating carpets of blossom; especially of Bluebell (*Endymion non-scriptus*), Primrose (*Primula vulgaris* and Oxlip (*Primula elatior*), which

35

are one of the glories of these forests, equalled only by the spectacular yellow, orange and red tints of the dying foliage in the fall. The early spring temporal niche is succeeded by a spring one, occupied by other herbs, for example Wood Sorrel (*Oxalis acetosella*), which flower at the time of leaf flush. In Asia and North America there are more genera and species in both tree and shrub layers, including magnolias, numerous maples (*Acer* spp), Tulip Tree (*Liriodendron tulipifera*), buckeyes (*Aesculus* spp) and hickories (*Carya* spp), as well as temperate outliers of mainly tropical families.

The Boreal Region encircles the globe at and beyond the northern limit of forests and covers major portions of North America and Eurasia as well as the islands of Newfoundland, Sakhalin and Iceland. It abuts southward on the temperate deciduous forest but the winters are colder and longer. Part of the region, between 45° and 70°N is occupied by the very extensive boreal coniferous forest, which covers 1 500 million hectares (3 700 million acres). In addition there are big areas of bog, peatland and swamp, known as muskeg, and in oceanic regions, such as Iceland, dwarf shrub vegetation known as heath. The main forest dominants are conifers with xeromorphic needle leaves, more resistant to winter cold and drought than broadleaved trees. Such trees can commence photosynthesis immediately conditions permit in the spring, so are better adapted to exploit regions where the growing season is short. Deciduous trees need about 120 days per year with mean temperature over 10°C, conifers can manage with 30 days, though there are differences between species. The narrow, conical, monopodial tree form with drooping branches is adaptive to regions of high snow fall. These forests have only a poorly developed shrub and herb layer: shade is greater, decay of falling leaves is slow so that undecomposed litter covers much of the surface, and the climate is worse. Spruces (*Picea* spp) with Norway Spruce (*P. abies*) merging eastward with Siberian Spruce (*P. obovata*) in Eurasia and White Spruce (*P. glauca*) in the New World, firs (*Abies* spp), pines (*Pinus* spp) and larches (*Larix* spp) dominate in different places. At its northern limit the boreal conifer forest merges into open parkland with scattered groves of trees, taiga. The northernmost forest in the world is in eastern Siberia at 72° 50′N, 105°E and is dominated by a larch *Larix gmelinii* (*L. dahurica*), which is highly productive in

the very short summer, but one of the few deciduous conifers, losing its needles each winter. The ground layer of boreal forests is predominantly of dwarf shrubs, for example bilberries and cranberries (*Vaccinium* spp), Leatherleaf (*Chamaedaphne calyculata*) and Labrador Tea (*Ledum palustre*), and is also richly mossy. Drier pine forests typically have herbs like *Linnaea borealis*, *Trientalis europaea* and the wintergreens (*Pyrola* spp) as well as saprophytes such as the orchids *Goodyera repens* and *Corallorhiza trifida*. There is no comparable belt of coniferous forest in the Southern Hemisphere, where indeed there is no land mass at the appropriate latitudes.

On north temperate mountains south of the boreal zone a conifer forest zone commonly occurs above the deciduous broadleaved forest, reaching up to the tree line. Resemblance extends to the herbs – several species are shared with boreal latitudes. Trees, though of the same genera, are mostly different species, for example the European Larch (*Larix decidua*) and in the Appalachians the Red Spruce (*Picea rubens*) and Fraser Fir (*Abies fraseri*).

Forest Dynamics. As we have seen, the species composition of a forest is dependent at the grossest scale on plant geography and within any region there is variation due to habitat, for example between swamp and dry land, and with different soil types. A further important variation arises from the complex structure of a forest community. At maturity a closed forest canopy casts dense shade. Plants can only grow up under the canopy which are able to succeed in conditions of low light and high root competition. In temperate deciduous forest many herbs to some extent avoid these limitations by making much or all of their growth (including flowering) before the trees come into leaf. Only certain tree species have seedlings which can grow up under a closed canopy. These are often called shade bearers. Sometimes gaps form in a closed forest canopy. A storm may blow down isolated trees or fell a swathe, fire may sweep through. A second group of tree species has seeds efficiently dispersed and (in the tropics) continually available, and these soon colonize such gaps. The seedlings are adapted to grow and succeed in the brightly lit, sometimes desiccating, conditions of gaps. These species are often known as light demanders. The seedlings cannot grow up in shade, so the trees cannot replace themselves *in situ*. They always colonize gaps and are also sometimes referred to as pioneer species. The

forests of pioneers are always seral. Familiar English examples are Scots Pine and birch. In fact there is a spectrum of types from obligate shade bearers to strict pioneers, especially in regions with a rich flora, and most markedly in the humid tropics. In the temperate deciduous forest of North America the pioneers *Pinus strobus*, *Quercus* spp and *Castanea* spp tend to be replaced in the absence of catastrophic forest destruction by the shade bearers *Acer* spp, *Tsuga* spp and *Fagus* spp. The two oaks native to England (*Quercus petraea* and *Q. robur*) are also both light-demanding species. In West Africa present-day extensive tall speciesrich rain forest containing much valuable timber in the form of several species of Meliaceae (African mahogany) is being replaced by a lower forest with fewer species of less commercial value. The principal timber species of Malaysia, the Philippines and Indonesia, light-wooded meranti (*Shorea* spp), are near-pioneers, favored by mild but not total forest disturbance. This dynamic aspect of forest composition, with different species adapted to different temporal niches in the canopy growth cycle, therefore has important ecological and commercial implications. The science of silviculture is based on understanding and manipulating it. Trees have long lives, and rare catastrophes leave their mark on forest composition for a century or more. Pioneers come up in large gaps as even-age stands and a rather coarse mosaic of large patches of different age develops. Shade bearers succeed the pioneers, replacing each other or themselves on smaller areas so that ultimately a mixed-age stand develops with a fine-scale mosaic pattern of gap, building phase and high mature forest. But it is doubtful if there is ever an equilibrium state, or constant species composition; a catastrophe, or indeed secular climatic change, sooner or later intervenes to cause gross alteration. In Western Europe Man's interference with the forests has been prolonged and profound and influences present-day structure and species composition. The dominance of light-demanding oak over much of England reflects its conscious selection by silviculture not its ecology.

T. C. W.

Opposite A European Beech (*Fagus sylvatica*) woodland bursting into full leaf is a classic example of temperate deciduous forest. Forest-floor herbs, such as this carpet of bluebells (*Endymion non-scriptus*), have to complete most of their annual cycle of growth and flowering before the leaf canopy becomes too dense.

Trees and Man

FORESTRY

As we have seen forests occupy over one-third of the earth's land surface. They are of immense variety, ranging from the dwarf trees with imperceptible growth in the Arctic regions, to the tropical rain forests, rich in species and varied in structure; from the vast areas of closely stocked coniferous forest in the North American continent, and in northern Europe, to the open savanna with a low stocking of trees which covers extensive areas in the tropics and subtropics.

The growing stock of trees is estimated to be 350 000 million cubic metres (1.24 million cubic feet) of which two-thirds is hardwood and one-third softwood. Total annual removals are of the order of 2 500 million cubic metres (88 000 million cubic feet) of which 45 percent is coniferous. Seventy percent of the hardwood removals are used for fuel.

For millennia the immense resource that these forests represent has been exploited by Man, whose activities have reduced their area to about half their greatest extent. Since ancient times the forest has been cleared for agriculture, for protection against wild beasts or human enemies, and to obtain its products. The main instruments of destruction have been fire and the grazing of domestic stock, supplemented at times by the deliberate introduction and release of nonindigenous species of herbivorous animals. It is reasonable to suppose that the net area of forest in the world is still decreasing by several million hectares per annum owing to continuing destruction and degradation chiefly by shifting cultivation in South America, Africa and parts of Asia.

Only in modern times has there arisen a concept of management of forests for the perpetuation of the renewable resource they represent and only in very recent times has the full scope and range of that resource begun to be realized.

Forests have always been exploited for the wood they provide for innumerable purposes through the ages – fuel, implements, shelter and housing, furniture and fencing. Today's industrial needs generate an increasing range of uses, often involving the breakdown of the structure of raw wood, and its reconstitution into paper or board, or its combination with plastics into new forms of material. With the predicted rise in world population from the present 4 000 million to 6 000 million by the end of the 20th century and an assumed annual increase in world consumption of wood of 2 percent, the need for management is evident; a continual increase in the supply of wood is required from a dwindling area of forest.

In addition to the production of wood it is now recognized that forests fulfill a wide variety of functions essential to Man's well-being. They protect the soil and so counter erosion and reduce flooding; they shelter and protect agriculture and influence local climatic extremes; they ensure clear water supplies and prevent

Opposite This mixed plantation of pine (*Pinus* sp) and larch (*Larix* sp) is situated above the native deciduous trees at Abergynolwyn, Wales, and encroaches on the natural moorland.
Right Tropical rain forest is being destroyed at an ever-increasing rate. In this picture, taken north of Kuala Trenggaro on the eastern side of the Malay Peninsula, the valuable timber trees have been removed and the remaining understory trees burnt to clear the land for an oil-palm plantation. The rate of decline of such tropical forests is causing great concern among conservationists.

Beech (*Fagus* sp) and pine (*Pinus* sp) trees growing
together under controlled silvicultural conditions.
The pines will eventually be systematically removed
to allow a mature beech forest to develop.

pollution; they provide a habitat for a vast
array of flora and fauna, a resource in
itself. Forests, woodlands and trees are
essential components of attractive landscapes and are becoming increasingly important for the recreational facilities they
can provide for the urban populations of
industrial countries.

The modern forester is therefore faced
with a dilemma: the necessity to increase
the sustained supply of wood from the
forests as rapidly and as economically as
possible and the need to protect the forest
ecosystem to maintain all the other benefits, often not quantifiable in economic
terms, which derive from the forest. This
challenge must be met within the framework of his government's economic planning. Their approach is now to select

practical patterns of action, supported by
scientific findings, on both biological and
mathematical grounds, in order to achieve
a balance between efficient production and
safeguarding the environment.

Silviculture is the art of creating and
tending a forest. It involves the application
of detailed knowledge of the life history
and general characteristics of trees, with
particular reference to environmental factors. Each tree species differs in its
requirements and its reactions to site
conditions, in its pattern of growth, and
in its ability to withstand extremes of
climate or terrain. It is by understanding
these factors for all the trees within the
climatic range that the silviculturalist con-
trols the development of the forests under
his care.

Some trees, such as pines (*Pinus* spp)
and birches (*Betula* spp), can be used as
pioneers on exposed and infertile sites,
while others, such as oaks (*Quercus* spp)

and ashes (*Fraxinus* spp) grow best in
more sheltered places and on rich deep
soils. Species such as larches (*Larix* spp)
and oaks need full light all around their
crowns for optimum growth; others such
as beeches (*Fagus* spp) and silver firs
(*Abies* spp), are shade bearers and can
remain growing slowly in the understorey
till eventually freed to grow into the upper
canopy of the forest.

Once a forest has been established it
needs continuous tending to maturity,
with periodical thinning to give more room
for the best stems, which are selected to
remain. As maturity approaches consideration must be given to the next generation.
Measures taken to achieve the desired
result include natural seeding, replanting
after clearing with the same or another
species or planting under the shelter of
the existing stand. Various silvicultural
systems have been evolved to secure the
regeneration of forests in different con-

ditions; the more diverse the structure, the more complex the system. The simplest system (though not necessarily the best) is clearcutting followed by replanting. The most complicated selection system is that in which single scattered mature trees are removed periodically to encourage continuous natural regeneration and the maintenance of a permanent uneven-aged structure, normally of mixed species. This system is often used in mountain regions to prevent erosion.

Afforestation is the creation of new areas of forest or woodland on sites that have been without tree cover for a long period, often hundreds of years or even since prehistoric times. Such sites may have been used for agriculture and allowed to deteriorate or they have changed because of climatic factors, as in the case of sand-dune invasion or as a result of industrial dereliction such as slag heaps in a mining area. In nearly all cases afforestation is in fact restoration of tree cover after a long interval and in conditions totally different from those when the forest was there before.

The purpose of afforestation is often to satisfy the growing demand for industrial wood but other objectives, such as flood control, shelter, prevention of erosion or the amelioration of the climate (particularly in arid countries) are also important. It is estimated that there are about 100 million hectares (250 million acres) of newly-created forest in the world and that this figure will be doubled by the end of the 20th century. Large programs of afforestation have been carried out in many countries; the Tennessee Valley scheme restored the 'dust-bowl' to fertility in the 1930's and in the EEC countries it is proposed to afforest 5 million hectares (12 million acres) of 'surplus' agricultural land. But it is in the USSR and China that really massive programs of afforestation for timber production and shelter are now taking place.

The techniques required for afforestation often differ considerably from those used in the regeneration of existing forests. The conditions are nearly always harsh, the soil impoverished, exposure to wind or sun severe, and the risk of damage by animals and pests much greater than in the more stable forest ecosystem. In wet uplands the land must be drained and impacted soils must be broken up by some form of cultivation to enable the small tree roots to penetrate. On the arid slopes of hills in hot climates terracing may be necessary to conserve any rain that may

fall and in rocky terrain it is sometimes essential to import soil to enable the newly-planted trees to make a start. Fertilization of the soil, particularly with phosphates, is nearly always necessary.

The species of tree selected for afforestation are not necessarily the same as those of the indigenous forests of the region. Fast-growing species are needed to satisfy industrial needs and they must also be hardy to withstand the rigorous conditions as pioneers. This normally means that conifers will form the bulk of the crop that is planted and these are often exotic species not present in the natural forests of the country. Thus Sitka Spruce (*Picea sitchensis*) from North America is the principal species used in afforesting the wet uplands in Britain. The Monterey Pine (*Pinus radiata*) from California is the main species used in New Zealand and Australia and the Cuban Pine (*Pinus caribaea*) from the southeastern United States is extensively used in South Africa.

In some countries where conditions permit, broadleaved trees such as oaks, poplars (*Populus* spp), *Eucalyptus*, alder (*Alnus* spp) and birches are included in the initial planting; the more rigorous the conditions, however, the less chance there is for the successful establishment of a diverse crop in the original planting. Normally afforestation must be regarded as the pioneer stage in the restoration of a forest ecosystem which may take 50 or 100 years to re-establish. Nevertheless, even a monoculture of a pioneer coniferous species brings a great environmental gain to the site. Protection from grazing and disturbance, from wind and erosion, and the conservation of moisture, start the chain of events in the ecological develop-

ment of the site from a plantation to a forest with its diversity of composition and structure and flora and fauna.

Improvement of Existing Forests. The need to conserve natural forest systems for their environmental value, rather than replace them with man-made forest, and at the same time increase their potential production of utilizable wood, has been receiving increasing attention from foresters. The tropical rain forests, threatened by exploitation for their valuable timbers and by destruction through shifting cultivation, pose many silvicultural problems. Management to increase the productivity of useful species without destroying the primeval ecosystem is a complex matter. Natural regeneration is difficult to ensure and the introduction of exotic species involves the progressive destruction of the ecosystem. Only if foresters and biologists can work together with substantial research facilities at their command, can a solution be found before it is too late.

In the past the need for a country to formulate a national policy has been mainly dependent on the need for a sustained or increased yield from its forests to supply established wood-using industries. Underdeveloped countries have tended simply to exploit the forest to obtain capital for other purposes or land for agriculture. Today the situation is different; the energy crisis, combined with a dwindling forest area and rapidly rising population, demands a purposeful statement of forestry policy for the sake of Man's economic and social well-being.

Weed killing in a young plantation is essential to prevent fast-growing weeds and shrubs competing 'unfairly' with the young trees.

FOREST PRODUCTS

In an effort to conserve at least some of the natural habitat of tropical forests, yet still be able to crop the trees, experiments such as the planting of fast-growing *Maesopsis eminii* (shown here in Uganda) within natural forests that are only partly felled are being performed. These trees are about three years old and will be felled at about 35 years of age.

Forests provide one of the most important renewable resources in the world. The forests themselves are the habitat of many plants and animals and the home of many people of many races, who depend on these plants and animals for food, clothes, building materials, fuel and other supplies. In many parts of the world they serve as a source of a wide range of raw materials for major forest industries and for minor forest products. Many forests provide a source of recreation for the local population, particularly for those living in large cities and their associated conurbations.

From the many statistics associated with forestry and forest products, perhaps the most remarkable fact to emerge is that about half the world's annual forest crop is used as fuel (either as firewood or as charcoal) and that 90 percent of the population in the developing countries depend on wood as their only source of fuel.

The major forest industries are concerned with timber and timber products, plywood, wood chips, wood pulp and paper. The so-called minor forest products include: vegetable products, such as leaf fodder and litter; bark for use as cork or tanstuffs; ornamental trees and shrubs; medicinal plants; edible fruits, seed and other plant parts; naval stores; oils, fats, resins, turpentine, gums, latex, dyestuffs and sap sugar; fibers, yarns and flosses; osiers, canes, bamboos, reeds, rushes and thatching materials. Plants have also given rise to mineral products in the form of peat, lignite and coal.

Wood and Timber. The major forest industries are based on the utilization of part or all of the forest tree. Mature trees are felled, the branches removed and the trunk (or stem) cut into logs from which solid timber components are cut. In the early 1970's the annual world consumption of wood was estimated at 2 300 million cubic metres (81 000 million cubic feet) of which some 1 100 million cubic metres (39 000 million cubic feet) were used as fuel. The rest was processed for industrial purposes of which sawn timber accounted for two-thirds, paper nearly a quarter and panel products (plywood and other boards) about a tenth. About two-thirds of all the sawn timber or about 44 percent of all industrial wood was used for building construction. Of the paper over half was used

There are a number of essential components required for a national forestry policy in this context. Efficiency of production and harvesting the raw materials of the forest must be balanced against safeguards for the environment. For example, modern chemical sprays give the forester a powerful yet destructive weapon if not controlled. The dominant use in multiple-use forests must be defined. This may be protective rather than productive, as in the Alps. There is a need to define how the forest is to fulfill the national aims and there must be an input of investment in trained experts and money to gain a con-

tinuing output in raw materials.

More research is needed and this is paramount if the joint problems of increased supply of wood is to be combined with conservation of the environment. Genetic research is particularly important in order to achieve better growth in each region. It has been calculated that improvements in this field could raise the potential global yield to more than ten times the present figure without depleting the growing stock. One side effect would be greater scope for conservation within the forest. Forest managers at all levels must be trained in the scientific basis for the application of forestry techniques, which will result in greater yields of wood without damaging the environment.

Governments must also recognize the long-term nature of forestry and maintain policies that ensure continuity.

P. F. G.

necessary as infrequently as possible.

Appearance becomes more important as the value of the end product increases and, for such things as carvings, veneers, paneling and high-grade furniture, it is paramount in importance. Appearance is not a single property but a combination of many; the difference between wood and its substitutes is primarily that no two pieces of wood are identical. Color is determined partly by the quantity of cell wall in relation to cell lumen but also by the colors of various substances contained in the cells, normally of the heartwood. Changes in color are provided by growth rings and the patterns produced can be varied by cutting the wood in different ways. Oak, for instance, is normally more attractive quarter-sawn and elm flat-sawn. Strong differences in color patterns are often found in softwoods with a large contrast between early wood and late wood. Douglas Fir, when flat-sawn or peeled as a veneer, for example, shows prominent 'contour' patterns. Some woods have dark and light patches within the wood, for example olive wood.

Grain is a collective term describing the appearance of the patterns of cells and

for wrapping and packaging papers and about a quarter for writing and printing papers while about 17 percent went for newspapers. The rates of increase in the manufacture of paper and panel products (especially particle board) over the previous ten years had been much higher than for sawn timber but sawn timber still retains its position as the largest single product of industrial wood and will do so for a considerable time to come. The annual rate of increase in the use of industrial wood over the previous decade had been about 3.5 percent per annum (simple interest on the 1964–1973 decade).

Taking the total known area of the world's forests and calculating the quantity of wood which could, at present rates of growth, be added per year, gives an increment which amounts to about twice what is at present being removed. This calculation, however, ignores the fact that large areas of forest (16 million hectares – 40 million acres) in many countries are being turned over to agriculture each year and many of the present exporters of timber are aiming to meet not more than their own needs in the long-term future. Moreover, much of the world's forest area is situated in very remote areas and its utilization is likely to become increasingly costly. Planted forest to date only amounts to about 3–5 percent of the total exploitable forest area, so the vast majority of the wood cut at present is being 'mined' from forests not planted by Man and in which little or no capital has been invested before the harvesting operation. There is a strong likelihood, therefore, that wood, along

Timber lorries, a familiar site in Johore in the Malay Peninsula in the mid-1960's, when the primary lowland evergreen rain forests were being felled. The timber is virtually all from trees of the family Dipterocarpaceae.

with many other raw materials, will become increasingly scarce and costly. There is also evidence to suggest that it will be the higher quality timber necessary for joinery, furniture and other uses, where it has to pass exacting specifications, which will rise in cost faster than the lower quality wood. It takes longer to produce and requires more care in growing than, for example, wood grown to produce paper. Wood for fuel is easier still to grow.

The suitability of the wood of a particular species of tree for a particular use depends both on the properties of the wood imparted to it by the mixture and nature of the different tissues of which it is composed and on the requirements of that use. Ebony is no more used for making model airplanes than balsa wood is used for high-class carving. Wood 'quality' is something that can be judged only in terms of the product to be made from it. If a wood is to realize its full potential and to be utilized in an optimum fashion, it needs to find the highest value use for which there is a market and to be manufactured into the finished article with a minimum of waste and in such a way as to render the finished articles as durable as possible in order to make replacement

Logging in Finland. The logs (whole tree trunks) are stripped and floated down the river, and are then hauled out and stacked, before being taken to mills for processing.

A plantation of teak trees (*Tectona grandis*). Trees are killed by ring-barking and left standing for two or three years to dry out so that the timber can be transported by water.

tissues in the wood. The patterns of vessels, rays and parenchyma give rise to the prominent rings in ash and elm (vessels), the fleck in beech (rays) and the pattern of light-color wood around vessels in *Iroko* (parenchyma). Changes in grain direction result in waves in the grain and in an interlocked grain which, on quarter-cut timber, is shown up as the well-known stripe in such timbers as mahogany. About a quarter of all wood used industrially is made into furniture and joinery. Not all needs to be of good appearance and high quality but a good proportion must be so.

About another quarter of all industrial wood is used structurally in building where strength is an important property. Here the wood must be used in its natural form to make use of its peculiar property of being strong in resisting forces at right angles to the grain direction. It is unlikely that reconstituted wood will ever improve

on solid wood, used structurally, because its alignment in the tree is as near ideal as it is possible to get. Wood density is closely related to strength and since it is easy to measure can be used to predict strength; but there are variations in the strength/density ratio and some trees have more efficient wood than others. Shrinkage and movement are particularly important where wood components need to fit closely together as in such uses as furniture, joinery and flooring. Wood is also a good insulator, electrically, thermally and against sound. In this respect, provided it is well treated against rot, it has considerable advantages over metal for such uses as window and door frames.

There are, therefore, good reasons for preferring wood for so many things. It is common, renewable and infinitely variable. What is sometimes forgotten is that, although it does 'grow on trees,' it takes a very long time to do so and there is by no means an inexhaustible supply.

Minor Forest Products. The relative importance of minor forest products has changed over the years due to the effects of industrialization and the development of technology. Naval stores provide a good example. The term first appears in England in the 16th century and covers the very important group of shipbuilding materials, that is pitch, tar and timber, all derived from species of pine. These commodities have always been of vital importance for the building and caulking of wooden ships and waterproofing their associated ropes, rigging and cordage. Much of the naval strategy of the seafaring nations from the 16th to the 19th centuries was based on a regular and reliable supply of these materials.

Naval stores today are generally one of three types, known as gum, wood and sulfate naval stores. Gum naval stores are produced by tapping or wounding certain resinous species of pine, collecting the oleoresin and treating it to produce rosin and turpentine. Wood naval stores arise from the slow burning (or destructive distillation) of pine species under carefully controlled conditions to produce turpentine, pine oil, rosin and pitch or tar. Sulfate naval stores form a by-product of the 'Kraft' process for the chemical production of wood pulp. The material produced is known as tall oil and contains resin acids and fatty acids. The greater portion of tall

Coconut harvest on the island of Zanzibar off the east coast of Africa. The whole fruits are being split to separate the familiar 'nuts' from the fibrous husks.

oil undergoes further processing to produce rosin and fatty acids.

Naval stores now form part of what has been called the silvichemical industry, which is concerned with the production of chemicals from trees. The industry covers a wide range of materials, such as lignin derivatives, vanillin, essential oils, maple syrup, oleoresins, alkaloids, tannins, rubber, true gums, ethanol, acetic acid, vitamins and waxes.

Many plants growing in forests produce extracts that have important medicinal properties. In the tropical forests *Cinchona* spp are a source of quinine; *Carapa* spp growing in America and Africa provide medicinal materials from both bark and seeds; *Strychnos* spp give rise to a number of alkaloids, which combine medicinal properties with deadly poisons, such as strychnine, brucine and curarine (the active principle of curare).

Of the forest plants that are edible or produce edible fruits and seeds cocoa, coconut, coffee, tea, bananas and spices are all important examples. Latex and rubber are tapped both from the forest tree and from plantation-grown crops. Chicle, the basis of chewing gum, is a natural product from a forest tree and is obtained by tapping the tree every five years to collect the exudate. Dyestuffs such as indigo and logwood are important locally, although synthetic dyes have largely taken over the world market.

The products of the forest are many and varied and have served to provide for many of the needs of Man since earliest recorded

A Cluster Pine (*Pinus pinaster*) being tapped for resin. The resin exuding from the tree turns white and hardens on contact with the air. Scars of previous tappings can be seen below the cup.

times. Great areas of forest have already been destroyed but the importance of this renewable resource underlines the necessity for the conservation and plantation of forests for the benefit of future generations. It is a matter which cannot afford to be overlooked.   J. F. L.

Sheets of crude latex from the Para Rubber Tree (*Hevea brasiliensis*) are pounded into sheets and hung up to harden before being shipped to the factory for processing.

AMENITY OR URBAN FORESTRY

USA	30.00	Belgium	18.20
Great		Norway	23.80
Britain	6.10	Denmark	9.30
Germany	26.80	Netherlands	6.10
France	19.10	Ireland	3.10

At the onset of the Iron Age the greater part of Western Europe was covered with forest – spruces, pines and birches in Scandinavia, pines, firs, beeches and oaks in central Europe and the oaks, birches and firs in the British Isles. Early man feared the forest, not only for its darkness and wild animals, but also for the outlaws who frequented its vastness. Nevertheless, he took such timber, vines and stakes as he needed to satisfy his simple domestic requirements and cleared away the trees for pastures and crop production.

From earliest times trees have been venerated, used in religious symbolism and for aesthetic purposes. The *yggdrasil* of Norse mythology, a huge spreading ash tree, was the very pillar of the world, binding together earth, heaven and hell. Trees and groves were sacred to the Greeks, often being associated with particular deities: the Oak with Zeus, the Olive with Athena, the Laurel with Apollo. Such veneration did not prevent trees being felled but when virgin forest was cleared individual trees or clumps would be left as holy relics – a custom worthy of resurrection today. Transplanting of trees is known to have been practised as early as 1500 BC in Egypt and in classical times Theophrastus and Pliny recorded methods of tree care – probably the first records of arboricultural practise. The regard that society has had for trees is reflected in the countless place names which owe their origin to the trees which grew in the vicinity, while in poetry, prose and song, tree imagery is to be found in every language.

With the increasing sophistication of society in the Middle Ages the demands on the forest estates of the developing countries of the world increased to provide the raw materials for manufacturing industry. The extent of the forest clearing since early days can be seen from the accompanying table in which the area of woodland is given as a percentage of the total area of land in 1968 – for most of these countries the 'natural' forest cover should be over 80 percent.

Up to the 13th and 14th centuries, the administration and exploitation of natural forests was often controlled by royal authority. However, this patronage waned concurrently with an increased demand for forest resources in the form of naval stores and fuel for the early iron-smelting industries. The 'gaps' produced by such exploitation were soon filled by increasingly sophisticated agricultural demands and practises. The result was the loss throughout Europe of vast tracts of natural forest that were never replaced. Concern over the depletion of European forests was constantly being voiced. For example, legislation was enacted in 1581 to try to control the destruction of the oak forests to the south of London which were being exploited for the production of charcoal for the iron-smelting industry.

From the view of amenity forestry there was, however, one clear benefit from this age. The period from the 15th to the 19th century was a time of naval powers, colonization and exploration – all made possible because of the forest resources of the homelands. With the opening up of new lands, thousands of new and curious plants were discovered, many of which were trees. This supply of unusual plants was further stimulated by their becoming fashionable among the new upper classes. The age of the landscape garden in which trees formed a primary part had started. Specimen tree collections in the form of arboreta and artificial landscapes began to appear in earnest during the 18th century, especially around the family residences of estates in Great Britain and in France, for example the work of Alphand in Paris. It reached its peak in the 19th century and even today we owe many of our landscape gardens to the endeavors of estate foresters a century or more ago.

The earliest manual on tree care both for their timber and their fruit was John Evelyn's *Sylva – a Discourse of Forest Trees and the Propagation of Timber* (1664), in which reference to previous work is made and detailed directions are given on the care of trees.

Following the ravages of two world wars the landscape of Europe needed to be rejuvenated and towns and cities rebuilt. At this time there was an increasing awareness of the contribution that trees make to the quality of life so that many government authorities at local and central level made resources available for the planting and maintenance of trees in both urban and rural areas. Many new towns also sprung up in which provision was made for new plantings while at the same time preserving the existing tree population, especially where they formed essential features of the landscape. Professional associations lobbied legislatures to enact regulations to provide for due consideration to the preservation and conservation of treed landscapes which were threatened by development. Fragile areas were given special status, for example the designation in Great Britain of Areas of Outstanding Natural Beauty and Sites of Special Scientific Interest, and the provision of Tree Preservation Orders. Tree planting grants to private individuals and organizations were made available from government-sponsored agencies such as the Countryside Commission in Great Britain. A further reflection of the growing interest in trees and the demand for instruction is to be found in the significant increase in the number of volumes that can be found in any bookshop.

Despite this increased public awareness and the protective legislation, the destruction of trees still continues, and this does not include just those forests and woodlands which are deliberately cropped for the timber that they produce. The systematic management of trees for the production of a raw material is just as essential for any society as the cropping of a field of grain, as both instances are examples of plants being used in the service of Man. The thoughtless parking of cars has been responsible for the loss of many elegant city and town trees. Vandalism in major cities contributes to pointless casualties, especially in new landscapes. Many authorities prefer to record their tree planting progress by the number of trees planted instead of those which become successfully established. In far too many cases new trees end up merely as supports for their stakes because there are not sufficient funds to allow for aftercare.

Discouraging as these disappointments

An example of good urban tree-planning from Ottawa, Canada. By careful planting of new trees and retention of existing ones, the harsh outlines of large buildings, such as the factory in the right background, have been softened. This sort of planning is sadly often not normally carried out.

are, far greater loss and mutilation of trees occur in the name of progress, perpetrated by sections of the community who should know better. Those involved with the development or use of land must carry a large share of the blame. Modern society requires houses, factories and roads and, except in a limited number of cases, rural areas and the parklands landscaped during past centuries are lost to urban and industrial demands. It is only when loud local protests have been mounted that, for example, motorway planners have been forced to realign routes which initially were carved through irreplaceable trees and wooded areas. An awareness of the damage to the landscape that motorway construction can cause has resulted in many fine planting schemes financed by central government. Trees are not necessarily just ornamental additions to our environment; trees lining a trunk road give protection from wind turbulence, thereby increasing highway safety. Other benefits include reduction in noise levels (in so far as tree noises, for example the rustle of leaves, mask traffic roar) and the alleviation of glare caused by buildings.

Housing development consumes large numbers of trees despite the conditions

Compaction of soil around the roots and reduced water availability can put roadside trees under stress. This scene in Oxford, England shows lime trees (*Tilia* sp) that were planted at the same time; the tall but sparsely branched street trees are clearly less healthy than the garden tree behind.

placed by planning authorities on their retention and protection. The alteration of the water table following disruption of the soil during building operations, the laying down of hard surfaces – concrete and tarmacadam – and the excavation and filling which alter the configuration of the land, deprive existing trees of their sources of moisture to the extent that they are placed under stress during a time when they are attempting to adjust to the changed environment they find themselves in. In this respect it is as well to remember that a tree has no option but to die when its environment changes for the worse. The provision of utility services involves digging trenches to lay down pipes for gas and electricity and when major roots are cut to allow their passage not only is the stability and nutrient source of the tree in jeopardy but fungal pathogens such as *Ganoderma applanatum* can gain entry into the cut surfaces. The resulting incipient growth goes unnoticed until spectacular bracket-shaped fruiting bodies appear as a precursor to the complete collapse of the tree. Badly-laid gas pipes which leak can kill trees in a very short time as has been found in Holland.

The tree can often be cited as a villain when this is far from the truth. The drought of 1976 in Western Europe caused clay soils to shrink which in turn caused structural failure of buildings. Because it has been shown that trees reduce the moisture content of soil, trees were blamed for the structural failures. Attempts were therefore made to limit tree growth to a distance from buildings equivalent to $1\frac{1}{2}$–2 times their mature height which, if enforced, would result in a treeless suburbia. While there is no denying the fact that trees in proximity to houses which have been built on shrinkable clays can be associated with structural failure during periods of dry weather, inadequate foundations are equally to blame.

Planners and local government agencies are often torn between the demands for housing and the demands for an acceptable living area. Local conservation groups are seen as interfering busybodies and the voices of protest have great difficulty in countering the economic or political arguments (spurious or real) which are presented for the destruction of trees. A compromise solution is usually arrived at when conflicting interests meet but these solutions are often overtaken by events. For example, trees may be retained so near to a new structure that their removal is necessitated within a twelve-month period of the completion of the building because they have deteriorated to such an extent, due to damage during construction, that they become a danger.

Individual owners of trees must also take a share of the blame for the mutilation of trees and their destruction. Many owners resort to the practise of lopping or pollarding in the mistaken idea that the pruning reduces the thickness of the branches or will stop, for example, the drip of honeydew from limes and sycamores which ruins the protective paint of cars. This practise of lopping to remove a 'nuisance' only alleviates the problem for a short time, as the rejuvenating processes produce a proliferation of branches which in a few years forms a denser growth than before and once again lopping is necessary. The cut ends or pollarding points develop areas of rot due to fungal infection of the cut surfaces and this rot slowly eats its way down the trunk. In the end a hideous tree looking like a hatstand in the winter and a lavatory brush in the summer is formed. Correct pruning procedures and skillful thinning of the canopy can alleviate the supposed nuisances without disfiguring the tree. In such instances it is essential to consult a professional tree surgeon if the best results are to be obtained. On new developments the correct choice of trees to enhance a property prevents the problem of trees overtaking the limited space available. The average suburban property is not large enough to support a tree of forest proportions and therefore it is wiser to plant the smaller type tree – birches (*Betula* spp) or rowans (*Sorbus* spp), for example, or some of the smaller maples, for example, *Acer griseum* or *A. hersii*, rather than the beeches, oaks, or monkey puzzles, which are best incorporated in special areas in the form of spinneys or copses. In rural areas, hedgerows have been the traditional site for trees since the loss of the true forest cover and are, in effect, linear nature reserves. The effects of diseases, such as Dutch Elm Disease, and the reduction of hedges are continuing to alter the landscape. The arable farmer complains of trees reducing his cropping areas or of the damage the roots of trees can cause to expensive machinery. He is justified in making these complaints but in every farm there are areas which cannot be cropped and where groups of trees could be planted to form spinneys and copses. Stock requires shade – protection in the summer and in the winter – and therefore good cattle husbandry includes the provision of trees in pastures. Having provided protection and shelter these same trees can produce timber for use in the estate or farm in the centuries to come.

With the greater mobility of city populations of the Western world, their demand for recreational areas has introduced the concept of amenity woodlands – areas of trees set aside for their aesthetic and recreational value as opposed to their timber production potential. The proximity of these woodlands to population centers dictates the frequency with which the woodlands are used. Their management, usually the responsibility of local authori-

Bad ground preparation, poor growing conditions and lack of social conscience have all contributed to this sad, but not infrequent scene, from Washington DC, United States, where the planted Maidenhair Trees (*Ginkgo biloba*) contribute little more to the landscape than the telegraph poles they mimic.

Proper tree maintenance is a job for experts, not only for the professional skill they employ, but also for the precautions required to undertake such hazardous tasks as trimming the end of a branch with reasonable safety.

ties, has to take into account the pressures which visitors place on the delicate balance of a woodland ecosystem. That local authorities should be expected to look after recreational woodlands would seem an obvious step when the organizational skills in the maintenance of public parks and street trees already exist. The concept of so-called 'urban forestry' has been with us for two decades and in the first instance this revealed the gulf in understanding between the management practises required for individual urban trees and the silvicultural practises required to manage a forest or woodland. Urban forestry, which was first developed in Canada, has been defined as a practise that 'does not deal entirely with city trees or with single tree management but rather with tree management in the entire area influenced and utilized by the urban population.' By definition, a forest or plantation managed for the production of timber comes within the above definition of the urban forest. Government forest departments have now realized the recreational value of the commercial forest. In Holland, forests are opened for recreational purposes once the initial establishment stage has been completed and in Great Britain forest walks are now to be found in all the large afforested areas. Even private forests have recently been opened to the public by provision of,

for example, nature trails. In North America and Scandinavia vast tracts of forest are open to the public for recreation purposes.

Amenity woodlands and commercial forests therefore require the same approach. Because the landscape of Europe has been manipulated by Man to the extent that natural forest is virtually nonexistent and is confined to the more remote areas, management of woodlands for amenity is essential. The forester aims at what is termed a sustained yield and hence income. For the amenity forester the value of woodlands is expressed in terms of social benefit, which means that external finance is required. However, there is no reason why woodland areas cannot be managed at two levels – the income from the true forestry used to subsidize the amenity facilities. In an amenity woodland, trees have to be replaced, and therefore silvicultural practises are demanded just as they are in the commercial forest.

Trees have been referred to as the furniture of the landscape and for their survival all members of society must take their share of responsibility. It is irresponsible for the public to demand both conservation measures from the public authorities and unrestricted access to woodlands. The compaction of the soil by many feet and the dumping of litter caused by open access, for example, will only hinder conservation measures. The task of maintaining a national heritage such as the country's rural and urban landscape is enormous and initiative rests with all, not just a few, if the inheritance is to be passed on to future generations.

T. H. R. H.

An example of typical 'lawnmower disease,' seen here on a maple (*Acer* sp) trunk. Careless control of mowing machines not only results in unsightly scars but the nutrition of the tree suffers, while the wounds are foci for fungal infection and/or insect infestation.

DISEASES AND PESTS OF TREES

From early times trees have played an important part in Man's technological development. This readily available natural resource was used for tools, fuel, shade, shelter and food. Much later, when Man came to raise trees under the less natural conditions of productive forestry, a need arose to concern himself with their diseases and pests. The early work on tree diseases was carried out in Germany by Robert Hartig in the late 19th century. Since that time science has provided a far greater understanding of both the tree and its disorders, and has often helped to minimize losses. Occasionally this has been achieved by direct control measures, but more often through disease avoidance.

Parasitic organisms causing disease (pathogens) are a legacy from the ancient natural forest. There they played an important role in a balanced ecosystem by assisting in the death and destruction of the old and the weaker trees, thus providing space and soil enrichment for the survivors. To a large extent Man has now taken over the role of natural selection by choosing his species and the individuals that he wishes to survive, but the pathogens remain, and are a potential threat to his trees. Trees can outlive all other plants; they have achieved this unique longevity by evolving highly efficient defenses against the entry of those organisms which seek to use them as a source of nutrition. A tree presents a veritable larder of food for those organisms that can overcome its defensive barriers or bypass them through wounds. Most pathogenic microorganisms attempt to gain entry by using a form of chemical and physical warfare. The tree's defense operates in a similar way, mostly employing complex chemicals which interfere with, or present a barrier to, the growth of the invader.

In any disease syndrome, three major factors are involved: the pathogen, the tree and the environment. These are constantly interacting and in any disease investigation no single factor should be considered in isolation. Different strains of a pathogen may vary in their aggressiveness, and individual trees of the same species can vary in their inherent ability to resist infection. Many pathogens have very specialized requirements, often having a very limited host range, and may flourish only under certain environmental conditions. Adverse environmental factors such as drought, water-excess, soil compaction and pollution can cause stress, sometimes weakening some part of the trees' defenses. Many fungal pathogens and insect pests can be quick to take advantage of weakened 'stressed' trees and their presence may cause sufficient further stress for the survival of the trees to be in jeopardy. However, a return to more favorable conditions for growth may enable a tree to overcome the pathogen or pest and recover, with the loss perhaps of only a small part of the tree.

Financial losses from diseases, pests and other adverse agents in the forest are enormous. It is estimated that around half these losses are caused by diseases (which cause mortalities, growth reduction and decay); the remaining losses are due to insect pests, fire, and other factors, in more or less equal proportions. However, in any locality at a particular time, any one of these agents can be of prime importance. Amenity trees grown for ornamentation or shade are normally less prone than forest trees to large-scale losses. This is mainly because the diversity of species used and their sporadic distribution make it more difficult for a pathogen to become widely established. However, the loss of a single tree growing in an important position can be as disastrous to the urban arborist as a hundred or more trees to the forester.

Control. Wherever possible the control of pests and diseases of trees should be achieved through good management rather than by employing more intensive chemical methods. This is because the longevity of trees may necessitate the repeated application of chemical treatments over long periods of time to give lasting protection. This could be uneconomic and may be damaging to the environment. Biological control methods, utilizing natural enemies or antagonists of pests and disease agents, have attracted much attention in recent years, especially with regard to insect pests, since they are cheap, nonpolluting and may be self-perpetuating. There are still, however, relatively few instances where such methods are used, although the use of insect pathogens, especially viruses, is now being assessed. With some insect pests, however, there may be no practical alternative to chemicals.

More intensive control methods become worthwhile for high value amenity trees. Such trees, growing along roads and in small gardens in towns, can experience a wide variety of stress factors. Frequently the arborist can only minimize physical damage and ensure an adequate supply of water, nutrients and air to the roots, so that the natural defense mechanisms can function effectively. To avoid disease problems it is important to select the most suitable species or variety of tree and to apply stringent regulations on the importation of plant material or timber, which may carry a foreign disease or pest into a country.

Diseases. Although the spore-bearing structures (sporophores) such as 'toadstools' and 'brackets' are conspicuous, the principal part of a fungus consists of a network of fine strands (hyphae) which individually are invisible to the eye. These hyphae ramify through the soil or other substrate, absorbing and transporting nutrients. Not all fungi produce such obvious sporophores; in some species they are microscopic, in others they appear as tiny pustules on leaves or twigs. Fungi are classified on the form these structures take. Most types of fungi rely on wind to transport their spores, but rain, insects and other animals may also facilitate their spread. Normally spores are produced in vast numbers, as only a small number ever reach their goal and initiate a new infection. When a spore reaches a suitable substrate it germinates, producing a hypha which attempts to penetrate the cells of the host. If the cells are susceptible, the fungus may continue to grow and thus establish a new infection. Most trees are, however, resistant to attack by most fungi. If a spore alights on a resistant plant, as is frequently the case, fungal development is prevented at an early stage. As well as dispersal by spores some fungi, in particular those infecting roots, may spread locally by means of extensive hyphal growth.

Diseases caused by microorganisms can be broadly characterized according to the parts of the tree where the infection occurs, although the more obvious symptoms of the disease may be manifested elsewhere. In particular, the first symptoms of root diseases often become apparent in the crown. This is well illustrated by the diseases caused by *Phytophthora cinnamomi*, a fungus of very wide host range and the agent of Littleleaf Disease of pines and the Jarrah Dieback of *Eucalyptus* in Australia. These diseases are seen as a slowing of growth or as death of parts of the crown, but the fungus infects and destroys the fine feeder roots of the tree. This fungus has motile spores which are actively attracted to suitable host roots. It is favored by wet soils, through which these spores readily move.

In contrast, other root-infecting fungi may attack the woody roots of their hosts. Such a pathogen is the Honey (or Shoestring) Fungus (*Armillariella mellea* = *Armillaria mellea*) which is very common throughout the world, attacking a wide range of trees and shrubs. The Honey Fungus can spread from a well-colonized root system for several metres through the soil by means of rhizomorphs. These are black shoestring-like strands of aggregated hyphae which are well suited to survive the rigors of the soil environment. On contacting a suitable host these rhizomorphs penetrate the bark of the roots and the hyphae grow through both bark and wood, killing and decaying the infected roots. As the proportion of infected roots gradually increases, crown symptoms may appear in the form of sparse or pale foliage. Large trees, however, often tolerate considerable amounts of root infection without noticeable symptoms, and succumb to lethal levels of invasion only after being weakened by an additional stress factor such as drought. The honey-colored toadstools of the fungus are often produced in clusters around the base of killed trees or old stumps, but the spores they produce rarely initiate new infections. The best means of control is the removal of infected stumps and roots from which the rhizomorphs are produced.

Heterobasidion annosum (*Fomes annosus*), another root-decaying fungus, can be particularly detrimental to many managed coniferous forests. Unlike the Honey Fungus, the spores of *Heterobasidion* are important in its spread. New centers of infection are initiated when spores colonize the stumps of recently-felled trees. The fungus then spreads down into the roots of the colonized stump, infecting neighboring living trees via root contacts, which occur frequently in forest plantations. In Britain the spread of this fungus has been greatly reduced by applying chemicals to the stumps to prevent the initial establishment of the pathogen. In the case of pines, which are frequently killed by the fungus, a biological control method is used; spores of a harmless saprophytic fungus are applied to the stumps. This fungus grows rapidly in the stumps and prevents establishment of the pathogen.

Both *Heterobasidion annosum* and the Honey Fungus can also spread into the bole of infected trees and cause decay. Some other decay-causing fungi, including *Poria weirii* and *Polyporus tomentosus*, both of which can cause extensive loss of timber in North America, also spread from tree to tree via root contacts. There are numerous other fungi which cause decay in standing trees. Many of these are incapable of attacking the living tissues of their hosts, but grow actively in the dead inner wood of trees. Such fungi usually require some form of wound to establish infection. Suitable wounds may be produced when branches die or break off, or may be made by humans either inadvertently, or deliberately in the process of pruning. Various fungi, such as *Ganoderma applanatum*, frequently cause decay in old ornamental trees, rendering them unsafe, while others like *Phellinus pini* can

cause considerable loss of timber. Such fungi do not affect the vigor of the tree, which may show no obvious outward sign that decay is present. The presence of sporophores of these fungi is, however, a sure indication of decay.

Other types of fungi can attack the living tissues of the bark, some giving rise to cankers. These may spread rapidly, girdling and killing the infected stem, or may attack only a more restricted area, sometimes persisting for many years. *Endothia parasitica*, which causes Chestnut Blight, is a pathogen of the former, more aggressive type. It also provides an example of the damage a pathogen can do when introduced by Man to a new, highly susceptible

host. The disease was first noticed in the United States in 1904 and is believed to have been imported with chestnuts from Asia. Once established it rapidly spread through the highly susceptible native population of American Chestnut (*Castanea dentata*), leaving few mature survivors. Attempts to eradicate the Chestnut Blight came too late, when the disease was already well established. Chestnut Blight has now reached southern Europe, but its effects there have been less severe than in North America. In contrast to the more aggressive bark pathogens, the canker on hardwoods caused by *Nectria galligena* has less overall effect on the vigor of infected trees, although small branches may be

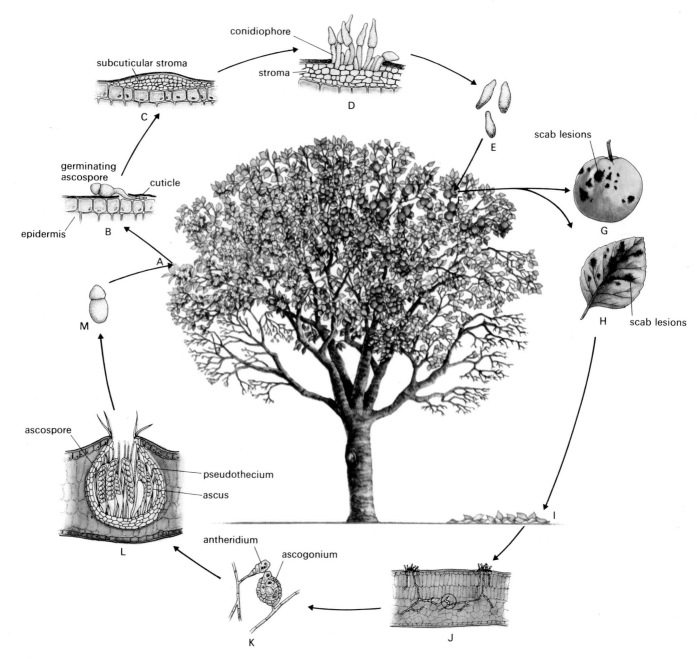

killed. The area of infected tissue extends slowly when the tree is inactive in winter, but in summer the tree puts on healing growth. These cankers may persist for many years.

Many of the rust fungi cause cankers. These fungi are specialized parasites, having a complex life-cycle, usually involving two different hosts. The most destructive is the White Pine Blister Rust (*Cronartium ribicola*) which causes spreading cankers and can kill susceptible pines. The spores produced on infected pines cannot directly reinfect pines, they must first infect currant plants (*Ribes* spp) on which spores are produced which can then infect other pines. In theory the eradication of *Ribes* in the vicinity of susceptible trees should control the disease, but this has proved impractical, and rust-resistant varieties of pine are being developed by plant breeders.

Some fungal pathogens may thrive in the conducting vessels of the tree, through which they can spread very rapidly. These diseases are called vascular wilts, and are seen as a more or less rapid wilting of the foliage, followed by death of the infected branches. These symptoms are caused by an interruption in the supply of water to the crown owing to the diseased condition of the vessels. Dutch Elm Disease, which, like the Chestnut Blight, has been inadvertently spread by Man, is a typical vascular wilt disease. The fungus (*Ceratocystis ulmi*) is spread from tree to tree by Elm Bark Beetles (*Scolytus scolytus*). These vectors become contaminated with spores of the fungus as they emerge from their

breeding galleries in the bark of infected trees. Before breeding again, the beetles feed on young elm twigs, and frequently introduce the spores into feeding-wounds. From these wounds the fungus rapidly spreads through the vessels to colonize the entire tree. Oak Wilt, caused by the fungus *Ceratocystis fagacearum*, is a very similar disease principally damaging red oaks. It too is spread by vectors, but these are less efficient than those of Dutch Elm Disease. Both Dutch Elm Disease and Oak Wilt can also spread on a local basis between the root systems of adjacent trees where root grafts may occur naturally. Oak Wilt is currently restricted to certain parts of the United States and stringent quarantine measures are in operation in an attempt to prevent the introduction of this disease into Europe. Sanitation felling and removal of diseased trees has been used to slow the spread of both these diseases and locally this has met with some success. Injection of fungicides to protect specimen trees has also been tried but generally success has been rather limited. The symptoms of Elm Phloem Necrosis are not readily distinguished from those of Dutch Elm Disease, but are probably caused by a mycoplasma-like organism which appears to be a specialized type of bacterium. This disease is also currently restricted to the United States.

In contrast to diseases of roots and stems, the diseases of leaves of trees are of relatively minor importance, except on very young trees. Many species of fungi can infect leaves, causing local areas of discoloration or death. One of the most striking is Tar Spot of maples (*Acer* spp) and the European Sycamore (*Acer pseudoplatanus*), which produces large black spots in the leaves in late summer. These are resting structures, enabling the fungus (*Rhytisma acerinum*) to overwinter on fallen leaves before producing its spores in spring to infect the new foliage. Overwintering is a major problem for fungi that infect the leaves of deciduous trees: most species overwinter on fallen leaves in this manner, but some may survive in the buds of their hosts. Infection of ornamental trees can often be reduced by the simple expedient of removing infected fallen leaves in winter. On conifers leaf diseases tend to be more serious as the needles are normally functional for several years. Although broadleaved trees can withstand quite extensive defoliation or leaf damage, loss of foliage in the case of conifers tends to be accompanied by a corresponding reduction in vigor.

Some diseases of leaves can also infect young shoots, killing them, though this progressive dying of twigs from their tips, commonly termed 'dieback,' can also be a secondary symptom of many other tree disorders. *Gnomonia veneta* causes a disfiguring dieback on plane (*Platanus* spp) trees, and *Scleroderris lagerbergii* can be damaging on certain conifers. The latter fungus typically only causes serious damage on weakened trees, and is unimportant on vigorous, healthy specimens.

Bacteria are very small single-celled microorganisms, typically a few thousandths of a millimetre long. They reproduce by dividing into two identical cells and these vegetative cells serve also for their dissemination, which is usually by rain splash or animal vectors. Bacteria are much less important than fungi as a cause of disease in trees, although a few notable exceptions exist, such as Fire-Blight, caused by *Erwinia amylovora*, and a canker on poplars (*Populus* spp) caused by *Xanthomonas populi* (*Aplanobacter populi*). This may be because their unicellular growth habit is less well adapted to colonizing solid substrates than the hyphae of fungi.

Viruses, which can also cause disease in trees, are as yet rather poorly understood, but it seems likely that they are of only minor importance. They are submicroscopic pathogens which require living host cells in order to reproduce. Virus spread usually requires vectors such as sap-sucking insects or nematodes, although they may also spread from place to place in seed and from tree to tree in pollen. Viruses normally cause only mild disfigurement of the foliage in the form of yellow mottling but may also reduce growth, sometimes without causing leaf symptoms. Although virus spread may be

Tar Spot lesions on a Sycamore (*Acer pseudoplatanus*) leaf caused by the microscopic fungus *Rhytisma acerinum*.

Opposite The developmental changes in a plant pathogen are critically adjusted to the seasonal growth of the host plant. Shown here is the disease cycle of the fungus *Venturia inaequalis*, the causal agent of scab of apples. Infections are established in the spring by ascospores that infect young leaves (A) while the tree is in blossom. The germinating ascospore (B) penetrates the cuticle of the leaf and grows to form a subcuticular stroma (C) that then produces flame-shaped conidia (D). This marks the start of the asexual stage of the life cycle. The conidia are dispersed by rain splash (E) to reinfect young apples and leaves (F). Further growth occurs as before (B-D), causing olive-colored scab lesions on the fruit (G) and leaves (H). The fruit also becomes misshapen and cracked. In the fall, infected leaves drop to the ground (I), and thread-like hyphae grow into the mesophyll of the dead leaf (J). Male reproductive organs (antheridia) and female reproductive organs (ascogonia) are formed and where hyphae from compatible strains meet, sexual reproduction occurs (K). The pseudothecia thus formed act as overwintering organs, forming in the spring mature perithecia containing ascospores (L). The ascospores thus formed (M) start the new cycle of infection.

reduced by removing infected trees and killing the vectors, infections cannot readily be cured, so healthy planting stock should always be used.

Pests. Trees may also be damaged by many insects, mites and eelworms (nematodes), which use trees as sources of food. Plant material is not very nutritious and these pests need to eat large quantities to survive, thus causing serious damage to trees. Most insects with a potential for causing such damage are kept in check by climate, the tree's defenses (for example leaf toughness and toxic chemicals), predators, parasites, and competition for food and space. If the balance of these factors is upset, for example by uniform planting of a single species (monoculture) which pro-

vides an extensive food supply, pest outbreaks may ensue. Similarly, insecticide usage may result in the breakdown of regulation by natural predators.

Often the most obvious insects to a casual observer are those which feed by chewing leaves, the defoliators. Many groups of insects, such as the larvae of moths (order Lepidoptera) and sawflies (order Hymenoptera) live in this way. Some beetles (order Coleoptera) and, in warmer climates, grasshoppers (order Orthoptera) and stick insects (order Phasmida) can also become pests. The Gypsy Moth (*Lymantria dispar = Porthetria dispar*) is arguably the most serious defoliator of broadleaved trees in North America. First introduced from Europe in 1869, the Gypsy Moth has spread to become a pest over 520 000 square kilometres (200 000 square miles); it has had few natural enemies to stop it and no problems of food shortage as the caterpillars feed on a large variety of both broadleaved and coniferous trees. Complete removal of the leaves each season results in death after two or three years.

Cycle of devastation – Dutch Elm Disease. *Left* This disease is caused by the fungus *Ceratocystis ulmi*, which is spread by the Elm Bark Beetle (*Scolytus scolytus*), seen here on a piece of bark bearing the mycelium and spore-bearing structures of the fungus. *Below Left* The disease kills the trees by blocking the water-conducting vessels in the wood with balloon-like enlargements (tyloses) as seen in this transverse section of a piece of elm wood. *Below Center* A typical bark gallery of the Elm Bark Beetle which can frequently be seen on pieces of dead elm bark. *Below Right* English Elms (*Ulmus procera*) showing the characteristic leaf yellowing that marks the onset of the disease.

Some insects feed directly on sap and have piercing or sucking mouthparts. These include capsid bugs, leaf hoppers, aphids, mealybugs and scale insects (order Hemiptera). One of the most common tree aphids in Western Europe is *Elatobium abietinum* (*Neomyzophis abietina*) the Green Spruce Aphid. Its effects are typical of many herbivorous Hemiptera: the leaf becomes discolored around the site of feeding. This discoloration may spread to produce large blotches, sometimes followed by total browning and leaf fall. Aphids rarely cause tree death, though growth may be diminished. Scale insects, as adults, live under protective layers of waxy wool or under hard shells. Some species feed on the stems instead of the leaves, as in the case of the Felted Beech Coccus (*Cryptococcus fagi*). This feeds on the bark of beech trees, covering the infected areas with a white 'wool.' The combined effect of the damage caused by this feeding, and the fungus *Nectria* sp, which may subsequently enter, often kills areas of the bark in a syndrome known as Beech Bark Disease, which may kill the tree.

Despite the environmental damage that may result from the use of chemicals, it is often necessary to control severe outbreaks of both 'chewing' and 'sucking' insect pests if extensive destruction of trees is to be avoided. Currently, research is progressing into breeding trees resistant to herbivores, as well as into biological methods for their control.

The larvae of certain small moths (order Lepidoptera) and flies (order Diptera)

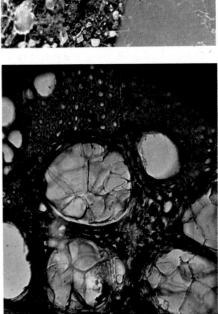

Some common diseases of apple: (1) Leaf Roller; (2) Apple Sawfly grub; (3) Woolly Aphid; (4) capsid bugs; (5) Apple Scab; (6) Apple Blossom Weevil; (7) Apple Worm; (8) Codling Moth; (9) wingless female of Winter Moth laying eggs; Looper Caterpillars behind; (10) apple mummified by Brown Rot.

burrow within leaves, feeding on the internal tissues and leaving visible tunnels. Nearly every holly bush in Britain shows the effects of the Holly Leaf Miner (*Phytomyza ilicis*). Galls are structures developed by the plant in response to feeding by certain insects and mites. Sycamores and maples frequently have their leaf surfaces covered with small bright red swellings, produced by mites of the genus *Eriophyes*. Although unsightly, leaf miners and galls rarely cause much economic damage.

Some insects live in shoots, bark and/or wood. Caterpillars of the Pine Shoot Moth (*Rhyaciona buoliana*) burrow into the buds and leading shoots of pines, killing the tips or distorting them. This species and its relatives are particularly troublesome in young plantations in Europe and North America.

The pests considered so far infest more or less healthy trees; however, bark and wood borers rely in the main on trees with

reduced vigor. Bark beetles (family Scolytidae) have been mentioned previously. The wood-boring larvae of woodwasps, moths, and especially beetles venture farther into the wood, although initially they may live just under the bark. In Europe and North America, one of the largest wood-boring beetle families is the Cerambycidae, the longhorn beetles. External signs of attack vary; when main trunks are infested no evidence is found until the bark begins to fall off, or adult exit holes appear in it. In those species which burrow into thinner stems, localized swellings and bark splittings can occur, as in the case of *Saperda populnea*, the Poplar Longhorn, a widespread pest over much of Europe, Asia and North America. The best control methods for bark and wood borers center around the removal of dead or unhealthy, including felled, timber before it can be used for breeding. Logs which cannot be processed in time can be protected with persistent insecticides.

Most species of tree benefit greatly from symbiotic relationships between their roots and fungi. Some nematodes, for example *Aphelenchus* sp feed on these mycorrhizal fungi. In forest nurseries, nematodes such as *Pratylenchus* feed as parasites on the roots of conifer seedlings, resulting in

stunted, sickly or dead plants. The roots of mature trees can also be attacked by nematodes, although the actual damage caused has rarely been assessed. Soil-inhabiting nematodes can be controlled by use of soil fumigants.

In addition to predisposing trees to diseases and insect pests, nonliving (abiotic) factors can alone cause considerable damage to trees. Droughts or excesses of water, extremes of temperature, wind, snow, fire and nutrient deficiencies can all weaken or damage trees. In the case of urban trees additional factors such as pollution, soil compaction and vandalism may be involved. Many of these can lead to the ingress of wood-decaying fungi. Additionally, trees weakened by root disease or decay may be more severely damaged by these environmental factors.

Despite the numerous pests and diseases that can attack trees, the majority survive to maturity and fulfill the purpose for which they were grown. It is only in exceptional circumstances, as, for example, with Dutch Elm Disease, that pests or diseases endanger the survival of whole tree populations. Such instances are generally attributable to the activities of Man upsetting the balance of natural systems.

D. K. B./R. B. P./M. R. S.

Trees of Every Kind

Three main types of trees are popularly recognized in terms of a single character – the leaf. They are the **conifers** with basically needle- and scale-like leaves, the **broadleaves** which primarily have flattened simple or compound leaves that are generally smaller than those of the third group, the **monocotyledon trees** such as the palms, in which they are also flattened but mainly fan-like or fern-like in appearance. Today there is no doubt that the broadleaves are the dominant natural tree-form throughout the world, except in the more extreme cooler climates where conifers still prevail. In temperate and warm temperate areas in particular, forestry policy is often to replace natural broadleaved forest or grassland with conifer monoculture under which conditions these trees thrive.

The palms are mainly tropical with only a few of the 2 800 species occurring in the subtropics and temperate regions. They are an ancient group and there is some evidence that their distribution was once wider even in the tropics, for example more species in Africa.

Today, the conifers are the only gymnosperms that occur in any quantity. Their history extends back some 300 million years but today they only dominate the cooler and cold areas of the world, such as the vast Boreal Region of the Northern Hemisphere and mountain habitats throughout the world. Their continuing success compared with other gymnosperm groups is probably due in part to the evolution of drought resistant features such as the needle- and scale-like leaves. Other gymnosperms with a tree-form are represented by two quite differing groups – the **cycads** and the **Maidenhair Tree** (*Ginkgo biloba*). Both these are the barest relicts of a flora that dominated the world during Mesozoic times, 225 to about 64 million years ago, although their evolu-

tionary history extends back at least as far as that of the conifers.

The only other primitive tree-like forms found today are the so-called **tree-ferns** which represent only a small proportion of the 12 000 species of all ferns and although the fossil record of tree-ferns extends back only about 190 million years the record of all ferns goes back 350 million years. It is interesting to observe the similarity in gross form between tree-ferns, cycads and palms, all groups that have evolved at quite different times and along vastly different lines, not the least in forms of reproduction.

The last group of tree-like species to be considered are the so-called 'tree cacti,' which are highly specialized plants adapted to harsh desert climates. In purely botanical terms they could be considered broadleaves, since they are dicotyledonous angiosperms, but because the majority lack true leaves, having spines instead, and because, at least in the young stage, mechanical support is given by the water

storage tissue of the photosynthetic tissues not the wood, these plants bear little resemblance to the conventional broad-leaved tree. Here we therefore give them separate treatment.

In this chapter 'Trees of Every Kind' we treat all these groups. Conifers, broadleaves and monocotyledon trees clearly take up to greatest space but tree ferns, cycads, the Maidenhair Tree and 'tree cacti' all have comprehensive coverage for their size. In the conifers section all genera found throughout the world have been included, despite the fact that many of the

Below Right Palms are a characteristic flora of the tropics and few people would fail to recognize the typical palm form, as with this *Livistona tahanensis*. However, this palm-like form has also evolved at other times and still exists today in two other vastly different groups – the cycads as with this *Lepidozamia hoperi (Below Center)* and tree-ferns like *Dicksonia antarctica (Opposite Bottom)*.
Opposite Top Conifers and broadleaves in cultivation. From left to right: Holly (*Ilex aquifolium*), Monkey Puzzle (*Araucaria araucana*), a golden-leaved privet (*Ligustrum* sp), Holly, Horse Chestnut (*Aesculus hippocastanum*) and Californian Redwood (*Sequoiadendron sempervirens*).

Asian and Southern Hemisphere genera only occur in temperate Northern Hemisphere cultivation as shrubs, rockery or alpine subjects. The dominant status, and consequent great variety, of the broadleaves makes it impossible to cover all genera to the same detail. Therefore in this chapter we have restricted our coverage to those broadleaved genera native

to or cultivated in the cool, temperate and warm-temperate (Mediterranean-type) climates; broadleaved trees of the tropics are covered in the chapter 'Trees of the Tropics.' Selection of genera to be included is difficult since there are many which comprise mostly shrubs but which include some trees. We have included such genera when they contain important trees even if the majority are shrubs or smaller. Once selected, coverage of species is comprehensive in that *all* important species are dealt with, whether trees or not. Thus, for example, under the entry 'Willows,' as well as the well-known trees, we also include the shrubby sallows and osiers and even the Arctic Willow which only grows to a height of a few centimetres.

A general account of monocotyledon trees, including the palms, is also given, highlighting their distribution, ecological and economic importance.

The text in 'Trees of Every Kind' falls into two groups: main text and concise tables. All entries have a discursive main text that gives details of number of species, distribution, diagnostic features of the genus, general horticultural and economic importance and diseases and pests where relevant, plus any specific interesting

information relevant to that genus. About 70 genera also have concise tables which, where possible, list all the species of the genus, for example the beeches (*Fagus*) with 8–10 species, or for the larger genera, for example *Rhododendron*, list the main species. The majority of these tables are accompanied by an artwork panel of representative species plus a map of native distribution, green for conifers, orange for broadleaves. The table entries give concise facts on common names, distribution and diagnostic features for each species, plus extra details of horticultural or economic importance where relevant. Wherever possible the species in each table are divided into natural divisions (**Subgenus, Section, Series** etc) but, where there is no such natural division available, but the species can be grouped, the general terms **Group I, II, III**... have been used. In some cases an entire table or parts of it have been constructed in the form of a key, coded by letters of the alphabet. Thus the first keyed entries will be under **A**, with the alternative **AA** and even **AAA**. Further keyed items work through the alphabet **B, BB**; **C, CC** etc.

In the main text, dimensions are given in metric measurements with Imperial measures in parentheses, but for conciseness only metric dimensions are used in the tables. When giving dimensions of, for example, a leaf it is often necessary to show both the normal parameters and extreme limits that may be found reasonably often; thus (10)12–15(17)cm long indicates normal dimensions of 12–15cm but with common extremes of as little as 10cm or as much as 17cm.

Most trees have a number of popular or common names and here we have given as many alternatives as possible. With regard to the scientific name or binomial there *should* of course be just one correct name. However, it is often not as simple as this since historically several names have been applied to a single species. Here we have always used the *currently* accepted scientific name, as far as is possible, throughout an entry but at first mention we have also given other synonyms either in parentheses or by using an = sign. Throughout this work, scientific terminology has been kept to a minimum, but inevitably some has had to be used for the sake of conciseness. For this reason a comprehensive illustrated Glossary has been provided at the end of the book and the chapter 'What is a Tree?' should be consulted for an account of the structure, reproduction and growth of trees.

TREE-FERNS

Unlike the other tree species mentioned in this book, tree-ferns are true ferns of the Class Filicopsida, related to the common Male Fern (*Dryopteris filix-mas*) and Bracken (*Pteridium aquilinum*). In most ferns, however, the stem is reduced to a compact rootstock, as in the Male Fern, or elongated, as in the rhizome of Bracken. In both cases the aerial foliage, both sterile and fertile leaves (or fronds as they are often called in ferns), arises, even in Bracken, at ground level direct from that stem.

'Tree-fern' is the name given to members of the family Cyatheaceae in which the rhizome is erect and stout and forming a trunk, with a crown of leaves at its apex. This arborescent growth is also developed in *Sadleria*, a genus of the Blechnaceae, and occasionally in other *Blechnum* species, for example *Blechnum braziliense*. It is only in the Cyatheaceae, however, that the plants reach any large size and ecological importance and the account below will be confined to those species.

Fossil tree-ferns have been found as far back as the Jurassic and that called *Coniopteris hymenophylloides* is most like *Dicksonia*.

The gross morphology of the tree-fern stem differs considerably from that of the angiosperm tree trunk. First, the tree-fern rarely branches; when it does, the stem divides dichotomously into two equal branches. Occasionally side branches may form, for example in *Cyathea mexicana*, from adventitious buds at the base of old petioles. Second, the tree-fern is without a true bark layer (periderm) although its outer surface is roughened by leaf-stalk remains and often covered with lichens, mosses and other epiphytes as in other trees of the tropical forest. Third, there is no massive root system as in true trees; the lower part of the stem has many adventitious roots which become entangled and form a tough covering often doubling the thickness of the trunk, thus supporting it. Tree-ferns may reach up to 25m (82ft) but at this height they are usually supported by surrounding vegetation.

The internal organization of tissues of the tree-fern is similarly less advanced although, at the cellular level, xylem (water-transporting cells) and phloem (sugar-transporting cells) are present and function as they do in higher plants but,

unlike conifers and broadleaved trees, there is no secondary tissue and the fern trunk cannot increase in girth. The xylem and phloem are associated in vascular bundles (*meristeles*) which are embedded in an often corrugated cylinder of lignified fibers (*sclerenchyma*) collectively called a *dictyostele*.

The leaves are arranged in a spiral arrangement around the stem and form a rosette at its apex which is protected by scales or hairs. The number of mature leaves in the crown varies with the species, being from five or six, as in *Cyathea contaminans*, to as many as 40, as in *Cyathea atrox*. In some species the leaf falls upon dying through the action of a rapid abcission layer leaving a characteristic scar on the trunk surface; in others, the petiole remains as a persistent covering for many years, for example *Dicksonia antarctica* and *Cyathea pseudomuelleri*. The leaf architecture is that of a typical fern, usually being twice to four times divided. The midrib (*rhachis*) and petiole (or *stipe*) may be covered in scales or thorns (as in *Cyathea*) or stiff bristles (as in *Dicksonia*). The leaf blade tissue is similar in anatomy to angiosperms but there is less ecological variation in thickness or adaption to drought. Along each side of the petiole are peg-like outgrowths called *pneumathodes*; on the young leaf they act as respiratory or water-control organs.

Like most other ferns reproduction is by spores formed on the backs of normal green leaves. In some species, such as *Cyathea lurida*, the fertile leaves are morphologically distinct, being reduced in area. The spores are produced in *sporangia* growing in clusters called *sori*, which are protected when young, or in some species until the spores ripen, by a membranous flap or cover called an *indusium*. Spores give rise to the sexual generation, which is a small wedge-shaped platelet of green cells (*gametophyte*), embedded in which are the sexual organs. On the fertilization of the female egg-cell by the motile male sperm a new tree-fern (*sporophyte*) plant develops, which may not reach maturity for 10 to 15 years.

The Cyatheaceae is divided into four subfamilies: *Dicksonia* and *Cyathea* are placed in the Cyatheoideae which also includes *Cnemidaria* and *Lophosoria*, two nonarborescent tropical American genera. Other genera in the family are *Cystodium* (closely related to *Dicksonia*), *Culcita*, *Thyrsopteris*, *Cibotium* and *Metaxya*; all are nonarborescent.

The main differences between *Cyathea*

and *Dicksonia* can be summarized as follows. *Cyathea* has scales on its stem apex, petiole, midrib and veins; its sori are in the middle rather than the edge of the leaf; they may lack indusia or more likely have a saucer- or cup-like one which may, in some species, enclose an entire sorus. *Dicksonia*, on the other hand, has stiff hairs or bristles and sori on the edges of the leaf which are protected by thin flap-like indusia on their inner face and the reflexed margin of the leaf on the outside.

Dicksonia comprises some 25 species distributed in the Southern Hemisphere. In New Zealand they grow from sea level to 600m (2 000ft) in the *Nothofagus-Podocarpus-Dacrydium* forests. In the southernmost latitudes *D. squarrosa* regularly withstands frost. In southeast Australia and Tasmania, *D. antarctica* is an important constituent in the *Nothofagus* forest where it forms a 3m (10ft)-high stratum beneath the dense canopy, young treeferns being able to grow even when receiving only 1 percent of the total light. If the forest is burnt dicksonias survive, their growing tips protected by dense hairs. *Dicksonia* spreads into the tropical areas of

Fronds of the Tasmanian Tree-fern (*Dicksonia antarctica*), one of the few tree-fern species that can be grown in temperate regions, where it still requires moist, shady sites; it is better known as a glasshouse subject.

New Guinea and the Malesian archipelago reaching Sumatra and Luzon (*D. blumei*) where they grow in mid-montane rain forest. Eight species are found in the Americas reaching as far north as Mexico (*D. cicutaria*). The genus is not found in Africa but one endemic species (*D. arborescens*) is found on the island of St. Helena.

Cyathea contains over 700 species, spread throughout the tropics, north to the Himalaya and North Honshu (*C. spinulosa*), south to Tasmania (*C. australis*) and the southern tip of New Zealand, where *C. smithii* grows in the *Metrosideros lucida* forest within a few metres of the ice of Franz Josef glacier. Elsewhere in south and southeast Asia tree-ferns are common throughout the everwet rain forest becoming a significant component in the mid- and upper-montane forest particularly where clouds regularly rest. Tree-ferns are a conspicuous member of open grassland above the tree line, about 3 000m (10 000ft) in New Guinea, Sumatra and Sulawesi. Surprisingly, although each plant must produce many grams of spores, germination or dispersal is low and species are not wide ranging, and almost each mountain range will have its endemics, for example *C. pseudomuelleri* of Mount Wilhelmina. A few species are widespread and common in secondary forest and near rivers throughout southeast Asia and islands, for example *C. contaminans*. The genus is less dominant in Africa and there *C. dregei*, a savanna species, can withstand periodic burning. In America the genus has its center of speciation in tropical South America, again mainly as a forest species, reaching Mexico in the north and Paraguay in the south.

Dicksonia fibrosa, called 'Whekiponga' by the Maoris of New Zealand, is used in the building of their huts and fences since the trunks last well in the ground and there is a belief that rats cannot gnaw their way through such tough material. It is also used both structurally and decoratively in ceremonial houses (runaga-houses) where the outer surface is shaved off to accentuate the gray and black pattern left by the leaf-scars.

Cyathea species are used for house building by native peoples throughout its range and living trees are often left for this purpose when forest is cleared for gardens. Maoris make jugs and vases from *C. dealbata* (called Ponga – hence Ponga ware) and other New Zealand species. When shaved the vascular tissue and leaf-gaps make an attractive pattern. The Maoris also use the pith from the upper

Today's tree-ferns are the merest remnant of a group of plants that once dominated the Earth. Shown here is a Soft Tree-fern or Katote (*Cyathea smithii*) in the Westland bush-country of South Island, New Zealand.

part of the trunk as a type of sago and they, as do natives in New Guinea, Borneo, Indonesia and elsewhere, eat the young unfurling fronds as a vegetable. Dried fronds are also used for bedding by Maoris. In Sabah, hollowed tree-fern stems are used as bee-hives.

The masses of adventitious roots at the bases of *Cyathea* trunks are used in orchid culture, either as sawn solid slabs or broken in potting mixtures. The trade in all species of *Dicksonia* and *Cyathea* is prohibited, without special license, by the Trade in Endangered Species Convention.

Tree-ferns are cultivated as ornamentals in parks in warm temperate and tropical areas, for example several *Dicksonia* species and *Cyathea medullaris*. Once established they require very little management; propagation from spores is slow and germination rate low. *Dicksonia antarctica* is grown in conservatories in Europe and is often established outside in the more oceanic areas. The slowness of growth is a deterrent to short-term landscapers.

C. J.

CYCADS

The cycads, comprising nine or perhaps ten living genera, are a group of very primitive woody plants which look like palms, although they are not at all closely related to this group. They represent the second largest order of living gymnosperms. They are distinguished from the conifers by a number of important characters, most conspicuously by their palm-like habit and large pinnately-compound leaves, but also by quite numerous structural and reproductive characters.

Perhaps more than any other group of plants, except *Ginkgo biloba* (Maidenhair Tree), the cycads deserve to be called 'living fossils,' for the group reached its climax of evolutionary development in the Mesozoic era (about 200 million years ago) and since then has apparently declined without undergoing any appreciable evolutionary change. The earliest fossil cycads are now known from the Permian period of the late Paleozoic (about 240 million years

Macrozamia riedlei, one of some 14 species of this temperate Australian genus of cycads. The unbranched stem and crown of palm-like leaves are typical cycad characters.

ago) and these, in the form of their seed-bearing organs and in other characters, were very like the living genus *Cycas*. In the succeeding Triassic and Jurassic periods, cycads enjoyed a widespread distribution and, judging from the abundance of fossilized leaves in many deltaic sediments laid down during these periods, the plants were often abundant. As fossil plants are nearly always preserved in a dismembered state – and cycads are no exception – few of these Mesozoic forms have yet been reconstructed, but those that have showed surprisingly little difference from some of the living representatives.

The geographical distribution of the living genera is interesting, suggesting that they are of ancient origin. *Cycas*, with about 20 species, is distributed most widely: it extends from Polynesia to Madagascar and northward to Japan; *Stangeria*, with only a single species, is confined to South Africa and *Encephalartos* (about 30 species) is more widely distributed in tropical and southern Africa. *Bowenia*, with only two species, is in northern Australia and *Macrozamia* (14 species), with *Lepidozamia* (two species), which is sometimes distinguished from *Macrozamia* as a separate genus, are also Australian. *Ceratozamia* (four species) and *Dioon* (three to five species) are found in Mexico and Central America. *Microcycas* (one species only) is confined to Cuba and *Zamia* (30–40 species) is more widely distributed in tropical America. This pattern of distribution is usually interpreted as meaning that the cycad genera are relict and happen to have survived in these relatively confined areas.

As cycads are very ancient plants it is not surprising that they exhibit many peculiar features, some of which may be of a truly primitive nature. In habit most are rather palm-like with an unbranched erect stem bearing a crown of leaves. It is not known if this is a truly primitive condition or whether it may represent a reduction from something more elaborate. It is difficult to ascertain the habit of the fossil forms. *Macrozamia hopei*, a native of Queensland, is reputed to be the tallest of the cycads, reaching a height of about 20m (65ft). Some living cycads have only a short subterranean stem; this is likely to be a modified and reduced condition. They are extremely slow-growing and long-lived plants. It has been estimated that some living specimens may be over 1 000 years old. They produce new leaves at rather prolonged intervals and may some-

Cycas revoluta growing in a public park at Naples, Italy. Cycads are regarded as being among the most 'primitive' of seed plants and have remained virtually unchanged for some 200 million years.

times enter a dormant phase when no new growth occurs for several years.

Like all other known gymnosperms, cycads are woody plants but their wood is peculiarly spongy. The leaflets of the pinnately-compound leaves in most cycads have a system of forking veins running more or less parallel but in *Cycas* there is only a single mid-vein and in *Stangeria* the leaflets have a fern-like venation with a mid-vein and forking laterals.

The root system is not without peculiarities. Some roots grow up to the soil surface and these branch profusely to form

Fossil leaves of the extinct cycad *Nilssonia compta* preserved in deltaic sediments of the Middle Jurassic period in Yorkshire, England.

soft, starch-rich tissues of the stem in some species, for example *Cycas circinalis* and *C. revoluta*, can be used to prepare a kind of sago. The large seed kernels can also be eaten but it is said that cycad tissues may be poisonous unless prepared in a certain way. Cycads, especially *Cycas* species, are cultivated as greenhouse ornamentals in temperate countries or outdoors in tropical gardens. The one most commonly grown as an ornamental is *Cycas revoluta*.

K. A.

Above *Encephalartos hildebrandtii* is a species of cycad from Africa. This specimen has produced a fine crop of male cones; each released pollen grain germinates to form two sperms that swim to the egg.

Right Seeds of the cycad *Dioon edule* have a high starch content and are eaten boiled, roasted or ground into flour in its native Mexico.

coralloid masses. These roots contain a microscopical plant, a blue-green alga, in a special layer of cells in the outer tissues. The cycad is believed to benefit by the fixing of atmospheric nitrogen by the alga.

All cycads have separate male and female plants. In all except the female plants of *Cycas*, the reproductive structures are borne in massive cones (usually terminally on the stem), growth of the stem then being continued from a bud near the cone base. In the female of *Cycas* there are no cones; instead the seed-bearing megasporophylls, which resemble the vegetative leaves to some extent, are borne in place of ordinary leaves and the stem therefore goes on growing and producing new leaves beyond.

There are a number of exceptional characteristics of the reproductive process but perhaps the most interesting of all is the production of swimming male sex cells (sperms). Two are produced in each germinated pollen grain after pollination of the ovules (young seeds). In only one other seed plant – the Maidenhair Tree – are motile sperms produced.

Cycads are of enormous scientific interest but of little economic value. They are sometimes called sago palms because the

THE MAIDENHAIR TREE

The Maidenhair Tree (*Ginkgo biloba*) is the only living representative of a large ancient Order of conifer-like trees. The name *Ginkgo* is derived from the Japanese name for the plant or its nuts, the latter being regarded as a delicacy in the East.

The Maidenhair Tree is sacred according to the Buddhist religion and has been cultivated for many centuries in both China and Japan, especially in the grounds of temples. It became known to Western science in the 18th century when the first specimens were planted in Europe. For some time it was believed that the species may have been saved from extinction only by cultivation in the Far East but there is now good evidence for believing that it occurs in a truly wild state at the borders of Chekiang and Anhwei provinces in eastern China. Within the last 200 years the tree has been planted widely and has been grown successfully under many different conditions of soil and climate. It is also remarkably free of disease and resistant to pests and air pollution.

The Order Ginkgoales flourished mainly during the Mesozoic era, especially during the Jurassic period (about 150 million years ago) when the great dinosaurs dominated the fauna. The genus *Ginkgo* itself probably extends back to this period but the group was very rich in species and some of them certainly represent distinct

Fossil remains of the leaves of *Ginkgo huttonii* in which the characteristic shape is quite clear. This is an extinct species, represented by fossil leaves from the Middle Jurassic of Yorkshire, England.

genera. *Ginkgo* enjoyed a world-wide distribution and the species were no doubt important constituents of the flora. Fossil leaf remains are often found abundantly in deltaic sediments laid down during Mesozoic times. Toward the end of the Mesozoic era *Ginkgo* declined and this continued during the Tertiary until today only the one species remains.

Ginkgo forms a massive tree and old specimens – some are believed to be more than 1 000 years old – attain a very large size. In the young tree there is usually a strong leader which forms the main trunk. The branches are somewhat straggly and these give the tree its rather distinctive appearance in the winter leafless condition. The leaves are especially interesting, with a wedge-shaped leaf blade borne on a long stalk (petiole); the venation is an open forking system without any vein fusions. It is the delicate fern-like foliage and the shape of the lamina that account for the tree's popular English name of Maidenhair Tree. In the fall the foliage turns a brilliant shade of yellow.

There are separate male and female

The Maidenhair Tree (*Ginkgo biloba*) is the only living member of the genus *Ginkgo*. This graceful specimen, planted in 1762, can still be seen at the Royal Botanic Gardens, Kew, England.

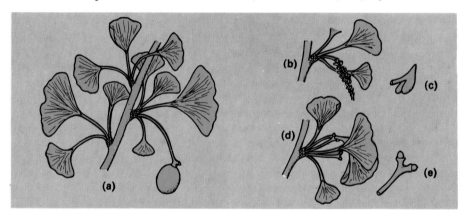

Foliage and reproductive structures of *Ginkgo biloba*. (a) Twig of a female tree showing dwarf-shoots with leaves attached and one bearing a fruit; (b) dwarf-shoot with a male cone; (c) a single microsporophyll from a male cone, showing the two pollen sacs; (d) and (e) young seed-bearing structures. Note that normally only one of the pair of young seeds reaches maturity.

trees. It appears that most of the earlier specimens planted in Europe were male, the first female one being recorded near Geneva in 1814. Some trees in cultivation have had branches of the opposite sex grafted onto them.

The pollen-bearing cones are not especially distinctive, being similar in a general way to the male cones of conifers. The seeds are borne usually in pairs but sometimes on stalks which appear to be equivalent morphologically to the male cones. Both are carried on leafy dwarf-shoots. Thus, there is no female cone in *Ginkgo* comparable with that in conifers.

One of the most remarkable features of the reproductive cycle in *Ginkgo* is the presence of swimming male cells (sperms) similar to those found in cycads. Indeed, there are several features of seed development which are similar in cycads and *Ginkgo*. It is believed that these do not indicate any close relationship but rather that they are primitive features which have been retained by these extraordinary ancient and primitive plants.

Ginkgoes grow well in most temperate regions except the cold northern regions. They seem impartial to soil type so long as it is fertile. They grow best in sunny positions. They make imposing specimen trees but are also often planted in avenues; they are tolerant of pollution and so are

One of the main benefits of growing a Maidenhair Tree as an ornamental, apart from being able to claim possession of a living fossil, is that the foliage turns brilliant shades of yellow in the fall.

useful trees for industrial areas. Cultivars available include 'Fastigiata,' a columnar form with semierect branches, 'Pendula' with weeping branches and 'Tremonia' which has a conical form.

The mature seed has a soft outer fleshy

layer which has the unpleasant odor of rancid butter. For this reason male trees are usually preferred for avenue planting. In the Orient the white seed kernel is regarded as a delicacy.

K. A.

CONIFERS

The living conifers and taxads (yews) comprise some 50 genera divided among seven families. They are the only numerically and economically important groups of gymnosperms, the other groups containing tree forms being the cycads and Maidenhair Tree (*Ginkgo biloba*) already dealt with.

Conifers are an ancient group, their fossil history extending back to the late Carboniferous period (300 million years ago). Several families are represented only by fossils. The living families themselves are mostly ancient. Thus, the monkey puzzle family (Araucariaceae) and redwood family (Taxodiaceae) extend back to the Jurassic period (195 million years ago) and the pine family (Pinaceae) at least to the Lower Cretaceous (135 million years ago).

Conifers are sharply divided into the Northern Hemisphere group and the Southern Hemisphere group. Although this general pattern of distribution probably has extremely ancient origins and may be related to the period in the past when there were two major land masses separated by the east–west running Tethys sea. Certainly other factors are involved. For example, there has undoubtedly been much extinction. There is good evidence that in the Jurassic and Cretaceous periods members of the Araucariaceae grew in Europe and other areas of the Northern Hemisphere. Many conifer genera now confined to relatively small areas once enjoyed a very much wider distribution. Thus, to give one example, *Sequoia sempervirens* (Coast Redwood), now confined to western North America, was in earlier geological times widely distributed in the Northern Hemisphere. There are several Far Eastern genera which were once widely distributed. The Pleistocene glaciations (2 million years ago) pushed many genera to the south, a contraction from which not all have fully recovered.

Most conifers are trees of cooler climates (either high latitude or high altitudes).

Few occur in tropical or subtropical lowlands. Large areas in higher latitudes are still naturally dominated by conifer forest, although the virgin forests have largely been exploited for timber. Many conifers of particular value as timber trees have been planted extensively well beyond their areas of natural distribution. *Pinus radiata* (Monterey Pine) which is confined as a native to a limited area of California, has been planted in many areas of Australia, New Zealand and South Africa and has become a very important timber tree.

The 'softwoods' of commerce are by definition the timbers produced by conifers. The term is not altogether appropriate, for the softest woods known are in fact obtained from broadleaved trees (dicotyledons), and some conifer woods are fairly hard, for example Yew (*Taxus baccata*). Softwoods, however, have a greater homogeneity than hardwoods (that is broadleaf tree woods) because they lack the same differentiation of their elements (see chapter What is a Tree?). Softwoods are used not only as an important constructional material, but also in various manufacturing industries (paper, textiles, synthetic board and packing materials, chemicals etc). Resins produced by conifers are important as the source of turpentine and various other substances used in the paint, pharmaceutical and perfumery industries. As a source of food, conifers are of little value. The seed kernels of a number of pines are eaten, especially the Stone Pine or Umbrella Pine (*Pinus pinea*) – the 'pignons' of Mediterranean regions.

Another use of increasing importance is in horticulture. There are very numerous horticultural varieties of many conifers which have been selected for their special ornamental value. Some members of the cypress and pine families (Cupressaceae and Pinaceae) are particularly rich in named horticultural varieties, many of them of dwarf form and prized for 'alpine' gardens. The only known intergeneric hybrids among conifers (× *Cupressocyparis*) have arisen in cultivation. The best-known hybrid is × *C. leylandii*, a cross between *Chamaecyparis nootkatensis* and *Cupressus macrocarpa*. This hybrid species is remarkably vigorous and is now widely grown as a hedge plant and screen-forming tree.

The conifers are generally considered to represent an Order Coniferales (= Coniferae) within the Class Coniferopsida. Living conifers (including the yews) comprise seven families, which are given in the accompanying table together with the

The yews, such as these Irish Yews (*Taxus baccata* 'Fastigiata'), and a few related genera are often separated from the 'pinoid' conifers and given the general name of 'taxoids.'

genera belonging to them. Here the Taxaceae is included within the conifers, but some botanists would regard these as representing a separate Order. One reason for this is that their seeds do not seem to be borne in cones in the manner of typical conifers, for example *Pinus*. In this, the Taxaceae is not alone – typical cones are not formed in the southern pine family (Podocarpaceae) and the cow's tail pine family (Cephalotaxaceae). These three families, because of the absence of typical (female) cones, are commonly and conveniently referred to as 'taxoids' to distinguish them from the remaining four families which have recognizable cones and are correspondingly known as 'pinoids.' The case of the junipers (*Juniperus* – Cupressaceae) may, at first glance, seem exceptional as a 'pinoid'; the fruiting cone is fleshy and commonly known as a 'berry.' Closer examination, however, soon reveals the characteristic cone structure and it is merely the fleshy scales which are misleading.

Some modern texts refer to the 'taxoids' as having 'imperfect cones' and the 'pinoids' as having 'perfect cones.' This raises the question of the term to be used for the female reproductive structure. The term cone is quite acceptable for the 'pinoids' but not for the 'taxoids' (for the reason already given). Traditionally the term 'female flower' has been used for both 'pinoids' and 'taxoids' and this is still used by some distinguished taxonomists, but others, equally distinguished, would restrict the term 'flower' to the Angiosperms (flowering plants) only, although even here the word has to be severely stretched to cover all cases. In this book, the practice has been adopted to use the words male cone for the male reproductive structures of both 'pinoids' and 'taxoids' and female cone for the female reproductive structures of the 'pinoids'; 'female cone' (within inverted commas) has been adopted for the female structures of the 'taxoids.' In other words, cone = perfect cone, 'cone' = imperfect cone, to use the other current expressions for the female structures.

In biological terms, this distinction between 'pinoids' and 'taxoids' is significant because the former group is adapted to wind dispersal of its seeds (except *Juniperus*) and the latter (including *Juniperus*) to animal dispersal.

K. A.

Diagnostic Features of the Conifer Families

PINOIDS
Pinaceae – the Pine Family
Leaves needle-like and, like the *cone-scales, spirally arranged but sometimes, by twisting, appearing two-ranked; buds scaly; male and female cones on the same plant (monoecious); cone-scales of two kinds – bract-scales and ovuliferous-scales, the latter separate from and borne in the axils of the bract-scales and bearing two inverted ovules on the upper surface, these giving rise to a distinctive type of seed with a membranous wing extending from the base; microsporophylls (stamens) of male cone with two pollen sacs; pollen grains with two bladder-like wings except in *Larix*, *Pseudotsuga* and *Tsuga*. Widespread in the Northern Hemisphere. Ten genera: *Abies* (firs), *Cathaya*, *Cedrus* (true cedars), *Keteleeria*, *Larix* (larches), *Picea* (spruces), *Pinus* (pines), *Pseudolarix* (Japanese Golden Larch), *Pseudotsuga* (Douglas firs), *Tsuga* (hemlocks or hemlock spruces). (*Cathaya* is a Chinese genus but as yet no material or data is available in the West.)

---

* *The word* cone-scale *is used here to mean the main contributor to the mature cone and may be the ovuliferous-scale, as in the Pinaceae, or the (supposed) fused bract- and ovuliferous-scale in the Cupressaceae, Taxodiaceae and Araucariaceae. Unless otherwise qualified, the word* cone *refers to the female (ovulate) structure.*

Taxodiaceae – the Redwood Family
Leaves linear to awl-shaped and, like the cone-scales, spirally arranged (except *Metasequoia*, where they are opposite); buds not scaly; monoecious; cone-scales not distinct as bract- and ovuliferous-scales, these, allegedly, being almost completely united to form a virtually single structure and each bearing two or more erect or inverted ovules which give rise to seeds which, in some genera, have marginal wings. Microsporophylls with two to nine pollen sacs; pollen without wings. Nine genera, eight in Northern Hemisphere, but *Arthrotaxis* is Southern Hemisphere: *Arthrotaxis* (Tasmanian cedars), *Cunninghamia*, *Glyptostrobus*, *Metasequoia* (Dawn Redwood), *Sciadopitys* (Japanese Umbrella Pine), *Sequoia* (Coast Redwood), *Sequoiadendron* (Big Tree, Giant Sequoia or Sierra Redwood), *Taiwania*, *Taxodium* (swamp cypresses).

Araucariaceae – the Monkey Puzzle Family
Leaves narrow to broad with parallel veins, and, as also the cone-scales, spirally arranged; monoecious or dioecious (sexes on separate plants); bract- and ovuliferous-scales not distinct, but allegedly, fused into a single structure and each bearing a single ovule, the subsequent seed being shed with the cone-scale. Male cone relatively large; microsporophylls with up to about 12 pollen sacs; pollen without wings. Two genera, mainly Southern Hemisphere: *Agathis* (kauri or kauri pines), *Araucaria* (monkey puzzles).

Cupressaceae – the Cypress Family
Adult leaves mostly small and scale-like (juvenile leaves sometimes needle-like) typically in opposite pairs, rarely in whorls of three; monoecious or dioecious; cones more or less globose, small, 2–3cm (0.8–1.2in) diameter, the scales in pairs and *either* peltate *or* flattened and imbricate, at least finally more or less woody (berry-like in *Juniperus*), the fertile scales with one to numerous erect ovules; seeds winged or not. In *Juniperus* the (ovulate) cone is much reduced to a single pair (or whorl of three to eight) fertile scales which coalesce and become fleshy. In the typical cone of this family the scale is commonly interpreted as resulting from the complete fusion of a bract- and an ovuliferous-scale. Seventeen genera: *Callitris*, *Calocedrus*, *Chamaecyparis* (false cypresses), × *Cupressocyparis*, *Cupressus* (cypresses), *Diselma*, *Fitzroya*, *Fokienia*, *Juniperus* (junipers), *Libocedrus*, *Neocallitropsis*, *Papuacedrus*, *Pilgerodendron*, *Tetraclinis*, *Thuja* (arbor-vitae), *Thujopsis*, *Widdringtonia*.

TAXOIDS
Podocarpaceae – the Southern Pine Family
Leaves spirally arranged in all except *Microcachrys* and scale-like or needle-like but in *Phyllocladus* the leaves are extremely reduced, their photosynthetic function being

Above Top Typical 'pinoid' conifers produce the familiar mature woody seed-containing cones which are made up of a number of distinct scales, as is shown on the right of this larch (*Larix* sp) twig, with young female cones on the left. *Above* In 'taxoids' the 'cone' is not in this form and in the case of the Common Yew (*Taxus baccata*) shown here, the mature 'cone' is surrounded by a red fleshy aril.

taken over by flattened stems (cladodes); monoecious or dioecious; cones much reduced to a few scales and maturing to contain only one seed (from an inverted ovule), which may be surrounded or embedded in a fleshy structure known as the epimatium – of doubtful homology, but commonly interpreted as an ovuliferous-scale; cones may be borne on a fleshy stalk or 'foot' (hence 'podocarp'); pollen grains mostly winged. The family is virtually confined to the Southern Hemisphere, only a few species extending north of the Equator. Seven genera: *Acmopyle*, *Dacrydium*, *Microcachrys*, *Microstrobus*, *Phyllocladus*, *Podocarpus* (podocarps), *Saxegothaea*.

Cephalotaxaceae – Cow's Tail Pine Family
Leaves spirally arranged on main shoots, but appearing in two opposite ranks on laterals; pollen sacs three to five; usually dioecious; cones much reduced comprising a few decussate pairs of simple bracts each subtending two ovules, but there is generally only one seed in the whole cone when it reaches maturity; the nature 'cone' is relatively large, protrudes beyond the original cones, and has an outer fleshy layer (aril) with a thin inner woody layer. *Cephalotaxus* is the only genus, the four to seven species being natives of the Northern Hemisphere.

Taxaceae – the Yew Family

Regarded by some authorities as a separate Class (Taxopsida) and Order (Taxales) of its own, Taxaceae being the only family. One reason is that the seeds are borne terminally on short axillary shoots which bear a few scales at the base. What may be regarded as normal for typical conifers is for seeds to be borne *laterally*. Evergreen trees or shrubs; leaves more or less linear, often appearing two-ranked, spirally arranged except in *Amentotaxus* where they are opposite; normally dioecious; three to eight (or nine) microsporophylls with pollen sacs; pollen grains wingless. 'Cones' axillary, comprising a single ovule without subtending bract, the seed finally surrounded by a colored fleshy aril. No resin ducts in wood. Five genera, four in the Northern Hemisphere, but *Austrotaxus* is Southern Hemisphere: *Amentotaxus*, *Austrotaxus*, *Pseudotaxus*, *Taxus* (yews), *Torreya*.

PINACEAE

Pines
(genus *Pinus*)

The true pines (genus *Pinus*) are a group of 70–100 species of evergreen conifers found almost exclusively in the north temperate zones of the Old and New Worlds. They range from just south of the equator in the Malay Archipelago, northward to the limit of the northern coniferous forests on the edge of the Arctic Circle.

Pines are predominantly trees of pyramidal habit but a few shrubs occur. The leaves in adult plants are of two types: bracts and adult leaves. The bracts are scale-like and are borne spirally, usually on lower parts of young shoots (long shoots). They are normally deciduous and bear in their axils so-called undeveloped or 'short shoots.' On these short shoots arise the adult leaves (needles) which are borne in clusters of two to five (usually two, three or five but at times up to eight or reduced to one). The needles spring from a basal sheath of 8–12 bud scales. These adult leaves persist for up to five years or more.

The male and female cones are separate but on the same tree. The male cones are short and cylindric, and are catkin-like. The female cones have a central axis bearing spirally arranged bract-scales, in the axils of which eventually arise the cone-scales (ovuliferous or fertile scales) each bearing two ovules on the lower surface. The apex of these cone-scales becomes en-larged and this enlargement (apophysis) may bear a more or less central spine or prickle. Part of the apophysis may be raised and differentiated to form what is called an umbo and this may bear a spine or prickle. The cones may be erect, inclined or pendulous.

Pollination is by wind and pollen is often so abundantly produced that it may become visible. Dispersal of pollen is aided by each grain having two bladder-like wings. At least a year elapses between pollination in the spring and fertilization, during which time the female cone remains small. After fertilization it grows rapidly to adult size, at first green becoming brown, and seeds are commonly ripe by about the following fall. Some species, however, require an extra year. The seeds in most species are winged, the wing almost always being longer than the seed.

The Bristle-cone Pine (*Pinus aristata*) is one of the most remarkable species. It grows in the Rocky mountains of Colorado, Utah, Nevada and Arizona. In these high-altitude conditions it grows extremely slowly, becoming gnarled and stunted with much dead wood. Some specimens are reckoned to be the oldest living things on earth today, reaching ages of up to 6 000 years.

Pines are subject to a number of fungus diseases, especially on acid soils with poor drainage. Amongst the rust fungi are: *Cronartium flaccidum* which causes blisters on the branches of the Weymouth Pine (*P. strobus*) and other five-needle pines. The alternate hosts are species of *Ribes* (currants). The disease is serious, causing stunting of the trees. Another rust disease is caused by *Coleosporium senecionis* on the Scots Pine (*P. sylvestris*) and produces similar blisters, but only on the needles. The alternate hosts are groundsels (*Senecio* spp). Amongst the larger parasitic fungi of pines are the bracket fungi *Heterobasidion annosum* and *Phaeolus schweinitzii*, both serious agents of disease in forests and plantations. There are also many insect pests, including pine shoot beetles (*Myelophilus* spp), Pine Shoot Moth (*Rhyacionia buoliana*) and the Pine Weevil (*Hylobius abietis*), which is particularly destructive.

The timber of pines is the most important of all the softwoods. The most widely planted forest species are the Scots Pine (*P. sylvestris*), Monterey Pine (*P. radiata*) and Corsican Pine (*P. nigra* var *maritima*). The timber is utilized in every kind of constructional work and carpentry. The resin helps to preserve the wood considerably and when coated with creosote it is ideal for outdoor use as telegraph poles, railroad sleepers and road blocks. The wood of the Scots Pine is known as yellow deal; its resin, obtained by tapping the trees, is distilled to give turpentine and rosin. Destructive distillation in closed (air-absent) vessels yields tar and pitch. Pine oils are obtained by distillation of leaves and shoots.

Pines are also planted extensively for ornament, either singly or in groups for landscaping, and as shelter trees. Notable tall ornamental pines are Lodgepole Pine (*P. contorta* var *latifolia*), Cluster Pine (*P.*

A wind-stunted Western Yellow or Ponderosa Pine (*Pinus ponderosa*) growing at an altitude of about 2 100m (7 000ft) on top of the granitic Sentinel Dome in the Yosemite National Park, California, USA.

The Main Species of *Pinus*

Subgenus *Strobus* – The Soft Pines
Leaves with one vascular bundle. Sheaths of short shoots (those bearing leaf clusters) deciduous. Base of scale leaves not decurrent. The wood contains little resin and the timber is soft.

A *Leaves in clusters of 5.*
B *Margin of leaves (lens) serrulate.*

P. cembra Swiss Stone Pine, Arolla Pine. Alps of C Europe, NE USSR and America. Tree 10–25(40)m. Shoots tomentose with thick brown hairs. Leaves dark green, 5–12cm long, lacking conspicuous white lines on the back. Mature cones 5–8cm long with unarmed terminal umbo; seeds without wings.
   'Aureovariegata' A form with yellow-tinged leaves.
   'Stricta' A columnar form with ascending branches.
P. lambertiana Sugar Pine. N America. Tree 50–100m. Shoots tomentose. Leaves 7–10cm long with conspicuous white lines on back. Mature cones (25)30–50cm long; seeds with wings longer than themselves.
P. peuce Macedonian Pine. Balkan mountains. Tree 10–20m. Shoots greenish, hairless and without bloom. Leaves 7–12cm long. Mature cones more or less cylindric, 8–15cm long; apophysis much swollen; seeds 8–10mm with longer wings.
P. strobus Weymouth Pine, White Pine. N America. Tree 25–50m. Shoots hairless, without bloom. Leaves 6–14cm long, soft and flexible. Mature cones often curved, 8–20cm long with flat apophysis; seeds mottled, 6–7mm long with longer wings.
   'Compacta' A slow-growing dwarf form with a dense habit.
   ''Contorta' A form with twisted branches and leaves.
   'Fastigiata' A form with erect branches and columnar habit.
   'Prostrata' A prostrate form with flat or slightly ascending branches.
P. wallichiana (*P. griffithii*, *P. excelsa*) Himalayan or Bhutan Pine. Himalaya and westward to Afghanistan. Tree usually about 35m, but sometimes 50m. Shoots hairless with evident bloom. Leaves 12–20cm long. Mature cones 15–25cm long with convex apophysis, its umbo touching the scale below; seeds 8–9mm with longer wings.

BB *Margin of leaves (lens) entire.*

P. aristata Hickory or Bristle-cone Pine. SW USA. Usually a bushy tree reaching 15m. Shoots pale orange, soon hairless. Leaves 2–4cm long. Mature cones 4–9cm long, the terminal umbo with a slender curved spine 6–8mm long.

AA *Leaves in clusters of 1–4.*

P. bungeana Lace-bark Pine. NW China. Tree 20–30m. Shoots hairless. Leaves 5–10cm long with entire (smooth) margins (lens); in clusters of 3. Mature cones 5–7cm long; apophysis with an umbo bearing a broad-based recurved spine; seeds 8–12mm long with short wings. The popular name derives from the exfoliating bark exposing striking multicolored areas of bare trunk.
P. cembroides Mexican Stone Pine. Arizona to Mexico. Tree 6–7m. Shoots dark orange, soon hairless. Leaves 2–5cm long with serrulate margin (lens), in clusters of 1–4. Mature cones almost globose, 2.5–5cm long with a broad umbo; seeds 15–30mm long with unusually narrow wings.

Subgenus *Pinus* – the Hard Pines
Leaves with two vascular bundles. Sheaths of short shoots persisting. Base of scale-leaves decurrent. The wood contains significant amounts of resin and the timber is comparatively hard.

C *Leaves in clusters of 3 (exceptionally otherwise, eg P. halepensis, P. radiata, leaves in 2's).*
D *Leaves not exceeding 15cm in length.*

P. halepensis Aleppo Pine. Mediterranean region and W Asia. Tree 10–15m. Leaves 6–15cm long, sometimes in clusters of 2. Mature cones 8–12cm long, the apophysis more or less flattened, the umbo obtuse and unarmed (ie with no prickle or spine).
P. radiata Monterey Pine. California. Tree 25–30m. Leaves 10–15cm long, occasionally in clusters of 2. Mature cones 7–14cm long, stout, asymmetric, sessile and reflexed, the apophysis rounded with a minute prickle.
P. rigida Pitch Pine, Easter Pine. E USA. Tree 10–15(25)m. Leaves firm, 7–14cm long. Mature cones symmetrical 3–7cm long, umbo prominent with a sharp, slender recurved prickle.

DD *Leaves more than 15cm long.*

P. coulteri Coulter or Big-cone Pine. S California and S Mexico. Tree to 25m. Shoots with bloom. Leaves 15–30cm long. Mature cones massive, 25–35cm long, the raised apophysis with a large umbo forming a stout, curved spine; wings thick and twice the length of the seeds.
P. palustris Longleaf or Pitch Pine. E USA. Tree to 40m. Bud scales white fringed. Shoots not bloomed. Leaves 20–45cm long. Mature cones 15–20cm long, almost without stalk, the umbo with a short reflexed prickle; seed wings membranous, about twice the length of seeds.
P. ponderosa Western Yellow Pine. W N America. Tree 50–75m. Shoots without bloom. Leaves (12)15–26cm long. Leaf clusters sometimes 2, 4 or 5. Mature cones yellowish-green, almost without stalks, 8–15cm long, the umbo with a stout recurved prickle.

P. jeffreyi Jeffrey's Pine. W N America. Tree similar to *P. ponderosa* but shoots with bloom. Mature cones larger and resin with a characteristic citronella-like smell.
P. taeda Loblolly Pine. E and SE USA. Tree 20–30(50)m. Shoots without bloom. Leaves (12)15–25cm long, bright blue-green. Mature cones sessile, 6–12cm long, the umbo projected as a stout triangular somewhat recurved spine; seeds 6–7mm long with wings about 25mm long.

CC *Leaves in clusters of 2.*
E *Leaves not exceeding 8cm.*

P. sylvestris Scots Pine, Scotch Fir. N and C Europe and W Asia. Tree 20–40m. Upper part of the trunk smooth and reddish. Leaves 2–7cm long, blue-green, often twisted. Mature cones 3–7cm long, the umbo almost symmetrical with a minute prickle. The subspecies *scotica* is broad-topped and native only in the highlands of N England and Scotland.
P. mugo Mountain Pine. Mountains of C Europe. Very similar to *P. sylvestris* but usually a shrub with leaves a brighter green. Very variable.
P. contorta Shore Pine. Coastal areas of W N America. Tree to 10m. Leaves 3–5cm long, firm and twisted. Mature cones very oblique, 2–5cm long; prickles of the umbo prominent but fragile. The var *latifolia* (Lodgepole Pine) is the inland representative.

EE *Leaves predominantly more than 8cm long.*

P. pinea Stone Pine, Umbrella Pine. Mediterranean region. Mushroom-shaped tree 15–25m. Leaves 10–20cm long. Mature cones almost globular, 6–9cm long. The species is known by its seeds, which are 12–18mm long, the wing only 6–7mm long and quickly falling off.
P. halepensis Aleppo Pine. Leaves also in 3's – see earlier description, under leaves in 3's.
P. radiata Monterey Pine. Leaves mainly in 3's – see earlier description, under leaves in 3's.
P. thunbergii Japanese Black Pine. Japan. Tree to 30m. Winter buds grayish-white, not resinous, with fimbriate scales free at the tips. Leaves (6) 8–11cm long, the basal leaf-sheath terminated by two long filaments. Mature cones 4–6cm long, the umbo with a prickle or not.
P. pinaster Cluster Pine. W Mediterranean region. Tree to 30m. Winter buds not resinous. Leaves 10–20cm long, firm; basal leaf-sheath without terminal filaments. Mature cones symmetrical, in clusters, 9–18cm long, the umbo with a prominent prickle.
P. nigra Austrian or Black Pine. Austria and eastward to the Balkan Peninsula. Tree 20–40(50)m. Bark characteristically dark gray and fissured into scaly plates. Leaves 9–16cm long and firm. Mature cones symmetrical, 5–8cm long, the umbo usually with a short prickle. The var *maritima* is the Corsican Pine, with lighter green, twisted leaves 12–18cm long.

P. sylvestris

P. contorta

P. strobus

P. nigra (var. maritima)

P. nigra (var. maritima)

P. wallichiana

P. ponderosa

P. radiata

P. halepensis

P. wallichiana

P. ponderosa

P. pinaster

P. radiata

67

pinaster), Stone Pine (*P. pinea*) and Weymouth Pine (*P. strobus*). Dwarf forms include the Lacebark Pine (*P. bungeana*), the Dwarf Mountain Pine (*P. mugo* var *pumilo*) and *P. sylvestris* 'Beuvronensis.'

The Monterey Pine (*P. radiata*) is outstanding as a windbreak, especially on sea coasts; these trees also remove salt from the atmosphere. It is very extensively planted in New Zealand especially on poor soils.

Propagation is usually from seed in the spring and is timed so as to avoid frost damage to the young seedlings. Cultivars are grafted. Young seedlings are transplanted about every two years to stimulate development of abundant fibrous roots. Most species are tolerant of a wide range of soils, provided they are well-drained, but some species are more or less calcicole, that is requiring a distinctly lime-rich soil.

Stone Pine seeds, which are large and soon lose their vestigial wing, are eaten as a delicacy in the Mediterranean region where they are known as 'pignons.'

The common name 'pine' has been applied to many pine-like trees which do not belong to the genus *Pinus* – indeed some are not even conifers. The accompanying table gives some examples.

F. B. H.

SOME PLANTS HAVING THE COMMON NAME 'PINE'

Common Name	Species	Family
Black Pine	*Callitris calcarata*	Cupressaceae
Bluegrass Pine	*Poa scabrella*	Gramineae
Brazilian Pine	*Araucaria brasiliensis*	Araucariaceae
Bush Pine	*Hakea leucoptera*	Proteaceae
Celery Pine	*Phyllocladus trichomanoides*	Podocarpaceae
Chile Pine	*Araucaria araucana*	Araucariaceae
Cypress Pine	*Callitris* spp	Cupressaceae
Ground Pine	*Ajuga chamaepitys*	Labiatae
Hoop Pine	*Araucaria cunninghamii*	Araucariaceae
Huon Pine	*Dacrydium franklinii*	Podocarpaceae
Japanese Umbrella Pine	*Sciadopitys verticillata*	Taxodiaceae
Kauri Pine	*Agathis* spp (especially *A. australis*)	Araucariaceae
King William Pine	*Athrotaxis selaginoides*	Taxodiaceae
Moreton Bay Pine	*Araucaria cunninghamii*	Araucariaceae
Murray Pine	*Callitris* spp	Cupressaceae
Needle Pine	*Hakea leucoptera*	Proteaceae
Norfolk Island Pine	*Araucaria heterophylla*	Araucariaceae
Parana Pine	*Araucaria angustifolia*	Araucariaceae
Parasol Pine	*Sciadopitys verticillata*	Taxodiaceae
Red Pine	*Dacrydium cupressinum*	Podocarpaceae
Rubber Pine	*Landolphia kirkii*	Apocynaceae
Screw Pine	*Pandanus* spp	Pandanaceae
She Pine	*Podocarpus elatus*	Podocarpaceae
Westland Pine	*Dacrydium westlandicum*	Podocarpaceae
White Cypress Pine	*Callitris glauca*	Cupressaceae
White Pine	*Podocarpus elatus*	Podocarpaceae

Spruces
(genus *Picea*)

The genus *Picea* comprises some 40–60 species of evergreen trees and is widely distributed over the cooler areas of the Northern Hemisphere of both the Old and New Worlds, from the Arctic Circle to the high mountains of the more southerly warm temperate latitudes of the Tropic of Cancer.

They form trees of more or less conical outline with irregularly branched horizontal to pendulous branches and reddish-brown furrowed bark. The branchlets are characterized by woody peg-like decurrent leaf bases, which are continuous with the cushion-like structures (pulvini) surrounding the shoots, separated from each other by grooves. Winter buds may be resinous or not. The leaves are needle-like, appearing either more or less radially arranged around the lateral shoots (leading shoots are less constant) or somewhat parted beneath to pectinate, that is the lower ranks of leaves, at least, are in two horizontal rows, one row on each side of the shoot. The leaves are of two types: diamond-shaped quadrangular with the width about equal to the height, or flattened with the width much greater than the height, so that there are essentially only two sides – an upper and a lower. Each leaf has typically two marginal resin ducts, sometimes one or rarely none.

Male and female cones are borne separately on the same tree, the male axillary in yellow or crimson catkin-like clusters, the female terminal. The young female cones are green or purple, each cone with numerous scales and each scale with two ovules at the base on the underside. Once fertilized, the cones ripen within the year and are pendulous and do not break up when ripe. The seeds are winged and more or less compressed.

Most species of *Picea* succeed in wet and cold soils, although in shallow soils they may not withstand much wind; otherwise they tolerate a lot of exposure and when firmly rooted can serve as windbreaks.

Propagation is usually by seed. For ornamental purposes the seedlings are transplanted every two years until final transplantation to the permanent position, which should be not later than when they are about 1m (3.3ft) high. For forestry purposes, it is usual to transplant at a height of about 30–40cm (12–15in). Young shoots are liable to late spring frost damage.

Spruces are susceptible to attacks by the rust fungus *Chrysomyxa rhododendri*, with the aecidial stage on *Picea abies* and *P. pungens*, the alternate host being *Rhododendron*. The imperfect fungus *Ascochyta biniperda* will attack two- to three-year-old species, especially of *P. abies*, as well as adult and old trees, causing defoliation. Bracket fungi, such as *Phaeolus schweinitzii*, *Phellinus pini* and others, also cause serious damage. *Phellinus pini* is particularly destructive, attacking mature trees, especially *Picea sitchensis*, causing Red-ring Rot.

The spruce aphid *Elatobium abietinum* causes defoliation in a number of spruces, including *P. sitchensis*. Plant lice also attack many spruce species forming so-called pineapple galls. Species of the genus *Adelges* are involved and have a complex life history requiring more than one coni-

ferous host. However, spruce are always the primary hosts and the ones bearing the galls. These are unsightly but do little harm to the tree.

Three North American species are of great economic importance – Red Spruce (*P. rubens*), Black Spruce (*P. mariana*) and White Spruce (*P. glauca*) – being widely used for paper pulp. In Norway and the United Kingdom the Norway Spruce (*P. abies*) is widely planted for afforestation, as also is the Sitka Spruce (*P. sitchensis*), the latter being particularly successful on a very wide range of soils from sandy to cold, wet and boggy. Each species occupies not far short of 10 percent of the total productive forest in these countries.

Spruce wood is soft and without odor, is easy to work and takes a good finish. It is used in general carpentry, for propping poles, packing cases and sounding boards and also for stringed instruments. The timber is also extensively turned into wood pulp for use in the manufacture of paper and rayon. The resin of the Norway Spruce is purified to yield Burgundy pitch and the leaves and shoots are distilled to give Swiss turpentine. Extracts of shoots and leaves (also of *P. abies*) mixed with various sugary substances, can be fermented to make spruce beer. The bark of *P. abies* is also used commercially in the tanning of leather.

Although various conifers may be sold as Christmas trees, the Norway Spruce is the most commonly chosen. Other spruces are extensively planted as ornamentals, notably cultivars of *P. pungens* (Colorado Spruce) and *P. engelmannii* (Engelmann Spruce). Dwarf spruces popular for planting in rock gardens include *P. glauca* 'Albertina Conica' and *P. abies* 'Clanbrassiliana,' 'Nidiformis' and 'Pumila.'

F. B. H.

The Main Species of *Picea*

Group I: Leaves flattened (showing virtually only 2 surfaces) with 2 white stomatic bands on the apparent lower surface (facing downward on horizontal branches), the apparent upper surface green, rarely with a broken stomatic line.

A *First-year lateral shoots hairy.*

P. omorika Serbian Spruce. Europe, especially Yugoslavia. Tree to 30m. Leaves on horizontal branches more or less parted below and exposing shoot (ie pectinate), thin, keeled on both surfaces, (8)12–18 × 2mm; abruptly pointed. Mature cones 3–6cm long, ovoid-oblong.
P. brewerana Brewer's or Siskiyou Spruce. W USA. Tree to 40m. Leaves radially spreading on pendulous shoots, 2–2.5 (3.0)cm long, slightly convex on both surfaces; apex pointed. Mature cones 6–12cm long, cylindric-oblong; cone-scales entire.

AA *First-year lateral shoots hairless. Leaves pectinate on lower surface of shoot. Cone scale with jagged margin.*

P. jezoensis Yeddo Spruce. NE Asia, Japan. Tree to 50m. Leaves 1–2cm long, the apex pointed but not horny and pricking. Mature cones 4–8cm long, cylindric-oblong. Variety *hondoensis*, with shorter leaves, often does better when cultivated than the type.
P. sitchensis Sitka Spruce. W coastal regions of USA from Alaska to California. Tree to 60m. Leaves 1.5–2.5cm long with sharp, horny, pricking apical point; convex and slightly keeled on both surfaces. Mature cones 6–10cm long, cylindric-oblong.

Group II: Leaves 4-sided and quadrangular diamond-shaped in cross-section, the width equal to or slightly less than the height; each side with (2)3–5(6) white (not banded) stomatic lines.

B *First-year lateral shoots hairless (sometimes hairy in* P. abies *and* P. asperata*) and at least the upper ranks of leaves bent forward over the shoot.*
C *Lower ranks of leaves parted laterally into 2 more or less horizontal sets (ie pectinate), those above overlapping.*

P. abies (*P. excelsa*) Norway or Common Spruce. C and N Europe. Tree to 50m. Leaves 1–2(2.5)cm long, green. Mature cones cylindric, 10–15cm long. Occasionally has faint pubescence on shoots. About 150 cultivars including many named dwarf forms.
P. glauca White Spruce. Alaska, Canada, N USA. Tree to 30m. Leaves 8–18mm, blue-green, glaucous, with a rank smell when bruised. Mature cones cylindric-oblong, 3.5–5cm long.

CC *Lower ranks of leaves not parted beneath but more or less pointed downward (ie radially arranged).*

P. smithiana Himalayan Spruce. The Himalaya. Tree 30–50m. Winter buds more or less resinous. Leaves 2–4(5) × 1mm; apex acute. Mature cones 12–15(18)cm long, cylindric.
P. asperata Chinese or Dragon Spruce. W China. Tree to 25m. Winter buds more or less resinous. Shoots yellowish-brown sometimes hairy. Leaves subradially arranged, 1–1.8cm long, sometimes curved; apex acute. Mature cones 8–10cm long, cylindric-oblong.
P. schrenkiana Schrenk's Spruce. C Asia. Tree to 35m. Winter buds not resinous. Shoots gray. Leaves radially arranged, 2–3.5cm long, sometimes curved; apex pointed. Mature cones 7–10cm long, cylindric-oblong; cone-scales entire.

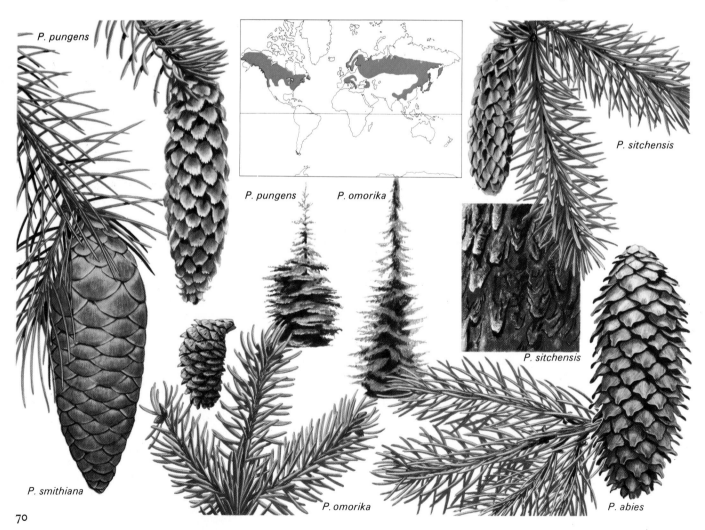

P. pungens

P. sitchensis

P. pungens　*P. omorika*

P. sitchensis

P. smithiana

P. omorika

P. abies

BB *First-year lateral shoots hairless but all ranks of leaves more or less spreading outward, radially or subradially at 45° to almost 90°, the upper ranks not bent forward over the shoot. Mature cones more than 5cm long.*

P. polita Tiger-tail Spruce. Japan. Tree to 40m. Leaves 1.5–2cm long, curved, very rigid and with sharp pricking point; shining deep green. Mature cones 8–10cm long.

P. pungens (glaucous cultivars) Colorado Spruce. SW USA. Tree to 50m with horizontal branches. Leaves 1.5–2.5cm, somewhat incurved, glaucous on all sides with waxy bloom obscuring the stomatic lines; rigid and stiff with sharp, prickly point, more leaves on upper than lower half of shoot. Mature cones 6–10cm long, cylindric-oblong. The above description covers the cultivars 'Glauca' (Blue Spruce) with horizontal branches and 'Kosteriana' with pendulous branches, both of which are commonly planted.

BBB *First-year lateral shoots hairy and lower leaves parted laterally into two horizontal sets (ie pectinate), those above overlapping. (In P. asperata and P. mariana the leaves are more or less radially arranged.)*
D *Terminal bud with basal ring of awl-shaped (acicular) scales; cones less than 5cm long.*

P. mariana Black Spruce. NW N America. Tree 20–30m. Young shoots glandular, hairy. Leaves 7–15mm long, somewhat glaucous with more stomatic lines on the sides next to the shoot; apex blunt. Mature cones ovoid.

P. rubens Red Spruce. Canada and southward to N Carolina. Leaves 1–1.5cm long, abruptly acute, deep to bright green, with about twice as many stomatic lines on the side next to the shoot. Mature cones 3–4(5)cm long, oblong.

DD *Terminal bud without basal ring of awl-shaped (acicular) scales. Cones more than 5cm long.*

P. engelmannii Engelmann Spruce. W N America. Tree 20–50m. First-year shoots yellowish-gray with glandular pubescence. Leaves 1.5–2.5cm long with acute apex, upper ranks bent forward over shoot; rank smell on bruising. Mature cones up to 8cm long. Rare in cultivation.

P. obovata Siberian Spruce. N Europe, N Asia. Tree to 50m. First-year shoots brown, pubescence fine. Leaves 1–1.8cm long, apex acute. Mature cones 6–8cm long, cylindric-ovoid; scales entire.

P. orientalis Oriental Spruce. Asia Minor and Caucasus. Leaves dark green, shining, 6–8mm (occasionally 12mm) long, with blunt apex. Mature cones 6–9cm long, cylindric-ovoid.

Group III: Leaves pectinately arranged and quadrangular but somewhat compressed from above downward so that, in cross-section, the width is greater than the height, with twice as many stomatal lines on the 2 sides next to the shoot (upper side) as on the other 2 (lower) sides (lens). Cones more than 5cm long.

P. bicolor Alcock Spruce. Japan. Tree to 25m. Primary shoots hairy, lateral ones not so; terminal bud without awl-shaped (acicular) scales at base. Leaves 1–2cm long, with 5–6 stomatic lines on each upper side and 2 on each lower side. Mature cones 6–12cm long, cylindric-oblong.

P. glehnii Sakhalin Spruce. Japan. Tree to 40m. Shoots reddish-brown, terminal bud with awl-shaped (acicular) scales at the base. Leaves 6–12mm long with 2 white stomatal bands above and 1–2 broken lines on each lower side; apex obtuse or acute. Mature cones 5–8cm long, cylindric-oblong.

P. likiangensis Likiany Spruce. W China. Tree to 30m. Shoots grayish-yellow. Upper 2 ranks of leaves imbricate and bent forward more or less parallel with the shoot. Leaves 8–15mm long, with 2 white bands above and 1–2(3, 4) broken stomatal lines on each lower side; apex acute, horny pointed. Mature cones 5–8cm long, cylindric-oblong.

Firs
(genus *Abies*)

Abies is a genus of evergreen trees comprising some 40–50 species widely distributed in the mountainous regions of the Northern Hemisphere: in central and southern Europe (southern Spain and the opposite region of North Africa), in Asia northward from, and including the Himalaya, as well as Japan and extensive areas of North America. The generic name occurs in classical Latin, referring to some kind of fir tree, although not necessarily a species of *Abies*. However, in the English language the word 'fir' is now restricted to species of this genus, except that Douglas Fir is the traditional name for species of the genus *Pseudotsuga* and Scotch Fir is a name traditionally given to the Scots Pine (*Pinus sylvestris*). Some authorities use the name silver firs for members of the genus *Abies* to distinguish them from other firs.

It is not difficult to distinguish the genus *Abies*. The erect cone, breaking up at maturity, the needles occurring singly, the rounded disk-like needle scar which is not raised above the level of the bark, thus giving a virtually smooth branchlet – this combination of characters readily identifies a conifer as a member of the genus *Abies*.

Some 30 species are planted outside their native regions but more for their fine and lofty appearance than as a commercial undertaking. The Common Silver Fir (*Abies alba*), Grand Fir (*A. grandis*), Noble Fir (*A. procera*) and Caucasian Fir (*A. nordmanniana*) are the commonest firs grown for ornament in parks and gardens, the first three also having some value on a limited scale as plantation trees. They require a moist, preferably deep soil and a moist climate and clean air, their susceptibility to atmospheric pollution rendering them unsuitable in or near industrial areas. Fraser's Balsam Fir (*A. fraseri*) and the Balsam Fir (*A. balsamea*) are used as Christmas trees in America and Canada.

Propagation is by seed usually in nursery beds, sometimes in a cold frame or propagating cabinet. Hybrids and varieties need to be grafted.

Firs are subject to attack by insects, aphid species of the genus *Adelges* being particularly serious. The extent of injury varies with the region. Thus, *Adelges picae* has little more than nuisance value in Europe, but in Canada it can kill trees of *Abies balsamea* at all stages. 'Silver Fir Dieback,' caused by *Adelges nuesslini*, is so serious in the United Kingdom on the Common Silver Fir that extensive planting of this tree has been abandoned. In general, treatment with an aphicide is only effective with young plants still at the nursery stage. No treatment is effective for badly affected trees. Such trees may be recognized by the development of gout-like swellings on the branches and the presence of the insects covered by a white, protective exudate.

Abies alba is sometimes disfigured by small so-called 'witches-broom' – a dense tuft of weak branches. Some of these appear to arise spontaneously but others are a response to attack by the rust fungus *Melampsorella caryophyllacearum*, whose alternate hosts are various species of the family Caryophyllaceae.

Abies wood is sold as (white) deal and varies from white to yellowish or reddish-brown with no obvious distinction between heartwood and sapwood. Resin canals are normally absent. This soft wood is easily worked, yielding a good surface, which readily accepts paint and polish. Its main use is for indoor work, but treated

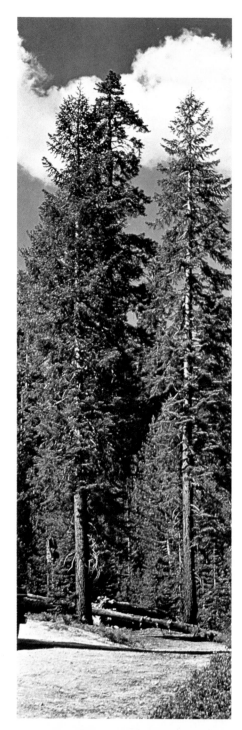

Above Left Red Firs (*Abies magnifica*) growing in the Yosemite National Park, California, USA.

Above Right A young shoot of the Himalayan Fir (*Abies spectabilis*). The reddish-brown branchlets bear long, densely-set needles which are notched at the apex, grooved above and with two white bands beneath. A cluster of young reddish, female cones is also visible.

Left The fan-like, pale green spring growth of the Giant Fir (*Abies grandis*) is an ornamental attraction of this fast-growing species.

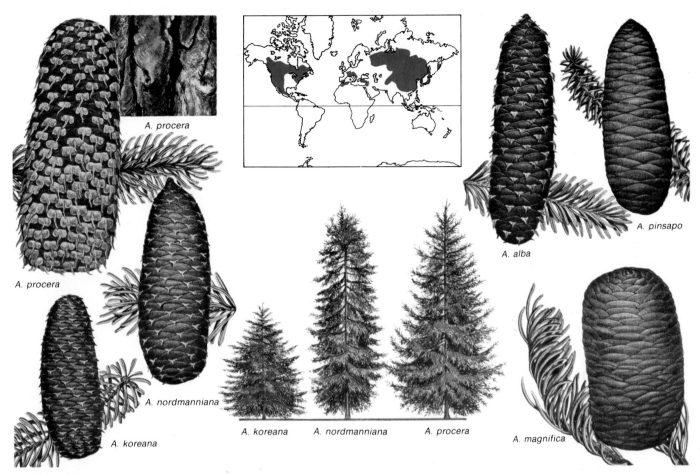

A. procera

A. procera

A. nordmanniana

A. koreana

A. koreana   A. nordmanniana   A. procera

A. pinsapo

A. alba

A. magnifica

The Main Species of *Abies*

Group I: Needles all arranged in one plane or at least some of them widely parted above (pectinate). Needles flat unless otherwise indicated.

A. alba (*A. pectinata*) Common Silver Fir. Mountains of C and S Europe. Tree to 50m. Branchlets hairy, not grooved; winter buds not resinous. Leaves 1.5–3cm long, notched at apex with two white stomatal bands on lower surface. Resin canals lateral.

A. balsamea Balsam Fir, Balm of Gilead. Common and widespread in N America, extending to Arctic Circle. A source of the resin Canada Balsam. Tree to 25m. Branchlets hairy, not grooved; winter buds resinous. Leaves 1.5–2.5cm long, notched at apex with 4–9 lines of whitish stomatal bands on lower surface only. Resin canals median.

A. concolor Colorado or White Fir. Mountains of Colorado to S California, New Mexico, Arizona and Mexico. Tree to 40m. Branchlets minutely hairy or hairless; winter buds resinous. Leaves 4–6cm long with white stomatal lines on both surfaces; not notched at apex. Resin canals lateral.

A. grandis Giant Fir. W N America. Tree to 100m; does well in cultivation, but then reaches only some 50m. Practically free from injury by disease or insect attacks and resistant to frost. Branchlets olive-greenish, minutely hairy to almost hairless; winter buds resinous. Leaves 3–6cm long, notched at apex; white stomatal bands only on lower surface. Resin canals lateral.

A. magnifica Red Fir. Oregon to California. Tree to 70m. Branchlets minutely rusty pubescent; winter buds resinous. Leaves 2.5–4cm long, quadrangular in section, not notched at apex; stomatal bands on all sides. Resin canals lateral.

A. procera (*A. nobilis*) Noble Fir. Cascade mountains, Washington to N California. Tree to 80m. Commonly planted under forestry conditions where it may reach 50m, but sometimes suffers serious attacks by *Adelges*. Branchlets minutely rusty pubescent; winter buds resinous. Leaves 2.5–3.5cm long, flat or grooved above, not or slightly notched at apex; stomatal bands on both surfaces. Resin canals lateral.

A. spectabilis Himalayan Fir. NW Himalayan mountains. Tree to 50m. Branchlets reddish-brown with pubescence in grooves; winter buds resinous. Leaves 2.5–6cm long, notched at apex; stomatal bands only on lower surface. Resin canals lateral.

Group II: Needles not pectinate as in Group I, but densely overlapping above. Branchlets hairy. Needles flat.

A. amabilis Red Silver Fir. Mountains of British Columbia, Alberta and Oregon to Washington. Tree to 80m, but only about 30m in cultivation and subject to aphis attack; winter buds resinous. Leaves 2–3cm long, truncate or notched at apex; stomatal bands white, only on lower surface. Resin canals lateral.

A. cilicica Cilician Fir. Mountains of Asia Minor, N Syria and Antitaurus. Tree to 30m. Winter buds with a few scales free at the tips, not or only slightly resinous. Leaves 2–3cm long, slightly notched at apex; stomatal bands whitish, only on lower surface. Resin canals lateral. Cone with hidden bracts.

A. nordmanniana Nordmann or Caucasian Fir. N Caucasus, Asia Minor. Tree to 50m. Very similar to preceding, but winter bud scales not free and cone with exserted and reflexed bracts.

Group III: Needles neither overlapping nor pectinate but directed upward and outward; flat.

A. koreana Korean Fir. Korea. Tree to 18m sometimes shrubby in cultivation. Winter buds slightly resinous. Leaves 1–2cm long, usually tapering downward with whitish stomatal bands only on lower surface. Resin canals median.

Group IV: Needles radially arranged around branchlets.

A. cephalonica Greek Fir. Mountains of Greece. Tree to 30m. Winter buds resinous. Leaves flattened, 2–3cm long, apex sharply pointed; white stomatal bands on lower surface only. Resin canals lateral.

A. pinsapo Spanish Fir, Hedgehog Fir. S Spain. Tree to 25m. Tolerant of lime. Winter buds resinous. Leaves 1.5–2cm long, thick rigid, apex not sharp pointed. Resin canals median.

with a preservative it has been used out doors, for example for telegraph poles. As the wood has no noticeable smell it has also been used for crating grocery and dairy products that might otherwise become tainted.

In certain American firs, the bark of young trees bears 'resin blisters' from which resin is obtained. Resins are non-volatile mixtures, insoluble in water, but soluble in organic solvents. Steam distillation removes turpentine, the residual solid being rosin, which is used in the manufacture of products such as plastics, soaps and varnishes. Canada balsam, extensively used as a permanent mounting medium in microscopical preparations, and in pharmacy, is obtained from the Balsam Fir and other North American species.

F. B. H.

Hemlocks or Hemlock Spruces (genus *Tsuga*)

Tsuga is a genus of about 10 species of evergreen trees (sometimes bushes) native to North America, Japan, China, Taiwan and the Himalaya. In habit they are broadly pyramidal, the branches being horizontal to somewhat pendulous. The leaves are flat, short-stalked (petiolate) and spirally inserted but appearing in two horizontal ranks by twisting of the petiole; the stalk is borne on a projecting decurrent leaf-base. The leaves persist for several years, finally falling off to leave a semicircular scar on the projecting leaf-base.

The spruces (*Picea*) are distinguished from *Tsuga* by the leaves being sessile (without stalks), with more prominent roughly diamond-shaped leaf-scars and the cones more than 2.5cm (1in) long, except that *Tsuga mertensiana* and the closely related supposed hybrid *T. jeffreyi* have cones to 7cm (2.8in) long. The male cones are minute, up to 5mm (0.2in),

yellowish-white, but more often a shade of red. The female cones are characteristically small, rarely exceeding 2.5cm (1in) long. They are pendulous and ripen in the first year but persist several years after shedding their seeds, which are small and winged, two occurring under each cone-scale.

Hemlocks like a good, fairly well-drained soil. Propagation is usually by seed, the varieties and forms by shoot cuttings or by grafting. In addition to the numerous varieties and forms, mostly of the species *T. canadensis* (Common or Canada Hemlock), there are a number of intergeneric hybrids, namely *Tsuga × Picea* (= *Tsugo-Picea*); *Picea × (Tsugo-Picea)*; *Tsuga × (Tsugo-Picea)*; *Keteleeria × Tsuga*.

The wood of the Common Hemlock is used for building construction generally and for ladder making. The resin is also useful and is known commercially as

Canada Pitch. The bark contains tannin which is extracted for tanning leather etc. The Western Hemlock (*T. heterophylla*) and Mountain Hemlock (*T. mertensiana*) are the species most frequently cultivated as ornamentals, the Western Hemlock also being found in forestry plantations particularly under hardwood crops.

F. B. H.

The Main Species of *Tsuga*

Group I: Leaves spirally arranged around branches, more or less rounded above or only slightly grooved. Cones 5–7.5cm long.

T. mertensiana Mountain Hemlock. W N America. Tree usually to about 30m, but up to 50m in its native habitat. Specific name formerly used for what is now known as *T. heterophylla* (see below). Cones spruce-like in clusters on shoot tip, 7 × 3.5cm, green when young, turning deep red-brown when mature. Bark brownish-orange with fine vertical fissures.

The largest of the hemlocks, the Western Hemlock (*Tsuga heterophylla*) makes a fine pyramidal ornamental tree with its horizontal and slightly drooping branches, in this specimen brushing the ground.

Douglas Firs
(genus *Pseudotsuga*)

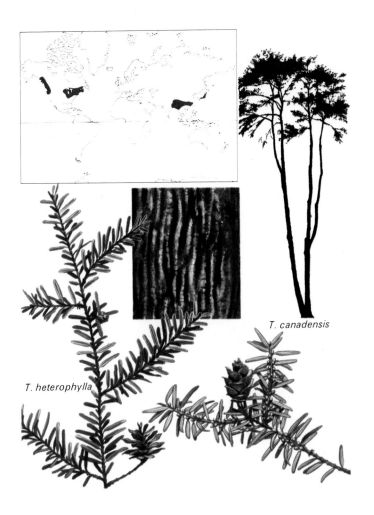

T. canadensis

T. heterophylla

Some 20 types of Douglas fir have been described but only five or six are recognized as 'good' species. They are natives of western North America, China, Japan and Taiwan and succeed on a wide range of soils but flourish in a damp climate on a moist, well-drained soil.

Douglas firs are evergreen trees, generally pyramidal in the early stages, finally somewhat widely spreading. The winter buds are characteristically spindle-shaped, not unlike those of the beech. The branchlets have slightly raised oval leaf-scars and the leaves are needle-like, grooved above, and spirally arranged. They have two white stomatic lines on the lower side and appear to be in one plane because the leaf-base is twisted (except in *Pseudotsuga japonica*). Each leaf has two marginal resin canals and one vascular strand. The male and female cones are separate but borne on the same tree. The male cones are short and catkin-like comprising numerous pollen sacs; the females are terminal, consisting of numerous persistent cone-scales, each scale with two ovules beneath. The mature cone is pendulous with the bract-scale prominently exserted (protruding), its apex being three-lobed. The seeds are winged.

The generic name *Pseutotsuga* (literally 'false hemlock') suggests a relationship with *Tsuga*, but the Douglas firs are easily distinguished by the plainly visible trifid exserted bract-scales of the mature cones and by the leaf-bases being not, or scarcely decurrent. The genus *Abies*, in which the Douglas firs were once placed, is distinct in its erect mature cones whose scales fall away from a persistent axis. In *Abies*, moreover, there is no exserted trifid bract-scale and the leaf-scars are circular and flat and level with the branchlet surface.

Douglas firs are susceptible to a number of fungus diseases. The gray mold fungus *Botrytis cinerea* affects seedlings and is able to flourish because of excessive damp and overcrowding. In older trees, *Rhabdoclyne pseudotsugae* causes brown patches on the leaves of *Pseudotsuga menziesii* (Oregon or Gray Douglas Fir) and its variety *glauca* (Blue Douglas Fir). More serious is canker and dieback caused by *Phomopsis pseudotsugae*. The main insect pest is the aphid *Adelges cooleyi*; the Douglas fir acts as the secondary host, the primary (sexual stage)

Group II: Leaves essentially in one plane (= pectinate), flat above and grooved. Cones 2–3cm long.

T. sieboldii Japanese Hemlock. S Japan. Tree to 30m in its native habitat, about half as high in Europe, where it is often little more than a large bush. Branchlets hairless (glabrous), leaves notched, margin entire. Cones pendulous, ovoid, 2.3 × 1.3cm, with flat-topped scales and dark brown when mature. Bark pink-gray, at first smooth with horizontal folds, later cracking into squares and becoming flaky.

T. canadensis Common or Canada Hemlock. E N America. Tree 25–30m. Branchlets covered in fine hairs (pubescent). Leaves with serrulate margins, distinct stomatal lines beneath and with distinct green edges. Cones numerous on side shoots, ovoid, 2 × 1cm, coffee-brown when ripe. Bark orange-brown on young trees, dark purplish gray-brown when mature. Many forms and varieties in cultivation.

T. heterophylla Western Hemlock. Coastal regions of W N America. Tree 30–60m. Branchlets pubescent. Leaves with serrulate margins, indistinct stomatal lines beneath and edges not obviously different. Cones pendulous and numerous on side shoots, blunt, ovoid, 2–3cm long, green to purplish

when young, becoming light brown. Bark gray-green and smooth when young, russet-brown and narrowly fissured when mature.

T. diversifolia Northern Japanese Hemlock. Japan. Tree to 25m in its natural habitat, but often a large shrub in cultivation. Branchlets pubescent all round. Leaves with entire margins, 8–15mm long, notched at apex. Cone cylindrical ovoid, 2–2.8cm, dark shiny brown. Bark orange-brown with pink fissures.

T. chinensis Chinese Hemlock. W China. Tree to 50m. Branchlets pubescent. Leaves with entire margins, up to 25mm long, notched at apex sometimes with a few marginal serrulations. Cone long-ovoid, 3 × 1.3cm, green turning to red-brown. Bark with curving patterns of dark gray-green scales becoming very flaky and fissured dark brown and gray.

T. caroliniana Carolina Hemlock. Mountains of SE USA. Tree to 15m occasionally to 25m. Branchlets pubescent. Leaves with entire margins, 8–18mm long, not or scarcely notched at apex with conspicuously white stomatal bands below. Cone long-ovoid, 2.5 × 1.5cm, orange-brown. Bark dark red-brown with yellow pores, becoming fissured and purple-gray.

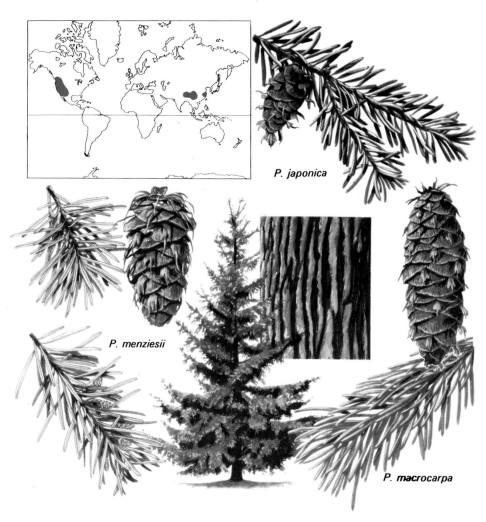

P. japonica

P. menziesii

P. macrocarpa

host being various species of *Picea*.

The timber of *P. menziesii* is in great demand and is the premier wood of North America. Although constituting half the standing timber of the western forests, its exploitation without replacement is leading to concern. Individual trees provide an immense quantity of timber which is, however, very variable in strength and grain, and requires careful grading to ensure reasonable uniformity. It is used for practically every type of constructional work – houses, bridges and boats, for general carpentry, rolling stock and all kinds of poles and posts including commemorative flagstaffs. A mature Douglas fir is also a fine sight as an ornamental tree, especially when cleared of the lower and dead branches. Single subjects are therefore extensively planted in rural areas and parks, while some dense stands can be found in forested areas.

F. B. H.

Larches
(genus *Larix*)

Larix is a genus of about 12 species of deciduous, commonly fast-growing trees, native to the cooler mountainous regions of the Northern Hemisphere – central and northern Europe, North America and Asia from the Himalaya to Siberia and Japan.

Larches are more or less pyramidal trees with spreading irregularly whorled branches. The leaves are borne spirally on the long shoots, but are most conspicuous as dense clusters on the very short shoots. The female cones are finally erect and are very attractive when young, with crimson bract-scales ('larch noses'). The cones mature within a year, becoming pale brown, but persist after the shedding of seeds. There are two seeds under each ovuliferous- or cone-scale, each seed having a thin well-developed wing. Mature cones are essential for species determination. In

Opposite A stand of larches (*Larix* sp) in the Black Forest, West Germany, showing their fall colors. Larches are unusual among the conifers in being deciduous. They are important timber producers.

The Main Species of *Pseudotsuga*

Group I: Leaf apices acutely pointed, or if somewhat blunt, then not broadly rounded or notched. Cones 5–18cm long.

P. menziesii (*P. douglasii*, *P. taxifolia*) Oregon or Gray Douglas Fir. W N America extending to N Mexico. Tree to 100m. Branchlets pubescent, rarely glabrous. Leaves 2–3cm, acute or blunt, dark green or bluish-green above. Cones 5–10cm, the trifid bract-scales usually erect, occasionally reflexed. The crushed leaves have a characteristic pleasant citronella-like smell.
var *glauca* E Rocky mountains from Montana to Mexico. Tree to about 40m. Leaves shorter and thicker than the type, bluntly pointed, glaucous, smelling of turpentine when crushed. Cones 6–7.5cm, the bracts usually with reflexed tips. Typical specimens are distinctive and known as Colorado Douglas Fir but a continuous chain of intermediates connects it with the type. More susceptible to fungus attack by *Rhabdocline pseudotsugae* than the type but more resistant to the aphid

Adelges cooleyi. It is planted for its decorative value and has no commercial potential.

P. macrocarpa Large-coned Douglas Fir. SW California. Tree 12–16(25)m. Leaves 2.5–3.5cm, light green. Cones 10–18cm, the bract-scales less exserted than in *P. menziesii*. The cone size at once distinguishes this species from all others.

Group II: Leaf apices broadly rounded or notched. Cones 3–6cm.

P. japonica Japanese Douglas Fir. SE Japan. Tree 15–30m. Branchlets glabrous. Leaves notched, directed forward but spreading in all directions, not obviously arranged in one plane, pale grayish-green. Cones 3–5cm, few-scaled (15–20).

P. sinensis Chinese Douglas Fir. W China. Tree about 20m. Branchlets hairy, reddish-brown. Leaves 2.5–3cm, arranged in one plane. Cones 5–6cm.

P. wilsoniana Taiwan and Mekong valley. Tree 20–30m. Branchlets at first reddish-brown becoming grayish, glabrous or sparsely and minutely hairy. Leaves to 5cm, arranged in one plane. Cones 5–6cm, the bract-scales with long reflexed central prong.

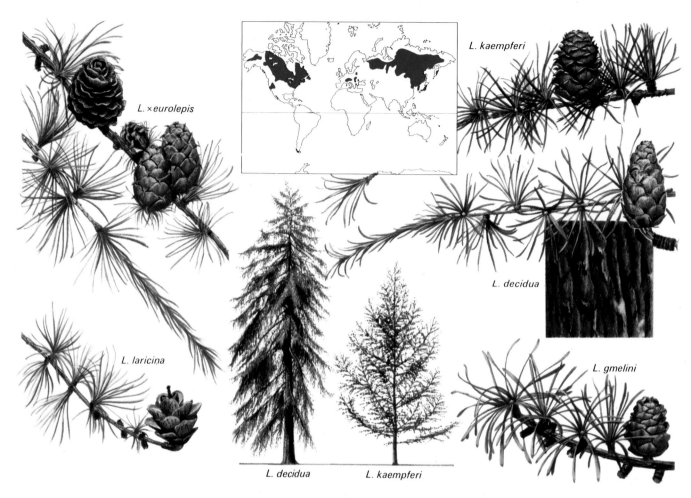

L. ×eurolepis

L. laricina

L. kaempferi

L. decidua

L. gmelini

L. decidua   L. kaempferi

the young cone and at the time of pollination the bract-scale much exceeds the ovuliferous-scale, but at maturity the bract-scale may or may not be hidden by the ovuliferous-scale.

Larches do best on well-drained light or gravelly loams and are intolerant of low-lying areas where water is liable to accumulate and which are subject to frost. Propagation is by seed; varieties are sometimes grafted.

Larch wood is strong and durable and used for posts, pit-props, barges etc. The relatively rapid rate of growth of most species is also an advantage when a quick return on investment is being sought. A disadvantage of larch cultivation, however, is that many are susceptible to a number of diseases. *Larix decidua* (European Larch) and *L. occidentalis* (Western Larch) suffer especially from Larch Canker or Blister caused by the ascomycete fungus *Trichoscyphella willkommii*, which flourishes where the trees are overcrowded or on poorly-drained soil. Infected trees are useless for timber and may be killed outright. Larch Chermes, a species of *Adelges* (related to aphids but much smaller) cause serious shoot damage thus retarding

growth. The larch is the secondary host for these insects, the primary host being species of *Picea* (spruce).

The bark has been used for tanning and dyeing and has medicinal properties and is mainly used in veterinary practise. Venice or Larch Turpentine, obtained by tapping, is so used. In summer months the leaves exude a whitish and sweet substance known as briancon larch manna which was also once used in medicine. It contains the unusual trisaccharide sugar melecitose.

F. B. H.

The Main Species of *Larix*

Unless otherwise stated all species below have an almost concealed bract-scale which does not project beyond the cone-scale (= ovuliferous-scale).

Group I: Leaves with two distinct white or greenish-white bands on under side.

L. *kaempferi* (L. *leptolepis*) Japanese Larch. Japan. Tree to 30m. Leaves 2–3.5cm, each white band beneath comprising five rows of stomata. Cones up to 3.5cm with tips of cone-scales recurved, reddish-brown and scaly sometimes with flakes that break

away. Makes rapid growth and is much planted.

L. *griffithiana* Sikkim Larch. E Nepal, Sikkim, Tibet. Tree to 20m. Leaves 3–4cm with greenish-white bands beneath. Cones erect, cylindric, abundant, purple-brown 6–11cm; bract-scales protruding as fine points, some depressed against cone. Bark reddish-brown with scales. Grows best in mild climates.

Group II: Leaves without white bands beneath.

L. *laricina* Tamarack, Eastern Larch. N America. Tree to 20m. Leaves 3cm. Branchlets hairless (glabrous). Cones 1.5 × 1cm with 12–15(16) scales, glabrous on outside and shining, with erect or slightly incurved tips. Bark dull pink or pinkish-brown, finely flaking but with no fissures. Tolerates wet peaty soils.

L. *gmelini* Dahurian Larch. NE Asia. Tree to 30m. Leaves 3cm. Branchlets usually covered in fine hairs. Cones 2–2.5cm with 20–40(50) scales, glabrous on outside and shining, with erect or slightly incurved tips. Bark reddish-brown and scaly.

L. *decidua* (L. *europaea*) European Larch. N and C Europe and Siberia. Tree to 35m. Leaves 2–3cm. Cone-scales 40–50 straight not incurved at apex and pubescent to shortly downy (tomentose) outside; bract-scales about half length of cone-scales. Bark greenish gray-brown and smooth when young later becoming fissured vertically.

L. russica (*L. sibirica*) Siberian Larch. E Russia and Siberia. Tree to 30m. Leaves 1.5–3cm. Cone-scales slightly incurved at apex and pubescent to shortly tomentose outside; bract-scales about one-third length of cone-scales.

L. × eurolepis Dunkeld Larch. This is a vigorous natural hybrid between *L. decidua* and *L. kaempferi*, pollen being supplied by the first species. What might be called typical specimens are intermediate between the parents, but seedlings from the hybrid itself show a wide range of variation between the original parents. Bark reddish-brown. Shows greater resistance to insect and fungal pests than other species.

L. occidentalis Western Larch. N America – British Columbia, Oregon, Washington, Idaho. Tree 43–55m high. Leaves 3–5cm. Cones tall ovoid, 3–5cm, purple-brown when ripe; bract-scales protrude as long spreading or down-curved points. Bark purplish-gray with deep wide fissures with flaky edges.

Golden Larch
(genus *Pseudolarix*)

The Golden Larch (*Pseudolarix amabilis* = *P. kaempferi*) is a splendid tree, the leaves turning a rich, golden yellow toward the end of the season whence the Chinese name 'chin-lo-sung' = Golden Deciduous Pine is derived.

Pseudolarix amabilis is the only confirmed species of the genus and is native to east China (Chekiang and Kiangsi provinces). A second species *P. pourtei* from central China has been proposed but this is known only from vegetative material; it has small quantitative differences from *P. amabilis* and may be the juvenile state of this species.

Pseudolarix is a deciduous tree reaching 40m (130ft). Its leaves are needle-like, about 4–6.5cm (1.6–2.6in) × 2–3mm (0.08–0.12in); they are produced either singly and spirally arranged on long shoots which are rough with persistent bases of shed leaves or in almost umbrella-like clusters on short shoots which are characteristically club-shaped and curved with persistent scales and distinct close-set, annual rings separated by constrictions. The cones are not unlike those of *Larix*, the males clustered in catkins about 2.5cm (1in) across, the females on the same tree about 5 × 1cm (2 × 0.4in) comprising thick, acuminate, woody scales which break up at maturity, releasing the seeds.

The Golden Larch differs from *Larix* (in which genus it was once placed) in the more robust leaves, the curved short shoots, the more or less pointed cone-scales (not blunt-rounded) and the cone breaking up at maturity (remaining intact in *Larix*).

The Golden Larch is quite hardy in the warmer parts of temperate regions but slow growing. It requires a good, deep, well-drained soil but is intolerant of lime. Propagation is best from seed which is often abundantly set in some cultivated areas, for example Italy.

F. B. H.

View of the underside of a shoot of the Golden Larch (*Pseudolarix amabilis*) showing a number of short shoots each with its distinctive annual rings and crowned by whorls of leaves that are beginning to show fall tints, which make a spectacular display at the end of the season.

Cedars
(genus *Cedrus*)

Cedrus is a genus of stately evergreens commonly regarded as comprising four species: *Cedrus atlantica*, *C. brevifolia*, *C. deodara* and *C. libani*. Some authorities consider them all to be geographical infraspecific taxa of a single species. This is probably true, but long-standing horticultural practise and convenience keeps them at the species level. They have a wide but discontinuous distribution in the Old World.

All species have long and short shoots, the latter with clusters of needle-like leaves, 0.5–5cm (0.25–2in) long according to species. Male cones are erect, ovoid or conic, up to 5cm (2in), opening September to November. Female cones are erect, up to 1cm (0.4in) borne terminally on short shoots. The fruiting cones, which take two or three years to mature, are oval to oblong, rounded at the apex and about 5–10cm (2–4in) long; the numerous flattened scales are finally deciduous from a central axis. On average, trees do not bear cones until they are 40 or 50 years old.

Cedars grow best in a well-drained rich loam or sandy clay. Propagation is from seed. Mature cones should be gathered in the spring and kept in a warm place. The cone-scales break away and free the seeds, which are then ready for germination; the seedlings are planted out in the following spring. Apart from *C. brevifolia*, which is little cultivated, all the species have numerous forms. Probably the best-known is the Blue Cedar (*C. atlantica* var *glauca*), which is prized for specimen planting and is probably the best colored of all 'blue' forms of conifer.

The wood of *Cedrus* is soft but durable and is widely used in building construction and for furniture. The resin has been used for embalming.

F. B. H.

The Species of *Cedrus*

C. atlantica Atlas or Atlantic Cedar. N Africa (Algeria). A pyramidal tree up to 40m with an upright leading shoot and lateral branches ascending, but not becoming horizontal. Needles 2.5cm long. Cones 5–7cm × 4cm, with a flat or slightly depressed apex. Variety *glauca* (Blue Cedar) has light blue or waxy leaves.

C. brevifolia Cyprus Cedar. Mountains of Cyprus. A broad dome-shaped tree up to 12m with spreading to recurved leading shoots. Needles 5–6mm long. Cones 7 × 4cm, with a depressed apex and short umbo.

C. deodara Himalayan or Indian Cedar, Deodar. W Himalaya. A pyramidal tree when young, although irregular when mature, growing up to 60m with a pendulous leading shoot and slightly drooping lateral branches with pendulous tips. Needles are 2.5–5cm with an apical spine. Cones 7–10cm × 5–6cm, barrel-shaped with a rounded apex.

C. libani Cedar of Lebanon. Lebanon, Taurus mountains, Syria. A dome-shaped tree up to 40m with an upright to spreading leading shoot and characteristic tiers of lateral branches ascending for a few metres then becoming horizontal. Needles 2.5–3cm. Cones 8–10cm × 4.6cm with a flat or depressed apex.

SOME TREES HAVING THE COMMON NAME 'CEDAR'

Common Name	Species
African Cedar	*Juniperus procera*
Alaska Cedar	*Chamaecyparis nootkatensis*
Atlantic or Atlas Cedar	*Cedrus atlantica*
Australian Red Cedar	*Toona* spp
Bastard Cedar	*Soymida febrifuga*
Bermuda Cedar	*Juniperus bermudiana*
Black Cedar	*Nectandra pisi*
California Incense Cedar	*Libocedrus decurrens*
Cedar Elm	*Ulmus crassifolia*
Cedar of Goa	*Cupressus lusitanica*
Cedar of Lebanon	*Cedrus libani*
Cyprus Cedar	*Cedrus brevifolia*
Eastern Red Cedar	*Juniperus virginiana*
Himalayan Black Cedar	*Alnus nitida*
Himalayan Cedar	*Cedrus deodara*
Himalayan Pencil Cedar	*Juniperus macrocarpa*
Incense Cedar	*Calocedrus decurrens*
Indian Cedar	*Cedrus deodara*
Japanese Cedar	*Cryptomeria* spp
Mahogany Cedar	*Entandrophragma candolei, E. cylindricum*
Manado Cedar	*Cedrela celebica*
Mlanje Cedar	*Widdringtonia whytei*
Oregon Cedar	*Chamaecyparis lawsoniana*
Pencil Cedar	*Juniperus* spp (especially *J. virginiana*)
Prickly Cedar	*Cyathodes acerosa*
Red Cedar	*Juniperus* spp (especially *J. virginiana*)
Sharp Cedar	*Acacia oxycedrus, Juniperus oxycedrus*
Siberian Cedar	*Pinus cembra*
Stinking Cedar	*Torreya taxifolia*
Western Red Cedar	*Thuja plicata*
Western White Cedar	*Thuja plicata*
West Indian Cedar	*Cedrela* spp
White Cedar	*Chamaecyparis* spp, *Chickrassia, Melia azedarach*
Yellow Cedar	*Chamaecyparis* spp

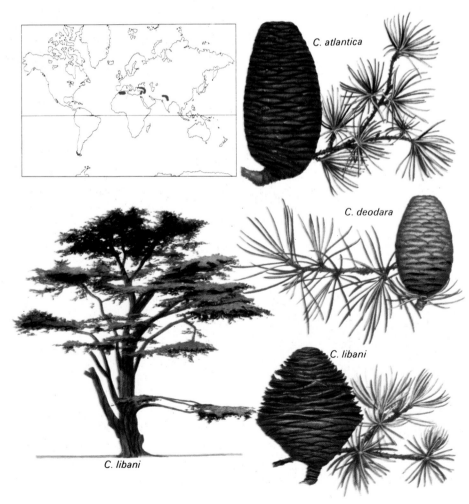

C. atlantica

C. deodara

C. libani

C. libani

Keteleeria

The genus *Keteleeria* contains about four 'good' species but segregates from these, by some authorities, raise this number to nine. Like *Abies* in its upright (not pendulous or reflexed) cones it differs mainly by the cone falling in one piece, whereas in *Abies* the cone-scales are deciduous from their axis. In *Keteleeria* the leaves are keeled above and (mostly) below, the under surface is pale yellowish-green as in yews (*Taxus* spp) and there are no whitish stomatal bands on the under surface, as there are in *Abies*.

Left The Cedar of Lebanon (*Cedrus libani*) is one of the most majestic of all conifers and many of our parks and open spaces rejoice in such magnificent specimens as this.
Below Young cones of the Atlantic or Atlas Cedar (*Cedrus atlantica*) take two or three years to mature so that most trees are clothed in cones throughout the year.
Right Foliage of *Keteleeria davidiana*, the leaves at the top clearly showing their twisted bases, which causes them to lie in one plane.

Keteleerias are evergreen trees native to southeast, central and western China extending to Indochina and Taiwan (Formosa). In form they are pyramidal to finally more or less dome-shaped with spreading branches in whorls. The leaves are needle-like, linear to slightly tapering, solitary, spirally inserted but are mostly twisted so as to lie in one plane (pectinate). The mature cones are large, upright and ripen in the first year. Each cone consists of numerous persistent broad woody scales, each in the axil of a forked bract-scale about half the cone-scale length. The seeds are winged and similar to those in *Abies* – two are produced for each cone-scale.

Keteleerias are only marginally hardy in temperate regions and thus distinctly rare in cultivation and even then only two of the species are represented: *K. davidiana* (central and west China, Taiwan) and *K. fortunei* (east China). The former is the most hardy of this generally 'unhardy' genus but the latter has survived in cultivation in Italy.

F. B. H.

Redwoods
(genera *Metasequoia*, *Sequoiadendron*, *Sequoia*)

The redwoods comprise three genera of living coniferous trees: *Metasequoia* (one living species; some 10 fossil representatives), *Sequoia* and *Sequoiadendron*, each with a single living species. Usually placed in the family Taxodiaceae, some Chinese authorities have suggested that all the *Metasequoia* species should be separated out as a separate family Metasequoiaceae. *Metasequoia* is unusual in that it is deciduous, shedding its leafy dwarf-shoots in the fall.

The Dawn Redwood (*Metasequoia glyptostroboides*) was originally described from fossil material in 1941 and appears to have been widely distributed in the Northern Hemisphere back to the Cretaceous period (136 million years ago) and extending through to the early and middle parts of the Tertiary period (down to about 26 million years ago). The living tree was described in 1945 from Hupeh and Szechuan provinces of China. It was introduced into cultivation in 1948 from seed received at the Arnold Arboretum and is now widely grown in temperate regions. It has proved quite hardy. In the British Isles trees have already exceeded 20m (65ft) tall and although female cones are produced they do not appear to set seed, possibly because of failure of male cones to produce fertile pollen. Its possibility as a forestry tree is being considered as it is a fast grower – 1m (3.3ft) a year in the first 10 years, but then slowing down. In cultivation, it favors well-drained sloping ground but is equally at home on moist land near a lake or stream or even in an average garden soil. Propagation is readily effected by cuttings, half-ripe ones being struck in the summer months; a cold frame is adequate for hardwood cuttings.

In general appearance and especially its deciduous habit, the Dawn Redwood resembles the Swamp Cypress (*Taxodium distichum*) but the Dawn Redwood has the leaves and shoots opposite (not alternate). Diseases and pests are not yet established.

The Sierra Redwood (*Sequoiadendron giganteum*), also known as Big Tree, Giant Sequoia, Mammoth Tree or Wellingtonia, is a native of the western slopes of the Sierra Nevada, California. It was formerly placed in the genus *Sequoia* along with *S. sempervirens* with which it shares the characteristic thick, spongy bark which can be 'punched' without injury to the fist. It is sometimes confused with the Japanese Red Cedar (*Cryptomeria japonica*) but this has leaves 1–1.5cm (0.4–0.6in) long with incurved points, whereas the leaves of *Sequoiadendron* are less than 1cm (0.4in) long, awl-shaped, with straight tips.

Propagation is best from imported seeds, but cuttings can be used toward the end of

Opposite Closely-packed trunks and profuse sucker growth are characteristics of Coast Redwood (*Sequoia sempervirens*) forest, as here in the Big Basin State Park, California.

Sequoiadendron giganteum

Sequoia sempervirens

Sequoiadendron giganteum

Metasequoia glyptostroboides

The Redwoods

Single sex coniferous trees with woody cones of spirally-arranged compound scales (the bract-scale is not distinct, but fused with the ovuliferous-scale). Leaves arise singly or in pairs and are either evergreen, needle or awl-shaped and alternately (spirally) arranged or deciduous, needle-shaped, opposite (as also are the shoots) and in the same plane.

Metasequoia glyptostroboides Dawn Redwood. Hupeh and Szechwan Provinces, China. Tree, in its native habitat, to about 40m tall; in cultivation, since its introduction, to more than 20m. Crown conical. Young bark orange-brown, flaking; older bark more brownish and somewhat furrowed. Leaves deciduous yellowish-green, all in one plane (pectinate) in opposite pairs along the shoots, flat and linear, 2–4 × 2mm. Male cones in small ovoid clusters, 2–5 at base of leaves; female cones more or less cylindric to 2.5cm on stalk to 5cm, each of about 12 green scales, somewhat swollen at the tips, seeds winged.

Sequoiadendron giganteum Sierra Redwood, Big Tree, Giant Sequoia, Mammoth Tree, Wellingtonia. California. Tree to 100m. Crown conical. Bark light brown, thick, soft, fibrous, deeply furrowed. Leaves evergreen, alternate, of one sort, ovate to lanceolate, 3–7mm long, sometimes to 12mm. Male cones sessile, 4–8mm long, yellow when mature in spring; female cones ellipsoidal, 5–8 × 4–5.5cm, very woody, finally pendulous, the scales flattened, diamond-shaped, each with 3–9 seeds and with slender spine when young; ripening second year. Seeds 3–6mm long, pale brown, winged.

Sequoia sempervirens Coast Redwood. S California. Tree to 120m. Crown conical. Bark brown, thick, soft, fibrous, furrowed. Leaves evergreen, dark green, alternate, of two sorts (dimorphic): on leading shoots more or less spirally arranged, ovate-oblong to 6mm long, tip incurved, while on lateral shoots more or less in two ranks, needle-like and often falcate, 6–18mm long. Male cones minute to 1.5mm long; female cones ovoid to 2.5cm long, finally pendulous, scales slightly flattened obliquely, ridged, often deciduous, each scale bearing 2–5 winged seeds.

summer. Erect shoots are best, but if side shoots are used, these should, after rooting, be cut back when dormant buds will be stimulated to give leading shoots. Cuttings can be struck in sandy soil and should root by spring.

Adult trees and certain specimens have so captured the American imagination that they have been assigned personal individual names. The General Sherman Tree, for example, which stands in the Sequoia National Park, is alleged to be more than 3 000 years old and is claimed, at 2 000 tonnes, to be the most massive (though not the tallest) tree in the world.

Sequoiadendron is relatively free from disease and pests but young trees and seedlings are susceptible to the common gray mold fungus *Botrytis cinerea*. Gray mold has a grayish-brown appearance and attacks many conifers, causing the shoots to curl and wither.

Supplies of timber are limited but when used it is mainly for farm buildings, posts and stakes since the wood is durable, especially in contact with soil. Although straight-grained, light and soft, the wood is not particularly easy to work.

This vigorous and long-lived tree is much grown in parks and gardens, either as specimen trees or, particularly imposing, lining roads and avenues. 'Aureum' is a slower-growing cultivar with a dense upswept crown and pale gold young foliage; 'Pendulum' has a weeping form with downswept side branches.

The Coast Redwood (*Sequoia sempervirens*) is now the only member of the genus *Sequoia*, the Sierra Redwood having been transferred to a separate genus *Sequoiadendron*. Native specimens of *Sequoia sempervirens* are immense and stately, more or less columnar, evergreen trees, found wild only on a narrow coastal belt – the 'fog belt' – on the Pacific coast of North America from southwestern Oregon through northern and central California to south of Monterey. It rarely extends inland for more than about 40km (25mi) and will not grow at an altitude of more than 1 000m (3 500ft). Trees of this species are probably the tallest in the world, the maximum height being about 120m (400ft); the diameter of the trunk at ground level may reach 10m (30ft). The Coast Redwood may live for nearly 1 000 years, the average range being 400–800 years.

The tree is at its best on a good, moist but well-aerated soil with considerable atmospheric moisture. In California it has successfully grown under such conditions to form pure forest with the huge trunks

unusually close to one another. It can also grow (but less impressively) in thin soil on rocky slopes. It is unusual amongst conifers in that it suckers freely and thus can readily regenerate by sprouts from the bases of felled trees. This is important because, although seeds are readily formed, the successful germination rate is low and, moreover, the seedlings are intolerant of shade.

The wood of *Sequoia* is in great demand being soft, fine-grained and easy to work. Long lengths are obtainable of up to 2m (6ft) wide without defects. It is used in building construction and carpentry generally, also for paneling, railway sleepers, telegraph poles, road blocks, fence poles etc. It takes a good polish. Excessive demand has denuded many of the original forests but some have been preserved by conservation efforts.

As with the Giant Sequoia, the Coast Redwood is an outstanding tree for single specimen planting in parks and large gardens. 'Adpressa' is a smaller-leaved cultivar which has creamy-white young foliage.

F. B. H.

Swamp Cypresses (genus *Taxodium*)

Taxodium is a genus of three closely related species of deciduous or more or less evergreen trees, all of which are popularly known as swamp cypresses. They are natives of southern and southeastern United States and Mexico. The shoots (branchlets) are either persistent with axillary buds near the end of each year's growth or deciduous without buds and falling within the current year or at irregular intervals. The leaves are pale green, flattened or awl-shaped, arranged essentially in one plane on the deciduous shoots or radially on the persistent shoots. The male and female cones are present on the same plants, the male in pendulous panicles. The female cones ripen in one year and when mature are globular, 25mm (1in) in diameter, comprising numerous peltate scales, which are irregularly four-sided on the outside. Each scale bears two angular three-winged seeds.

The most commonly cultivated species, *Taxodium distichum* (Swamp or Bald Cypress), is a tall handsome tree whose pale green foliage gives it a surprisingly delicate feathery appearance. It usually favors swamps and streams, but will grow equally well on drained soil. Under swamp conditions the roots will produce upright protuberances or 'knees,' which rise above the level of the water and so assist in root aeration. These 'knees' are comparable to the specialized roots (pneumatophores) of

T. mucronatum

T. distichum

T. ascendens   T. distichum

the mangroves and other tropical swamp inhabitants.

Taxodium ascendens (Pond Cypress or sometimes also Bald Cypress) and *T. mucronatum* (Montezuma or Mexican Cypress) are both less hardy than *T. distichum* and so are not cultivated so much. *Taxodium mucronatum* is evergreen in its native Mexico but becomes deciduous in cooler climates. One particular specimen, in the Mexican village of Santa Maria del Tule near the city of Oaxaca, is

The Species of *Taxodium*

T. distichum Swamp or Bald Cypress. SE USA and westward to Illinois and Missouri; Arizona. Tree to 30–50m. Branches more or less horizontal, conical at first becoming round-headed at maturity. Leaves spreading, a characteristically delicate pale green, 8–18mm long, spirally arranged but twisted at the base and, as a result, appearing in one plane; reddish-brown at the end of the season and falling separately or with the deciduous branchlets. In wet ground roots produce upright 'knees' to assist in root aeration.

T. ascendens Pond Cypress, Upland Cypress or Bald Cypress. SE USA and westward to Alabama. Tree rather similar to *T. distichum*, but smaller, reaching about 25m, the trunk swollen at the base, the branches spreading, but the ultimate branchlets more or less erect. Leaves awl-shaped, not in 2 ranks but arranged all around the shoots, adpressed, 5–10mm long, bright green, turning to a rich brown in the fall.

T. mucronatum Montezuma or Mexican Cypress. Mexico. Tree much the same size as *T. distichum* but not well-known outside its native Mexico. It differs from *T. distichum* in being half-evergreen to evergreen with longer male cones, the pollen sacs opening in the fall and not in spring as in the other species.

Bald Cypresses (*Taxodium distichum*) in winter, established in a swamp near the River Mississippi, Illinois, United States. The open water marks the former course of the river. Note the broad buttress roots at the base of the trunk.

named *El Gigante*. It has become a historic landmark and is viewed locally with great pride. The Spanish conquistador Hernán Cortés wrote about this same tree which he saw during his expedition of the 1520's. For a long time this tree was believed to have the thickest trunk in the world until it was revealed that its massive size was the result of three trees having grown and fused together.

The timber most commonly used is from *T. distichum*; the wood is soft and does not shrink, is resistant to insect attack and is little affected by damp conditions. These qualities make it a suitable packaging material and useful for piping, ventilators, fencing and garden furniture.

F. B. H.

Chinese Firs
(genus *Cunninghamia*)

Cunninghamia (Chinese or China firs) is a genus of two, perhaps three, species native to China and Taiwan. The Chinese Fir (*Cunninghamia lanceolata*) is infrequently found in cultivation but in its native China it is an important timber tree. They are evergreen trees with spread-

Fine specimens of the Chinese Fir (*Cunninghamia lanceolata*) displaying their reddish bark, glossy, irregularly arranged, emerald-green foliage and rounded immature fruiting cones. They are infrequently found in cultivation, but are important timber trees in their native China.

ing branches. The leaves are stiff, decurrent, linear-lanceolate with serrulate margins, white-banded beneath and spread in two ranks, but arise spirally. Male cones are oblong, borne in terminal clusters. Females occur on the same tree as the males and are subglobose, comprising rather thin, leathery, overlapping, serrate, pointed scales without distinct bract-scales. There are three inverted ovules per scale, each maturing to a narrowly-winged seed.

Chinese firs are not particularly hardy except in the milder/warmer parts of temperate regions, hence are not often seen in cultivation, and then only in sheltered positions on a good soil. They will regenerate from stool shoots of felled trees. Propagation is best from seed, but cuttings from erect shoots may be used.

Two species have been positively identified. *Cunninghamia lanceolata* (south and west China) grows to 25m (82ft) and has leaves 3–6cm × 2–6mm (1.2–2.4 × 0.08–0.2in) with two broad, white stomatal lines beneath. The mature cones are 2.5–5.0cm (1–2in) long. The timber is much used for coffins. *Cunninghamia konishii* (Taiwan) reaches 25m (82ft) or more and differs from the previous species by having smaller and narrower leaves, 1.8–2.8cm × 2mm (0.7–1.1 × 0.08in); stomatal bands are absent or not clearly marked. The mature cones are up to 2.5cm (1in) long. The doubtful species is *C. kawkamii* also from Taiwan, which is intermediate in form between the two previous species and is probably a variety of *C. konishii*.

F. B. H.

Japanese Umbrella Pine
(genus *Sciadopitys*)

The Japanese Umbrella Pine or Parasol Pine (*Sciadopitys verticillata*) is an evergreen pyramidal tree reaching 40m (130ft) in its native habitat of central Japan, where it sometimes forms forests up to an altitude of 1000m (3300ft).

The bark is almost smooth but separates into thin shreds. The leaves are of two types. The main ones are in whorls of (10)20–30 paired leaves 8–12 × 0.2–0.3cm (3–5 × 0.08–0.12in), each pair united along their whole length by their sides; stomata are found only over a small area in the groove on the lower surface. The appearance of each whorl is very much like that of the 'stays' of an open umbrella. Along the internodes between these whorls are triangular, somewhat overlapping, scale-like leaves which are green at first, becoming brown in the second year. Male cones are in terminal clusters, each cone with spirally-arranged pollen sacs. The female cones are solitary, on same tree as the males, each comprising numerous (ovuliferous) scales, which, in the young state,

are much smaller than the subtending bract-scales, but greatly exceed them in the mature cone when they become woody

Below The Japanese Umbrella Pine (*Sciadopitys verticillata*) makes a fine and unusual ornamental pyramidal tree for parks and gardens. *Bottom* It is so named since the leaves (each actually two leaves united along their lengths) are arranged like the stays of an umbrella.

and more or less wedge- or fan-shaped. Each scale bears seven to nine seeds in the second year, the cone then ovoid and 8–12 × 3.5–5.0cm (3–5 × 1.4–2in), the upper margin of each scale being slightly recurved. Seeds are compressed ovoid, 12mm (0.48in) long and narrowly winged.

This species is a slow grower and hardy in temperate regions where it readily produces seed by which it is propagated. However, it is uncommon in cultivation and grown only for its unique appearance – quite unlike any other conifer.

The wood is durable and water resistant which makes it useful for boatbuilding.

F. B. H.

Tasmanian Cedars
(genus *Athrotaxis*)

Athrotaxis comprises three species of evergreen trees or shrubs all from the mountains of Tasmania. The leaves are spirally arranged and scale-like or awl-like. Cones are unisexual, the females finally woody, ripe within one year, more or less globose and comprising 5–20(25) spirally-arranged scales, each subtending a bract which is fused with its scale except at the tip. The scales are swollen at their free (outer) end, tapering to the base at the point of attachment. The seeds are winged.

The Smooth Tasmanian Cedar (*Athrotaxis cupressoides*) is a tree to 6–12m (20–40ft) in its native habitat of the mountains of central and western Tasmania where it grows at altitudes in excess of 1 000m (3 300ft), but it reaches about half this height in cultivation. The branchlets are rounded and concealed by the densely-packed adpressed, decussate scale-like leaves, about 3mm (0.12in) long, which are rhombic in outline, with a translucent, finely serrate margin. The leaf bases overlap and on larger branches the leaves are larger. Female cones are finally about 12mm (0.48in) across, comprising five or six scales, the free tip of each bract-scale projecting as a short, spiny point. It is distinguished from the other two species by the scale-leaves being closely adpressed along all their length to the branchlets and the absence of stomatal bands on the ventral surface.

The King William Pine (*A. selaginoides*)

Above Top Foliage of the King William Pine (*Athrotaxis selaginoides*) showing the stomatal bands on the upper surface. *Above* Foliage, young (green) and mature (brown) fruiting cones and short spikes of male cones of the Japanese Red Cedar (*Cryptomeria japonica*).

tops 33m (108ft) in its native habitat of western Tasmania. The leaves are 7–12mm (0.28–0.48in) long, lanceolate to awl-shaped, curved toward but free of the branchlet, pointing forward at about a 30° angle. They are much less densely arranged than in the previous species from which it is also distinct in having two stomatal bands on the ventral surface of the leaf and lacking translucent margins.

The Summit Cedar (*A. laxifolia*) is intermediate in form between the previous species, growing to a height of 10m (33ft) in the western mountains of Tasmania. Its leaves are slightly spreading, 4–6mm (0.16–0.24in) long, the margin translucent and entire; two stomatal bands are present on the upper (ventral) surface.

The wood of Tasmanian cedars has some value in cabinet-making and lighter types of carpentry. All three species are marginally hardy in temperate zones.

F. B. H.

Japanese Red Cedar
(genus *Cryptomeria*)

The Japanese Red Cedar (*Cryptomeria japonica*) is the only member of its genus but exists in two distinct, geographically isolated varieties. The one seen most frequently in cultivation is var *japonica* from Japan, while var *sinensis* is native to China. Cryptomerias are evergreen trees with reddish-brown bark which detaches in longish shreds. The leaves are spirally arranged in five ranks and more or less awl-shaped, 6–12mm (0.24–0.48in) long, the base decurrent on the shoot. Male and female cones occur on the same branch, the male in short spike-like clusters each with numerous pollen sacs, the female solitary and maturing in one year into a woody, erect, stalked cone 2–3cm (0.8–1.2in) across comprising 20–30 wedge-shaped composite scales. The outer edge of each of the composite scales (cone-scales) appears disc-like and has a more or less central recurved spine with the upper margin bearing three to five short rigid processes.

Variety *japonica* is of more compact appearance, the branches more spreading and the leaves stouter; the female cones comprise some 30 scales, each fertile scale maturing to bear five seeds. In var *sinensis* the habit is more open with the ultimate branchlets tending to droop; the female cones rarely have more than 20 scales, each fertile scale maturing to bear two seeds.

Variety *japonica* is commonly favored as an ornamental forming a bright green narrowly conical crown with a rounded apex. It is fully hardy, growing best in cool damp areas with good deep alluvial soil. Propagation is by seeds or cuttings. There are numerous cultivars; 'Elegans' is often planted but despite its name is sometimes an untidy sight. Its leaves are 2–3cm (0.8–1.2in) long and of the juvenile type; they are of a fine green color in summer changing to reddish-bronze as winter approaches. Cones are rarely produced in this cultivar.

In Japan about one-third of the area under afforestation is devoted to var *japonica*. It is also planted by temples and at the sides of many celebrated avenues to which it has contributed much of their fame. The wood is durable, easy to work and resistant to insects. It is much used in building construction and for furniture and the bark is valuable as a roofing material. F. B. H.

Chinese Swamp Cypress
(genus *Glyptostrobus*)

The Chinese Swamp Cypress or Chinese Water Pine (*Glyptostrobus lineatus* = *G. pensilis*) is a small deciduous tree native to south China. Like the Swamp Cypress (*Taxodium distichum*) it is characteristic of damp places in its native China where it appears to be mainly a cultivated tree, possibly because it is believed to bring luck to the home and rice crops.

Glyptostrobus is closely related to *Taxodium*, differing in its pear-shaped, stalked female cones comprising thin, elongated nonpeltate scales which are coarsely-toothed at their apices; the seeds are oval to oblong with a single wing and not, as in *Taxodium*, three-angled and appearing

Below Persistent and deciduous shoots of the Chinese Swamp Cypress (*Glyptostrobus lineatus*).

as if with three thick wings.

The Chinese Swamp Cypress is scarcely hardy in temperate regions and is hence rarely seen in cultivation. The shoots are hairless and of two types: either persistent (usually terminal) and spirally arranged with axillary buds, or deciduous, falling with leaves in the fall and without axillary buds. The leaves on persistent shoots are scale-like, 2–3mm (0.08–0.12in) long, spirally arranged and overlapping while those on deciduous shoots are more or less needle-like, 8–12mm (0.32–0.48in) long and about 1mm (0.04in) wide and arranged in the same plane, one row on each side of the shoot (pectinate) and falling with the shoot in the fall. The sexes are separate but on the same tree, the male cones in hanging clusters, the females finally about 18mm (0.7in) long on a 12–18mm (0.5–0.7in) long stalk. F. B. H.

Taiwania

The genus *Taiwania* comprises three very closely related species of evergreen trees, which may in fact be geographical subspecies of a single species, namely *Taiwania cryptomerioides*. They are native to north Burma, southwest China, Taiwan and Manchuria.

Taiwania cryptomerioides is a tree to about 60m (195ft) but rarely reaches more than 15–16m (49–52ft) in cultivation. Its leaves are of two types; on juvenile and sterile shoots they are awl-shaped, 12–18mm (0.5–0.8in) long, curved and much like those of *Cryptomeria* with a broad glaucous stomatal band on each surface; leaves on adult and fertile shoots are scale-like, smaller to about 6mm (0.2in) long, triangular and overlapping with stomatal lines on all surfaces. Female cones are sub-globose, 10–11(15)mm (0.4–0.45(0.6)in) long, comprising numerous rounded and mucronate scales. Each scale bears two ovules which mature into winged seeds. *Taiwania* is related to *Cunninghamia* but this has three ovules per scale.

Taiwania cryptomerioides is scarcely hardy in temperate regions, but has survived with winter shelter.
F. B. H.

Left Awl-shaped leaves, each with broad stomatal bands, of the Coffin Tree (*Taiwania flousiana*), which is possibly just a geographic variant of *T. cryptomerioides*.

Monkey Puzzle
(genus *Araucaria*)

Araucaria is a genus of evergreen coniferous trees comprising some 18 species all confined to the Southern Hemisphere, notably in South America, Australasia and the islands of the South Pacific. The genus includes the well-known Monkey Puzzle Tree or Chile Pine (*Araucaria araucana* = *A. imbricata*), the Norfolk Island Pine (*A. heterophylla* = *A. excelsa*) and the Parana Pine or Candelabra Tree (*A. angustifolia*).

Members of *Araucaria* are tall imposing trees with branches in regular whorls. The bark of the old trees is ridged with the remains of old leaf-bases or rough and peeling off. The leaves persist for many years and are flat and broad or awl-shaped (acicular) and curved; some species have awl-shaped juvenile leaves. Male and female cones are usually borne on different trees but sometimes on separate branches of the same tree. The male cones grow in large cylindric terminal or subterminal

A fine specimen of the Norfolk Island Pine (*Araucaria heterophylla*) seen here planted by the seafront in Napier, North Island, New Zealand. These trees are also popular as house and glasshouse pot plants and are very attractive when small.

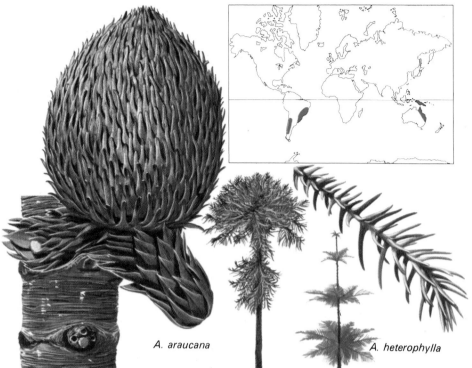

A. araucana

A. heterophylla

The Main Species of *Araucaria*

Group I: Leaves broad and flat, about 1·5cm long. Cone-scales without or with only vestigial wings.

A. araucana (*A. imbricata*) Chile Pine or Monkey Puzzle Tree. Chile and W Argentina. Tree 30–50m with spreading, stout, upwardly curved branches of striking appearance. Leaves 2.5–5 × 2.5cm, densely imbricated, ovate-lanceolate but with a broad base, firm and with a sharp, pointed apex. Male cones in catkin-like clusters, cylindric, 8–12cm long; mature cones more or less globose up to 15(20)cm across; seeds somewhat compressed, 2.5–3.5cm long, adnate to scale, each with recurved apical appendage.

A. bidwillii Bunya-Bunya. Coastal district of Queensland, Australia. Tree to 50m and fast-growing. The main branches horizontal, younger branchlets pendulous. Leaves on sterile shoots 18–25 × 4.5–11mm, lanceolate, with a narrow base, the apex tapering to a long stiff point; leaves on fertile shoots (and the upper branches) stiffer and incurved, 15–25mm long. Sexes usually on separate plants (dioecious), the male cones in clusters 15–18 × 1.3cm, cylindrical and catkin-like; mature cones elliptical, up to 30 × 23cm and weighing up to 5kg; scales large with a long recurved point; seeds large and pear-shaped up to about 6.5 × 2.5cm with a rudimentary wing.

A. angustifolia Parana Pine or Candelabra Tree. Brazil and Argentina. Tree to 35m with a flat crown, the branches in whorls of 4–8. Leaves with long points, stiff and leathery, the stomata on lower surface; leaves of sterile branches 3–6 × 0.6cm and appearing opposite, those of fertile branches shorter and arranged spirally. Cones 17cm across, 12cm high, each scale with a recurved, stiff appendage; seeds 5 × 2cm, light brown. Allied to *A. araucana* but differs in the leaves being softer and less crowded. The wood is soft and commercially valuable.

Group II: Leaves either more or less awl-shaped to broadly ovate or less than 1cm long. Cone-scales obviously winged.

A. heterophylla (*A. excelsa*) Norfolk Island Pine. Restricted to Norfolk Island in the South Pacific. Handsome tree to 70m, main branches horizontal, lateral branches sometimes pendulous. Leaves on young lateral and sterile shoots 8–13(15)mm long, spreading, not crowded and those on older and fertile shoots incurved, crowded and overlapping, 6–7mm long with incurved horny point, the midrib hardly visible. Male cones in clusters, 3.5–5cm long and catkin-like; mature cones more or less globose about 10–12cm across; seeds with well-developed wings, the adherent scales each with a flat triangular incurved spine. Much cultivated in the Mediterranean area and places of similar climate as an ornamental tree. Many cultivars.

clusters, each with numerous pollen sacs. The females mature in two to three years, often as very large globose or ovoid cones of woody overlapping scales, which break up when the seeds are ripe. There is one seed on each scale and adherent to it, with a marginal wing on all edges, in most species.

The genus is very closely related to the kauri pines (*Agathis*) but an essential difference is that the seeds are free from the cone-scale in this genus and not adherent as in *Araucaria*.

Propagation is mainly by seed but cuttings of terminal shoots from well-established plants can also be used.

The wood of *Araucaria* is resinous, straight-grained and easy to work. *Araucaria araucana*, *A. bidwillii* (Bunya-Bunya) and *A. cunninghamii* (Moreton Bay Pine or Hoop Pine) are the most important timber trees although the latter is susceptible to serious attack from the Hoop Pine Borer, a species of *Calymmaduus*. The timber is mainly used for general indoor joinery and carpentry and for boxes and masts as well as pulp for papermaking. For all practical purposes it can be used as a substitute for the Scots Pine (*Pinus silvestris*).

The striking appearance of the Monkey Puzzle Tree has made it a popular subject for cultivation in parks and gardens. It was most popular during the late 19th century and is not frequently planted these days.

The tree was introduced to Britain by Archibald Menzies in 1795, who removed some of the edible seeds when dining with the Viceroy of Chile. It became popular after a good supply of seed was sent back by William Lobb in 1844. Its fascination led to much planting in highly unsuitable places, especially suburban gardens where it rarely does well, looks out of place, and generally bedraggled and unhappy through loss of the lower branches at an early stage – a response to poor soils and atmospheric pollution. It does best on moist but adequately drained soils in a humid and clean atmosphere. It is, and looks at its best in arboreta and parks especially when in pure stands rather than randomly distributed amongst other trees.

In addition to *A. araucana*, the seeds of *A. bidwillii* are an important article of diet of Australian aborigines and for this reason there are government restrictions on felling in certain areas.

The Norfolk Island Pine is, amongst others, commonly grown as an indoor plant and does well when planted in a large tub with a good fibrous loam – leaf mold and sand mixture. There is, however, one fine specimen of this plant growing outdoors in the famous subtropical gardens at Tresco, one of the Isles of Scilly, about 50km (30mi) west of Land's End in Cornwall, England.

F. B. H.

A. cunninghamii Moreton Bay Pine or Hoop Pine. Mainly in New South Wales and Queensland, Australia and also in New Guinea. Tree 60–70m. Bark characteristically cracking into horizontal hoops or bands, peeling. Branches horizontal, the branchlets mostly concentrated at the ends. Leaves on sterile lateral branches and young trees in general lanceolate 8–15(19)mm long, straight and spreading with a sharp, pointed apex; on older trees and fertile branches, leaves more crowded, shorter, incurved with a short pointed apex. Male cones in clusters, 5–7.5cm long and catkin-like; mature cones broadly ellipsoidal about 10 × 7.5cm with exserted (protruding) stiff, recurved apices of the cone-scales; seeds with narrow membranous wings.

A. columnaris New Caledonian Pine. New Caledonia and Polynesia. Tree closely allied to *A. heterophylla* under which name it often appears. Fertile and older branchlets with densely overlapping, incurved leaves, each with a distinct midrib, giving a characteristic and distinctive whip-cord appearance; leaves on sterile and young branchlets triangular or lanceolate.

A. balansae New Caledonia. Tree 12–18m, the branches more or less horizontal and turning down at the ends. Leaves densely crowded, broadly awl-shaped about 3mm long with stomata on inner surface. Mature cones at the apex of short shoots, oval, 6–7.5 × 5–6.5cm, each scale with a hard bristle 8mm long. Close to *A. columnaris* which has larger leaves. Of little or no commercial value.

Kauri Pines
(genus *Agathis*)

The kauri or kauri pines (genus *Agathis*) are the most tropical genus of all the conifers. Some 20 species have been described but five (or more) may be, at most, subspecies. Representatives are found in the wettest tropical rain forests of the Malay archipelago, Sumatra, the Philippines and Fiji, with outliers in the subtropical forests of Queensland in Australia and northernmost New Zealand.

They are imposing evergreen trees with massive columnar trunks and large spreading crowns. Male and female cones are borne on separate trees. Kauri pines differ from *Araucaria* by the seed being free from the (ovuliferous) scale and not adnate to it, the larger leaves which are broad and flat rather than more or less awl-shaped or lanceolate and the seeds being mostly unequally winged whereas in *Araucaria* they are wingless or about equally winged.

Agathis timber is one of the most valuable softwoods in the world and is highly prized for boatbuilding, as a decorative veneer and for household utensils and drawing boards. The wood of most species is strong, durable and of excellent quality and because of the shedding of lower branches in young specimens, is remarkably free from knots.

All parts contain a resin (kauri gum) and in several species it exudes spontaneously and from injuries, accumulating on branches, trunks and at the base of trees. It has been extensively used in the manufacture of varnishes, linoleum and paints, being also known as an animé and more specifically as copal, damar or dammar, these last two a reference to *Agathis dammara* formerly known as *Dammara alba* and *A. alba*. Other sources are from *A. robusta* and the very important *A. australis*, the Kauri (or Cowdie) Pine from the North Island of New Zealand. In addition to the freshly-exuded resin, there are large quantities of fossil resin preserved in peat bogs where kauri pines no longer grow. This supply is even more esteemed, sought after and commercially exploited. The preserving peat has also been distilled to yield a petroleum spirit and turpentine.

A plantation of *Agathis dammara*, one of the species of kauri pine, on the southern slopes of Gunung Slamet in central Java. The trees, which are being felled for timber, are 30 years old. *Agathis* timber is one of the most valuable softwoods.

Kauri pines have been so over-exploited for their products that Government action was required to conserve them. Most *Agathis* timber now comes from small groves or isolated trees scattered through primary forest but the plantations on Java promise to be a major timber source when the virgin rain forests have disappeared.

F. B. H.

CUPRESSACEAE

Cypresses
(genus *Cupressus*)

Cupressus – the true cypresses – is a genus comprising, as now understood, about 20 species. Cypresses are widely distributed in the New and Old Worlds, from Oregon to Mexico in North America, the Mediterranean area, western Asia, the western Himalaya and China.

They are evergreen trees, rarely shrubs; the branchlets are densely clothed with small overlapping scale-like decussate leaves with minute denticulate-fringed margins (lens). On older branches the leaves are more awl-shaped (acicular), larger and spreading. Male and female cones are terminal and solitary on separate branches of the same tree. Mature female

cones are globose to broadly elliptic, mostly more than 1cm (0.4in) across, with 6–12 finally woody, peltate scales, each bearing 6–12 (sometimes as many as 20) more or less winged seeds, which may be smooth or beset with a few resinous tubercles. The cone requires 18 months to mature.

The limits of the modern genus have been reduced by the transfer of a number of species to *Chamaecyparis* known as false cypresses. In almost all cases trees and shrubs of both genera are easily distinguished. In *Chamaecyparis* the ultimate branchlets are usually flattened in one plane and these flattened foliar-like sprays (phyllomorphs) are commonly horizontally (sometimes more or less vertically) disposed. In *Cupressus* the ultimate branchlets are not generally so flattened but diverge in various directions so no phyllomorphs are evident. It is also interesting to note that, generally speaking, the species of *Chamaecyparis* are much more hardy than those of *Cupressus*, which, in much of northern Europe at least, are regarded as 'semi-tender.' There is no doubt that the two genera are closely related and this is

borne out by the existence of the intergeneric hybrid × *Cupressocyparis.*

In suitable climatic conditions, including reasonably clean air, cypresses are not particular as to soil type, succeeding on light to heavy loams and even on a highly sandy soil, provided adequate moisture is maintained. This is true of *C. macrocarpa* (Monterey Cypress), the most commonly planted species in the United Kingdom, which does well by the sea in the southwest, where the high relative humidity no doubt significantly reduces transpiration and thus equally the demand for water. Propagation of species is mainly by seeds and the cultivars by cuttings and sometimes by grafts on the appropriate stock.

Cypresses are susceptible to bacterial and fungal diseases, notably *Bacterium tumifaciens*, which can cause galls on the stem and root, especially near soil level, and stem canker caused by species of the imperfect fungus *Pestalotia* (*Pestalozzia*). Amongst insect pests, the aphid *Cinara* (*Cupressobium*) *cupressi* can weaken trees of *C. macrocarpa* by feeding in vast numbers on the sap. It also excretes 'honeydew' on which disfiguring growths of sooty molds

can occur. The Conifer Spinning Mite (*Oligonychus ununguis*) also attacks the genus, causing, amongst other things, an unsightly chlorosis.

The wood of many cypresses is valuable, being durable and easily worked. It is used in general building construction, carpentry and for posts and poles of all sorts, but not for packing cases since the often spicy odor of the wood may contaminate susceptible contents. The most commonly used timbers are those of *C. macrocarpa* and *C. sempervirens*. These two species are also widely planted as ornamentals but their 'semi-tenderness' restricts them to the mildest areas and they are likely to suffer in anything approaching a severe frost. In more subtropical areas of the world, plantations, especially of *C. macrocarpa*, have been established. This species is also increasing in popularity as a screening or hedging plant.

F. B. H.

The Main Species of *Cupressus*

Group I: Leaves conspicuously resinous and glandular on the back, the ultimate branchlets typically diverging at all angles and not flattened into one plane as phyllomorphs.

C. macnabiana Macnab Cypress. Mainly N California. Shrub or small tree to about 12m. Branchlets compressed dorsiventrally; leaves rich green or glaucous, about 1mm long, densely set, the apices enlarged and blunt. Mature cones 12–19mm across with 6–8 scales.

C. arizonica Rough-barked Arizona Cypress. Arizona, Mexico and New Mexico. Tree 15–25m. Bark rough reddish-brown, graying, not exfoliating. Branchlets not compressed; leaves acute, deep green to grayish-green, about 2mm long, the margin (lens) finely toothed. Mature cones 12–25mm across with 6–8 scales.

C. glabra Smooth Arizona Cypress. C Arizona. Tree 7–18m. Bark cherry-red, smooth and exfoliating each year. Branchlets not compressed. Leaves 1.5–2mm, long, white-spotted with resin, acute, finely toothed margin (lens), gray to grayish-green, keeled. Mature cones 20–26mm across, with usually 8(5–10) scales, each with a prominent umbo. Tolerates calcareous soils and is drought-resistant.

Group II: Leaves not conspicuously resinous or glandular on the back, but sometimes with a faint nonresinous 'slit' or 'pit,' and then ultimate branchlets flattened in one plane.

A *Ultimate branchlets flattened in one plane (phyllomorphs), more or less horizontally disposed. Cones subglobose, 8–16mm across.*

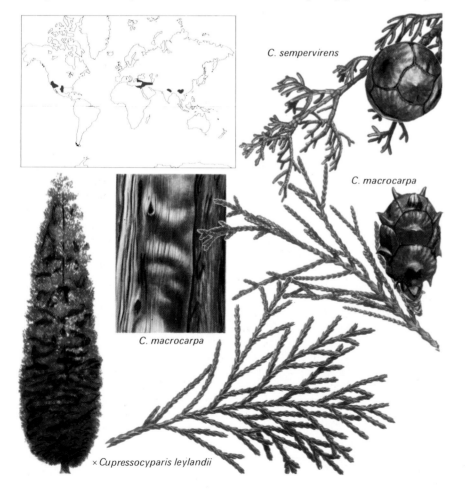

C. sempervirens

C. macrocarpa

C. macrocarpa

× *Cupressocyparis leylandii*

C. lusitanica var *benthamii* Mexican Cypress, Cedar of Goa. Mexico. Tree to about 33m. Leaves shining, dark green, with central dorsal 'pit' and acute apex. Mature cones about 12–15mm across with 6–8 scales, each scale with a prominent umbo, slightly, or not reflexed; seeds smooth.

C. torulosa Bhutan or Himalayan Cypress. W Himalaya and Szechwan, China. Tree to 50m. Ultimate branches more or less flattened, curved and characteristically whip-like. Leaves about 1.5mm long, somewhat blunt at the apex, usually with a dorsal, central 'pit.' Mature cones about 11(12)mm across with 8–10 scales; seeds relatively few, 6–8 per scale with tubercles.

AA *Ultimate branchlets not flattened in one plane, but diverging at all angles. Cones 1–4cm wide or long.*

C. macrocarpa Monterey Cypress. California. Tree to about 25m, at first pyramidal, finally with a broad crown. Leaves 1–2.5mm long, densely packed, apices adpressed, rather blunt; bruised foliage with citronella-like smell. Mature cones subglobose, 2.5–4 × 1.75–2.5cm, with 8–12(14) scales, each with a short, stout and blunt umbo; seeds minutely tubercled. Distinguished by its large cones from all other commonly cultivated species except *C. sempervirens*, which has smaller leaves and smooth seeds. Useful as a windbreak in exposed places by the sea.

C. sempervirens Italian Cypress, Mediterranean Cypress, Funeral Cypress. The 'classical' cypress of the ancients. Mediterranean area including Crete, Cyprus and Sicily; Switzerland, USSR and the mountains of N Iran. Tree usually 20–30m, but up to 50m in the Mediterranean area. Branches either spreading (var *horizontalis*) or fastigiate (var *sempervirens*). Leaves dark green, 1mm long, diamond-shaped but apices bluntish; bruised foliage with little or no smell. Mature cones subglobose to broadly elliptical, 2.5–3 × 2cm with 8–14 scales, the central umbo inconspicuous; seeds smooth. The type is var *sempervirens* and is very striking with its erect, fastigiate branches, the whole tree being lanceolate to narrowly pyramidal in outline. This variety is also known as 'Stricta'.

C. goveniana Gowen Cypress. California. Shrub or small tree to 20m. Leaves 1–2mm long, sometimes with a 'pit,' gray to blackish-green; bruised foliage with distinct, pleasant, resinous smell; shoots purplish-brown. Mature cones globose, 10–15mm across with 6–10 scales, each with a low blunt umbo.

C. lusitanica Mexican Cypress, Cedar of Goa. Mexico, extending to the mountains of Guatemala. Tree reaching 30m but variable. Branches commonly spreading and pendulous at the ends; ultimate branchlets not flattened in one plane but diverging at all angles (compare with *C. lusitanica* var *benthamii* above). Leaves acute, glaucous to gray-green, the tips spreading, 1.5–2mm long; bruised foliage with little or no smell; shoots pinkish-brown. Mature cones subglobose, 12–16mm across with 6–8 scales, the umbo pointed and often hooked; seeds smooth, the wing sometimes little developed.

The Monterey Cypress (*Cupressus macrocarpa*) is now confined in the wild to a few miles of coastline south of Monterey in California, United States. Under cultivation it is a rapid-growing, tall, pyramidal tree used extensively for coastal windbreaks and for hedging.

Hybrid Cypresses
(genus × *Cupressocyparis*)

The genus × *Cupressocyparis* (hybrid cypress) is a natural bigeneric hybrid – × *Cupressocyparis leylandii* – between *Cupressus macrocarpa* (Monterey Cypress) from California and *Chamaecyparis nootkatensis* (Nootka Cypress or Yellow Cypress) from the Pacific coast of northwestern America.

× *Cupressocyparis* is thought to have arisen in cultivation in England at Leighton Hall, Welshpool, Shropshire in 1888 when a number of seedlings of the Nootka Cypress were being raised from seed. A Monterey Cypress was growing in the same garden. In 1911 further seedlings were raised at Leighton Hall, this time from seed taken from *Cupressus macrocarpa*. From these original seedlings a number of clones have now been established numbering some 10 or 11, with some differences in growth habit, color and texture.

The hybrid cypress only really began to attract widespread attention in the 1950's for fast-growing shelter belts and hedges; by the 1960's demand began to outstrip limited supplies largely due to this hybrid needing to be propagated vegetatively from cuttings. Today × *Cupressocyparis leylandii* is widely planted as a very fast-growing, hardy and adaptable conifer. A tree planted in 1916 is now over 33m (110ft) high with a girth of 2.5m (8ft). From a distance it resembles the Nootka rather than the Monterey Cypress in general appearance but is usually far more columnar and erect in habit. However, the leaves and branches are less flattened than Nootka and resemble more the filiform shape of Monterey. Cones are produced on more mature trees and they are somewhere between the cone structures of the two parents, with tubercles on the cone-scales.

The hybrid cypress seems to inherit its hardiness from the Nootka parent and its fast growth from the Monterey. It withstands clipping and can be made into a dense hedge from 2m (6.6ft) in height but it is not suitable for dwarf hedging. In the last ten years or so, research and further selection of the original seedlings from Leighton Hall and also from others found elsewhere, have produced the following clones:

'Green Spire' (Clone 1). Dense and narrow with bright green foliage.
'Haggerston Gray' (Clone 2). Probably the commonest clone; green foliage but slightly grayer than 'Green Spire.'
'Leighton Green.' Another widely-grown clone.
'Naylor's Blue.' A narrow column tree with gray-green foliage.

'Stapehill.' This has a more flattened type of green foliage.

Two other *Cupressocyparis* hybrids have also emerged: × *C. notabilis* (*Chamaecyparis nootkatensis* × *Cupressus glabra*) (Arizona Cypress) and × *C. ovensii* (*Chamaecyparis nootkatensis* × *Cupressus lusitanica*) (Mexican Cypress).

The timber of the Leyland Cypress is of good quality and since the tree can be readily grown under forestry conditions it is likely to become widely planted.

T. W. W.

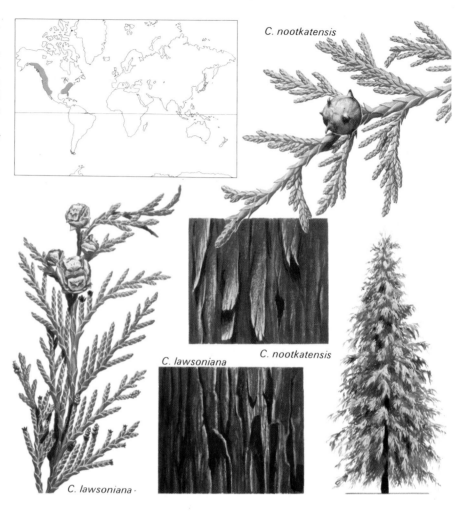

C. nootkatensis

C. lawsoniana

C. nootkatensis

C. lawsoniana

False Cypresses
(genus *Chamaecyparis*)

The false cypresses comprise seven species of evergreen conifers of the Northern Hemisphere. They are found mainly in the western and southeastern coastal regions of North America and in Japan and Taiwan. In cultivation, they are not particular as to soil provided it is not too calcareous and is moist without being waterlogged.

The false cypresses are hardy, mostly pyramidal trees with a habit very similar to that of the true cypresses (*Cupressus*) except that the young shoot systems or sprays (phyllomorphs) are flattened and in one plane, a characteristic they share with species of the genus *Thuja* (arbor-vitae). The leaves are scale-like, opposite and decussate, but the juvenile leaves are sometimes awl-shaped. The two sexes are found on the same tree but on separate branches. The female cones are globose and very small – up to 1cm (0.4in) across. They mature in a year except in *Chamaecyparis nootkatensis* (Nootka Cypress), which requires about 18 months. The seeds are somewhat compressed, each with a thin broad wing.

The timber of most of the species of *Chamaecyparis* is of high quality, being generally light, durable, easily worked and resistant to fungus decay and insect

Chamaecyparis lawsoniana cultivars planted in 1926 at Bedgebury National Pinetum, Kent, England, including 'Stewartii' (left foreground), 'Pottenii' (middle left and right, pale green, conic), 'Lutea' (bright gold), 'Triumph of Boskoop' (middle, blue), 'Intertexta' (background, pendulous).

The Main Species of *Chamaecyparis*

Group I: Underside of phyllomorphs partially whitish or at least glaucous, especially on leaf margins (lens). Lateral leaves significantly larger (twice as long) than facial ones and all closely adpressed – except *C. pisifera* where leaves are about the same size (and length) with acute more or less spreading tips.

C. formosensis Formosa Cypress. Taiwan. Tree reaching 65m with a girth of 24m in its native habitat. Lateral and facial leaves of equal length, about 1.5mm, keeled or with glandular pit, dull green, bronze-tinged, often whitish beneath, smelling of rotten seaweed when crushed. Mature cones 8–9mm across but ellipsoidal, with 10–11 scales, the outer surfaces more or less wrinkled; seeds 2 per scale, oval with narrow wings and conspicuous resin tubercles. The species is close to *C. pisifera* but differing in color, shape and the smell of the crushed leaves. It forms pure forests in Taiwan on Mount Morrison at 2 300–3 300m in association with *C. obtusa*. It is a valuable timber tree in its native land (the wood is resistant to insect attack and decay) but it is in danger of extinction through over-felling.

C. lawsoniana Lawson Cypress. Extreme W USA. Tree 25–50m, spire-like with spreading branches, pendulous at the tips. Lateral leaves of ultimate branchlets 2.5–3mm long; facial leaves about half as long, all acute and with glandular dots appearing conspicuously translucent when examined under lens against light. Male cones characteristically crimson. Mature cones about 8mm across with usually 8 scales, each with 2–4 seeds. Much planted and with 200 or more named cultivars.

C. obtusa Hinoki Cypress. Japan, with var *formosana* in Taiwan. Tree to 40m, pyramidal. Leaves distinctly obtuse, without glands, the white markings beneath somewhat Y-shaped; lateral leaves about twice as long as the facial ones. Mature cones 8–10mm across with 8–(10) scales, each with up to 5 seeds. Numerous cultivars. Intolerant of lime and a dry climate.

C. pisifera Sawara Cypress. Japan. Tree to 50m. Leaves with spreading acute tips, the facial and lateral leaves about the same size and obscurely glandular. Mature cones 6(8)mm across with 10(12) scales, each scale with 1–2 seeds. Numerous cultivars.

Group II: Underside of phyllomorphs the same color as the upper side or slightly paler, without whitish or glaucous marking. Lateral leaves about the same size as the facial leaves or only a little longer.

C. thyoides White Cedar (sometimes also known as White Cypress). E N America. Tree to 25m. Branchlets distinctly compressed and phyllomorphs less uniformly disposed in the horizontal plane. Leaves bluish-green on both sides, conspicuously glandular. Mature cones 6(7)mm across.

C. nootkatensis Nootka or Yellow Cypress. W N America. Tree 30–40m, more or less conical with spreading branches, pendulous at the tips. Phyllomorphs horizontal and characteristically drooping at the sides, giving the appearance of a short circle segment; branchlets not obviously compressed; leaves green above, paler beneath, virtually without glands. Mature cones 10(12)mm across with 4–6 scales and 2–4 seeds on each scale.

Arbor-vitae
(genus *Thuja*)

There are six species (some with numerous varieties) in the genus *Thuja*, and all are generally known as arbor-vitae. They are evergreen trees and shrubs from China, Japan, Taiwan and North America.

The trees are usually of pyramidal habit and the young shoots (phyllomorphs) are characteristically flattened in one plane and bear scale-like decussate leaves. Male and female cones are borne on the same plant. The male cones are very small and borne terminally on the smallest shoots. The female cones are erect, solitary with imbricate cone-scales; only the middle two or three pairs of scales are fertile and each bears two seeds on the lower surface.

Arbor-vitae are often grown as ornamentals, growing well on well-drained loams, also on light moist sandy soils and in peat. Propagation is by seeds or cuttings, the cultivars by cuttings rather than by grafting. The large cultivars, such as those of the White Cedar (*Thuja occidentalis*), the Chinese Arbor-vitae (*T. orientalis*) and the Western Red Cedar (*T. plicata*) make excellent single specimen trees for large gardens, and are finding some use as hedging, particularly the latter which withstands clipping well although *T. occidentalis* does better in cold climates. The numerous slow-growing, dwarf cultivars are particularly suitable for some gardens and rock gardens.

Scale insects are about the only serious pest and are controlled by spraying every eight days for six weeks with a soft-soap and paraffin wash.

The wood, which is light, easy to work and without resin canals, is used for general building, furniture, telegraph poles etc. The outer bark makes a useful roofing material. There is an inner, more fibrous bark which serves as a stuffing for upholstery. In the United States timber of the Western Red Cedar (*Thuja plicata*) is used for roofing tiles. This same species has also proved a successful timber tree in Scotland but in the warmer, southern parts of England it is unsatisfactory, mainly because of extensive shrinkage during the seasoning process, which causes significant gaps to occur between the annual rings. Trunks of the Western Red Cedar were those most frequently used by the North-American Indians as totem-poles.

F. B. H.

attacks. The wood of most species has its own pleasant distinctive odor and color. *Chamaecyparis formosensis* is one of the most valued timber trees in Taiwan where it grows at an altitude of 2 000–3 000m (6 500–10 000ft). Specimens can reach 50m (165ft) high and some are estimated to be about 3 000 years old. This is one of the woods without a distinctive odor. The wood of *C. lawsoniana* is no less useful and has an odor that can be described as 'spicy.' It is used for general building, for floors, furniture and fence posts, railway sleepers and in boatbuilding. The wood of *C. nootkatensis* is also of excellent quality and is used in much the same way. It is known in the trade as 'yellow cypress,' though this popular name is also used for the wood of the Swamp Cypress (*Taxodium distichum*). The excellent wood of *C. obtusa* is much prized in its native country of Japan and is probably unsurpassed for the highest quality work in all kinds of construction. It is very straight, evenly grained and often beautifully marked. *Chamaecyparis pisifera*, another Japanese species, is perhaps the least exploited of the false cypresses but is nevertheless extensively used for less ornamental kinds of carpentry.

Outside their native habitats, several species of *Chamaecyparis* and their numerous cultivars are planted for ornamental purposes, including *C. pisifera*, *C. obtusa* and *C. nootkatensis*. As well as being popular ornamentals for parks and large gardens, there are many dwarf cultivars of these species suitable for growing in small gardens and rock gardens. However, the best-known cultivated species is the Lawson Cypress (*C. lawsoniana*) from southwestern Oregon and northwestern California. The number of cultivars is in excess of 200, ranging from dwarf shrubs grown in rock gardens to tall, columnar trees with many different color forms. It also makes an excellent hedging or screening subject and will grow in a wide range of conditions, including shaded or exposed sites.

F. B. H.

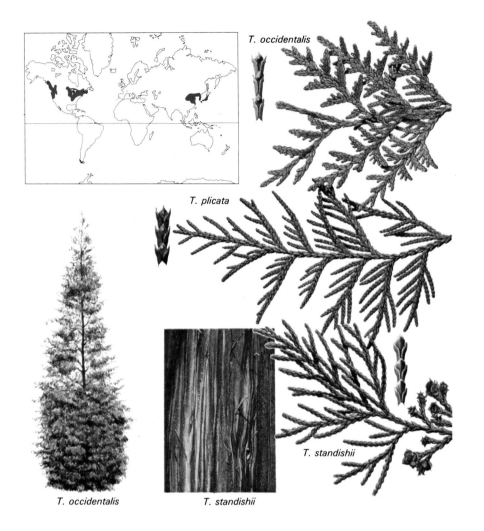

T. occidentalis

T. plicata

T. standishii

T. occidentalis   *T. standishii*

Hiba
(genus *Thujopsis*)

This genus has been separated from *Thuja* to accommodate the single species *Thujopsis dolobrata* (Japan) which differs from *Thuja* in having much more flattened branchlets and each fertile cone-scale maturing three to five seeds and not just two.

The Hiba Arbor-vitae is a pyramidal tree to 15m (50ft) but it is often shrubby in cultivation. The scale leaves are decussate, 4–6mm (0.16–0.24in) long, the lateral more or less spreading and acute, the facial obtuse, both virtually white beneath except for a thin green margin. Female cones are broadly ovoid to 15mm (0.6in) long, comprising six to eight scales each with a subapical boss or mucro on the outside; the upper pair of scales are sterile and bear winged seeds.

In cultivation the Hiba is hardy in temperate regions where it thrives on well-drained soils. It is much planted for its handsome and pleasing appearance, differing at a glance from typical species of *Thuja* by its broader branchlets, often much denser habit toward the base, much more rounded cones and thicker cone-scales. Several cultivars have been developed including the golden-yellow-leaved 'Aurea,' variegated 'Variegata' and dwarf 'Nana.'

The soft, durable wood is used locally in Japan for general construction work and the bark for caulking boards.

F. B. H.

The Main Species of *Thuja*

Subgenus *Biota*
Shoots (phyllomorphs) predominantly in vertical planes and green on both sides. Cone-scales thick, recurved at the apices; seeds without wings. This subgenus is sometimes regarded as a separate genus.
T. orientalis Chinese or Oriental Arbor-vitae. N and W China. Tree 5–10m, sometimes more or less shrubby. Leaves with small gland on the back. Mature cones 1.5–2.5cm long, usually with 6 scales. Easily recognized by the subgeneric characters. Numerous named varieties.

Subgenus *Thuja*
Phyllomorphs predominantly in horizontal planes and often white-streaked on underside of leaves. Cone-scales thin, the apices not recurved; seeds winged.
T. occidentalis American or White Cedar. E N America. Tree to 20m. Underside leaves of phyllomorphs without white streaks or markings, usually yellowish or bluish-green, each leaf at least of main axis with conspicuous glandular dot on the back (lens). Cones 8–12mm with 8–10 scales, only half of them fertile. Numerous named varieties.
T. plicata Western Red Cedar. W N America. Tree 30–60m. Underside leaves with more

or less X-shaped white streaks and any glands inconspicuous; bruised foliage strongly aromatic. Mature cones about 12mm long with 10–12 scales, each with a small spine; about half the scales fertile. Numerous named varieties.
T. standishii Japanese Arbor-vitae. Japan. Tree to 18m. Phyllomorphs not obviously flattened; leaves without glands, the underside ones with more or less triangular white markings; bruised foliage not aromatic. Mature cones with 8–10 scales, only the middle 4 fertile.
T. koraiensis Korean Arbor-vitae. Korea. Usually a somewhat sprawling shrub, but sometimes a slender conical tree to 9m. Phyllomorphs much flattened; leaves with conspicuous glands, dark green on the upper surface of the phyllomorphs, contrasting with the almost white lower surface; bruised foliage not aromatic. Mature cones 8–10mm with 4 pairs of scales, the middle 2 pairs fertile.
T. sutchuenensis, from NE Szechwan in C China, is little known and is not yet in cultivation.

A broadly-conical specimen of the Hiba Arbor-vitae or Japanese Hiba (*Thujopsis dolobrata*) native to Japan contrasts well with the golden-yellow foliage of the English Yew, *Taxus baccata* 'Aurea,' in the left background.

Southern Incense Cedars (genus *Libocedrus*)

As now understood, the genus *Libocedrus* (*sensu restricto*) comprises five species, two native to New Zealand and three to New Caledonia.

They are evergreen trees and shrubs with the branchlets flattened into spray-like phyllomorphs. The juvenile leaves are short and needle-like, the adult ones scale-like, arranged in decussate pairs and mostly dimorphic. Male and female cones occur on the same trees. Mature cones comprise two pairs of decussate, woody, valvate scales but only the upper pair are fertile. Each scale is more or less dorsally spined, the fertile scales producing one or two unequally winged seeds.

Only two species are found in cultiva-

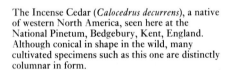

The Incense Cedar (*Calocedrus decurrens*), a native of western North America, seen here at the National Pinetum, Bedgebury, Kent, England. Although conical in shape in the wild, many cultivated specimens such as this one are distinctly columnar in form.

A spray (phyllomorph) of *Libocedrus bidwillii* with each twig densely clothed in scale-like, decussate, adult leaves.

tion and then only rarely. Pahautea (*Libocedrus bidwillii*) comes from New Zealand, where it grows at altitudes of up to 2 000m (6 500ft) and reaches a height of 25m (82ft). Its ultimate branchlets are flattened and the juvenile leaves markedly dimorphic – the facial about 1mm (0.04in) long, the lateral about 3mm (0.12in). Adult leaves are scale-like, adpressed, triangular and all about 2mm (0.08in) long. Female cones are ovoid, about 10mm (0.4in) long, the four scales each with a spine-like horn and the two fertile scales each maturing a single seed. Kawaka (*L. plumosa = L. doniana*) also from New Zealand, reaches a height of 33m (110ft). Its branchlets are distinctly flattened and the juvenile leaves very dimorphic – the laterals to 5mm (0.2in) long, the facial barely 1mm (0.04in). The adult scale leaves overlap and are adpressed, subequal, the laterals about 3mm (0.12in) long, the facial just over 1mm (0.04in). Female cones are ovoid, finally 10–15mm (0.4–0.6in) long, each of the four scales with a curved dorsal spine. One seed is produced on each fertile scale. Both these species are only marginally hardy in temperate areas. The wood is of some economic value, fragrant and durable.

The following species remain in the genus *Libocedrus* (*sensu restricto*): *L. austrocaledonica*, *L. bidwillii*, *L. chevalieri*, *L. plumosa*, *L. yateensis*. Changes to new genera are as follows:

L. arfakensis becomes *Papuacedrus arfakensis*
L. papuana becomes *P. papuana*
L. toricellensis becomes *P. toricellensis*
L. chilensis becomes *Austrocedrus chilensis*
L. decurrens becomes *Calocedrus decurrens*
L. formosana becomes *C. formosana*
L. macrolepis becomes *C. macrolepis*
L. uvifera becomes *Pilgerodendron uviferum*

F. B. H.

Northern Incense Cedars (genus *Calocedrus*)

Calocedrus comprises three species respectively from the Pacific coast of North America, China and Taiwan. They are evergreen trees with their ultimate branchlets (sprays or phyllomorphs) flattened. The leaves are scale-like, flattened, decussately arranged, with the edges of the lateral ones overlapping and virtually equal in length to the facial ones; both sets are adpressed except at their slightly recurved pointed apices. The cones are unisexual and typically on different branches of the same tree, rarely on separate trees. The male cone is oblong comprising 6–16 decussate pollen sacs. The female cone is elliptic-oblong comprising three pairs of finally woody, imbricate scales, each scale with a subapical recurved thorn-like process. Only the middle pair of scales are fertile each bearing two ovules; the innermost pair of scales are fused together, and the outermost (lowest) pair much shorter and recurved. The cone matures in one year, each seed with two very unequal wings.

The three species were formerly included under *Libocedrus* (*sensu lato*), one character separating them out being that the facial and lateral scale leaves are nearly equal in length. The Incense Cedar (*Calocedrus decurrens*) (formerly *Libocedrus decurrens*) grows to 45m (148ft) in its native habitat and has an elongated conical canopy in the wild state. Its bark is deeply furrowed and reddish-brown. The leaves are long decurrent, those on the ultimate lateral branches about 3mm (0.12in) long, but up to 12mm (0.48in) on the main branches with juvenile leaves even longer. Male cones are 6mm (0.24in) long, the females ovate, 18–25mm (0.71–0.98in) long, pendulous, fleshy at first, finally woody. It is native to Oregon and western Nevada to lower California, growing at altitudes between 1 000 and 2 750m (3 280 and 9 020ft).

The Incense Cedar is by far the best known of the species and is widely planted in temperate regions, being fully hardy. There are some four cultivars, but 'Columnaris' with its narrow columnar canopy is the commonest in cultivation. It is not particular as to soil, but flourishes best in a moist, well-drained loam away from atmospheric pollution. Propagation is best from seeds, but cuttings may be taken. The wood is light, resistant to decay and fragrant. It is used for pencils and general carpentry, boxes, fence posts etc.

Calocedrus macrolepis is a tree to 35m (115ft) which differs from the previous species by its larger leaves on the ultimate lateral branchlets – 6–8mm (0.24–0.32in) long – and only one seed is usually produced on each fertile scale. It is rare in its native habitat of south China to the Burmese border and not really hardy in cultivation, but may be grown in warmer parts of temperate regions.

Calocedrus formosana is very close to *C. macrolepis* in form but its leaves are only 2mm (0.08in) long, with two stomatal lines on the lateral leaves, whereas there are typically four in *C. macrolepis*. It is native to the broadleaved forests of Taiwan ascending to altitudes of nearly 2 000m (6 560ft) and it is little known in cultivation.

F. B. H.

Chilean Incense Cedar (genus *Austrocedrus*)

Austrocedrus is a genus of one species, the Chilean Incense Cedar (*Austrocedrus chilensis*) native to Chile and Argentina; it was formerly included under *Libocedrus*. It differs from this genus in having scale leaves that are much more strongly dimorphic – the facial ones being one-quarter (or less) the length of the lateral ones (one-half in *Libocedrus*) – blunter and rhombic to ovate as against triangular, and

cones comprising four valvate scales, only two of which are fertile, each with one or two unequally winged seeds.

It is an evergreen tree to about 25m (82ft) in its native habitat, but little more than 15m (50ft) when cultivated in temperate regions. The shoots are compressed, frond-like (phyllomorphs) with the leaves arranged in decussate pairs, the lateral ones 2–4.5mm (0.08–0.18in) long, the facial (upper and lower) ones rarely more than a quarter of this length. The male cones are about 3mm (0.12in) long, and comprise numerous pollen sacs. The female cones are solitary and finally woody, each of the four valvate scales with a minute subterminal dorsal tubercle. Only the upper two scales are fertile, these being about 8–12mm (0.32–0.48in) long and therefore much longer than the lower two sterile scales.

The Chilean Incense Cedar is reasonably hardy in temperate regions, where it favors moist but well-drained soils. However, since it has few attractive qualities, it is not much planted outside botanical collections. Propagation is usually by cuttings, but seeds can be used. The wood is scented and durable and has been used for general carpentry purposes.

F. B. H.

Papuacedrus

The three doubtfully distinct species of this genus of evergreen trees from the Moluccan Islands and New Guinea were formerly placed in *Libocedrus* (*sensu lato*), but they differ from *Libocedrus* (*sensu restricto*) in leaf form and anatomy and cone structure. Male cones comprise numerous

whorled bracts that are not decussately arranged. Female cones have four valvate scales each with a dorsal, short, stumpy spine; only the upper, much larger pair of scales is fertile and these mature four very equally winged seeds. The main species is *Papuacedrus arfakensis* from the Arfak mountains of New Guinea where it grows up to an altitude of 1 000m (3 300ft). It is a tree up to 35m (115ft) with a more or less pyramidal form and red, scaly bark. The juvenile leaves are up to 2cm (0.8in) long, almost herbaceous, with a slender spreading point. The facial pair are more or less overlapped by the lateral pair, both pairs tapering downward; the greatest width of about 10mm (0.4in) occurs just below the spreading point. The adult leaves are smaller, darker green, widening upward to an erect blunt apex. Female and male cones occur on different branches of the same tree. The two upper (inner) fertile scales are narrowly ovate, each about 12 × 8mm (0.48 × 0.32in).

None of the species is extensively cultivated.

F. B. H.

Pilgerodendron

Pilgerodendron contains a single evergreen species which was formerly placed under *Libocedrus* from which it differs in leaf form and arrangement, and cone structure. *Pilgerodendron uviferum* is restricted to the Andes of southern Chile and Argentina including Patagonia and Tierra del Fuego. It is a tree to 25m (82ft), rarely a shrub. The branchlets are quadrangular in outline. Leaves are scale-like, boat-shaped, 3–8mm (0.12–0.32in) long, opposite and decussate. They are all essentially similar

Sprays (phyllomorphs) of the Chilean Incense Cedar (*Austrocedrus chilensis*), the twigs clothed in decussate pairs of scale leaves.

Papuacedrus arfakensis showing its red scaly bark and dark green scale leaves with white bands on the underside.

Pilgerodendron uviferum grows up to 25m (82ft) in its native South America but is rare in cultivation when it is most often grown as a rockery subject.

in size, overlapping and adpressed to the shoots except at the somewhat spreading bluntish, slightly incurved tips to which they taper from a broad base. The cones are 8–12mm (0.32–0.48in) long, ovoid and comprise two pairs of woody, valvate scales, each scale with a subapical curved, dorsal spine. Only the upper pair of scales are fertile, each scale with one, rarely two, ovules; the lower sterile pair are much smaller. The seeds have very unequal wings. *Pilgerodendron uviferum* is sometimes mistaken for *Fitzroya cupressoides*, which has leaves wider above, narrowing to a decurrent base and the cones have three pairs of scales.

This species only occasionally survives in temperate regions and is thus rare in cultivation. The timber is extensively used in its native area.

F. B. H.

Cypress Pines
(genus *Callitris*)

Callitris is a genus of some 14–16 species which are native to Australia, Tasmania and New Caledonia, particularly dry and arid regions. They are evergreen trees or shrubs with sexes on the same plant. The

adult leaves are scale-like, arranged in alternating whorls of three and adpressed, except at the tips; the juvenile leaves are 6–12mm (0.24–0.48in) long arranged in whorls of four. Male cones are either solitary or clustered, small and cylindrical to oblong. Female cones are mostly 2–3cm (0.8–1.2in) long, globular to narrowly pyramidal, solitary or clustered and comprising six to eight thick, woody, often pointed, unequal valvate scales that are grossly warted, veined or smooth on the back. Two to nine seeds are produced per scale, each with one to three wings.

Tetraclinis and *Widdringtonia* are closely related genera and in both the cones are normally composed of not more than four scales. *Tetraclinis* also has the leaves in fours whilst in *Widdringtonia* they are arranged alternately in opposite pairs.

In north temperate zones, for example Europe, cypress pines require a cool greenhouse except in the warmest parts, such as southwest England and Ireland and southern France. Propagation is by seed or cuttings. The most frequently cultivated cypress pines include the following species. The Murray River Pine or White Cypress Pine (*Callitris columellaris* = *C. arenosa*) from New South Wales and the southern coast of Queensland, is a shrub or slow-growing tree to 25m (82ft). Its wood is very fragrant, insect resistant and is much used for panels and cabinet-making. The Black or Red Cypress Pine (*C. endlicheri*) from New South Wales, northeastern Victoria and Queensland, is a tree to some

Scrubland in Wyperfeld National Park, New South Wales, Australia, dominated by cypress pines (*Callitris* spp).

25m (82ft). Its polished wood is finely figured and hence much used for paneling. The Rottnest Island Pine or Common Cypress Pine (*C. preissii* = *C. robusta*) from southern and western Australia, is a low shrub or tree to 30m (100ft). The Oyster Bay Pine or Port Jackson Pine (*C. rhomboidea*) is a tree to 10–15m (33–50ft). It is widely distributed in Australia but only locally frequent; it is also naturalized in New Zealand. The Tasmanian Cypress Pine (*C. oblonga*) from Tasmania is a bush or small tree to 8m (26ft).

In general cypress pine wood is close-grained, hard, fragrant, and takes a good polish, the grain patterns often being quite striking. The presence of natural preservatives no doubt adds to its resistance to insect and fungal attack. It is used for building purposes, furniture, turnery and general carpentry. The bark can be slashed for resin and is also an economic source of tannins, whilst the cones, leaves and shoots can be distilled for the fragrant principles they contain.

F. B. H.

Junipers
(genus *Juniperus*)

There are about 60 species of evergreen trees and shrubs in the genus *Juniperus*, commonly known as junipers. They are widely distributed throughout the Northern Hemisphere, from the mountains of the tropics as far south as the equator and

ranging as far north as the Arctic. The Common Juniper (*Juniperus communis*) is extremely widely spread in temperate regions, forming dominant scrub on chalk, limestone and slate.

Junipers have leaves of two kinds: the normal adult leaves are small, scale-like and decussate, closely pressed to the shoot, crowded and overlapping; the juvenile leaves are larger and awl-shaped (acicular), growing in three's or opposite pairs at a node. In a number of species the awl-shaped, juvenile leaves are the only ones present. They do not always connect smoothly with the stem (on which, in some species, they are decurrent) but sometimes there may be some kind of constriction at the junction with the stem, as in *J. communis*, where the leaf base is swollen, the swollen tissue being virtually free of the stem. There is thus a constriction between the swollen leaf-base and the stem, the actual connection between the two being much narrower. Such leaves are referred to as 'jointed.'

The scale-like leaf margin (lens) is denticulate in some species but smooth (entire) in others. Cones are unisexual, borne either on different plants or separately on the same plant. The male cones are solitary or in more or less crowded catkins; the female cones consist of three to eight fleshy, pointed scales which coalesce and finally form a more or less globular body or 'berry.' This so-called juniper berry is often coated and bloomed, with subtending scaly bracts; it matures in the second or third year. There are between one and 12 seeds according to species.

Propagation is readily effected from seed but germination may be delayed up to about one year. Cultivars and varieties are increased by cuttings from the current year's shoot or by grafting on the appropriate stocks.

The most serious fungus disease that junipers are likely to suffer is from the rust *Gymnosporangium*, which forms large unsightly gelatinous yellow patches around the stems. These rusts are heteroecious, ie two hosts are required to complete the life history. Eradication of the alternate hosts – members of the rose family (Rosaceae) – is the best control measure.

Insect pests include the Juniper Webber (*Dichomeris marginella*), so-called because it spins foliage together which subsequently turns brown and dies. The Juniper Scale Insect (*Caralaspis* spp) and the Conifer Spinning Mite (*Oligonychus ununguis*) also do serious damage.

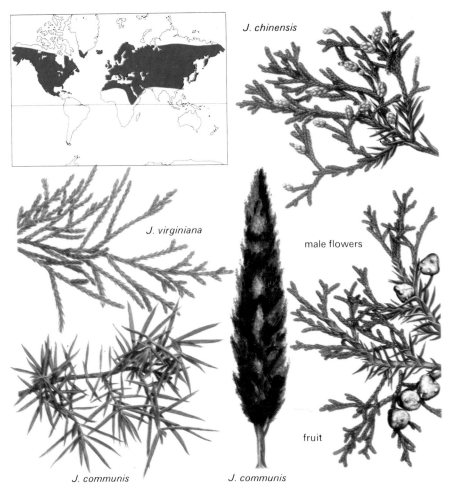

J. chinensis

J. virginiana

male flowers

fruit

J. communis

J. communis

Juniper wood is generally durable and easy to work; the presence of oils is probably responsible for the juniper's resistance to many insect attacks. The timber is used in general building, for roof shingles, furniture, posts and fences. In Burma *J. recurva* var *coxii* is the favored wood for coffins. *Juniperus virginiana*, generally known as the Pencil Cedar, is extensively used in the manufacture of pencils. Cedar wood oil is obtained from a distillation of the sawdust, shavings etc and, until recently, was the main 'immersion oil' used in the highest power light microscopy. *Juniperus oxycedrus* (Prickly Juniper) yields Oil of Cade (Oleum cadinum) or juniper tar by distillation of the wood. This oil has been used as a treatment for skin diseases, especially psoriasis, but is now largely replaced by coal-tar products, which prove more effective. It is also used in the perfumery industry. Oil of juniper is distilled from the fully grown but unripe berries of *J. communis* and is responsible for the characteristic flavor of gin. It is either added to the rectified spirit obtained after fermentation of the mixed grain mash or the spirit is redistilled together with the berries. The word 'gin' is a corruption of Geneva, derived from the French word *genévrier*, meaning juniper, and has nothing to do with the famous Swiss town. Oil of Savin, from *J. sabina*, is obtained by distilling fresh leaves and shoots. It is a powerful diuretic and has been used as an abortifacient.

Junipers are slow-growing and hardy and a number of species are frequently grown as ornamentals in parks, large gardens and often in graveyards. The most popular species are the Chinese Juniper (*J. chinensis*) and Pencil Cedar. Dwarf and prostrate forms suitable for ground cover and in rock gardens include the Creeping Juniper (*J. horizontalis*), the Procumbent Juniper (*J. procumbens*) and dwarf cultivars of the Common Juniper, for example 'Compressa' and 'Stricta.'

F. B. H.

The Main Species of *Juniperus*

Group I: *Caryocedrus* Leaves always awl-shaped (acicular) and spreading, in 3's, jointed at base and decurrent on the shoot; white-banded (from stomata) on upper surface. Cones axillary, sexes on separate plants; seeds usually 3.

J. drupacea Syrian Juniper. Greece, Asia Minor, Syria. Tree 10–12m, usually narrowly pyramidal. Leaves decurrent on stem, narrowly lanceolate, 15–25 × 3–4mm, with 2 white bands on upper side, separated by green midrib, except sometimes at apex. Berries globose to broadly ovoid, 1.5–2.5cm long.

Group II: *Oxycedrus* Leaves always awl-shaped (acicular), in 3's and jointed at base but not decurrent on the shoot, white-banded (from stomata) on upper surface.

J. communis Common Juniper. Cosmopolitan. Shrub or tree to about 12m. Leaves more or less awl-shaped, hard-pointed and skin-piercing, 10–15 × 1–2mm, the upper surface with a single white band, broader than the green margins but divided at the extreme base by the midrib. Berries globose to broadly ovoid, 5–6mm long, bluish-black.

'Hibernica' ('Stricta'), the Irish Juniper, has very dense foliage and short branches bending outward so that the upper surface, in the mass, presents a deep blue-green appearance.

montana (var *nana*, *J. sibirica*) is the Mountain Juniper, a prostrate shrub about 30cm high, the leaves scarcely prickly; it is characteristic of windswept areas – roughly arctic alpine Europe.

Note: A number of other very closely related species have been described but are now regarded as geographical variations, eg var *depressa* from E N America and var *hemisphaerica* from S Europe.

J. rigida Needle Juniper. Japan, Korea, Manchuria. Tree to 13m, sometimes a shrub, with pendulous branches. Leaves narrowly awl-shaped, 13–25 × 1mm, sharply pointed, deeply grooved on upper surface with the single white band narrower than the green margins; keeled below. Berries globose, about 6–8mm across, brownish-black.

J. oxycedrus Prickly Juniper. Spain, N Africa through Syria to the Caucasus. Shrub or small tree to 10m. Leaves linear-lanceolate, 12–18 × 1–1.5mm, apex piercing sharp, the upper surfaces with 2 white bands separated by a narrow green midrib and surrounded by a narrow green marginal band. Berries globose, 6–12mm in diameter, distinctly reddish-brown.

Group III: *Sabina* Leaves predominantly scale-like, at least on adult plants, but sometimes wholly awl-shaped (acicular); awl-shaped leaves, when present, always decurrent on the shoot and in opposite pairs or 3's. Cones terminal.

J. recurva Drooping Juniper. Burma, SW China, E Himalaya. Shrub or small tree to 10m, with spreading, pendulous branches. Leaves only awl-shaped and in 3's at a node, crowded and overlapping,

3–6 × 1mm, sharp-pointed, white-banded above without a green midrib; not jointed at base. Berries ovoid, 8–10mm long, dark purplish-brown to black.

coxii (Coffin Juniper) is a large tree with larger, less crowded leaves, about 1cm long, the upper surface of each leaf with 2 whitish bands on upper surface. It is sometimes considered a distinct species but, when typical, is probably only an extreme form of a variable species; there are intermediates.

J. phoenicia Phoenician Juniper. Mediterranean region including Algeria, Canary Islands. Shrub or tree to 6m. Leaves predominantly scale-like, imbricate and closely adpressed, in 3's or opposite pairs, 1mm long, blunt-tipped, the margin denticulate; awl-shaped leaves (rarely present) about 6mm long, 3 at a node. Berries more or less globose, about 8mm across, brown or reddish-brown.

Note: Specimens on the Canary Islands reach an exceptional size and may be 1 000 years old. They have been described as a separate species (*J. canariensis*), but this is not generally accepted.

J. thurifera Spanish Juniper. SW Europe, N Africa, Asia Minor and the Caucasus. Tree to 12m. Scale leaves more or less diamond-shaped, opposite and decussate, imbricate and closely adpressed, sometimes in 3's on leading shoots; awl-shaped leaves in opposite pairs, 5–6mm long with 2 whitish bands on each upper surface; margin denticulate. Berries globose, about 8mm in diameter, blue or bluish; seeds about 4.

J. chinensis Chinese Juniper. The Himalaya, China, Mongolia, Japan. Tree to 20m, sometimes a low shrub. Leaves either wholly scale-like, diamond-shaped, crowded, imbricate and closely adpressed, 1.5mm long with blunt tip, or with a few awl-shaped leaves 8–12mm long, 3 at a node (less often in opposite pairs), with 2 white bands on upper surface, separated by a green midrib; margin entire; apex spiny and skin-piercing. Berries more or less globose, 6–8mm across, brown. A variable species with numerous cultivars.

J. sabina Savin. C Europe. Shrub to 5m, the bruised foliage having an unpleasant smell and a bitter taste. Leaves predominantly scale-like, diamond-shaped, imbricate and closely adpressed, about 1mm long with a dorsal gland; awl-shaped leaves 4mm long, sharply pointed, each with a glaucous upper surface and prominent green midrib; margin entire. Berries globose to ovoid, 5–6mm across, brownish or bluish-black, pendulous. Numerous cultivars.

J. virginiana Red or Pencil Cedar. E and C USA. Tree to 30m, with ascending or spreading branches, ultimate branchlets not reaching more than 1mm thick. Leaves predominantly scale-like, imbricate and closely adpressed, 1.5mm long, apex pointed, diverging and with a small dorsal gland; awl-shaped leaves spiny-pointed, opposite or 3 at a node, 5–6(8)mm long and glaucous above; margin entire. Berries ovoid or subglobose, about 6mm long, bluish-glaucous. Numerous cultivars.

Patagonian Cypress
(genus *Fitzroya*)

Fitzroya comprises a single evergreen species (*Fitzroya cupressoides*) from Chile and Argentina where it may live up to an age of 3 000 years. It grows to 50m (164ft) in the wild and the trunk has a diameter of 9m (30ft), with characteristic reddish, furrowed bark. The leaves are spreading and typically arranged in whorls of three (rarely opposite). They are ternate, dark green, obovate, about 3mm (0.12in) long narrowing into flat decurrent bases, the free end more or less spreading, but with an incurved tip. Male and female cones occur separately on the same trees or on different trees, although some cones may be bisexual. The solitary male cones have up to 24 pollen sacs. The female cones comprise three alternating whorls, each whorl of three valvate scales, the lower smallest whorl sterile, the uppermost always fertile and the middle whorl sometimes fertile. They are finally woody, globose, 6–8mm (0.24–0.32in) in diameter, the fertile scales bearing two to six seeds each with two or three wings. The mature cone bears a terminal gland which secretes a fragrant resin.

The Patagonian Cypress is reasonably hardy when cultivated in temperate zones, but then it is often shrubby. Propagation is usually from cuttings taken toward the end of summer, since many cultivated trees are only female, thus setting no seed. The wood yields a valuable timber not unlike that of the redwoods and is used for general construction work locally.

F. B. H.

The leaves of *Fitzroya cupressoides* are arranged in three's and have distinct white bands that run down their decurrent bases.

African Cypresses
(genus *Widdringtonia*)

Widdringtonia comprises five species from tropical and southern Africa. They are mostly evergreen trees, rather like *Callitris* but the adult leaves are smaller and decussate (three-ranked in *Callitris*) and the slender, adpressed base of each scale leaf suddenly expands into an obtuse, incurved, broad mucronate apex. The leaves of juvenile plants are needle-like and spirally arranged. Male and female cones occur on separate trees. Mature cones are woody, more or less globose, mostly comprising four similar cone-scales, each with five or more ovules. The seeds are two-winged.

Cypress pines are not generally hardy in temperate regions although the following two species are marginally hardy in warmer parts of this region. The Berg Cypress (*Widdringtonia cupressoides*) from Table Mountain to Drakensburg in South Africa is a shrub to 3–4m (10–13ft). Its main branches are 10–20cm (4–8in) in thickness, the juvenile leaves 12 × 1mm (0.48 × 0.04in) and the adult leaves scale-like. The cones comprise virtually smooth scales that are 12–18mm (0.48–0.71in) long; 20–30 seeds are produced by each cone.

The Clanwilliam Cedar, Cape Cedar or Cedarboom (*W. juniperoides*) from the Cedarberg mountains, South Africa up to an altitude of 1 300m (4 300ft), is a tree to nearly 20m (66ft) although it is smaller and more bushy in cultivation. The juvenile leaves are 15–18 × 1mm (0.6–0.71 × 0.04in) and the adult leaves are scale-like. Mature cones are solitary, borne on short laterals, globose, 8–18(25)mm (0.32–0.71(1)in) across, comprising four, exceptionally six, rough and spine-tipped scales. The timber of this species has some commercial value for furniture and cabinet-making, whilst its good resistance to insect attack makes it suitable for fencing posts.

F. B. H.

Neocallitropsis

The single member of this genus, *Neocallitropsis araucarioides* from New Caledonia, is related to *Callitris*, but has the habit of *Araucaria*. It is a tree to 10m (33ft), its branchlets clothed with eight vertical rows of stiff, incurved leaves so that each branchlet has a cylindrical shape. Each leaf is about 6 × 5mm (0.24 × 0.2in), keeled below with a pointed apex and serrulate margin. The male cones are ovoid, 12 × 6mm (0.48 × 0.24in) comprising about eight rows of bracts bearing sessile pollen sacs. The female cones are terminal, borne on short laterals, each cone consisting of two alternating whorls of four narrowly-pointed bracts, each bract maturing a single seed. (In *Callitris* there is only one whorl of six or eight alternating long and short scales.)

This species is very rare in cultivation.

F. B. H.

Tetraclinis

Tetraclinis articulata is the only member of this genus and is native to southern Spain, North Africa and Malta. It is related to *Callitris* and *Widdringtonia*, but differs at a glance from these two genera by having the branchlets (phyllomorphs) distinctly flattened and by its scale leaves which are arranged in decussate pairs. It

Left The Alerce (*Tetraclinis articulata*) is a rare drought-resistant tree native to parts of the Mediterranean region which has its branchlets clothed in scale leaves.

is an evergreen tree growing up to 15m (50ft) and has erect, articulated branches. The lateral scale leaves somewhat exceed the length of the facial ones, but both have long decurrent bases, the upper free parts more or less boat-shaped with pointed tips. Female cones are solitary, terminal, globose and 8–12mm (0.32–0.48in) in diameter. They are composed of two pairs of nonpeltate woody scales, that are triangular in outline, with a blunt or pointed apex; all the scales are finally grooved or furrowed on the outer surface after separating and bear a very small subapical spine. Only the upper (inner) pair of scales are fertile, each producing two to nine broadly-winged seeds.

Its ability to withstand high temperatures and extended periods of drought has led to the replanting of this species in its native areas. In cultivation it is only hardy in the warmest parts of the north temperate zone.

The wood has been much esteemed, probably from Roman times; it is hard, sweet-smelling, often with attractive markings and has been much used for cabinet-making and high-class furniture. The trunk also yields a resin (Sandarac) which is extensively used for the manufacture of varnish.

F. B. H.

Diselma

Diselma comprises a single species (*Diselma archeri*) which is endemic to western Tasmania and Lake St. Clair, where it grows at altitudes of a little over 1 000m (3 300ft). It grows to about 8m (26ft) and is characterized by minute, decussate or whorled, closely adpressed scale-like leaves which

are blunt, about 1mm (0.04in) long and pear-shaped. Male and female cones are borne on separate plants. The female cones are subglobose, about 2mm (0.08in) across comprising four scales, only the upper (inner) pair of which are fertile. Each fertile scale gives rise to two three-winged seeds. *Diselma* is of no known economic value and is very rare in cultivation. It was formerly placed in the genus *Fitzroya*.

F. B. H.

Fokienia

Fokienia probably contains a single species (*Fokienia hodginsii*) which is native to China, extending westward into Indochina. *Fokienia maclurei* is considered to be a synonym, while *F. kawaii* is doubtfully distinct. *Fokienia hodginsii* is an evergreen tree to 13m (43ft), with flattened branchlets arranged in one plane (phyllomorphs). Leaves are scale-like, 3–8mm (0.12–0.32in) long and dimorphic – the shorter ones on older trees. Their apices are pointed or blunt and they are arranged in four ranks, each set of four leaves of equal length, but with the facial pair narrower than the lateral pair. The female cones are globose, about 25mm (1in) in diameter, comprising 12–16 peltate scales, the outside of each scale with a small papilla in a central depression. They ripen during the second year with two seeds per fertile scale. This unusual species is very rare in cultivation. F. B. H.

Both *Diselma archeri* (*Opposite Right*) and *Fokienia hodginsii* (*Below*) are extremely rare in cultivation; the former has slender branchlets clothed in scale leaves, the latter attractive sprays of branchlets. Both species are the only members of their genus.

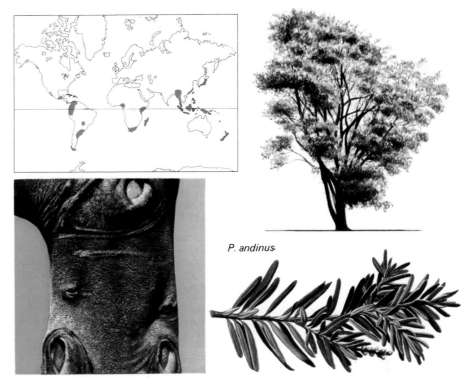

P. andinus

PODOCARPACEAE

Podocarps and Yellow Woods
(genus *Podocarpus*)

Podocarpus is a genus of evergreen trees and shrubs commonly called podocarps or yellow woods. Some species were formerly placed in the genus *Taxus* (yews) on account of their similar fleshy edible aril-covered seed. *Podocarpus andinus* of southern Chile, in fact, is known as the Plum-fruited Yew. Sectioning of the genus is not easy and interpretation of the structure of some species is often difficult. In fact, *P. palembanicus* has been regarded as a flowering plant (angiosperm) by some authorities in the past. The genus is unique in having the only known coniferous parasitic species, *P. ustus* which parasitizes *Dacrydium taxoides*, also in the family Podocarpaceae.

About 115 species have been described of which 100 are generally accepted as 'good.' They are natives of the tropics, subtropics and warm temperate regions of the Old and New Worlds, mainly the Southern Hemisphere, especially of South and East Africa, South America and New Zealand, with a few species extending to Central America, China, India, the West Indies, Japan, Malaysia and the Philippines.

Their leaves are mostly alternate, very variable in form from small and scale-like up to 35cm (14in) long and 5cm (2in) wide with an equally variable anatomy which is used in sectioning the genus. The sexes are typically on separate plants, rarely on the same. Male cones are either solitary or clustered. Female 'cones' are often reduced to a short, stout stalk with two to four 'bracts' of which only one is fertile then bearing one, sometimes two, inverted ovules fused to these scale-like bracts. The latter either remain small or become more or less expanded above into an aril-like structure – the epimatium. In many species the sterile 'bracts' fuse with the upper part of the stout stalk to give an often brightly colored fleshy receptacle on which the seed matures. In some species this fleshy receptacle is edible. The seed is commonly ovoid or globose and resembles a drupe or nut with an outer layer which may be skin-like or more or less fleshy, surrounding a hard inner shell or 'kernel.' The homologies of this 'cone' structure are not clear: the 'bract' is thought to be a bract-scale and the epimatium an ovuliferous-scale.

Podocarps are important timber trees in their native areas. Fine timber – known as yellow wood – is obtained from the South African species *P. falcatus* and *P. latifolius*, the Australian *P. elatus* and *P. amarus* and in New Zealand from *P. totara* – locally known as 'Totara,' which is deeply rooted in the traditions of the Maoris.

Most species are not hardy in temperate regions, although there are some clear exceptions to this rule. The Plum-fruited Yew forms a bushy tree which makes an excellent hedge, often being a welcome alternative to the Common Yew (*Taxus baccata*). It grows well on good soils overlying chalk. Other hardy species include *P. salignus*, *P. totara*, *P. alpinus* and *P. nivalis* – the Alpine Totara which is normally seen as a low-growing shrub forming a mound of prostrate stems. Other species, such as *P. dacryoides* and *P. elatus*, grow well in conservatories.   F. B. H.

The Main Species of *Podocarpus*

Section *Dacrycarpus*
Leaves awl-shaped or flattened or both. Bract fused with outer seed coat and as long as seed; receptacle fleshy.
P. dacrydioides White Pine. New Zealand. Tree to 50m. Leaves of young trees soft, flat, to 8mm in a single row on each side of shoot (on mature trees scale-like, spirally arranged – trees may show both types). Seed a black nut, 4–6mm, on red fleshy stalk. Important timber tree.

Section *Microcarpus*
Leaves scale-like only and overlapping. Bract free from outer seed coat and shorter than seed.
P. ustus New Caledonia. Densely branched shrub to 1m. Scale leaves to 2mm, coppery-red to purple. Seeds globose, 2.5mm in diameter, purplish, without fleshy receptacle. Parasitic on *Dacrydium taxoides*.

Section *Nageia*
Leaves many-nerved, to about 5 × 2.5cm, about half as broad as long; opposite or almost so.
P. nagi China, Japan, Taiwan. Tree to about 25m, but mostly a bush in cultivation. Leaves leathery, ovate, 5 × 2.5cm. Seeds plum-like about 1.25cm across on slightly thickened stalk.

Section *Afrocarpus*
Leaves alternate, more or less spirally arranged; stomata on both leaf surfaces.
P. dawei Uganda. Tree to 33m. Leaves leathery, 1.25–4.75 × 0.3–0.4cm. Seeds brown to purple, bloomed, subglobose, about 2cm long. Important timber tree.

Section *Polypodiopsis*
Leaves opposite and decussate, but appearing mostly in one plane of 2 ranks; stomata on both leaf surfaces. This section contains species from widely different areas including S America, S Pacific Islands, New Guinea, New Caledonia and Fiji. They are of little economic value and little known in cultivation.

Section *Sundacarpus*
Leaves lacking a hypoderm and at least 5 × 0.6cm, more or less spirally arranged around the branchlets; transfusion tissue present. Receptacle little developed and typically not fleshy. Species from NE Australia (Cape York Peninsula), New Guinea, Philippines and Indonesia (East Indies). Of no economic or ornamental importance.

Section *Stachycarpus*
Leaves lacking a hypoderm and not exceeding 3.6 × 0.5cm, typically appearing to be arranged in 2 ranks; transfusion tissue absent. Receptacle little developed and typically not fleshy.
P. andinus Plum-fruited Yew. Andes region of S Chile. Tree to about 17m but mostly a much-branched shrub in cultivation. Leaves linear, 2–3 × 0.5–0.7cm, often distinctly 2-ranked with 2 glaucous bands beneath. Female 'cone' arising from upper leaf axils on a scaly stalk; seeds with yellowish-green, white-speckled outer fleshy coating, subglobose, about 2cm across.
P. spicatus New Zealand. Tree 20–25m with dense, finally erect shoots. Leaves somewhat scale-like, 6–12mm long, glaucous on each side of midrib below. Male cones sessile, each about 4mm long, about 20 grouped together on short (2.5cm) stiff shoot; seeds globose, about 8mm across, black with glaucous bloom and without fleshy base. Wood like ordinary deal and in general use.
P. ferrugineus New Zealand (mainly South Island). Tree 17–30m. Leaves like those of the Common Yew (*Taxus baccata*), 18–30 × 2mm (about half this size on old trees), the margins more or less revolute. Male cones 6–18mm long, borne singly; female 'cones' subsessile, also borne singly, about 18mm long, with short point, bright red with waxy bloom. Wood strong and hard and much used for indoor purposes, but requires treating with preservative for outdoor staking etc.

Section *Podocarpus*
The typical section of the genus. Leaves *either* with hypoderm, hypodermal fibers *or* well-developed transfusion tissue. Receptacle typically well developed, more or less fleshy to leathery.
AA *Leaves linear to narrow lanceolate, rarely reaching 25 × 12mm, typically yew-like.*
B *Typically shrubs. Leaves rounded to slightly mucronate, not tapering; not in spikes.*
P. alpinus Mountains of Victoria, New South Wales (Australia) and New Zealand. Dense shrub (rarely low tree 4–5m). Leaves 6–12mm with essentially blunt apex; arranged in 2 ranks. Seed ovoid, 5–6mm long, single or paired, red, on fleshy receptacle.
P. nivalis Alpine Totara. Mountains of New Zealand. Dense shrub to 2m. Leaves irregularly arranged, 6–18mm long, essentially mucronate. Seed a small nutlet on red, fleshy base.
BB *Trees with stiff, tapering and acutely pointed leaves.*
P. totara Totara. New Zealand. Massive tree to over 30m. Leaves irregularly arranged or 2-ranked, 10–20mm long by up to 4mm wide on adult trees, almost sessile. Seeds mostly solitary, more or less globose, about 12mm across, on a red swollen receptacle. var *hallii* (sometimes regarded as a distinct species) is similar, but smaller and with longer leaves and the seed acute rather than rounded.
AA *Leaves lanceolate to oval, exceeding 25mm in length and not yew-like.*
P. macrophyllus China, Japan. Small shrub or tree to nearly 20m. Leaves densely and irregularly arranged 10(15) × 0.5cm, with prominent midrib above. Male cones in clusters, female 'cones' solitary; seeds elliptic-ovoid, about 1cm long on purple, fleshy receptacle. There are a number of varieties.
P. salignus Chile. Tree to about 20m. Leaves 5–10(12) × 0.4–0.6cm, with prominent midrib above, often slightly falcate. Male cones solitary or few but not in spikes; female 'cones' solitary; seeds more or less oblong about 8 × 3mm, red, on slender-stalked fleshy receptacle. Valuable timber tree.
P. nubigenus Chile, S Argentina. Tree to about 25m (in cultivation sometimes a bush) and densely branched. Leaves irregularly arranged but sometimes in 2 ranks, 2.5–3.5 × 0.3–0.4cm, with apical spine, straight to somewhat falcate and glaucous beneath. Male cones in clusters; seeds ovoid-oblong, about 8mm long on a swollen, fleshy receptacle.

Opposite In their native habitats many podocarps are tall trees such as this magnificent Outeniqua Yellow Wood (*Podocarpus falcatus*) in the Tsitsikama forest, South Africa.

Red Pines
(genus *Dacrydium*)

Dacrydium is a genus of evergreen trees and a few shrubs represented by 20–25 species. These conifers are natives of New Zealand, Tasmania, Australia, New Caledonia, New Guinea, Malaya, the Philippines, Fiji and Chile. The trees bear two types of foliage – juvenile which is soft and awl-shaped (acicular) and adult which is of small, densely-arranged, overlapping, leathery scale-like leaves. Both types of foliage often occur on the same tree simultaneously. The two sexes occur on different plants. The male cones are produced in catkins in the axils of upper leaves, and female 'cones' at or near the tips of branchlets. The seeds have an aril.

The genus, whilst including many stately trees of ornamental value, for example *Dacrydium cupressinum* and *D. franklinii*, also includes smaller species, for

The drooping branchlets of *Dacrydium verticillata* are densely clothed in overlapping scale leaves, which cover up the stems.

example *D. taxoides*, a shrub or small tree to 15m (50ft) from New Caledonia (parasitized by *Podocarpus ustus*), *D. bidwillii*, the Mountain Pine of New Zealand, an erect or prostrate shrub of 0.6–3m (2–10ft) and with very widely spreading branches, and *D. laxifolium*, another prostrate shrub of New Zealand, but attaining only a few centimetres in height.

Several species produce timber of economic value, for example the Red Pine (*D. cupressinum*) a native of New Zealand; this tree has a pyramidal shape reaching 18–34m (60–100ft) high with *Cupressus*-like branchlets and produces a wood used for building, railway sleepers, furniture and cabinet work. The Huon Pine of Tasmania (*D. franklinii*), which also attains a height of 34m (100ft), is an attractive tree with pendulous branchlets. The red timber is fragrant and similarly used for building, furniture and cabinet work. The timber of the Westland Pine (*D. colensoi*) of New Zealand is also of economic value.

F. B. H.

Prince Albert Yew
(genus *Saxegothaea*)

Saxegothaea comprises a single species, the Prince Albert Yew (*Saxegothaea conspicua*) from Chile. It is a remarkable evergreen more or less conical and bushy tree to 13m (45ft) which has yew-like foliage. The shoots are drooping and either opposite or in whorls of three or four. The leaves are more or less two ranked, spirally inserted, linear, 12–25mm (0.5–1in) long each with a sharp, distinct horny point. Male and female cones are found on the same tree. The male cones are about 1mm (0.04in) long and borne near the shoot apex. The female 'cones' are solitary, terminal and comprise overlapping spine-tipped fleshy scales. The mature structure is cone-like but fleshy, subglobose, 12–20mm (0.5–0.8in) in diameter, the bluish-gray scales more or less connate, the upper ones each with two inverted ovules that ripen into broadly ovoid seeds that are about 4mm (0.16in) long with a small arillate edge.

The Prince Albert Yew is hardy in the warmer parts of the north temperate zone, but shelter is advisable elsewhere. Propagation can be effected by cuttings, but it is a slow grower. The timber is durable and easy to work so that it is used locally for general carpentry.

F. B. H.

The yew-like foliage and 'cones' formed of fleshy spine-tipped scales of the Prince Albert Yew (*Saxegothaea conspicua*), which is native to Chile.

Microstrobos

This genus comprises two species of evergreen shrubs characteristic of wettish habitats in Tasmania and southeast Australia. Their leaves are scale-like, overlapping and spirally arranged in four or five rows. Female cones are very small, comprising four to eight glume-like bracts.

Both species are rare in cultivation with *M. fitzgeraldi* (New South Wales) the most hardy in temperate zones and hence the most frequently seen. This species is a bushy shrub up to 2m (6.6ft) tall and bears numerous long slender shoots. The leaves are 2–3mm (0.08–0.12in) long, diverge from the stem and are keeled, with an incurved tip. The female 'cone' is 2–3mm (0.08–0.12in) long and the seed about equal in length to its subtending bract.

The second species *M. niphophilus*, from the mountains of Tasmania, is a shrub to 2m (6.6ft) and is distinguished by its compact, bushy habit and even smaller leaves which are more densely clustered.

F. B. H.

Acmopyle

Acmopyle comprises three species of evergreen trees with yew-like foliage that are native to New Caledonia and Fiji. They are not hardy in temperate zones, although *Acmopyle pancheri* (New Caledonia) is sometimes grown as a glasshouse subject. It is a tree up to 16m (50ft) tall with erect branches. The leaves are linear lanceolate, 8–20 × 2–3mm (0.32–0.8 × 0.08–0.12in) with obtuse apices and borne in two ranks. The upper leaf surface has broken white stomatic lines and the under surface is more or less silvery. Male cones are 3–4cm (1.2–1.6in) long borne terminally in clusters of one to three. The female cones are also terminal, each comprising up to nine sterile bracts and a single fertile apical bract which are all fused together to form a fleshy, more or less warty, receptacle. The fertile bract bears a single globose seed that is longer than the receptacle. This genus is related to *Dacrydium* and *Podocarpus*, differing mainly in fruiting cone character, although some authorities place it in the yew family, Taxaceae.

F. B. H.

Below Foliage and cones of *Microcachrys tetragona*. *Opposite Left* The flattened leaf-like appendages of *Phyllocladus trichomanoides* are in fact modified stems which function as leaves.

Microcachrys

This genus comprises a single species, *Microcachrys tetragona* from the mountains of Tasmania. It is a straggling bush with a prostrate habit and slender four-angled branchlets. The leaves are scale-like with hairy margins, overlapping, 1–2mm (0.04–0.08in) long and arranged in four ranks. Individual trees may be unisexual or bisexual. Male cones are ovoid, borne terminally, about 3mm (0.12in) long; female 'cones' are finally 6–8mm (0.24–0.32in) comprising numerous bracts. The mature cones are finally fleshy and a translucent red color – each bract with an inverted seed with a fleshy scarlet aril (or epimatium).

This species is marginally hardy in temperate zones although not common in cultivation, when it is sometimes staked for upright habit. It is particularly unusual in its attractive fruits which yield fertile seeds.   F. B. H.

Celery-topped Pines
(genus *Phyllocladus*)

Phyllocladus comprises some seven species of evergreen trees and shrubs native to the Philippine Islands, Borneo, the Moluccan Islands and Australasia. The striking feature of these plants are the flattened and expanded short shoots which look like and function as leaves (phylloclades as in Butcher's Broom, *Ruscus* spp). The true leaves are scale-like and borne on the long

shoots. Some authorities place the genus in its own family – the Phyllocladaceae.

The following species are more or less hardy in the warmest parts of temperate regions. They are only marginally hardy and, at the limit of cultivation, are often stunted with great reduction in size of the phylloclades. The Alpine Celery-topped Pine (*P. alpinus*) from the mountains of North and South Islands of New Zealand is a bush or tree to about 10m (33ft). The phylloclades are crenate to somewhat lobed, roughly diamond-shaped, 6–38 × 3–18mm (0.24–1.5 × 0.12–0.7in). The female 'cones,' each with three or four ovules, mature to a globose red fruit 6mm (0.24in) in diameter.

The Celery-topped Pine or Tanekaha (*P. trichomanoides*) is found locally up to altitudes of 800m (2600ft) throughout New Zealand. It grows to 20m (66ft) with a trunk up to 3m (10ft) in diameter. The branches are arranged in whorls with the phylloclades often reddish-brown when young, up to 25mm (1in) long, ovate to oblong in outline, more or less lobed. The sexes are borne on the same plant, the female 'cones' in groups of about seven appearing mostly near the apex of terminal phylloclades. The fruit comprises a nut-like seed with a swollen, basal fleshy cup formed of fused scales. The wood of this species is of good quality and durability and the bark is rich in tannin from which a red dye is obtained.   F. B. H.

CEPHALOTAXACEAE

Cow's Tail Pines
(genus *Cephalotaxus*)

The genus *Cephalotaxus* comprises seven species of evergreen trees and shrubs, native to China, Japan and India (Khasi hills and Assam). The genus resembles *Torreya*, but the leaves are not spiny. The branches are opposite or whorled with the young branchlets grooved and minutely white-pitted by stomata. The leaves are yew-like, spirally inserted but, at least on lateral shoots, mostly appearing in two ranks, the upper leaf surface with a prominent midrib, the lower with two wide stomatic bands. The sexes are typically on separate plants, sometimes on the same, with male cones in globose heads in leaf

axils and female 'cones' at the base of branchlets, each comprising a few pairs of scales, and each scale bearing two ovules. Usually only one fertilized ovule in the whole 'cone' matures in the second season to form a stalked, protruding, green to purple, ellipsoid, drupe-like seed up to 2.5cm (1in) long, the outer layer finally fleshy and enclosing an inner woody 'kernel.'

The Chinese Plum Yew (*Cephalotaxus fortunii*) from central China is a small tree to 13m (43ft) in the wild but in cultivation tends to be a rather untidy shrub. It is grown for its evergreen foliage and the reddish-brown bark which peels away in flakes. The leaves are 5–8cm (2–3in) long, tapering gradually to a point in two horizontal ranks.

The Japanese Plum Yew (*C. drupacea*) is a similar tree to the above and likewise mostly shrubby in cultivation. The leaves are abruptly pointed, 2–5cm (0.8–2in) long, in a V-shaped arrangement on the shoot. The variety *prostrata* provides useful ground cover. The species is regarded by some authorities as a variety of *C. harringtonia*, a species not found wild but long cultivated in Japan and known by its irregularly pectinate, straight or curved leaves up to 6.5cm (2.5in) long.

The species are hardy in temperate regions and require much the same conditions as yews (*Taxus* spp) although somewhat less tolerant of chalk. Propagation is by seed or cuttings. They stand pruning well and are useful as hedging. The wood has some value, but the yield is low.
                          F. B. H.

Foliage and green fruiting 'cones' of *Cephalotaxus harringtonia*, a species of plum yew long cultivated in Japan.

TAXACEAE

Yews
(genus *Taxus*)

Yew is the popular name for the 10 species (regarded by some as varieties of one species) of *Taxus*, a genus of evergreen trees, shrubs and subshrubs (used for ground cover). Yews are widely distributed throughout the north temperate zone of the Old and New Worlds, with one species, the Chinese Yew (*Taxus celebica*) virtually on the equator on the Indonesian island of Sulawesi (Celebes). Although placed by many authorities in the order Coniferales, the yews and other genera of the family Taxaceae lack the typical seed-bearing cone structure and do not have resin canals in the wood and leaves. For these and other reasons, including fossil evidence, the family is sometimes excluded from the Coniferales and transferred to a separate order – Taxales.

The leaves of yews are linear and more or less spirally arranged on erect shoots but appear mostly two-ranked on horizontal shoots. Male and female cones are normally borne on different plants and are small and solitary. When ripe the seed is nut-like and surrounded by a fleshy cup (aril) which is conspicuous by its usually scarlet color and is commonly referred to as a 'berry' (strictly only angiosperms have berries). In the absence of its seeds, *Taxus* is often confused with *Abies* and *Tsuga*. It is at once distinguished by the underside of the leaves being uniformly yellow-green without conspicuous white stomatal lines, always evident in the other two genera.

All parts of the plant, except the scarlet aril, are highly poisonous. The enclosed seed or 'stone' of the aril also contains poison, so that children in particular should be discouraged from eating the tempting red fruit in case they swallow the stone. The poison is a mixture of alkaloids collectively referred to as taxine. Yew poisoning, resulting in gastroenteritis, heart and respiratory failure, is extremely serious, and fatal results in both humans and animals are well documented. In many temperate countries veterinary surgeons

consider the yews to be the most dangerous of all native trees and shrubs.

A grim comment on yew poisoning is that the main symptom is sudden death – within five minutes following some sort of convulsion. Thus, countermeasures are difficult and, in cattle, dangerous: opening the rumen, removing the contents and replacing them with normal foodstuffs. The best approach, as always, is prevention. The poison is also found in dried parts of the plant, so these should be cleared away and burnt.

Yews succeed well on almost any soil from peaty to calcareous, provided it is not liable to waterlogging, which may be fatal. Propagation is by seed, and for the cultivars by cuttings, grafting (on stocks of *Taxus baccata*) or by layering.

Apart from Yew Leaf Scorch, caused by *Sphaerulina taxi*, fungus diseases are not especially serious. Amongst insect pests, the Yew Gall Midge (*Taxomyia taxi*) attacks terminal leaves resulting in up to about 80 leaves becoming closely bunched together like an artichoke head, hence the name 'artichoke' gall. The attacks do little harm but are unsightly. 'Big bud' is another gall, caused by the mite *Phytopus*

The fleshy scarlet covering (aril) to the seed of yews is the only part of the plant that is *not* highly poisonous.

psilaspis. Only the buds are infected and these become enlarged and discolored with large numbers of mites at the center. Much more serious are attacks by the Yew Scale

Opposite The Common Yew (*Taxus baccata*) makes an excellent hedging plant and one of the most magnificent, over 6m (20ft) high, is seen here at Blenheim Park, England. *Right* Male cones of the Common Yew, which are short-lived and normally occur on separate plants from the females.

T. cuspidata

T. baccata
(underside)

T. baccata
(topside)

T. baccata

Insect (*Parthenolecanium pomeranicum*). White eggs may be found under females on almost any part of the plant at about midsummer. 'Honeydew' is excreted by the insects and this forms a favorable medium for the growth of 'sooty molds.'

The wood of yews is close-grained, durable and hard but elastic. In Britain it was the traditional material for making bows and is still used today for archery sports, being combined with hickory (*Carya*), the latter for the side facing the 'string,' the former on the side away from it. In spite of its high quality, the wood is less popular now than formerly; it is used mainly for floor blocks, panels, fence posts, mallet heads etc, and as a veneer in cabinet-making.

About five species are known in cultivation, the most common being the Common or English Yew (*Taxus baccata*). In Britain this species has been associated with cemeteries and graveyards and many of these trees are of great age, around a thousand years old. Whatever other reasons may be suggested for this association – religious, bow-making etc – there is the highly practical one that these places are least likely to be frequented by cattle and unaccompanied children who might otherwise be victims of its poisonous properties.

The English Yew is also planted for ornament throughout Western Europe and some of its cultivars make excellent hedges. It is a favorite subject for topiary work.

F. B. H.

The Main Species of *Taxus*

Group I: Leaves gradually tapering, not abruptly pointed (but see *T. celebica*). Winter bud scales not keeled.

T. baccata Common or English Yew. Europe, N Africa, W Asia. Tree 12–20m with rounded head, sometimes with a few erect stems from the base as well as a main stem. Leaves 1–2.5cm, usually in one plane on either side of stem, suddenly contracted into very short petiole. Seeds with a conspicuous scarlet fleshy edible cup (aril) surrounding an olive-brown poisonous seed 6mm long. Very many garden forms and cultivars.

'Fastigiata' (Irish Yew) is a distinctly compact and columnar cultivar with upwardly directed branches.

Group II: Leaves abruptly pointed (but see *T. celebica*). Winter bud-scales keeled.

T. cuspidata Japanese Yew. Japan. Tree 16–20m. Leaves 1.5–2.5cm × 2–3mm, not obviously in one plane, but ascending on either side of the stem in a V-shape. Seeds much as in *T. baccata*. Several cultivars.

T. canadensis Canada Yew. Canada and NE USA. Low, somewhat straggling shrub about 1m tall. Leaves 1.3–2cm × 1–2mm, arranged horizontally in 2 ranks. Seeds as in *T. baccata*.

T. brevifolia Western or American Yew. W N America, British Columbia, Washington, Oregon, California. Tree 5–15(25)m, rarely shrubby. Leaves 1–2.5cm × 2mm, arranged horizontally in 2 ranks. Seeds as in *T. baccata*.

T. celebica (*T. chinensis*) Chinese Yew. Widely distributed in China but extending to Taiwan (Formosa), the Philippines and Sulawesi (Celebes) although there is doubt whether the extra China distributions represent the same species. Shrub or tree to about 12m. Leaves 1.5–4cm × 2–4mm, straight or slightly curved, tapering at the apex or more or less abruptly pointed, the lower surface densely covered with minute papillae. Seeds much as in *T. baccata*. This species is sometimes labeled *T. chinensis*.

Note: Two hybrids are also in cultivation: *T. × hunnewelliana* (*T. cuspidata* × *T. canadensis*) and *T. × media* (*T. cuspidata* × *T. baccata*).

The so-called 'artichoke' gall of yews caused by the Yew Gall Midge (*Taxomyia taxi*).

Nutmeg Trees
(genus *Torreya*)

The genus *Torreya* comprises six or eight species of evergreen trees from East Africa and the United States of America. They are closely related to the yews (*Taxus* spp), but the branches and branchlets are opposite or almost so, the leaves are pungent with a sharply pointed apex and the lower side, which has a single resin canal, shows two narrow but distinct whitish to off-whitish stomatal bands. The sexes are mostly but not always on separate plants. The seed is drupe-like, being wholly surrounded by a thin fleshy layer, and requires two years to mature. In *Taxus*, the seed has a basal aril and the lower sides of the needles are uniformly pale yellowish-green and there is no resin canal. Nutmeg trees are scarcely hardy

Branchlets of the California Nutmeg (*Torreya californica*) with a comb-like (pectinate) arrangement of linear, spine-tipped leaves which have a strong aroma when crushed.

except in the warmest parts of temperate regions.

The California Nutmeg (*T. californica*) is a tree growing to 20m (66ft) in its native habitat, coastal regions of California, ascending to nearly 2 000m (6 600ft) in the Sierra Nevada. The second-year shoots are reddish-brown, the crushed leaves strongly aromatic, 3–6cm × 3mm (1.2–2.4 × 0.12in). The seed is ovoid to 3.5cm (1.4in) long and purple streaked.

The other main American species is the Florida Torreya or Stinking Cedar (*T. taxifolia*) which is a tree to 13m (43ft), rarely 18m (60ft), growing in southwestern Florida. The second-year shoots are yellowish-green. The leaves are 2.5–3cm × 3mm (1–1.2 × 0.12in), pungent but not unpleasantly so when crushed and the stomatal bands are not obviously in grooves. The seeds are obovoid, 2.5–3cm (1–1.2in) long, with the same peculiar smell. It is the least hardy species, not surviving in temperate regions.

The Chinese Torreya (*T. grandis = T. nucifera* var *grandis*) from eastern and central China, is a tree growing to 25m (82ft) in China, but mostly a shrub in cultivation. The second-year shoots are yellowish-green. The leaves are virtually without smell when crushed and the stomatal bands are in grooves. The seeds are ellipsoidal.

The hardiest species is the Japanese Nutmeg or Torreya (*T. nucifera*), which is a tree growing to 25m (82ft) but, like the previous species, generally shrubby in cultivation. The second-year shoots are reddish-brown. The leaves are very aromatic when crushed and the stomatal bands are in grooves. The seeds are more or less ovoid, green tinged purplish-red, and are edible.

F. B. H.

Amentotaxus

The genus *Amentotaxus* comprises one to four species which were formerly placed in the Cephalotaxaceae. They are evergreen shrubs to small trees, native to Assam and China (including Hongkong). The shoots are opposite and the leaves decussate (opposite with each pair at right angles to the ones above and below it), needle-like, conspicuously keeled beneath, with a single whitish stomatal band on either side of the keel. The male and female cones are borne on separate plants, the male in sessile pendent groups of two to four (rarely one or five), the female stalked, solitary, in the axil of a bract, maturing to a drupe-like structure, the seed, which is surrounded by a more or less orange aril, open above with persistent scales at the base.

The type species is *Amentotaxus argotaenia*, a shrub growing to 4m (13ft), with leaves 4–7cm × 6mm (1.6–2.8 × 0.24in). It has probably not been cultivated. Other recorded species are *A. cathayensis* (western China), *A. formosana* (Taiwan and China) and *A. yunnanensis* (Yunnan province of western China).

F. B. H.

Austrotaxus

The genus *Austrotaxus* comprises a single evergreen species from New Caledonia with the foliage of *Podocarpus*, but a seed like that of yews (*Taxus* spp). Its male cones are in spikes like some species of *Podocarpus*, but unlike *Taxus* where they are in small stalked heads of some 6–14 pollen sacs.

Austrotaxus spicata is a tree growing to 25m (82ft) with a bushy crown. The leaves are linear, spirally arranged, 8–12 × 4mm (0.3–0.5 × 0.16in), with revolute margins, keeled below, grooved above, and with the apex pointed. The male cones are axillary in dense spikes up to 15mm (0.6in) long; the females are solitary, giving rise to a single stone-like elliptical seed 12–16mm (0.5–0.6in) long, with a fleshy, yellowish, aril-like sheath. It grows in moist woods on slopes to about 400–1 000m (1 300–3 300ft) and has probably not been cultivated.

F. B. H.

Pseudotaxus

The genus *Pseudotaxus* comprises a single species from China, differing from *Taxus* in leaf epidermal structure, there being no papillae surrounding the stomatal openings, and in the presence of sterile scales in the male cone and a white, not red, aril surrounding the seed.

Pseudotaxus chienii is an evergreen shrub growing to 2–4m (6.5–13ft), with the sexes borne on separate plants. In the female cone there is a short stalk with about 15 decussately arranged scale-like bracts, the uppermost and longest one 4–5mm (0.16–0.2in) long, concealing the young ovule.

F. B. H.

BROADLEAVES

The term 'broadleaved tree' is a popular and convenient one used to distinguish trees belonging to the class Angiospermae (the flowering plants) from those belonging to the class Coniferae (the Conifers). Even within the flowering plants, broadleaves are normally considered as being only those trees belonging to the dicotyledons (subclass Dicotyledoneae), that is those that have two seed leaves within each seed. Broadleaved trees typically have leaves that are flattened, although in some species this shape is considerably modified, and their reproductive structures are borne in flowers, compared to the conifers where the leaves are typically needle-like and the reproductive structures are borne in cones. The structure of the wood also differs (see the chapter What is a Tree?) so that the timber of broadleaves is commercially known as hardwood and that of conifers softwood. Another microscopic, but vital, difference is that the female egg-containing body – the ovule – is enclosed in an ovary in all flowering plants whereas in conifers it is not enclosed in an ovary but lies naked on the cone-scales.

Apart from the broadleaves, tree-like forms also occur in the other subclass (Monocotyledoneae) of flowering plants. These so-called monocotyledons (seeds with one seed leaf) differ from the 'true' broadleaved trees in having typically fan-like leaves and 'wood' produced by a completely different process. The main representatives are the palms (see the later chapter on Monocotyledon Trees).

Flowering plants are the dominant and most successful plants of the present world's flora. In the course of evolution angiosperms and gymnosperms (including Conifers) have diverged from a common stock, but the angiosperms are much more recent than the gymnosperms. However, the fossil evidence is very scanty and incomplete. The earliest evidence of angiosperms is from the middle Jurassic period of the Mesozoic era, some 136–190 million years ago and their greatest development took place within the tropics primarily as trees. Even today the tropical forests of the world are the richest in flowering plant species and contain the greatest diversity of broadleaved trees. These forests are characterized by abundant, almost daily, rainfall, a high and constant temperature throughout the year and soil enriched by a very considerable animal population – a combination of factors which is favorable to evergreen plant life. Thus many tropical trees are in fact evergreen despite the popular conception of people from temperate regions that they are deciduous. From this center of evolution many species have, as it were, 'emigrated' to temperate regions north and south of the equator where there are seasonal changes of weather including reduced and intermittent rainfall with alternating warm and cold periods of different intensity limits. Many broadleaved trees have adapted to such changes in the environment by evolving the deciduous habit, so that they pass the winter period in a state of dormancy, to grow again with the return of the warmth in spring.

Today broadleaved trees are of vital importance in the economies of most countries. Their products are innumerable – they are sources of food, fuel, construction materials, newsprint, drugs, coloring and flavoring matters, to name but a few – and of course their value as ornamentals has been recognized for thousands of years. For many centuries, the exploitation of such products has been of great significance in the rise of civilizations and even today many countries look to the exploitation of their one remaining resource – the tropical rain forests – as a means of attaining a 'developed' economy. The present increasing rate of destruction of tropical forests is a matter of grave concern to conservationists. It is known that such forests contain many species, both plant and animal, which have yet to be described and most people would deplore the extinction of any species. It is disturbing to be told that, at the present rate of tropical forest destruction, there will be none left in about 30 years' time. The problem of the conservation of tropical forests is that they must be properly managed on an international basis for the overall good. However, it is understandably difficult to persuade underdeveloped nations of the need to conserve this last resource when the Western World has already destroyed its own natural forests. Therefore, hand in hand with conservation must go the curbing of the ever increasing demands of rich nations of the Western World for the products of such forests.

The classification of broadleaved trees is more complex than that of the conifers where all the families are made up of trees or shrubs (arborescent). Altogether there are some 300–400 families of flowering plants but only a relatively small number (approximately 60) are purely arborescent. Many families contain herbs as well as trees. In evolutionary terms, trees are more primitive than herbs, so we find that the most primitive families, the Magnoliaceae and Winteraceae, contain only trees and shrubs. A number of other so-called primitive traits can be recognized, a number of which are (with advanced conditions in parentheses): large regular flowers with numerous free parts (small irregular flowers with fewer and fused parts); superior ovaries of free carpels (inferior ovaries of fused carpels); dehiscent fruits (indehiscent fruits). One major branch of evolution has been the development of the wind-pollinated trees in which the petals and sepals are either absent or reduced and the flowers are typically arranged in pendulous catkins. These so-called anemophilous trees produce copious quantities of pollen rather like the conifers, which are also wind-pollinated. Some experts at one time considered that such wind-pollinated species were primitive but it is now considered that they have evolved from an angiosperm stock which had typical insect-pollinated flowers.

The following section details those broadleaved genera whose members are either mainly native or cultivated in temperate and warm temperate regions such as the Mediterranean. Each genus is placed within its family, with the families arranged in order of increasing evolutionary sophistication. The system of arrangement adopted is based upon that of G. L. Stebbins in his *Flowering Plants – Evolution Above the Species Level*. At the end of this volume, under the chapter heading 'Identification of Trees' we have provided keys to the broadleaved genera found in this volume. The first key separates the families and subsequent keys for each family separate the individual genera.

F. B. H.

Opposite To the majority of 'temperate' readers this picture of the leaves of the Copper Beech (*Fagus sylvatica* forma *purpurea*) summarizes their image of the foliage of a typical broadleaved tree – a relatively large and flimsy structure comprising a flattened lamina supported by a main central midrib and associated veins, which is lost from the tree during the cold winter months. Although this is the basic form, numerous variations occur. Many temperate broadleaves are also evergreen, while those of dry habitats and climates, such as the Mediterranean region, typically have leaves that are reduced in size and leathery. The greatest diversity of broadleaved trees occurs in the tropics where a mixture of deciduous and evergreen species occurs depending on the precise climatic factors, although the 'average' shape and size does not differ greatly from those of the temperate region.

MAGNOLIACEAE

Magnolias
(genus *Magnolia*)

The genus *Magnolia* has over 80 species distributed in southeast Asia and America. It is well known in horticulture, and provides some of the most popular ornamental trees and shrubs, some of the species when in full bloom being unsurpassed in beauty. The geographical range of the genus is of the same discontinuous type as those of *Talauma* and *Liriodendron* (Tulip Tree) in the same family. In Asia *Magnolia* species occur in a roughly triangular area extending from the Himalaya in the west to Japan in the east and southward through the Malay Archipelago to Java. In America they are found in the eastern United States and extreme southeast Ontario, and range southward into the Greater Antilles and through Mexico and Central America to northern South America. The majority of the species (over 50) are Asian, the remainder (about 26) being American. Most of the species are montane, though a few are found at low altitudes. Rather more than half the species are tropical. Only the temperate species are suitable for outdoor cultivation in northern latitudes.

The name of the genus commemorates Pierre Magnol (1638–1715), an early Director of the botanic garden at Montpellier, France, and Professor of Botany and Medicine.

Magnolias have large simple alternate leaves and the flower buds are enclosed in a single scale. The large showy flowers are solitary and borne terminally on the shoots. The entire perianth is petaloid and comprises six or nine segments (exceptionally more) which are arranged in whorls. These perianth segments, being neither distinctly sepals nor petals, are often referred to as 'tepals,' although in some cases the outer whorl may be reduced and sepal-like. The fruit is conical.

Magnolias have long been in open-air cultivation in Europe, the first to arrive being the American *Magnolia virginiana* in 1688. However, some of the Asian species had been cultivated in China and Japan long before that. Four more American species were brought to Europe by 1786, including *M. grandiflora*, an evergreen species which is now widely planted in tropical countries as well as in temperate regions. The first Asian species to be

The purple tulip-shaped flowers of *Magnolia liliflora* 'Nigra', a Japanese cultivar of a Chinese species, show just why magnolias are among the most popular ornamental shrubs and trees. The green spathe-like bracts fall off as the flower opens to reveal the whorls of showy petal-like tepals.

The Main Species of *Magnolia*

Subgenus *Magnolia*
Eight sections of temperate and tropical flowering trees with anthers that shed pollen introrsely. The flowers appear after the leaves; the tepals are in similar whorls. The leaves are evergreen or deciduous and the fruits variously shaped.

Section *Gwillimia* 18 evergreen species with stipules adjoining the leaf stalks and short, nonflattened beaks on the carpels.
M. delavayi Yunnan, China. Large bushy tree up to 12m. Leaves ovate to oblong and very leathery, up to 30cm long and 16cm wide. Flowers with 6 greeny-white tepals; anthers straw-colored.
M. coco SE China. Erect shrub 2–4m high. Leaves oblong 9–15cm long, leathery, shining above. Flowers nodding with 3 green outer tepals, and 6 white, fleshy inner tepals.
M. henryi Yunnan, N Thailand. Tree 6–8m tall. Leaves wedge-shaped, 20–65cm long, 7–22cm wide, leathery. Flowers white with 8 or 9 tepals.
M. championi Hong Kong. Shrub or small tree, up to 4m high. Leaves elliptic, 7–16cm long and 2.5–5cm wide, leathery. Flowers globe-shaped, cream-colored and very fragrant, with 10 tepals.

Section *Lirianthe*
M. pterocarpa India, Burma. A tall tree similar to *M. henryi* of the previous section but differing by the remarkable long flattened beaks on the carpels.

Section *Rytidiospermum* 9 evergreen species with a whorl-like arrangement of leaves at the end of the branches.
M. macrophylla SE USA. Tree or large shrub to 10–15m. Leaves oblong-ovate, extremely large, 30–100cm long with auriculate-subcordate bases. Flowers large,

up to 35cm in diameter, the 6 tepals white with a purple blotch at the base.
M. tripetala Umbrella Tree. E USA. Small branching tree up to 12m. Leaves obovate, 30–60cm long and 18–30cm wide. Flowers large, white and unpleasantly scented. Fruit slightly rose-colored. Closely related species include *M. ashei* (USA), *M. fraseri* (S USA), *M. dealbata* (S Mexico).
M. hypoleuca Japan. Large tree, up to 30m. Leaves obovate, up to 45cm long and 20cm wide, deciduous. Flowers with 2 distinct whorls of tepals – outer ones red-brown, tinged with green, inner ones large, fragrant, pale creamy-yellow.
M. officinalis E China. Large tree up to 22m. Leaves elliptic-obovate, up to 35cm long and 18cm wide. Flowers large, fragrant with creamy-white, fleshy tepals.
M. rostrata China, Tibet, Burma. Tree up to 24m. Leaves obovate-oblong, up to 50cm long and 20cm wide. Flowers with green fleshy tepals in the outer whorl and white tepals within.

Section *Magnoliastrum*
M. virginiana Sweet Bay, White Laurel. E USA. A semievergreen tree up to 20m. Leaves oblong-ovate, 5–10cm long, shining green above, bluish-white below. Flowers globular, creamy-white, very fragrant, with a bright red fruiting cone.

Section *Oyama*
M. sieboldii Japan, Korea, China. A slender deciduous tree up to 7m. Leaves obovate or oblong-obovate 9–15cm long. Flowers on a long stalk, cup-shaped, pure white, with a rich, crimson rosette of stamens.
M. sinensis W China. A large spreading shrub 4–6m tall. Leaves sparse, elliptic-oblong, 8–12cm long, 3–5cm wide. Flowers cup-shaped, fragrant, white, with 12 tepals; anthers with red filaments and red carpels.
M. wilsonii China. A spreading shrub or small tree to 8m, with leaves and flowers like those of *M. sinensis*.
M. globosa Sikkim, Yunnan. A small tree up to 8m tall. Leaves membranous, 10–25cm long, oval, with acute or mucronate apex and cordate base. Flowers white, with 9 tepals and a purple bract.

Section *Theorhodon* A section of 15 tropical evergreen trees mostly confined to the Caribbean islands. Flowers have sessile carpels.

M. cubensis Cuba. A tree up to 20m. Leaves narrowly ovate, 6–8cm long and 2.5–4cm wide, leathery. Flowers small, with white tepals.

M. domingensis Haiti. A tree 3.3–4m tall, with spreading branches. Leaves obovate, thick and leathery, 7–11cm long and 4–7cm wide. Flowers unknown.

M. grandiflora Laurel Magnolia, Bull Bay. SE USA. A tall pyramidal tree up to 30m. Leaves oval to oblong, 12–25cm long and 6–20cm wide. Flowers very large, up to 30cm in diameter, with thick, creamy-white tepals, purple stamens and rusty-brown fruits. Many varieties are cultivated. Related species include *M. emarginata* (Haiti), *M. ekmannii* (Haiti), *M. pallescens* (Dominican Republic), *M. hamori* (Dominican Republic), *M. portoricensis* (W Puerto Rico), *M. splendens* (E Puerto Rico).

Section *Gynopodium*

M. nitida NW Yunnan, SE Tibet, NE Burma. A shrub or tree 6–15m high. Leaves ovate-oblong, up to 10cm long and 2.5–5cm wide, evergreen, very glossy. Flowers creamy-white or yellow with a short-stalked fruit and bright golden-red seeds.

M. kachirschira Formosa. The only other member of this section and very similar to *M. nitida*.

Section *Maingola* 10 tropical Asiatic species, with short, stalked leaves and free stipules.

M. griffithii Assam, Burma. A large tree (of unrecorded size). Leaves elliptic-oblong and pointed, 18–30cm long and 8–12cm wide. Flowers white-yellow, small and leaf-opposed.

M. pealiana Assam. Similar to the previous sp but with smaller, hairless leaves.

Subgenus *Pleurochasma*

Three sections of temperate trees with anthers that shed their pollen from lateral or sublateral openings. The flowers are either precocious, appearing before the leaves, or with a reduced calyx-like outer whorl of tepals and appearing with the leaves. The leaves are deciduous and the fruits are cylindrical or oblong and usually more or less distorted.

Section *Yulania* 5 species with 9 subequal tepals appearing before the leaves.

M. denudata Yulan. C China. A tree up to 18m, with wide spreading branches and a trunk up to 2.5m in circumference. Leaves obovate-oblong 8–18cm long and 8–12cm wide. Flowers large, pure white, bell-shaped with 9 fleshy tepals. The earliest cultivated garden magnolia known from the Tang dynasty in China. Closely related Chinese species include *M. sprengeri*, *M. dawsoniana*, *M. sargentiana*.

Section *Buergeria* 5 temperate species with a reduced outer whorl of tepals. Flowers appear before the leaves.

M. kobus N Japan. A large somewhat round-headed, deciduous tree up to 20–35m. The slender branches and young leaves are scented when crushed. Leaves obovate, 8–12cm long. Flowers white, with 6 tepals.

M. salicifolia Mount Hakkoda region, Japan. Slender, pyramidal tree up to 5–7m. Leaves narrowly oval to lanceolate, up to 10cm long. Flowers like *M. kobus*.

M. stellata Star Magnolia. Japan. A much-branched shrub up to 5m tall and equally broad. Bark aromatic when young. Leaves narrow oblong, up to 9cm long. Flowers pure white with 12–18 tepals. Lesser known related species include *M. biondii* (E China), *M. cylindrica* (N and C China).

Section *Tulipastrum*

M. acuminata Cucumber Tree. E USA. A large pyramid-shaped tree up to 20–30m. Leaves oblong, bright green, 12–25cm long, hairy below. Flowers greenish-yellow, cup-shaped, erect and slightly fragrant. Fruit like a cucumber.

M. cordata E USA. Shrub or tree up to 10m. Leaves broadly ovate, 8–15cm long. Flowers cup-shaped, yellow, the inner tepals marked with reddish lines.

M. liliflora China. A large sturdy bush, 2–4m tall. Leaves oblong-ovate, 9–20cm long, tapering to a point, dark glossy green above, downy below. Flowers with vinous purple and white tepals.

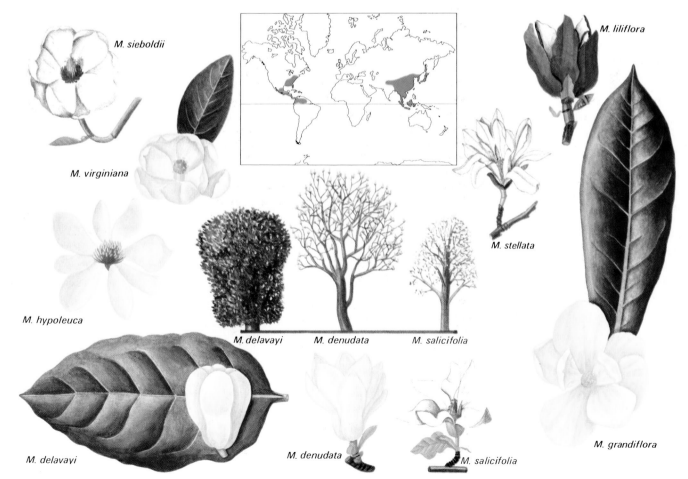

M. sieboldii

M. virginiana

M. hypoleuca

M. delavayi

M. delavayi

M. denudata

M. denudata

M. salicifolia

M. salicifolia

M. stellata

M. liliflora

M. grandiflora

Perhaps the most stunning of all magnolia groups are the pink-flowered species which produce magnificent shows, particularly in the early spring. Shown here is *Magnolia campbellii mollicomata*, a native of southeast Tibet and Yunnan.

introduced into Europe was *M. coco* (1786) from Java, a nonhardy evergreen shrub to about 1m (3.3ft) with flowers very fragrant at night, commonly grown in southeast Asia. This was soon followed by the precocious-flowered *M. denudata* (the Yulan of the Chinese) and the semi-precocious *M. liliflora*, two species already cultivated in China and Japan. By the end of the 19th century seven more species had been introduced from North America and Japan, as well as the magnificent *M. campbellii* from the Himalaya; but it was not until the present century, largely as the result of the botanical exploration of west and central China, that it was possible to complete the fine array of species now available for cultivation in temperate gardens. At present the number of *Magnolia* species in outdoor cultivation in Europe and North America is about 28, of which three are evergreen and the rest deciduous.

The ever-rising popularity of magnolias as garden subjects is due mainly to the striking beauty of such deciduous, precocious-flowered species as *M. campbellii*, *M. sargentiana*, *M. dawsoniana*, *M. sprengeri*, *M. denudata*, *M. salicifolia*, *M. kobus* and *M. stellata*. There are now also hybrids in increasing numbers, some of which have arisen spontaneously by accident, others the results of deliberate cross-fertilization. The most frequently grown hybrid is *M. × soulangiana* (*M. denudata × liliflora*) which was first grown in Europe in the 1820's and is now represented by many cultivars.

Propagation is easiest by layering or by grafting and for the latter, *M. acuminata* is one of the better stocks. Magnolias like a well-drained soil with ample humus. Some species are lime tolerant, others not.

The leaves of many species readily yield 'skeletons' and these have been used to 'set off' bouquets; the bark has been used as a tonic and general stimulant.

Several species produce useful commercial timber, such as the Southern Magnolia (*M. grandiflora*) from the eastern United States, the Japanese Cucumber Tree (*M. hypoleuca*) (often wrongly known as *M. obovata* – an illegitimate name) from Japan, and Campbell's Magnolia (*M. campbellii*) from the eastern Himalaya.

J. E. D.

Tulip Trees
(genus *Liriodendron*)

Liriodendron is a genus with two species of deciduous trees, *Liriodendron tulipifera* (Tulip Tree) from North America and *L. chinense* (Chinese Tulip Tree) from central China. The Tulip Tree is a fast-growing, stately tree, in its native habitats reaching heights of 50–60m (160–200ft). It was one of the first introductions to Europe from America in the 17th century and some fine specimens may be seen as ornamental trees in large gardens.

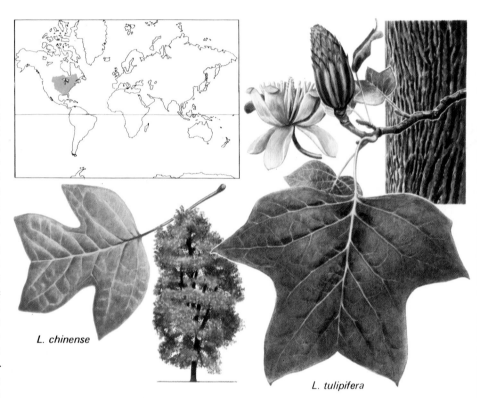

L. chinense

L. tulipifera

The Species of *Liriodendron*

L. tulipifera Tulip Tree, Yellow Poplar, Whitewood. Native to North America where it occurs from Nova Scotia south to Florida and into the Middle West, reaching its finest development in the South Alleghany region. A hardy, stately ornamental, deciduous tree of lofty pyramidal habit reaching up to 60m. Leaves are alternate, 7.5–20cm in length, with long mobile leaf stalks and truncated apex. Flowers greenish-white with orange-stained base to the petals, somewhat resembling a tulip flower. The carpels mature to winged, 1- or 2-seeded nutlets densely packed on a spindle-shaped column.

L. chinense Chinese Tulip Tree. Found in limited regions of C China; first noticed in 1875 in the Lushan mountains. A more densely growing, smaller tree than *L. tulipifera*, reaching up to 20m. Leaf shape is somewhat similar but the undersides of the leaves are covered with minute hairs which are visible with a hand lens. The flowers are smaller and more greenish.

Opposite A massive Tulip Tree (*Liriodendron tulipifera*), with its so characteristically shaped leaves clearly visible, spreads its branches over a lake at Stourhead, England.

The leaves are alternate and very characteristically truncate at the apex. The tulip-like flowers are borne singly at the ends of short branchlets. Each flower is greenish-yellow with orange blotches, with three deflected sepals and six petals. The stamens are numerous and surround a densely-packed tapering column of carpels. Flowers are usually produced from May to July on trees of some maturity (20–30 years).

The trees flourish best on a rich, deep soil. They should be given a permanent site at an early stage and do not like being transplanted. Both species are hardy in temperate climates.

Also known as the Yellow Poplar or Whitewood, the Tulip Tree makes splendid specimen trees in parkland and amenity areas. The leaves are a bright fresh green throughout the summer, turning gold and lemon in the fall. *Liriodendron tulipifera* 'Fastigiatum' is a more erect cultivar. The Chinese Tulip Tree is rarely found in cultivation and was first introduced to Europe at the beginning of the 20th century.

The Tulip Tree has important timber value, producing a soft, fine-grained, light yellow wood much used for carpentry, furniture and boat-building. It does not split easily and is readily worked. The inner bark is said to have medicinal properties.

T. W. W.

produced in axillary clusters, rarely solitary, usually less than 5cm (2in) across.

In cultivation *Drimys* species are only hardy in the warmer parts of temperate regions, and cannot survive prolonged freezing conditions in winter. Outside such areas they require a cool conservatory.

The best-known species in cultivation is Winter's Bark (*Drimys winteri*). This species has considerable horticultural potential for arboreta and parks in warmer regions of temperate zones. It is most often seen as a tree, 8–16m (26–52ft) in height although sometimes it only reaches the stature of a large shrub. The leaves are more or less elliptic to oblanceolate, reaching up to 20cm (8in) in length. The flowers are white, fragrant, each up to 4cm (1.5in) across with 5–20 narrow petals. The fruits finally take the form of fleshy berries. *Drimys winteri* var *andina* (from the Andes) is of dwarf habit reaching about 1m (3.3ft) in height and very floriferous at an early stage. If a wide view is taken of this species, its range is from Tierra del Fuego to Mexico. It was named after one Captain Winter who sailed with Sir Francis Drake. He collected the highly aromatic bark from a tree in the Magellan Straits area and used it on the ship's crew as a treatment against scurvy.

The Mountain Pepper (*D. lanceolata* = *D. aromatica*) is also sometimes found in cultivation. It is a shrub or small tree up

to 5m (16ft) and is native to Tasmania and eastern Australia. Its branchlets are a fine red color and the leaves elliptic to oblanceolate, 1.5–7cm (0.5–3in) long, with short petioles that are also red. The white flowers are borne in fascicles, each flower about 13mm (0.5in) across. The sexes are on separate plants, the male flowers with 20–25 pinkish-buff stamens, the female with a single carpel. The fruit is a pungent black berry which when dried has been used as a pepper.

F. B. H.

LAURACEAE

True Laurels
(genus *Laurus*)

The true laurels belong to the genus *Laurus* which contains just two species – the Sweet Bay, Bay Laurel, or just Bay (*Laurus nobilis*) and the Canary Island Laurel (*L. azorica* = *L. canariensis*). Both species are evergreen shrubs or trees with hairless branchlets. The leaves are also hairless, entire and highly aromatic when bruised. The flowers are unisexual and borne on separate plants in small axillary clusters. They have a whorl of four sepals, the male flowers with usually 12 (8–14) stamens with the anthers opening by valves, the females with four staminodes. The fruit is a berry surrounded by a persistent perianth.

The Sweet Bay is much cultivated outside its native Mediterranean, the aromatic leaves being used for flavoring in many culinary operations. It is generally hardy in most temperate regions and is not particular as to soil, but this should be well drained and open to the sun. Many plants are grown in tubs and kept clipped; they are particularly suitable for growing near the seashore. Propagation is from cuttings.

Laurus nobilis is the classical laurel, sacred to Apollo, the symbol of victory and honor in the form of crowns and garlands. In the Middle Ages distinguished men were crowned with a wreath of this berried laurel, whence the term Poet Laureate. University undergraduates were known as Bachelors from the Latin *baccalaureus* meaning laurel berry. They were forbidden to marry as this would distract

WINTERACEAE

Winter's Bark
(genus *Drimys*)

Drimys is a genus of evergreen shrubs and small trees, the bark and other parts of which are aromatic and/or acrid – hence the generic name from Greek *drimus* = acrid. Some 20 species have been described, but about five (at the most 10) are what could be called 'good' species, the others simply being the same species given a different name. They are natives of eastern Australia (including Tasmania), New Caledonia, Malaysia, South and Central America (Mexico). Their leaves are entire, hairless, and the stipules are either absent or minute. The flowers are

The glossy evergreen foliage and flower buds of the Winter's Bark (*Drimys winteri*).

Spring foliage and remains of flowers of the Bay Laurel (*Laurus nobilis*). This is the best known member of the aromatic laurel family (Lauraceae), but most members have aromatic foliage.

them from their studies. By extension of this, all unmarried men are now referred to as bachelors. The leaves were once used medicinally and contain about 2 percent of the essential oil cineole – a terpene with a smell like camphor. This oil is widely distributed, being found also, for example, in the oil of *Eucalyptus globulus*, *Melaleuca leucadendron* (cajuput oil), both in the family Myrtaceae, and in various worm-seed oils, for example, *Artemisia* species (Compositae).

The Canary Island Laurel forms trees to nearly 20m (66ft) in the wild. It differs from the previous species in its larger leaves, 6–12cm (2.4–4.8in) long, and its downy branchlets. A native of the Canary Islands and the Azores, it is less hardy than *L. nobilis* and is rarely seen in cultivation.

The term 'laurel' is, perhaps, more commonly associated with the Cherry Laurel (*Prunus laurocerasus*) and Portugal Laurel (*Prunus lusitanica*), both in the rose family (Rosaceae), as well as the Spotted or Japanese Laurel (*Aucuba japonica*) in the family Cornaceae. The first two species have the same dark green, leathery, elliptical entire leaves. This is also true of healthy *Aucuba japonica*, the spotted form of the leaves being due to localized destruction of chlorophyll pigments by virus infection which does not affect the associated yellow carotenoid pigments. The True Laurel is readily distinguished from

all the above species if a leaf is held against the light, when the translucent margin of the leaf is plainly visible.

F. B. H.

Californian Laurel
(genus *Umbellularia*)

The Californian Laurel (*Umbellularia californica*), also known as the Californian Bay, Californian Sassafras, Oregon Myrtle and Headache Tree, is the only species of its genus and is an evergreen, strongly aromatic tree reaching heights of 20–40m (66–132ft), although sometimes it is only a shrub in cultivation. It is a native of the Pacific Coast region of California and Oregon (western United States).

The leaves are particularly pungent when crushed, painfully irritating to nose and throat and reputed to cause headaches even to people merely sitting under the

The strong aroma emitted by the Californian Laurel (*Umbellularia californica*) is reputed to cause headaches in those who sit under its branches for too long!

SOME PLANTS HAVING THE COMMON NAME 'LAUREL'

Common Name	Species	Family
Alexandrian Laurel	*Calophyllum inophyllum*	Guttiferae
Bay Laurel	*Laurus nobilis*	Lauraceae
Bog Laurel	*Kalmia polifolia*	Ericaceae
Californian Laurel	*Umbellularia californica*	Lauraceae
Camphor Laurel	*Cinnamomum camphora*	Lauraceae
Canary Island Laurel	*Laurus azorica*	Lauraceae
Cherry Laurel	*Prunus laurocerasus*	Rosaceae
Chilean Laurel	*Laurelia serrata* (*L. aromatica*)	Antherospermataceae
Ecuador Laurel	*Cordia alliodora*	Ehretiaceae
Great Laurel	*Rhododendron maximum*	Ericaceae
Indian Laurel	*Terminalia alata*	Combretaceae
	Persea indica	Lauraceae
Japanese Laurel	*Aucuba japonica*	Aucubaceae
Mountain Laurel	*Kalmia latifolia*	Ericaceae
Portugal Laurel	*Prunus lusitanica*	Rosaceae
Sheep Laurel	*Kalmia angustifolia*	Ericaceae
Spotted Laurel	*Aucuba japonica*	Aucubaceae
Spurge Laurel	*Daphne laureola*	Thymelaeaceae
Swamp Laurel	*Magnolia virginiana*	Magnoliaceae
Tasmanian Laurel	*Anopterus* spp	Escalloniaceae

tree – hence Headache Tree. Handling the foliage may cause skin irritation and running of the eyes, etc, in some people.

The leaves are alternate, glossy, more or less ovate-oblong, 6–12cm (2.4–4.8in) long, tapering toward the apex. The flowers are small, yellowish-green, bisexual and arranged in many-flowered stalked axillary umbels 15–18mm (0.6–0.7in) across (racemose in the closely related *Sassafras*). They open in late winter and early spring. Each has a calyx of six lobes, petals are absent and stamens are arranged in four whorls, the innermost whorl sterile (staminodes). The anthers have four locules, a distinction from *Laurus* which has two locules. The ovary is single and the resulting fruit is a plum-like ovoid drupe 2–2.5cm (0.8–1in) long. The Californian Laurel is only occasionally grown as an ornamental. It is hardy only in the less extreme parts of temperate regions and tolerant of shade in its early years. It is not particular as to soil provided it is reasonably fertile and free from chalk. Propagation is from seed or by cuttings. The timber is extremely hard and heavy, being used for making wooden ornaments.   F. B. H.

Sassafras
(genus *Sassafras*)

Sassafras is the common and genus name of three species of deciduous trees, with one species in each of North America, China and Taiwan. Best known is the American Sassafras (*S. albidum = S. officinale*) which can reach a height of 30–35m (100–125ft) in its native eastern United States.

All species have leaves that are entire or one- to three-lobed at the apex depending on age. The flowers are yellowish-green borne in short racemes before the leaves emerge. They are either unisexual, the sexes on different plants, or sometimes bisexual. Petals are absent but there are six sepal lobes. Males have nine stamens, the four-celled anthers opening by flaps; females have a single ovary and style and occasionally functional stamens are present. The fruit is an ovoid blue-black drupe.

The American Sassafras has gray bark that is vertically fissured with numerous horizontal breaks at fairly regular inter-vals. The leaves are three-nerved from near the base, variable in shape from more or less entire wedge-shaped (young) to three-lobed at the apex (adult). They produce a sweet, strong aroma of oranges, lemons and vanilla when crushed. Old trees have only a few lobed leaves. The fruit is 1cm (0.4in) long, bluish-black and borne on a bright red stalk. This species is hardy in temperate regions and is planted as an ornamental for its fall foliage which is yellowish-pink, finally orange to scarlet. It succeeds on rich, moisture-retaining soil. Propagation is from seed, by root suckers or by taking cuttings.

The fragrant principle is widely distributed throughout the plant and has been used for flavoring tobacco and root beer, the latter an American beverage.

Sassafras oil is extracted from the dried inner bark of the root. It contains about 80 percent of the phenolic compound safrole and has been used to destroy lice, and to treat insect stings and bites. The older trivial name (*S. officinale*) recalls its use in medicine (Oleum sassafras) – it has been prescribed as a carminative and stimulant, presumably where these two requirements are not in conflict! It has been dropped from western pharmacopoeias, its use being now restricted to perfumery and cosmetics. The British Government recommended its prohibition as a flavoring agent in 1965, no doubt influenced by

A young sucker of the American Sassafras (*Sassafras albidum*) in fall colors, growing in the woodlands of Michigan. Each shoot bears both entire and lobed leaves – a characteristic of this species.

the report that 0.5–1.0 percent of the oil in the diet of rats could result in hepatomas.

The timber is also fragrant, and durable enough to be used for fence posts as well as for fuel. In the past American Indians hollowed out the trunks to make canoes of excellent durability.

Sassafras tzumu, from Central China, is found rarely in cultivation.   F. B. H.

CERCIDIPHYLLACEAE

Katsura Tree
(genus *Cercidiphyllum*)

An ornamental of increasing popularity, the Katsura Tree (*Cercidiphyllum japonicum*) is a graceful deciduous tree native to China and Japan. The only member of its genus, it was originally described from Japan where it is the largest native deciduous tree, reaching up to 30m (100ft). However, it is represented in China by variety *sinense* which may reach 40m (130ft) and has a single main trunk. In cultivation it usually produces more than one main stem and it is smaller.

The leaves are heart-shaped like those of the Judas Tree (*Cercis siliquastrum*), typically in opposite pairs, appearing as if arranged in layers. They turn to magnificent shades of scarlet-crimson, orange and finally yellow in the fall, but are variable in their color changes. The flowers are solitary, insignificant, lack petals, and the sexes are on separate trees. The males have a minute calyx and 15–20 stamens, while the females have four slightly larger, fringed, green sepals and four to six (rarely three) carpels with long purplish-red styles. The fruit is a many-seeded dehiscent green to yellowish pod and the seeds winged.

Hardy in temperate regions (but may be nipped by a spring frost), the Katsura Tree is one of the most attractive of shade ornamentals although it will still grow in semi-shade or full sun. They prefer moist, fertile soil and are ideal for woodland settings. The timber is fine-grained and used for making furniture and interior fittings for houses and other buildings.

The taxonomic position of the genus is not certain and this derives largely from the interpretation of the female flower:

Graceful weeping shoots of the Katsura Tree (*Cercidyphyllum japonicum*) in outstanding fall colors.

whether it is considered to be a single flower or a condensed inflorescence, in which case the number of individual flowers corresponds to the number of carpels. A common solution is to relegate it to its own Family (Cercidiphyllaceae) in the Order Magnoliales and probably related to *Liriodendron* (Tulip Tree).

F. B. H.

PLATANACEAE

Planes and Buttonball Trees
(genus *Platanus*)

Planes, also known as sycamores or buttonball trees in America, are tall deciduous trees with often very characteristically scaling bark, as in the London Plane. The genus comprises some 10 species, all natives of America except *P. orientalis* (southeast Europe to the Himalaya) and *P. kerrii* (confined to Indochina). Not all species are hardy in temperate regions (some of these are noted later in the species list).

All parts of the plants are covered with stellate (star-shaped) hairs. The leaves are alternate, simple, palmately three- to nine-lobed (except *P. kerrii* where the leaves are elliptic-oblong with pinnate veins). The long petiole is swollen at the base and forms a hood over the axillary bud; the stipules are large and embrace the shoot but soon fall away. The flowers are unisexual, borne on the same plant in one to several globose heads on separate long stalks. There are three to eight small sepals which are free and hairy. The male flowers have three to eight stamens and as many petals which are spoon-shaped and the females have three to eight separate ovaries, each with a basal tuft of long hairs. The fruit comprises a dense hanging cluster of one-seeded nutlets, each shed with its basal tuft of hairs.

The planes are grown predominantly for ornament. Propagation is mainly by seeds, layers or cuttings in the fall. A deep loam is required. Most of the cultivated specimens are probably of hybrid origin. They form magnificent trees and, for example, in the Balkan peninsula *P. orientalis* is frequently planted in public squares for the shade it gives – 'and plane trees large enough to afford shade to quaffers' (Virgil: *Georgics*, translated by H. Gilbert-Carter). The Buttonwood or Buttonball Tree or American Plane (*P. occidentalis*) is one of the two major ornamental species. It is a fast-growing, beautiful and massive tree, reaching 40–50m (130–165ft). It is commonly grown in North America, particularly the southeastern United States, both for ornament and timber, but does not grow well in Europe.

The London Plane (*P. acerifolia = P. hispanica*, *P. hybrida* of some authors) is famous for its tolerance of grime and its ability to grow in the paved streets of cities, being also equally at home at water edges. It is a common sight in many European town squares and avenues. It has been London's most popular tree since the 18th century, shortly after its appearance in the Oxford Botanic Gardens, probably as a result of a cross between *P. orientalis* and *P. occidentalis*. Like the Buttonwood, the London Plane has a tall trunk with attractively scaling bark and a beautiful winter silhouette characterized by arching branch tracery and the hanging fruiting balls. Against this, as with other species, there is a long-held and widespread belief that the stellate pubescence and especially the pappus-like hairs on the seed can cause not insignificant irritations of the upper respiratory tract, resulting in 'catarrhal' conditions, and even affect the lungs. The wood is hard and fine textured and has been used for fancy goods, as a veneer and for decorative purposes generally. It burns very well in open grates.

The fungus *Gnomonia platani* (*G. venata*) causes Plane Tree Scorch or Anthracnose and is a well-recognized disease of London Plane. It attacks leaves and twigs causing discoloration of leaf tissue and finally death and defoliation at an early stage; it also causes a canker. The disease is rarely fatal, the affected leaves being soon replaced by a second crop. The Oriental Plane (*P. orientalis*) is believed to be immune but the susceptibility of the different species is confused because of misidentification of the host tree. The disease is most prevalent in the United States.

The species of *Platanus* are very similar, so much so that at least one worker regards them all as varieties of one species. This is rather extreme and, if adopted, would result in a loss of convenience (see table of main species for further details).

F. B. H.

A London Plane (*Platanus acerifolia*) in winter, clearly showing the attractive scaling bark.

The Main Species of *Platanus*

Group I: Fruiting heads 3–7, rarely 2, on each stalk. Leaves mostly deeply lobed.

P. orientalis Oriental Plane. Europe (Balkan peninsula), Crete, Asia and the Himalaya. Tree to about 30m. Bark scaling, pallid, tinged gray or green. Leaves 20cm wide,

5–7 lobed, the cleft reaching at least to half-way, usually coarsely toothed, glabrous on lower surface. Fruiting heads 2–6, each up to 2.5cm. Of the few named varieties, some are probably of hybrid origin. Variety *insularis* (Cyprian Plane) is sometimes incorrectly attributed to this species, but is now considered a variety of *P. acerifolia*.

P. racemosa (*P. californica*) Californian Plane. California. Tree to 40m. Leaves 15–30cm across, 5 lobed, rarely 3, tomentose, at least beneath, the lobes virtually entire or with a few teeth. Fruiting heads 2–7, each 2.5cm across. A rare and much less

vigorous species outside SW America.

P. wrightii Mexico and adjoining S USA. Tree to 25m. Leaves deeply divided into 3–5 lanceolate, entire or almost entire lobes, at first tomentose on both sides, the underside becoming hairless. Fruiting heads 2–5, mostly stalked and smooth, the achenes truncate or rounded with an often deciduous style. Very closely related to *P. racemosa*, of which it is sometimes regarded as a variety, but the leaves are more deeply divided with an often cordate base and the fruiting heads do not exceed 4. Hardiness about the same.

London Planes (*Platanus acerifolia*) are widely grown as town and city trees, as with this avenue of trees at the Albert Memorial in London's Hyde Park.

Group II: Fruiting heads 1 or 2, rarely more, on each stalk. Leaves mostly with shallow lobes.

P. occidentalis Buttonwood, Buttonball, American Plane, American Sycamore. E and SE USA. Fine tree to 40–50m. Bark creamy-white, scaling, much darker at base especially in older trees. Leaves 10–22cm wide, about the same or less in length, typically 3 lobed, rarely 5; clefts shallow. Fruiting head about 3cm across, usually single, rarely 2.

P. acerifolia (*P. hispanica*, *P. hybrida*) London Plane. Extensively planted in Europe and N America. Tree to 35m with characteristic scaling bark. Leaves 12–25cm across, 3–5 lobed, the cleft extending about one-third leaf length, middle lobe about as long as broad; petiole 3–10cm long. Fruiting heads typically 2, rarely more. Fertile seed is set, but the germination rate is low. Seedlings said to be variable, as would be expected from a hybrid. Origin unknown, but was once thought to be a variety of *P. orientalis* stabilized by cultivation, although the prevailing view is that it is a hybrid between *P. orientalis* and *P. occidentalis* which arose in the Oxford Botanic Gardens around 1700, probably some years before. A successful cross between the putative parents was made in 1968 in the USA, so that detailed comparisons will be possible as this seedling reaches maturity. Earlier names, still in use for the London Plane, are *P. hybrida* and *P. hispanica*, but no authentic specimens exist to clinch the identity. The binomial *P. hispanica* was, however, applied by Augustus Henry to a plant received from a Belgian nursery in 1878. It differs markedly from *P. acerifolia* both in habit and foliage, the latter being on average larger, and of a lighter almost sea-green color, the lobe margins more toothed and the whole leaf tending to turn downward at the edges. It is now distinguished under the name *Platanus* 'Augustus Henry.' It may be another hybrid variant from the same parentage as *P. acerifolia* (*P. orientalis* × *P. occidentalis*).

P. occidentalis

P. orientalis

P. acerifolia

The Oriental Plane (*Platanus orientalis*) (*Top Right*) and American Plane (*P. occidentalis*) (*Center Right*) are geographically isolated in their native range, so they cannot hybridize unless deliberately grown together. When this is done the result is the London Plane – a highly vigorous and fertile hybrid.

HAMAMELIDACEAE

Witch Hazels
(genus *Hamamelis*)

The genus *Hamamelis* comprises four or five (perhaps six) species of deciduous shrubs or small trees native to eastern Asia and eastern North America. They are deservedly popular with gardeners, for most of the species and their hybrids and cultivars produce spider-like yellow or rusty-red flowers from December to March (except *H. virginiana*: see below) which stand up to the severest weather. Petals, sepals and stamens are typically in fours, but sometimes in fives. The leaves resemble those of the Common Hazel (*Corylus avellana*) and usually turn an attractive yellow or red in the fall. This resemblance to hazel led early settlers in North America to use the twigs for water divining, and because of the branches' pliant properties, the popular name arose. Witch Hazel is a name used also for the Witch Elm (*Ulmus glabra*) and Hornbeam (*Carpinus betulus*), the term 'witch' or 'wych' being an old English word used to denote any tree with particularly pliant branches. The Common Witch Hazel (*H. virginiana*) of the eastern United States and Canada is a large spreading shrub or tree to 7–10m (23–33ft) whose leaves turn yellow in the fall. The small yellow flowers are produced in the fall and are particularly resistant to cold weather. The bark, leaves and twigs yield the witch hazel of pharmacy which is widely used as an astringent and coolant, and can be applied to cuts and bruises. The extract contains substances which tend to constrict the blood vessels with the effect of preventing bleeding.

The Japanese Witch Hazel (*H. japonica*)

from Japan, is a shrub or small tree to 10m (33ft) and has slightly scented wavy-petaled flowers in roundish heads; leaves turn yellow in the fall. This species is somewhat variable in form – var *arborea* is taller growing, var *flavopurpurascens* has reddish petals, cultivar 'Sulphurea' has much crumpled pale yellow petals and cultivar 'Zuccariniana' pale yellow-lemon flowers produced in March.

The Chinese Witch Hazel (*H. mollis*), from western and western central China, is the most handsome of the genus. It is a shrub or small tree to 10m (33ft) producing very fragrant flowers, the petals of which are not wavy. The best cultivar is 'Pallida' with large sulfur-yellow flowers produced in January and February.

Hamamelis × intermedia is a hybrid between the above two species, with many good named cultivars. It was first produced at the Arnold Arboretum in the United States. The Ozark Witch Hazel (*H. vernalis*) is a shrub to 2m (6.5ft) and has small scented flowers varying in color from pale yellow to red produced in January to February. S. L. J.

Sweet Gums
(genus *Liquidambar*)

Liquidambar is a genus of three, possibly four, species of resinous trees of scattered distribution: eastern North America, Asia Minor and southeastern China and Taiwan. Their leaves are palmate, long-stalked with three to seven lobes, much as in maples (*Acer*) but distinguished from that genus by being alternate and not opposite. The flowers are unisexual but on the same tree, inconspicuous, greenish to yellowish, the males in short clusters, each flower having stamens only, the females in globose heads, each flower with more or less closely adpressed ovaries. The fruits are capsules containing winged seeds.

Sweet gums are grown mostly as ornamentals for their splendid fall colors, although only *Liquidambar styraciflua* is seen at all extensively. It grows best in good, deep, not too moist soil and is propagated by seed, although germination may not

Above Top The Chinese Witch Hazel (*Hamamelis mollis*) is the most popular of the cultivated witch hazels. *Above* It produces the weather-resistant yellow to red flowers between January and February which are a welcome splash of color in these winter months.

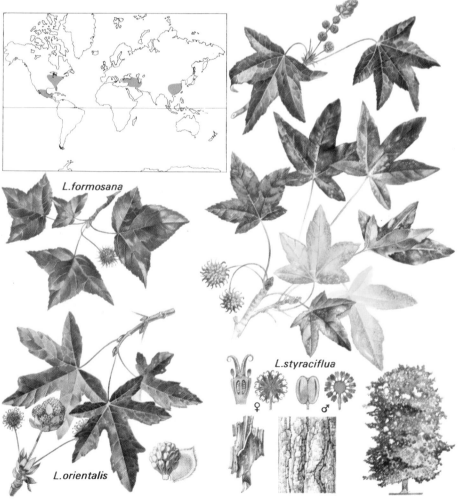

L.formosana

L.orientalis

L.styraciflua

occur until the second year. The fall coloring can be magnificent, from scarlet through to dark red, but its quality and quantity can vary immensely.

The timber of this species is of value and known commercially as satin walnut; it is used for furniture, cabinet-making and veneer. Fragrant resinous gums known as American storax and liquid storax are obtained from the bark of *L. styraciflua* and *L. orientalis* respectively. They are used in perfumery primarily to scent soap, as an expectorant in cough pastilles and as a fumigant in the treatment of skin diseases such as scabies. The old-fashioned Friar's balsam contains liquid storax and is used as an inhalant in bronchial upsets. The word 'storax' is also the popular name derived from a quite different group of resinous flowering plants of the genus *Styrax*, family Styracaceae.

Liquidambar formosana is rare in cultivation but in its native regions the wood is used for making tea chests and the leaves to feed silk worms.

M. C. D.

The Species of *Liquidambar*

L. styraciflua Sweet Gum. E USA, Mexico, Guatemala. Deciduous tree to 45m in the wild state but nearer 10–15m in cultivation. Leaves 10–18cm wide, 5–7 lobed, turning a fine red color in the fall. Fruiting head with small, blunt scales.
  'Levis.' Branches without corky bark. Leaves brilliantly colored in the fall.
  'Variegata.' Leaves marked with yellow.
  'Rotundiloba.' Leaves with 3–5 short rounded lobes.
  'Pendula.' Branches deflexed, pendulous, forming a narrow crown.

L. orientalis Asia Minor. Deciduous tree to about 30m in the wild, but under 10m in cultivation, where it is less common than the previous species. Leaves (4)5–7(9)cm wide usually with 5 inconspicuously toothed smallish lobes.

L. formosana Taiwan, S and C China, Indochina. Deciduous tree to about 40m in the wild. Leaves 3 (rarely 5) lobed, (8) 10–15cm wide. Fruiting head with slender awl-shaped bristles.
  var *monticola* Leaves hairless, usually truncate at the base, cordate only in young seedlings, plum purple when unfolding, later bronzy-crimson, then finally dull green, crimson again in the fall.

Persian Ironwood
(genus *Parrotia*)

The Persian Ironwood (*Parrotia persica*) is a small deciduous tree that is too infrequently found cultivated in parks and large gardens in temperate regions. In its native northern Iran and the Caucasus it forms dense thickets with interlacing main stems and branches which may fuse together. Such natural grafting is also seen in cultivated specimens. In the wild it reaches 15–20m (50–65ft) but only 5–8m (16–28ft) in cultivation and then sometimes shrubby.

The Persian Ironwood is the only member of its genus. All parts are covered with star-shaped hairs (stellate). The bark is flaking, rather similar to that of the London Plane and the leaves alternate, sinuous and toothed. The flowers are small, bisexual and borne during early spring in dense clusters surrounded by large bracts. Petals are absent, but there is a five- to seven-lobed calyx. The five to seven stamens are conspicuous for their size and red color. The fruits comprise three to five nut-like capsules, which open at the top. The seeds are 8–9mm (0.34–0.4in) long and shining brown.

The Persian Ironwood (*Parrotia persica*) is an ornamental that offers something for all seasons, particularly the winter when (*Below Center*) its attractive scaling bark is shown to good effect, which is then complemented in early spring by (*Bottom*) dense clusters of red-stamened flowers.

The Persian Ironwood is fully hardy in temperate regions and its value as an all-the-year-round ornamental is underestimated. It is particularly attractive for its early spring flowers which open before the leaves and the splendid golden to crimson foliage in the fall. The leaves often have a reddish tinge in spring and the attractive bark stands out well in the winter. In summer the flower buds are deep brown and characteristically downcurved at the tip. It grows well in a sunny or partly shaded position on fertile, well-drained soil. Propagation is by layering in spring or by cuttings in summer. Cultivar 'Pendula' has a weeping habit and exceptional fall colors.

F. B. H.

FAGACEAE

Oaks
(genus *Quercus*)

Quercus is a large and economically important genus including many trees prized for their noble aspect and fall colors. Specimens have been recorded up to 700 years old.

In the wider sense, as accepted here, the genus includes about 500 species, predominantly of the Northern Hemisphere, the majority in North America, but a large number in Europe, the Mediterranean and western and eastern Asia. In South America, oaks occur only in the Andes of Colombia. The relatively small tropical distribution is virtually confined to high mountains. The altitudinal range of oaks is from sea level to 4 000m (13 000ft) in the Himalaya. They like a reasonably rich soil, not too sandy or too dry.

Oaks are predominantly trees, but some are shrubs. They may be evergreen, half-evergreen (that is leaves surviving in the winter, but falling by springtime) or deciduous. The leaves are rarely entire, and the margins are usually cut or lobed in various ways. Male and female flowers are borne on the same tree, the males in pendulous catkins, the females solitary or in spikes of two or more flowers. The fruit is a large, solitary, characteristic nut (acorn) more or less enclosed from the base upward by a cup (cupule) composed of variously shaped scales more or less imbricate, less often connate to form concentric rings. Oaks are wind-pollinated, and interspecific hybridization is extensive; this greatly complicates identification.

Oaks provide the finest hardwoods and this wood is in the forefront of all timbers because of its great strength and durability. It is not easy to distinguish the various commercial oak timbers, but a distinction is made between the white oaks and the red oaks, the former being somewhat harder and more durable. Both kinds are used for the same purposes: furniture, and bridge, ship and many other types of construction. The wood will take a high polish and when radially cut it is a favorite for paneling because of the fine 'silver grain' formed by the wood rays. Important white oak species are *Quercus alba*, *Q. macrocarpa*, *Q. robur*, *Q. sessiliflora*; important red oaks are *Q. rubra* (*borealis*), *Q. velutina*, *Q. palustris*.

Live Oak is the name given to *Q. virginiana*, which is considered to be the most durable of all oak timbers. It is used for trucks, ships and tool-making, but unfortunately is now in short supply. The timber of some oaks is used for inlay work,

The Kermes Oak (*Quercus coccifera*) is a Mediterranean shrub. This specimen, heavily infested with galls (red), is growing on the island of Corfu.

Male flowers of oaks (*Quercus* spp) are clustered in catkins and produce copious quantities of wind-dispersed pollen.

for example, 'brown oak,' which is oak timber stained by the mycelium of the bracket fungus *Fistulina hepatica*. Similarly, oak timber may be stained a deep emerald green by the mycelium of the cup fungus *Chlorosplenium aeruginascens*. The green coloring substance has attracted considerable attention and it has been isolated and characterized as a rare type of green pigment named xylindein.

Cork is obtained from the outer bark of the Cork Oak (*Q. suber*). Trees are first stripped at about 20 years and subsequently at nine-year intervals. The freshly stripped bark is dried and then boiled in water to remove impurities and soften it. It is finally cut either parallel to the lenticels giving corks that are permeable, or at right angles to them so that the resulting corks are airtight. Cork oaks survive this 'surgery' for anything from 100 to 500 years.

The Kermes Oak or Grain Tree (*Q. coccifera*) is the host for a scale insect, *Coccus ilicis*, which since medieval times has been extracted to give a fine, scarlet, cochineal-like dye. 'Kermes' is the Arabic name for the insect. 'Grain' is from 'grana tinctorum,' the Latin equivalent.

Various oak species, such as *Q. lusitanica* and the closely related *Q. infectoria*, are important sources of tannins. The tannins are extracted from the bark and from galls by chopping the material into fragments, which are then cooked and ex-

tracted by steam. In addition to leather tanning, tannins are used to make the 'blue-black' type of ink used in fountain pens.

Acorns are not generally of much economic importance, but they are eaten by small game birds and have been used to fatten pigs and poultry. They are not much used for human consumption but those of *Q. rotundifolia* are quite palatable.

It seems paradoxical that a timber as nearly indestructible as oak should come from a tree that, when growing, is host to a

A Durmast or Sessile Oak (*Quercus petraea*) spreads its branches in a field in South Wales. The oaks are perhaps the best-known members of the family Fagaceae and provide some of the world's most valued timber.

large number of invaders, especially fungi and insects. For example, the powdery mildew *Microsphaera alphitoides* is a serious parasite on oak leaves, especially of young trees. It is particularly prevalent in continental Europe because European oaks are more susceptible than American species. Control is mainly by spraying.

The Oak Leaf Roller Moth (*Tortrix viridana*) can cause serious defoliation and it is sometimes necessary to resort to airplane dusting as a means of controlling the pest. Rarely serious but more numerous invaders of living oak trees are the gall-forming insects. More than 800 gall-forming insects have been recorded in oak, some 750 of these being gall wasps. Galls are composed of hypertrophied host tissue, which forms as a result of stimulation by the egg-laying insect. The resulting grubs eventually feed on this tissue, which also attracts other secondary insect invaders. One of the commonest galls is the Oak Spangle Gall caused by the gall wasp *Neuroterus quercusbaccarum*. This gall takes the form of numerous, reddish shield-like disks on the lower leaf surface in late summer. Some galls are, in fact, of economic importance. Thus, the Oak Apple or Oak Marble Gall, which is caused by the gall wasp *Andricus kollari*, contains tannin

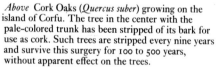

Below It is often difficult to identify oak trees growing in England either as the Common Oak (*Quercus robur*) or the Durmast Oak (*Q. petraea*) because of hybridization which results in many intermediate forms, a process known scientifically as introgressive hybrization.

Above Cork Oaks (*Quercus suber*) growing on the island of Corfu. The tree in the center with the pale-colored trunk has been stripped of its bark for use as cork. Such trees are stripped every nine years and survive this surgery for 100 to 500 years, without apparent effect on the trees.

used for making 'blue-black' ink.

Oaks have a long history in mythology, being associated with Zeus, the god of thunder. It is often held that oak trees are particularly susceptible to being struck by lightning and Shakespeare refers to 'oak-cleaving thunderbolts' in *King Lear*. Plants with supposed magical properties are regarded as being especially superior if found growing on oak. Thus, Mistletoe (*Viscum album*), with an extensive mythology of its own, is much prized when found on oak, which is a rare host for this semi-parasite.

Outside their native ranges many oaks are grown as ornamentals. Most are hardy, long-lived trees often producing attractive fall colors. They grow best in well-drained soils and produce a better crown if grown in an open position in full sunlight. Some of the better-known cultivated species are Red Oak (*Q. rubra*) for its crimson to red-brown fall foliage, the Turkey Oak (*Q. cerris*) for its rapid growth, the Scarlet Oak (*Q. coccinea*) for its scarlet fall foliage and the Holm Oak (*Q. ilex*) for its evergreen foliage. The Holm Oak is also used for screens and windbreaks and for hedging, particularly in coastal areas.

F. B. H.

The Main Species of *Quercus*

Group I: Leaves evergreen, persisting more than 1 year, hairless beneath when mature.

Q. coccifera Kermes Oak, Grain Tree. Mediterranean. Usually shrub to 2m, rarely a small tree. Leaves dentate, broad elliptic to 5cm, the teeth spine-tipped. Cupular scales spreading.

Q. myrsinaefolia China, Japan. Tree to 18m. Smaller in cultivation. Leaves lanceolate, 5–12cm, serrate. Cupular scales in concentric rings.

Group II: Leaves evergreen (half-evergreen in *Q. × hispanica*) persisting more than 1 year, white or grayish-downy beneath when mature.

Q. suber Cork Oak. S Europe, N Africa. Tree to 20m, bark corky. Leaves more or less ovate-oblong, 3–7cm with mucronate teeth and 5–7 pairs of veins.

Q. × hispanica (*Q. cerris × suber*) Spanish Oak. Occurs naturally in S Europe. Tree to 30m with thick but only slightly corky bark. Leaves persisting through fall to

Many oaks produce attractive fall colors, but few can rival those of the Scarlet Oak (*Quercus coccinea*); cultivar 'Splendens' is shown here.

spring, ovate to oblong, 4–10cm long with 4–7 pairs of shallow mucronate, triangular lobes.

Cultivar 'Lucombeana' or Lucombe Oak belongs to this hybrid group, one striking form of which is recognized by the main branches being much swollen where . they join the main trunk and the terminal buds are surrounded by subulate bristles which are absent from the lateral buds (a useful distinction from *Q. cerris* in which all buds have subulate bristles).

Q. ilex Holm Oak, Evergreen Oak. Mediterranean, N Spain, W France. Tree to 20m. Leaves ovate-lanceolate, apex acute, 3–7cm, entire or more or less serrate with 7–10 pairs veins. Acorns bitter and unpalatable.

Q. rotundifolia SW Europe. Very similar to *Q. ilex*, which it replaces in SW Spain, but lateral veins of leaf make wider angle with midrib. Acorns sweet and edible.

Q. virginiana Live Oak. S USA, Mexico. Tree to 20m. Leaves oblong, apex rounded, 4–13cm, typically entire and margin revolute. The finest evergreen oak. Wood much prized.

Group III: Leaves deciduous or half-evergreen, not persisting more than one year; entire.

Q. phellos Willow Oak. N America. Tree to 30m. Leaves lanceolate, 5–10cm, pale green fading to yellow.

Group IV: Leaves deciduous as above, but lobed, the lobes bristle-tipped.

Q. marilandica Blackjack Oak. SE USA. Tree to about 10m. Leaves markedly obovate, 3–5 lobed, 10–20cm, rusty pubescent below.

Q. velutina (*Q. tinctoria*) Black Oak. N America. Tree 30–50m. Leaves ovate to oblong, 10–25cm, with 7–9 lobes which are toothed and more or less wavy, hairy beneath. Bark and acorns yield a yellow dye 'quercitron.'

Q. rubra (*Q. borealis*) Red Oak. E USA. Tree to 25m. Branchlets dark red. Leaves oblong, 12–20cm with 7–11 lobes, the lobes cut less than half-way to midrib, hairless below except for axillary tufts of hair.

Q. palustris Pin Oak. N America. Tree to 30m. Leaves elliptic-oblong, 10–15cm, 5–7 lobed to more than half-way to midrib, hairless below, but with conspicuous axillary tufts of hair. Fall leaves a duller red than following species.

Q. coccinea Scarlet Oak. N America. Tree to 25m. Branchlets scarlet red. Leaves elliptic-oblong, 8–15cm, 7–9 lobed almost to midrib, hairless below except for inconspicuous axillary tufts of hair. Much admired for its brilliant scarlet fall leaf colors.

Group V: Leaves deciduous as before but with bristle-tipped serrations, not lobes.

Q. libani Lebanon Oak. Syria, Asia Minor. Tree to 10m. Leaves oblong-lanceolate, 5–10cm; veins 9–12 pairs.

Q. acutissima China, Japan, Korea, Himalaya. Tree about 15m. Leaves oblong-obovate, 8–18cm; veins 12–16 pairs.

Group VI: Leaves deciduous as before, but no bristle-tips to teeth or lobes, but these may be mucronate.

Q. cerris Turkey Oak. S Europe, W Asia. Tree to 38m. Leaves elliptic-oblong, toothed; blade without basal auricles, 5–10cm, with 4–10 pairs of narrow lobes. Cupular scales conspicuously long, filiform and spreading.

Q. robur English Oak, 'Pedunculate Oak.' Europe, N Africa, Asia Minor. Tree to 45m. Leaves obovate-oblong, lobed, with basal auricles, 5–12cm, the 3–7 rounded lobes cut less than half-way to midrib. Fruiting stalk 2–7cm long.

Q. petraea Durmast Oak, 'Sessile Oak.' Europe, Asia Minor. Tree to 40m. Leaves obovate-oblong, 8–13cm, the 5–9 rounded lobes cut less than half-way to midrib; basal auricles absent. Fruits virtually sessile.

Q. alba White Oak. E USA. Tree 45–50m. Leaves obovate-oblong with 5–9 rounded lobes, some lobes cut more than half-way to midrib.

Q. bicolor Swamp White Oak. E N America. Tree to about 30m. Branchlets hairless. Leaves oblong-obovate, 10–16cm, sinuate-dentate, hairy beneath, 6–8 lobed. Cupule much shorter than acorn.

Q. macrocarpa Burr Oak. N America. Tree usually to 25m, sometimes reaching 55m. Branchlets hairy (at first). Leaves more or less obovate, lyrate-pinnatifid, 10–25cm, hairy beneath, terminal lobe large, more or less crenate to twice-lobed. Rim of cupule with filiform fringe of scales.

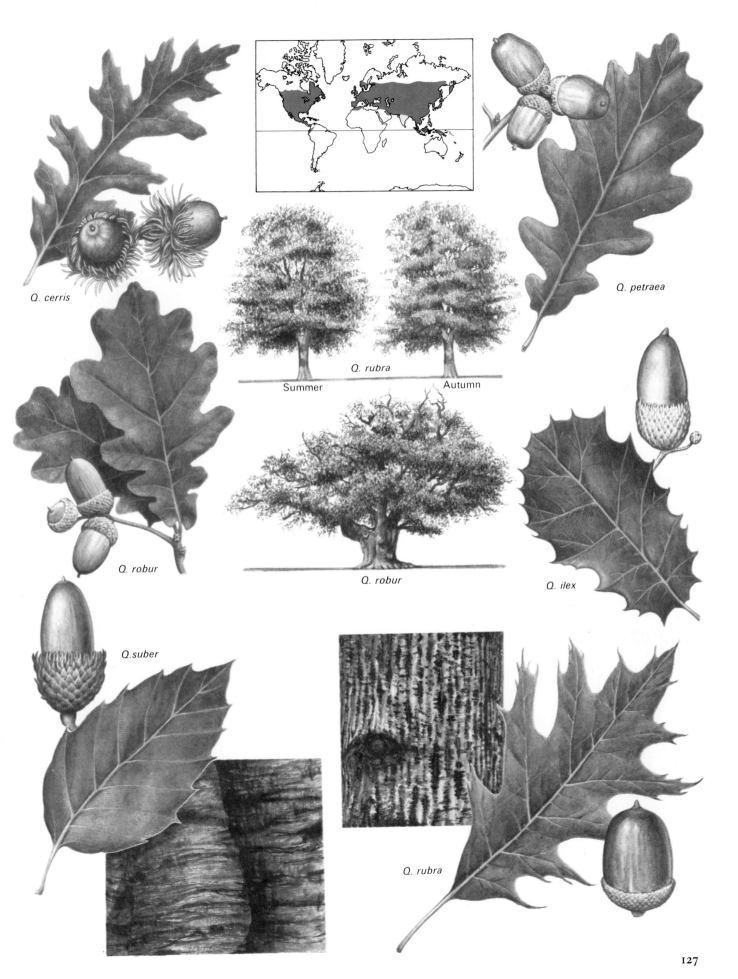

Q. cerris

Q. petraea

Q. rubra

Summer

Autumn

Q. robur

Q. robur

Q. ilex

Q.suber

Q. rubra

Beeches
(genus *Fagus*)

Beeches are a closely-knit group of 8–10 species of deciduous trees belonging to the genus *Fagus*. They grow to a height of 30–45m (100–150ft) and occur throughout the Northern Hemisphere, being found in all three continents, where they are frequently dominant or codominant in temperate forests. Tertiary fossils, said to be beeches, have been reported as far north as Iceland, but further studies are required for confirmation. Pre-Roman peats in Great Britain have yielded pollen of the Common Beech (*Fagus sylvatica*), in spite of Julius Caesar's statement that it did not occur. It is likely that he was referring to the Sweet Chestnut (*Castanea sativa*). The southern beeches belong to the closely-related genus *Nothofagus* and are native to regions of the Southern Hemisphere.

Beeches have rounded, spreading canopies and smooth, gray bark. The leaves are alternate, more or less ovate, acute, with coarsely dentate to wavy margins, and are usually thin and shining green; the slender, elongated winter buds are a very distinctive feature of the trees. The flowers are unisexual and appear on the same tree after the leaves have opened. The numerous male flowers are crowded into slender-stalked globose heads, each flower having a four- to seven-lobed perianth (calyx)

The characteristic appearance of Common or European Beech (*Fagus sylvatica*) during winter; there is a dense layer of leaf litter and a complete lack of a shrubby understorey.

surrounding 8–16 stamens. The female inflorescence has two flowers, each flower with three styles and a perianth of four or five lobes. The fruit is an ovoid-triangular nut, and one or two nuts are wholly or partly enclosed in the involucre of fused bracteoles which becomes woody and four-valved and is then referred to as the cupule. It is borne on a stout and short (up to 2.5cm; 1in) or slender and longer (up to 7cm; 3in) peduncle. The cupule is covered with prickly, bristly, bract-like or short, deltoid appendages.

The species are quite hardy, lime-tolerant and flourish on a light to medium soil. The Common Beech is the characteristic woodland species of many calcareous soils. Such woods are often remarkable for their absence of ground flora because of the dense mosaic of leaves which effectively reduces the light. In the fall, however, beechwoods are some of the best areas for finding many fine species of gill fungi (Agaricales), especially of the genus *Cortinarius*.

Beech timber, for example that of Common Beech, is valuable as it is strong, tough, hard and of high compressive strength and has many uses where these qualities are important, such as ships' wedges, plane blocks, furniture and flooring, but it deteriorates when exposed to the weather. The nut of some species is sufficiently rich in oil to provide valuable food for stock such as pigs.

Beeches are hosts to parasitic attacks by representatives of most of the fungus groups. Some serious examples recorded for Common Beech include 'damping off' caused by the oomycete fungus *Phytophthora cactorum* (*P. fagi*) (Perenosporales). This is prevalent in nurseries and control may require sterilization of the seedbed. Another species, *P. cambivora*, attacks the roots. Unpleasant cankers on branches have been caused by the pyrenomycete, *Nectria galligena*. Less serious, perhaps, and more an indication of previous wounding, old age or a generally unhealthy plant are the bracket fungi *Fomes fomentarius*, *Phellinus igniarius* (= *Fomes igniarius*) and *Ganoderma applanatum* (Aphyllophorales). The well-known hymenomycete, *Auricularia auricula* (Auriculariales) or Judas' Ear Fungus (erroneously known as Jew's Ear Fungus), although mainly confined to the Common Elder (*Sambucus nigra*), is also sometimes found on the Common Beech. It is some compensation that the fungus is edible. Among gill fungi (Agaricales) are *Oudemansiella mucida* (= *Armillaria mucida*),

The male flowers of the Common or European Beech (*Fagus sylvatica*) emerge at the time of leaf expansion in crowded, long-stalked, globose heads, which shed wind-dispersed pollen.

which is not particularly serious and has a rather beautiful white sheen, and *Pleurotus ostreatus*, the Oyster Mushroom, an excellent edible fungus, which is commercially cultivated in some countries.

Pests of beeches are numerous. Again only a selection can be made. Widely distributed is the Woolly Beech Aphid, *Phyllaphis fagi*, which feeds on the leaves, turning them brown, the aphids covering themselves with dense masses of white woolly threads. They can be found on the underside of leaves during spring and early summer. Serious also is the homopterous Felted Beech Coccus, *Cryptococcus fagi*. Attacks by this pest may open the way to subsequent fungus infections which may eventually kill the tree. There is also a weevil, the Beech Leaf-miner, *Rhynchaenus fagi*, whose grubs feed on and cause a leaf blotch, which may give the whole tree a scorched appearance. Control of these pests is mainly by appropriate insecticides, but in the case of the Beech Leaf-miner, the grubs should be crushed or picked off and burnt. The grub lives and finally pupates in its 'mine' in the leaf mesophyll. Action should be taken as soon as these 'mines' are noticed.

Several beeches are widely cultivated for their handsome shape and foliage. For the species, propagation is from seeds, but cultivars have to be grafted. The Common Beech is particularly rich in varieties and cultivars. The Fern-leaved Beech (*F. sylvatica* 'Asplenifolia') has leaves varying between narrowly strap-shaped to shallowly to deeply pinnately lobed, sometimes down to the midrib. Dawyck's Beech (*F. sylvatica* 'Dawyck') is a fastigiate form which arose in Scotland in 1860 and is planted by roadsides and in avenues. The Cut-leaved Beech (*F. sylvatica* 'Heterophylla') exists in two forms: forma *laciniata* has ovate-lanceolate leaves tapering at both ends, the margin with seven to nine deep serrations on each side, extending about one-third of the way to the midrib; forma *latifolia* has larger leaves than the type – in young trees up to 8 × 14cm (3 × 5.5in), rather less in older trees. 'Weeping' beeches ('Pendula') come in various forms – some with horizontal main branches draped with pendulous branchlets and others with the main branches also pendulous. The Purple or Copper Beeches (forma *purpurea*) are forms in which the chlorophyll of the leaves is masked by an anthocyanin pigment which colors them varying shades of purplish, purplish-black or almost dark red. They are commonly planted and admired by many, reviled by some. *F. sylvatica* 'Zlatia' has golden-yellow young leaves which later turn green.

F. B. H.

The Species of *Fagus*

Group I: Nut 1/3–1/2 its length longer than the cupule; peduncle 2–3 times longer than cupule. Leaves glabrous beneath.
F. japonica Japanese Beech. Japan. Tree 21–25m. Leaves elliptic to ovate, acuminate, 5–8cm, more or less glabrous beneath, margin almost entire to sinuate-crenate; veins (9)10–14(15) pairs. Cupule processes short deltoid.

Group II: Nut not exceeding its cupule; peduncle stout, shortly hairy, 5–25mm long. Leaves green beneath.
F. grandifolia American Beech. E N America. Tree 21–25m, suckering. Leaves ovate to oblong, 6–12cm, with coarse serrations; veins (9)11–14(15) pairs. Cupule appendages awl-shaped.
F. sylvatica Common or European Beech. C and S Europe, including British Isles, extending to Crimea. Tree 30(45)m. Leaves ovate to elliptic, 5–10cm, margin remotely denticulate, mostly more or less wavy; veins 5–9 pairs. Cupule appendages prickly awl-shaped.
F. orientalis Oriental Beech. Asia Minor, the Caucasus, N Iran. Tree to 30m. Leaves widest above middle, ovate to obovate-oblong, 6–11(12)cm, margin entire, slightly wavy; veins 7–12(14) pairs. Cupule appendages bract-like linear to spathulate (spoon-shaped) below, more bristle-like above, peduncle 2–7.5cm.
　F. moesiaca and *F. taurica* are binomials for two beech populations intermediate

in (mainly) fruit and leaf characters between *F. sylvatica* and *F. orientalis* and generally occurring where these species overlap.
F. crenata (*F. sieboldii*) Siebold's Beech. Japan. Tree to 30m. Leaves widest below middle, more or less ovate, 5–10cm, margin somewhat crenate; veins 7–10(11) pairs. Cupule appendages linear and bristle-like above, more spathulate below, peduncle 5–15mm.
F. lucida Hupeh Province (E China). Tree 6–9(10)m. Leaves elliptic to ovate, 5–8cm, shiny-glossy on both sides, margin weakly sinuate; veins (8)10–12(14) pairs, exserted as small prickle in leaf-margin sinus. Cupule woolly, the appendages scale-like, deltoid, adpressed.

Group III: Nut not exceeding its cupule but peduncle slender, glabrous, rarely slightly pubescent, 2.5–7cm. Leaves more or less glaucous or glossy beneath.
F. englerana Chinese Beech. China. Tree 6–15(23)m. Leaves elliptic to ovate (4)5–8(11)cm, margin sinuate, the nerves of lower surface with silky hairs, otherwise glabrous; petiole to 10mm; veins 10–14 pairs. Cupule appendages bract-like, more or less linear.
F. longipetiolata C and W China. Tree to 25m. Leaves ovate to somewhat oblong, 7–12cm, margin with a few teeth, the lower surface finely but conspicuously pubescent; petiole 1–2cm; veins 9–12(13) pairs, extending to leaf margin teeth. Cupule with slender, curled, bristle-like appendages.

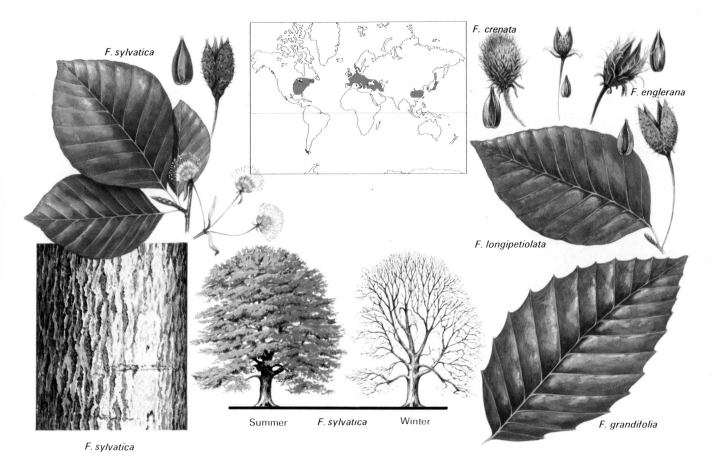

F. sylvatica　*F. crenata*　*F. englerana*　*F. longipetiolata*　*F. grandifolia*

Summer　*F. sylvatica*　Winter

F. sylvatica

Southern Beeches
(genus *Nothofagus*)

Nothofagus is an important genus of shrubs and trees with a discontinuous distribution between the Old World and the New. It comprises 18 temperate species ranging in South America from about 33°S latitude to Cape Horn and from New Zealand northward through Tasmania to Eastern Australia, and 18 species in the more tropical islands of New Guinea and New Caledonia. Many species are dominants or codominants in the cool temperate and tropical montane forests of the Southern Hemisphere, although some grow in subtropical lowland conditions.

There has been much speculation on the causes of the discontinuous distribution of *Nothofagus*, with the Old and New World ranges separated by the broad wastes of the Southern Oceans and Antarctica. The fruits have poor powers of dispersal so ruling out long-distance transport by birds, wind or ocean currents, which have been shown to be responsible for similar discontinuities in other plants. However, fossil *Nothofagus* of Cretaceous age (about 100 million years ago) have been found in Antarctica, showing that the southern beeches were present at a time when Australasia, South America and Antarctica were joined together in the supercontinent of Gondwanaland which subsequently fragmented by plate tectonics into the modern southern continents, thus explaining the discontinuous distribution of *Nothofagus* and, perhaps, other ancient groups.

The southern beeches are deciduous or evergreen shrubs or, more usually, trees up to 50m (165ft), having nonpersistent stipules and separate male and female flowers on the same plant. The male flowers are solitary, in pairs or in groups of three (rarely five), with numerous nonpersistent bracts, a campanulate perianth and 5–90 stamens. The female flowers, which have a minute dentate perianth, are solitary or in groups of three (rarely seven) surrounded by a two- or four-partite cupule, derived from a lobed extension of the flower-stalk (pedicel), which hardens in fruit. The fruit is a one-seeded nut.

The genus, which is most closely related to the Northern Hemisphere beeches (*Fagus* spp), is divided into two sections: section *Calucechinus* (eight species) is deciduous and, apart from one Tasmanian species, is entirely South American; section *Calusparassus* (28 species) is evergreen, with all but three species in the Old World, mostly in New Guinea and New Caledonia.

The temperate species of *Nothofagus* are parasitized by 'mistletoes' – by members of the genus *Elytranthe* (Loranthaceae) in New Zealand, while *Misodendrum*, the only genus in its family, is restricted to the South American beeches. The latter are also hosts for the fungus *Cyttaria darwinii*, which induces large cankers on the stems and branches. On poor soils, cankers also result from frost damage and rapid growth, causing bark splitting. Seed yields are frequently severely depleted by insect larva attack.

Left Nothofagus antarctica on Navarino Island, Tierra del Fuego. This southern beech grows closer to Antarctica than any other tree. The amount of dead wood clearly indicates the severity of the conditions. *Opposite* The Black Beech (*N. solandri*) has fan-like branches and 'loose' canopy of small, evergreen leaves.

Several of the temperate species of *Nothofagus*, particularly those from South America, produce a hardwood timber which, although somewhat softer than *Fagus*, finds a wide range of uses in furniture manufacture, building construction, fencing and so on. *Nothofagus procera* ('Rauli'), *N. obliqua* ('Roble'), *N. glauca* and *N. alessandri* (the latter two used for boat-building in Chile) have the best timber quality, whilst that of *N. dombeyi* and *N. pumilio* is slightly poorer. Some temperate species, principally *N. antarctica* ('Ñire'), *N. obliqua* and *N. procera*, have been grown as garden ornamentals for their form and splendid fall coloring. However, since the earliest forest plots were set out in Britain in the 1930's, there has been increasing interest in planting *Nothofagus* for timber production. *Nothofagus obliqua* and *N. procera* have demonstrated their ability to outyield all the native hardwoods on a wide range of soils and rainfall regimes and there is currently much work being carried out on testing species from a variety of natural habitats to extend the *Nothofagus* plantations in Britain.   D. M. M.

The Main Species of *Nothofagus*

Section *Calucechinus*
Deciduous trees. Leaves plicate (folded like a fan) in bud.

Subsection *Antarcticae* Cupule 4-partite (in 4 parts). Female flowers in 3's (or rarely 7's).
N. alessandri 'Ruil.' C Chile. Tree to 40m. Leaves 55–135 × 80–90mm, ovate-oblong, finely dentate, glabrous. Male flowers in 3's, with 10–20 stamens. Nuts 6.5–7.5mm, having 3 acute angles and 3 concave surfaces (triquetrous), winged and glabrous.
N. alpina 'Rauli' or 'Reuli.' C Chile. Tree to 30m. Leaves 20–30 × 10–15mm, ovate-lanceolate, shallowly serrate. Male flowers solitary, with 20–30 stamens. Nuts about 6mm, pubescent, the lateral 3-winged, the central 2-winged.
N. antarctica 'Ñire' or 'Guindo.' S Chile, S Argentina. Tree to 18m or small shrub. Leaves 13–45 × 5–22mm, oblong to ovate-suborbicular, somewhat lobed, crenate, usually glabrous but slightly pubescent (puberulent) on veins beneath. Male flowers solitary, in 2's or 3's, with 8–13 stamens. Nuts about 6mm, triquetrous and glabrous.

N. glauca 'Roble de Maule' or 'Hualo.' C Chile. Tree to 40m. Leaves 45–80 × 30–50mm, ovate-oblong, doubly serrate, glabrous but fine-haired (ciliate) on veins beneath. Male flowers solitary, with 40–90 stamens. Lateral nuts 15–16mm, triquetrous, not winged.
N. obliqua 'Roble Pellin,' 'Coyan' or 'Hualle.' C and S Chile, C and S Argentina. Tree to 35m. Leaves 20–75 × 12–35mm, elliptic-oblong, doubly-serrate, subglabrous. Male flowers solitary, with 20–40 stamens. Nuts 5–6(10)mm, distinctly winged.
N. procera 'Rauli.' C and S Chile, C and S Argentina. Tree to 30m. Leaves 40–120 × 20–40mm, oblong to narrowly ovate, finely denticulate; male flowers solitary, with 20–30 stamens. Nuts about 6mm, pubescent or glabrous, the lateral 3-winged, the central 2-winged.
N. gunnii Tanglefoot Beech. Tasmania. Tree or shrub 1.5–2.5m. Leaves 10–15 × 10–15mm, orbicular-ovate, crenate, with long adpressed hairs on veins beneath. Male flowers solitary in 2's or 3's, with 6–12 stamens. Nuts about 8mm, the lateral broadly 3-winged, the central flat and 2-winged.

Subsection *Pumiliae* Cupule 2-partite. Female flower solitary.
N. pumilio 'Lenga' or 'Roble Blanco.' S Chile, S Argentina. Tree to 25m or small shrub at higher elevations. Leaves 20–35 ×

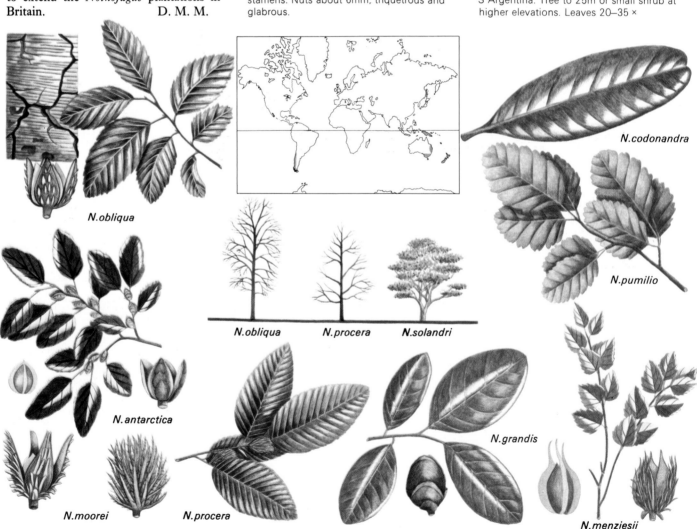

N.obliqua

N.codonandra

N.pumilio

N.obliqua   N.procera   N.solandri

N.antarctica

N.grandis

N.moorei   N.procera

N.menziesii

10–25mm, broadly ovate to broadly elliptical, obtusely doubly-dentate, subglabrous. Male flowers solitary, with 20–30 stamens. Nuts about 7mm, triquetrous and puberulent.

Section *Calusparassus*
Evergreen trees. Leaves not plicate in bud.

Subsection *Quadripartitae* Cupule
4-partite. Female flowers in 3's, lateral flowers with parts in 3's, central with parts in 2's. Leaves subentire to lobed or deeply-divided.

N. betuloides 'Coigüe de Magallanes.' S Chile, S Argentina. Tree to 30m. Leaves 12–25 × 6–19mm, ovate-elliptical, serrate, glabrous. Male flowers solitary, with 10–16 stamens. Nuts 5–6mm, triquetrous and glabrous.

N. dombeyi 'Coigüe.' C and S Chile, C and S Argentina. Tree to 50m. Leaves 20–30 × 7.5–15mm, ovate-oblong to lanceolate, unevenly denticulate and glabrous. Male flowers in 3's, with 8–15 stamens. Nuts about 6–7mm, sparsely pubescent, the lateral 3-winged, the central 2-winged.

N. nitida 'Roble de Chiloe.' C Chile, C Argentina. Tree to 30m. Leaves 22–35 × 12–20mm, ovate-oblong to triangular, coarsely dentate and glabrous. Male flowers in 3's, with 5–8 stamens. Nuts about 6mm, triquetrous, winged and sparsely pubescent.

N. cunninghamii Myrtle Beech. SE Australia. Tree to 50m. Leaves 6–20 × 6–20mm, suborbicular, distantly crenate and glabrous. Male flowers solitary, rarely in 3's, with 8–12 stamens. Nuts about 6mm, glabrous, the lateral 3-winged, the central 2-winged.

N. moorei Australian Beech. E Australia. Tree to 50m. Leaves 15–115 × 8–60mm, ovate-oblong, serrate, glabrous but with hairs on midvein above. Male flowers solitary, with 15–20 stamens. Nuts about 6mm, lateral triquetrous and 3-winged, central flattened and 2-winged.

N. menziesii Silver Beech. New Zealand. Tree to 30m. Leaves 6–15 × 5–15mm, broadly ovate to suborbicular, doubly crenate, glabrous except on veins beneath. Male flowers solitary, with 30–36 stamens. Nuts about 5mm, puberulent, the lateral triquetrous and 3-winged, the central flat and 2-winged.

N. fusca Red Beech. New Zealand. Tree to 30m. Leaves 25–35 × 12–25mm, broadly ovate to ovate-oblong, rather deeply serrate, glabrous except on veins beneath. Male flowers solitary, in 2's and 3's, rarely in groups of 5, with 8–11 stamens. Nuts 7mm, glabrous, triquetrous or flat, winged.

N. truncata Hard Beech. New Zealand. Tree to 30m. Leaves 25–35 × about 20mm, broadly ovate to elliptic-oblong or suborbicular, shallowly, coarsely and obtusely serrate, glabrous or subglabrous. Male flowers solitary, in 2's or 3's, with 10–13 stamens. Nuts about 8mm, puberulent.

Subsection *Tripartitae* Cupule 3-partite.
Female flowers in 3's, lateral flowers with

parts in 3's, central flower with parts in 2's. Leaves entire.

N. cliffortioides Mountain Beech. New Zealand. Tree to 15m or a shrub. Leaves 10–15 × 7–10mm, ovate to ovate-oblong, glabrous above, densely grayish, white- or brownish-tomentose beneath. Male flowers solitary, in 2's or 3's, with 8–14 stamens. Nuts 6–7mm, glabrous or puberulent, wings with acute tips.

N. solandri Black Beech. New Zealand. Tree to 25m. Leaves 10–15 × 5–10mm, narrowly to elliptic-oblong, glabrous or subglabrous above, densely grayish white-tomentose beneath. Male flowers solitary or in pairs, with 8–17 stamens. Nuts up to 7mm, with broadly-based wings.

Subsection *Bipartitae* Cupule 2-valved.
Female flowers solitary or in 3's, all with parts in 2's.

Series *Triflorae* Cupule with 3 nuts.
N. perryi New Guinea. Tree 14–40m. Leaves 30–80 × 12–35mm, ovate-oblong, crenate in upper part, glabrous. Male flowers in 3's, with 13–15 stamens. Nuts 5–8mm, ovoid, more or less winged near apex.

N. nuda New Guinea. Tree about 20m. Leaves 80–100 × 30–40mm, elliptical, shallowly-crenate toward apex, glabrous.

N. balansae New Caledonia. Tree. Leaves 47–80 × 20–30mm, obovate-elliptical, glabrous. Male flowers in 3's, with 12–30 stamens. Nuts 13–15mm, orbicular, narrowly-winged.

N. discoidea New Caledonia. Tree. Leaves about 80 × 25–40mm, lanceolate, glabrous. Male flowers in 3's, with 12–30 stamens. Nuts 16–19mm, more or less orbicular, narrowly-winged.

N. starkenborghi New Guinea. Tree 16–45m. Leaves 30–80 × 12–35mm, elliptical, rarely obovate, glabrous. Male flowers in 3's, with about 12–14 stamens. Nuts about 6mm ovoid, more or less winged.

N. aequilateralis New Caledonia. Tree. Leaves 85–100 × 30–40mm, elliptical, glabrous. Male flowers in 3's, with 12–30 stamens. Nuts orbicular, narrowly-winged.

N. brassii New Guinea. Tree 25–45m. Leaves 25–90 × 15–40mm, elliptic- to ovate-oblong, glabrous. Male flowers in 3's, with about 15 stamens. Nuts 6–10mm, ovoid to subglobose, winged toward apex.

N. baumanniae New Caledonia. Tree. Leaves 60–120 × 25–55mm, more or less oblong, glabrous. Male flowers in 3's, with 12–30 stamens. Nuts 20–30mm, more or less orbicular, narrowly-winged.

N. codonandra New Caledonia. Tree. Leaves 90–125 × 28–55mm, oblong, glabrous. Male flowers in 3's, with 12–30 stamens. Nuts 17–20mm, more or less orbicular, narrowly-winged.

Series *Uniflorae* Cupule with 1 nut.
N. pullei New Guinea. Shrub 2–4m or tree 20–50m. Leaves 10–45 × 7–28mm, broadly elliptical to elliptic-oblong, glabrous above, sparsely hairy on midvein beneath. Male flowers solitary, with 10–15 stamens. Nut 5–6mm, orbicular to elliptical.

N. crenata New Guinea. Tree to 40m. Leaves 25–50 × 12–20mm, ovate-oblong, crenate

toward apex, glabrous. Male flowers solitary. Nut about 5mm, more or less orbicular, narrowly-winged.

N. resinosa New Guinea. Tree 15–50m. Leaves 40–100 × 25–50mm, elliptical, minutely dentate near apex, glabrous. Male flowers solitary, with 13–15 stamens. Nut 9–10mm, broadly ellipsoid, winged, puberulent.

N. pseudoresinosa New Guinea. Tree 30–45m. Leaves 25–55 × 12–25mm, elliptic-oblong, glabrous. Male flowers solitary. Nut 7–8mm, ovoid.

N. carrii New Guinea. Tree 20–45m. Leaves 20–60 × 10–30mm, obovate, rarely elliptical, glabrous. Male flowers in 3's, with about 10 stamens. Nut 7–11mm, ellipsoid to ovoid-oblong.

N. flaviramea New Guinea. Tree 15–45m. Leaves 50–120 × 27–50mm, ovate-oblong, glabrous. Male flowers in 3's; nut 8–10mm, obovate.

N. grandis New Guinea. Tree (12)25–48m. Leaves 45–100 × 20–50mm, broadly elliptical to elliptic-oblong, glabrous. Male flowers in 3's, with 10–17 stamens. Nut 7–10mm, rhomboid, narrowly-winged.

N. rubra New Guinea. Tree 17–45m. Leaves 25–95 × 15–45mm, ovate-oblong to elliptical, glabrous. Male flowers in 3's. Nut 4–6mm, orbicular to broadly ovoid.

N. womersleyi New Guinea. Tree about 20m. Leaves 50–90 × 25–40mm, ovate-oblong, glabrous. Nut 7–10mm, ovate-oblong, flat, winged toward apex.

Chestnuts
(genus *Castanea*)

Castanea is a genus of about 10–12 'good' species from the Northern Hemisphere. The Sweet Chestnut (*Castanea sativa*) is a native of the eastern Mediterranean countries but is now naturalized in the north and has been in Britain since Roman times.

The chestnuts are fast-growing, long-lived deciduous trees, often growing to a great size, branching low down and spreading horizontally. The trunk has a characteristic spirally ridged bark. The leaves are elliptical, serrate, with a polished surface which makes the tree readily identifiable from a distance even in dense mixed woodland. The flowers are small and are borne in catkins in the axils of the leaves, the upper part of the catkin with groups of male flowers, the female flowers below in groups of three, yielding three nuts enclosed in a prickly capsule.

The most serious disease of chestnuts is, without doubt, Chestnut Blight caused by the sac fungus (Ascomycotina) *Endothia parasitica* (Sphaeriales). This parasite has more than decimated the eastern United

States forests of *Castanea dentata*. It was first noticed in 1904 and thought to be a local parasite. It is now clear that it was introduced from China and Japan where it occurs on other locally indigenous species of chestnut, doing little harm. The parasite appeared in Europe in 1938, being observed on *C. sativa* in Italy, whence it has spread with serious results. For example about one-third of trees are infected in Turkey. Invasion takes place only through wounds, killing bark and sap wood. The tree usually dies in the matter of a few years. The fruits themselves may also become infected and this probably contributes to the spread of the disease. Control of spread is virtually impossible, the spores being very effectively carried by birds, insects, rain and wind. The treatment of infected trees by fungicides is not yet a practical proposition. Hopes have been entertained of making use of hypovirulent strains. Such a strain of low virulence, when injected into a tree prevents attacks from the more virulent forms. Attempts are also being made to produce disease-resistant hybrids by crossing the American species with resistant oriental species.

The nut of *C. sativa* is also liable to attack from the sac fungus *Sclerotinia pseudotuberosa* (Helotiales) (conidial stage *Rhacodiella castaneae*). This results in the cooked nuts turning brown and developing an unpleasant taste which renders them inedible. Various methods, mostly chemical, have been suggested to minimize this disease, but such methods are not a substitute for sensible storage.

Less serious diseases include the sac fungus *Microsphaera alphitoides* (Erisiphales), the Oak Mildew, which also attacks the leaves of *C. sativa*. Still another sac fungus parasite is *Phytophthora cambivora* (Peronosporales) causing the Ink Disease of chestnut trees. The roots are attacked, become discolored and exude a fluid rich in tannin, which reacts with iron in the soil, to produce a blackish ink. The infected tree may die within months or after a few years.

In southern Europe chestnuts form an important article of diet, and can also be variously processed to produce such diverse delicacies as *marrons glacés* and chestnut stuffing for turkey. The timber of young trees is used for hop-poles and hoops for barrels, but older wood is too weak for exploitation. The bark is used in tanning.

Other species of *Castanea* also supply timber which is often used for railway sleepers; many of these species also produce edible nuts. Best-known are the American Chestnut (*C. dentata*) from eastern North America, the Japanese Chestnut (*C. crenata*), and two species from China, *C. henryi* and *C. mollissima*. Some of these species are also among the most popular ornamental trees of the genus. They are all hardy, but like warm situations, tolerating drought well. Although of basically a similar structure to *C. sativa*, they can be distinguished mainly on leaf-characters. *Castanea henryi* and *C. pumila* have a possibly more fundamental difference: the nuts are solitary rather than the usual three or more (rarely two) in the other species.

I. B. K. R.

The Main Species of *Castanea*

Group I: Leaves hairless or with only a few hairs on the veins beneath.
C. dentata American Chestnut. E N America. Tree to 30m. Leaves hairless beneath. Catkins 15–20cm.
C. henryi China. Tree 20–25m. Leaves with a few hairs on the veins beneath. Catkins about 10cm. Fruit with solitary nut.
Group II: Leaves hairy on the lower surface. Fruits usually with solitary nuts.
C. pumila Chinquapin. E USA. Shrub or tree to 20m. Hairs on leaves whitish.
C. alnifolia SE USA. Shrub less than 1m tall. Hairs on leaves brownish.
Group III: Leaves hairy on the lower surface. Fruits with 2–3 nuts.

C. molissima Chinese Chestnut. China. Tree to 20m. Young twigs remaining hairy. Leaves lacking scaly glands beneath, the margins with triangular teeth.
C. sativa Sweet or Spanish Chestnut. S Europe, N Africa and Asia Minor. Tree about 30–40m. Young twigs soon losing their downiness. Leaves with scaly glands beneath, the margins with pointed, coarse teeth.
C. crenata Japanese Chestnut. Japan. Tree to 10m. Young twigs soon losing their downiness. Leaves with scaly glands and hair beneath, the margins with pointed but small teeth.
C. seguinii China. Shrub or tree to 10m. Leaves with scaly glands beneath, but hairs only on veins, margin coarsely toothed.

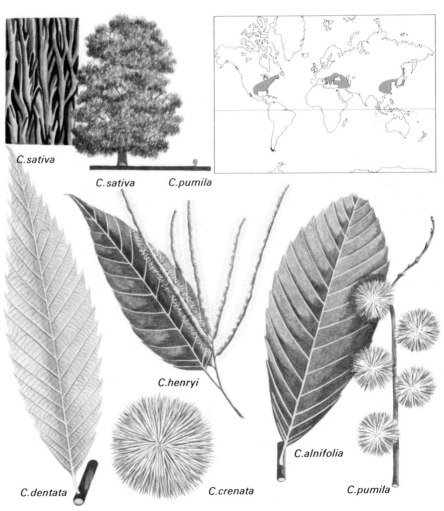

C.sativa

C.sativa　　*C.pumila*

C.henryi

C.dentata

C.crenata

C.alnifolia

C.pumila

Opposite Sweet chestnuts (*Castanea sativa*) strewn on the ground in an English wood. The edible 'nuts' (strictly they are seeds) are encased in a spiny capsule which splits open when they are ripe.

Golden Chestnut, Chinquapins
(genera *Chrysolepis/Castanopsis*)

The taxonomy of this group of evergreen trees has been, and continues to be, a matter of considerable debate. *Chrysolepis*, *Castanopsis* and also *Lithocarpus* are considered living links between the oaks (*Quercus* spp) and chestnuts (*Castanea* spp). The system followed here is as follows. *Chrysolepis* is a genus of two species from the west coast of the United States. These species were originally placed in the genus *Castanea*, subsequently transferred to *Castanopsis* and then moved again to *Chrysolepis*. *Castanopsis* is now a genus of some 120 species exclusively native to the subtropics and tropics of Asia. Chief differences between the genera are: *Castanea* is deciduous and its fruit matures in one year; *Chrysolepis* and *Castanopsis* are evergreen and in the former the fruit takes two years to mature; in *Castanopsis* the inflorescence spikes are unisexual, but in the other genera the sexes are mixed in a single spike. To confuse the matter even more, the popular name Chinquapin is also applied to *Castanea pumila*.

The Giant Chinquapin or Golden Chestnut (*Chrysolepis chrysophylla*, formerly *Castanopsis chrysophylla*) has shiny green leaves that are covered with persistent golden yellow scales below. It is sometimes found in cultivation for this attractive foliage but as with the other members of the genus it is not hardy in cold climates, although at its northern limits it will form a shrub. It grows to almost 35m (115ft) in the wild, but only to about 10m (33ft) in cultivation and then it is sometimes shrubby. It is intolerant of lime-rich soils. The Bush Chinquapin (*Chrysolepis sempervirens*, formerly *Castanopsis sempervirens*) is a shrubby plant growing to about 4m (13ft) but spreading to about 6m (20ft) in cultivation.

The best-known Asian species is the Japanese Chinquapin (*Castanopsis cuspidata*) which has a grayish hairy covering on the undersides of the leaves. In Japan this tree is valued for its timber and edible nuts and is hence much planted in gardens and parks. Logs of this species are also used in Japan to cultivate edible fungi. In north temperate regions it is hardy but makes poor growth. The remaining *Castanopsis* species are widespread in tropical forests and are valued for their timber and as sources of food, for example the Greater Malayan Chestnut (*Castanopsis megacarpa*) yields top quality wood much used for cabinet-making in the Orient.

F. B. H.

Tanbark Oak
(genus *Lithocarpus*)

Virtually unknown in Europe, the genus *Lithocarpus* comprises tropical, evergreen oak-like trees and shrubs native to Asia

(300 species) with a single species – the Tanbark Oak (*Lithocarpus densiflorus*) – native to California and Oregon. The leathery leaves and young shoots are covered by a pale orange down. The leaves and erect male catkins with female flowers below are much like those of chestnuts, but the fruit is an oak-like acorn which takes two years to mature. A few of the Asian species, such as *L. chinensis* and *L. corneus*, are grown as ornamentals in the southern United States. Tannins used in the leather industry are obtained from the bark of the Tanbark Oak. The genus is very closely related to *Quercus* (the oaks) and is sometimes included in it, but the male flowers are in erect spikes (pendulous in *Quercus*) and there are other differences.

F. B. H.

BETULACEAE

Birches
(genus *Betula*)

Birch is the common name for the genus *Betula* which provides trees outstanding for their beauty and usefulness. The birches comprise about 50 species of trees and shrubs native to the north temperate and Arctic regions. Most species are extremely hardy, *Betula nana* reaching the tree limit in the Northern Hemisphere.

The birches are deciduous, wind-pollinated trees or shrubs. The bark is often extremely handsome, particularly in the White Birch (*B. pubescens*), the Silver Birch (*B. pendula*) and the Paper Birch (*B. papyrifera*) in which it peels off in papery layers. Some species are characterized by trunks of yellow, orange, reddish-brown or almost black shades. The lenticels are horizontal and the leaves alternate and serrate. The flowers, which appear with leaves, are borne in unisexual 'catkins' on the same plant. Each catkin-bract has three flowers. The male flower has a perianth of four minute calyx lobes and two stamens, the catkins being produced in the fall and overwintering; the female flower has a single ovary with two styles and a three-lobed bract. The fruit is a two-winged nutlet with a membranous wing on each side for wind dispersal. The

Below A shoot of the Golden Chestnut (*Chrysolepis chrysophylla*) clearly showing the evergreen foliage with a dense covering of golden hairs below, the chestnut-like fruit and remains of the male flowers at the shoot tip. *Right* The lanceolate, slender-pointed, evergreen leaves of *Lithocarpus henryi* from China, one of the few members of this genus found in cultivation, albeit rarely.

Opposite This graceful silhouette of a Silver Birch (*Betula pendula*), pictured at dawn, leaves little doubt as to why this fast-growing species and its many cultivars are popular ornamentals.

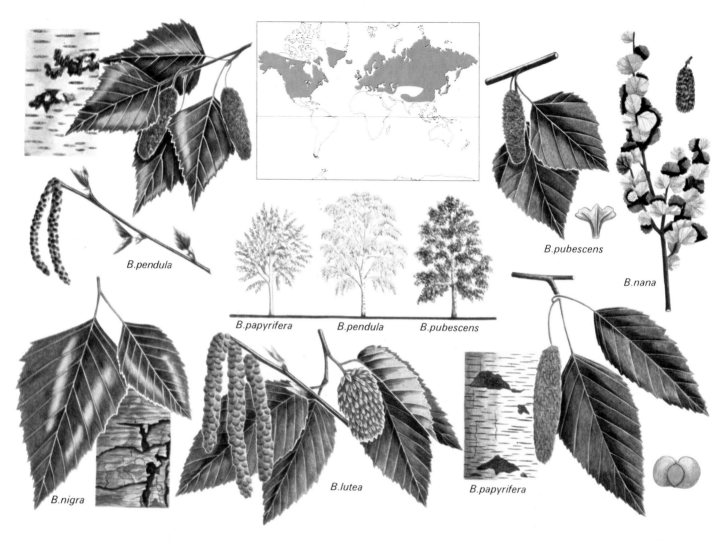

B.pendula

B.pubescens

B.nana

B.papyrifera   B.pendula   B.pubescens

B.nigra

B.lutea

B.papyrifera

The Main Species of *Betula*

Section *Betula*

Fruiting inflorescences subglobose or ovoid or shortly cylindrical and solitary. Wings of the nutlets entirely or almost hidden by the fruiting bracts.

Subsection *Nanae* Shrubs to 2m, though often prostrate. Leaves small, 0.5–4.5cm, distinctly reticulate with 2–6 veins. Male inflorescences situated on shortened leafless branchlets; fruiting female inflorescences small and erect.

B. nana Dwarf Birch. North temperate regions in moist places on mountains. Bush 50–100cm, with erect downy branches, not warty. Leaves orbicular, 0.5–1.5cm diameter, with round teeth, dark green above, glabrous at maturity; veins in 2–4 pairs. Fruiting catkins 5–10mm, scales with lobes of equal length.

Subsection *Costatae* Trees or largish shrubs. Leaves large, 25–100mm, 7 to many pairs of veins, not or only indistinctly reticulate. Male inflorescences terminal on elongated branchlets, more rarely on laterals as well; fruiting female inflorescence erect or pendulous, bracts often elongated.

B. nigra River Birch. C and E USA. A graceful pyramidal tree, 15–30m, with striking blackish curling shaggy bark. Shoots warty and downy. Leaves rhomboid-ovate, cuneate at base, 4–9 × 2–6cm, double-toothed, glaucous beneath; veins underneath hairy in 6–9 pairs. Female catkins 2.5–4cm, scales downy, middle lobe smallest.

B. utilis Himalayan Birch. The Himalaya and China. Tree to 20m with peeling creamy-white bark. Twigs very downy becoming reddish-brown. Leaves ovate, 5–7.5cm, irregularly toothed; veins in 9–12 pairs. Fruiting catkins cylindrical, 3.5 × about 1cm; scales ciliate, middle lobe longer and rounded.

B. lenta Black, Cherry or Sweet Birch. E N America. Tree 20–25m, bark very dark, not peeling. Young branches softly hairy, soon becoming glabrous. Leaves 7–15 × 3–9cm, ovate to oblong, cordate at base, toothed; veins in 10–12 pairs, bearing silky hairs underneath. Petiole 1–2.5cm. Female catkins about 2.5 × 1cm; scales glabrous. The young bark has a sweet aromatic smell when bruised. Attractive in the fall when the leaves turn yellow.

B. lutea Yellow Birch. E N America. Tree to 30m, bark smooth and shining, yellowish-brown and peeling prettily. Young shoots hairy with bitter aromatic bark. Leaves 6–12 × 3–6cm, apex pointed, base cordate, margin doubly toothed, ciliate; veins in 9–12 pairs, hairy underneath. Fruiting catkins 2.5–4 × 2cm, erect; scales downy on outside and margin. A handsome tree with leaves turning rich yellow in the fall.

Subsection *Albae* Leaves large, 2.5–10cm, usually with 5–7(8) pairs of veins, not or only indistinctly reticulate. Male inflorescences usually situated terminally on elongated branchlets; female fruiting inflorescences usually cylindrical, bracts short.

B. pendula Silver, White or Common Birch. Europe, N Asia and N Africa. Tree to 25m with a silvery-white peeling bark and more or less pendulous branches. Twigs glabrous with pale warts. Leaves 2–6 × 2–4cm, ovate-deltoid, acuminate, cuneate at base, sharply doubly serrate. Fruiting catkins 1.5–3.5 × 1cm; scales glabrous, central lobe smallest. There are a number of forms and cultivars sold commercially, including one, 'Purpurea,' with deep purple leaves.

B. pubescens Downy Birch. Europe and N Asia. Tree to 20m with peeling white bark, becoming dark and rugged at the base. Twigs covered in down and wartless. Leaves ovate, 3.5–5cm, rounded at base, downy; veins in 5–7 pairs. Fruiting catkins 2.5cm; scales ciliate, center one larger and pointed, lateral rounded. Hybrids between this species and *B. pendula* occur but are

rare. There are a number of cultivars.
B. papyrifera Paper or Canoe Birch. N
America. Tree 15–30m of thin graceful
habit. The bark is one of the whitest among
all the birches, peeling off in papery layers.
Young shoots warty and hairy when young.
Leaves 4–9 × 2.5–7cm, ovate, cordate at
base, margins doubly toothed, upper and
lower surfaces hairy; 6–10 pairs of veins
and small black glands present on lower
surface. Fruiting catkins drooping, 4 × 1cm;
scales glabrous, lateral lobes broader than
middle. The most widespread of all the
American birches, used for fuel, roofing and
canoe making. A number of varieties are
recognized and cultivated.

Section *Betulaster*
Female fruiting inflorescences cylindrical in
conspicuously elongated racemose heads or
solitary through abortion. Wings of the nutlets
markedly wider than the fruiting bracts.
B. maximowicziana Japan. Tree reaching
30m in its native habitat. Bark orange-
brown becoming grayish. Leaves heart-
shaped, pointed, 7.5–15cm (the largest in
the genus) turning a lovely clear butter-
yellow in the fall.

genus is distinguished from *Alnus* by the
fact that the fruiting catkins disintegrate
when ripe.

In cultivation, *Betula* species grow well
in good well-drained loam, although *B.
pendula* likes a poor sandy soil. *Betula
pubescens* flourishes on acid heathland
among heather, spreading rapidly over
clearings and wastelands by means of vast
numbers of wind-dispersed seeds. *Betula
nana* and *B. nigra* occur normally on wet
ground. Birches are best propagated from
seed.

Birches are attacked by two parasitic
bracket fungi. Rotting of the wood is
caused by *Fomes fomentarius* with large,
hard fruiting bodies, and *Piptoporus betulinus* (*Polyporus betulinus*) with fruiting
bodies up to 30cm (12in) in diameter,
fleshy at first and becoming corky with
age. Both these fungi usually gain entry to
the tree through wounds and are therefore
most commonly seen on old or mutilated
trees. Often witches-brooms, conspicuous
dense formations of crowded shoots looking like large birds' nests, occur on the
branches. These are caused by the ascomycete fungus, *Taphrina betulina* (Taphrinales), which upsets the tree's hormone
balance. Old brooms may be 1m (3.3ft) or
more in diameter and composed of many
hundreds of twigs.

Useful timber is obtained from the
Black Birch (*B. lenta*), the Himalayan
Birch (*B. utilis*), the Silver or Common
Birch (*B. pendula*) and the White Birch (*B.

pubescens). This timber is too soft for use
in the building construction trade, but the
handsome grain makes it valuable for
furniture. It turns and works easily and
is employed in chairs, coopering, clog-
and spoon-making. It provides valuable
firewood, particularly in parts of Russia,
and considerable quantities of charcoal.
The wood is exceptionally durable when
wet, so can be used for piles in certain
places, but it decays quickly if exposed to
alternate wetness and dryness. The flexible
branches, cut in winter, are made into
besom brushes, still much used by gardeners. The bark is impermeable to water
and can therefore be used for roofing,
household utensils, and to make a variety
of containers. The bark of the Canoe or
Paper Birch (*B. papyrifera*) is used by the
North American Indians in the construction of canoes; these are made from sheets
of bark tied together with root-fibers of
the White Fir and smeared with resin from
the Balsam Fir. Birch twigs and bark also
yield an oil which is used as a preservative
and gives the fragrance to Russian leather.

S. L. J.

Alders
(genus *Alnus*)

The genus *Alnus* comprises some 35
species, predominantly natives of north
temperate regions, with one or two species
extending down the Andes of South
America to Chile, Peru and Argentina.
The species are mainly characteristic of
cool climates as well as being moisture-
loving. This tolerance of wet soils gives
rise to a particular type of alder scrub or
woodland. This is an association of plants
on predominantly alkaline (or very slightly
acid), more or less permanently wet peat
commonly known as *fen*. Above the winter
water level and thus free from standing
water, plants, notably alders, become
established. Such woods are known locally
as *carrs*, associated with the Icelandic word

In its natural habitat the Silver Birch (*Betula
pendula*) is a fast-growing colonizer of woodland
spaces and is often the first tree-species to appear
in the sequence of natural woodland rejuvenation.

Alders are best known as waterside plants, either forming woodland known as *carr* in damp habitats or lining lakes and rivers as with this Common Alder (*Alnus glutinosa*) pictured in early spring and still displaying the previous year's fruiting 'cones.'

kjarr, meaning a fenwood.

Alders are deciduous trees and shrubs, with alternate, simple leaves, usually serrate or dentate. The flowers are unisexual and occur in catkins with both sexes on the same plant. The pendulous male catkins are borne at the tips of the previous year's shoots and overwinter unprotected by bud-scales; the female catkins are erect or pendulous with a four-lobed perianth of one whorl (calyx). After fertilization,

the female forms a characteristic woody fruit looking somewhat like a small pine cone. These 'cones' persist after the seed is shed and can normally be seen throughout the following winter.

Most of the alders in cultivation are hardy, and include Italian Alder (*Alnus cordata*), Common or Black Alder (*A. glutinosa*), Gray Alder (*A. incana*) and Red Alder (*A. rubra*). Their ability to flourish in wet soil conditions makes them popular for planting by rivers, streams and ponds.

An important feature is the presence of large nodules on the roots housing a symbiotic bacterium known as *Frankia alni*, which is capable of vigorous nitrogen

fixation, from which the alders benefit.

Alders do sometimes succumb to leaf-spot disease fungi, but none is serious. Old trees may be attacked by various bracket fungi: here prevention is the best treatment and normal precautions should be taken whenever tree 'surgery' is being resorted to. The frequent occurrence of root nodules, already referred to, must be regarded as beneficial.

The wood is used for decorative purposes, clog-making and some toy manufacturing. Alder bark, obtained from various *Alnus* species such as *A. glutinosa* and *A. incana*, has long been used for its tannin content. The tannins have the property of coagulating proteins and this is the basis for their use in converting raw hides into leather. Alder tannin is similar to oak tannin, obtained from the so-called oak-apple galls. Alder tannin has also been used for dyeing linen, using a suitable mordant.

F. B. H.

The Main Species of *Alnus*

Subgenus *Alnaster*
Winter buds sessile. Female catkins terminal, appearing with the leaves in spring, on short, few-leaved branches. Fruit with wing.

A. pendula Japan. Shrub or small tree 8–13m. Leaves not lobed, oblong-lanceolate; acuminate, 5–12cm, the base cuneate to rounded, margin sharply serrate; veins in 12–18 pairs. 'Cones' 2–5, pendulous, 8–15mm, peduncle 3–6cm.

A. viridis European Green Alder. Europe, especially mountainous districts. Shrub 1–3m with sticky branchlets. Leaves not lobed, more or less roundish-ovate, 2.5–6cm, apex acute, base more or less cuneate, margin finely serrate; veins in 5–10 pairs. 'Cones' 1cm, in racemes. Very hardy, thriving in cold and heavy soils.

A. crispa American Green Alder. Mountains of E N America from Labrador to N Carolina. Eastern American counterpart of *A. viridis*. Shrub to 3m. Young leaves sticky and pleasantly aromatic. Leaves 3–8cm, not lobed, more or less roundish-ovate, the base more rounded than *A. viridis* to subcordate, margin finely serrate; veins in 5–10 pairs. 'Cones' 3–6 in racemes, each 1–1.5cm long.

A. sinuata W N America from Alaska to N California. The western American counterpart of *A. viridis*. Shrub or small tree to 13m. Leaves also with 5–10 pairs of veins but distinct by being more or less lobed. 'Cones' 3–6, each about 1cm long, peduncle to 2cm.

Note: Both *A. crispa* and *A. sinuata* are regarded by some authorities as subspecies of *A. viridis*.

Subgenus *Cremastogyne*
Winter buds stalked. Male and female catkins solitary in the axils of leaves, the peduncles 2–3 times longer than the catkins. Female

flowers naked. Spring-flowering.

A. cremastogyne China. Tree 25–30m. Leaves at first off-whitish, pubescent beneath in vein axils, soon glabrous, more or less oblong-obovate, 7–14cm, apex acute, base rounded to slightly cuneate, margin toothed; veins in 8–9 pairs. 'Cones' 1.5–2cm, pendulous, peduncles 2–6cm. Fruit with broad wings. Rare in cultivation.

A. lanata Similar to previous species and from same area, but leaves reddish-woolly beneath.

Subgenus *Clethropsis*
Winter buds sessile. Female catkins single or racemose in leaf axils, the 'cone' mostly longer than its peduncle. Male catkins long and slender, the flower perianth lobes mostly free to the base or, if connate at base, then with fewer than 4 lobes. Fall-flowering.

A. nitida W Himalaya. Tree to 30m in its native habitat. Leaves more or less oblong-ovate, 8–14cm; veins in 9–10 pairs, anastomosing at the weakly serrulate margin. Male catkins to 15cm. 'Cones' 2–3cm, single in a leaf axil. Seed with thick leathery wing.

A. nepalensis The Himalaya, Nepal to W China (Yunnan). Tree 15–20m with silvery bark. Leaves ovate-lanceolate, 8–12(17)cm, sharply serrate; veins in 12–14(16) pairs. Seed with membranous, thinner wing than previous species.

Subgenus *Alnus (Gymnothyrsus)*
Winter buds sessile. Leaves conspicuously serrate. 'Cone' typically longer than its peduncle, single or racemose in the axils of leaves. Male flowers with 4-partite perianth connate at base and, like the female catkins, formed on previous year's wood, over-wintering to flower in spring.

A. glutinosa Black Alder or Common Alder. Europe, extreme N Africa, Asia Minor and Caucasus to Siberia, locally naturalized in E N America. Tree 25–35m. Leaves plicate in bud, green beneath, more or less oval to broadly obovate, 4–9(10)cm, coarsely and doubly serrate, the rounded apex notched, lateral veins in 5–7(8) pairs. Catkins 3–5, the 'cone' about 1.5–2cm. Many named varieties, those with variously cut or divided leaves – var *laciniata*, var *incisa* – being particularly striking.

A. rubra (*A. oregona*) W N America. Tree 20–25m. Shoots soon bright red. Leaves plicate in bud, more or less oblong-ovate, 7–12cm, apex acute, almost truncate at base, somewhat lobed, glaucous beneath; veins in 12–15 pairs. 'Cones' 1.5–2.5cm, peduncle present, orange-colored.

A. incana Speckled or Gray Alder. Europe (not Great Britain), Caucasus and N America. Tree to 20m, occasionally shrubby, with grayish bark. Leaves plicate in bud, more or less glaucous beneath, broad elliptic to obovate, 4–10(12)cm, apex acute; veins in 9–12 pairs. 'Cones'

4–8, each about 1.5cm, sessile or almost so. European specimens are sometimes known as var *vulgaris*. Numerous named varieties: var *acuminata* has leaves lobed to about halfway.

A. cordata Italian Alder. Corsica and S Italy. A handsome pyramidal tree to 15m. Shoots and leaves glabrous. Leaves not plicate in bud, orbicular to broadly ovate, 5–10cm, apex more or less acuminate, cordate at base; veins in 6–10 pairs. 'Cones' 1.5–2.5cm.

Note: There are a number of hybrids, for example: *A. glutinosa* × *incana* = *A. hybrida*; *A. cordata* × *glutinosa* = *A. elliptica*.

Hornbeams
(genus *Carpinus*)

The hornbeams are a distinctive group of some 6o species distributed throughout the temperate regions of the Northern Hemisphere. They are deciduous, wind-pollinated trees of moderate size with conspicuously ribbed alternate leaves and

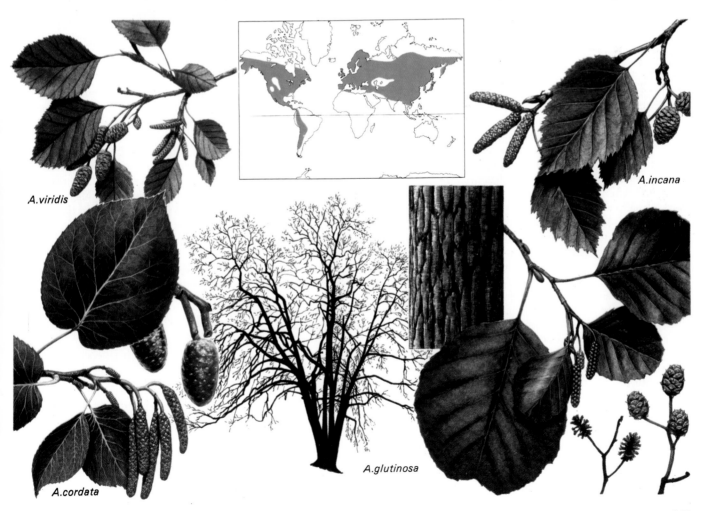

A.viridis

A.incana

A.cordata

A.glutinosa

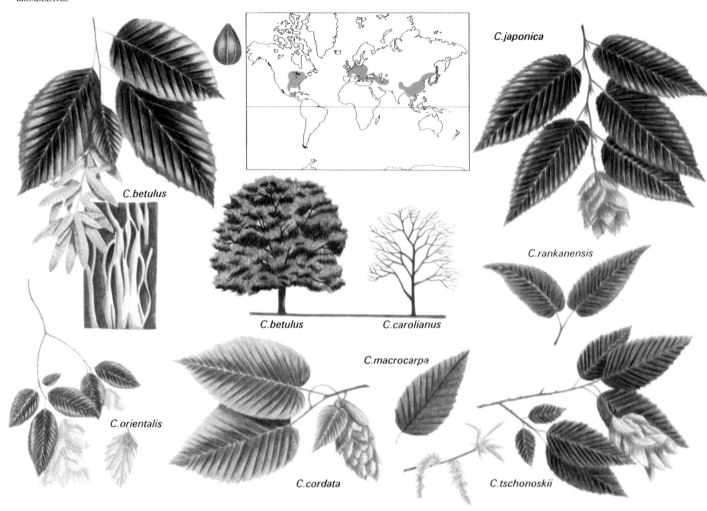

C.betulus

C.japonica

C.rankanensis

C.betulus

C.carolianus

C.macrocarpa

C.orientalis

C.cordata

C.tschonoskii

branches ascending at an angle of 20–30°. The flowers are pendulous, unisexual and borne in catkins, with both sexes occurring on the same tree: male catkins arise on the old wood, and the slender female catkins occur in loosely constructed cones terminating the young shoots. At the base of each flower is a small, three-lobed, hairy bracteole. After fertilization the small ovary becomes woody to form a ribbed nut and the large collar-like bracteole serves as a wing for dispersal.

Hornbeams are extremely hardy trees and very handsome, especially when in flower and fruit. For this reason, about half of the species have been brought into cultivation, including several of the more widespread American and Asiatic species.

The spring-flowering Common Hornbeam (Carpinus betulus) is often cultivated. Ranging in height from 1.5 to 25m (5–80ft) in its mature state, it looks something like a beech tree, for which it is commonly mistaken. However, its stalked leaves are much more pointed than those of the beech, with double-toothed margins and prominent parallel veins emerging from the midrib, its winter buds are very much shorter and more squat, and the flattened,

ridged and fluted trunk is much duller in appearance. It is a native of Europe and southwest Asia. The timber is very tough with almost a horny texture and is very difficult to fashion into artifacts. However, its hard texture is valued for the manufacture of piano-key movements and for wooden axles and spokes. It burns very well and makes excellent charcoal for burning and for the manufacture of gunpowder. During the Middle Ages, hornbeams were coppiced and pollarded for firewood and charcoal, as evidenced by the old pollards which can still be found in woodlands today. Hornbeam coppices well, retaining its leaves after clipping, and because it branches profusely, like beech, it makes an excellent hedge. About seven well-known cultivars are grown in Europe, varying in color, leaf shape, tree shape and branching habit.

The American Hornbeam or American Muscle Tree (C. caroliniana), a native of the eastern United States, is somewhat similar to the Common Hornbeam, but is usually a smaller tree differing in its whitish, hair-covered leaves, which turn orange-yellow or scarlet in the fall. Another well-known species, the Japanese Horn-

beam (C. japonica), is a widely cultivated, sturdy, pyramidal tree which grows to a height of 12–15m (40–50ft). It is particularly valued for its large, handsome leaves and the large bracteoles on its pendulous female catkins. Less frequently cultivated, but nonetheless beautiful trees include the Oriental Hornbeam (C. orientalis), the very hardy and vigorous Chinese Henry's Hornbeam (C. henryana) and the Cordate Hornbeam (C. cordata).

C. J. H.

The Main Species of *Carpinus*
Subgenus *Carpinus*
Scales of male flowers ovate and scarcely stalked. Bracts of fruiting catkins loosely packed and thus little infolded, leaving the nut exposed. Veins of leaves in 10–17 equal or subequal pairs. 54 species.

C. betulus Common Hornbeam. Eurasia. Tree 15–25m. Leaves oval, 4–9 × 2.5–5cm, their bases rounded or heart-shaped, one side longer than the other, shortly pointed at the apex, unequally and doubly toothed, dark green and initially downy above, underside more downy, especially on the midrib, but both sides becoming glabrous by the fall; veins in 10–13 pairs, petiole 0.5–1cm. Fruiting catkins 3–8cm, with large, conspicuous, 3-lobed bracts, the central lobe 2–4cm and often toothed, produced in facing pairs, each with an ovate, ribbed nut at the base.

C. caroliniana American Hornbeam, American Muscle Tree. E N America. Somewhat similar to *C. betulus* but grows more slowly and never attains such a size. Its leaves turn a much deeper color in the fall. In winter, the best distinctions between the two species come from bud characters. In *C. betulus* they are slender and spindle-shaped and about 7cm long, in *C. caroliniana* the buds are egg-shaped and only 0.5cm long.

Closely related species (all from China) include *C. tientaiensis, C. lanceolata, C. londoniana, C. macrostachya, C. davidii, C. kempukwan, C. viminea, C. kweichowensis, C. poitanei,* and *C. tropicalis.*

C. macrocarpa Iran. Tree to 20m, becoming rounded when mature. Leaves narrow, oblong-acute to rounded acuminate, 6–11 × 3–5cm, densely hairy on the veins and with woolly axils; veins in 10–15 pairs, petioles 1–1.6cm. Fruiting catkins about 8 × 4.5cm when mature, with long peduncles up to 6cm; bracts semi-ovate, 3–3.5 × 2cm, unevenly serrate toward the apex, the bases unlobed, and the margin conduplicate. Ripe nut ovoid and hairy with a hairy coronate apex.

Morphologically similar species include *C. schuschaensis* (SW Asia), *C. geokczaica* (Russia), *C. grosseserrata* (Iran) and *C. hybrida* (Caucasus).

C. orientalis Oriental Hornbeam. SE Europe. Usually a small tree or large shrub but sometimes a shrubby bush. Leaves ovate, 2.5–5 × 1–2.5cm, rounded to somewhat wedge-shaped at the base, pointed at the apex, having a sharply and regularly double-toothed margin, dark, glossy green above and with silky down on both surfaces of the midrib; veins in 12–15 pairs, petiole 5–7mm. Fruiting catkins 3–6cm when mature, with short stalks, bracts more or less ovate, slightly longer on one side, coarsely and irregularly toothed but not lobed, each enclosing a tiny nut up to 0.5cm long. Its small leaves and unlobed bracts distinguish it from *C. betulus* and *C. caroliniana*

Morphologically related species include *C. turczaninowii* (China), *C. paxii* (China), *C. chowii* (China) and *C. coreana* (Korea).

C. tschonoskii Japan and NE Asia. A small, deciduous tree to 10m. Leaves ovate, 4–8 × 2–4cm, with a tapered apex, unequally and doubly toothed margins, a rounded base, dark green upper surface and flattened hairs on the midrib; veins in 9–15 pairs, petiole slender, downy, about 7mm. Ripe fruiting catkins develop to 5–6cm on long silky stalks with narrowly ovate bracts 1–2cm, toothed on one side, silky-hairy especially on the veins and at the base where they become slightly boat-shaped to accommodate the ovoid nut in the hollow.

The allied species include *C. tsiangiana, C. chuniana, C. polyneura, C. henryana, C. seemeniana, C. faginea, C. rupestris, C. kweitingensis, C. austrosinensis, C. bandelii, C. tungtzeensis,* *C. yedoensis, C. fargesiana, C. sungpanensis, C. huana, C. putoensis, C. pubescens* and *C. monbeigiana* (all from China), *C. fauriei* and *C. tanakeana* (Japan), *C. examia* and *C. coreensis* (Korea), *C. multiserrata, C. kawakamii, C. hogoensis, C. sekii* and *C. hebestroma* (Taiwan).

Subgenus *Distegocarpus*
Scales of male flowers narrow-oblong with distinctive stalks. Bracts of fruiting catkins closely packed together, thus overlapping and infolded at the base to enclose the nut. Veins of leaves in 15–25 prominent equal pairs. Five species.

C. japonica Japanese Hornbeam. Japan. Tree to 18m. Leaves ovate or oblong, 5–10 × 2–5cm, mostly heart-shaped at the base, but sometimes rounded or wedge-shaped, sharply double-toothed and often with an alternating large and small tooth.

C. cordata and **C. mollis** China. Both distinguished from *C. japonica* by their large, deeply cordate leaves and enormous winter buds. They are very similar, however, in the curious manner in which the nut is protected by basal portions of the bract infolding over it.

C. rankanensis and **C. matsudai** Taiwan. Both species are deciduous trees to 20m. Leaves ovate-oblong, 8–10 × 3–4cm, membranous, papery in texture, with caudate bases and the margins irregularly serrate becoming serrulate toward the acuminate apex; veins in 20–24 distinct pairs.

Hazels
(genus *Corylus*)

Corylus is a genus of about 15 species of trees or shrubs from the temperate Northern Hemisphere including Europe, Asia and North America. They are deciduous, wind-pollinated shrubs, less often trees. The leaves are soft, alternate and singly or doubly toothed. The flowers, which appear before the leaves in late winter or early spring, are unisexual with both sexes on the same plant, and the perianth is absent. The male flowers are borne in the familiar clusters of two to five pendulous catkins ('lambs' tails'), each bract (scale) subtending a single flower with four to eight stamens, branched almost to the base, and two bracteoles. The female cluster is bud-like, the upper bracts each with two flowers and associated bracteoles, and each flower has a single ovary surmounted by two styles, their stigmas strikingly red at pollination. The fruit is an edible nut enclosed in a leafy involucre or husk originating from the enlarged bract and associated bracteoles. The hazels are a very hardy group, with economic and decorative value.

The European Hazel (*Corylus avellana*) is a vigorous shrub or small tree up to 7m (23ft), forming dense thickets of erect, much-branched stems. It was formerly an important economic species, grown in coppices to supply wood for making hurdles and walking sticks, and also nuts (hazelnuts, cobnuts, filberts) for fall cropping. It is still grown commercially, but the true Filbert is *C. maxima* from southeastern Europe and Asia Minor, which is widely cultivated for its nuts, both in its native areas and elsewhere, for example in southeast England, where the chief commercial variety is known as 'Kentish Cob.'

European Hazel is subject to a few fungus diseases. The mildew *Phyllactinia corylae* (Erysiphales) commonly occurs on its leaves and may cause defoliation. More serious are attacks from *Nematospora coryli* (Endomycetales) which causes malformation of hazelnuts in Italy. This parasite is the cause of the so-called stigmatomycosis of tropical and subtropical seeds as well as the fruits, the fungus being carried by plant bugs. It is particularly destructive. Control includes removal of the bugs' food plants. Hazelnuts are also attacked by the well-known Brown Rot of apples and pears, *Sclerotinia fructigena* (Helotiales), the infection entering through punctures caused by *Balaninus nuceum*, the Nut Weevil. Control is essentially by sprays to keep down the weevil.

European Hazel (*Corylus avellana*) catkins with a female flower at the shoot tip. Each catkin contains numerous male flowers, consisting only of stamens. Such 'reduced' flowers were once thought primitive, but the absence of sepals and petals is now considered a highly evolved condition.

In North America, the main native cultivated species are American Hazel (*C. americana*) and Beaked Hazel (*C. cornuta*); *C. avellana* has also been introduced from Europe.

Hazels do well in a loam soil and are especially good in chalky areas. Propagation is best by seeds for the trees and by layering for the shrubs. Where suckers are produced these can be used.

Species that are cultivated both for their nuts and ornamental value are Chinese Hazel (*C. chinensis*), Turkish Hazel (*C. colurna*) and Tibetan Hazel (*C. tibetica*). Ornamental cultivars include *C. avellana* 'Aurea' with soft, yellow leaves, *C. avellana* 'Contorta' (Corkscrew Hazel) with strangely twisted branches and *C. maxima* 'Purpurea' with purple leaves.

T. W. W.

The Main Species of *Corylus*

Group I: Involucral lobes free or partly united at the base, not forming a distinct tube, but rather a deeply-lobed, wide-spreading campanulate husk. The following three species are closely related and could be regarded as the local representatives of one 'macro' species.

C. avellana Common or European Hazel, Cobnut. Europe, W Asia, N Africa. Typically a much suckering, bushy shrub to 6m. Leaves more or less broadly ovate, cuspidate, hairy, 5–10cm. Male catkins yellow, 3–5cm, very conspicuous in early spring. Female flowers minute, crimson-scarlet. Fruit in clusters of 1–4, each 18mm long nut barely enclosed in its campanulate involucre, divided to about halfway by more or less lanceolate toothed lobes.

　C. avellana 'Contorta' (Corkscrew Hazel) is a unique slow-growing variety with twisted stems.

C. americana American Hazel. Canada, E USA. Similar to above. Shrub 2–3m. Leaves 5–13cm. Nut about 1.5cm, concealed by an irregularly lobed involucre, connate at the base, about 3cm long.

C. heterophylla China, Japan. Shrub or small tree to about 7m. Leaves variable in shape, mostly widest above the middle, 5–10cm long. Involucre campanulate, 18–24mm long, somewhat longer than the nut, deeply divided into 6–9 triangular teeth with essentially smooth margins, about 4–6mm deep.

Group II: Like Group I but involucre like a small round-bottomed flask (more conical in *C. maxima*), the 'bulb' enclosing the nut, the 'neck' somewhat grooved, as long as, but mostly 2–3 times longer than the bulb, more or less toothed above.

C. cornuta (*C. rostrata*) Beaked Hazel. E and C USA. Shrub to about 3m. Leaves more or less ovate to obovate, 4–11cm, irregularly toothed to slightly lobed, petiole less than 1cm. Involucre with distinct

'bulb,' conspicuously bristly. The nuts are said to be inedible.

　var *californica*, from the western states of North America has the involucral 'neck' only about as long as the 'bulb.

C. maxima Filbert. S Europe (not British

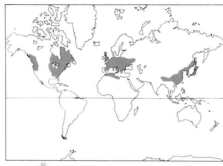

Isles). Bushy shrub or tree to 7m. Leaves broadly ovate, widest above the middle, 5–13cm long. Involucre downy, without bristles, more conical without evident 'bulb,' the free end more deeply toothed. Extensively cultivated for its nuts, and parent of the cultivated English Filbert, of which there are a number of varieties.

C. sieboldiana Japanese Hazel. Japan. Shrub to 5m. Leaves elliptic to obovate, 5–10cm, petiole 1.5–2.5cm. Involucre bristly and with distinct 'bulb,' its 'neck' only $1\frac{1}{2}$ times longer.

　var *mandshurica* (Manchurian Hazel) has leaves to 15cm and the involucre with more spreading bristles, its 'neck' about twice as long as the 'bulb.'

Group III: Species with unusual features either of bark or fruits, but the latter quite unlike fruits of Group II.

C. colurna Turkish Hazel. E Europe, Asia Minor. Pyramidal tree to 25m. Bark strikingly furrowed on shoots more than 2 years old, soon becoming corky. Leaves broadly ovate, (7)8–12(15)cm, margin more or less lobed, petioles 2.5–4.5cm, at first downy and with glands. Involucre of fruit with numerous linear, pointed, somewhat curved, hairy lobes with gland-tipped bristles.

C. chinensis Chinese Hazel. China. Similar to *C. colurna*, of which it was once made a variety. Tree approaching 30m in the wild, about half that in cultivation. Leaves (10)15–18cm, uniformly serrulate, not lobed. Involucre strikingly constricted above the enclosed nut into a tube with slender, sometimes forked lobes.

C. tibetica Tibetan Hazel. Tibet. Tree, sometimes shrub-like, to about 7m. Leaves more or less ovate, 5–13cm, petiole 2.5cm. Fruit a group of 3–6 nuts, the involucres quite unique with their slender, branched, glabrous spines, the whole looking like a burr, commonly recalling the fruit of Sweet Chestnut (*Castanea sativa*).

Hop Hornbeams (genus *Ostrya*)

The genus *Ostrya* comprises 10 species of medium-sized deciduous trees with wide-spreading horizontal branches. They are found throughout the temperate regions of the Northern Hemisphere, extending in Central America south to Guatemala and Costa Rica.

The leaves of hop hornbeams are alternate, more or less oval, with parallel veins and a toothed margin. The flowers appear with the leaves in spring. The male flowers, which occur in pendulous catkins, exposed throughout the winter, have 3–14 stamens and no perianth. The female flowers are borne in erect bracteate catkins, with two flowers per bract. The calyx

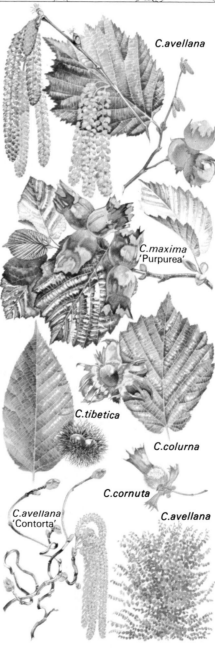

C.avellana

C.maxima 'Purpurea'

C.tibetica

C.colurna

C.cornuta

C.avellana 'Contorta'

C.avellana

Foliage and fruit of the European Hop Hornbeam (*Ostrya carpinifolia*), so named because the inflated, cone-like fruit resembles a Hop (*Humulus lupulus*) cone.

is adherent to the ovary and this is enclosed in an open involucre (husk) which closes after fertilization and then expands to form a bladder-like casing enclosing a nutlet, the whole fruiting catkin not unlike a Hop (*Humulus lupulus*) 'cone.' The species resemble the true hornbeams (*Carpinus* spp), but here the involucre surrounding the nutlet remains open and the male catkins are not exposed during winter.

Some three species are occasionally cultivated as ornamentals and are quite hardy in temperate regions, the two most common being the European Hop Hornbeam (*Ostrya carpinifolia*), which is native to southern Europe and Asia Minor, and the American Hop Hornbeam (*O. virginiana*) which occurs in the eastern United States. They are not particular as to soil, and are normally propagated from seed. The European Hop Hornbeam is a tree growing to 20m (66ft), with gray bark. The leaves are acuminate, 4–12cm long, with 11–15 pairs of veins and the ovoid nutlet is 4–5mm long. The American Hop Hornbeam or Ironwood is a tree growing to 20m (66ft), with dark brown bark and leaves similar to *O. carpinifolia*. The nutlet is spindle-shaped and 6–8mm long. The wood of this species is extremely hard and tough – hence its popular name – and is widely used for tool handles and fence posts. It is very similar to the Japanese Hop Hornbeam (*O. japonica*), native to southeast Asia, which produces a timber valued for flooring and in making furniture.

F. B. H.

She Oaks
(genus *Casuarina*)

This group of highly distinctive semi-evergreen to more or less deciduous trees and shrubs are the only members of the family Casuarinaceae, which comprises some 45 species native to northeast Australia and neighboring southeast Asia (Malaysia), New Caledonia, Fiji and the Mascarene Islands. They are mostly tall trees with a characteristic weeping habit and shoots that are slender and wiry recalling the horsetails (*Equisetum* spp). The leaves are reduced to form whorls of many-toothed sheaths surrounding the articulations of the jointed stems. The flowers are also highly reduced and usually unisexual with the sexes on the same or different plants. The male flowers are borne in simple or branched terminal spikes, each flower with a single conspicuous stamen and one or two perianth lobes, and the females in dense, spherical or oval heads, each a single one-celled ovary without perianth. The fruits occur in globular clusters, each fruit a winged nutlet enclosed in two hard bracts which later open to reveal the fruits, so that the whole fruiting structure resembles a pine cone. The whole appearance is more that of a conifer rather than a flowering plant.

Casuarinas are well-adapted to very dry

She oaks in general have a conifer-like appearance and this Horsetail Tree (*Casuarina equisetifolia*) growing on the shore of the island of Rodriguez, Indian Ocean, is no exception.

habitats, and although not able to survive sustained frost a number of species are grown as ornamentals outside their native regions. They will grow in a sandy loam, in alkaline and brackish soils. The usual method of propagation is by cuttings of half-ripened wood. Species such as *Casuarina campestris*, *C. cunninghamiana*, *C. littoralis* and *C. sumatrana* are grown in parks and as street trees in frost-free regions of southern Europe and the United States. The Horsetail Tree (*C. equisetifolia*), also known as the South Sea Ironwood or Mile Tree, is a pioneer colonizer of seashores in its native Pacific regions and this tolerance has been exploited by its use for hedges and windbreaks in seaside resorts. It is widely cultivated in tropical America (California, Florida) and Africa.

The larger species of *Casuarina* yield a hard, conspicuously grained wood, used for constructional work and ornamental furnishings. The popular name Beefwood refers to the reddish color of the wood.

F. B. H.

THEACEAE

Camellias
(genus *Camellia*)

First a note on pronunciation – the middle syllable should be pronounced to rhyme with *fell* and not with *feel*. Camellias, about 80 species in all, are natives of tropical and subtropical Asia, where their decorative value and economic importance as the source of tea and oil has long been recognized. Ancient Chinese and Japanese literature contains many references to the beauty and uses of camellias and as early as the 6th century AD descriptive lists of varieties were published.

It was the search for the elusive tea plant which led to the introduction of camellias to the western world: the first authentic record is of *Camellia japonica* growing in Britain shortly before 1739. From 1792 onward camellias from the Orient reached Europe and subsequently America in increasing numbers. The first half of the 19th century proved to be a period of immense popularity and many hundreds of new seedlings were raised in Italy, France, Belgium, Britain and

Not all camellias are small shrubs, there are also some fine examples of scramblers, and one of the most spectacular and best proven is *Camellia japonica* 'Adolphe Audusson' shown here giving a fine display of blood-red blooms on a building wall.

America. In all but the most favored regions they were grown under glass and it was many years before camellias were universally acknowledged as one of the finest evergreen flowering shrubs for general garden use.

They are, in fact, not fully hardy in much of the north temperate zone, a slight frost causing the flowers of many kinds to scorch.

Camellias are evergreen trees or shrubs with leaves that are often dark green and shiny. They are alternately arranged and have toothed margins. The flowers *either* have a clear stalk with five sepals obviously differentiated from the two to five bracteoles (sometimes absent) *or* they appear to lack a stalk, because, if there is any suggestion of one it is concealed by overlapping, mostly deciduous bracteoles and sepals, the latter not differentiated from the former and together being referred to as bud-scales or perules. Each flower has 5–12 sepals and numerous stamens which are mostly free and adherent to the petals, although sometimes they are united into a tube. The ovary is superior, comprising three to five fused carpels. The fruit is a dehiscent capsule containing large oily seeds, one or two in each of the chambers.

For ornamental purposes *C. japonica* stands supreme. In its native Japan and Korea it bears single red flowers but after centuries of cultivation it shows as great a diversity of habit, foliage, floral form and color as any single member of the plant kingdom. New variations arise annually from seed and by mutation and at least 14 000 names have been applied to cultivars of this species, which is spring-flowering and bears blooms in every combination from white to red and from single form to complete double. Another popular Japanese camellia, *C. sasanqua*, has scented flowers which appear in the fall and winter. It prefers warmer areas and is extensively planted in America and Australia, often to form hedges.

The aristocrat of the family is *C. reticulata*, from the Yunnan province of China, the cultivated forms bearing flowers 18cm (7in) in diameter. Also from Yunnan comes *C. saluenensis*, which has proved such an excellent parent in the production of the modern hybrid race of camellias. There is little doubt that ornamental camellias are on the verge of a new era with the production of hybrids of improved quality and hardiness ensuring their continued popularity and cultivation in many areas of the world.

In cultivation, camellias prefer a loam with peat admixed, but lime must be absent. Propagation is by seeds, or stem and leaf-bud cuttings; side grafting is also used.

Camellias, particularly under glass, are liable to attack by piercing and sucking insects which deposit 'honeydew' and this forms a substratum for the development of 'sooty molds,' for example, species of *Capnodium*. The imperfect fungus, *Pestalotia guepini* can cause a leaf-spot disease, especially in glasshouse plants.

The Tea Plant (*Camellia sinensis*) is the most widely cultivated member of the genus and the most important economically. There are many forms, some hardier than others, but all when pruned produce great quantities of young shoots – the basis of the tea industry which has spread far from the traditional centers in India, China and Sri Lanka. *Camellia oleifera* is cultivated in China for the valuable seed oil which is used for cooking and hair dressing; in Japan *C. japonica* seeds are utilized for the same purpose. Camellia wood is often used as fuel and for carved utensils and souvenirs.   C. P.

The Main Species of *Camellia*

Group I: Flowers with an evident, unconcealed stalk. Sepals distinct and differentiated from the sometimes deciduous associated bracteoles.

A *Ovary glabrous.*
C. cuspidata China. Bushy shrub to 2m with erect slender branches to 2m. Shoots without hairs. Leaves lanceolate-elliptic, 3–8.5cm, with marginal gland-tipped teeth, copper tinted when young, finally deep green. Flowers solitary, white up to 4cm, stalk 6–8mm; stamens without hairs. Reasonably hardy.
C. fraterna E China. Very like *C. cuspidata*, but shoots, flower stalk and calyx densely hairy to woolly. Flowers white or with pink flush. Glasshouse subject.
C. tsaii SW China, Burma. Shrub to 5m. Shoots densely adpressed, hairy. Flowers white, numerous, each 2.5cm across; calyx more or less without hairs. Also like *C. cuspidata*, but the shoots are hairy, the leaves softer and flower stalk to 10mm. Hardy in warmer parts of north temperate region.

AA *Ovary hairy.*
C. sinensis Tea Plant. See introductory remarks for origin. Shrub or small tree. Shoots with or without hairs. Leaves lanceolate up to 11cm. Flowers with 7–8

Tea is a stimulant beverage made from the leaves of the evergreen shrub *Camellia sinensis*. As shown here, plucking is done by hand, and only new shoots are taken. The terminal bud and top two leaves yield the best tea; the quality is lower if more leaves are plucked. After plucking, most of the crop is processed to give either green tea or black tea; in the latter the withered, crushed leaves are allowed to ferment before final drying, while in the former the leaves are not fermented but steamed, which prevents blackening of the leaves.

white petals; stamens 8–13mm. Var *assamica* has leaves to 20cm, more bluntly acuminate and is a tree to 16m. Glasshouse subject.

C. taliensis China. Shrub to 3m or more. Shoot with hairs. Leaves more or less elliptic, (8)10–15cm long. Flowers white, 5–6.5cm across, 1–3 in a cluster; petals 8–10(11); stamens 1cm. Not dissimilar to *C. sinensis* and somewhat hardier, surviving a fairly hard winter in the warmer parts of the north temperate regions.

Group II: Flowers appearing without a stalk (sessile). Sepals not distinct nor differentiated from the associated, sometimes caducous (nonpersistent), bracteoles (these envelopes also referred to as bud scales or perules).
C. japonica cultivars belong to this group and are known by their wholly petaloid flowers, stamens and ovary appearing as petals or petal-like structures.

B *Flower bud scales (perules) falling as flower opens. Stamens virtually free.*
C. sasanqua Japan. Shrub or small tree to 6m. Leaves more or less broadly elliptic, 4–9cm. Flowers white or flushed pink, stamens wide-spreading. Very popular in Japan, and flowers from the fall to spring. About as hardy as *C. japonica* but the flowers are more susceptible to frost.
C. oleifera China. Shrub to 8m, rarely a tree. Leaves stiff, often wider above the middle, 4–7.5cm. Flowers white, 5–6.5cm across; stamens erect, cohering. Fairly hardy, flowering from mid fall to early spring.

BB *Flower bud scales (perules) persisting until flowers are open or fruit forms. Stamens more or less united.*
C. granthamiana Hongkong. Shrub to 5m. Leaves broadly oblong-elliptic, 7.5–10cm, leathery and deeply veined on upper surface. Flowers white, solitary, 12–14cm across; style of ovary with 5 lobes. Glasshouse subject rare in cultivation.
C. hongkongensis Hongkong. Tree to 10m. Leaves more or less free to base, oblong, 7.5–12.5cm, almost entire. Flowers red, styles 3, the perules persisting to fruit. Glasshouse subject.
C. japonica Common Camellia. Japan, Korea. Shrub or well-branched tree, 10–12m. Leaves oval to ovate, 7.5–10cm, with corky black dots on lower surface. Flowers red, solitary, 6.5–10cm across, the numerous stamens united in a tube below to about halfway; ovary without hairs, with single style divided into 3 lobes. Extremely variable in cultivation with its very numerous variations, for example, 'Lady Vansittart' and 'Apple Blossom.' 2 subspecies are worthy of note: *rusticana*, a native of Japan growing at a higher altitude toward the northern limit and often covered with snow, has downy leaf petioles, and *macrocarpa*, a form from the coastal regions of the south, has narrow

leaves and large apple-sized fruits.
C. saluenensis W China. Bushy shrub 3–5m. Leaves elliptic to lanceolate, 4–6.5 × 2cm, marginal teeth tipped with black glands. Flowers 1–2 together, pale pinkish; ovary hairy with a 3-lobed single style. Fairly hardy.
C. reticulata W China. Shrub or tree to 11(15)m. Leaves elliptic to obovate, upper surface net-veined, 5–11cm long. Flowers solitary, of a soft rose-red, 7.5cm across (almost double this in cultivated forms); perules velvety; ovary hairy with a 3-lobed single style. Many fine forms: 'Mary Williams,' 'Superba,' 'Trewithen Pink.'
C. pitardii Very close to *C. reticulata* but leaves sharply acuminate, narrow, not exceeding 4cm wide, the margin more deeply toothed. In cultivation as var *yunnanica* with leaves acute and light crimson flowers.

In recent years much work has been done on interspecific hybrids and the selection of new cultivars etc. Outstanding are:
C × williamsii (*C. japonica × C. saluensis*) with variants such as 'November Pink', the earliest of the group to flower, 'C. F. Coates', sometimes known as the 'Fishtail Camellia' from its peculiarly three-lobed leaf apex, and 'Donation', often considered the most beautiful camellia of the century with its large, pink semi-double flowers and vigorous habit.
Camellia Cornish Snow (*C. cuspidata × C. saluensis*) with variants such as the white-flowered 'Michael' and almond-pink-flowered 'Winton'.

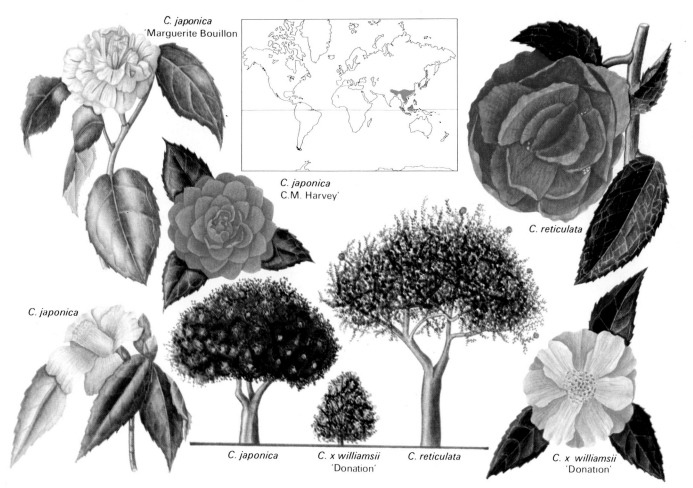

C. japonica 'Marguerite Bouillon'

C. japonica C.M. Harvey'

C. reticulata

C. japonica

C. japonica

C. x williamsii 'Donation'

C. reticulata

C. x williamsii 'Donation'

Stewartias
(genus *Stewartia*)

The eight to ten members of the genus *Stewartia* are native to eastern Asia and eastern North America. They are small deciduous trees or shrubs, with characteristic, attractive, smooth flaking bark. The leaves are alternate, simple, ovate to obovate, toothed dark green and shiny turning shades of red, orange and yellow in the fall. The showy cup-shaped, bisexual white flowers are borne singly over a long period of the summer.

A number of species of *Stewartia* are planted as ornamentals, preferring humus-rich, well-drained neutral or slightly acid soil. They can be propagated from seeds, by layering in spring or from cuttings taken in late summer. The best-known species in cultivation are the Japanese Stewartia or Deciduous Camellia (*S. pseudocamellia*) from Japan, and *S. koreana* from Korea, both trees to 18m (60ft), and the Chinese Stewartia (*S. sinensis*) from central China, a shrub or small tree to 10m (33ft). American species are represented in cultivation by the Silky Camellia (*S. malacodendron*) and the Mountain Camellia (*S. ovata*), both shrubs growing to 5–6m (16–20ft).

F. B. H.

TILIACEAE

Limes, Lindens, Basswoods
(genus *Tilia*)

The genus *Tilia* is singularly uniform, all 30 limes or lindens being trees of moderate to large size with long-petioled, ovate-acuminate leaves, toothed and with an abrupt point, and small cymes of fragrant flowers from a pedicel which is fused to about halfway along a pale green bract. The flowers are white or yellow with five petals alternating with five sepals and five bundles of stamens and often five petaloid scales or staminodes. The fruit is indehiscent and nut-like. The genus is widespread in the north temperate zone but is absent from western America, central Asia and the Himalaya. There are two species

The main attraction of stewartias, such as these Chinese Stewartias (*Stewartia sinensis*), is the strikingly colored and peeling bark which provides a year-round show.

native to limestone cliffs and damp woods in the west of Britain. One is the Small-leafed Lime (*Tilia cordata*), which is long-lived, like most limes, and can grow to a height of 35m (115ft). It bears elegant, small, cordate leaves, slightly silvered beneath, and numerous small flowers spreading or erect from their bracts. In North America it is abundant as a tree of city streets from St. Louis and Atlanta north and east to Montreal. The other British native is the Large-leafed Lime (*T. platyphyllos*), which makes a good clean tree with a hemispheric crown until very old, when it can be 33m (110ft) tall. The cymes bear only three to five large flowers which open early. This lime is used as an understock for grafts of some rarer species and for cultivars.

The Common Lime (*T. × europaea* = *T. vulgaris*) is a natural hybrid between the two foregoing species and grows to be the tallest broad-leaved tree in Great Britain at 46m (150ft). Although often planted in town streets it has the disadvantages of sprouting continually around the base and weeping honeydew from the aphids that infest it throughout the summer. Because of these defects, the Caucasian Linden (*T. euchlora*) is now often planted instead of the Common Lime. It has insect-free, handsome glossy leaves but tends to make a crown like a mushroom. The American Lime or American Basswood (*T. ameri-*

cana) makes a splendid conic tree in most American cities, with deep, rich green, large leaves with white veins, but it seldom flourishes in Europe, unlike its hybrid with the Silver Pendent Lime which arose in Berlin, *T. × moltkei*. This has very large leaves with fine white down beneath and on the petiole. The Silver Pendent Lime (*T. petiolaris*) is a fine tall tree with leaves silvered beneath and outer branchlets pendulous. The Silver Lime (*T. tomentosa*) is a more sturdy, domed tree with harder leaves, darker above, which thrives in cities. The Mongolian Lime (*T. mongolica*), which is rare but in demand, has red-stemmed dark leaves cut into acute lobes. The choicest Lime is the Oliver's Lime (*T. oliveri*) from China, with large pale leaves with sharp whitish teeth and a silvered underside, held out level from a drooping petiole.

Limes thrive on any moderately damp soil that is not too acid or peaty, and many tolerate considerable exposure. Propagation can be by seeds, but these are sometimes difficult to obtain and often infertile, so that layering is commonly resorted to, with grafting for rare species and cultivars.

Pests of limes include the sac fungi *Ustulina deusta* (*U. vulgaris*) and *Nectria cinnabarina* (Coral Spot), the latter gaining entry through wounds and causing subsequent dieback. The honeydew from aphids is also a suitable substrate for various 'sooty molds' (Capnodiaceae), also belonging to the sac fungi.

The timber from *Tilia* species is light, soft and pale-colored. It is used for furniture, carving, paneling, for making matches and boxes and especially for the manufacture of pianoforte keys. The main timber-yielding trees are the American Basswood, the Small-leafed Lime and Japanese Linden (*T. japonica*). The inner bark fibers of these three species and the Tuan Linden (*T. tuan*) are used for making mats, cordage and, when plaited, for shoes. Lime timber is also used to produce charcoal for drawing and burning.

A. M.

The Main Species of *Tilia*

Group I: Leaf green beneath, glabrous but for veins and vein axillary tufts, pubescent in *T. platyphyllos* but hairs simple.

T. cordata Small-leafed Lime. *Europe, Caucasus mountains. Domed, broad, densely-crowned tree to 35m. Leaves 5cm, cordate-ovate or narrow triangular, pale beneath, slightly glaucous; orange tufts of hair in vein-axils. Flowers erect or at any

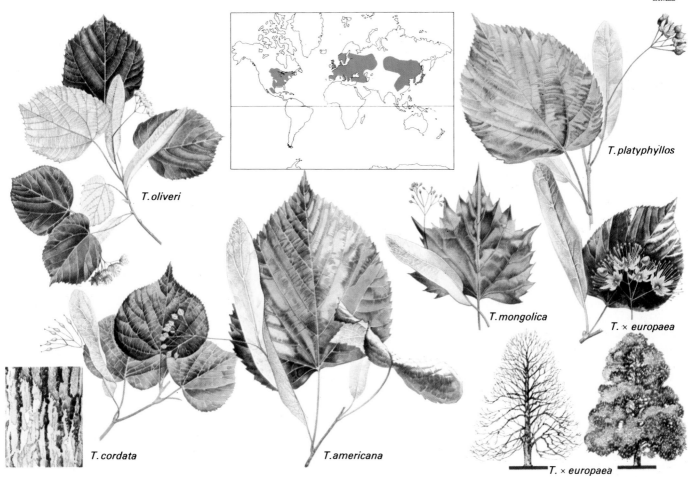

T. oliveri

T. platyphyllos

T. cordata

T. mongolica

T. × europaea

T. americana

T. × europaea

angle, whitish, 5–10 from each pale green bract. Common in American city streets from Virginia to Colorado and Washington and in S Canada.

'Green Spire,' a neatly conic form with orange shoots, is now grown in N USA.

T. americana American Basswood or Linden. *NE USA, SE Canada. Conic until mature, when broadly domed. Peculiarly luxuriant rich green foliage, with big leaves, 12 × 10cm, but some sprout-leaves to 20 × 18cm. Underside same color but veins white. Flowers 10–12 from big pale green bract. Widely planted in streets and squares beyond its natural range in midwestern states, Colorado, South Dakota, Manitoba, and in the west, Montana to Washington and British Columbia.

'Fastigiata' is a narrowly conic-columnar occasional in the streets in the USA.

T. euchlora Caucasian Linden. *Caucasus mountains. Related to *T. cordata*. Domed and pendulous crown when maturing. Leaves bigger than *T. cordata*, 10(15)cm, glossy deep green above. Shoots yellow-green. Flowers 3–7, rich yellow from greenish-white bract. Patches of bright yellow leaves in the fall. Infrequent in streets and parks in Europe; rare in collections in America.

T. × europaēa (*T. vulgaris*) Common Lime or Linden. *Europe. Natural hybrid *T. cordata* × *T. platyphyllos*. Very tall tree to 46m, with narrow domed crown opening toward the top and numerous sprouts from base and bole, rarely clean. Leaves dull green above, a little paler beneath with small tufts of white hair in all vein-axils. Flowers 4–10,

pale yellow, hanging from yellow-green bract. Abundant in streets, parks and gardens in Europe; in America, a few in New York, New England and British Columbia.

T. mongolica Mongolian Lime. *N China, Mongolia. Medium-sized domed tree. Leaves on red petiole, small, hard, dark shiny green, unique in genus for deeply and jaggedly toothed lobes. Very hardy but scarce. Planted where available in Europe and in NW USA in cities.

T. platyphyllos Large-leafed Lime. *Europe. Tree with hemispherical crown to 32m. Leaves softly hairy above and below (hairs simple), as are shoot and petiole. Flowers 3(4–6), yellowish-white from whitish bract, large and early. Common in Europe, frequent in American cities from Baltimore to St. Louis; occasional in Virginia, Washington, British Columbia.

'Laciniata' Cut-leaf Lime. Tree to 15m with leaves small, acuminate, toothed and lobed deeply, nearly to midrib. 'Rubra' Red-twigged Lime. Tree to 25m. Shoots dark red in winter, green in summer. Foliage denser and paler than type and flower-bract cream-white.

Group II: Leaves silvery-white beneath with typically fascicled or stellate hairs.
T. × moltkei Hybrid *T. americana* × *T. petiolaris*. Vigorous tree to 25m with somewhat pendulous crown. Leaves big, 20–25cm, coarsely toothed like *T. americana* but with dense, soft gray-white pubescence beneath. Arose in Berlin, before 1880.

T. heterophylla White Basswood. *E USA. Probably a form of *T. americana* with intermediates but striking in some roadside woods in Ohio as wind shows silver underside of leaves. Leaves only to 12cm, more finely toothed, densely white-haired beneath.

T. oliveri Oliver's Lime. *China. Tall, narrowly domed tree to 23m. Shoot and bud apple-green and pink, leaves big, 13–20cm, pale green above with whitish sharp teeth, silvered beneath, flowers 2–4 from big pale green bract. Very handsome.

T. petiolaris Silver Pendent Lime. Perhaps from the Caucasus. Tall, narrow-domed pendulous tree to 33m, usually grafted at 2m onto *T. platyphyllos*. Shoot, petiole and underside of leaves closely matted with white simple hairs. Leaves very oblique at base, 12 × 12cm, dark green, sharply toothed, on slender petiole 6–12cm. Flowers 7–10, cup-shaped, broad-petaled, fragrant and late.

T. tomentosa Silver Lime. *SW Asia. Broadly domed tree to 30m with stout branches when old, regular hemispheric crown when young. Leaves broad, dark, hard, crinkled, very oblique, 12 × 10cm on 5cm petiole. Flowers cup-shaped, yellow, fragrant. Scarce in cities and big gardens in N USA, mostly in New York, and New England; frequent in European cities.

Many species of Tilia are cultivated well beyond their natural range. The geographical distribution given at the beginning of each entry refers to the natural distribution.

Elms
(genus *Ulmus*)

The genus *Ulmus*, to which the various elms are allocated, comprises some 20 species of deciduous trees. It has a good continuous fossil record from the Upper Cretaceous onward, and its salient characters have shown little variation during its long geological history. It has always been a north temperate genus, although three species are found in the tropics. It now occurs throughout Europe as far north as Scotland and Finland. It is absent from most of Siberia but present in Turkey, Israel, Iran, Afghanistan, parts of central Asia and the Himalaya. In the Far East it is widespread in China (possibly its center of origin), Japan, the Soviet Far East and Korea, and extends south through Malaya to Sarawak and Sulawesi. In Africa, it is confined to northern Algeria. In North America it is confined to the eastern states, and extends south through Mexico and Central America to Colombia.

Although the species are difficult to distinguish, the genus is usually readily identifiable by two salient leaf characters: bilateral asymmetry and bidentate leaf margins. The flowers may be stalked as in the American White Elm (*Ulmus americana*) or sessile as in the European Field Elm (*U. minor*). In most species, the flower buds develop in the spring after the leaves, in whose axils they had been produced, have been shed – the vernal flowering

The weeping Camperdown Elm (*Ulmus glabra* 'Camperdownii') is a cultivated form of the Wych Elm, often grown in parks.

The Main Species of *Ulmus*

Group I: Flowers in fall, stalked. Fruit hairy, wing narrow.
U. crassifolia Cedar Elm. SE USA. Tree to 25m with broad round-topped head, branches often with 2 corky flanges. Leaves ovate, rough above, 2.5–5cm. Fruit oval, about 1cm.
U. serotina SE USA. Spreading tree to 20m. Leaves oblong, smooth above, 5–8cm. Fruit oval, 1–1.5cm.
U. monterreyensis An imperfectly known species from Nuevo Leon, Mexico. Tree to 15m. Leaves elliptic, shiny but rough above, 2–4cm. Mature fruits not observed.

Group II: Flowers typically in the fall, sessile. Fruit glabrous, wing conspicuous.
U. parvifolia Chinese Elm. China, Korea, Japan, SE Asia. Tree to 20m with rounded head. Leaves lanceolate, smooth above, 2–4cm, 30–50 secondary teeth, sub-evergreen in the south. Fruit oval, about 1cm.
U. lanceifolia E Himalaya, SW China, Burma, SE Asia, Sumatra, Sulawesi (Celebes). Spreading tree to 45m. Leaves lanceolate, smooth above, 4–6cm, 50–70 secondary teeth. Fruit orbicular, sometimes markedly asymmetrical, about 2.5cm.

Group III: Flowers vernal, stalked. Fruit densely hairy throughout, no wing.
U. mexicana Mexican Elm. Mexico, through C America to Colombia. Tree to 20m. Leaves elliptic, smooth above, 8–10cm, fewer than 100 secondary teeth. Fruit elongate oval, about 1cm.
U. villosa W Himalaya. Tree to 25m. Mature leaves usually on long shoots, elliptic, smooth above, 7–9cm, more than 100 secondary teeth. Fruit elongate oval, 1.2–1.5cm.

Group IV: Flowers vernal, stalked. Fruit densely hairy throughout, wing narrow.
U. alata Wahoo, Winged Elm. SE USA. Round-headed tree to 15m. Branches usually with 2 corky flanges. Leaves oblong, smooth above, 3–5cm. Fruit elongate oval, about 1cm.
U. thomasii Rock Elm. E Canada, NE USA. Tree to 30m with rounded head. Leaves elliptic, smooth above, 5–8cm. Fruit oval, 1.5–2cm.

Group V: Flowers vernal, stalked. Fruit hairy along the edge only.
U. laevis European White Elm. E Europe, as far north as S Finland and as far west as NE France. Tree to 30m of irregular habit. Trunk often bossy with buttressed roots. Leaves elliptic, tapering abruptly, often highly asymmetrical at the base, smooth above, 6–12cm. Fruit oval, 1–1.5cm.
U. americana American White Elm. SE Canada, E USA. Regular, wide-spreading tree to 40m. Leaves elliptic, tapering abruptly, smooth or rough above, 7–12cm. Fruit oval, about 1cm. The only species known to be tetraploid (56 somatic chromosomes).
U. divaricata Only known from Nuevo Leon, Mexico. Spreading tree to 10m. Leaves elliptic, rough above and below, subsessile,

3.5–8cm. Fruit oval, 0.5–0.8cm; styles persistent.

Group VI: Flowers vernal, sessile or subsessile. Fruit broadly winged, seed central in fruit. Leaves large.
U. rubra Slippery Elm. SE Canada, E USA. Tree to 20m with spreading, open canopy. Leaves oblong, tapering gradually, rough above, 10–12cm. Fruit orbicular, hairy over the seed only, 1–2cm.
U. macrocarpa N China, Soviet Far East, Korea. Bushy tree to 10m. Leaves elliptic, tapering abruptly, very rough above, 4–8cm. Fruit orbicular, hairy over the entire surface, 2–2.5cm.
U. wallichiana W Himalaya. Tree to 30m with spreading crown. Leaves elliptic, tapering abruptly, rough above, 9–12cm. Fruit orbicular, hairy throughout or only over seed, 1–1.3cm.
U. uyematusi Taiwan and the Chinese hinterland opposite. Tree to 25m. Leaves elliptic, tapering abruptly, subsessile, rough above, about 10cm. Fruit oval, glabrous, about 1cm; fruit stalks about 0.6cm.
U. bergmanniana C China. Tree to 25m. Leaves elliptic, tapering abruptly, subsessile, rough above, 8–11cm. Fruit orbicular, glabrous, about 1.5cm; fruit stalks 0.2–0.4cm.
U. glabra Wych Elm. N Europe. N China, Korea, Soviet Far East, N Japan, Sakhalin, mountains further south. Spreading tree to 40m. Leaves elliptic, tapering abruptly, subsessile, rough above, 9–12cm. Fruit orbicular, usually glabrous, sessile, about 2cm.
    'Horizontalis' Weeping Wych Elm. Originated at Perth, Scotland, in the early 19th century and frequently planted in cemeteries in the British Isles. Main branches spread horizontally in a low flat crown; lesser branches pendulous.
    'Camperdownii' Camperdown Elm. Originated at Camperdown House, Scotland, around 1850 and used as the previous elm. Another weeping elm, but main branches grow upward and form a round head; lesser branches pendulous.
    'Exoniensis' Exeter Elm. Originated in a nursery at Exeter, England, about 1826, and now widespread in parks in N Europe. Branches grow upward to constitute a narrow columnar head. Leaves coarsely toothed, wrinkled and twisted.
    var *elliptica* Caucasus and SE Russia. Differs from typical *U. glabra* in having hairs over the seed on the fruit.

Group VII: Flowers vernal, sessile. Fruit broadly winged, seed central in fruit. Leaves usually small.
U. pumila Siberian Elm. C Asia, Mongolia, Soviet Far East, N China, Korea, Tibet. Tree to 25m. Mature leaves often on long shoots, elliptic, smooth above, 2–5cm. Fruit orbicular, 1–1.5cm.
U. glaucescens Mongolia and N China. Tree to 25m. Leaves ovate, smooth above, 3–4cm. Fruit oval, 2–2.5cm.
U. chumlia W Himalaya. Tree to 25m with spreading branches. Leaves elliptic, smooth above, 6–8cm. Fruit orbicular, 1–1.2cm.

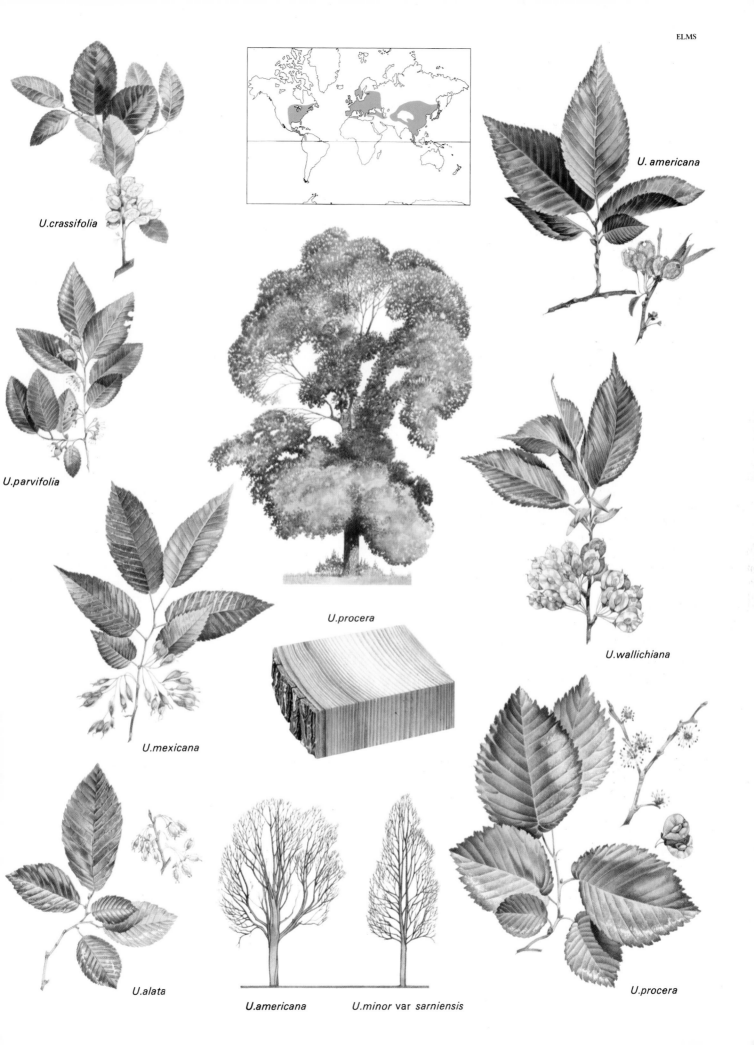

U.crassifolia

U. americana

U.parvifolia

U.procera

U.wallichiana

U.mexicana

U.alata

U.americana   *U.minor* var *sarniensis*

U.procera

Group VIII: Flowers vernal, sessile. Fruit broadly winged, seed displaced to apex of fruit.

U. davidiana China, Korea, Soviet Far East, Japan, Sakhalin. Tree to 30m. Leaves elliptic, rough above, 5–10cm; petioles densely hairy. Fruit oval, glabrous or hairy over the seed, about 2cm.

U. wilsoniana SW China. Tree to 25m. Leaves elliptic, smooth or rough above, 5–8cm. Fruit oval, glabrous, about 1.5cm.

U. castaneifolia C China. Tree to 20m. Leaves narrow, lanceolate, rough above, 12–14cm. Fruit oval, glabrous, about 2cm.

U. minor (*U. carpinifolia*) European Field Elm. C and S Europe, E England, Algeria, Near East. Tree to 30m of variable habit; canopy open. Leaves elliptic, often highly asymmetrical at the base, usually smooth above, 5–8cm; petioles glabrous or hairy. Fruit oval to orbicular, glabrous, 1–2cm.

'Modiolina' Orme Tortillard, Cross-grained Elm. France. Small tree with gnarled and twisted branches. Leaves variable. Timber extremely cross-grained and formerly used for wheel hubs.

'Umbraculifera' Widely distributed in Soviet C Asia and N Iran. Habit highly characteristic, the head formed of a dense network of branches with an almost spherical perimeter. Leaves elliptic, 3–6cm. One of the most distinctive landscape elements of C Asia, trees often marking shrines and wells. Propagated by grafting.

'Viminalis' Originated in Kent, England, in 1817. Branches ascending; crown narrow. Leaves lanceolate, 2–5cm.

var *cornubiensis* Cornish Elm. The principal elm in Cornwall and W Devon, England. Tall tree with straight bole and narrow crown. Leaves elliptic, about 5cm.

var *sarniensis* Guernsey Elm. The predominant elm of Guernsey, Channel Islands, and extensively planted as a roadside tree in England. Medium-sized tree of stiff pyramidal habit. Leaves ovate, 4–6cm.

var *lockii* (*U. plotii*) Lock's Elm. N midlands of England. Trunk crooked; crown narrow; leading branch characteristically drooping to one side like an ostrich feather in outline. Mature leaves often on long shoots, oblong, about 3cm.

U. procera English Elm. S and C England, NW Spain. Tree to 40m with stout, straight bole and figure-of-eight or violin-shaped silhouette; canopy dense. Leaves orbicular, highly asymmetrical at the base, usually rough above, 5–6cm; petioles hairy. Fruit orbicular, glabrous, about 1–2cm.

Group IX: Hybrids between members of Groups VI and VIII.

U. × hollandica (*U. glabra* × *U. minor*) Numerous hybrids of this parentage occur in Europe, and in many regions, such as the Netherlands and parts of E England, they outnumber either parent. Vigorous trees to 40m; habit variable. Leaves large, usually petiolate, typically more than 8cm. Fruit variable, tending to be intermediate between that of the parental species.

'Major' Dutch Elm (of England).

Introduced from France to the Netherlands by nurserymen, and taken from the Netherlands to England in the time of William III. No longer common in the Netherlands, but still frequent in NE France. Planted extensively in exposed places in the British Isles such as Land's End and the Scilly Isles; also frequently planted in Ireland. Irregularly branched and of open, scraggy habit. Leaves ovate, usually rough above, with characteristic black blotchy discoloration toward fall, 8–11cm.

'Belgica' Dutch Elm (of the Netherlands). Of Belgian origin, apparently first recorded at Bruges in the 18th century. Mainly planted in the Netherlands, where it is the most frequent elm, and in Belgium. Tidy habit and broad, rounded head. Leaves narrow elliptic, 8–12cm.

'Vegeta' Huntingdon Elm. Originated in Hinchingbrooke Park, near Huntingdon, England, about 1750. Mainly planted in S England. Trunk usually divides into a radiating fan of principal branches. Leaves elliptic, smooth above, 9–11cm.

'Hoersholmiensis' Hørsholm Elm. Originated at the Hørsholm nursery, Denmark, around 1885 and planted as a street tree in Denmark and S Sweden. Leaves narrow lanceolate, 10–12cm.

Note: Leaf descriptions normally apply to well-developed leaves on dwarf shoots.

habit. In some subtropical species, for example, the Chinese Elm (*U. parvifolia*), the flowers develop from the buds while the leaves which subtend them are still attached – the fall flowering habit. The fruit is the principal character used in specific discrimination, in particular the distribution of hairs upon it. Hybridization between most of the elm species can be accomplished artificially and it also occurs frequently in nature.

Throughout their natural range, elms show a preference for riverain sites. It is, however, difficult to ascertain the exact natural distribution of several species, as their areas have been much extended by human planting over the past 2 000 years, particularly in Europe, central Asia and China.

The elms, in particular the English Elm (*U. procera*), American Elm (*U. americana*), Slippery Elm (*U. rubra*) and Rock Elm (*U. thomasii*), are of manifold utility. The foliage has been a preferred cattle feed over wide areas. This use is frequently mentioned in the Roman agricultural writers and persisted in parts of Europe until the beginning of the present century. It is still important in the Himalayan species *U. wallichiana*. Extensive lopping

for cattle by prehistoric man is a possible explanation for the widespread 'elm decline' that occurred in northwest Europe about the time when neolithic agriculture was spreading.

Elm timber has a number of special characteristics. In particular it is cross-grained and resists splitting. Consequently it has been the timber of choice for wheelwrights for the hubs of spoked wheels, a use which goes back as far as Mycenean Greece. The polished wood of elm shows a beautiful zigzag pattern, the so-called partridge-breast grain so skillfully exploited in the wooden sculptures of Arp, Moore and Hepworth.

Another characteristic of the timber is its resistance to decay under continuously waterlogged conditions. This accounts for its choice for underwater piles, the wooden water mains in former urban use, and the floats of water wheels.

A local use of elm, more widely known from its frequent mention by the Roman poets, is as a support for the vine. This practise was important in central Italy only.

The principal medicinal product of the elms is the mucilaginous bark of the Slippery Elm (*U. rubra*), which is used as a demulcent for inflamed states of the alimentary canal.

The elms have associated with them a large flora and fauna of species found nowhere else. The flora mainly comprises fungi, most of which cause little harm. Exceptional, however, in its destructive effect is the so-called Dutch Elm Disease caused by the fungus *Ceratocystis ulmi*. Dutch Elm Disease was first recognized as such in 1918. It caused widespread death of elms in much of Europe between the World Wars, whence it was introduced into North America. In Europe, the disease attenuated after this outbreak, but another flare-up began after 1965, perhaps through reintroduction of virulent strains from North America. The fungus kills by inducing blockage of the vessels. It is distributed by bark-boring beetles, mainly *Scolytus* spp.

The elm fauna mainly comprises insect and mite species, most again causing little damage. Some insect stocks have evolved on and with the elms and the taxonomy of each throws light on the evolution of the other. The Eriosomatidae, for instance, are a family of gall-inducing aphids living principally on elms.

Elms have been widely cultivated as ornamentals, particularly in avenues and formal plantings.   R. H. R.

Caucasian Elms
(genus *Zelkova*)

The genus *Zelkova* comprises six or seven species from the eastern Mediterranean, the Caucasus, Iran and western and eastern Asia. They are deciduous trees or shrubs with smooth peeling bark and alternate leaves with conspicuously toothed margins and a short petiole. The flowers are bisexual, unisexual (and then borne on the same plant) or polygamous (unisexual and bisexual flowers on the same plant), with a four- to five-lobed calyx but no petals. The male flowers are borne in groups of two to five in the axils of the lowermost leaves and have four to five stamens. The female or bisexual flowers are solitary or few in the axils of the uppermost leaves and have a single ovary and excentric style. The fruit is unwinged, nut-like (or like a dry drupe) with a wrinkled surface subtended by the persistent calyx and crowned by the remains of the style, forming two minute beaks. Zelkovas are hardy in temperate regions and succeed on any well-drained, deep, good soil. Flowering occurs in spring when the leaves appear. Propagation is by seed or by grafting onto elm stocks.

Hemiptelea davidii, the only species of its genus, is sometimes included in *Zelkova* but this species has hairy shoots with long, stout spines and a broadly ovoid, stalked, winged fruit. It is a native of China, Mongolia and Korea and is hardy in temperate regions.

Wood from all species is used in cabinet-making and inlay work. *Zelkova serrata*, a native of China and Japan, forming lowland forest with maple, beech and oak, produces a hard, fine-grained wood like that of English Elm (*Ulmus procera*) and is highly valued in Japan for special building purposes such as temples. The Asiatic name for the wood is 'Keaki.' It resists moisture well because of its high oil content, but this imparts flavor to the wood and makes it unsuitable for food containers or vessels. In Korea it is highly prized for the rims of wagon wheels. The species was introduced into Britain in 1862 and is grown for ornamental purposes. The Caucasian Elm (*Z. carpinifolia*) was introduced in 1760 and has been used as a replacement tree for elms lost through Dutch Elm Disease. Unfortunately, it is now evident that zelkovas are also subject to the disease.

The foliage of zelkovas is cut in summer, dried and used as winter feed for livestock. The Caucasian word *zelkoua* translates as 'stonewood,' a reference to the hardness of the timber.

S. A. H.

The Species of *Zelkova*

Group I: Bark pinkish to orange or with close-set horizontal pink stripes. Shoots glabrous or more or less pubescent but not hispid (ie without rough bristly hairs).
Z. serrata (*Z. acuminata*) Keaki. Japan. Tree to 40m in the wild, much less in cultivation. Bark gray, horizontally striped with pink. Shoots pubescent, soon glabrous. Leaves more or less ovate, 3–10(12)cm, with about 10 mucronate teeth on each side, veins 8–12(14) pairs. Fruit roundish, 3–5mm across.
Z. sinica Chinese Zelkova. C and E China. Tree to 15(17)mm. Bark orange or pink, not striped. Shoots gray-woolly. Leaves ovate to oval, 2–7cm, margin entire toward cuneate base but shallowly crenate-toothed toward apex, veins 6–8 pairs. Fruit 5–6mm across.

Group II: Not the characters of Group I. Crown unique in its ovoid-oblong shape formed by very numerous branches vertically ascending from apex of 1–3m trunk.
Z. carpinifolia (*Z. crenata*) Siberian or Caucasian Elm. Caucasus. Tree to 25m. Shoots pubescent. Leaves more or less elliptic, 2–5(9)cm, margin broadly crenate, ciliate, veins 6–12 pairs, petiole 1–2(3)mm. Fruit 4–6mm across.

Group III: Not the characters of Groups I or II. Branches spreading to give a more or less dome-shaped crown.
Z. abelicea (*Z. cretica*) Cretan Zelkova. Rocky mountains in Crete, possibly endemic. Recorded from Cyprus in 1840 by a competent botanist (Kotschy) but not since re-collected; possibly extinct. Shrub to 5m or tree to 15m. Shoots slender, at first with short bristles which soon fall off. Leaves subsessile, ovate to oblong, 1–2.5(4)cm, rough above, pubescent or glabrescent beneath, the margin with 7–10 broad rounded crenations. Flowers white, sweet scented. Fruit pubescent.
Z. verschaffeltii Cut-leaf Zelkova. Possibly Caucasus. Shrubby bush or small tree. Leaves subsessile, oval to lanceolate, rough above, 3–6(8)cm, the margin with 5–8(9) coarsely triangular teeth on each side and as many paired veins. Fruit globose, green, 4–5mm across, grooved. Very close to *Z. carpinifolia* and perhaps a form of that species, differing mainly in habit.

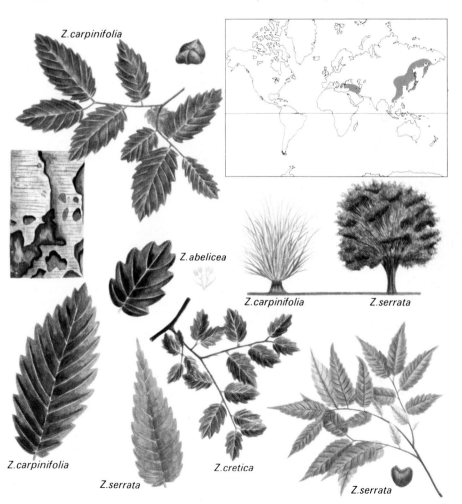

Z.carpinifolia

Z.abelicea

Z.carpinifolia

Z.serrata

Z.carpinifolia

Z.serrata

Z.cretica

Z.serrata

Hackberries
(genus *Celtis*)

The genus *Celtis* comprises some 60–70 species from North America, southeastern Europe, and the Near and Far East (China, Korea, Japan). They are related to the elms from which they differ in having leaves with three main veins

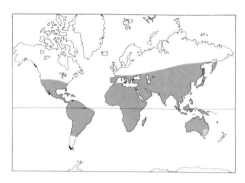

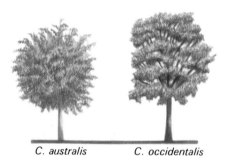

C. australis   C. occidentalis

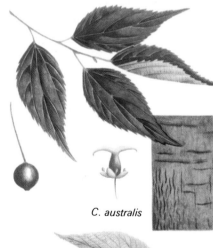

C. australis

C. occidentalis

instead of one and globose fleshy fruits (dry and winged in elms).

Hackberries are mainly deciduous, hardy trees with decorative leaves, the tropical and subtropical species often evergreen. The flowers are green, with a perianth of one whorl (calyx) usually produced in the spring with the young leaves, and are either bisexual or male, both occurring on the same tree. The male flowers occur in clusters (below the bisexual), with four or five calyx segments and stamens; the bisexual flowers (above the males) are typically solitary (sometimes up to three), borne in the young leaf axils. The fruit is a globose drupe with a central stone covered by a thin pulp, which may be edible, and a thick skin usually colored red or purple.

A few more or less hardy species, for example, the Common Hackberry (*Celtis occidentalis*), are grown in temperate regions but are not outstanding, apart from the bright yellow fall leaves of some species. They like a well-drained, loamy soil. Propagation is by seeds or by grafts on stocks of *C. occidentalis*.

The fruit of *C. australis* is said to have been the 'Lotus' of the Homeric Lotus-eaters, consumption rendering them unmindful of home and family. Pliny used the name *Celtis* for an African species of *Lotus*, perhaps because of the sweet berries. The timber is used for manufacturing utensils, walking sticks and fishing rods. It is also claimed to make the best whip-handles.

Other species of *Celtis* yielding usable timber of medium to low quality, which is used locally, are *C. brasiliensis* from Brazil, the Stinkwood (*C. kraussiana*), Africa from the Cape to Ethiopia, *C. mildbraedii* from west and central tropical Africa and *C. philippinensis*, from the Philippines to New Guinea. The Granjeno (*C. iguanaea*), from tropical Central America, also has edible fruits, and *C. cinnamomea* from the Indian subcontinent and Indonesia has strongly-scented wood which when powdered is known as 'kajoo lahi.' This is used medicinally as a blood purifier and tonic.

B. N. B.

The Main Species of *Celtis*

Group I: Leaf margins toothed or serrate at least in upper half.
A *Lower surface of leaves plainly pubescent. Fruit with pitted stone.*
C. australis European Hackberry. Mediterranean region: S Europe, N Africa,
SW Asia. Tree to 25m, girth to 3m. Bark gray, like a beech (*Fagus*). Shoots hairy. Leaves ovate-lanceolate, bases wedge-shaped, upper surface with short, stiff hairs at first, falling later. Fruit globose, 9–12mm across, finally (purplish) black. Reputed to reach 1 000 years. Timber valuable, tough.
C. caucasica Caucasian Nettle Tree. Caucasus, Afghanistan, India. Tree to 20m. Closely related to *C. australis*, but leaves shorter and wider and fruit yellow. Hardier than *C. australis*.
AA *Lower surface of leaves glabrous, at least between the veins, rarely with a little sparse down. Fruit with pitted or smooth stone.*
C. occidentalis Sugarberry, Common Hackberry. S USA. Tree to 40m. Bark gray, rough, corky. Leaves ovate with cordate base, 5–10cm, petiole 1cm or more. Fruit globose, 8–9mm across, at first more or less orange, finally dark purple; stone pitted.
  var *crassifolia* has larger and thicker leaves, (9)11–15cm.
C. sinensis Chinese Hackberry. E China, Korea, Japan. Tree to 20m in the wild, little more than half that in cultivation. Leaves broadly oval, shiny, dark green, deeply toothed toward apex, petiole less than 1cm. Fruit rich orange; stone pitted.
C. bungeana Mountains of N China. Tree 10–14m. Leaves ovate to lanceolate, 5–9cm, toothed only toward apex, petiole less than 1cm. Fruit ovoid, 6–7mm across, black; stone smooth.
C. glabrata Caucasus, Asia Minor. Shrub or small tree to 4m. Shoots at first downy, quickly glabrous. Leaves ovate, 2.5–6(7) × 15–34mm, margins of upper half with coarse, deep, incurved teeth; entirely hairy and rough to the touch. Fruit globose, 4–5mm across, rusty brown; stone very slightly pitted.
C. tournefortii Balkans, Asia Minor, Crimea, Sicily. Shrub or small tree, 6–7m. Leaves ovate, 3–7cm, margins of upper half with wide, blunt teeth. Fruit orange; stone smooth. Both this and the previous species are closely related to *C. bungeana*.

Group II: Leaf margins more or less entire or slightly wavy. Fruit with pitted stone.
C. mississippiensis (*C. laevigata*) Mississippi Sugarberry or Hackberry. S USA. Tree 20–25m. Bark warty. Leaves more or less ovate, 5–10cm, the apex long, drawn out and tapering (long acuminate). Fruit (5)6–7mm across, orange, finally dark purplish, its stalk 1–2cm long, longer than the 6–10(12)mm leaf stalk.
  var *smallii* has sharply serrate leaves.
C. reticulata SW USA. Tree 10–12(15)m, sometimes shrubby. Leaves more or less ovate, 3–8(10)cm, apex typically acute. Fruit 8–9mm across, orange-red; its stalk 1cm long, about equal to length of leaf-stalk, not longer.
C. pumila SW USA. Shrub or small tree to 4(5)m. Leaves more or less ovate, 3–8cm, apex acute, larger leaf margins sometimes with a few wider spaced teeth in upper half of leaf. Fruit 6–8mm across, orange to purplish. Resembles a small *C. occidentalis*.

MORACEAE

Figs
(genus *Ficus*)

Ficus is a large pantropical genus of approximately 2000 species, mostly from the Old World but some from the New World, for example *Ficus paraensis*. Members vary from small shrubs to large trees up to 45m (150ft) tall, and they are important constituents of many upland tropical forests. They are frequently evergreen in tropical zones, but tend to become deciduous in temperate zones. Some species are glabrous (eg *F. elastica*), others hairy, or with stinging hairs (*F. minahassae*) or with silica bodies in the leaves (*F. scabra*). Leaf arrangement is usually alternate, occasionally opposite (*F. hispida*). The leaves vary from 4cm (1.5in) (eg *F. pumila*) to 50cm (20in) (eg *F. gigantifolia*) long, undivided or lobed, venation palmate or pinnate, and in shape may be asymmetrical about the midrib (*F. tinctoria*) or dimorphic; for example, in *F. pumila* the young leaves are cordate and sessile, while the older ones are large, elliptic and petiolate. Caducous stipules are universally present, usually in pairs. Also universal is the presence of latex vessels throughout the plant: the India-rubber Fig (*F. elastica*) was used extensively in rubber manufacture up to the mid-19th century.

Figs have a characteristic inflorescence, termed a *syconium* – a flask-shaped fleshy container with many minute flowers densely arranged on the inner walls. Fig flowers may be of three types: male flowers with one or two short stamens (rarely three or six), and female flowers which may be either long- or short-styled, each type with one ovary containing one ovule. The long-styled flower is capable of being fertilized to produce seed. The short-styled flower is infertile and known as a 'gall flower,' because in it the female fig insect lays her eggs and there the young insect develops to maturity inside the ovary of the flower. The difference in style length is adapted to the egg-laying habits of the insect, whose ovipositor is too short to reach the ovary of the long-styled flower. However, in her attempts, the insect effectively pollinates the stigma with pollen picked up from the male flowers she has already crawled over. The common fig insect is the gall-wasp *Blastophaga psenes* (Hymenoptera), but

it is thought that each *Ficus* species may support its own species of *Blastophaga*. The male of *Blastophaga* is small (less than 1mm), blind, and never leaves the syconium. The female is slightly larger, more mobile and after mating may leave the syconium through the pore or through the wall. Both sexes develop similarly in the ovary of the flower, which expands to form a case around the growing insect. The insect hatches by burrowing through the wall of the ovary.

Several species of fig are classed as 'strangler' figs, where the fig grows around a host plant, slowly enclosing it and often eventually killing it. This strange habit is common in tropical species, for example *F. pertusa* and *F. cordifolia*. The strangler fig begins from a seed dropped in the fork of a twig by a fig-eating mammal or bird. As the seed germinates it begins to grow downward, the roots wrapping round the host. The effect is to crush the bark, thus ringing the tree and destroying its food-bearing vessels. Eventually the fig survives as a free-standing tree.

The Edible Fig (*F. carica*) has a long history of cultivation, beginning in Syria probably before 4000 BC. Since then it has held an important place in folklore and literature. The art of fig culture was first documented by the Greek poet Archilochus, around 700 BC, and there are many references to the fig in the Bible. It grows successfully in many tropical and some temperate habitats, usually on dry, higher ground. The main areas of cultivation are California, Turkey, Greece and Italy. The Common Fig is a small tree, less than 10m (33ft) tall, with large palmately-lobed leaves 10–20cm (4–8in) long. There are two fruiting types, Adriatic and Smyrna. The more common Adriatic Fig does not have male flowers and the fig fruits develop from the female flowers without the need for pollination and fertilization. Its seeds are undeveloped and infertile. The Smyrna Fig also has no male flowers, but differs in that the female flowers require pollination. To achieve this, branches of wild figs with male flowers are attached to Smyrna Fig trees at the time fig wasps are expected to emerge, thus allowing cross-pollination. The Wild Fig with male flowers is known as the Caprifig.

There are many species of *Ficus* with edible fruits, for example *F. glomerata*, a common tree of eastern Asia. Although edible, the fruits are hardly palatable by Western standards, the figs being full of insects or hard seeds. *F. religiosa* (Peepul Tree) and *F. pertusa* are Indian species

The normal first colonizers of bare rock surfaces are microorganisms and bryophytes and although some of these lower plants are apparent as brown mats on this bare rock, a seedling wild fig (*Ficus* sp) has managed to gain a foothold, using the crevices as anchorage points and drawing up water through long adventitious roots from the river below. The original seed almost certainly reached this position and germinated during a flood period when the water level was much higher.

which are often planted as shade trees because of their dense spreading crowns. Several species are used as host trees for the lac insect, for example *F. cunia* and *F. rumphii*. The insect secretes a resinous substance (lac) which in its purified form (shellac) is used for several industrial purposes, particularly in the manufacture of varnish and for electrical insulation. In temperate zones some species are grown as houseplants. The commonest is the Rubber Plant, which is a sapling of *F. elastica* var *decora*. Also grown are the Climbing Fig (*F. pumila*) and the Weeping Fig or

Java Willow (*F. benjamina*). A number of species can be grown outside in warm temperate areas, for example the Moreton Bay Fig (*F. macrophylla*).

Several species of the genus are called banyans, the best known being *F. benghalensis*. This species is a large tree which though indigenous to the Himalayan foothills is now widespread throughout India, as for centuries it has been planted in many villages for the excellent shade it provides. The Hindus also regard it as sacred, for it is said that Buddha once meditated beneath a banyan tree.

Perhaps its most interesting botanical features are its pillar-like aerial roots. These roots grow vertically downward from the branches and, once established in the ground below, quickly thicken, so that the tree assumes the unusual appearance of being supported by pillars. By this manner of growth the tree is able to spread outward almost indefinitely and many examples are of immense size and great antiquity. Some specimens probably cover the largest area of all the living plants; one giant tree growing in the Andhra Valley in India is quoted as having 'a crown measuring 600m (2 000ft) in circumference' and being supported by 320 aerial pillar-roots. There was at one time a very old specimen growing in the Calcutta Botanic Garden which had over 460 such roots around its main trunk, and also another in Sri Lanka with over 300 pillars, whose umbrella-like crown provided enough shade to cover an entire village.　　　　　　　　　　　S. W. J.

The Main Species of *Ficus*

Section *Urostigma*
Monoecious. Figs with small bracts around the apical pore and at the base. Flower tube 3-, rarely 4- or 2-lobed; 1 stamen. Fruits usually in axillary pairs. A large group from Asia, Australia, Africa and America, many of which are climbers and/or epiphytic ('stranglers').

F. elastica India-rubber Fig, Caoutchouc Tree. India, SE Asia. Seedlings epiphytic, becoming large trees to 60m with thick, buttressed, multiple trunks and spreading surface roots. Leaves thick, 12–30 × 6–15cm, elliptic, apex and base more or less rounded, surface smooth and glossy. Terminal bud sheathed by only 1 stipule (instead of the more usual 2 stipules). Figs sessile, spherical, about 1cm diameter, surface smooth, pale green with darker flecks.

F. religiosa Bo-tree, Peepul Tree. India. Seedlings epiphytic, becoming large trees with many trunks and dense leaf canopies. Leaves thin, to 17 × 12cm, more or less triangular, the apex drawn out into a slender tip to 6cm. Figs sessile, cylindrical, surface smooth, green to purple with bright red flecks.

F. benjamina Weeping Fig, Benjamin Banyan, Java Willow. India, SE Asia. Several distinct varieties:

> var *benjamina* Tree to 30m with aerial roots, trunks never buttressed, branches drooping. Leaves thin, leathery, to 11 × 5cm, elliptic, broader toward the base, the apex drawn out to a long curving tip. Figs on short stalks, spherical to cylindrical, about 1cm long, surface smooth, green, bright red and/or black flecked with white. Cultivated for its ornamental value.

> var *comosa* Tufted Fig. As above but leaves in dense clusters at the tips of shoots. Figs on short stalks, more or less spherical, 2cm, surface yellow to orange.

> var *nuda* As above but leaves narrow. Figs pale green to reddish-brown, the bracts at the base of the fig falling before the fruit is mature.

F. benghalensis Banyan Fig. India. Large trees with multiple, buttressed trunks supporting dense leaf canopies. Spreading surface roots. Leaves leathery, 15–25 × 12–17cm, ovate, the apex rounded or tipped by a short point, base more or less rounded, surface with soft velvet-like covering of short hairs. Figs sessile, spherical to cylindrical, about 2cm long, surface hairy, bright red flecked with white. Prominent yellow bracts at base of fig.

F. thonningii C and W Africa. Common trees, epiphytic as seedlings, becoming large trees with multiple buttressed trunks and dense leaf canopies. Leaves leathery, smooth, about 14 × 5cm, elliptic, apex and base broadly rounded, upper surface dark green, lower surface light green. Figs sessile, sometimes solitary, more or less cylindrical, about 1.5cm long, surface sparsely hairy, green flecked with white.

F. rubiginosa Rusty-leaved Fig. Australia. Seedlings epiphytic, becoming large trees with multiple trunks which are buttressed, though not conspicuously so. Leaves leathery, to 17 × 6cm, elliptic, apex and base rounded, both surfaces rough in texture, red-brown when young, becoming smooth when mature. Figs on short stalks, spherical, about 1.5cm diameter, surface smooth to very rough, green, yellow or rust-colored, flecked with green or white.

F. pretoriae Wonderboom. S Africa. Tree to 23m with a broad, spreading crown, supported by many trunks. Leaves stiff, papery, elliptic, 7.5–20cm long, up to 7cm wide, apex more or less acute, base rounded to shallowly cordate, surface dull above without hydathodes (water-secreting glands) or hairs. Figs singly or in pairs in leaf axils or clustered in the axils of leaf scars, very short-stalked, spherical to broadly pear-shaped, approximately 0.7cm diameter, surface green to reddish-brown, hairy, flecked with greenish-white. Basal bracts green, becoming red with age.

Section *Pharmacosycea*
Monoecious. Figs usually solitary and lacking basal bracts. Flower tube 4-lobed; stamens 1–3, usually 2. Trees, never climbers or stranglers. Mainly tropical America, but a few species in Asia and one in Madagascar.

F. maxima C America, W Indies, Amazon basin. Fairly common. Tree to 30m. Leaves thin, papery, 6–20 × 2–9cm, variable in shape, usually elliptic, apex blunt or pointed, base continuing into short petiole. Figs short-stalked, spherical, 1–2cm diameter, surface smooth, sometimes sparsely hairy, green or yellowish-green, apical pore 1–2mm diameter.

F. insipida C America, from Mexico to S Brazil. Tree to 40m, trunk buttressed. Leaves thick, leathery, 5–25 × 1–11cm, narrowly to broadly elliptic, apex blunt or pointed, base narrowing into petiole. Figs sessile or short-stalked, spherical, 1.5–3cm diameter, green or yellow, apical pore 2–4mm diameter.

F. gigantoscyce Colombia. Tree to 20m. Leaves 13–28 × 5–15cm, elliptic, apex acute, sometimes with a distinct tip, base deeply cordate forming 2 deep lobes. Figs very large, spherical, 3–8cm diameter, yellow or reddish.

Section *Sycomorus*
Monoecious. Figs pear- or top-shaped, in clusters on leafless stems, branches and on the main trunk. Stamens 1 or 2, rarely 3. Africa, SW Asia and Australia.

F. sycomorus Mulberry Fig, Pharaoh's Fig. N to E Africa, SW Asia. Small tree to 15m. Leaves rough, leathery, to 15 × 13cm, broadly ovate, margins undulate, the apex bluntly rounded, the base cordate, upper surface glabrous, dark green, lower surface paler, slightly hairy. Figs on slender stalks, pear-shaped, to 3cm long, surface green with dense velvet-like covering of white hairs.

F. racemosa Cluster Fig. India, SE Asia, Australia. Tree to 25m with spreading crown. Leaves thin, leathery, margins undulate, elliptic or ovate, to 20 × 8cm, apex pointed, base cordate, surface smooth and glossy with a silvery appearance. Figs in large clusters borne directly on the trunk and leafless parts of branches, shortly pear-shaped, to 3cm long, green becoming bright red flecked with white at maturity.

Section *Ficus*
Dioecious. Figs in clusters or pairs on leafless branches or behind leaves. Female flowers with styles much longer than those of gall-flowers. 2 stamens (4 in *F. carica*). Trees and climbers. Many species, in Africa, Asia and Australasia.

F. carica Edible Fig, Cultivated Fig. Native of SW Asia. Small spreading tree to about 4m, deciduous in temperate climates. Leaves broadly lobed, large, 10–20 × 10–20cm, base truncate or rounded, lower surface sometimes sparsely covered with rough hairs. Male flowers with 4 stamens. Figs usually in pairs or singly on leafless branches or behind leaves, pear-shaped; surface usually green, sometimes tinged with purple or brown. Extensively cultivated; many varieties. The Wild Fig, var *caprificus*, is very variable.

F. pumila Climbing Fig. Asia, common in China and Japan. Vine-like, attaching itself to rocks, buildings etc by short sticky roots

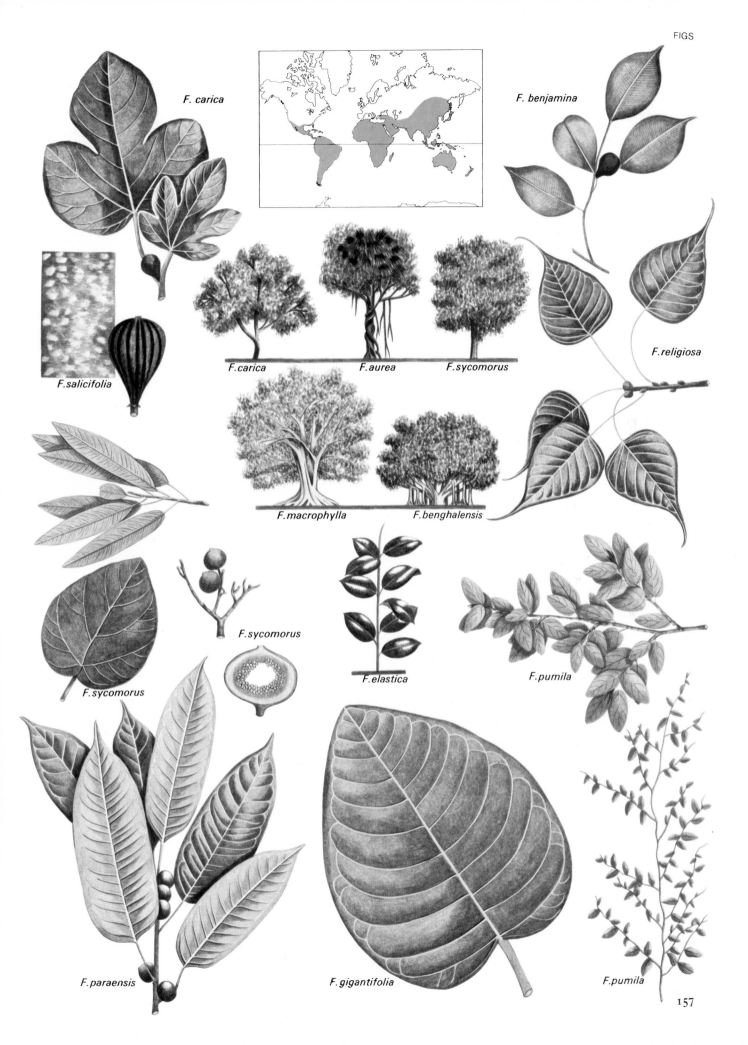

F. carica

F. benjamina

F.salicifolia

F.carica   F.aurea   F.sycomorus

F.religiosa

F.macrophylla   F.benghalensis

F.sycomorus

F.sycomorus

F.elastica

F.pumila

F.paraensis

F.gigantifolia

F.pumila

which develop at the nodes. Leaves dimorphic, ie young leaves sessile, small, heart-shaped; older leaves petiolate, larger, to 11 × 4cm, elliptic, surface smooth, glabrous, or lower surface sparsely hairy. Figs on short, thick stalks, mostly solitary, more or less cylindrical with a prominent apex, large, to 6 × 3.5cm, surface pale green or gray flecked with white, densely hairy. Cultivated. Young specimens popular as house plants.

F. hispida Opposite-leaved Fig. India, SE Asia and N Australia. Shrub or small tree with hairy twigs. Leaves opposite on some branches, alternate on others, large, ovate, to 31 × 11cm, apex blunt or sharply pointed, base rounded, both surfaces very rough, the upper surface having a dense covering of rigid hairs, hydathodes present, margins toothed. Figs on short stalks, in axillary pairs, more or less spherical, very hairy, green or yellow flecked with white. 3 bracts prominent at the base of each fig. The fruits of this species are reputed to be poisonous.

F. auriculata Roxburgh Fig. India, SE Asia into China. Shrub. Leaves with long petioles, ovate, very large, up to and sometimes exceeding 46 × 35cm, base deeply cordate, the 2 lobes sometimes overlapping or becoming united, apex acute, upper surface with scattered hydathodes, lower surface hairy. Figs in clusters on the main branches and trunk, on thick stalks, pear-shaped, very large, up to 6.5cm diameter, 5cm long, surface greenish-white to brown with red flecks, hairy. 3 large bracts at the base of each fig.

F. tinctoria Dye Fig, Humped Fig (on account of the asymmetry of the leaves). SE China, Philippines, Indonesia, N Australia. Leaves thin, approximately ovate, the blade unequal in shape about the midrib, to 18 × 7cm, apex acute, base rounded or narrowing into petiole, margins angular, as in holly (*Ilex*), surface hairless with scattered hydathodes. Figs axillary, singly or in pairs, more or less sessile, spherical, about 1cm diameter, surface sometimes rough and hairy, yellowish-green flecked with paler green. The juice from the fruits is used as a base for a green dye. The bark fibers are used to make poor quality cordage and those of young shoots to make fishing nets.

F. minahassae Philippines, Sulawesi (Celebes). Tree. Young twigs with sharp stinging hairs. Leaves ovate, to 20 × 12.5cm, apex rounded to acute, base deeply cordate, the lobes meeting or overlapping, margins finely toothed and fringed with hairs, both upper and lower surfaces with rigid hairs and many scattered hydathodes. Fruits in clusters on long rope-like spurs arising from the main trunk and up to 3m long. Figs very small, less than 0.5cm diameter, red.

F. pseudopalma Palm-like Fig. Philippines. Small tree to 7.5m. Leaves papery, obovate, large, to 100 × 15cm, margin coarsely toothed near the apex, entire at the base, upper surface glossy with scattered hydathodes. Figs short-stalked up to 4 × 2cm, surface ribbed lengthwise, dark brown to green/purple, with raised white flecks. Basal bracts prominent.

Mulberries
(genus *Morus*)

The genus *Morus* is best known for its fruit, the mulberry. All its members are deciduous and most are tropical. There are probably about 12 distinct species of *Morus*, although over 100 have been described, on the basis of the large variation found in the fruits. The cultivated forms are of Asiatic and American origin.

In common with the rest of the Moraceae, the milky sap from cut *Morus* stems contains latex. The leaves are cordate, simple or lobed, with three to five veins originating at the junction of the leaf blade with the petiole. Leaf shapes may vary from tree to tree, or even on the same branch. The flowers are unisexual, small and individually inconspicuous with male and female on the same tree. They are clustered into green, pendulous, male or female catkins. The mulberry fruits form around a central core in blackberry-like clusters, in which the colored juicy parts have developed from the perianth segments of the individual flowers. The seeds are small, hard and are embedded in the flesh. Cultivated mulberries may be about 2cm (0.8in) long, but those from the wild are usually less than 1cm long.

The White Mulberry (*Morus alba*) was probably the parent of the original American 'Downing' Mulberry, selected for its fruit yield. It forms a wide-spreading tree up to 15m (50ft) tall, with gray bark and small leaves, 5–15cm (2–16in) long, which are shiny above and may be hairy beneath, with coarsely-toothed margins. The fruits are red. It is thought to have escaped from China, its country of origin, to North America. In China its primary functions were to provide silk-worm fodder from the soft tender leaves and also to provide timber. It was not selected for its fruit until it became established in America. With *Catalpa ovata*, the White Mulberry used to be considered one of the two most important timber trees of China, and most Chinese homesteads had one or two of each planted nearby. The expression 'Sang Tzu' means literally 'Land of the mulberry and catalpa,' and is still a common phrase in Chinese usage meaning 'home' or 'homeland.'

The Russian Mulberry (*M. alba* var *tatarica*) is a very hardy variety not grown for its fruit but as an ornamental low-growing shrub in cold northerly climates.

The Red or American Mulberry (*M. rubra*) is a native of North America and a common tree of American woodland. It may reach 12–20m (40–65ft) in height and has larger, more bluntly-toothed leaves than *M. alba*. The fruits are red to purple, and drop from the branches when ripe. The fallen fruit is juicy and very sweet, and is collected to make pies, jams and jellies. From American literature it is known that the mulberry was an important food source of the North American Indians and the early explorers and settlers. It also provides useful timber.

The Black, Persian or English Mulberry (*M. nigra*) is the most commonly cultivated species in Europe. It attains a height of no more than 10m (33ft), the bark is brown and the leaf has a rough upper surface and blunt-toothed margins. The fruits are purple to black. A native of Persia, it was introduced into Europe in the early 16th century, some time before *M. alba*. *Morus nigra* is reputedly slow-growing and long-lived, with specimens recorded to be 300 years old.

In Africa, large tree species are more common than shrubs. *Morus mesozygia* is a central African species, up to 30m (100ft) tall. It is utilized as a shade tree; the top branches are removed and the lateral branches are weighted, to produce an umbrella-shaped crown. It yields edible mulberries, but they are small and not usually harvested.

S. W. J.

The Main Species of *Morus*

M. alba White Mulberry. A native of China; escapes have become naturalized in N America and Europe. Tree to 15m with spreading, umbrella-shaped crown, branches gray to yellow-gray, bark smooth, young twigs slender. Leaves thin, small, 5–15cm, broadly ovate, sometimes almost orbicular, or triangular, apex pointed; surface pale green, smooth and rather glossy above, hairy beneath, particularly on veins and in vein-axils; margins irregularly lobed, coarsely toothed. Fruit on short stalks as long as fruits, white to pinkish-purple, usually red when ripe, globose, 2cm diameter, often smaller in wild specimens; sweet. Widely cultivated, the leaves being used as food for silkworms. There are numerous varieties, some useful as ornamental shrubs and trees.

var *heterophylla* Variously lobed leaves on same plant.
var *laciniata* Leaf margins jaggedly toothed.
var *macrophylla* Large leaves to 30cm.
var *pendula* Pendulous habit.
var *tatarica* Hardy, shrubby form.

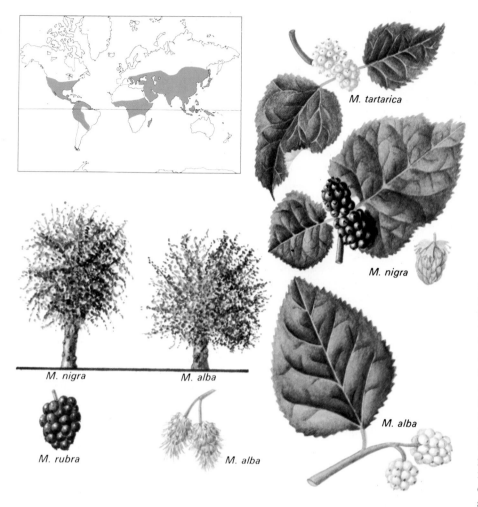

M. tartarica

M. nigra

M. alba

M. nigra

M. alba

M. rubra

M. alba

Osage Orange
(genus *Maclura*)

The Osage Orange (*Maclura pomifera*) – the only member of its genus – is a fast-growing spiny, deciduous tree, up to 18m (6oft) tall. It is native to the fertile lands of Arkansas and Texas, and naturalized elsewhere in the United States. The name Osage derives from the Osage river, the largest tributary of the Missouri river, and is also the name of a tribe of North American Indians. It is distinguished by its orange, fissured bark and the sharp spines on the young shoots and leaf stalks (var *inermis* has no spines on the shoots). The leaves are alternate, ovate, with pointed tips, and glossy green above with whitish veins below. The leaves turn bright yellow in the fall. Crushed leaves and shoots yield a sticky milky latex that can be a mild skin irritant. The flowers are unisexual, with male and female occurring on separate trees in inconspicuous globose clusters. The fertilized female flowers fuse together to form a globose, yellow-green, orange-like false fruit up to 13cm (5in) in diameter which contains many hard true fruits (drupelets) and is full of milky latex. It is inedible.

var *venosa* Leaves broadly diamond-shaped with conspicuous pale yellow or white veins.

The following five species are closely related to *M. alba*.

M. serrata NW Himalaya. Similar to *M. alba*, but young shoots and leaves with velvet-like covering of short hairs. Styles longer, hairy, united below (styles free in *M. alba*). Fruit not juicy.

M. laevigata E India. Fruit more or less cylindrical in shape, to 5cm long.

M. macroura Widespread in Java and Sumatra. Similar to *M. laevigata*.

M. indica A component of secondary forests in C Africa. Young shoots hairy. Leaves small, 3–12 × 2.8cm, surface dark green, rough.

M. celtidifolia C America from Mexico to Peru. Bears edible fruit.

M. rubra Red or American Mulberry. Common in woods throughout N America. Tree to 20m with wide, spreading crown. Leaves larger than those of *M. alba*, 8–20cm, ovate to oblong, surface dull green, rough above, hairy beneath, margins bluntly toothed. Fruits globose, 3–4cm diameter, reddish-purple, very sweet. A popular source of edible fruit.

'Nana' A slow-growing, dwarf form with a compact habit.

M. nigra Black, English or Persian Mulberry. Native of Iran, cultivated and perhaps also naturalized in parts of Europe. Small spreading tree to 10m. Young twigs thick, dark brown with a velvet-like hairy covering. Leaves thick, 5–20cm long, ovate with deeply cordate base and abruptly acute apex; surface dull, dark green, rough above, hairy beneath; margins sometimes lobed, coarsely and sharply toothed. Fruits more or less sessile, dark purple, about 2cm diameter, acid, becoming sweet only when completely ripe; of good quality, although considered inferior to that of *M. rubra*. In the past the leaves have been used for silkworm fodder.

M. mesozygia Fairly common in C Africa, planted to provide shade. Large tree to 30m with spreading umbrella-shaped crown. Young shoots hairless, reddish-brown. Leaves rather thin, 7–11 × 3–7cm, elliptic, base shallowly cordate, surface hairless above, sparsely hairy on veins and in axils beneath. Fruits on long stalks, about 1cm diameter, sweet, rather dry in texture.

Fruits and foliage of the Osage Orange (*Maclura pomifera*), a native of Arkansas and Texas, United States. The remarkable orange-like fruits are in fact 'false fruits,' each mass comprising a large number of true fruits fused together. These fruits may be attractive but are not edible.

Outside its native range the fruits are less frequently seen, since trees of opposite sex are rarely close enough for the female flowers to be fertilized.

The Osage Orange was once very widely used as a thorny hedging plant throughout America, and although still used as such, its decline was in part due to the introduction of more efficient, barbed-wire fences. It grows well in a wide range of soils, including those that are poor, its spreading roots making it resistant to drought. It is propagated by seeds, layering or root cuttings. The timber is hard, strong and flexible, and is used for fence posts. When first cut, the wood is bright orange, later discoloring to brown. It was once used by the North American Indians for making bows and fighting clubs (hence its other popular name – Bow wood) and is still valued as such by present-day archers.

F. B. H.

Paper Mulberry
(genus *Broussonetia*)

Broussonetia comprises two species of deciduous plants, one a tree, the other shrubby. They are natives of northeastern Asia (China, Japan, Korea), allied to the mulberries (*Morus* spp), but with male and female flowers on different plants.

The Paper Mulberry (*B. papyrifera*) from China and Japan is the only species that is cultivated. It is a tough, quick-growing tree reaching 12m (40ft), with a milky latex. It is tolerant of city pollution and moisture-sapping winds of hot, dry regions. Characteristic features are its rounded crown, twisted trunks and large, 7–20cm (2.8–8in), alternate, ovate, toothed leaves that are woolly beneath. The petiole is 3–10cm (1.2–4in) long. However, leaf shape is variable, some being distinctly lobed; several shapes may appear on the same shoot. Trees are unisexual with male and female flowers on different plants, the males in 3.5–7.5cm (1.4–3in) pendulous catkins and the females in rounded clusters. After fertilization, the female flowers turn into red, globular fruits which are produced in such profusion and have such a high viability that seedlings become a problem around a mature tree.

Shoot and trunk of *Broussonetia kazinoki*, a rare shrub in cultivation and native to China and Japan. Leaf shape, even on a single shoot, is highly variable.

Broussonetia kazinoki is a shrub to about 4m (13ft) which is much less attractive than the previous species. It differs by having male catkins not reaching 2cm (0.8in) long and glabrous or virtually glabrous leaves and petioles to only 2cm (0.8in) long.

The Paper Mulberry is frequently grown throughout eastern Asia, less commonly in southern Europe and eastern North America. It will grow in almost any soil but must have full sun. In southeast Asia the bark is used to make paper and cloth, whence the popular name.

F. B. H.

Willows, Sallows, Osiers
(genus *Salix*)

Salix is a large, well-known genus of 300 or more species popularly known as willows, sallows and osiers. The great majority of species occur in cool temperate or colder situations in the Northern Hemisphere; they are rare in most parts of the tropics and the Southern Hemisphere, and are totally absent from Australasia.

Willows vary from creeping shrubs a few centimeters high to tall trees up to 18m (60ft) or more, but very few are forest trees. Most occur in rather open places, the larger species usually in swampy areas or along streams and rivers, the smaller species more often in boggy places on heaths and moors or in damp, stony ground on mountains and in the Arctic. Some species send masses of rootlets into

Below Osiers are cut willow twigs (*Salix* spp) used for basket-making. First they are dried, as here, but before being used they are soaked in water to make them supple. *Opposite* Magnificent specimens of Crack Willow (*Salix fragilis*) spread their branches over a river. Many of the larger willows grow in swampy or riverside situations.

water by the side of which they grow. In the White Willow (*Salix alba*) they are whitish and in the Crack Willow (*S. fragilis*) red. The small seeds, each with a tuft of hairs, are easily scattered by the wind and many species of *Salix* are strong colonizers of wasteland or newly exposed, neglected or reclaimed ground, in some cases quickly forming dense thickets.

The flowers are borne in rather stiff catkins, the male and female on different trees. Each flower is borne in the axil of a scale, and consists of a single ovary with two stigmas in the case of the female and a small group of two to about 12 stamens in the case of the male, together with one or two small, club-shaped glands which secrete nectar and are considered by some to represent the vestiges of a perianth. These characters, among others, are used to divide the genus into three major groups or subgenera, all of which are well represented in most north temperate regions. In the main, subgenus *Salix* (*Amerina*) consists of trees or tall shrubs with narrow and pointed leaves (true willows), subgenus *Caprisalix* of tall or short shrubs with narrow and pointed or broad and rounded or blunt leaves (osiers and sallows respectively), and subgenus *Chamaetia* of dwarf, creeping mountain or Arctic shrubs with small, broad and rounded or blunt leaves (dwarf willows).

Hybridization between different species of *Salix* is a very widespread phenomenon and many artificial hybrids have been made, to add to the considerable number of natural ones. At least 180 hybrids have been listed, about 40 of these being triple or quadruple ones. Since most of these hybrids are fully fertile, and can cross with their parental species or with other species or hybrids, the boundaries between many species have become somewhat blurred and the identification of specimens of *Salix* can be very difficult. Any one species is able to cross successfully with many others but, in general, species of subgenus *Salix* (true willows) do not hybridize with species of the other two subgenera, although the latter do interbreed. A notable exception is the Almond-leaved Willow (*S. triandra*) which, although a true willow, hybridizes with certain species of osier and sallow. In the past, much *Salix* hybridization has been carried out by taxonomists and geneticists in Sweden, and one plant has been obtained with 13 different species in its parentage.

Propagation of willows is easily effected by leafless cuttings and by seeds, but because of the ease with which hybridiza-

The Main Species of *Salix*

Subgenus *Salix (Amerina)*
The true willows. Male flowers with 2 to about 12 stamens and 2 nectaries. Catkins long and narrow, arising from lateral buds of the previous year, appearing with or after the leaves.

S. alba White Willow. Lowland regions from W Europe to C Asia. Tree to 25m with upward-growing main branches, forming a rather narrow shape, and often with pendulous twigs. Leaves long and narrow, with white silky hairs on both surfaces. Male flowers with 2 stamens.

> var *coerulea* Cricket-bat Willow. Differs in its more erect growth-habit and bluish-gray leaves which lose their silky hairs during the summer. Most cricket-bat willows are female and may belong to a single clone.

> var *vitellina* Golden Willow. Differs in its bright yellow or orange first-year shoots, and the leaves also lose their hairs during the summer. It is most often pruned hard to produce thickets of colored suckers. A commonly grown form known as 'Chermesina' (Coral-bark Willow) has bright red shoots. The pendulous form of this variety is held to be one of the parents of the most commonly cultivated weeping willow, known as *S. × chrysocoma*. The other putative parent is *S. babylonica*.

S. babylonica One of the so-called 'weeping willows,' uncommon and not particularly hardy in Europe. Probably native to Iran. Tree to 15m with widely spreading main branches and long, pendulous ('weeping') twigs. Leaves long and narrow, smooth. Male flowers with 2 stamens.

S. fragilis Crack Willow. Europe, W Asia. Tree to 27m with spreading main branches, forming a broad crown, and twigs which are very fragile at their joints. Leaves long and narrow, deeper green than those of *S. alba* and losing their hairs when still

The Dwarf Willow (*Salix herbacea*) is a creeping shrub no more than 5cm (2in) tall. This arctic and temperate mountain species forms a close mat of short shoots from an underground stem.

very young. Male flowers with 2 stamens, but most trees are females. Hybrids between this and *S. alba* are common.

S. pentandra Bay-leaved Willow. Europe, W Asia. Tree to 18m. Leaves long and pointed but broader than in other species of this group (up to 5cm wide). Male flowers with usually 5(12) stamens. A very handsome species, which commonly hybridizes with *S. alba* and *S. fragilis*.

S. triandra Almond-leaved Willow. Europe, Asia. Tall shrub or small tree to 9m. Leaves long and pointed, smaller than in other species of this group, dark green and smooth. Male flowers with 3 stamens. An attractive shrub, commonly grown also as an osier, which forms hybrids with species not only of this group but also with *S. viminalis* and others in subgenus *Caprisalix*.

S. nigra Black Willow. N America. Tree to 30m. Leaves long and narrow, with sparse hairs especially near the main vein. Male flowers with 3–7 stamens. Quite commonly cultivated in Europe, where it usually reaches only 9–12m and resembles a small, densely branched *S. alba*. There are related species in S America and S Africa, where the genus as a whole is rare.

Subgenus *Caprisalix*
The osiers and sallows. Male flowers with 2 stamens and 1 nectary. Catkins short, arising from lateral buds of the previous year, appearing with or before the leaves.

S. viminalis Comon Osier. Europe, Asia. Tall shrub or small tree to 6m with very long, gray to yellowish, straight twigs which are very hairy when young. Leaves very long and narrow, smooth above but with dense silky hairs beneath. Stamens separate. This species hybridizes with many others, particularly *S. triandra*, *S. purpurea* and various sallows, and several hybrids involving 3 species occur.

S. elaeagnos Hoary Willow. C and S Europe, W Asia. Shrub to 5m, resembling a slender *S. viminalis* but with less hairy twigs and partially fused stamens. A characteristic species of mountain rivers in C Europe.

S. purpurea Purple Willow. Europe, Asia. Shrub to 5m with slender, smooth, yellowish to reddish twigs. Leaves long and narrow, smooth, very pale beneath, distinctive among the genus in that at least some of them are borne oppositely rather than alternately. Stamens fused, appearing as if one but with two anthers. Hybrids occur with various sallows and with *S. viminalis*. In the latter hybrid the stamens are intermediate between those of the parents, being fused in the bottom half and separate above.

S. daphnoides Violet Willow. Europe (but not Britain) to C Asia, the Himalaya. Tall shrub or tree to 9m with long, straight, purple twigs covered with a whitish, waxy bloom. Leaves long and rather narrow, soon smooth. Stamens separate. Commonly cultivated for its attractive twigs, for which it is pruned hard.

S. caprea Sallow, Goat Willow, Pussy Willow. Europe and W Asia. Shrub or small tree to 9m with strong twigs at first hairy but soon smooth. Leaves broad, blunt at the apex, densely and softly hairy beneath. Stamens separate. A very familiar plant in NW Europe, the twigs with male catkins being collected for decoration in the spring, especially on Palm Sunday. There are two common and very closely related species which often hybridize with each other and with *S. caprea*: *S. cinerea* (Gray Sallow), differing in its narrower leaves with sparser hairs, more persistently hairy twigs, and raised striations under the bark of two-year-old branchlets; *S. aurita* (Eared Sallow), a smaller plant, differing from *S. cinerea* in its wrinkled leaves and widely spreading twigs.

S. nigricans Dark-leaved Willow. N and C Europe, Asia. Shrub to 4m with hairy, dull twigs. Leaves broad, blunt at the apex, more or less hairy beneath, becoming blackish when dried. A characteristic upland species, only on mountains in the south of its range.

S. phylicifolia Tea-leaved Willow. N and C Europe. Shrub to 4m with smooth twigs. Leaves oval, pointed, hairless when mature. A plant which grows in similar habitats to, and often with, *S. nigricans*, with which it very often hybridizes and forms a range of intermediates.

S. repens Creeping Willow. Europe, Asia. Small shrub to about 1.2m, with creeping (often underground) main stems and usually ascending, somewhat hairy twigs.

Leaves small, very variable in shape and hairiness, usually oval and at least slightly hairy. This variable species occupies a wide range of habitats. The more distinctive forms are considered by some to be separate species, eg *S. rosmarinifolia*, from C Europe, with very narrow leaves and short catkins, and *S. arenaria* (*S. argentea*) from damp sand-dunes on the Atlantic coasts of Europe, with very hairy twigs and dense silvery hairs on the leaves. Both the latter are popular with gardeners.

S. lanata Woolly Willow. Arctic and subarctic Europe and Asia. Small shrub to 1.2m with stout, densely hairy twigs. Leaves oval, pointed, with dense white hairs on both surfaces. Catkins cylindrical, with golden-yellow hairs so that even the female plants are very attractive in flower. A very popular garden shrub.

Subgenus *Chamaetia*
The dwarf willows. Male flowers with 2 stamens and 1 or 2 nectaries. Catkins short, arising from terminal buds of the previous year, appearing with or after the leaves.

S. herbacea Dwarf Willow. Arctic lowlands and temperate mountains of Europe and N America. A very dwarf shrub rarely over about 5cm high. Leaves about 13mm long, often almost circular, smooth and shining with rather prominent veins. Catkins very short, few-flowered. A characteristic plant

of mountaintops in temperate Europe, often forming large patches by its creeping underground stems. Commonly described as the smallest shrub, though in reality there are many other equally dwarf shrubs in *Salix* and other groups. It hybridizes with many other dwarf willows.

S. arctica Arctic Willow. Arctic regions. Dwarf shrub a few centimeters high with small, broad, pointed, more or less smooth leaves with slightly prominent veins. Catkins cylindrical. Representative of a large group of dwarf arctic willows, differing from *S. herbacea* in that the stems creep on the surface of the ground, but also often forming large patches.

S. retusa Mountains of C Europe. Similar to *S. arctica* but the leaves often rounded or notched at the apex and the catkins shorter. This and some related species more or less replace the *S. arctica* group on the mountains of the temperate zone.

S. reticulata Reticulate Willow. Arctic lowlands and temperate mountains of Europe, Asia and N America. Dwarf shrub a few centimetres high with broad, rounded, slightly hairy leaves with prominent veins beneath but with impressed veins above. Catkins narrow, on long stalks. Another patch-forming dwarf willow with surface-creeping stems, this is very distinctive and prized by rock-gardeners.

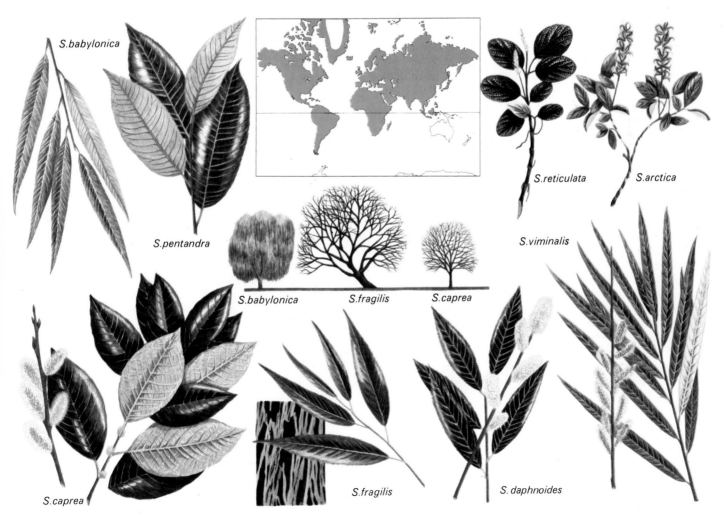

S.babylonica

S.reticulata S.arctica

S.pentandra

S.viminalis

S.babylonica S.fragilis S.caprea

S.caprea

S.fragilis

S.daphnoides

tion takes place, seeds should only be used if the parentage is beyond doubt. 'Weeping' forms can be grafted on tall stems. Any average soil, provided there is an ample water supply, is suitable – for example a deep heavy loam by a waterside.

The stems of willows, whether a year or two old or ancient trunks, show remarkable powers of regeneration, particularly in the winter and early spring before the leaves appear. *Salix* sticks pushed into the ground will quickly take root, and this characteristic, together with a very rapid growth rate, is much exploited.

Diseases and pests are numerous and only a selection can be mentioned here. Amongst fungus diseases are: *Uncinula aduncta = U. salicis* (Erysiphales), which attacks the leaves; *Rhytisma salicinum* (Phacidiales), which forms raised blackish scabs on leaves of *S. caprea*, *S. alba* and other species; *Venturia chlorospora* (Pleosporales) (Willow Scab), which infects leaves and twigs, especially of *S. fragilis* var *decipiens*, turning them black and in wet weather causing defoliation. More serious is *Physalospora miyabeana* (Black Canker of willow). This attacks especially *S. alba* var *vitellina* and causes a canker on the stems, rendering them useless for basketmaking. Amongst rust fungi (Uredinales) are species of *Melampsora* which infect osiers and make the stems unfit for basketmaking. Watermark disease of Cricket-bat Willow is caused by the bacterium *Erwinia salicis* (*Bacterium salicis*) which penetrates the vascular system, causing dieback. Infected wood is deeply stained and of no value for making cricket bats. Bracket fungi (Aphyllophorales) causing rotting of the stem include *Leitiporus sulphureus* (*Polyporus sulphureus*), *Polyporus varius*, *P. squamosus*, *Trametes suaveolens* and *Pseudotrametes gibbosa* (*Trametes gibbosa*).

Insect pests of willows are unusually numerous. They include Willow aphids which cause wood staining, distortion of all parts and, ultimately, death. *Pterocomma populea* and *Melanoxantherum salicis* are just two species liable to occur in vast colonies. Aphids can be controlled by a number of the new insecticides, including systemic ones, but the old nicotine-soap wash is still very effective. Willow leaf beetles and Willow moths are also known, the leaves being the main sufferers. There is also a Willow weevil or borer, *Cryptorhyncidius lapathi*, which is more serious on young trees, including the Cricket-bat Willow. The grubs rupture the tissues and the lesions can be secondarily infected by bacteria and fungi. Finally, willows are liable to gall formation, which occurs on leaves, in buds and on shoots. Galls are the plant's response to attacks from various insects and other invertebrate animals (mites etc). In general galls are not particularly harmful to the host plant, but they may be considered unsightly.

Willow timber is light, fairly soft, but tough and elastic and not given to splintering when subjected to strain. It is thus useful for making boxes, polo balls, steamer paddles, tool handles and, because it is relatively nonflammable, for the brake blocks of railway stock. Cricket bats are made from the Cricket-bat Willow (*Salix alba* var *coerulea*), which can be harvested about 12 years after planting. Baskets and other wickerwork (including lobster pots) are made from the young (mostly one-year-old) sucker shoots of the Common Osier (*S. viminalis*) and other osiers and true willows. These species can be encouraged to put out long, straight, flexible suckers by severe pruning (pollarding) of old trunks, from which the suckers can be harvested annually.

Willow thickets are commonly associated with mammals which eat bark, branches and leaves, while the buds and catkins may provide food for a number of bird species. The glucoside salicin, which has mild analgesic properties, is widely distributed in the genus and is extracted from the bark of, for example, *S. purpurea* and its hybrid with *S. viminalis* (*S. × rubra*). The use of salicin has now been virtually abandoned in favor of acetylsalicylic acid (well-known as aspirin) and other synthetic analgesics.

Willows generally may be cultivated for their rapid growth (*S. alba* has been measured to grow 20m (65ft) in 15 years) and as attractive waterside and ornamental trees. The 'weeping' forms are particularly popular, but quickly outgrow small gardens. Most of them are hybrids which obtain their weeping habit from *S. babylonica*, variously considered to be a native of the Middle East or of China.

Hybrids of *S. babylonica* with *S. alba* and *S. fragilis* are grown extensively. The commonest weeping willow in Europe is *S. alba* var *vitellina × S. babylonica*, which has pale to bright yellow twigs and a beautiful weeping habit. It has received a wide range of names, such as *S. alba* 'Tristis,' and *S. alba* 'Vitellina Pendula,' but botanically it is correctly known as *S. × sepulcralis*. Most of the forms of weeping willow in cultivation are derivatives of the two above hybrids, but the American Weeping Willow is *S. purpurea* 'Pendula.' *Salix babylonica* itself is a brown-twigged tree of poor growth in Europe. It is traditionally associated with Psalm 137 of the Old Testament ('We hanged our harps upon the willows . . .'), but the tree in question is now believed to have been *Populus euphratica*. Other ornamental willows include the Violet Willow (*S. daphnoides*) with purple twigs overlaid by a white bloom, the Coral Bark Willow (*S. alba* 'Chermesina') with twigs at first dark red, finally bright orange-red, the Golden Willow (*S. alba* var *vitellina*) with yellowish twigs, and the Japanese Willow (*S. melanostachys*) with black and scarlet catkins. Dwarf rock garden plants include the Woolly Willow (*S. lanata*) with long, silky pubescence and large golden catkins, and the Dwarf Willow (*S. herbacea*) which forms little more than a carpet over the ground. A striking cultivar of a distinctly rare species is the Contorted Willow (*S. matsundana* 'Tortuosa') with unmistakable twisted and contorted 5–8cm (2–3in) long narrow-lanceolate leaves.

C. A. S.

Poplars, Aspens, Cottonwoods
(genus *Populus*)

The poplars, aspens and cottonwoods belong to the genus *Populus* which comprises 34 species of trees. They are found from Alaska to Mexico, from North Africa through Europe, Asia Minor and the Himalaya to China and Japan. They are nearly all fast-growing trees which can grow to a large size. All poplars have resinous buds and alternate leaves with long stalks, and in many the stalks are flattened laterally. The flowers are on pendulous catkins which open before the leaves and have a cup-shaped disc at the base. The two sexes are on separate trees, except in some (not all) specimens of the Chinese Necklace Poplar (*P. lasiocarpa*), which was introduced by the distinguished plant hunter E. H. Wilson. Some of these bear catkins which have male flowers below, bisexual and female flowers above.

Poplars are wind-pollinated and the

The leaf stalks are long and flattened so that the leaves 'tremble' in the slightest breeze, as in the American Quaking or Trembling Aspen, (*P. tremuloides*). The White Poplar (*P. alba*) makes a medium-sized domed tree, rarely straight, and is conspicuous in the summer because the underside of the leaf is densely matted with brilliant white hairs, as are the shoots. It grows dense thickets of suckers which can help stabilize blowing sands, and the trees withstand severe exposure to sea winds. The Gray Poplar (*P. canescens*) is the giant of this section, often attaining 30–35m (100–115ft) rapidly. It is a hybrid or intermediate between the two species just mentioned and differs from the White Poplar mainly in its stature; the leaves also differ slightly, being grayer beneath than the dense bright white of *P. alba*.

The Chinese Necklace Poplar is a rather sparsely branched small tree with shaggy dark gray bark, noted for its very large fresh green leaves with midribs, veins and (usually) the petioles, red; it is rare.

The balsam poplars are native to North America, Siberia and eastern Asia and have large, sticky buds and usually large leaves, hairless but whitened beneath. Many species give out a delicious aroma as the buds burst, especially following rain. The Western Balsam or Black Cottonwood (*P. trichocarpa*) can be 60m (almost 200ft) tall in its native range on the Pacific coast of North America and can grow 2.5m (8ft) in a year in Britain, where it is commonly planted. The firm, thick leaves are long-triangular to 25cm (10in) long and turn yellow in the fall. The recently introduced decorative poplar, *P. × candicans* 'Aurora,' is a balsam and the only variegated poplar seen, the dark green of its leaves being often replaced by white, cream or pink over much of their surface.

The true European Black Poplar (*P. nigra*) is native to Britain in the form var *betulifolia* (Downy Black Poplar). This is now rare in the wild, but is much planted in industrial areas. The Lombardy Poplar (*P. nigra* 'Italica') is the narrow columnar tree common throughout northern Europe and North America. By 1750, the Eastern Cottonwood (*P. deltoides*), which is so common throughout the eastern United States of America and has luxuriant large deltoid leaves, was growing in France and had hybridized with the Black Poplar, giving rise to the group known as *P. × canadensis* (*P. × euramericana*). The oldest and commonest of these is the Black

The Quaking Aspen (*Populus tremuloides*) is widespread on bare soils, and, as shown here, is capable of surviving in very precarious situations. It probably reached this position by a wind-dispersed seed.

fruits are capsules containing numerous seeds which are surrounded at the base by long silky hairs, hence the American vernacular name cottonwood. Because these form a carpet of cottonwool around a fruiting tree in midsummer when the seeds are shed, male trees are preferred in public places.

Poplars are classified into four distinct sections: *Populus* (*Leuce*), white poplars and aspens; *Leucoides*, a small group which includes *P. lasiocarpa*; *Tacamahaca*, the balsam poplars; and *Aegiros*, the black poplars. Poplars hybridize readily within their own section, but there are important hybrids between species of balsam and black poplars. Many of the hybrids exhibit even greater vigor than the parent species, and are the fastest-growing trees in regions too cool for eucalypts to grow at their best. For timber production these hybrids are planted in most places to the exclusion of the parent species. The sections to which these hybrids belong comprise species most easily raised from cuttings.

Members of the aspen group are propagated by seed or from their abundant root-suckers and are hard to grow from cuttings. The Aspen itself (*P. tremula*) is a dainty small tree, common throughout Europe. Its leaves are gray-green during the summer, turning yellow in the fall.

Italian Poplar 'Serotina,' a male form of great vigor, making a huge tree with an open crown and leaves which unfold very late, orange-brown at first turning grayish-green. A similar but more shapely, recently introduced hybrid is 'Robusta,' a conic tree with larger leaves opening weeks earlier and orange-red for a few days. Its bright red male catkins are profuse in early April. The Berlin Poplar, *P.* × *berolinensis* (*P. laurifolia* × *P. nigra* 'Italica') is often seen in Germany, and has an upswept, dense crown of leaves which taper to their bases and are whitish beneath.

Propagation of poplars by seed is not recommended; hybrids are likely to arise since male and female plants of the same species rarely grow in close proximity. The polygamous *P. lasiocarpa* will come true from seed; otherwise propagation is mainly by cuttings of leafless wood stuck in open ground. To produce new hybrids, cuttings from the two parent species can be grown in water and brought to flower under glass. With simultaneous flowering, cross-pollination can be effected and seed obtained in a matter of weeks. This should be sown without delay.

Like willows, poplars are prey to many diseases, most serious being bacterial canker caused by the bacterium *Aplanobacter populi*. Cankers arise on stem and branches and growth is badly retarded. Infection is usually through injury caused by wood-boring insects and through the scars left from recently fallen leaves. *Populus trichocarpa* 'Fritzi Pauley' is resistant to bacterial canker.

A serious foliage disease is caused by *Marssonina* (*Marssonia*) *brunnea* (Melanconiales) which has led to premature defoliation and ultimate death of large numbers of trees, especially of *P.* × *canadensis* 'Gelrica.' *Marssonina populinigri* is also serious on Lombardy Poplar. The only rust fungi that attack poplars are species of *Melampsora*. Defoliation may occur, leading to retarded growth, but lasting damage is not usual. Nursery stock is especially liable. *Dothichiza populea* (Sphaeropsidales) is responsible for a dieback condition and may be mistaken for bacterial canker but it is not so serious. Other fungus parasites are *Taphrina populina* (*T. aurea*) (Taphrinales), the Poplar Leaf Blister and *Cytospora chrysosperma* (Sphaeropsidales). Poplar trunks may also be attacked by bracket fungi (Aphyllophorales), for example *Phellinus igniarius*, and by the agaric *Armillaria mellea* or honey fungus.

The control of all these diseases is predominantly one of prevention: the planting of resistant cultivars, the rapid removal of infected trees; in other words, good management.

The main pests include the Poplar borers, species of Longhorn beetles of the genus *Saperda*. They can penetrate bark and enter the wood, which they can effectually girdle, and kill the tree. *Chrysomela populi* is the Poplar Leaf Beetle, the grubs of which can reduce a leaf to its skeleton, thus seriously retarding growth. Spraying with appropriate proprietary insecticides is effective.

Finally, a number of unsightly but hardly damaging insect galls are found on poplars, for example, the gall midge *Harmandia globuli* forms reddish galls, rather smaller than a garden pea, on the midrib and veins of *P. tremula* and *Pemphigus spirothecae*, an aphid, causes a curious spiral gall on the petioles of the Lombardy Poplar.

Poplars are unusually rapid growers, but this is best achieved in sheltered conditions when there is a warm summer and on a reasonably good soil with ample water supply but no danger of waterlogging. The Lombardy Poplar is commonly used for shelter purposes and as a screening to hide unwanted sights such as factories, and in recent years balsam hybrids, for example *P. tracamahaca* × *trichocarpa*, are being increasingly used for the same purpose. Poplars are not favoured for planting in confined areas, such as towns. Furthermore, in clay soils the extensive root system and high transpiration rate can result in soil shrinkage with damage to road and building foundations. Other disadvantages of poplars are their relatively short lifespan, the untidiness of the shed female catkins and seeds and the extensive suckering of many species. For growing on a large scale, planting should be at intervals of about 8m (26ft), as poplars are notoriously intolerant of competition. In spite of this limitation there is increasing interest in poplar cultivation and much effort is expended in producing ever better cultivars for particular purposes.

Poplar wood is soft, pale in color and virtually without smell, this last property making it useful for food containers. Being relatively nonflammable, it is much used for flooring and brake blocks of railway stock. As it does not readily splinter, it is useful for containers of various sorts. It is extensively used for matches, its relative nonflammability being countered by dipping in paraffin wax. For outside work, the wood must be treated with preservative.

A. M.

The Main Species of *Populus*

Subgenus *Populus* (Leuce)
White and gray poplars and aspens. Young trunks and branches of older trees smooth and gray, pitted with dark, diamond-shaped lenticels. Leaves toothed or lobed, petioles rounded, quadrangular or laterally flattened.

A *White and gray poplars. Petioles rounded or quadrangular, not or scarcely flattened. Leaves on long shoots densely tomentose (woolly) beneath; other leaves less so to glabrous and of different shape.*

P. alba White Poplar. *Europe (excluding Britain). Medium-sized tree rarely to 18m, usually with leaning bole. White patches on bark of old trees, pitted black. Shoot, leaf stalk and underside densely felted bright white. Leaves on strong shoots with angular lobes; on old shoots nearly round, shallowly toothed. Frequently cultivated in Europe; less common in N USA as an introduction.
    'Pyramidalis' Large tree with erect branches and resembling the Lombardy Poplar, but broader.
    'Richardii' A less vigorous tree with golden-yellow leaves that are white beneath.

P. canescens Gray Poplar. *Europe (excluding Britain). Vigorous, very large tree to 38m with many-domed crown somewhat pendulous with age. Leaves as in *P. alba* but grayish-white beneath and less often lobed. Commonly cultivated and naturalized across USA, especially in Gulf states, fewer in NE and to Montreal. Naturalized in England and Ireland, forming big trees in chalk and limestone valleys.

AA *Aspens. Petioles much laterally flattened. Leaves glabrous beneath or almost so, without translucent margin, uniform in size and shape and characteristically rounded.*

P. grandidentata Big-toothed Aspen. *NE USA, SE Canada. Slender tree to 17m with smooth pale gray-green bark. Leaves solid to touch, orbicular, 10 curved teeth each side, fresh green, 10 × 8cm on pale yellow 9cm petiole. Very rarely cultivated in Europe.

P. tremula Aspen. *Europe. Conic, lightly branched, often leaning tree to 20m with pale gray-green, smooth but pitted bark, and suckering widely. Leaves round, slightly pointed with incurved teeth, gray-green above, paler beneath.

P. tremuloides Quaking Aspen. *Mexico to Alaska and Newfoundland. Narrow small tree usually in dense stands with pale gray-green to clear white bark. Leaves abruptly pointed with fine blunt teeth, fresh green above, whitish beneath, bright yellow in the fall.

Subgenus *Leucoides*

Small section of 4 species. Bark roughened and scaly. Petioles rounded or quadrangular.

P. lasiocarpa Chinese Necklace Poplar. *C and W China. Gaunt, broad-conic tree to 22m with few level branches and peeling, flaking gray-green bark. Leaves 20–35cm, cordate base, broadly ovate and finely toothed, finely hairy beneath, red midrib and veins, on pink flattened petiole 20cm long. The only poplar with male and female flowers on the same tree. They are often on the same catkin, 5 or 6 females at the base of a male catkin.

Subgenus *Tacamahaca*

Balsam poplars. Trunk with furrowed bark. Unfolding leaves gummy, pale or whitish beneath without pubescence, appearing early, margin translucent, cordate to subcordate at base; petioles rounded or quadrangular, often grooved above. Winter buds very viscid, perfuming the air on bursting.

P. balsamifera (*P. tacamahaca*) Balsam Poplar. *Alaska, Canada, N USA. Upright narrow tree to 30m. Long brown resinous buds fragrant in spring. Leaves to 15cm, thickly whitened beneath but smaller, less whitened in the wild. Suckers freely.

P. × candicans (*P. gileadensis*) Balm of Gilead. Hybrid balsam of unknown origin growing wild in NE USA and SE Canada.
　‘Aurora’ Variegated Poplar. Fairly recent cultivar with dark green leaves 10 × 8cm and more, variably splashed with or very largely cream, white and pink on red or white petiole.

P. trichocarpa Western Balsam Poplar, Black Cottonwood. *W N America. Very vigorous, untidy, rather erect tree to 37m (60m in America) with a few suckers at base of some trees. Leaves highly variable in size, 10–30cm, thick to touch, whitened like paint beneath. Males bear thick green and dull crimson catkins; females bright green, soon setting, fruit covered in white wool. The cultivar ‘TT 32’ is a hybrid between this and *P. balsamifera* with a narrowly erect crown and of great vigor.

Subgenus *Aegiros*

Black poplars, cottonwoods. Trunk with furrowed bark (smooth in *P. nigra* ‘Italica’). Leaves more or less triangular (rhomboid to cordate), green on both sides, margins translucent, more or less coarsely crenate; petioles laterally flattened.

P. deltoides Eastern Cottonwood. *E USA. Big leafy tree to 45m with gray bark and heavy branches. Leaves to 20 × 20cm, rich, shiny green; incurved teeth to near abrupt tip. Many minor variants in the wild.

P. nigra Black Poplar. *Europe, SW Asia. Broad-domed tree to 35m with burry bole and heavy branches. Foliage in dense upswept tufts. Leaves 8 × 8cm.
　‘Italica’ Lombardy Poplar. *N Italy; other forms further east. Fastigiate, columnar-conic tree to 36m (40m in W USA). Male only.

P. × canadensis (*P. euramericana*). A series of garden hybrids between *P. deltoides* and *P. nigra* arising in S Europe since 1750.
　‘Robusta’ Tree to 40m with conic, regular crown. Exceptionally vigorous. Leaves similar to *P. deltoides*, orange at first. Male only.
　‘Serotina’ Black Italian Poplar. Tree to 46m with wide cup-shaped crown on clean bole and pale gray, vertically fissured bark. Very late in leaf, brownish-orange at first. Male only.
　‘Serotina Aurea’ Golden Poplar. Tree to 32m with dense, many-domed crown; less vigorous. Foliage a good yellow. Good in towns.
　‘Marilandica’ Tree to 36m with rounded dome, dense when young, more open and heavily branched when mature. Leaves small, very triangular, coarsely toothed. Female only.
　‘Regenerata’ Vase-shaped tree with arching branches and slender hanging shoots. Leaves opening early, pale brown soon green. Female only.
　‘Eugenei’ Very vigorous and neat tree to 35m, conic until old when broad-columnar, hanging shoots. Male only.

Many species of Populus are cultivated and naturalized well beyond their natural range. The geographical distribution given at the beginning of each entry refers to the natural distribution.

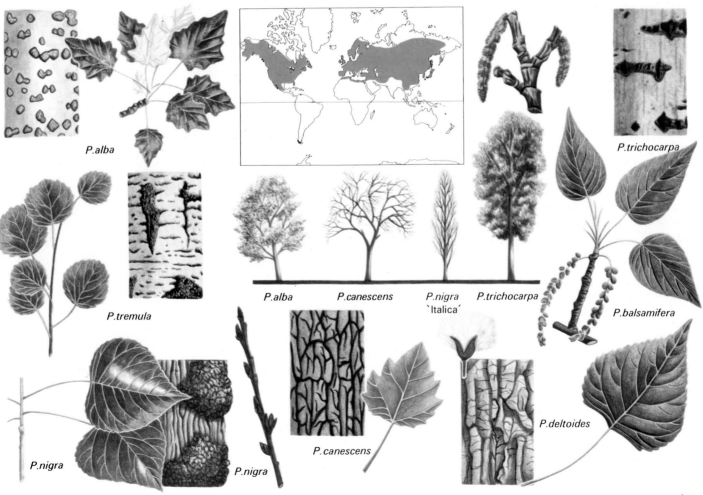

P.alba

P.tremula

P.nigra

P.nigra

P.alba　　*P.canescens*　　*P.nigra* ‘Italica’　　*P.trichocarpa*

P.canescens

P.trichocarpa

P.balsamifera

P.deltoides

Rhododendrons, Azaleas
(genus *Rhododendron*)

The genus *Rhododendron* is one of the largest in the plant kingdom. Over 1000 species have been described but recent work has reduced the number to about 800 'good' species. Many species are very closely related to each other and may merge botanically and distributionally. There are in fact more of these merging species than there are really distinctive ones, and people have rightly remarked that rhododendrons are a taxonomist's nightmare.

The abundance of species is matched by a very wide distribution, mainly in the Northern Hemisphere, including much of the west and east seaboards of North America, several isolated parts of Europe and much of southeast Asia and the East Indies right down to the northern tip of Australia. The altitudinal zones of distribution can vary from subtropical rain forest at little above sea level to almost the limit of vegetation in the Himalaya at 5800m (over 19000ft) and also to arctic tundra.

Rhododendron, from the Greek 'rhodos' (rose) and 'dendron' (tree) = rose tree, may create a delightful imaginative picture of what a rhododendron should look like but in practise it hardly begins to describe the diversity of form the genus offers. They are mostly erect shrubs to about 10m (33ft) but they may form 30m (100ft) forest giants (*Rhododendron giganteum* and *R. arboreum*) or tiny creeping 2.5cm (1in) alpine shrublets (*R. forrestii* and *R. keleticum*). In their favorite habitats in the centers of distribution on the China, northeast Burma and southeast Tibet frontiers and New Guinea, the variation in species is prodigious. Every possible habitat is occupied: the forest floor, stream sides, marshes, ridges, glades, cliffs, rocks and boulders, open meadows and thickets, screes and mountain tops and even the trees themselves, where many species grow epiphytically in the moss and debris at all levels from trunks to the very topmost branches. These plants nearly all occur on acid soil, rich in slowly decaying organic matter. Rhododendrons will not grow on calcareous soils or more or less neutral soils with high lime status.

The leaves vary considerably in size, ranging from 6mm (0.25in) to 1m (3ft) in length. They are alternate, linear to orbicular in shape, with entire margins and may be evergreen to completely deciduous and dark, light or glaucous green. The undersides of the leaves (and sometimes other parts) have glandular or nonglandular hairs which may form a thick felt-like layer known as the indumentum. This can be white to rich rusty-brown in color. Sometimes the glandular hairs are modified to form minute scales (lepidote species), a character important in the classification of rhododendrons (see later).

The roots are usually fibrous but with no root hairs, these being replaced by fungal mycelial threads (mycorrhiza) in normal soils. The root systems are commonly compact but certain species found wild under dry conditions have more spreading roots to search for moisture.

The first flowers open at low elevations in the wild (and in gardens) in midwinter, carrying on into summer and fall, and the seeds may take nearly a year to mature. In the high mountains, the growing season can be as short as four months. Here the

Few plants can rival the blaze of color produced by members of the genus *Rhododendron* in the spring. Seen here are crimson azaleas, which all belong to the genus *Rhododendron*, and flowering cherries (*Prunus* sp) in full bloom at the Strybing Arboretum, which is part of the Golden Gate Park, San Francisco, United States.

flowers may have no chance to open before July and have to ripen their seeds under the fresh snow in October.

The size of the flowers varies from the enormous scented trumpets of *R. nuttallii*, about 12cm (5in) across the spreading lobes, the huge multiflowered trusses of *R. sinogrande*, both from southeast Asia, the great tubular funnel-shaped flowers of *R. leucogigas* from west New Guinea to the minute flowers of some of the high mountain species of the lepidotes under 12mm (0.5in) long.

The flower shape varies from the narrow tubes of *R. keysii* to the saucer-shaped *R. aberconwayi* and *R. souliei*. The inflorescences are usually terminal, rarely axillary as well, and exclusively axillary in subgenus *Azaleastrum*; each may contain anything from 1 to 30 or more individual flowers.

The flowers are bisexual and usually have a well-developed five-partite calyx (sometimes 6–10), variously shaped but never urn-shaped. There are usually 5–10 stamens (sometimes 16 or up to 25), the anthers without appendages and dehiscing by pores. The ovary is superior and five-celled (sometimes more) and the style is single with a capitate or discoid stigma.

The flowers are often heavily spotted and/or blotched in the throat and their color ranges from pure white to pink, orange, red, crimson to almost black, many shades of yellow, mauve, purple to almost blue and sometimes different intensities and combinations of these colors. The fruit is a capsule splitting at the septa and the very small and light seeds, often winged or tailed, are produced in great quantities and are usually wind-dispersed.

As adopted here, rhododendrons are classified into four groups: the scaly rhododendrons (subgenus *Rhododendron*); 'true' rhododendrons (subgenus *Hymenanthes*); the azaleas, which comprise the subgenera *Azalea* and *Tsustsia*; and the 'false azaleas' (subgenus *Azaleastrum*).

The majority of rhododendrons are easily cultivated in climates with somewhat similar temperatures to those of the wild, provided they are given acid soil with plenty of organic matter, shelter and abundant free-draining moisture during the growing season. The common *R. ponticum* has naturalized itself all too successfully in many parts of Europe and has become a serious arboricultural weed in places. Most rhododendrons now cultivated are hybrids and these have been raised in great variety over the years, especially in Western Europe, North

America, Japan, Australia and New Zealand. Propagation can be by seed, cuttings, grafting or layering. For evergreen hybrids, the majority are now propagated by cuttings. Formerly they were grafted on *R. ponticum* stock. Likewise deciduous hybrids are now rooted from softwood cuttings and *R. lutum* was formerly used as an under stock.

Fungal diseases include Bud Blast caused by the imperfect fungus *Pycnostysanus azaleae*. It is indigenous to eastern North America but is now fairly widespread in Europe. If only a few buds are infected, as shown by brown patches on fall flower-buds, these may be picked off and burnt. Hybrids with the *Ponticum* series as one parent are the main victims. Spraying is only really effective against the Rhodendron Leaf-hopper, the females of which puncture the buds thus facilitating entry by the fungus.

On evergreen azaleas, the fungus *Exobasidium vaccinii* (Hymenomycetes) is not uncommon. The leaves become blistered and finally almost white from extension of the fungus. Picking off infected leaves and burning them is the best treatment. Although unsightly, the disease is not very serious.

A more serious disease of azaleas is Petal Blight, caused by the cup fungus *Ovulinia azaleae*, which originated in Asia and spread to the United States. The corollas are attacked and in a matter of days are reduced to a slimy mess. Light infections can be dealt with by picking off and burning the flowers as soon as small dot-like patches appear. For large-scale prevention, the use of a currently approved systemic fungicide is advocated.

Finally, it is wise to remove all dead wood whenever this becomes apparent, as this may be caused by the hymenomycete fungus *Stereum purpureum*, a fungus which also causes the serious Silver Leaf Disease of plums.

Among insect pests, the Rhododendron Leaf-hopper (*Graptocephala coccinea*) has already been noted as being responsible for facilitating attacks of Bud Blast Disease. Other pests include the Rhododendron Bug or Fly (*Stephanitis rhododendri*), a North American pest which has now reached Europe. Its sucking activities result in mottling and rusty-brownish spots on the leaves and under favorable conditions for the bug there is inevitable weakening of the plant, especially in a dry summer. Both these insect pests can be contained by the appropriate currently recommended sprays. However, mild

attacks of the Rhododendron Bug can be dealt with by picking off the leaves and burning them.

It is appropriate at this point to note that attempts to grow rhododendrons in a more or less calcareous soil by planting them in peat may, sooner or later, result in lime-induced chlorosis, more especially if the peat includes incompletely rotted material from a compost heap or leaf mold likely to be rich in calcium (lime) such as that derived from leaves from chalk-inhabiting trees.

Rhododendrons are largely grown for their beauty although some drugs have been extracted from them (especially from *R. chrysanthum* from eastern Asia) and in their native areas young leaves are sometimes cooked. The wood of some species is occasionally used (regrettably many wild stands are destroyed for firewood). The dwarfer varieties are marvelous subjects for modern small gardens when grown in peat beds while the larger species are best in woodland conditions.

Azaleas have for long been included botanically in the genus *Rhododendron* although Linnaeus regarded *Azalea* as a separate genus on the strength of the number of stamens (five in azaleas, usually 10 or more in rhododendrons). Azaleas are divided into two main groups, the so-called evergreen azaleas (subgenus *Tsustsia*) and the deciduous azaleas (subgenus *Azalea*). The former include the free-flowering 'Japanese' azaleas and the less hardy 'Indian' azaleas so extensively grown as pot plants. Colors here vary from several shades and combinations of red, pink and mauve to white, and many are double. All are native to southeast Asia. Their chief characteristic is the adpressed hairs on leaves and stems.

The deciduous azaleas are mostly hardier and the flowers range from red through orange and yellow and pink to white; they are often scented. *Rhododendron luteum* (*R. flavum*, *Azalea pontica*) is the common yellow species from around the south Black Sea coast, while the other species mostly come from North America and Japan and its adjacent areas. The 'Exbury,' 'Mollis' and 'Knaphill' hybrids are well known and the leaves mostly color in the fall.

Few rhododendrons were known before Hooker visited Sikkim in 1849, and the bulk of species from southeast Asia were introduced between 1910 and 1950. There is little doubt that many species are yet to be discovered in the Tibet–northeast Indian frontier. P. A. C.

Representative Species of *Rhododendron*

Scaly Rhododendrons (subgenus *Rhododendron*)

Lepidote. Mostly evergreen shrubs, sometimes epiphytic, rarely small trees. Nonglandular hairs on leaves always unbranched (simple). Inflorescence typically terminal with 5 or more flowers, rarely only axillary and then with 1–4 flowers; stamens 5–10(25).

Section *Rhododendron* Mostly evergreen shrubs. About 200 species in SE Asia, E USA and S Europe.

R. augustinii Szechwan (W C China). To 7m. Leaves to 12cm long, midrib hairy below, usually lanceolate. Flowers in trusses of 2–6, usually pale to rosy-purple in the wild but selected forms in cultivation are shades of lavender-blue, midseason. Hardy to −15°C. The best-known of the 'Triflorums' and as near to a true blue as any rhododendron species in the selected forms.

R. campylogynum Yunnan (W China) to SE Tibet. To 50cm. Leaves to 2.5cm long, obovate. Flowers 1–3 per cluster, black-purple to creamy-white, midseason to late. Hardy to −18°C. One of the prettiest and best of the dwarfs with very variable thimble-shaped flowers on long pedicels.

R. carolinianum E USA. To 1.8m. Leaves to 8cm long, obovate-elliptic. Flowers in trusses of 4–8, pink to white, late midseason. Hardy to −40°C. The hardiest lepidote species and therefore most useful as a plant and parent for very cold areas.

R. cinnabarinum The Himalaya. To 5m. Leaves to 9cm long, usually evergreen, obovate-elliptic to broadly lanceolate. Flowers in trusses of about 5, white, pink, through yellow, apricot, orange to plum-crimson or purple, very variable, midseason to late. Hardy to −18°C. Has very unusual waxy, tubular, pendent flowers.

R. dauricum E Asia. To 2.5m. Leaves to 3.5cm long, deciduous or semievergreen. Flowers 1–3 per cluster, rosy-purple, rarely white, very early. Hardy to −25°C, often the first species to flower in winter or early spring. Closely related is *R. mucronulatum* with longer, narrower leaves.

R. ferrugineum Mts of S Europe. To 1.2m. Leaves to 3.6cm long, oblanceolate. Flowers several per truss, rosy-crimson, rarely white, late. Hardy to −25°C. The well-known 'Alpenrose.' Closely related is *R. hirsutum* with hairy leaves, which grows wild on limestone.

R. glaucophyllum The Himalaya. Small shrub to 1.2m with peeling brown bark. Leaves to 9cm long, glaucous below, aromatic. Flowers pink to white in a small, loose truss, midseason. Hardy to −20°C. Attractive and free flowering.

R. impeditum Yunnan and Szechwan. To 30cm. Leaves about 1.3cm long, broadly elliptic. Inflorescence 1–2, flowers purplish-blue, midseason. Hardy to −23°C. One of the best of the 'Lapponicums' which take the place of heather on the Chinese mountains.

R. lindleyi E Himalaya to Manipur. A straggly, sometimes epiphytic shrub to 9m.

Leaves to 24cm long. The beautiful, widely tubular, scented flowers are in small loose trusses, white, often tinged with pink, midseason. Hardy to −12°C. One of the loveliest scented species, unfortunately only suitable for mild areas.

R. nuttallii The Himalaya to Kweichow (S China). To 10m. Leaves to 20cm long, elliptic, bullate. Flowers 3–9 per truss, 12.5cm or more long, creamy-yellow, often flushed pink, usually fragrant, midseason. Hardy to −2°C. It is sad that this magnificent species is so tender; does well in parts of California, New Zealand and Australia.

R. racemosum Yunnan and Szechwan. 15cm to 4.6m. Leaves to 5.4cm long, usually elliptic, glaucous below. Flowers axillary, 1–4 per leaf axil, shades of pink or rarely white, early to midseason. Hardy to −20°C. A floriferous easily grown plant, adaptable to warm and dryish conditions.

R. russatum Yunnan and Szechwan, W China. Compact to straggly shrub to 1.8m. Leaves to 8cm long. Flowers in tight little trusses of deep blue to reddish-purple, early midseason. Hardy to −22°C. One of the richest colored of the dwarfs, free flowering and hardy.

Section *Vireya* Evergreen shrubs with long-tailed seeds, mostly epiphytic; from the Malesian regions. About 300 species.

R. yunnanense SE Tibet to Kweichow. Shrub, often rather straggly, to 5m. Leaves evergreen to deciduous, to 10cm long. Flowers in small trusses, white to pale pink, midseason. Hardy to −17°C. An exceptionally free-flowering plant from a young age. Vigorous and easily grown.

R. laetum NW New Guinea. To 1.5m. Leaves to 9.5cm long, broadly elliptic. Flowers in trusses of 6–8, usually deep, pure yellow. All tropical species in this section need heated glasshouse treatment wherever there is frost and they bloom spasmodically through the year. Similar is *R. zoelleri* with yellow and orange flowers.

'True' Rhododendrons (subgenus *Hymenanthes*)

Elepidote. Mostly evergreen shrubs or trees. Nonglandular hairs on leaves and other parts almost always branched. Inflorescence normally terminal; stamens mostly not less than 10. About 200 species.

R. arboreum The Himalaya and neighboring areas. Shrub or tree to 25m often with single trunk. Leaves to 17cm long, leathery. Flowers in compact trusses; red forms tender, hardy to only −8°C, pink and white forms to −16°C. Blooms early. Makes a splendid long-lived specimen.

R. barbatum The Himalaya. Large shrub to 9m with a lovely reddish-plum to purple bark. Leaves to 20cm long; petiole often bristly. Flowers in compact truss, scarlet. Hardy to −16°C. Makes a fine sight in early spring in milder localities.

R. bureavii Szechwan. Shrub to 7.5m. Leaves to 20cm long, elliptic, shoots and leaf underside covered with rusty-red indumentum. Flowers in trusses of 10–20, white flushed rose, spotted, midseason. Hardy to −20°C. A magnificent foliage plant.

R. campanulatum The Himalaya. Shrub or tree to 10m. Leaves to 16cm long, usually elliptic. Flowers in trusses of 6–12, white to purple-red, spotted, midseason. Hardy to −18°C. Bluish and white forms are the best.

R. catawbiense E USA. Shrub to 3m or more. Leaves to 15cm long, usually oval. Flowers in trusses of 15–20, lilac-purple to occasionally white, late. Hardy to −40°C. One of the hardiest of all species and is included in the parentage of many of the popular hardy hybrids. The common *R. ponticum*, from Western Europe to the Caucasus, is closely related.

R. decorum Burma to Szechwan. Shrub or tree to 9m. Leaves to 18cm long, usually oval. Flowers in trusses of 8–14, white to pale rose, scented, midseason to late. Hardy to −18°C, some forms more tender. A fine, vigorous, easily grown species.

R. falconeri E Himalaya. Tree to 12m. Leaves to 30cm long, oblong-oval, rugose above and rusty indumentum below. Flowers cream-colored in compact trusses, fleshy, midseason. Hardy to −13°C. A majestic species in foliage and flower, needs shelter.

R. forrestii var *repens* SE Tibet to Yunnan. Prostrate creeping shrub. Leaves to 5cm long, broadly obovate. Flowers single or in pairs, bright scarlet, fleshy, early. Hardy to −15°C. A beautiful but often shy flowering alpine species which is the parent of many useful low red hybrids.

R. fortunei SE China. To 10m. Leaves to 17cm long, oblong-elliptic, petiole purplish. Flowers in trusses of 6–12, pink to lilac-white, fragrant, midseason to late. Hardy to −28°C. The hardiest scented species and a valuable plant for cold areas.

R. degronianum (*R. metternichii*) Japan. To 3.5m. Leaves to 15cm long, oblong-lanceolate. Flowers in trusses of up to 15, usually pink to rose, sometimes tinged blue, midseason. Hardy to −28°C, many forms being very hardy and heat resistant. Closely related is *R. yakushimanum*, which forms a beautiful compact low bush with lovely foliage and flowers. This is being used extensively for hybridization.

R. macabeanum Manipur and Nagaland, India. Large shrub or tree to 10m. Leaves to 30cm long, dark and shiny above, white to gray indumentum below. Flowers produced early in huge trusses of up to 30, yellow with purple blotch. Hardy to −16°C. Perhaps the finest large yellow-flowered species.

R. neriiflorum Yunnan to SE Tibet. Shrub to 3m or more. Leaves to 10cm long, oblong-oval. Flowers in trusses of 5–12, usually scarlet, midseason. Hardy to −15°C. This fine species has many relations with shades of red, orange and pink flowers.

R. sinogrande Yunnan to Assam. To 11m. Leaves to 90cm long, oblong-lanceolate, the largest in the genus. Flowers in huge trusses of up to 52, usually cream with crimson blotch, midseason. Hardy to −12°C. The splendid foliage needs sheltered conditions.

R. souliei Szechwan. Shrub to 5m. Leaves to 8cm long, ovate, flowers pink to white, saucer-shaped in trusses of 5–8, late midseason. Hardy to −22°C. One of the most beautiful of all species which grows

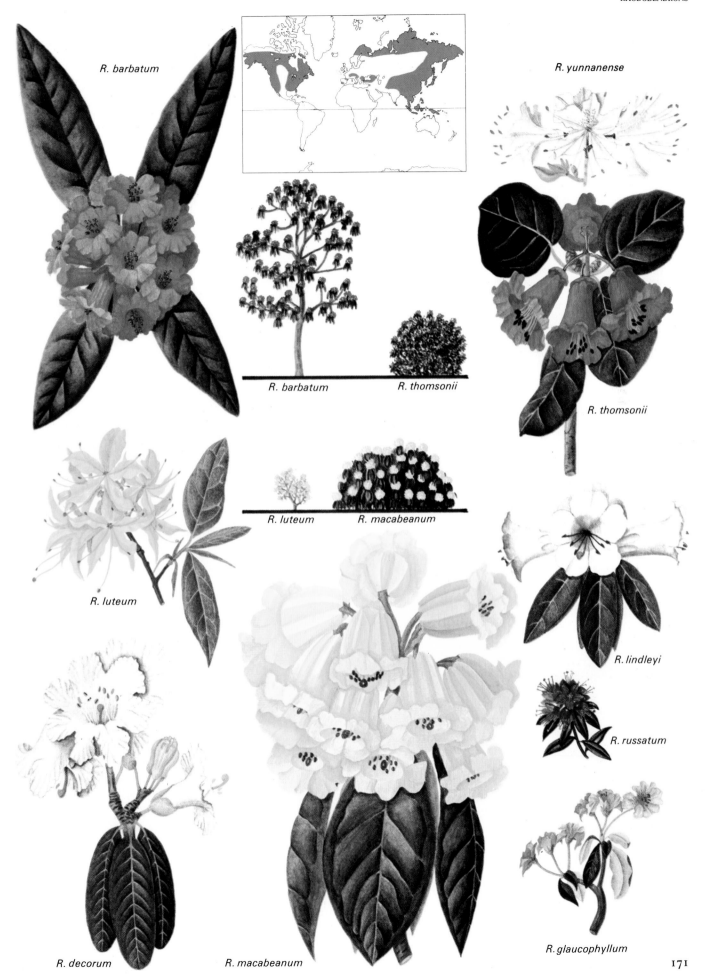

R. barbatum

R. yunnanense

R. barbatum   R. thomsonii

R. thomsonii

R. luteum   R. macabeanum

R. luteum

R. lindleyi

R. russatum

R. decorum   R. macabeanum

R. glaucophyllum

best in drier areas. The closely related *R. wardii* is the best yellow species for general planting.

R. thomsonii The Himalaya. To 10m. Fine smooth, flaking bark. Leaves to 9cm long, orbicular. Flowers in loose trusses of up to 12, deep blood-red, waxy, early midseason. Hardy to −14°C. A grand plant in and out of flower.

R. williamsianum Szechwan. To 1.5m, forming a dome-shaped compact bush. Leaves to 4cm long, usually orbicular, bronzy when young. Flowers in trusses of 2–3 or more, loose, pink, midseason. Hardy to −20°C. A unique species in foliage and flower and a parent of many useful low hybrids.

Azaleas

Elepidote. Often deciduous or partly deciduous, rarely evergreen. Nonglandular hairs on leaves and other parts unbranched (simple). Inflorescence terminal and umbellate; stamens usually less than 10, often 5. About 65 species in 2 subgenera.

Subgenus *Azalea* (*Pentanthera*)

Buds normally producing flowers or shoots (not both). All species deciduous. About 25 species.

R. luteum E Europe to Caucasus. To 4m. Leaves to 10cm long, deciduous, oblong-lanceolate. Flowers in trusses of about 12, yellow, fragrant, midseason. Hardy to −28°C. Naturalized in many parts of Britain.

R. occidentale W USA. To 5m. Leaves to 10cm long, usually oblanceolate, deciduous. Flowers in trusses of 40 or more, commonly white, tinged pink with yellow flair but very variable, fragrant, late. A beautiful species, especially fine in the coastal forms which should be much more cultivated. There are several hybrid strains in this section.

Subgenus *Tsustsia* (*Tsutsutsi*)

Buds appearing to produce both flowers and shoots. Includes species with leaves only

partly deciduous. About 40 species.

R. schlippenbachii Korea. To 5m. Leaves to 10cm long, obovate, in whorls at ends of branchlets, deciduous. Flowers in trusses of 3–6, precocious, pink with red spots, midseason. Hardy to −35°C. A beautiful azalea, especially suited to cold, continental climates.

R. simsii Burma, through S China to Taiwan. To 1.8m. Leaves to 5cm long, elliptic, with adpressed hairs, usually evergreen. Flowers 2–6 per truss, rose to dark red, midseason. Hardy to −7°C. This azalea is the chief parent of the so-called 'Indian,' 'Indica' or indoor azaleas, so popular as house plants. Other species, mostly from Japan, give rise to the hardier types usually grown out of doors.

'False' Azaleas (subgenus *Azaleastrum*)

Elepidote. Shrubs or small trees, mostly evergreen. Nonglandular hairs on leaves and other parts unbranched. Inflorescence always axillary, 1–5-flowered; stamens 5–10. About 20 species.

R. ovatum The type species of the subgenus. E and C China. Evergreen bushy shrub to 3m. Leaves variable in shape to 10cm long, ovate to rhombic-elliptic, apex mucronate. Flowers solitary, corolla almost rotate, white, pink to pale purple, about 3cm across; stamens 5. Not particularly hardy.

Hybrids

'Blue Diamond' (*augustinii* × 'Intrifast') To 2m. A small-leaved hybrid, one of the nearest to blue, midseason, hardy to −18°C.

'Bowbells' ('Corona' × *williamsianum*) Low habit, coppery-bronze new growth, flowers pink, midseason, hardy to −18°C.

'Christmas Cheer' (*caucasicum* hybrid) Light pink flowers over a long period, early, hardy to −21°C.

'C.I.S.' ('Loders White' × 'Fabia') Flowers a mixture of yellow, apricot and crimson, midseason, hardy to −15°C.

'Crest' (*wardii* × 'Lady Bessborough') Tall, flowers good yellow, large trusses,

midseason, hardy to −21°C, slow to bloom.

'Curlew' (*ludlowii* × *fletcherianum*) Dwarf, small leaves, flowers yellow, freely produced, midseason, hardy to −18°C.

'Cynthia' (*catawbiense* × *griffithianum*?) Tall, flowers rosy-crimson in a conical truss, late midseason, hardy to −24°C. Raised before 1870 but still a good plant.

'Elisabeth Hobbie' ('Essex Scarlet' × *forrestii* var *repens*) Low, compact, flowers glowing red, midseason, hardy to −30°C, but not heat resistant. One of a whole group of German hybrids of considerable garden value.

'Elizabeth' (*griersonianum* × *forrestii* var *repens*) Low, compact, flowers bright red, midseason, hardy to −18°C, very free flowering.

'Fastuosum Flore Pleno' (*catawbiense* × *ponticum*) Tall, flowers lavender-mauve, double, late, hardy to −25°C.

'Fragrantissimum' (*edgeworthii* × *formosum*) Leggy habit, flowers white, sweetly scented, midseason, hardy to −10°C. One of a number of tender scented hybrids.

'Furnivals Daughter' (seedling of 'Mrs Furnival') Medium, flowers pink, heavily spotted, late midseason. A fine new blotched hybrid.

'Halfdan Lem' ('Jean Mary Montague' × 'Red Loderi') Medium, flowers glowing scarlet in huge trusses, midseason, probably hardy to −20°C. A grand new American hybrid.

'Hotei' ((*souliei* × *wardii*) × 'Goldsworth Orange') Medium, flowers rich yellow, midseason, probably hardy to −15°C. A new American introduction, the deepest yellow yet raised.

'Lady Chamberlain' (*cinnabarinum* var *roylei* × 'Royal Flush') Medium, flowers bright orange to salmon-pink according to clone, midseason, hardy to −15°C. A showy group with waxy tubular semi-pendent flowers.

'Linda' (*williamsianum* hybrid) Low, flowers rose-red, midseason, probably hardy to −25°C. A new Dutch hybrid.

'Loderi' (*griffithianum* × *fortunei*) Tall, huge flowers, pink to white, fragrant, midseason, hardy to −18°C. There are various clones of this sumptuous hybrid.

'May Day' (*haematodes* × *griersonianum*) Low habit, flowers scarlet in loose trusses, free flowering, midseason, hardy to −15°C.

'Moonstone' (*campylocarpum* × *williamsianum*) Low and compact, flowers pale yellow to pink, loose truss, midseason, hardy to −20°C.

'Nobleanum' (*caucasicum* × *arboreum*) Medium, flowers scarlet, rose-pink or blush-white, very early, hardy to −18°C.

'Nova Zembla' ('Parson's Grandiflorum' × red hybrid) Medium, flowers dark red, midseason, hardy to −30°C.

'Penjerrick' (*campylocarpum* × *griffithianum*) Tall, flowers cream or pink, large, in loose trusses, midseason, hardy to −12°C.

'Pink Pearl' ('George Hardy' × 'Broughtonii') Tall, flowers blush-pink in tall trusses, late midseason, hardy to −20°C. One of the most popular rhododendrons.

The variety of color available in *Rhododendron* species is well shown in this display at Windsor Great Park, England.

'Polar Bear' (*diaprepes × auriculatum*) Tall, flowers white, fragrant, very late, hardy to −22°C.

'Praecox' (*ciliatum × dauricum*) Medium, small leaves, flowers rosy-lilac, early, hardy to −20°C. Very popular early hybrid.

'Purple Splendour' (*ponticum* hybrid) Medium, flowers dark purple with black blotch, late, hardy to −24°C. The best of its color.

'Roseum Elegans' (*catawbiense* hybrid) Tall, flowers rosy-lilac, late, hardy to −40°C, a favorite for cold climates.

'Sappho' (unknown) Tall, leggy, flowers white, heavily spotted maroon, late midseason, hardy to −20°C.

Strawberry Trees

(genus *Arbutus*)

The genus *Arbutus* comprises 12 species of evergreen trees and shrubs native to North and Central America, southern Europe and western Asia. They are evergreen trees or shrubs, the bark of some species exfoliating to reveal a smooth underbark of a splendid reddish-brown or reddish-cinnamon color. The leaves are alternate and leathery. The flowers, which resemble those of Lily of the Valley (*Convallaria majalis*), are borne in terminal clusters. They are pale greenish or pinkish, urn-shaped with a five-lobed calyx, white corolla and 10 stamens. The fruit is a characteristic strawberry-like subglobose berry with mealy flesh and a warted surface.

Strawberry trees are cultivated for their attractive green foliage, the beautiful underbark of some species and the clusters of flowers sometimes appearing together with the red fruits. They do well on peaty or loamy soils, but some of the best, unlike so many ericaceous plants, are equally at home on a calcareous soil. Propagation of species is best from seed, otherwise by grafting onto *Arbutus unedo* as stock. As soon as new plants are established they should be planted in their permanent places as quickly as possible as they do not transplant easily.

The berries of *Arbutus unedo* are edible, but do not taste a bit like strawberries and some people find them unpalatable. In Corsica they have been fermented into a wine. The American species *A. menziesii* yields a useful wood.

S. A. H.

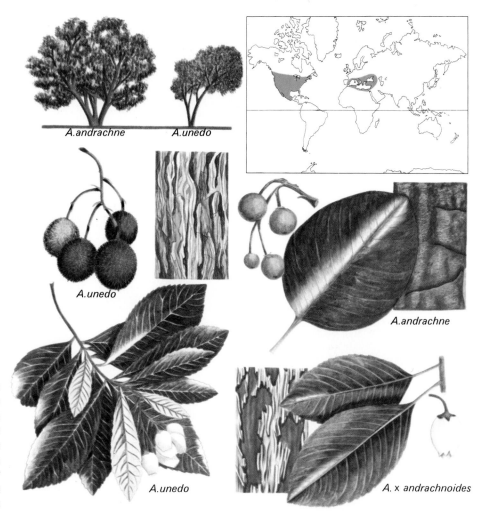

A.andrachne A.unedo

A.unedo

A.andrachne

A.unedo

A. × andrachnoides

The Main Species of *Arbutus*

Group I: Young leaves tomentose beneath and flowers (spring or early summer), white to pinkish, in more or less erect panicles. Leaf margin entire or serrate, the petiole more than 1.5cm long. Species from SW USA.

A. xalapensis SW USA, Mexico, Guatemala. Shrub or small tree to 15m. Underbark reddish-brown. Leaves more or less oval-oblong, (3.5)4–10(11) × 1.2–4.5cm, the lower surface brown-tomentose when young. Flowers in an erect to nodding cluster, each flower with an inflated basal ring. Fruit dark red.

A. arizonica Mts of Arizona (USA) south into Mexico. Tree to 15m. First-year twigs hairy and reddish-brown, but older wood with grayish or whitish bark. Leaves narrowly oval, 4–8 × 1.5–3cm. Sometimes regarded as a variety of previous species.

Group II: Leaves at no time tomentose beneath (may be a few hairs on veins or petioles); adult leaves of mature plants normally serrate, tapering below into a less than 1cm long petiole (but see *A. × andrachnoides*). Flowers white or with greenish tinge in pendulous or nodding panicles. Young plants (1–2m) may have some entire leaves as also does forma *integerrima* of *A. unedo*.

A. unedo Strawberry Tree. SW Ireland, SW France, Spain and Mediterranean region, including Balkan peninsula, Asia Minor. Tree (5)10(13)m. Bark soon grayish-brown, fibrous. Leaves elliptic to obovate, blackish-green above, paler green below, 5–10 × 2–3cm. Flowers in hairy not glandular clusters, corolla white to pinkish or pale greenish-white, 8mm across, appearing toward midfall as the previous season's fruits ripen. Fruit subglobose, about 18 × 15mm, warty. A fine fall and winter sight. Lime tolerant.

forma *integerrima* Leaf margins entire. Occurs as a wild plant.

A. × andrachnoides (*A. unedo × A. andrachne*) Greece. May reach 10m. Underbark smooth and reddish-brown. Flowers in spring or late fall. Distinguished from *A. unedo* by leaves sometimes with virtually smooth margin but base always rounder and less tapering, underside paler, fruit less warty, about 10mm across; and from *A. andrachne* by leaves almost always toothed, flower clusters nodding. Frequent in cultivation, its underbark a striking color.

A. canariensis Canary Islands. Shrub or small tree 9–15m. Leaves 5–12 × 0.5–4.5cm. Rather like *A. unedo*, but has drooping to suberect glandular-hairy, somewhat leafy clusters of greenish-tinged flowers, each flower corolla a little longer, 8–9mm against 6–7mm in *A. unedo*. Fruit 2–3cm across, yellow-orange, warty. Half-hardy only.

Group III: As Group II but adult leaves normally entire (some leaves serrate in *A. andrachne*), the base broadly or narrowly rounded and not tapering into the (1.3)1.5–3cm long petiole. Flowers white or pinkish or white with pale greenish tinge, in erect panicles. Bark more or less reddish-brown.

A. andrachne SE Europe (E Mediterranean). Tree 9–12m in the wild, in cultivation mostly a shrub to about 6m. Leaves oval, 5–10 × 2.5–5cm, dark, shining green above, paler below. Flowers (spring) on glandular hairy stalks, in hairy pyramidal clusters about 7 × 5cm, corolla pale yellowish-green. Fruit globose, 12–13mm across. Tolerant of lime, but rarely seen in cultivation.

A. menziesii Madrona. W N America (British Columbia to California). Tree to over 30m in the wild, some 10–15m in cultivation. Leaves oval, 5–13cm long, dark shining green above, pale glaucous to almost white below. Flowers (spring) in glabrous pyramidal clusters about 15 × 12cm, corolla virtually pure white. Fruit orange to red, ovoid, 10–13mm long. Hardy and universally admired for its white flowers, almost terra-cotta colored underbark and reddish fruits.

Arbutus unedo, popularly called the Strawberry Tree, has creamy white flowers, similar to those of the Lily of the Valley, borne in terminal panicles (*Above Middle*). The fruits (*Above Right*), which mature at the same time as the next seasons flowers, can be used for jams, jellies and desserts. In Portugal they are the main constituent of *medronho*, a very strong 'firewater' spirit with a unique flavor.

Sorrel Tree
(genus *Oxydendrum*)

The Sorrel Tree (*Oxydendrum arboreum*), also called Sourwood, is the only member of its genus and is native to the southern United States of America. Its best known features are the yellow, red and purple colors of the fall foliage, and the leaves are apparently pleasantly acid-tasting – for those who wish to try them! It is a small deciduous tree or a shrub, growing to 25m (82ft) in the wild but to about 7–8m (23–26ft) in cultivation. The leaves are alternate, elliptic-oblong, finely serrated and glossy green, the flowers bisexual, in terminal one-sided panicles developing

The fragrant hanging clusters of flowers and glossy-green foliage of the Sorrel Tree (*Oxydendrum arboreum*) make it an attractive ornamental.

from midsummer on the end of branches to form fragrant hanging clusters up to 20cm (8in) long. There are five sepals and the petals are urn-shaped, white, with five short lobes, not unlike Lily of the Valley (*Convallaria majalis*). The fruit is a five-valved capsule containing numerous reticulate seeds.

The Sorrel Tree is a fairly popular park and garden tree for lawns in temperate regions, growing most vigorously in a sheltered, semi-shaded position on acid, humus-rich soil, although the best flowers and fall colors occur in a sunny position. It can be propagated from seed, by layering or by taking cuttings. The leaves have some medicinal properties, having been used to treat heart complaints and by some people to allay thirst.

F. B. H.

EBENACEAE

Persimmons
(genus *Diospyros*)

Diospyros is an economically important genus of 400–500 tropical and subtropical species including the persimmons which yield edible fruits and the ebonies which

yield valuable timber. They are deciduous or evergreen trees and shrubs with shoots without terminal buds. The sexes are normally on separate plants and the flowers are inconspicuous, whitish, with calyx and corolla usually four-lobed (sometimes three- to seven-); there are one to four times as many stamens as there are corolla lobes. The fruit is a large, juicy berry with an enlarged calyx.

Ebony is the heavy, hard, dark heartwood derived from several species of *Diospyros*, the dark color being caused by deposition of resins; the sapwood is usually uncolored. It has been valued since earliest times and two inlaid ebony stools were found in the tomb of Tutankhamun. It has always been carved into images and being reputed to be antagonistic to poison it was used in India for royal drinking cups. It takes a high polish and in more recent times has been used principally for small objects such as piano keys, knife handles, chessmen, hairbrushes and walking sticks. Most trade names refer to country or port of origin. Although the word is synonymous with black, ebony wood can be other colors. Coromandel and calamander ebonies have brown or gray mottling.

Although several species of *Diospyros*, including *D. reticulata* (Mauritius) and *D. ebenum* (Sri Lanka), are described as the producers of the best ebony, *D. virginiana* is the only species of commercial value in timber production. The sapwood is white when fresh, deteriorating

The Main Species of *Diospyros*

Group I: Native to USA.

D. virginiana American Persimmon. E and C USA; fields and woodland. Stately evergreen tree to about 15m, in primeval forest sometimes to 30m. Bark dark gray-black cracked into small rectangular plates. Leaves on long petioles, very variable even on individual shoots, from 1cm oval to 20cm oval-ovate with sizes mixed along shoot; fine fall colors. Anthers slender. Edible fruits 2–4cm in diameter, green, yellow or red; seeds flat, thin-skinned, much longer than wide.

var *pubescens* has branches villous, leaves pubescent below.

D. mosieri E and C USA; pinelands. Shrub, similar to *D. virginiana* but smaller overall. Anthers stout. Seeds turgid, only slightly longer than wide.

Group II: Native to Africa.

D. abyssinica E Africa. Forest tree to 30m. Bark black with oblong plates, wood beneath bark orange. Leaves 10 × 2.5cm, veins prominent. Fruit glabrous, yellow becoming red or black, small and one-seeded on saucer-shaped 3-lobed calyx; calyx much shorter than fruit, lobes with flat margins.

D. barteri W Africa. Forest scrambler. Stems rusty hirsute. Leaves brown, hairy below.

D. mannii W Africa, Congo, Angola. Forest tree to 20m. Red-brown bark. Distinctive densely bristly hairy twigs, flowers (lobes with flat margins) and fruit. Fruit orange with dense red bristles on calyx of long starfish-like lobes.

D. mespiliformis W African Ebony, Swamp, Calabar or Lagos Ebony. Widespread throughout tropical Africa in lowland rain forest. Tree to 30m. Bark with rectangular plates, black outside, pink inside. Leaves elliptic, 15 × 5cm. Male flowers in stalked clusters, female flowers single. Fruit round, yellow, surrounded at base by small cup-shaped calyx of 4 or 5 distinctive lobes with wavy margins.

D. monbuttensis Yoruba Ebony, Walking-stick Ebony. Forest tree with bark red, papery, peeling; spines on trunk. Fruit glabrous, round on much shorter cup-shaped calyx with flat margins.

D. soubreana W Africa. A shrub of drier rainforests.

D. tricolor W Africa. Thick-stemmed shrub with zigzag rusty silky branches; forms a dense thicket immediately behind beaches on coast.

Group III: Native to Asia.

D. ebenum Ceylon or East Indian Ebony. India and Ceylon. Large evergreen forest tree. Leaves thin leathery, with minutely netted raised venation on both surfaces.

Male corolla hairless; female flowers usually solitary, calyx much enlarged and reflexed in fruit. Heartwood jet black, not streaked.

D. kaki Kaki, Chinese or Japanese Date Plum, Persimmon. China, Japan, Burma and India. Similar to *D. lotus* but branchlets and leaves softly hairy; leaves with depressed midrib. Male and female flowers similar, female flowers usually solitary; calyx deeply 4-lobed with silky hairs, corolla downy at apex. Fruit yellow or red, hanging on the tree long after the leaves have fallen.

var *sylvestris* is smaller, distinguished by smaller female flower, densely hairy ovary and smaller fruit.

D. kurzii Andaman Marble, Zebra Wood. Andaman, Nicobar and Coco Islands, Ceylon, India. Large evergreen tree with smooth gray bark. Only female flowers known, in short-stalked cymes, with 2–10 flowers; calyx almost hairless, corolla velvety outside.

D. lotus Date Plum. China, Japan to W Asia. Tree to 25–30m, deciduous, with dome-shaped crown, often forked lower down. Foliage very glossy dark green, glaucous and hairy on veins beneath, petiole pubescent (with fine hairs); male and female flowers on separate plants, the female usually solitary; calyx lobed to halfway down, slightly pubescent; corolla hairless outside. Fruit finally yellowish or purplish.

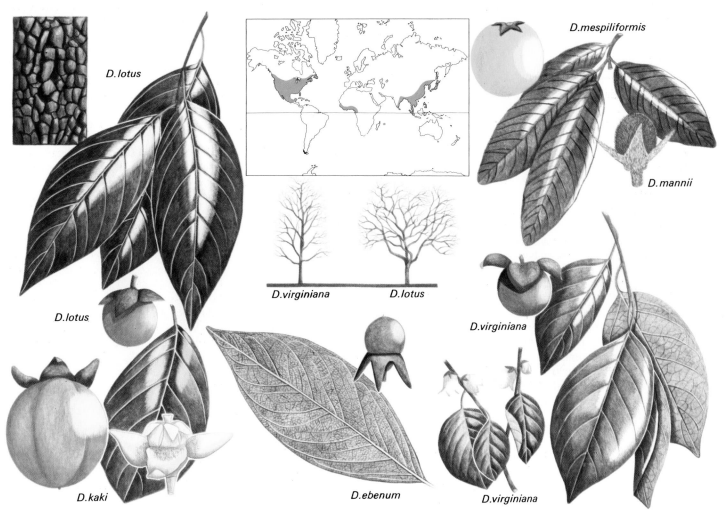

D. lotus

D. lotus

D. mespiliformis

D. mannii

D. virginiana   D. lotus

D. virginiana

D. kaki

D. ebenum

D. virginiana

D. melanoxylon Coromandel Ebony. India. Tree to 15m. Dark gray bark with rectangular scales. Leaves thickly leathery. Male calyx cup-shaped, woolly, corolla woolly; female flowers usually solitary, calyx with broad edges recurved. Fruit yellow. Heartwood streaked jet black.

D. tomentosa Very similar to *D. melanoxylon* and often included with it, but smaller leaves.

The Mauritius Ebony (*Diospyros tesselaria*) with straight dark trunk (*Center Right*), growing among other trees on Mauritius.

to reddish or bluish. Local tribes in Africa use a bark extract as a fish poison.

The persimmon is the round, usually orange, edible fruit of certain species of *Diospyros*. The warm temperate fruit crop known as the Kaki, or Chinese, Oriental or Japanese Persimmon (*Diospyros kaki*), is grown in the subtropics throughout the world. The wild North American species *D. virginiana* (Common or American Persimmon) is present in hardwood forests from New Jersey to Texas.

The Kaki Persimmon was first cultivated in China. In Japan it is now the national fruit, with a total crop approaching that of the citrus fruits. In 1796 it was introduced into Europe but was of little commercial importance outside China and Japan until its introduction into the

United States (where it is now mostly concentrated in California) following Commodore Perry's expeditions to Japan (1852–1854). The scaly-barked trees thrive on well-drained lighter soils and grow to a height of 14m (46ft). They have dark green ovate leaves and produce yellowish-white flowers two or three years after being grafted. The flowers may be male or female or bisexual. Male pollinator varieties are usually needed to obtain fruit production on female types, but some female varieties produce fruit parthenocarpically (without fertilization) and hence need no pollination to produce fruit.

Persimmons need very little winter chilling to induce satisfactory flower and fruit development. The orange to bright yellow fruit 3–7cm (1.2–2.8in) across must be fully ripe and soft before being ready to eat fresh or with cream. The jelly-like ripe flesh is sweet and yellow. Earlier, while the fruit is still hard, it has a very astringent taste due to the presence of tannin which disappears as the fruit ripens.

In the United States *D. virginiana* is often used as a rootstock to produce dwarf trees which are convenient to handle but often last as little as 10 years. The strong, hard wood (North American ebony) is also used, often in golf-club heads. In China and Japan local seedlings are used as rootstocks to give large trees which are very long lived.

D. armata, *D. lotus* and *D. virginiana* are hardy in temperate regions, but *D. kaki* only in the warmer parts.

R. W.

STYRACACEAE

Snowbell Trees
(genus *Styrax*)

Styrax comprises about 130 species from the tropics and subtropics of North America, Europe and Asia. They are deciduous or evergreen trees or shrubs with alternate, entire or slightly serrated leaves which are somewhat mealy with stellate pubescence. The flowers are typically bisexual, white, bell-shaped, and borne in pendulous simple or branched racemes. The calyx is shortly five-toothed, the corolla five-lobed (sometimes eight), and there are 8–10 (sometimes 16) stamens inserted on the corolla base. The ovary is superior or nearly so. The fruit is a dry or

fleshy drupe with a pericarp that is sometimes dehiscent.

Some species are sufficiently hardy to be cultivated in temperate regions for their attractive white, pendulous clusters of bell-like flowers. They like a good but lime-free soil, even one verging toward the peaty, in a sheltered frost-free site. Propagation is best from seed, otherwise by layers and cuttings, the last best taken in summer and placed in a sand-frame.

The most commonly cultivated are *Styrax hemsleyana* from central and western China, an attractive tree growing to 6m (20ft) with racemes of white flowers in early summer, and the Snowbell Tree (*S. japonica*) from China and Japan, a shrub or small tree growing to 10m (33ft) with masses of elegant snowdrop-like flowers appearing even earlier than those of *S. hemsleyana*. The Snowbell Tree also has a fine-grained wood which is used for making umbrella handles. Another hardy species is the Big Leaf Storax (*S. obassia*) from Japan, also a shrub or tree to 10m (33ft), with broad elliptic to obovate leaves, 7–20cm (2.8–8in) long, somewhat obscuring the long racemes of white fragrant flowers. *Styrax americana* from the southeastern United States is a shrub growing to 3m (10ft) with one to four flowers in a pendulous cluster. It is not very hardy in temperate regions.

Styrax benzoin from Bolivia and southeast Asia (Sumatra, Thailand), is a tree yielding a resin, gum benzoin or Sumatra benzoin, which is used medicinally as a constituent of Friar's balsam. This is placed in a steam kettle, the ensuing pleasant-smelling antiseptic steam having

View from underneath the canopy of the Snowbell Tree (*Styrax japonica*) showing the mass of fragrant flowers which hang down from the shoots.

a soothing effect on the breathing of patients suffering from respiratory troubles. It is also made up into throat pastilles as well as being used as incense. Chemically, benzoin is a mixture of various esters of benzoic and cinnamic acids together with free acids. The resin is not normally produced in the intact bark, but is only produced by careful and regular stimulation by incision of the bark. *Styrax benzoin* is not hardy in temperate regions. Storax (*S. officinalis*) from southeast Europe and Asia Minor is a shrub or small tree growing to 6m (20ft) and is the source of a resin used as incense (medicinal storax is derived from the unrelated *Liquidambar orientalis* and *L. styraciflua*). It is hardy in the milder areas of temperate regions, being grown for its large and fragrant summer flowers. F. B. H.

Snowdrop Trees
(genus *Halesia*)

Halesia (pronounced Hailś-ia after Stephen Hales, 1677–1761, an outstanding English experimental biologist) is a genus of four species native to the eastern states of North America. They are deciduous trees with simple, serrate leaves. The flowers are bisexual, occurring in axillary fascicles, white or, less often, pale pinkish. The calyx and corolla each consist of four segments, the latter more or less lobed; there are 8–16 stamens and the ovary is inferior. The fruit is a ribbed drupe with two to four wings. Formerly, the genus also included species from China and Japan, now transferred to *Pterostyrax*, which, amongst other differences, have perianth members in fives and the flowers arranged in panicles.

The plants are grown for their very attractive snowdrop-like flowers, produced abundantly in the spring. The best known species are the Snowdrop Tree or Silver Bell (*Halesia carolina* = *H. tetraptera*) from the southeastern United States, a beautiful small, spreading tree which grows well in cultivation in sheltered, limefree sites, and the much taller pyramidal Mountain Snowdrop Tree or Silver Bell Tree (*H. monticola*) from the mountains of southeastern United States. This species has some value as a timber tree. Propagation is by seed or by layering.
T. W. W.

The Species of *Halesia*

Group I: Corolla lobed to less than halfway, except in *H. carolina* forma *dialypetala*. Fruit with 4 prominent wings.

H. carolina (*H. tetraptera*) Silver Bell, Snowdrop Tree. SE USA. Dense, rounded, twiggy shrub in cultivation, 7–8m high, but a tree to 15m in the wild. Leaves oval to obovate, 5–10cm long, covered beneath with gray stellate hairs. Flowers abundant in spring, pendulous, bell-shaped, white like the Snowdrop (*Galanthus nivalis*,

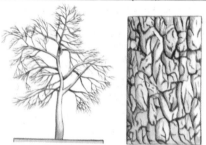

H.monticota var *vestita*

H.carolina

H.carolina

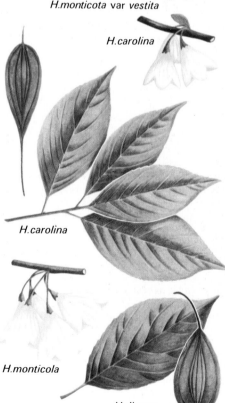

H.monticola

H.diptera

G. elwesii), 1–1.5cm long. Fruit club-shaped, 2.5–3.5(4)cm long. Very fine; the best-known in cultivation.
  forma *dialypetala* Corolla divided well beyond middle of petals.
H. monticola Mountain Snowdrop Tree or Silver Bell Tree. Mts of SE USA, ascending to about 1 000m. Tree to 30m with trunk up to 1m across, carrying a high canopy of branches; bark separates from trunk in large, loose, plate-like scales. Leaves more or less glabrous, otherwise, like the flowers, much as in *H. carolina*, but corolla larger, 1.5–2.5cm. Fruit 3.5–5.0cm long.
  var *vestita* Leaves distinctly tomentose, at least to begin with, especially dense on the veins; forma *rosea* has pale pink flowers.
H. parviflora Small-flowered Snowdrop Tree. E USA (S Georgia, Florida). Shrub. Flowers only 10–12mm long; style exserted. Fruit club-shaped, 2.5–4.5cm long, wings 4, narrow. Like *H. carolina*, but smaller in all its parts. Rare in its native habitat, little known in cultivation. Sometimes described with 2-winged fruit.

Group II: Corolla lobed well below middle. Fruit with 2 prominent wings.
H. diptera SE USA. Usually a small shrub in cultivation to 2.5–5m, but sometimes a small tree to 10m in the wild. Leaves elliptic to obovate. Flowers with corolla (18)20–25mm long. Fruit usually club-shaped, 3.5–5.0cm long, with 2 prominent wings. Less attractive than *H. carolina*; less free-flowering.

PITTOSPORACEAE

Pittosporums
(genus *Pittosporum*)

Pittosporum is a genus of 150–200 species which are natives predominantly of Australia and New Zealand but with representatives in Macaronesia (Canaries etc), West Africa, East Africa, Hawaii, Polynesia, the Himalaya, China and Japan. They are evergreen shrubs and trees with alternate, leathery, entire leaves. The flowers are never blue, with the sepals, petals and stamens each of five parts, the respective whorls alternating, the petals mostly united below. The ovary ripens to a capsular fruit of two to five leathery to woody valves, containing numerous seeds which are covered with a viscid resinous layer, to which the generic name refers (*pittos* = pitch). An unusual feature of *Pittosporum tenuifolium* and *P. crassifolium* is that the seedlings have three or four cotyledons not the normal two.

Propagation is by cuttings from half-ripened wood; where seeds are formed, these can also be used.

In their native areas, the wood has some value, but outside such areas they are grown mainly for ornament. In the climate of most of Europe few species are hardy except in the south and more especially the southwest including areas such as the Isles of Scilly where they are 'at home.' The hardiest species, generally, is *P. tenuifolium* (from New Zealand) which may grow to a tree of 10m (33ft). The evergreen, elliptical leaves have a pronounced but shallowly wavy margin and are of an attractive pale grass-green color; branchlets of such leaves are often used as a background for cut flowers. The flowers, which are produced abundantly in the spring, are of a fine, very dark purple and are very sweet-smelling as dusk begins. It is said that the flowers of the genus as a whole are inconspicuous. This may be true at a distance of some meters, but close-to, once the flowers are recognized, the effect is very pleasing.

Pittosporum crassifolium from New Zealand is also grown for ornament but is less hardy than the previous one. It has the same very dark purple, but larger, flowers and the ripe dehisced capsules produce smooth, sticky and shiny black seeds that are equally attractive. It has a special interest in coastal areas, such as the Isles of Scilly, because it is very resistant to salt spray and is used as a very successful windbreak for enclosing small plots of land where bulbs are cultivated. Locally, these wind-breaks are called 'fences.' It is one of the introductions of the remarkable Augustus Smith who became the first Lord Proprietor of the Isles of Scilly (1834) and who laid out the famous Tresco Gardens there. For those who appreciate

A capsule of *Pittosporum crassifolium* which has opened to reveal the brown mucilage-covered seeds that have given the genus its name.

variegated plants, *P.* 'Garnettii' is interesting in that the variegated leaf margins become tinged pinkish toward winter. Its exact status is not clear and though usually regarded as a cultivar of *P. tenuifolium* it may prove to be a hybrid between that species and *P. ralphii*. Another interesting species is *P. bullata* which has puckered leaves that look like an eiderdown quilt.

A species with perhaps more conspicuous flowers is *P. tobira*, a bushy shrub to 5 or 6m (16–20ft) It has obovate leaves and the flowers are white and fragrant, about 2.5cm (1in) across. It is a native of the Far East (China, Taiwan, Japan). Again, it is not really hardy, but is commonly grown in southern Europe.

F. B. H.

EUCRYPHIACEAE

Eucryphias
(genus *Eucryphia*)

Eucryphia, the only genus of its family, comprises five species from the temperate zone of the Southern Hemisphere: two from Chile and three from Australasia. There are also five hybrids. They are evergreen or semievergreen trees, sometimes shrubby, with leaves that are opposite and simple or pinnate; the stipules are connate. The flowers are white, very abundant, bisexual, axillary, with the sepals and petals in fours; the stamens are numerous. The fruit is a tough dehiscent capsule which ripens after one year. The trees are very attractive in flower.

In cool temperate regions, only *Eucryphia glutinosa* is generally hardy, the others, including the hybrids, being suitable only for the warmer temperate regions. In general they prefer a moist soil on the acid side of neutrality with no free lime. Exceptions are the hybrid *E. × nymansensis* and *E. cordifolia*, although the latter is distinctly tender and few calcareous areas have a sufficiently mild climate for it to survive a cold winter. Woodland protection is helpful. Propagation is best effected by cuttings and layers.

In its native Chile, *E. cordifolia* makes a fine tree to some 24m (79ft), and the timber has been used for railway sleepers, telegraph poles, canoes, oars and cattle yokes. Indoor uses include furniture and

The Species of *Eucryphia*

Group I: All the leaves simple, ie not made up of paired leaflets.

E. cordifolia Chile. Evergreen shrub or tree to about 24m with pubescent branchlets. Leaves oblong with wavy margins, 3.8–7.6cm long, base cordate, densely pubescent beneath (the leaves of young specimens are longer, more pointed at the apex and with the margin distinctly toothed). Flowers white, 5cm across, each with 4 petals arising in terminal leaf axils; stamens numerous, the anthers reddish-brown. Native of rain forests of Chile.

E. lucida (*E. billardieri*) Leatherwood. Tasmania. Evergreen tree commonly 7–17m, occasionally topping 30m with a 3m girth. Branchlets pubescent. Leaves opposite, resinous (as are the young shoots), oblong, 3.8–7.6 × 1–1.5cm, margin entire; petiole 3mm. Flowers white, 2.5–5cm across, scented, pendulous on a 1.25cm pedicel and arising singly in leaf axils; stamens numerous, the anthers yellow.

E. milliganii Tasmania. Very similar to *E. lucida* of which it has been regarded as a mountain variety, differing by being a shrub to 4m high having smaller flowers and leaves only 8–19mm long. In its native habitat found at higher altitudes than the previous species.

E. (*lucida* × *cordifolia*) A hybrid which arose

flooring. The bark is a source of tannin. The timber of the Tasmanian species *E. lucida* is pinkish and used for general building as well as for cabinet making. *Eucryphia moorei* from New South Wales (Australia) has similar applications.

Outside their native areas, those species hardy enough to be cultivated are planted for their attractive evergreen leaves which enhance the beauty of the white flowers.

F. B. H.

The outstanding beauty of eucryphias derives from the large white flowers with prominent stamens, as with this flower of *Eucryphia glutinosa*. Few plants can rival the display of one of these specimens when in full blossom.

in southwest England, with the leaves larger than *lucida*, the margin wavy and somewhat toothed toward the apex.

E. × hybrida (*lucida × milliganii*) A hybrid recognized in the wild state in Tasmania but not yet in cultivation.

Group II: All the leaves compound, ie with mostly 2–3 pairs of leaflets and an odd terminal one (imparipinnate) or trifoliolate (one pair of leaflets and an odd terminal one).

E. glutinosa (*E. pinnatifolia*) Chile. Evergreen or half-evergreen (occasionally deciduous) tree, 3–5m high with upright branches; branchlets pubescent. Leaves clustered toward ends of shoots with 3–5 leaflets each more or less oval, 3.8–7.6cm long with marginal teeth; petiole pubescent. Flowers in 1's or 2's toward ends of shoots, about 6cm across, each with 4 white petals and numerous stamens having, normally, yellow anthers. Generally considered to be the finest in the genus, it is now rare in its native habitat.

E. × hillieri (*E. lucida × moorei*) More or less intermediate between the parents. Leaflets 2–3 pairs, rarely trifoliolate, wider and more rounded at apex than in *E. moorei*, margin entire. 'Winton' and 'Penrith' are 2 named cultivars.

E. moorei Plumwood. New South Wales (Australia). Evergreen tree to about 18m in cultivation, the branchlets with short, brown hairs. Leaves of 5–13 leaflets, somewhat hairy above at first, subsessile,

with oblique base, narrowly oblong, 1.7–7.6 × 0.3–1.5cm, with entire downy margins, the midrib protruding beyond the lamina as a short spine, veins of underside shortly hairy. Flowers pure white, 2.5cm across, with 4 petals and arising singly in leaf axils; pedicel hairy, 1.8cm long; stamens numerous, white.

Group III: Hybrids bearing both simple, pinnate and trifoliolate leaves.

E. × intermedia (*glutinosa × lucida*) Evergreen tree, the branchlets faintly grooved. Leaves simple, subdentate, up to 6.5cm long, with small apical mucro; trifoliolate leaves with terminal leaflet to 6.5cm, the lateral ones sessile and to 2.5cm. Flowers pure white, 2.5–3.0cm across, with 4 petals, arising singly at the ends of branches. A vigorous hybrid which arose spontaneously in NE Ireland.

E. × nymansensis (*glutinosa × cordifolia*) Erect shrub or small tree to 16m, the branchlets grooved. Intermediate between the parents, having both simple and compound leaves, but mostly trifoliolate, the odd terminal leaflet the largest, 3.8–9.0 × 2.5–3.8cm, all with rather pointed marginal teeth; flowers pure white, 6.4cm across, mostly with 4 petals, a few with 5; stamens numerous, pinkish-purple when ripe. This much admired fertile hybrid arose at 'Nymans' in Sussex, England, and is frequently seen although not as hardy as *E. glutinosa*.

ROSACEAE

Thorns
(genus *Crataegus*)

Crataegus is a genus of about 200 'good' species commonly known as thorns, hawthorns or mays. It is predominantly a genus of eastern and central North America and some 1 000 binomials have been published, but it is now certain that most of these are either synonyms, hybrids or variants of one sort of another. Of the 'good' species about 100–150 occur in North America, 10–15 in Europe, 20–30 in central Asia and Russia, and 5–10 in the Himalaya and the Far East (China and Japan).

They are deciduous, rarely semievergreen shrubs or trees, usually thorny, with leaves that are alternate, simple or variously lobed. The flowers are small, rarely more than 1.5cm (0.6in) across, mostly white, rarely more or less reddish and sometimes fragrant, with five sepals and petals arising from a disk at the

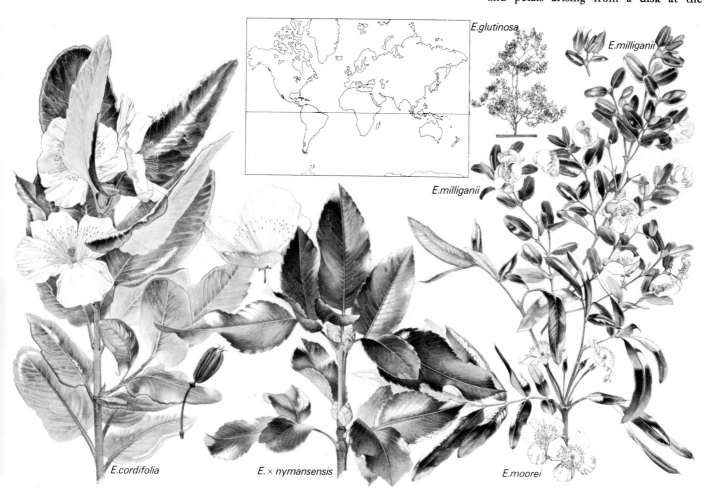

E.glutinosa

E.milliganii

E.milliganii

E.cordifolia

E. × nymansensis

E.moorei

margin of the receptacle (hypanthium); there are 5–25 stamens, the anthers variously colored, and a single ovary adnate to the receptacle with one to five chambers, each with one ovule. The fruit (haws) is a red, yellow or blackish pome falling with the receptacle and maturing one to five hard nutlets. The number of styles and nutlets is typically the same.

The genus is of great taxonomic difficulty partly because of extensive hybridization and partly because the species do not fall into easily differentiated sections. Good material comprising foliage, flowers and fruit is essential. Leaf venation, stamen number, anther color and nutlet characteristics are important features to have available.

As living plants, species of *Crataegus* are widely used for hedges and as ornamentals; many are prized and planted for their abundance of flowers – often fragrant – and the red and scarlet fruits. A few species have pleasing fall colors.

Diseases of hawthorns are few and not particularly serious. The Hawthorn Mildew (*Podosphaera oxycanthae*), a sac fungus (Erysiphales), is not uncommon in the British species but it is doubtful if the perithecia (fruiting bodies) can overwinter. Another sac fungus, *Sclerotinia crataegi* (Helotiales), is sometimes found on *C. monogyna*. The most striking disease is the rust fungus *Gymnosporangium clavariaeforme* (Uredinales) where the aecidial stage occurs on Hawthorn and may distort the shoots (the more prominent teleutospore stage is found as conspicuous yellow club-like protrusions on *Juniperus communis*).

The wood of *Crataegus* species is very hard and has been used for engraving. The Cockspur Thorn (*C. crus-galli*) from the eastern and southeastern United States of America produces a heavy wood used for tool handles, and that of the European Midland Thorn (*C. laevigata*) is used for a variety of articles from wheels to walking sticks. Many species are popular ornamental trees, grown for their blossom and their fruit. The best known is the Pink May, a variety of *C. laevigata*.

The fruits of several species are made into jellies or preserves and those of *C. cuneata* are used for the treatment of stomach complaints in China; *C. laevigata* provides a leaf-infusion tea to reduce blood pressure, a coffee substitute from the seeds and a tobacco substitute from the leaves.

I. B. K. R.

The Main Species of *Crataegus*

Group I: Leaves large, at least on long shoots, with veins extending to base of sinuses as well as lips of lobes. Included here are those species with small fruits 4–6mm across.

A *Nutlets variously pitted on ventral side.*

B *Styles and nutlets 1–2(3). Fruit yellow or red, 6–9mm across. (Section Oxycanthae.)*

C. laevigata (*C. oxycantha, C. oxycanthoides*) May, Midland Hawthorn. Europe, N Africa. Shrub or tree to 5(6)m; thorns to 2.5cm. Leaves obovate with 3–5 lobes, base wedge-shaped, soon glabrous. Inflorescence glabrous, 5–12-flowered; stamens typically 20, anthers red; styles 2–3. Fruit red, broadly oval with 2 nutlets. Extensively cultivated.

C. monogyna Common Hawthorn. Europe, W Africa, W Asia. Shrub or tree to 10m, similar to previous species but leaves larger, more deeply lobed with 3–7 lobes, thorns more numerous, style 1(2), fruit subglobose with 1 nutlet. Extensively cultivated.
  'Biflora' Glastonbury Thorn. Will flower a second time in mild winter months.

BB *Styles and nutlets 4–5. Fruit black or purplish-black. (Section Nigrae = Pentagynae.)*

C. pentagyna SE Europe, Caucasus, Iran. Shrub or small tree to 6m. Leaves 3–7-lobed, hairy beneath but finally glabrous. Flowers in pubescent clusters, anthers pink. Fruit oval not shiny.

C. nigra Hungarian Thorn. SE Europe (Hungary). Tree to 6(7)m. Leaves with 7–11 lobes, hairy on both sides. Flowers in densely hairy clusters, anthers yellow. Fruit subglobose, shiny.

AA *Nutlets smooth on ventral side.*

C *Fruits small, 4–6mm across. Sepals more or less deciduous. Styles and nutlets 3–5. Leaves glabrous or quickly so.*

C. phaenopyrum Washington Thorn. SE USA. Tree to 10m; thorns to 7cm. Leaves broadly triangular, 3–5-lobed. Fruit oblate, red, persisting through winter. Pleasing scarlet and orange fall colors. (Section Cordatae.)

C. spathulata S and SE USA. Shrub or small tree to 8m. Leaves of flowering shoots obovate, sometimes broadly 3(5)-lobed at apex, base tapering. Fruit subglobose, red with reflexed sepals, ripening late and persisting through fall. (Section Microcarpae.)

CC *Fruits more than 1cm across with persistent sepals.*

D *Shoots and/or inflorescence at least virtually glabrous. Leaves more than (5)6cm long, more or less deeply lobed, the lowest lobe pair divided almost to midrib; petioles more than 1cm. Fruit ovate, 2–3 × 1–2.3cm, red with whitish dots. (Section Pinnatifidae.)*

C. pinnatifida N China. Tree to 6m; thorns short or absent. Leaves more or less triangular, 5–10cm long, with 5–9 lobes, the lowest pair cut almost to midrib, dark shiny green above; petioles 2–6cm. Flowers with 3–4 styles. Fruit red, 1.5cm across.

Exposure to wind is the most serious test of the mechanical strength of the stem of a plant. This windswept hawthorn (*Crataegus* sp), growing at 180m (600ft) on Cader Idris in North Wales, has increased its chances of survival by developing its trunk and branches on the side away from the prevailing wind.

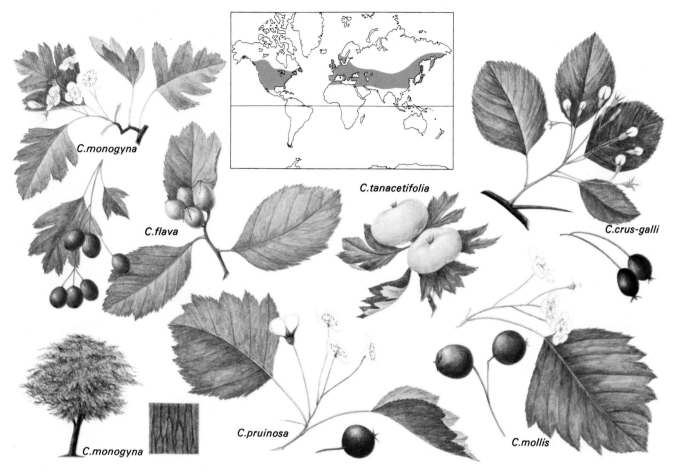

C.monogyna

C.flava

C.tanacetifolia

C.crus-galli

C.monogyna

C.pruinosa

C.mollis

var *major*, with larger leaves and fruits to 2.3cm across, and glabrous inflorescence is the better ornamental.

DD *Shoots, leaves and inflorescence more or less densely hairy. Leaves 3–7cm long; petioles less than 1cm. Fruits almost round or smaller than previous Section, yellow to orange-red without dots. (Section* Azaroli, *formerly* Orientales.)

C. laciniata (*C. orientalis*) SE Europe, Spain. Tree to 6(7)m, almost thornless. Leaves with 5–9 pinnatifid lobes, more or less hairy on both sides, tapering or flat at base. Flowers with 3–5 styles. Fruit oblate to 2cm across; nutlets 4–5. Much planted for its attractiveness in flower and fruit.

C. tanacetifolia Tansy-leaved Thorn. Asia Minor. Tree to 10m, sometimes a shrub. Young shoots woolly-tomentose, mostly without thorns. Leaves rhomboid-ovate to obovate, 2–5cm long with 5–7(8) deepish lobes, the margins glandular-serrate. Flowers 2–2.5cm across, 5–8 in a densely woolly corymb; stamens 20, anthers red, styles 5; calyx woolly, glandular-serrate. Fruit globose, 2–2.5cm across, yellow to red with characteristic laciniate bracts below; nutlets 5.

Group II: Large leaves at least of long shoots, with veins extending to lobes or teeth and not to base of sinuses. Leaves not or only shallowly lobed, except section *Sanguineae*.

E *Nutlets variously pitted on ventral surface.*

F *Fruit black or purplish-black. Stamens 10. Nutlets (3)4–5.*

C. douglasii N America. Tree to about 12m, often without thorns; young shoots glabrous reddish-brown. Leaves 3–8cm, more or less ovate, sometimes slightly lobed, base tapering. Flowers with 2–5 styles. Fruit shining black. (Section *Douglasianae*.)

C. chlorosarca comes here with its black fruit but is referred to section *Sanguineae* having distinctly lobed leaves (see GG below).

FF *Fruit yellowish, orange or (bright) red. Stamens (8)10–20.*

G *Leaves entire or slightly lobed. Sepals finely serrate often with glands, or incised, longer than receptacle (hypanthium). (Section* Macrantha.)

C. succulenta E N America. Tree to 6m, thorns 3–5cm. Leaves 5–8cm, more or less obovate, doubly serrate, base tapering. Flower clusters densely hairy, sepals glandular serrate, stamens 15–20, anthers pink, styles 2–3. Fruit globose, 1.5cm across, red.

GG *Leaves obviously lobed, sharply serrate. Sepals typically entire shorter than receptacle. (Section* Sanguineae.)

C. wattiana C Asia (Altai Mts to Baluchistan). Small tree with shining

mahogany-colored shoots, often without thorns. Leaves broadly oval, 5–9cm long, base rounded-flat to somewhat tapering, lobes 3–5 pairs divided almost to halfway. Flowers with 15–20 stamens, anthers whitish to pale yellowish. Fruit globose, orange to reddish, 8–12mm across.

C. altaica is very close to above with leaves lobed beyond halfway, the lowest pair almost to midrib and resembling *C. pinnatifida*.

C. chlorosarca E Asia. Small tree with warted shoots. Leaves broadly ovate, 5–9cm long with 3–5 pairs of short, broad lobes, base broad. Flowers with serrulate calyx lobes, styles 5. Fruit oblate, 1cm across, black (untypical for its section).

C. sanguinea Siberia, SE Russia. Shrub or tree to (6)7m, usually without thorns; shoots soon brownish-purple, shiny. Leaves broad ovate with tapering base and 2–3 pairs of shallow distinct lobes. Flowers with 20 stamens, anthers pinkish to purple. Fruit globose, 1cm across, bright red. Widespread in its native habitat where it is much used for hedgerows. A variable species; determination difficult because of hybridization with closely allied species.

EE *Nutlets smooth on ventral surface.*

H *Flowers typically solitary, rarely 2–5. Leaves to 1.5cm long, tapering at base not or only slightly lobed, margin more or less toothed above middle. Calyx lobes foliaceous laciniate or deeply glandular-serrate. (Section* Parvifoliae.)

C. uniflora SE USA. Shrub or low tree to 2.5m, with numerous thorns. Leaves obovate to 3.5cm, with coarse, blunt teeth. Flower clusters with woolly pedicels and calyces. Stamens 20 or more with whitish to pale yellow anthers. Fruit subglobose, yellow or with greenish tinge, 10–13mm across; nutlets 3–5.

HH *Flowers in simple or slightly branched clusters of 4 or more. Lobes of calyx not foliaceous, either entire or glandular-serrate.*

I *Leaf blades at least, and flowers somewhat, conspicuously glandular. Flowers in clusters of 4–7(8).*

J *Leaves with 1–3 pairs of shallow lobes in upper part and variable in shape on flowering shoots of same plant, mostly less than 2cm wide, base tapering into a less than 2cm long, densely glandular petiole. (Section* Flavae.*)*

C. aprica SE USA. Shrub or tree to 6m, with zigzag shoots; thorns to 3.5cm. Leaves oval to obovate, toothed and sometimes slightly lobed in upper part. Flowers with 10 stamens, anthers yellow. Fruit globose, 12mm across, orange to red.
C. flava is very similar but flowers have 20 stamens and purple anthers.

JJ *Leaves mostly with 4–5 pairs of pointed lobes, rarely unlobed, more or less uniform in shape on flowering shoots of same plant, mostly more than 2cm wide, base tapering or more abruptly narrowing; petiole virtually without glands and/or more than 2cm long.*

C. intricata N America. Shrub to 4m with curved thorns to 4cm. Leaves elliptic to ovate, 2–7cm long, margin doubly serrate, lobes 3–4 pairs. Flowers with 10 stamens, anthers yellow, the bracts densely glandular. Fruit broadly oval, 9–13mm across, bronze-green or brownish; nutlets 3–5. (Section *Intricatae*.)
C. coccinioides N America. Tree to about 6(7)m; thorns 3–5cm. Leaves 5–8cm long with 4–5 pairs of pointed lobes. Flowers (4)5–7 in a cluster, stamens 20, anthers pink. Fruit subglobose, 15–18mm across, red; nutlets 4–5. Pleasing orange to red fall colors. (Section *Dilatatae*.)

II *Leaf blades and flowers, except sometimes the sepals, virtually without glandular hairs. Petioles sometimes more or less glandular. Flowers few or many in a cluster.*

K *Flowers 2–6(7) in a cluster. Leaves unlobed, rarely slightly so, typically tapering at base.*

L *Young shoots, at least rough-warty. Thorns less than 1cm long.*

C. cuneata Japan and C China. Bushy shrub to 1.5m. Leaves obovate, 2–6cm long. Flowers hairy, styles 5, stamens 20, anthers red. Fruit more or less subglobose, 12–15mm across, red with 5 nutlets. (Section *Cuneatae*.)

LL *Young shoots smooth. Thorns longer than 1cm.*

C. aestivalis SE USA. Tree to 10m; thorns 2–3.5cm. Leaves oblong to obovate, to 3cm long; petiole 6mm–2cm long, sometimes 3-lobed. Flowers in glabrous clusters appearing before or with the leaves. Fruit red, 8mm across, with 3 nutlets. (Section *Aestivales*.)
C. triflora Shrub or tree to 7m. Leaves 2–7cm long with a few shallow lobes. Flowers 2–5 in a cluster, 2.5–3.0cm across, sepals glandular serrate, stamens 20, anthers yellow. Fruit globose, 12–15mm across, red; nutlets 3–5. (Section *Triflorae*.)

KK *Flowers numerous in a cluster (more than 7). Leaves tapering at base, lobed or not.*

M *Petiole up to 1cm long, rarely to 1.5cm. Leaves unlobed or only slightly lobed, tapering at base.*

N *Fruit large, 2–3 × 1.5–2cm. Leaves ovate-lanceolate, unlobed, tapering at base, hairy on both sides.*

C. stipulacea (*C. pubescens* forma *stipulacea*) Mexico. Tree to 6m; thorns mostly absent. Leaves 4–10cm long, sometimes with a few glandular serrations in upper part. Flowers with hairy pedicels and calyx, stamens 15–20, anthers pink, styles 2–3. Fruit yellowish or orange, speckled, with 2–3 nutlets. (Section *Mexicanae*.)

NN *Fruit smaller. Flowers appearing with or after the leaves. Leaves oblong to obovate.*

O *Leaves typically unlobed on flowering shoots, leathery, dark green and shining above, veins inconspicuous or slightly impressed above, fruit hard, inedible; nutlets 1–3, rarely 5. (Section* Crus-galli.*)*

C. crus-galli Cockspur Thorn. E and C N America. Shrub or tree to about 12m, less in cultivation; thorns 4–7.5cm. Leaves obovate, 2–5(10)cm long. Styles 2, stamens 10, anthers pink. Fruit subglobose, red, 10mm across, persisting through winter.
C. × lavallei (?*C. crus-galli × stipulacea*) Tree to (6)7m; thorns few, stout, 2.5–4(5)cm. Leaves 5–10cm long, mostly oblong to obovate. Flowers 2–2.5cm across, styles 1–3, stamens 15–20, anthers yellow-orange to reddish-brown. Fruit ellipsoidal, 13–15mm long, orange-red with brown dots, persisting through winter; nutlets 2–3.

OO *Leaves sometimes slightly lobed above middle, more or less papery, not shining above; veins typically and obviously impressed above. Fruit fleshy, edible; nutlets 3–5, rarely 2. (Section* Punctatae.*)*

C. punctata E N America. Tree to 10(12)m; thorns 5–7.5cm, sometimes absent. Leaves more or less ovate, 5–10cm long. Flowers with 5 styles and 20 stamens. Fruit subglobose, about 2cm across.

MM *Petiole, at least of some leaves on long shoots, 1.5–3cm long. Leaves tapering or broad at base.*

Crataegus × prunifolia is a small tree that is out-outstanding for the brilliant fall coloration of its foliage and its persistent fruits. This species is known only in cultivation.

P *Inflorescence, flowers and both surfaces of leaves more or less densely hairy (but see* C. ellwangeriana*). Leaves more or less lobed and truncate to subcordate at base. (Section* Molles.*)*

C. mollis C USA. Tree 10–12m; thorns 2.5–5.0cm. Leaves leathery, broadly ovate, 6–11cm long, with 4–6 pairs of shallow lobes. Flowers 2.5cm across, styles 4–5; stamens 20, anthers pale yellow. Fruit subglobose, hairy, red, 12–15mm across.
C. submollis NE USA, SE Canada. Similar to previous species, but leaves more papery and stamens 10.

PP *Inflorescence and flowers glabrous or almost so. Leaves sparsely hairy only when young, soon virtually glabrous.*

Q *Leaves not or only slightly lobed and with tapering base.(Section* Virides.*)*

C. viridis E and S N America. Tree to 12m; thorns to 3.75cm. Leaves ovate to oval, 4–9cm long, usually 3-lobed above. Flowers with 2–5 styles, stamens 20, anthers pale yellow. Fruit globose, 6–8(9)mm across, red.

QQ *Leaves obviously lobed, base broad, not gradually tapering.*

C. pruinosa USA. Tree to 6m or large shrub; thorns stout, 2.5–3.8cm. Leaves more or less ovate, 3–5cm long, with broad cuneate base with 3–4 pairs of triangular lobes and unfolding reddish. Flowers 2–2.5cm across; stamens 20, anthers pink. Fruit roundish, 1.0–1.5mm across, long remaining green, finally purplish with sweet yellow flesh; nutlets 5. (Section *Pruinosae*.)

F. B. H.

Medlar
(genus *Mespilus*)

Medlar is the common name for *Mespilus germanica*, a small spreading deciduous tree growing to about 7m (23ft), found in southeastern Europe extending eastward to central Asia. It is the sole representative of the genus *Mespilus* and is related to the hawthorns (*Crataegus* spp) although differing in its solitary flowers, and fruits with five carpels. *Mespilus* and *Crataegus* are so closely related that both graft and sexual hybrids have been synthesized between the two. The branches are often armed with hard spines to 2.5cm (1in) long and the leaves are hairy, subsessile, oval to ovate, 5–10(12)cm (2–4(5)in) long. The flowers are white, about 3cm (1.2in) across, and appear in late spring. Medlars often persist in cultivation as old, gnarled but attractive specimens.

The brownish apple-shaped fruits are traditionally eaten with wine after frosting or 'bletting' (rotting) has softened the hard fruit tissues. Jellies and preserves can also be made from the fruits. The taste is rather an acquired one.

The leaves color well in the fall following the showy flowers, and the medlar is as much cultivated for its ornamental appearance as for its fruits. It prefers an open sunny position on well-drained soil. Cultivar 'Nottingham' has an erect habit and produces small richly-flavored fruits, while 'Dutch' has a spreading habit with larger fruits. It is very hardy and grows in any reasonable soil.

B. M.

The fruits of the Medlar (*Mespilus germanica*) are quite unmistakable. They are edible but are normally only palatable after a period of exposure to frost.

Common Quince
(genus *Cydonia*)

The Common Quince (*Cydonia oblonga*) is the only species of its genus. Other species, formerly placed in this genus and conveniently distinguished as flowering quinces are now transferred to the genus *Chaenomeles*. This has involved a number of nomenclatural changes, sometimes confusing, the more important ones being dealt with under *Chaenomeles*. The two genera are closely related. *Cydonia* differs by its entire (not toothed) leaf margin, the free styles (not united below) and the almost invariably solitary flowers (solitary or clustered in *Chaenomeles*).

The Common Quince is a densely branched, thornless, deciduous tree growing to 5–6m (16–20ft). The leaves are alternate, elliptical to ovate, 6–10cm (2.4–4in) long, with an entire margin, more or less woolly beneath and with glandular hairy stipules. The flowers are white or pink, 2–3(5)cm (0.8–1.2(2)in) across, with numerous stamens. The fruit is usually pear-shaped, 6–10cm (2.4–4in) long, very fragrant, with numerous seeds in each of its five chambers (in apples and pears, each of the chambers has only two seeds).

The place of origin of the Common Quince is uncertain; it appears to be wild (or naturalized) in parts of the Near East and central Asia and may have originated in northern Iran and Turkestan (USSR). In Europe it has been cultivated for centuries for its fruit which, although quite unpalatable raw, can be made into a jelly and used as an excellent flavoring for pies and tarts etc. The seeds contain a bassorin-type gum which is used as a mucilage in toilet preparations. An infusion of the seeds is listed in some pharmacopoeias.

The Common Quince grows best in a deep moist loam in warm sheltered sites, either as a freestanding tree or trained on walls. It may live to a great age. Propagation is by cuttings, stools, layers and suckers. It also serves as a stock for grafting pears. Cultivars include 'Lusitanica' (Portuguese Quince), which is very vigorous and floriferous but less hardy, and 'Maliformis' with the fruits apple-shaped.

The Common Quince is subject to a number of diseases. A common and

Foliage and pinkish flowers (*Top*) and characteristic pear-shaped, woolly fruit (*Middle*) of the Common Quince (*Cydonia oblonga*). The fruit is quite unpalatable raw but has been used for centuries in pies and tarts etc.

serious one is Quince Leaf Blight, caused by the sac fungus *Fabraea maculata* (Helotiales). It can cause defoliation and is not uncommon on quince stocks used for grafting pears. *Sclerotinia cydoniae* (also Helotiales) is a leaf blotch producing brown blotches on the leaves and can be serious. The Common Quince is also liable to mildew attacks and to various rots. The rust fungus *Gymnosporangium confusum* has its cluster cup (aecidial) stage on the Common Quince, the teleutospore stage being found on a juniper tree, *Juniperus sabina*.

T. W. W.

Flowering Quinces
(genus *Chaenomeles*)

Chaenomeles comprises three or four species from China and Japan, very similar to *Cydonia* in which genus they were formerly placed. They are deciduous or half-evergreen shrubs or trees, often suckering, with alternate, more or less toothed leaves (entire in *Cydonia*). The flowers are solitary or clustered with the parts in fives, except the stamens which may number 20 or more, and the styles are united below (free in *Cydonia*). The fruit is a pome (false fruit), each of the five chambers containing numerous brown seeds (apples and pears have only two seeds per chamber).

The species are hardy and do well on any average well-drained loamy soil, preferably in a sunny position. Propagation of species is best from seed; for varieties, cultivars or hybrids, cuttings or some form of layering must be used.

Perhaps the most widely cultivated species is *Chaenomeles speciosa* (formerly *C. lagenaria*), commonly known in the United States as the Japanese (Flowering) Quince and in Britain as 'Japonica'. This has been, and in some quarters still is, the center of nomenclatural confusion. *Pyrus japonica* was described by Thunberg from the Hakone mountains in Japan in 1784. Long before its introduction into Europe, a different species from China had

The Japanese Flowering Quince (*Chaenomeles speciosa*), known to many simply as the 'Japonica,' is a popular early-flowering shrub often grown against walls.

been introduced and was wrongly taken to be identical with Thunberg's species. This became known as 'Japonica.' The Chinese species was, in 1818, shown to be distinct from Thunberg's Japanese species and renamed *Pyrus speciosa*. The specific part of the name (*speciosa*) has been retained despite the transfer first to genus *Cydonia* and then to *Chaenomeles*. The Japanese Quince or Japonica is a profusely branching, suckering shrub growing to 2m (7ft) with single or double scarlet flowers, 3.5–5cm (1.4–2in) across, appearing in early spring. The fruits are aromatic, more or less ovoid, 3–7cm (1.2–2.8in) long, yellowish-green with white speckles, and can be used in the same way as those of the Common Quince.

Maul's Flowering Quince (*C. japonica*) is a thorny, deciduous, widely spreading shrub growing to about 1m (3.3ft) with orange-red to scarlet flowers and a red-blotched yellow fruit like an apple, 4cm (1.6in) across. The Chinese Quince (*C. sinensis*) is a deciduous tree growing to about 13m (43ft) with pinkish flowers, a deep yellow, woody, egg-shaped fruit, 10–15cm (4–6in) long, and leaves that turn red in the fall. All the species are adaptable as wall shrubs or in borders or hedges.

A number of hybrids are in cultivation including *C. × superba* (*C. japonica × C. speciosa*) and *C. × vilmoriana* (*C. cathayensis × C. speciosa*), both of which exist as a number of cultivars.

T. W. W.

Whitebeams, Mountain Ash
(genus *Sorbus*)

Sorbus is a genus of approximately 100 species of deciduous trees and shrubs of the Northern Hemisphere. They are found as far south as Mexico and the Himalaya. The genus includes the rowans or mountain ashes, the whitebeams and the service trees. Many of the species are grown as ornamentals and can tolerate shade and atmospheric pollution.

The branches bear alternately arranged leaves; in whitebeams these are simple but in the rowans they are pinnately compound with ovate leaflets. However, every kind of intermediate shape from simple through lobed to compound is found in representatives of the genus as a result of inter-specific hybridization. The inflorescence consists of tight flattened clusters (compound cymes) of flowers with five white, or occasionally pink, petals. The 15–20 stamens surround a semi-inferior ovary which ripens into a pome (a false fruit, commonly called a 'berry'), which is white, yellow, orange, pink or red according to species. The seeds are small and scattered in the pulp of the fruit.

One of the most attractive trees is the Rowan, European Mountain Ash or Quickbeam (*Sorbus aucuparia = Pyrus aucuparia*), which grows wild at altitudes of up to 600m (2 000ft) in its native Scottish Highlands. It is often planted elsewhere as an ornamental in parks and gardens where it attains a height of about 12m (40ft). The leaves are pinnate with seven pairs of leaflets, each with a serrated margin. It produces large clusters of bright orange-red fruits, which in var *edulis* are edible and used for making jams and jellies. The berries, like those of other species, are particularly attractive to birds who digest the pulp and excrete the seeds; these may subsequently germinate in a variety of habitats, including clefts on cliff faces and even in the hollow trunks of old trees. At one time rowan wood was used as firewood and for making furniture and tools in the more barren and relatively treeless districts of northern Scotland.

Sargent's Rowan (*S. sargentiana*), a native of western China, is a thick-shooted bushy tree which grows to a height of about 5m (18ft). It is very common in parks and gardens, most often as a graft on the stem of *S. aucuparia*. It is recognizable by its very large pinnate leaf, up to 40cm (16in) long, with 9–11 leaflets, its large sticky red winter buds and very small bright red fruits. Other Asian rowans are much less commonly grown, including the Kashmir Rowan (*S. cashmeriana*), the Japanese Rowan (*S. commixta*) and Vilmorin's Rowan (*S. vilmorinii*).

The Common Whitebeam or Chess Apple (*S. aria*) is a native of Europe, found on chalky or sandy soils, growing to a height of 15m (50ft). It bears ovate toothed leaves, covered on the lower side with white downy hairs. The flowers are large and white, the fruits ovoid and scarlet. The Swedish Whitebeam (*S. intermedia* = *S. suecica*) usually grows to a height of 4.5m (15ft) and is commonly used for planting in town streets and parks. The leaves are deeply lobed and covered on the underside with grayish hairs. Large clusters of white flowers are followed in August and September by conspicuous scarlet fruits.

The Wild Service Tree (*S. torminalis*) is native to southern England, rarely exceeding 12m (40ft) in height and recognizable by its five-lobed leaves, which are very similar to those of the maples although they are not borne in opposite pairs. The flowers are white and the fruits globose and brown with dull reddish speckles. Although the fruits are rather acid they are edible and at one time were sold in Kent as 'chequers berries.' The true Service Tree (*S. domestica*) is found all over Europe, growing to a height of about 18m (60ft). The flowers are creamy-white and the fruits are large, pear-shaped, brownish-red and edible. In some areas the fruits are fermented with grain to produce an alcoholic beverage and the bark is used for tanning leather.

Species of *Sorbus* hybridize readily and a number are grown as ornamentals, such as the Bastard Service Tree (*S. × thuringiaca*), which is the result of a cross between *S. aucuparia* and *S. aria*, and the Service Tree of Fontainbleau (*S. × latifolia*), which is a hybrid of *S. aria* and *S. torminalis*.

S. R. C.

The Main Species of *Sorbus*

Group I: Leaves pinnate with at least 4 pairs of leaflets.

S. americana (*Pyrus americana*) American Mountain Ash, Dogberry, Missey-moosey, Roundwood. E N America. Shrub or tree to 10m. Leaflets 11–17, narrowly oblong-lanceolate, 5–12cm long, acuminate (narrowing to a point), sharply toothed (serrated) on margins, bright green and glabrous above, paler below. Fruits shining red, globose, 4–6mm.

S. aucuparia (*Pyrus aucuparia*) Rowan or European Mountain Ash, Quickbeam. Europe and W Asia. Shrub or tree to 18m. Leaflets 11–15, oblong-lanceolate, 3–6cm long, more or less rounded, serrated on margins, dark green above, grayish below. Fruits orange-red (yellow in 'Xanthocarpa'), subglobose, 6–9mm.

S. domestica Service Tree. S Europe, N Africa and Asia Minor. Leaflets 11–21, narrow, oblong-lanceolate, 16cm long, acute, the margins sharply serrated from near the base. Fruits brownish, tipped with red, pear-shaped, about 3cm long.

S. scopulina Rocky Mts, USA. Shrub to 4m. Leaflets 11–13, glossy, lanceolate or oblong-lanceolate, 3–6cm long, cuneate (wedge-shaped) at the base and shortly acute or acuminate at the apex. Fruits bright red, subglobose, 8–10mm.

S. sargentiana Sargent's Rowan. China. Shrub to 5m. Leaflets 7–11, oblong-acute, 4–6cm long, mid-green turning to red in the fall. Fruits orange-red, globose, 6–8mm.

S. vilmorinii Vilmorin's Rowan. W China. Shrub to 4m. Leaflets 19–25, narrow ovate with serrated margins. Fruits rose-red, ripening to whitish-pink, 6–8mm.

S. decora E USA and Canada. Shrub or small tree to 10m. Leaflets 11–17, oblong, sharply acute, 4–8cm long but the lowermost pair usually smaller, margins coarsely serrated from the tip to the middle below. Fruits glossy red, subglobose, 6–10mm.

S. californica California. Small shrub 1–2m. Leaflets 7–9, oblong-oval, simply or doubly serrate from the tip to below the middle, 2–4cm long, glabrous on both sides, glossy above. Fruits scarlet, globose, 7–10mm.

S. cascadensis British Columbia to N California. Shrub 2–5m. Leaflets 9–11, oval but sharply acute at the apex, somewhat rounded at the base, sharply serrate from the apex to below the middle. Fruits scarlet, globose, 8–10mm.

Group II: Leaves simple, serrate, lobed, sometimes basally pinnate.

S. pseudofennica (*S. fennica*) Scotland. Small tree to 7m. Leaves oblong or ovate, 5–8cm long with 1–2 pairs of free leaflets at the base, sharp serrated margins, dark yellowish-green above, grayish and felty below. Fruits scarlet, subglobose, 7–10mm.

S. × hybrida (*S. aucuparia* × *S. intermedia*)

A European Mountain Ash or Rowan (*Sorbus aucuparia*) growing in its natural setting on the slope of a hill in the Scottish Highlands. This small tree and its cultivars are popular garden subjects.

Scandinavia. Small tree up to 10m. Leaves lobed ovate, 6–15cm long with 2–3 pairs of oblong, serrate, mid-green (grayish and felty below) leaflets at the base; fruits red, subglobose, 6–8mm.

S. × *thuringiaca* (*S. aria* × *S. aucuparia*) Europe. Tree to 13m. Leaves oblong, 7–11cm long, with 1–3 pairs of free leaflets at the base (sometimes they are not free and the leaf is merely lobed at the base, with no free leaflets), serrated margins, dull green and glabrous above, grayish and felty below. Fruits red, subglobose, 8–10mm.

Group III: Leaves entire, without true leaflets.

S. aria Common Whitebeam, Chess Apple. Europe. Tree to 12m. Leaves ovate-elliptic to elliptic-oblong, toothed or shallowly lobed, 5–13cm long, acute rounded or cuneate at the base, often more than twice as long as broad, whitish when young, turning to dark green (yellow in 'Aurea') and finally red in the fall. Fruits scarlet, subglobose, 8–15mm.

S. torminalis Wild Service Tree. Europe, N Africa, Asia Minor. Tree to 20m. Leaves broad ovate, 5–15cm long, cordate to broad cuneate at the base, deeply lobed with 3–5 angular, serrated lobes, the lowest pair much deeper than the rest. Fruits brown, ellipsoid, 12–16mm.

S. intermedia Swedish Whitebeam. N Europe. Small tree to 9m. Leaves deeply lobed, serrate, 7–12cm long, elliptic, 1.5–2 times as long as broad, rounded or broad cuneate at the base, mid-green, but gray and hairy on the underside. Fruits bright red, oval or oblong, 12–15mm.

S. leptophylla Endemic to Wales. Small shrub to 3m. Leaves obovate, 6–12cm long, 1.5–2.5 times as long as broad, acute, cuneate at the base, doubly serrate, dark green above, greenish-white below. Fruits scarlet, subglobose, 20mm.

S. rupicola British Isles and Scandinavia. Small shrub to 2m. Leaves obovate or oblanceolate, 8–14cm long, 1.4–2.4 times as long as broad, unequally toothed, dark green above but white and felty below. Fruits green-red, subglobose, 12–15mm.

S. vexans Endemic to SW England. Small tree to 8m. Leaves obovate, 7–11cm long, up to 2 times as long as broad, cuneate at the base, coarsely serrate, yellowish-green above but white and felty below. Fruits scarlet, subglobose, 12–15mm.

S. subcuneata SW England. Endemic. Small tree to 9m. Leaves elliptic, acute, cuneate or rather rounded at the base, 7–10cm long, lobed in the upper parts (the lobes being rather triangular) and sharply toothed, bright green above but grayish and felty below. Fruits brownish-orange, subglobose, 10–13mm.

Serviceberry, Shadbush
(genus *Amelanchier*)

Amelanchier is a genus of 25 species often cultivated for their abundant white flowers in spring and brilliant red fall foliage. About 20 species are found in North

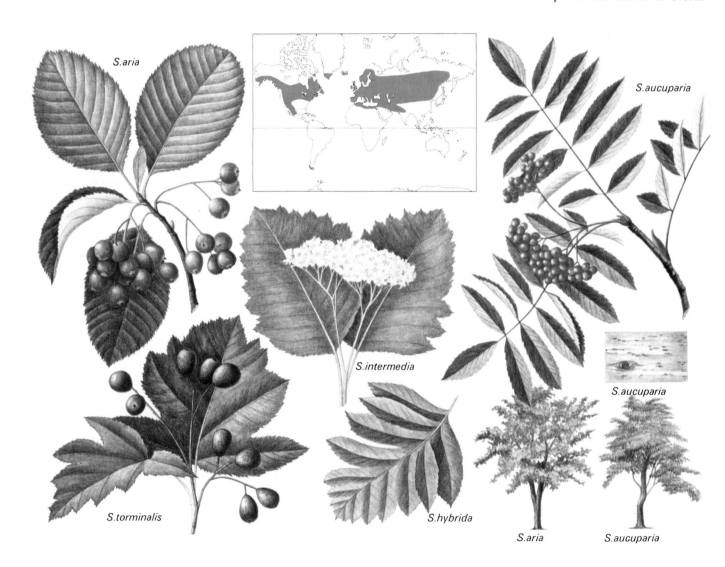

S.aria

S.aucuparia

S.intermedia

S.aucuparia

S.torminalis

S.hybrida

S.aria   S.aucuparia

The Juneberry, Shadbush or Serviceberry (*Amelanchier arborea*) from North America is cultivated for its snow-like but short-lived flowers and bright red fall foliage. Very similar in appearance to *A. canadensis*, with which it is often confused, this species has bronze-tipped and edged leaves as they emerge, which can be seen here.

America, extending as far south as Mexico, with the remainder distributed throughout central and southern Europe and parts of Asia, including China, Japan and Korea. Popular names for the genus are numerous and are often indiscriminately applied to various species, the most common being shadbush, shadblow, serviceberry, juneberry and snowy mespilus.

They are deciduous shrubs or trees, sometimes stoloniferous or suckering. The leaves are alternate, simple, and the stipules soon fall away. The flowers are bisexual, white, borne in terminal racemes of 6–20, rarely only one to three, before or with the leaves. The calyx-tube (hypanthium) is bell-shaped with five small lobes, and there are five petals and 10–20 stamens. The ovary is solitary with two to five chambers and two to five styles. The fruit is a small, purplish to black, often juicy and sweet, pome containing 5–10 seeds.

The species are generally hardy in temperate regions and are not particular as to soil as long as it is not waterlogged. Propagation is by seed, layering or division. Grafting on hawthorn (*Crataegus* spp) stock has been practised but is not recommended. They are cultivated chiefly for their abundant white flowers produced in the spring. Some species, for example *Amelanchier laevis* and *A. lamarckii*, have an attractive bronze or purplish tinge to their leaves, especially the young ones, while *A. asiatica* and *A. lamarckii*, among others, give pleasing reddish leaves in the fall. The sweet and juicy fruits of some species are much sought after by birds, whilst those of *A. canadensis* and *A. stolonifera*, especially the 'Success' strain of the latter are made into jellies for human consumption.

The genus is taxonomically difficult both nomenclaturally and species-wise. There are perplexing intermediates, many no doubt from natural hybridization. This is especially true for the binomial *A. canadensis*, which covers four different species: *A. arborea*, *A. canadensis sensu restricto*, *A. laevis* and *A. lamarckii*, all with their ovary tops glabrous and not hairy-woolly. This is an important character to note. Others are examination of just opened leaves for any indumentum or bronze or purplish tints, and the number of styles and whether they are free to the base or more or less joined from the base upward.

F. B. H.

Apples
(genus *Malus*)

Malus is a genus of 25–30(35) species of deciduous, fruit-bearing trees and shrubs, the fruits of some being known as crabs or crab apples. The genus also includes the many varieties of the long-cultivated Edible Apple (*Malus pumila* – see table for synonyms), which are probably the result of crosses between several species (see table). They are characterized by simple, more or less lobed leaves and bisexual flowers in clusters, ranging from white through pink to purplish, with five petals, five sepals, 15–50 stamens, the anthers typically yellow, and two to five styles united toward the base.

The Cultivated or Edible Apple is an upright or spreading tree with dark, gray-brown, irregularly fissured, scaly bark and gray to reddish-brown twigs. The leaves are simple, ovate or oval, broad cuneate or rounded at the base, crenate-serrate, and generally hairy on the under-surface. The flowers are white, usually suffused with varying degrees of pink, and are formed in clusters of four to seven. They arise sometimes on one-year-old wood (axillary fruit buds), on apical buds of most one-year-old shoots (cultivars known as 'tip-bearers') but more generally on tips of short, about 7cm (2.8in), vegetative growths ('dards' and 'brindilles') and from simple or compound spurs on wood more than two years old. Most cultivars are partially self-sterile and are pollinated by insects such as bees and flies. The fruit is a pome (a false fruit, the greater part of which is developed from the receptacle of the flower, and not from the ovary), green or yellow to red, having five leathery chambers (loculi), each normally containing two seeds or pips.

As with many cultivated plants the origin of the Cultivated Apple, and other species of *Malus* that have contributed to its hybrid constitution, remains uncertain. Available evidence indicates that it originated in the upland regions between the Black Sea, Turkestan and India. Some of the better forms spread westward to be established elsewhere as varieties still capable of future variation.

Apple cultivars have arisen as chance seedlings, by deliberate selection from seedlings of unknown parentage or from naturally occurring bud-sports. Scientific breeding only began when Thomas Andrew Knight (1759–1835) demonstrated that desirable characters in different parents could be combined by their controlled cross-pollination, an approach now being pursued with vigor on a worldwide basis.

Varieties of cultivated apple. *Top* 'Golden Delicious'; *Bottom* 'Belle de Boskoop.'

Irradiation techniques are also being increasingly used to induce desirable mutations. It is interesting to note, however, that 'Cox's Orange Pippin,' 'Bramley's Seedling,' 'Golden Delicious,' 'Granny Smith,' 'Ribston Pippin' and 'Discovery' all originated as chance seedlings.

Today, the apple has developed into one of the most economically important fruits. The worldwide interest in, and importance of, this crop is demonstrated by the existence of over 2 000 named cultivars.

Economically, apples can be classified into four main groups: dessert, cooking, cider and ornamental. Worldwide emphasis has been on the development of dessert types, which are normally cultivars producing average-sized fruits, about 6–7cm (2.4–2.75in) in diameter. They are mainly red and/or yellow (rarely green), with a high sugar content, the particular flavor being largely imparted by the amount of aromatics present. Cooking types are normally large-fruited cultivars, on average 10cm (4in) in diameter, mainly green, with a high acid content. When cooked with sugar the flesh is reduced to a frothy consistency with a well-developed sharp flavor, as in 'Bramley's Seedling.' In England, it has been suggested that the large, ribbed, green early cultivars, such as the 'Costard' (first recorded in 1292 and which gave rise to the term 'costermonger') and 'codlins,' and the smaller, more rounded, sweeter 'pippins' (imported by Henry VIII's gardener, Richard Harris in 1609) were, respectively, the forerunners of present-day cooking and dessert types.

Cider varieties are grown mainly in the United Kingdom, northern France and other northern European countries. They are subdivided into sweets, sharps, bitter-sweets and bitter-sharps, depending on the proportions of sugars, acids and tannins in their expressed juices, all of which, along with certain organic and aromatic substances, have a profound effect on the 'vintage' quality of the cider produced. Most commercial ciders are made by mixing juices from the different cultivars to produce the desired blend of sweetness, acidity or astringency.

Present-day demands cannot be met by the juice from true cider varieties so they are normally supplemented from quantities of downgraded dessert types.

Other apple products are unfermented apple juice, wine, liqueurs, vinegar, fillings for tarts, pies and sauces and pectin from dried apple pulp after juice extraction. More than 23 million tonnes of apples are

Varieties of cultivated apple. From the top: 'Cox's Orange Pippin,' 'Granny Smith,' 'Bramley's Seedling.'

grown annually throughout the world.

A number of *Malus* species, particularly the so-called crab apples, are grown exclusively for their decorative character – the profusion of spring blossom and attractive leaves, shoots and bark. Particularly notable are the hybrids *Malus* 'Eleyi' and *M. × purpurea*, the latter with many fine forms. Many produce quantities of small fruits, of little use other than for making jelly, but they add distinctive splashes of color in parks and gardens in the fall. Recently, their potential as pollinators in commercial orchards and for providing useful characters for apple breeding has aroused considerable interest.

Apples can be grown only in regions where winter temperatures are sufficiently low to provide the chilling required to break bud dormancy. Without it, bud-break in spring fails or is erratic, so making the crop an uneconomic proposition. Distribution, therefore, is confined to the northern and southern temperate zones and the higher altitudes of warmer regions.

Conversely, however, excessive winter cold, which is most likely to occur in regions centered on large land masses, such as Russia and North America, can cause injury or death of buds, bark-splitting, root damage and withering of the stigmas, thus preventing pollination. It is possible to reduce such losses by using rootstocks and cultivars selected for resistance to low temperatures. Soils with adequate depth, drainage, texture, structure and fertility are required.

Many of the pests and diseases that formerly, singly or collectively, caused serious annual losses are now readily controlled by efficient spray chemicals, assisted by cultivars resistant to specific pests or diseases and by improved cultural techniques. However, the comparatively few that remain difficult to control can be extremely destructive unless adequate precautions are taken, for example Powdery Mildew (*Podosphaera leucotricha*), Scab (*Venturla inaequalis*), Fruit Rot (*Phytophthora cactorum*) and Canker (*Nectria galligena*).

The most ubiquitous pest is *Panonychus ulmi* (Fruit Tree Red Spider Mite) which has survived most modern pesticides because of its capacity to develop resistant strains. The Codling Moth (*Laspeyresia pomonella*) is also widely dispersed but is more serious in drier, warmer regions.

E. H. W.

The Main Species of *Malus*

Section *Malus* (*Calycomeles*)
Calyx usually persistent.

Subsection *Malus* No stone cells in fruit; leaves entire.

M. pumila (*M. domestica, M. communis, M. sylvestris* ssp *domestica, M. pumila* ssp *domestica*) Cultivated or Edible Apple. *Malus pumila* is used here to cover only varieties cultivated for their fruit and does not include the main wild ancestors. The main species contributing to the Cultivated Apple have been *M. sylvestris, M. orientalis* and *M. sieversii* with significant contributions from *M. baccata, M. prunifolia* and *M. robusta* and lesser contributions from other species, such as *M. floribunda, M. atrosanguinea, M. zumi* and *M. micromalus*. Through controlled breeding, some of the latter species are now making significant contributions to resistance to diseases and pests. The Cultivated Apple has been distributed throughout the temperate zones of the Northern and the Southern Hemisphere. Chromosome numbers range from diploids ($2n = 34$) via triploids ($2n = 51$) to tetraploids ($2n = 68$).

M. sylvestris ssp *sylvestris* Wild Crab. C, N and E Europe. Small tree. Leaves much less hairy than those of *M. sylvestris* ssp *paradisiaca*. Fruits 2–4cm in diameter and usually acid. It is used as a rootstock; the fruits are used in the production of jelly. Chromosome number is $2n = 34$ and 51. The name 'Crab Apple' as distinct from Wild Crab is sometimes used to distinguish crosses between various cultivated apples and so-called Siberian crabs such as *M. × robusta*. *Malus × astracanica*, the Astrakhan Apple, and *M. prunifolia* have also been involved in such crosses.

M. sylvestris ssp *paradisiaca* (*M. praecox*, *M. paradisiaca*, *M. dasycarpa*) Types include 'Paradise' and 'Doucin.' Leaves more hairy than those of ssp *sylvestris*, fruits usually much sweeter and less acid. Chromosome number is $2n = 34$ and 68. It has been widely used throughout Europe as a dwarfing rootstock for many hundreds of years but is rarely found growing wild. It is possibly a hybrid between ssp *sylvestris* and *M. orientalis* and/or *M. sieversii*.

M. orientalis The Caucasus, especially in sparse oak forest areas. Closely related to *M. pumila*. The tall not very winter-hardy trees produce late-ripening sweet fruit which transports well. Involved in the origin of some Caucasian, Crimean and Italian cultivars.

M. sieversii Closely related to *M. pumila*.

M. sieversii ssp *kirghisorum* Valleys of the Pskem, Ugam and Kok-Su rivers (E USSR). Introgressed into cultivars. Found in the underbush of the Wild Walnut (*Juglans regia*) in W T'ien Shan (W China).

M. sieversii spp *turkmenorum* Kopet-Dag Mts, Turkmenistan (S USSR). Large early-maturing fruit. The cultivar 'Babaarabka' is characterized by the death of the main trunk at about 20 years of age, followed by rejuvenation from soboles (creeping underground stems).

M. sieversii ssp *niedzwetzkyana* Sometimes regarded as a distinct species or a variety of *M. pumila*. SW Siberia, Turkistan (S USSR), T'ien Shan Mts (W China). Small tree with red leaves, dense purple-red flower clusters giving rise to large conical dark red fruits. A parent of many very attractive ornamentals. Chromosome number is $2n = 34$. The hybrid species *M. × purpurea* (*M. atrosanguinea × niedzwetzkyana*) has produced attractive types, such as 'Eleyi,' 'Aldenhamensis' (a useful pollinator for cultivars) and 'Lemoinei.' The cross 'Lemoinei' *× M. sieboldii* gave rise to the fine ornamental 'Profusion' with wine-red scented flowers borne in large clusters, copper-crimson young leaves, small ox-blood-red fruits.

M. prunifolia Chinese Crab Apple, Plum-leaf Crab. N China, E Siberia. Small tree bearing white-pink flowers (rose-crimson in the bud), 3cm in diameter; fruits yellow-red, globose and about 2cm across. The trees are very resistant to frost and drought. It has been used in the breeding of numerous cultivars, including 'Bellefleur-Kitaika' and 'Saffran Pippin.' The chromosome number of the species includes diploids ($2n = 34$), triploids ($2n = 51$) and tetraploids ($2n = 68$). It has been suggested that *M. prunifolia* has arisen as a result of hybridization between *M. baccata* and some other species.

M. prunifolia ssp *rinki* (*M. asiatica*, *M. ringo*) Ringo Crab. China, Korea, Japan. Cultivated for its abundant bright red or yellow fruit. Dwarf almond-pink double-flowered selections are prized as ornamentals. The trees prefer sunny dry limestone outcrops, mountain slopes or hillsides and are not adapted to moist bottom lands. Chromosome number is $2n = 34$. Segregation pattern of seedlings suggests hybrid origin.

M. spectabilis Hai-Tang Crab Apple, Chinese Crab, Chinese Flowering Apple. China, Japan. Cultivated in China as an ornamental and for its fruit, which is used to make the confection called 'Tang-Hu-Lu.' Flowers semidouble–single, rose-red to blush-pink, 4–5cm in diameter. There is a diversity of fruit types, including deep red, pink or purple forms that are angular, long or flat. In China the selections are usually propagated on *M. baccata* rootstocks. The species is not found growing wild. Chromosome number is $2n = 34$ or 51. The *M. × micromalus* (*M. spectabilis × baccata*) hybrid forms a small

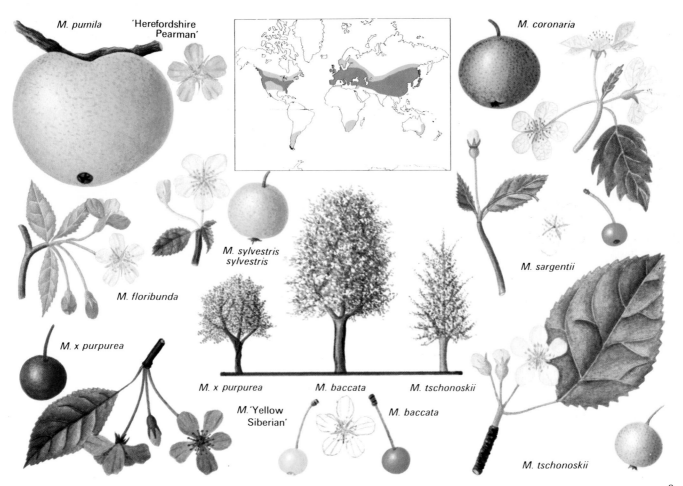

M. pumila 'Herefordshire Pearman'

M. coronaria

M. sylvestris sylvestris

M. floribunda

M. sargentii

M. x purpurea

M. x purpurea

M. baccata

M. tschonoskii

M. 'Yellow Siberian'

M. baccata

M. tschonoskii

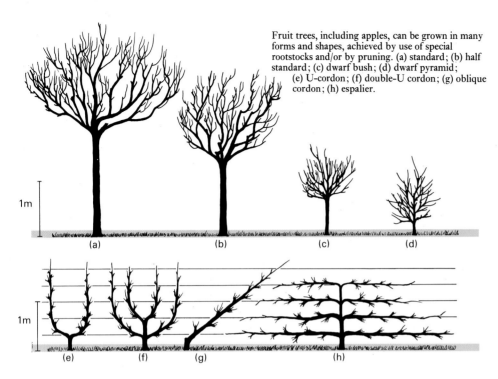

Fruit trees, including apples, can be grown in many forms and shapes, achieved by use of special rootstocks and/or by pruning. (a) standard; (b) half standard; (c) dwarf bush; (d) dwarf pyramid; (e) U-cordon; (f) double-U cordon; (g) oblique cordon; (h) espalier.

tree of upright habit with pink flowers, 4cm in diameter and roundish red fruit, 1.5cm in diameter, with a calyx that is either deciduous or persistent.

Subsection Chloromeles No stone cells in fruit; leaves dissected; fruits green. Native to N America.

M. ioensis Prairie Crab. C USA. One of the few diploids (2*n* = 34) in this subsection, the remainder being mostly triploids or tetraploids. Leaves coarsely serrated or shallowly lobed. Flowers 4cm in diameter. Fruits 3cm in diameter, waxy and green. *M. ioensis* 'Plena' (Bechtels' Crab) is an attractive ornamental tree with violet-scented double flowers. The hybrid *M.* × *soulardii* (*M. pumila* × *ioensis*) – Soulard Crab – is another very attractive ornamental with large almond-pink flowers and yellow (red-flushed) fruit, 5cm in diameter. Another hybrid is 'Red Tip Crab' (*M. ioensis* × *sieversii* ssp *niedzwetzkyana*) characterized by red young leaves and reddish-purple flowers.

M. glaucescens E USA. Tree or shrub forming a wide dense head. Leaves with short triangular lobes (most deeply lobed on the vegetative shoots). When mature the leaves are glabrous and turn an attractive yellow to dark purple in the fall. Flowers 4cm in diameter, with styles that are shorter than the stamens. Fruits waxy, yellow-green, fragrantly scented, 4cm in diameter. Chromosome number is 2*n* = 68. The species is related to *M. glabrata* (2*n* = 68), which differs in having styles that are longer than the stamens.

M. angustifolia Southern Crab. E USA (Virginia to Florida and Mississippi). Slender tree or shrub remaining semi-evergreen in favorable locations. Leaves sharply lobed on vigorous shoots but narrow and toothed on mature shoots. Flowers salmon-pink, violet-scented, 2.5cm

in diameter. Fruits yellowish-green, roundish, 2.5cm in diameter. Chromosome number is 2*n* = 34 or 68. *Malus angustifolia* ssp *pendula* has slender weeping branches.

M. platycarpa SE USA (N Carolina to Georgia). Low spreading tree, characterized by leaves with several pairs of triangular lobes. Flowers large and pink. Fruits pale yellow-green, 5cm in diameter. The fruit is sometimes used to make preserves. Chromosome number is 2*n* = 51 or 68.

M. coronaria Garland Crab. E and C USA. Strong-growing tree. Leaves slightly lobed and short and broad on vigorously growing shoots. Flowers scented, 3.5cm in diameter. Fruits green, 3cm in diameter and slightly ribbed at the apex. Chromosome number is 2*n* = 51 or 68. *M. coronaria* 'Charlottae' has large lobed leaves which become richly colored in the fall. It also has interesting large, shell-pink, semidouble violet-scented flowers which open in late May or early June. *M. bracteata* (2*n* = 51) is a closely related species, which usually has less lobed leaves.

M. lancifolia USA. Medium-sized spreading, often spiny, tree. Leaves rather thin, lanceolate (especially on flowering shoots), slightly lobed on vigorous shoots and glabrous at maturity. Flowers shell-pink, 3.5cm in diameter. Fruits waxy, green, round, 2.5cm in diameter. Chromosome number is 2*n* = 51 or 68.

Subsection Eriomeles Stone cells in fruit; leaves not, or slightly, lobed.

M. prattii C and W China. Tree growing to 10m. Leaves 6–15cm long, red-veined, nonlobed, attractively colored in the fall. Flowers white, 2.5cm in diameter, occurring in many-flowered clusters. Fruits red or yellow, roundish, 1.5cm in diameter. *M. ombrophila* is a related species with fewer styles per flower and slightly larger fruit.

M. yunnanensis W China. Tree similar in size to *M. prattii* but having pointed leaves with 3–5 pairs of short, broad lobes. Flowers white, 1.5cm in diameter, up to 12 per cluster, with 5 or more styles. Fruits deep red, round, 1–1.5cm in diameter, with a reflexed calyx. The crimson and orange fall leaf coloring makes it an attractive ornamental.

Subsection Eriolobus Stone cells in fruit; leaves lobed; very late flowering.

M. trilobata W Asia, E Mediterranean, NE Greece. Tree or shrub. Leaves maple-leaf-like, deeply 3-lobed and sublobed, toothed. Flowers 3.5cm in diameter, opening very late and often failing to set fruit. Fruits (if present) yellow or red.

Subsection Docyniopsis Stone cells in fruit; leaves not, or slightly, lobed.

M. tschonoskii Japan. Large tree. Leaves slightly lobed, 7–12cm long, turning yellow, orange, purple and scarlet in the fall. Flowers white, pink-tinged, 3cm in diameter. Fruits yellow-green, purple-tinged, round, 3cm in diameter. This species, which rarely sets fruit, is an attractive ornamental often planted in public parks for its attractive foliage.

M. doumeri (*M. formosana*) Taiwan. Tree growing to 15m. Leaves slightly lobed, finely serrated, glabrous, 9–15 × 4–6.5cm, without lobes. Flowers 2.5–3cm in diameter. Fruits about 5.5cm in diameter, with a relatively large core. In its native Taiwan the species is found at 1 000–2 000m above sea-level. It is tolerant of warm, moist climatic conditions. *M. laoensis* (*M. laosensis*), from Laos and neighboring areas, is probably related to *M. doumeri*.

M. melliana China. Tree growing to 10m. Leaves pointed, finely serrated, hairy, 5–10 × 2.5–4cm, without lobes. Flowers about 2cm in diameter. Fruits about 2.5cm in diameter, consisting almost exclusively of core. In its native China the species is found at 700 and 2 400m above sea-level.

Section Gymnomeles
Calyx usually deciduous.

Subsection Baccatae Leaves entire; fruit soft-fleshed.

M. baccata Siberian Crab. N and E Asia, N China, E Siberia. Tree growing to 15m; very frost resistant. Leaves 3–8cm long, with finely serrated leaf margins. Flowers white, about 3.5cm across, with styles that are usually longer than the stamens. Fruits red or yellow, berry-like, roundish, about or just under 1cm in diameter. Chromosome number is 2*n* = 34, 51 or 68. The species usually grows at 50–1 500m above sea-level. It is used as a rootstock for fruiting apples and flowering crab apples and as an ornamental for its showy flowers and handsome foliage. The species *M.* × *robusta* is a hybrid between *M. baccata* and *M. prunifolia*. *M.* × *robusta* 5 is a Canadian selection from this hybrid and is used as a very cold hardy rootstock for commercial apple cultivars. The ornamental hybrid *M.* × *hartwigii* (*M. halliana* × *baccata*) forms a small tree with semidouble pink-white flowers, 5cm in diameter.

M. baccata var *mandshurica* Manchurian Crab. C China, Korea, Japan, E Siberia. Tree similar to *M. baccata* but with styles scarcely as long as the stamens and fruit to about 1.2cm in diameter. It grows at 100–2 100m above sea-level. It is cultivated for its fragrantly-scented flowers and also serves as a hardy rootstock.

M. baccata ssp *sachalinensis* Sakhalin Apple.

M. baccata ssp *gracilis* Small pendent-branched tree. Leaves small, 1.5–3cm long, on long stalks. Fruits to 3cm in diameter.

M. baccata ssp *nickovsky* In some cases only growing to 1m in height in 100 years.

M. rocki (*M. himalaica*?) Himalayan Apple. W China, the Himalaya. Closely related to *M. baccata*. Leaves 12cm long, pubescent on the lower surface. Fruits more or less round, about 1cm in diameter, with a calyx that is very slow to dehisce. Chromosome number includes types with $2n = 68$. The species grows at between 2 400–3 800m above sea-level.

M. sikkimensis Sikkim Apple. The Himalaya. Closely related to *M. baccata*. Small tree with stout branching spurs at the base of the branches. Flowers white or at most slightly pink. Fruits often slightly pear-shaped, dotted and about 1.5cm long. Reported to be a triploid with 51 chromosomes.

M. hupehensis (*M. theifera*) Hupei Apple. China, Japan, Assam (NE India). Medium-sized tree with stiff branches. Flowers fragrant, pink then white, 4cm in diameter. Fruits yellow-green (red-tinted), about 1cm in diameter. Chromosome number is $2n = 51$ or 68. The species grows at 50–2 900m above sea-level.

M. ×halliana Hall's Apple. China, Japan. Small tree. Leaves dark, glossy, glabrous (except for the midrib), sometimes colored slightly purple. Flowers red in the bud but becoming paler when open, 3cm in diameter. Fruits purple, 8mm in diameter. Chromosome number is $2n = 34$ or 51. 'Parkmanii' is an attractive ornamental selection with pendulous semidouble, rose-red to shell-pink flowers on crimson pedicels.

Subsection *Sorbomalus* Leaves dissected; clusters of red or yellow fruit.

Series *Sieboldianae* Styles with long weak loose hairs at base; calyx and pedicels glabrous or slightly pubescent.

M. sieboldii (*M. toringo*) Toringo Crab. Korea. Shrub 2–10m high, with a profusely branching, spreading (or semi-weeping) habit. Leaves 3–5-lobed. Flowers pink or red in the bud, fading to white when open, 2cm in diameter; often self-fertile. Fruits red (or sometimes yellow-brown) and about 6–8mm in diameter. Chromosome number is $2n = 34$, 68 or 85. The species is tolerant of salt. The dwarf types are cultivated in Japan as ornamentals; they are also of some value as a dwarfing rootstock. *M. ×sublobata* (*M. prunifolia × sieboldii*) is a small pyramidal tree with slightly lobed leaves, pink flowers and yellow fruit. *M. ×zumi* (*M. baccata* var *mandshurica ×sieboldii*) – Zumi Crab – is similar to *M. sieboldii* but has larger flowers

(3cm) and bright red fruit (1.2cm). *M. zumi* 'Calocarpa' is a variant with a more spreading habit, attractive small leaves and flowers, and fruit which stays on the tree through the winter. *M. ×atrosanguinea* (*M. halliana × sieboldii*) – Carmine Crab – is an attractive hybrid forming a small tree with green, glossy, nearly glabrous leaves and a profusion of flowers which are crimson in the bud and rose-colored when open. It looks much like *M. floribunda* and

produces red-tinted yellow fruit. A selection from *M. atrosanguinea* has been used in breeding for resistance to Apple Scab (*Venturia inaequalis*) in commercial apples.

M. sargentii Sargent's Apple. Japan. Shrub growing to 2m, producing a mass of white flowers and red cherry-like fruit.

Children picking apples in an orchard near Wandiligeng, Victoria State, Australia.

Chromosome number is $2n = 34$, 51 or 68.

M. floribunda Japanese or Showy Crab. Japan. A very attractive tree flowering abundantly. Flowers deep carmine-red in the bud, fading to pale blush and eventually to white when open, 3cm in diameter. Fruits red (or sometimes yellow), round, 8mm in diameter. Chromosome number is $2n = 34$. A selection has been very widely used as a source of a major gene for Apple Scab (*Venturia inaequalis*) resistance in commercial apple breeding programs. The hybrid *M. × arnoldiana* (*M. baccata × floribunda*) is a small floriferous tree produced in the Arnold Arboretum in the USA in 1883. It has red buds, white flowers and red-tinted yellow fruit (1cm in diameter). Another hybrid, *M. × scheideckeri* (*M. floribunda × prunifolia*) is a slow-growing tree with a profusion of semidouble fragrant pale pink flowers, 3.5cm in diameter, and yellow fruit, 1.5cm in diameter. The trees do not do well on thin alkaline soils. The species *M. brevipes* ($2n = 34$) is related to *M. floribunda* but has a more compact habit.

Series *Florentinae* Styles with long weak loose hairs at the base; calyx and pedicels hairy; leaves distinctly lobed.

M. florentina (*M. crataegifolia*) Italy. Small tree with hawthorn-like foliage; under-surface of the leaves hairy; flowers white, 3cm in diameter; fruits 1.2cm long. In the fall the orange and scarlet leaves make a fine ornamental display.

Series *Kansuenses* Styles glabrous.

M. toringoides China. Very attractive small tree with flowing wide-spreading branches. Flowers creamy-white, 2.5cm in diameter, occurring in subsessile umbels. Fruits red and yellow, round or pear-shaped, 1.2cm long. Chromosome number is $2n = 51$ or 68. *M. transitoria* (NW China) is related to *M. toringoides* but is more elegant in general appearance and with much more deeply lobed leaves and smaller, rounder yellow fruit. Both species have attractive fall leaf coloration.

M. kansuensis NW China. Small tree. Leaves with hairs on the veins of the lower surface. Flowers creamy-white, 1.5cm in diameter, each having a hairy calyx. Fruits red or yellow, 1cm long. The related species, *M. honanensis* (NE China), has dotted roundish fruits, 8mm in diameter.

M. komarovii China. Small tree growing to 3m. Leaves lobed as in *M. kansuensis*, 4–8 × 3–7cm. Flowers 3.5cm in diameter. Fruits 8–10mm in diameter. In its native China the species is found at 1 100–1 300m.

M. fusca (*M. diversifolia*, *M. rivularis*) Oregon Crab. USA (mainly Washington and Oregon but also California to Alaska). Large shrub or small tree with vigorous dense growth, often producing a dense almost impenetrable thicket. Flowers white or pink, 2–5cm in diameter. Fruits red or yellow, 1.5cm long. R.W.

Note: The distribution map also shows major areas of fruit cultivation (yellow) outside the native regions (brown).

Pears
(genus *Pyrus*)

Pears are popular edible fruits produced by the 15–20 species of the genus *Pyrus*. They are deciduous shrubs or trees, sometimes with spines, and the leaves are simple and alternate. The flowers are bisexual, occurring in simple umbel-like corymbs. They have five sepals and petals, 20–30 stamens with typically red to purplish anthers, and two to five styles, free to the base; the ovary is inferior, consisting of two to five cells united together and with the receptacular calyx-tube (hypanthium). The fruit is a pome (false fruit), mostly pyriform (pear-shaped), the enlarged receptacular tissue forming the edible flesh with its numerous grit cells (stone cells) and surrounding the papery to cartilaginous ovary wall which with its seeds comprises the true fruit, popularly the core.

In the past, it was not uncommon to unite apples (*Malus*) and pears (*Pyrus*) in one genus, *Pyrus*. In fact, Linnaeus himself wrote *Pyrus malus* for the Wild or Crab Apple. This is quite unjustified. Apples have typically yellow anthers, the styles are united below and the edible flesh is typically without grit cells. Moreover, grafts, either way, between apples and pears are not successful.

Pears have evolved over a period of more than 2 000 years from a primary center in central Asia with secondary centers arising in both China and the Caucasian region. In China and Japan *Pyrus pyrifolia* (*P. serotina*), a species with hard crisp fruit, formed the population from which that region's cultivated varieties were selected, these being known by the various group names of Oriental, Chinese, Sand or Japanese pears. They are distinctly gritty (from stone cells), have little flavor and are mostly used for culinary purposes. These Oriental pears have not spread beyond China and Japan to any significant extent except as rootstocks or as parents in breeding programs.

The European or Common Pear (*P. communis*) is an aggregate species with a center of origin in Asia Minor and complex history of hybrid origin, believed to involve ancestral wild species such as *P. pyraster*, *P. syriaca*, *P. salvifolia*, *P. nivalis*, *P. austriaca*, *P. cordata* and possibly

Apple blossom in full bloom. Some *Malus* species are grown purely as ornamentals.

The unmistakable fruit of the cultivated Pear (*Pyrus communis*); this cultivar is 'Merton Pride.'

others. From this 'mixture' have been derived the cultivated or orchard pears. More than 1 000 different kinds of cultivated pears are known. These have frequently escaped back to wild conditions and 'back-crossed' with one or other of the above supposed ancestors. It is thus not possible to distinguish with any certainty how really 'wild' the present descendants of the supposed ancestors are. These are sometimes treated as subspecies of *P. communis*, but recent treatments maintain their specific rank and this is followed here. *Pyrus communis* may thus be taken as a species which has 'bred itself back' into natural habitats. *Pyrus pyraster* is little more than a form with a greater frequency of spines, smaller flowers and fruits, the last not really sweet tasting. Some authorities would regard *P. pyraster* as the correct name for the nearest thing to a

wild pear. Unlike some of the ancestral species, the leaves of the Common and Wild Pear are virtually always shallowly crenate.

Pears have been cultivated since ancient times. Homer spoke of their cultivation in 1 000 BC, Theophrastus described grafting of selected varieties in 300 BC and Pliny and Cato recorded the widespread continuation of the use of grafting for pears throughout the Roman Empire.

Following the fall of the Roman Empire little or no progress was made in the cultivation of pears until interest revived in France in the early 17th century. Pear breeding was first initiated in 1730 by the Abbé Nicolas Hardenpont in Belgium. He was the first person to select varieties with the soft melting flesh that is a feature of most modern commercially produced pears. Jean Baptiste Van Mons (1765–1842), one of the many enthusiasts who continued Hardenpont's breeding work,

at one time had 80 000 seedlings under test in his nursery and released several dozen new varieties during his lifetime.

In Europe, pears were grown mostly in gardens and propagated by grafting, but when they were first taken to North America most of the propagation was by seed. Only in the 19th century, when pressure to produce uniform commercial (rather than garden) products developed, did it become the general practise in North America to select varieties for propagation by grafting. The selections chosen were often of European origin. Historically, European pear breeders have been given credit for adding quality to the fruit while North American breeders have added cold hardiness and resistance to disease.

Fireblight caused by the bacteria *Erwinia amylovora* has made it impossible to grow pears in large areas of the central United States of America where the summers are very warm and humid. Following the spread of the disease to Europe some 30 years ago there has been concern as to its effect on the very important European pear industry. However, because of differences in climate, it seems unlikely that the disease will have more than a minor impact in northern Europe although it still remains to be seen what effect it will have if it spreads to more southerly regions.

The Oriental Pear (*P. pyrifolia*) crossed with the European or Common Pear (*P. communis*) gave rise to important commercial varieties, such as 'Le Conte,' 'Kieffer' and 'Garber.' These are more resistant to fireblight than the standard European pears but have fruit of poorer quality, which makes them more suitable for canning than for fresh consumption. Resistance to fireblight has also been obtained from Chinese varieties such as 'Ba Li Hsiang' (*P. ussuriensis*).

In North America, pears have usually been grafted on pear seedlings obtained from commercial varieties such as 'Winter Nelis,' 'Bartlett' (known in Europe as 'Williams' Bon Chrétien') and 'Beurre Rose.' On such rootstocks large trees are produced which, although relatively slow to come into fruit production, are able to withstand cold winter conditions. In contrast, in Europe the Quince (*Cydonia oblonga*), including vegetatively propagated selections such as 'Quince A,' are used as rootstocks because of their ability to dwarf and induce trees to fruit early in their life. When the quince/pear graft union is incompatible, as is the case with varieties such as 'Williams' Bon Chrétien,' it is necessary to insert a piece of a com-

Most pears are grown for their fruit but a few have ornamental value. Perhaps the best is the Willow-leafed Pear (*Pyrus salicifolia*); cultivar 'Pendula,' with its elegant weeping branches and silvery-gray foliage is the best form.

patible pear variety such as 'Beurre Hardy' or 'Old Home' between the quince root-stock and the incompatible scion variety.

Pear decline caused by a mycoplasma spread by the Pear Psylla (*Psylla pyricola*) has caused the death of millions of trees in the United States of America. Most of these trees were being grown in the Pacific Coast region on oriental rootstocks such as *P. pyrifolia* (*P. serotina*) and *P. ussuriensis*. Seed from the Chinese species *P. calleryana* and *P. betulaefolia* and from European pear varieties has provided a source of rootstocks that render the grafted tree resistant to the mycoplasma. 'Old Home,' used as a vegetatively propagated rootstock, appears to give complete protection against pear decline.

The present world production of pears is over 7 million tonnes per year. Major producers are Italy, China, West Germany, the United States, France and Japan.

A few pear species are grown as ornamentals, the most notable being three closely related species, all characterized by abundant pure white flowers, whitish leaves with entire margins and a tapering leaf base: *P. salicifolia* 'Pendula,' *P. nivalis* and *P. elaeagrifolia*. R. W.

The Main Species of *Pyrus*

Section *Pyrus*

Fruit typically with persistent calyx (but finally deciduous in *P. cordata*). Species native to Europe, N Africa through to C Asia, Manchuria and Japan.

P. communis Common or European Pear. Europe, W Asia; doubtfully native in Britain. Tree to 15(20)m. Shoots with variable number of spines. Leaves more or less ovate, 2–8 × 1–2cm, margin finely crenate, rarely smooth. Flowers 3cm across. Fruits roundish to pyriform (pear-shaped), 6–16cm long, finally soft-fleshed and sweet-tasting. An important contributor to cultivated pears, these being sometimes referred to as var *culta*.

P. pyraster Wild Pear. W Asia, C Europe. Very similar to previous species, but more constantly thorny and flowers smaller. Fruits less than 6 × 2cm and somewhat sour to taste. Possibly one of the most important contributors to the cultivated pears.

P. nivalis Snow Pear. S Europe, especially W Switzerland, France. Thornless small upright tree to 16m. Leaves elliptic to obovate, 5–8 × 2–4cm, white tomentose at first (as also the young shoots), finally glabrous above. Flowers white (April); in full flower seen from a distance the tree appears like a giant snowball. Fruits sweet (when overripe), yellow-green, round, 2–5cm across, on long stalks. Sometimes cultivated as an ornamental and for the production of perry (pear cider); it is also used as a rootstock. The hairy leaves and high stomatal density suggest a relationship with some south European cultivars.

P. salvifolia Poirier Sauger. This is possibly related to *P. nivalis* (and native to the same area) but has pyriform fruit. Considered by some to be a hybrid between *P. nivalis* and *P. communis*.

P. cordata W Europe (France, Spain, Portugal). Smaller in all parts than *P. communis* and *P. pyraster*, especially the round, white-speckled brown fruits only 9–12(15)mm across. Untypically for its section, the calyx is finally deciduous. It is found in hedges and sometimes cultivated for its wood.

P. longipes Algeria. Shrub or small tree with fine-toothed leaves. It is closely related to *P. communis* but has a partly deciduous calyx. Fruits brown and dotted, round and about 1.5cm in diameter. It was probably involved with *P. communis* in the origin of some cultivars. *Pyrus boissieriana* is a closely related Persian species.

P. syriaca Armenia through W Asia to Cyprus. Forms a small thorny tree with glossy green leaves. The species is closely related to *P. communis* and was probably involved in the origin of some cultivars where *P. communis* is the main contributory species.

P. balansae W Asia. Long-stalked turbinate (top-shaped) fruit borne on a long stalk. It is related to *P. communis*.

P. caucasia Caucasus (forest zone). Vigorous tree that spreads rapidly in open areas. The lowland type is vigorous, frost- and drought-resistant; the highland type is less vigorous and susceptible to frosts and drought. The species was involved in the origin of some E European cultivars.

P. turcomanica This species is related to *P. communis* and *P. caucasia*. Well characterized by the snow-white pubescence of all young parts and sepal lobes adpressed to the fruit.

P. korshinskyi W T'ien Shan (W China), Pamir region of Tadzhikistan (S USSR). Fruits roundish, 2cm in diameter, with a stout stalk. The species is related to *P. communis*.

P. armeniacaefolia China. This species was first reported in 1963 and is similar to *P. communis* in some respects but with apricot-like leaves.

P. salicifolia Willow-leafed Pear. W Asia, SE Europe. Young leaves covered with silvery hairs but becoming glabrous (hairless) and grayish-green on the upper surface later. Fruits pyriform, 2.5cm long, with a short stalk. The species is involved in the origin of some cultivars. It makes an attractive ornamental and is a graft-compatible drought-resistant rootstock.

'Pendula' is a graceful tree to 8m with slender pendulous branches; leaves narrow-lanceolate, 3–9 × 0.7–2cm, appearing whitish when young from a dense matting of silvery hairs, finally shining green above.

P. × canescens (*P. nivalis × salicifolia*) is a fine small, silver-leafed hybrid.

P. glabra is a related subglobose-fruited species from Persia.

P. amygdaliformis W Asia, S Europe. Shrub or small tree, sometimes thorny. Leaves narrow, silvery and hairy when young but becoming sage-green and less hairy later. Fruits yellow-brown, globose, 3cm in diameter, borne on stout 3cm long stalks.

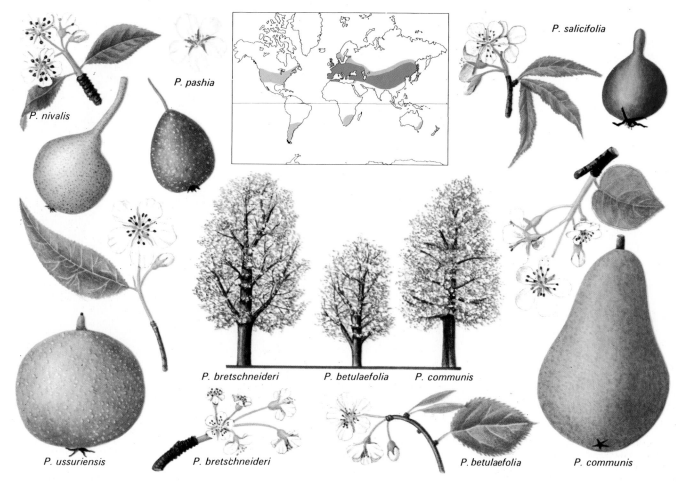

P. salicifolia

P. pashia

P. nivalis

P. ussuriensis

P. bretschneideri

P. betulaefolia

P. communis

P. bretschneideri

P. betulaefolia

P. communis

The hairs and high stomatal density of the leaves suggest an involvement in the origin of some S European cultivars. The *P. × michauxii* (*P. amygdaliformis × nivalis*) hybrid forms a small tree with gray to glossy green leaves.

P. elaeagrifolia Asia Minor. Small, usually thorny tree with attractive grayish-white hairy leaves. Fruits green, short-stalked, rounded or turbinate (top-shaped), about 2.5cm in diameter. Very closely related to *P. nivalis*.

P. regelii Bukhara region of Uzbekistan and Pamir region of Tadzhikistan (S USSR), W T'ien Shan (W China). Shrub or small tree, very resistant to drought. Leaves very variable, more or less unlobed and coarsely serrate or with 3–7 narrow lobes almost to the midrib. Fruits nearly pyriform, 2.5cm long.

P. takhtadzhiani W Asia. Tree with same growth habit as Common Pear cultivars but now found only in the wild, although formerly cultivated.

P. ussuriensis Ussurian Pear. Manchuria, especially the valley of the Ussuri River. Small to medium-sized tree that is very winter-hardy and adapted to cold dry areas. Leaves glabrous, turning crimson-bronze in the fall. Flowers 3.5cm in diameter, appearing very early in the spring. Fruits green-yellow, short-stalked, roundish, 4cm in diameter. This species was possibly involved with *P. communis* in the origin of some ancient cultivars. It often lacks resistance to Pear Scab (*Venturia piri*) but includes types resistant to Fireblight

(*Erwinia amylovora*). It is used as a rootstock (although inducing susceptibility to pear decline disease), as an ornamental and widely as a parent in scion variety breeding programs. *Pyrus ussuriensis* ssp *cuoidea* (N China, Korea) has ovoid-round fruits. The long-stalked species, *P. lindleyi*, is closely related to *P. ussuriensis*.

P. hopeiensis Hopeh Province (NE China). The species was first reported in 1963 and is probably related to *P. ussuriensis* but has fewer seeds, smaller fruit, very short stamens and long styles.

P. pseudopashia China. The species was first reported in 1963 and is possibly related to *P. xerophila*.

P. xerophila China. The species was first reported in 1963. Leaves small, pointed, with only a few small serrations; fruits round, 1.5cm in diameter, with a very large core; stamens extending well beyond the ends of the styles. It is adapted to a hot dry climate.

Section *Pashia*

The calyx is typically deciduous (but see *P. cordata* in section *Pyrus*). The species are native to China and the Himalaya.

P. pyrifolia (*P. serotina*) Chinese, Japanese, Oriental or Sand Pear. Widely cultivated in China and Japan and named 'Sand' for the stone cells, which give the fruit a firm crisp texture. The collective name for the numerous cultivated pears is var *culta*. The roundish brown fruit travels and stores well. It has been hybridized with the

Common Pear to improve the storage and Fireblight (*Erwinia amylovora*) resistance of Western cultivars. *Pyrus × lecontei* (*P. communis × pyrifolia*) hybrids include 'Kieffer' and 'Le Conte.' The Japanese selection 'Twentieth Century' is one of the best cultivars. As a rootstock, however, *P. pyrifolia* induces susceptibility to pear decline disease. *Pyrus bretschneideri* (*P. betulaefolia × pyrifolia*), from N China, is slightly less hardy than the very winter-hardy *P. ussuriensis*. It bears medium-sized fruit of better flavor and texture than other Oriental pears.

P. betulaefolia N and C China. Small, slender and graceful tree. Fruits 1cm in diameter, borne in long-stalked cherry-like clusters. Some selections are resistant to Pear Scab *Venturia piri*). The species is used as a rootstock for which it has the advantage of inducing resistance to pear decline disease.

P. phaeocarpa N China. The brown pyriform fruit rapidly becomes soft after harvest.

P. calleryana China, Japan, Korea. Medium-sized tree. Leaves glabrous, glossy green. Flowers with as many as 20 stamens but normally only 2 styles. Fruits brown, dotted, about 1cm in diameter. The species is used as a rootstock, which induces resistance to pear decline disease. 'Bradford' is a nonthorny selection producing dense blooms in late March or early April and attractive colored leaves in the fall.

P. pashia W China, the Himalaya. Fairly large spiny tree, although some selections are small. Leaves hairy when young but becoming nearly glabrous when older;

vigorous shoots sometimes have 3-lobed leaves. Flowers with up to 30 stamens (with red anthers) and 3–5 styles. Fruits brown, round, about 2.5cm in diameter. The species is used as a rootstock and is sometimes cultivated for its fruit.

P. serrulata China. Fruits brown (with pale dots), rounded, with a calyx that is sometimes more or less persistent.

P. sinkiangensis Sinkiang region (W China). The species was first reported in 1963 and is possibly closely related to *P. serrulata*.

Note: The distribution map also shows major areas of fruit cultivation (yellow) outside the native regions (brown).

Plums, Apricots, Almonds, Peaches, Cherries
(genus *Prunus*)

A Peach Tree (*Prunus persica*) in fruit. Formerly included in a separate genus (*Amygdalus*), it now belongs to a subgenus within *Prunus*.

The commercially important stone fruit crops (plums, apricots, peaches, cherries) together with the almond, ornamental cherries and cherry laurel all belong to the genus *Prunus* which comprises about 200 species mainly of the north temperate zone, a few extending to the Andes mountains of South America. They are mostly deciduous, less frequently evergreen, shrubs or trees with alternate leaves that are typically serrate, with stipules. The flowers are bisexual, solitary, fascicled or in racemes with five sepals and petals, the latter mostly white, sometimes pink to red. There are usually more than 15 stamens situated on the edge of a calyx-tube (hypanthium) which surrounds the single two-ovuled ovary with a single style. The fruit is a drupe that typically matures one seed.

There are almost countless cultivars, varieties and hybrids including plants selected for their ornamental value of spring blossoms, fall colors, edible fruits (the fleshy mesocarp of the drupe) and sometimes the edible seed (kernel) which is surrounded by a stony endocarp – seed and endocarp being commonly called a 'stone.'

The genus is divided into five subgenera (treated by some as separate genera) which fall into two broad groups. The first group, in which the fruit typically has a longitudinal furrow (sulcate) extending more than halfway on one side and the skin has a bloom, comprises the subgenera *Prunus = Prunophora* (plums and apricots) and *Amygdalus* (peaches and almonds). The second group, in which the fruit is sometimes furrowed but to less than halfway and the skin has no bloom, comprises subgenera *Cerasus* (cherries), *Padus* (bird cherries) and *Laurocerasus* (cherry laurels).

Plums are remarkable among orchard fruits for their very great diversity of tree vigor, habit and fruit shape. There is good evidence, including genetical evidence, that plums, bullaces, damsons and greengages should be referred to the binomial *Prunus domestica* agg as subspecies, and that this taxon has resulted from a cross between *P. spinosa* (Sloe, Blackthorn) and *P. cerasifera* (Cherry Plum, Myrobalan). The latter species is known only in cultivation but there is little doubt that it has arisen from the very closely related *P. divaricata*, a genuinely wild species from western Asia which forms natural but sterile hybrids with *P. spinosa*. Plums have been cultivated in the Old World for at least 2000 years.

Subspecies *domestica*, with its cultivars, is the plum proper, which can be eaten fresh, cooked or preserved in various ways. Where the climate permits, many cultivars are dried and marketed as prunes, which are often consumed for their mild purgative action, a property shared to some extent by all plums. In cooler areas the cultivars tend to bear smaller fruits, more suitable for canning and making into jams. In Yugoslavia *slivovitz* (plum brandy) is produced by distillation of fermented juices of such plums. The annual world production of plums is about 4 million tonnes, the main producing areas being Europe and North America.

The Bullace and Damson (ssp *insititia*) are found wild in many parts of Europe (naturalized in Britain) and Asia. The fruits are astringent, purplish, more or less globose in the Bullace, oval in the Damson. The name Damson derives from Damascus where they were cultivated before the Christian era. A group of clones of this subspecies known as St. Julien is used extensively as rootstocks for the European plums.

The Greengage (spp *italica*) originated from the cultivar 'Reine Claude,' itself a cross between subspecies *domestica* and subspecies *insititia*. It is widely cultivated for the delicate and sweet flavor of its yellowish-green fruits, which is subtly distinct from that of plums.

The Sloe or Blackthorn (*P. spinosa*) is a dense suckering shrub with spiny branches and small white flowers, usually single or in pairs, appearing in early spring before the leaves. The black, globose fruits, 1cm across, are very astringent but are used for flavoring, for example in sloe gin, a well-known liqueur. The plant is native and widespread throughout Europe, extending to parts of northern Asia.

The Japanese Plum (*P. salicina*) is grown mainly in those areas enjoying freedom from spring frosts, such as parts of the United States of America, Italy and South Africa. Cultivars of this species flower very early in the year, before the European types. Despite its common name, it is not indigenous to Japan, although extensively cultivated there, and is thought to have originated in China. Most cultivars produce very large (5–7cm long) highly colored fruits of inferior quality to the best European types. Their lower perishability, however, permits export of fresh fruit over long distances. In Europe it is probably only planted for its flowers.

The Cherry Plum or Myrobalan (*P. cerasifera*) is known only in cultivation, but is undoubtedly derived from the very closely related *P. divaricata* which is genuinely wild from the Balkans to central Asia. It is only occasionally grown for its cherry-like fruits and is perhaps more appreciated for its very early spring flowering. A group of types known as the Myrobalans is frequently used as rootstocks for plums where trees of high vigor and tolerance to heavy soil conditions are required. The variety *pissardii* ('Atropurpurea') is commonly planted for its reddish-purple leaves which appear before the pinkish flowers in early spring.

Other ornamentals include *P. × blizeana* of supposed parentage *P. cerasifera* var *pissardii × P. mume*, with double rose-pink flowers, and *P. × cistena*, another hybrid involving *P. cerasifera* var *pissardii* this time with *P. pumila* or, possibly, *P. besseyi*: it has crimson to bronzy-red leaves and white flowers appearing in spring before the leaves.

The Apricot (*P. armeniaca*) is an important fruit crop that is believed to have originated in western China and to have been brought to Italy about 100 BC, reaching England in the 13th century and America in 1720. The fruit is smaller than a peach, typically orange-yellow when ripe, and with drier flesh. Its food value ranks higher than most common fruits, particularly in vitamin A as well as proteins and carbohydrates. The United States of

America is the largest producer, others being Hungary, Turkey, Spain and France. The annual world production is about 1.3 million tonnes. About half the commercial crop is dried with smaller quantities canned or sold fresh. A well-drained soil is required and freedom from spring frost. A too warm winter encourages flower bud fall and a more or less semi-arid locality is important in the ripening season as maturing fruits tend to split during heavy rain.

The main all-purpose cultivar is 'Royal.' Propagation is by budding onto apricot and peach seedling stocks. Nearly all cultivars are self-fertile. Fruits are produced on one-year-old shoots and short-lived spurs. Biennial bearing is sometimes a problem so pruning to renew spur systems and also fruit thinning is often necessary. Trees usually fruit after the third year and may be productive for up to 20 years.

Sweet and Bitter Almonds (*P. amygdalus* = *P. dulcis*). *Prunus amygdalus* var *dulcis* includes those grown for their flowers as well as those cultivated primarily for their sweet almonds which are the most widely consumed of all edible nuts. Italy is the main exporter, but almonds are also grown in North Africa, South Africa and California. The annual world production is about 0.7 million tonnes. Sweet almonds contain the enzyme complex commonly called emulsin and exceedingly small amounts of the glucoside amygdalin. When enzyme and glucoside are brought together by crushing, chewing or any

Sweet Almonds (*Prunus amygdalus* var *dulcis*); the hard outer shell is the inner wall of the fruit within which is the seed.

other sort of injury, for example exposure to organic solvents such as chloroform, then eventually benzaldehyde and prussic acid are formed. As is well-known, prussic acid (hydrogen cyanide) is a powerful and deadly poison, about 65 milligrams (1 grain) being sufficient to kill an adult. A possible trace of amygdalin in sweet almonds yields so little prussic acid that some 900 almonds weighing about 567g (1¼lb) would have to be consumed at one sitting to produce this fatal dose of cyanide; and this is on the assumption that the maximum amount of prussic acid is produced by the enzyme under these conditions. This poison is rapidly destroyed in the human body and is not cumulative, so that over an extended period a far greater quantity would have to be consumed before death occurred. On the other hand, the amygdalin content of bitter almonds (var *amara*) is about 2–3 percent and only about 28g (1oz) or some 45–50 kernels could yield enough prussic acid, if chewed and ingested, to prove fatal. Equivalent poisonous doses for children are, of course, much smaller and it is suggested that a young child should not consume more than about 20 sweet almonds at any one sitting or not more than 50 for an older one, and never at any time should children eat bitter almonds. Because of the potentially dangerous amounts of prussic acid in bitter almonds (var *amara*), commercially ground almonds used in the making of marzipan and for flavoring macaroons should not contain any bitter almonds. Medicinal almond oil or *Oleum amygdalae* is obtained by expressing it from both sweet and bitter almonds, but more especially the latter, the amygdalin remaining behind. It is used for toilet preparations, food flavoring and in the treatment, by injection, of haemorrhoids (piles).

The Peach (*P. persica*) is closely related to the almond and much prized for its delicious fleshy (furry) fruit, of which there are many varieties, as well as for the numerous so-called 'flowering' peaches. The variety *nectarina* is the Nectarine, differing by having a smooth skin like a plum. The peach originated in China (still the area of greatest diversity) under conditions that gave a selective advantage to self-pollination. Consequently, peach varieties can normally be planted without pollinators. Peaches have been cultivated in China since at least 2000 BC. It seems likely that the Nectarine arose as a mutant and was selected for cultivation at a later date, after the Peach had spread to the

The Main Species of *Prunus*

Subgenus *Prunus* (*Prunophora*)

Fruit with external longitudinal groove (sulcate), typically hairless and with bloom. Often spring-flowering before the leaves. No terminal bud, axillary buds solitary.

Section *Prunus*

Typically 1–2-stalked flowers per cluster. Leaves in bud convolute. Ovary and fruit glabrous.

P. spinosa Blackthorn, Sloe. W Asia, Europe, N Africa. Very thorny shrub or small tree to about 4m. Flowers solitary before the leaves. Fruit blue-black with distinctive bloom, globose, 1–1.5cm, very astringent. Generally accepted as involved with *P. cerasifera* in the ancestry of *P. domestica*.

P. domestica agg (*P. spinosa* × *P. cerasifera*) Plums, Bullaces, Damsons, Greengages. Natural hybrids of this parentage occur in the Caucasus. The cultivated plants grown for their fruits and widely naturalized.

ssp *domestica* European or Garden Plum. W Asia, Europe. Tree 10–12m, spines absent. Flowers in pairs, greenish-white, about 2cm across. Fruit 4–7.5cm, longer than wide, bluish-black, purple, red. Widely cultivated in temperate zones.

ssp *insititia* Bullace, Damson, St. Julien. W Asia, Europe. Shrub or tree to 6m, often with thorns. Flowers white, about 2.5cm across. Fruit 2–5cm long, blue-black; round and sweet in Bullace, oval and astringent in Damson (originating near Damascus).

ssp *italica* (ssp *domestica* × ssp *insititia*) Greengage ('Reine Claude'). ?Armenia. Introduced into England by the Gage family between 1494 and 1547. Fruit more or less globose, greenish, taste sweet, very characteristic.

P. cerasifera Myrobalan, Cherry Plum. W Asia. Shrub or tree 8–10m, often spiny. Flowers solitary, about 2.5cm across, appearing with or a little before the leaves, mostly white. Fruit globose, cherry-like, 2–3cm across, red. Only known in cultivation, more as an ornamental, only to a limited extent for its fruit, but important as rootstock for other plum species.

var *pissardii* has leaves reddish, purple-tinged, with pinkish flowers is much more common as an ornamental. *P. divaricata* is the wild form of the species differing virtually only by smaller fruits which are yellow. Caucasus east to Asia.

P. × *syriaca* (*P. cerasifera* × *P. domestica*), the Mirabelle Plum, with subglobose yellow fruits is known in a semi-wild state in Europe.

P. salicina Salicine, Japanese Plum. China. Tree to about 12m. Flowers white, about 2cm across, typically in clusters of 3, appearing well before the leaves. Fruit sweet, more or less globose, 5–7cm long, depressed at stalk end, varying (greenish) yellow, orange, red. Long cultivated in Japan and elsewhere in 19th century, especially USA but fruit inferior in quality to most other cultivated plums.

Section *Prunocerasus*

2–5 flowers per cluster. Leaves mostly conduplicate in bud, rarely convolute. Ovary and fruit glabrous. Stone mostly smooth.

P. americana American Red Plum. N America. Tree to 10m. Flowers white, about 3cm across. Fruit virtually round, about 2.5cm across, usually finally red, rarely yellowish. Hybrids with *P. salicina* have been made in America to produce new varieties.

Section *Armeniaca*

Shrubs or trees, thornless. Flowers appearing before leaves, usually sessile or subsessile. Leaves convolute in bud. Ovary and fruit pubescent.

P. mandshurica Manchurian Apricot. Korea and Manchuria. Tree to 5m with pendulous and somewhat spreading branches. Flowers pink, solitary, about 3cm across. Fruit nearly round, 2.5cm, yellow. Selections are widely cultivated as ornamentals.

P. armeniaca Apricot. W Asia. Tree to 10m. Bark reddish. Flowers white or pink, mostly solitary, 2.5cm across. Fruit round, 4–8cm, short velvety, yellow with red blush, stone smooth but furrowed along one margin. Widely cultivated in warmer parts of temperate zones of both hemispheres.

P. brigantina Briançon Apricot. SE France. Shrub or tree to 6m. Flowers white in clusters of 2–5. Fruit clear yellow, almost round, about 2.5cm, quite smooth and glabrous. An inflammable, perfumed oil, 'Huile de Marmotte,' is expressed from the seeds.

Subgenus *Amygdalus*

Fruit with external groove, more or less pubescent. Terminal bud present; axillary buds 3; leaves conduplicate in bud. Flowers typically sessile, rarely stalked, in clusters of 1–2, appearing before leaves.

Section *Amygdalus*

Calyx-tube cup-shaped and about as long as its sepal lobes.

P. amygdalus Almond. W Asia. Tree to 8m. Flowers subsessile, pale pink, 3–5cm across, usually solitary. Fruit velvety, compressed roundish to 6cm long; stone smooth but with pits. Widely cultivated in S Europe, California etc, and as an ornamental for its early spring flowering.

var *dulcis* Sweet Almond of commerce. In Britain only planted as an ornamental. var *amara* Bitter Almond. Very bitter to taste with potentially lethal amounts of prussic acid.

P. persica Peach. China. Tree 6–7m. Flowers solitary, pink, to 3.5cm across. Fruit globose, velvety, 5–7cm, yellowish tinged reddish on exposed side; stone furrowed, deeply pitted. Widely and long cultivated in temperate zones.

var *nectarina* Nectarine. Fruits quite glabrous like a plum skin.

Section *Chamaeamygdalus*

Calyx-tube (hypanthium) much longer than its sepal lobes.

P. tenella Dwarf Russian Almond. SE Europe to W Asia and E Siberia. Bushy shrub to almost 2m. Flowers in clusters of 1–3, a fine rose-red, 1–2cm across. Fruit like a small almond, velvety, 2.5cm long, ovoid. Used in breeding and several ornamental types have been selected.

Subgenus *Cerasus*

Fruit virtually without groove or bloom. Flowers 1–10(12), sometimes in short (to 5cm) racemes of less than 10 flowers. Terminal bud present; leaves conduplicate. Stone either smooth or furrowed and pitted.

Section *Microcerasus*

Flowers solitary or in short few-flowered (less than 10(12)) racemes. Leaf axils with 3 buds.

P. tomentosa Downy Cherry. China, Japan, ? the Himalaya Sprawling shrub to about 3m, rarely tree-like. Flowers white or pink-tinged, 1.5–2cm across. Fruit almost round, 1cm across, bright red, edible, may be slightly hairy. Ornamental value short-lived. Himalayan collections possibly from cultivated plants.

P. glandulosa Dwarf Flowering Almond. China, Japan. Bushy shrub to about 1.5m. Flowers white or pinkish. Fruit round, red, 10–12mm across. Double-flowered plants 'Alba Plena' (white), 'Rosea Plena' (pink) are of much greater ornamental value.

P. pumila Dwarf American Cherry, Sand Cherry. N America. Shrub 1–2.5m. Flowers (almost) white in clusters of 2–4. Fruit subglobose, purplish to black, 8–12mm long, too bitter to be really palatable. The species has been hybridized with plum species such as *P. cerasifera*.

P. besseyi Rocky Mountain Cherry, Western Sand Cherry. N America. Similar to previous species but with slightly larger flowers and edible sweet fruits of commercial promise. Both species have potential in rootstock breeding.

Section *Pseudocerasus*

As section *Microcerasus* but sepals upright or spreading and buds solitary. Flowers in bunches of few-flowered short racemes. A high proportion of the ornamental flowering cherries are derived from Chinese and Japanese species of this section or from their hybrids.

P. subhirtella Wild Spring or Higan Cherry. Japan. Tree to 9m. Flowers in clusters of 2–5, each about 2cm across, pale pinkish, tending to fade with age. Includes many attractive ornamentals, especially cultivar 'Autumnalis,' flowering late fall to early spring.

var *ascendens* The wild mountainous form of the species in W China, Japan and Korea. Tree to 20m and leaves larger. Of interest essentially for its involvement in cultivated varieties.

P. canescens Gray Leaf Cherry. China. Bushy shrub to 2(3)m. Of little ornamental value except as parent, with *P. avium*, of the hybrid *P.* × *schmittii* with pale pink flowers and polished bark.

P. incisa Fuji Cherry. Japan. Bushy shrub to 5m, sometimes tree to 10m. The female parent with *P. campanulata* of the very fine floriferous, hardy hybrid 'Okame.'

P. nipponica Japanese Alpine Cherry. Japan. Bush or bushy headed tree to 6m. Another fine early flowering cherry.

P. 'Kursar' is raised from seed of *P. nipponica* var *kurilensis*.

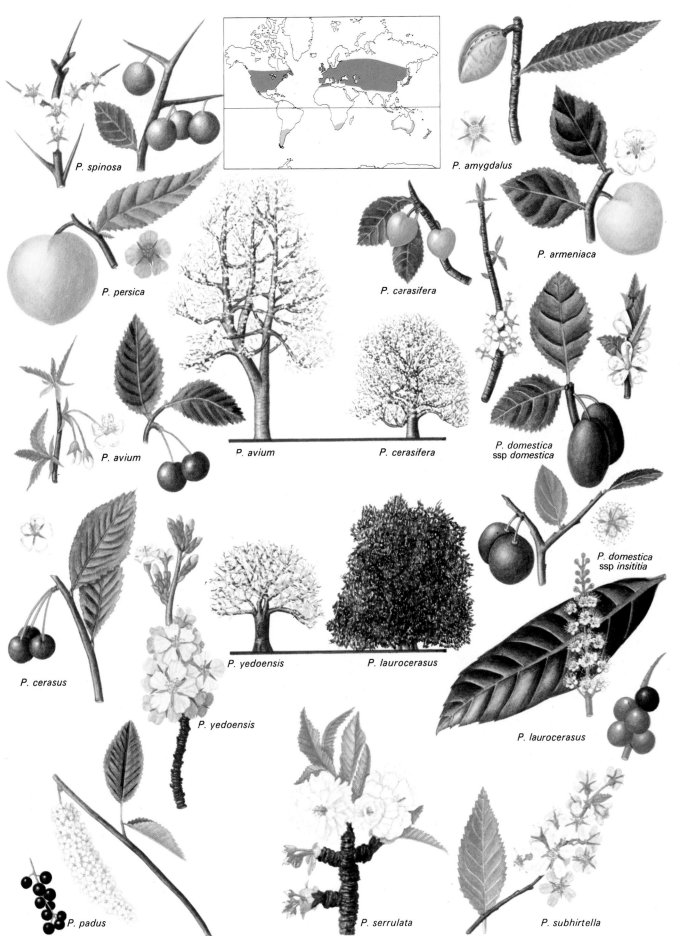

P. spinosa

P. amygdalus

P. persica

P. cerasifera

P. armeniaca

P. avium

P. avium

P. cerasifera

P. domestica
ssp domestica

P. cerasus

P. yedoensis

P. laurocerasus

P. domestica
ssp insititia

P. yedoensis

P. laurocerasus

P. padus

P. serrulata

P. subhirtella

P. campanulata Bell-flowered Cherry. Formosa and S Japan. Tree to 9m, less hardy than other species of this section. The pollen parent of 'Okame' – see *P. incisa* above.

P. rufa A Himalayan pink-flowered type, closely related to *P. tricantha* from Sikkim.

P. serrula W China, Tibet. Tree 10–16m, prized for its fine flaky bright brown bark. Flowers white in clusters of 1–3.

P. concinna China. Produces a profusion of white flowers before the leaves appear.

P. conradinae China. Includes some semi-double flowered selections.

P. yedoensis Yoshino Cherry. Japan. A source of several attractive ornamental selections. Origin uncertain; not known wild. Possibly a hybrid *P. speciosa* × *P. subhirtella*. See *P. speciosa.*

P. sargentii Sargent Cherry. North Japan, Sakhalin (Sachalin, a USSR island N of Japan). Tree to 25m. Flowers rose-pink, 3–4cm across, 2–6 in an umbel. Fruit almost black, subglobose, 8–10mm across. Very attractive both in flower and its orange to red fall foliage.

P. serrulata Now regarded as a garden form, with scentless double white or pink flowers, of the Hill Cherry, a native of China and Japan, distinguished as *P. serrulata* var *spontanea* which is the national tree of Japan reaching 20m. Some 60 Japanese Flowering Cherries ('Sato Zakura' in Japanese, meaning 'Domestic Cherries') are commonly listed under it and some are thought to have their origin from *P. serrulata* but the majority of them probably derive from *P. speciosa* (*P. lannesiana* var *albida*), the Osiima Cherry

P. speciosa Oshima Cherry. Japan. Very closely related to *P. serrulata* and included by some authorities under that species but not synonymous with it. Flowers single, white and fragrant.

P. sieboldii Japan. Generally regarded as a hybrid (*P. speciosa* × ?). Tree reaching 8m with 2–4 large, often double flowers on each short peduncle.

Section *Lobopetalum* As section *Pseudocerasus* but with reflexed sepals. Petals notched at apex or 2-lobed. Chinese species.

P. cantabrigiensis Cambridge Cherry. Tree with 3–6 pink flowers in each short stalked umbel. Fruit like a bright red cherry, 1cm across. Often confused with the following species.

P. pseudocerasus Similar to previous species but the 2–6 flowers are in a raceme and there are gland-toothed bracts at the base of each pedicel.
A selection intermediate between this and *P. cantabrigiensis* was hybridized with *P. avium* to produce the new rootstocks 'Colt' (for sweet and sour cherries) and 'Cornflower' (for ornamental cherries).

Section *Eucerasus* As section *Lobopetalum* but petals not notched or lobed. Flowers usually in sessile umbels with persistent bud-scales at the base.

P. avium Mazzard, Gean, Wild (Sweet) Cherry. Europe, SW Russia, N Africa (mountains). Tree 20–24m. Flowers pure white, 2.5cm across, calyx-tube (hypanthium) constricted above. Fruit globose, 9–12(18)mm across, typically blackish-red, sweet or bitterish but not sour (acid). The ancestor of most of the sweet cherries.

P. cerasus Sour Cherry. Not known as a wild plant. Widely cultivated and often naturalized over Europe and W Asia. Similar to preceding species but often shrubby and not exceeding 10m; commonly suckering. Calyx-tube (hypanthium) not constricted above. Fruit bright red, sour (acid) but not bitter. The ancestor of Morello cherries.

P. fruticosa Ground Cherry. Europe to parts of Siberia. Dwarf, spreading shrub to 1m. Flowers white, 1.5cm across. Fruit dark red, round, nearly 1cm across, of cherry-like taste but scarcely palatable. Long cultivated in Europe.

Section *Mahaleb* As section *Eucerasus*, but basal scales at base of flower clusters dropping before flowers open. Flowers mostly in racemes of 12 or fewer, less often in umbels. Bracts deciduous and leaf teeth rounded.

P. mahaleb St. Lucie Cherry, Mahaleb Cherry. C and S Europe. Tree to 10(12)m. Flowers white, 12–18mm across, fragrant, in 6–10(12)-flowered racemes 3–4cm long. Fruit black, ovoid, 8–10mm long. Used as rootstock for grafting cherries, although the resulting trees have a short life.

P. pennsylvanica Pin or Wild Red Cherry. N America. Shrub or tree to 12m with very slender red shiny often pendulous branches. Flowers white, 12mm across in 2–5(10) umbels or short racemes. Fruit round, 6mm across, red, abundantly produced.

Section *Phyllocerasus* As section *Mahaleb*, but bracts persistent, leaf teeth pointed, and 1–4 flowered umbels.

P. pilosiuscula C and W China. Shrub or tree to 12m. Flowers white, 18–20mm across. Fruit ellipsoidal, 8–9mm long, red.

The fruit of the Wild Cherry (*Prunus avium*).

Section *Phyllomahaleb* As section *Mahaleb*, but flowers in (4)5–10 flowered racemes.

P. maximowiczii Japan, Korea, Manchuria. Tree to 16m. Flowers dull yellowish-white, 1.5cm across, 6–10 in the raceme. Fruit round, 5mm across, red finally black. Foliage often strikingly red in the fall.

Subgenus *Padus*

As subgenus *Cerasus* but flowers in long (6cm or more) racemes of (10)12 or more flowers. Leaves deciduous.

P. padus European Bird Cherry. Europe to Japan. Tree 10–15m (or more). Flowers white, 8–13mm across, petals 6–9mm long, fragrant, in pendulous racemes with leafy peduncle. Fruit round, black, 6–8mm across, calyx deciduous; taste astringent.

P. serotina Rum Cherry. N America. Tree to 30m, usually about 15m in cultivation. Flowers white, 8–10mm across, petals 2–4mm long; peduncle of raceme leafy; fruit round 8–10mm across, finally black, with persisting calyx.

Subgenus *Laurocerasus*

As subgenus *Padus* but leaves evergreen. Peduncles of racemes always leafless.

P. lusitanica Portugal Laurel. Portugal, Spain. Shrub or tree to 6(15)m. Shoots and petioles red. Leaves shining, elliptical, 7–13cm long. Flowers white, 8–13mm across. Fruits dark purple, rounded cone-shaped to 8mm long, very unpalatable.

P. laurocerasus Cherry Laurel. Asia Minor, SE Europe. Shrub or tree to 6m. Shoots and petioles pale green. Leaves more or less obovate-oblong, (5)10–15cm long, margin more or less serrate. Flowers white, 8–9mm across. Fruit purplish-black, rounded cone-shaped, about 8mm long, palatable (makes an acceptable jam).

Note: The distribution map also shows major areas of fruit cultivation (yellow) outside the native regions (brown).

more westerly parts of central Asia. It was reported in Greece between 400–300 BC, but the Romans did not begin its cultivation until about the 1st century AD. It was taken to North and South America by the early Spanish and Portuguese colonists, who continued the seed method of propagation used by the Romans, although both Greeks and Romans knew about grafting and used it widely for other tree fruit crops.

During the 19th century there was an increased interest in high quality fruit for commercial distribution and this brought about a switch from seed to vegetative propagation to ensure a uniform product. Thus, the best seedlings were selected and grafted following procedures long used for peaches grown in walled English gardens. In current practice most rootstocks are grown from seeds – either wild types or selected commercial varieties. Various other *Prunus* species may be used such as *P. tomentosa* (dwarfing). In France peach × almond (*P. amygdalus*) hybrids have done well as rootstocks for peaches on soils subject to lime-induced iron deficiency. Dramatic changes in varieties have occurred over the last century owing to the massive efforts of fruit breeders, especially in the United States of America. New genetic material from China has been a major contributor to this change. Thus Chinese Cling, introduced to America from China via England in 1850, was the parent of such well-known varieties as 'Elberta' and 'J. H. Hale' and involved in the ancestry of a high proportion of present-day varieties.

Problems associated with extending the area of commercial fruit production include lack of winter hardiness (in colder regions) and chilling limitations; varieties need 500–1000 hours with temperatures below 7°C (45°F) during the winter to promote normal flowering and fruit setting.

Peaches are of two main types – freestones (used mostly for fresh consumption) and clingstones (used mainly for canning). Since peaches can only be stored for a few weeks, a very high proportion is processed. The annual world production is about 5.5 million tonnes.

Cherries belong to the subgenus *Cerasus*. The Sweet Cherry, Gean or Mazzard (*P. avium*) is one of the ancestors of the commercial fruiting cherries, more especially the black ones. The center of origin is now believed to be northwest and central Europe. Variety *duracina* is the Bigarrean Cherry with its firm flesh; var

juliana, the Heart Cherry, has soft flesh.

The sour cherries are derived from *P. cerasus*, which is not known as a genuinely wild plant but is naturalized in Europe including Britain. Variety *austera* is the Morello Cherry, cultivars of which are much used for cooking and preserving.

Sweet cherries, with the exception of the recently bred variety 'Stella,' are self-incompatible and therefore two compatible varieties must be grown together to produce fruit crops. Most sour cherries, however, are self-compatible and fruit well without special pollinators. The annual world production of sweet and sour cherries is about 2.5 million tonnes.

The Dwarf or Ground Cherry (*P. fruticosa*) is a low spreading deciduous shrub growing to about 1m high. It is a native of Europe, extending northward to eastern Siberia and has been cultivated in England for some 300 years. Its fruits have a cherry flavor, but are too astringent to be palatable. Hybrids between this species and *P. cerasus*, known as *P. × eminens*, occur naturally and are sometimes found in gardens under the name *P. reflexa*.

Hybrids between *P. avium* and *P. cerasus* are known as *P. × gondovinii* and are cultivated in Europe as 'Duke' cherries. Breeders are now in a position to produce a new range of cherry varieties, rootstocks and ornamentals since, for the first time, the necessary breeding techniques and the rull range of species are readily accessible.

The so-called flowering cherries are the most outstanding and widely cultivated of all ornamentals in the genus *Prunus*. The number of cultivars and selections in cultivation run into hundreds from *P.* 'Plena,' the finest of the geans (*P. avium*) to the outstanding Japanese flowering cherries such as *P.* 'Kanzan' with its massive clusters of double purple-pink flowers. These Japanese cherries are mostly derived from the white-flowered Oshima Cherry (*P. speciosa* or *P. lannesiana* forma *albida* which is held by some to be the same thing and has priority) or from the very closely related *P. serrulata*. Whatever the species involved in the cultivars, no confusion arises if the generic name is simply followed immediately by the cultivar name in single inverted commas, for example, *Prunus* 'Kanzan.' In English texts they are commonly treated under the binomial *P. serrulata*, principally to maintain a long-standing practise. Again no confusion arises.

The Bird Cherries and Cherry

Laurels belong to the subgenera *Padus* and *Laurocerasus* respectively. Both are characterized by having flowers in racemes of more than 10 flowers each about 1–1.5cm (0.4–0.6in) across or slightly less. They are sometimes treated as a single subgenus (*Laurocerasus*), but the bird cherries are typically deciduous and the cherry laurels always evergreen. The species commonly known as the Cherry Laurel (*P. laurocerasus*) is a vigorous shrub with leathery obovate to lanceolate leaves up to 15cm (6in) long, white flowers and small black fruits. It is widely planted for hedging and screening and is tolerant of shady positions. The leaves yield hydrocyanic acid on injury and when torn into small pieces are used as the active agent in killing-bottles for small insects.

R. W.

LEGUMINOSAE

Acacias
(genus *Acacia*)

Acacia is a large genus comprising about 700–800 species native to the tropics and subtropics, about half of them in Australia. Many species are highly attractive, with feathery silvery-gray foliage and yellow flowers in large conspicuous clusters, and some are economically important.

They are mostly evergreen trees and shrubs, rarely herbs, but a few are twiners and hook climbers. Most species can withstand prolonged drought (xerophytic). The leaves are typically bipinnate, often silvery, without terminal leaflets, and sometimes remarkable in being reduced to a more or less expanded petiole which functions as a leaf (phyllode). The stipules are sometimes thorn-like. The flowers are unisexual or bisexual, predominantly yellow, rarely whitish, minute but borne in dense globose or cylindrical heads of 20–30, each flower with five (rarely four) blunt tooth-like sepals, five (rarely four) petals about 1.5mm (0.06in) long and numerous protruding yellow stamens making each head attractively conspicuous; the sepals and petals are sometimes absent. The ovary is sessile or stalked and the fruit is a roundish to elongated pod (legume). The phyllode-bearing species (section *Phyllodineae*) are mostly native to Australia.

The species are not in general particularly hardy, but about two dozen, of which the Silver Wattle or 'Mimosa' (*Acacia dealbata*) is the most popular, can be grown in the milder parts of temperate regions, but even these may succumb in a hard winter. Any reasonably good soil is adequate, but most species, except *A. longifolia* and *A. retinodes*, will not tolerate free lime. Propagation of species is by seed, otherwise cuttings from half-ripened wood should be used.

Acacias are an important component of the widespread scrub found in Australia where they are called wattles following their use by early settlers for building huts of wattlework plastered with mud. Other species form a conspicuous part of the landscape in desert areas and dry savannas of Africa and dry plains of India, where they are frequently the only trees found. They are often called thorns or thorn-trees in Africa and tropical America, a reference to the large thorns found in many species which serve as a protection against grazing animals. These thorns are mostly modified stipules and may be swollen at the base.

In the Bull-horn Acacia (*A. cornigera*) from Mexico and Central America (and widely naturalized in the West Indies) a remarkable association has been developed with the ant *Pseudomyrmex ferruginea*. At the base of each leaf the acacia has a pair of massive swollen thorns 2–3cm (0.8–1.2in) long. They are inhabited by colonies of the ants, which bore into them and hollow them out. The ants are attracted to the trees by nectaries at the base of the petioles, which provide them with sugars, and by curious sausage-shaped food organs called Beltian bodies at the tips of the leaflets, which provide them with a diet of oils and proteins. This remarkable association, an example of symbiosis between plants and ants, known as *myrmecophily*, was first described by Thomas Belt in his book *The Naturalist in Nicaragua* (1874) and has since been found in a number of other species, such as *A. drepanolobium*. There has been considerable debate as to what benefit, if any, the acacia obtains from the presence of the ants. Recent work has shown that the acacia obtains protection from herbivores through the action of the worker ants which swarm over the tree, stinging and biting any predators and at the same time protecting their own territory. In addition, the ants cut away any branches of other plants that touch their host acacias and thereby ensure a tunnel through the foliage to the light above, allowing the acacia to grow rapidly and compete effectively with other vegetation.

The Main Species of *Acacia*

Group I: Leaves bipinnate.

AA *Nutlets smooth on ventral side.*

A. baileyana Golden Mimosa, Bailey's Mimosa or Cootamundra Wattle. Australia. Small graceful tree. Leaves gray-glaucous with 2–4 pairs of pinnae. Flowers in globose heads in racemes. Pods glaucous.

A. dealbata Silver Wattle. Australia. Tree to 30m with silvery-gray bark. Leaves downy with (8)15–20(25) pairs of pinnae. Flowers strongly scented in globose heads borne in long panicles. Cultivated in S France for perfumery and florists' 'Mimosa.' Produces a gum arabic substitute.

A. drummondii W Australia. Shrub or small tree to 3m. Shoots furrowed. Flowers lemon-yellow in dense, solitary, cylindrical, drooping spikes.

A. mearnsii (*A. mollissima*) Black Wattle. Tasmania. Tree with softly hairy shoots and leaves. Flowers in heads borne in leaf-axils. Pods strongly constricted between the seeds. A source of tannin. Similar to previous species, but pinnules (leaflets on pinnae) much smaller (to 2mm) and young shoots and leaves yellowish.

AA *Plants spiny.*

B *Flowers in spikes or spike-like racemes.*

A. catechu Black Catechu, Cutch, Black Cutch or Khair. W Pakistan to Burma. Small to medium-sized deciduous tree with short hooked spines. Flowers in solitary spikes or 2–3 together. Pods flat. The heartwood is a source of tannin and dyeing extract.

A. albida Tropical and subtropical Africa, Syria and Palestine. Wide-spreading tree to 30m with straight spines in pairs. Leaves blue-green. Flowers cream-colored in long spikes. Pods bright orange, indehiscent, curved or curled into a circular coil.

A. cornigera Bull-horn Acacia. Mexico to Costa Rica. Shrub or small tree with large, swollen, twisted spines, the latter partly hollow and inhabited by biting ants which protect the plant from herbivores.

A. gummifera Morocco or Barbary Gum. Morocco. Tree to 10m. Pods white-tomentose, constricted between the seeds.

A. horrida Cape Gum Tree. India, tropical E Africa, Somalia and Sudan. Low tree or shrub, usually flat-topped. Spines 2.5–10cm long. Flowers creamy-yellow. Material in cultivation under this name is usually misidentified and is probably *A. karroo*.

A. senegal Gum Arabic Tree. Tropical Africa. Shrub or tree to 12m with spiny prickles in 3's, the middle one recurved, or solitary. Flowers white or creamy-yellow, in axillary spikes. Pods flat. The source of 'true' gum arabic of commerce.

BB *Flowers in globose heads (capitate).*

A. farnesiana Opopanax, Popinac, Huisache, Sweet Acacia, West Indian Blackthorn or Cassie. Tropical and subtropical America and Australia but widely introduced in other tropical areas and cultivated. Deciduous shrub or small tree to 6m, much branched. Flowers very fragrant, bright golden-yellow. Widely grown as an ornamental and for the essential oil from its flowers used in perfumery.

A. giraffae Camel Thorn. South Africa, Rhodesia. Tree to 13m with straight stout paired spines. Flower-heads in clusters. Pods curved, velvety-gray, indehiscent.

A. karroo Karroo Thorn. South Africa. Deciduous shrub or small tree with pungent ivory-white spines, 5–10cm long on older parts of plant. Flowers fragrant, the heads in clusters of 4–6 in leaf-axils. Pods flattened. Used as a hedging plant or sand-binder.

A. nilotica (*A. arabica*) Gum Arabic Tree, Babul or Egyptian Thorn. Tropical and subtropical Africa and Asia extending to India. Variable tree to 25m with long straight spines. Flowers bright yellow on axillary pedunculate heads. Provides a gum arabic substitute, tannin and hard, durable timber.

A. seyal Gum Arabic Tree or Tahl Gum. Tropical and subtropical Africa, Sudan to Rhodesia. Tree to 12m with straight spines (with or without ant galls). Flowers bright yellow on axillary pedunculate heads. Pods curved, constricted between seeds. Source of good quality gum arabic.

A. woodii (*A. sieberana* var *woodii*) Paperbark Thorn. S Africa. Large tree. Young shoots golden-tomentose. Spines very short. Flowers cream, in solitary or paired heads.

Group II: Adult leaves apparently simple, modified to phyllodes, occasionally with a few pinnate leaves.

C *Flowers in globose heads (capitate) which may be solitary, clustered or in racemes.*

A. acinacea Gold Dust. Australia. A branching shrub to 2.5m with oblong phyllodes. Flowers yellow in solitary, golden heads or 2 together.

A. alata W Australia. Shrub to 2.5m. Phyllodes narrowly triangular or ovate-lanceolate, 1-veined, with decurrent linear-oblong wing, tipped with a slender spine. Flowers creamy-yellow in axillary solitary or paired, heads.

A. armata Kangaroo Thorn. Australia. Shrub to 3m; young shoots ribbed, spiny at the apex. Stipules spine-like. Phyllodes semi-ovate, 12–25 × 3–6mm, curved at the tip, each node with its 2 stipules modified as forked spines to 12–13mm long. Flowers bright yellow in heads which are simple or paired in axillary stalks.

A. melanoxylon Blackwood Acacia. S Australia, Tasmania. Large tree 20–40m. Stipules not spine-like. Phyllodes 3–5 veined, oblong-lanceolate, curved; some bipinnate leaves produced. Flowers cream-colored; heads in axillary racemes. Important timber tree.

A. pycnantha Golden Wattle. Australia. Shrub or medium-sized tree to 7m. Stipules not

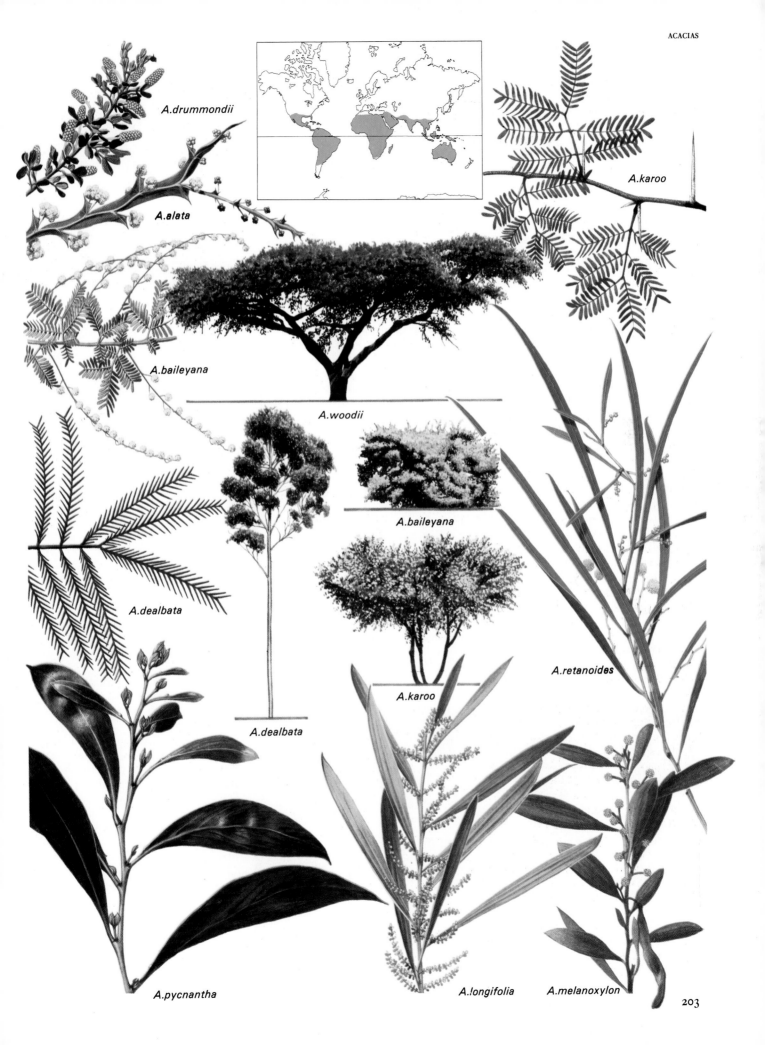

A.drummondii

A.alata

A.karoo

A.baileyana

A.woodii

A.baileyana

A.dealbata

A.karoo

A.retanoides

A.pycnantha

A.dealbata

A.longifolia

A.melanoxylon

spine-like; phyllodes 1-veined, lanceolate-curved. Flowers fragrant, bright yellow; heads in racemes. Widely used for tanning.

A. retinodes Wirilda. Tasmania, Australia. Shrub or small tree to 10m. Stipules not spine-like. Phyllodes linear-lanceolate-curved. Flowers pale yellow; heads in branched racemes. Widely cultivated.

CC *Flowers in cylindrical spikes.*

A. acuminata Raspberry Jam Tree. Australia. Tree to 10m or shrub. Phyllodes linear, 10–25cm × 4–8mm. Flowers in axillary spikes. Wood scented like raspberry jam, hence its popular name.

A. longifolia (inc. *A. floribunda*) Sydney Golden Wattle. Australia, Tasmania. Shrub or tree to 10m. Phyllodes oblong-lanceolate, 7.5–15cm × 9–18mm. Flowers bright yellow in lax, axillary spikes. Often cultivated for ornament.

There is clearly mutual advantage gained from this acacia–ant relationship.

The best ('genuine' or 'true') gum arabic is obtained from *A. senegal*, a native of tropical Africa from Senegal to Nigeria, the gum exuding largely from the branches. Certain other species, such as *A. nilotica* and the Whistling Thorn (*A. seyal*), yield an inferior gum arabic. It is used in pharmacy, confectionery and as an adhesive. Black catechu or cutch, a dark extract rich in tannin, is obtained from *A. catechu* by steeping the wood in hot water. The original khaki cloth is said to have been dyed and shrunk in this tanning agent. Other tannin-producing species include the Australian Black Wattle (*A. mearnsii*), the Golden Wattle (*A. pycnantha*) and Silver Wattle (*A. deal-bata*), which are planted in southern Europe (Spain, Portugal, Italy) for this purpose. The latter species is also widely cultivated for timber, ornament and soil stabilization in southern Europe and is the 'Mimosa' of florists which is used as a winter cut-flower. It is conspicuous on the Cote d'Azur in the south of France, where whole hillsides are covered by it, although it is occasionally devastated by a combination of drought, frost and fire. Several species, such as Australian Blackwood (*A. melanoxylon*), yield valuable timber used for a wide range of purposes including furniture, boomerangs, boats and spears, and are planted in southern Europe. Others are planted for ornament, as shade trees, or for stabilizing coastal dunes.

Ornamental plants (all Australian) for the milder parts of temperate regions include *A. dealbata* which has already been mentioned, the combination of silvery, feathery foliage and conspicuous, globose clusters of fragrant flowers being particularly attractive. *Acacia podalyriifolia* is a splendid shrub growing to 3m (10ft), with more or less ovate, mucronate phyllodes, 2.5–3cm (1–1.2in) long, and abundant racemes of stalked, globose heads of fragrant flowers. The Sydney Golden Wattle (*A. longifolia*) is conspicuous for its cylindrical heads of strongly perfumed flowers and the Wirilda (*A. retinodes*), with fragrant flowers in globose heads, can flower at all times of the year. The Kangaroo Thorn (*A. armata*), which is unusual in its ribbed young shoots, spiny at the apex, has deep yellow flowers and is popular as a glasshouse, hedging or sand-binder plant. Planted for soil stabilization, as well as for ornament, in southern Europe is *A. cyanophylla* (the Orange Wattle or

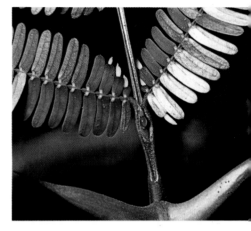

Several species of *Acacia* have a unique relationship with ants which live among and within the thorns – the ants obtain food from the host plant while the plant is thought to obtain protection from browsing animals by the action of their stinging and biting swarm of ants. This association is known as myrmecophily. The photograph here shows part of a leaf of the myrmecoptytic species *Acacia cornigera* (Bull-horn Acacia), from Mexico and Central America. It shows nectar glands, exuding a drop of red fluid, at the base of the leaflet stalks. The ants feed on this fluid which is rich in carbohydrates. They also bore into and live within the pairs of enlarged thorns which occur at the base of each leaf stalk. This example of symbiosis has now been discovered in several other *Acacia* species.

Blue-leaf Wattle), a western Australian plant, with more or less lanceolate to oblanceolate, blue-green phyllodes which may reach 30cm (12in) long, and globose flower heads.

The Karroo Thorn (*A. karroo*) from South Africa is grown in southwest Europe (sometimes becoming naturalized) and has striking whitish, piercing spines 5–10cm (2–4in) long.

The Opopanax (sometimes spelt Opoponax) (*A. farnesiana*) is naturalized in all tropical countries and much cultivated in the subtropics, but is believed to be a native of tropical and subtropical America. It is prized for its fragrant violet-scented flowers – Cassie flowers – which are extracted by the perfume industry. It is also known as Huisache, Sweet Acacia, Popinac and West Indian Black Thorn. *Opopanax* is also a valid generic name for two or three herbaceous species of the family Umbelliferae (Apiaceae), natives of southern Europe including Greece, gum opopanax being obtained from *Opopanax chironium*.

V. H. H.

The globe-like inflorescences of *Acacia lanigiera*, one of the Australian wattles. Most acacias have yellow flowers; the main element of the display is the masses of long-stalked stamens.

Judas Trees
(genus *Cercis*)

Cercis is a genus of about seven species from North America and southern Europe to eastern Asia (China). They are deciduous shrubs or trees, some species with characteristic dark red buds. The leaves are more or less round with a cordate base, alternate and entire with five or seven prominent veins arranged fan-wise. The flowers are rose-purplish borne in clusters, sometimes directly on the trunk (cauliflorous) and appear before or with the leaves. The calyx is bell-shaped, shortly and bluntly-toothed, and the corolla has five petals, the upper three smaller; there are 10 stamens. The fruit is a flat pod, green to pinkish, finally brown, with several flat seeds.

They are mostly hardy species grown for the beauty of their flowers and their

characteristic and pleasing leaf shape. The best known is the Judas Tree (*Cercis siliquastrum*) which is one of two trees (the other is an elder, *Sambucus* sp) on which Judas is said to have hanged himself – the cauliflorous flowers being no doubt sym-

The flowers of the Judas Tree (*Cercis siliquastrum*) grow directly from the branches – an example of cauliflory.

bolic of blood. This legend explains the frequent occurrence of the species beside churches and in graveyards. It is a tree of

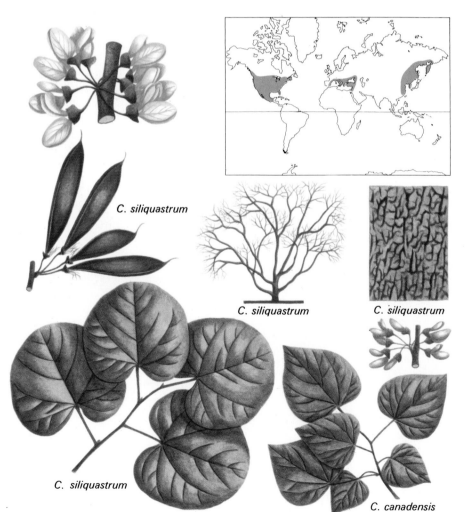

C. siliquastrum

C. siliquastrum

C. siliquastrum

C. siliquastrum

C. siliquastrum

C. canadensis

The Main Species of *Cercis*

Group I: Leaves rounded or notched at apex, 6–10cm wide.

C. siliquastrum Judas Tree. S Europe and Asia. Tree to 12m but generally less, with spreading, irregular habit. Leaves almost round, not quite so long as wide, sinuate at base, apex usually rounded, very rarely pointed, brightish green above, glaucous below. Flowers bright purplish-rose, 1–2cm long, in clusters of 3–6 produced in great quantities. Pods up to 15cm long.
    var *alba* White-flowered.

C. reniformis Texas, New Mexico. Tree to 12m. Leaves broadly ovate to reniform, leathery, sometimes downy beneath. Flowers rose-pink, 1cm long. Pod about 6cm long.

Group II: Leaves shortly pointed at apex.

C. canadensis Redbud. C and E N America. Usually shrubby but occasionally tree to 12m. Leaves broadly ovate to cordate, 8–12cm wide, heart-shaped, dull beneath and downy at vein axils, thinner and brighter green than *C. siliquastrum*. Flowers in clusters of 4–8, pale rose-pink, smaller and paler than *C. siliquastrum*.
    var *alba* White-flowered.
    var *pubescens* Leaves downy beneath.

C. chinensis (*C. japonica*) China. Tree to 12–15m but shrubby in cultivation. Leaves rounded, 8–12cm long, glossy green on both surfaces. Flowers in clusters of 4–10, purple-pink, larger than those of *C. canadensis*. Pods 9–12cm long.

C. racemosa China. Shrub or small tree to 12m. Leaves 6–12cm long, broadly ovate, bright green above, downy below. Flowers rosy-pink, borne in very distinctive racemes 10cm long. Pod 9–12cm long.

low and irregular spreading habit, usually 5–6m (15–20ft) high, and with a spread of similar dimensions. Old trees often become one-sided with branches bending to the ground. The bark, which is purplish and ridged when young, becomes grayish-red and fissured on mature trees.

Cercis racemosa, from China, is unique amongst the species in that its flowers are arranged in a raceme, that is the flowers in the unbranched cluster are stalked.

The name Redbud, also an alternative common name for the whole genus, is more properly applied to *C. canadensis*, a popular ornamental in North America, although much less popular in Europe than the Judas Tree.

Judas trees like a good average loamy soil. Adult specimens do not transplant easily and so should be given their permanent position at an early stage. Propagation is best by seed; stocks for grafting are usually *C. canadensis* or *C. siliquastrum*. The Coral-spot Fungus (*Nectria cinnabarina*) is a serious disease and attacked wood should be cut back to sound wood and the stumps scalded.

S. A. H.

Honey Locusts
(genus *Gleditsia*)

Gleditsia (incorrectly, *Gleditschia*) is a genus of 10 species of deciduous trees from eastern North America, China, Japan and Iran. The trunk and branches are armed with simple or branched spines which are stem structures arising from the leaf-axils and can be very aggressive. The leaves are bipinnate or pinnate and the flowers are inconspicuous small, green, in racemes 5–15cm (2–6in) long. Unlike those of most legumes, the petals are uniform. Nearly all species have numerous seeds embedded in pulp in pods 30–50cm (12–20in) long. Seeds are dispersed in the pod, which is often spirally twisted to aid wind dispersal.

Many species are cultivated for their attractive fern-like foliage, for example the

The fern-like golden-yellow foliage of the Honey Locust (*Gleditsia triacanthos*) cultivar 'Sunburst.'

Honey Locust (*Gleditsia triacanthos*). Its cultivar 'Sunburst' has golden yellow foliage in both spring and fall while 'Moraine' (a clone of forma *inermis*) lacks the spines and is sterile, with the result that the pods do not rattle when dry. Also cultivated is the spineless hybrid *G. texana*, which arose naturally where populations of *G. aquatica* and *G. triacanthos* grew together in Texas. The pods of *G. texana* are many-seeded but without pulp and thus intermediate between *G. aquatica*, which has one-seeded pods with pulp, and *G. triacanthos*, which has many-seeded pods with pulp. They succeed in all types of well-drained soil and are finding favor as town trees since they tolerate atmospheric pollution.

Some species have domestic uses. The pulp from *G. triacanthos* is sweet (hence the common name) and pods may be fermented to make 'beer' or fed to stock. Pods of the Caspian locust (*G. caspica*) and also of *G. japonica* (Japan) and *G. macracantha* (China) are used in soap. Pods of the latter are also used in tanning. The wood of many species is hard and durable.

M. C. D.

G.triacanthos   G.triacanthos

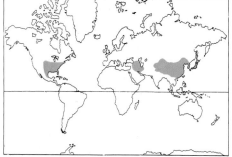

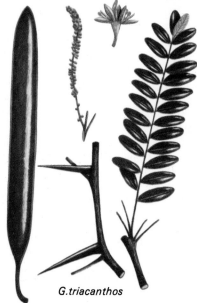

G.triacanthos

G. aquatica

G.sinensis

Group III: Pods many-seeded and straight. Trunk usually without spines.

G. ×texana Texas. Natural hybrid tree, arising from the cross *G. triacanthos × G. aquatica*. It grows to 40m and has smooth, pale bark and glabrous young shoots. Leaves 5–20cm long, dark green and glossy, pinnate or bipinnate with 12–14 pinnae. Male flowers in dark orange-yellow racemes 8–10cm long. Pods, without pulp, 10–13cm long, dark chestnut brown.

Group IV: Pods 2–3-seeded. Leaflets entire and pubescent beneath.

G. heterophylla NE China. Shrub or small tree. Spines slender, simple or trifid and up to 35cm long. Leaves pinnate with 10–18 oblong pinnae 1–3cm long, gray-green. Pods 3.5–5.5cm long, thin, glabrous.

Group V: Pods 1–2-seeded. Leaflets crenulate, glabrous beneath.

G. aquatica Water Locust. SE USA. Tree to 20m, in Europe only reaching shrub size. Trunk bears branched spines 10cm long. Leaves 20cm long, glabrous, pinnate with 12–18 ovate-oblong pinnae 2–3cm long or bipinnate with 6–8 pinnae. Pod, thin, 2.5–5cm long, usually with only one seed.

Laburnums
(genus *Laburnum*)

Laburnum is a genus of small trees and shrubs with attractive foliage and pendulous racemes of bright yellow flowers, but poisonous leaves and seeds. As now conceived, there are two species, and their hybrid, native to southern Europe.

The leaves are alternate and trifoliolate, with petioles but without stipules. The flowers are bisexual, yellow, pea-like on slender pedicels and borne in terminal pendulous racemes. The calyx is bell-shaped and two-lipped, the lips not longer than the corolla tube, which is yellow, with the petals all free. The filaments of the 10 stamens are united into a tube. The style is slender, with a small, upcurved terminal stigma. The ovary is short-stalked. The narrow oblong pod is constricted between each of the one to eight seeds, the upper suture thickened or more or less winged. The seeds are kidney-shaped.

Both species (*Laburnum anagyroides* and *L. alpinum*) are much planted as ornamentals. They are not particular as to soil, provided it is not waterlogged. Pods are freely formed which, if removed early, will prolong the life of what are relatively short-lived plants. They are reasonably free from disease, that caused by *Pleio-*

The Species of *Gleditsia*

Group I: Pods many-seeded, flat, usually twisted, not dotted. Spines compressed at least at the base.

G. triacanthos Honey Locust. N America. Tree to 45m. Trunk and branches usually armed with simple or branched spines 6–10cm long. Leaves 14–20cm long, dark and glossy, pinnate with more than 20 oblong-lanceolate pinnae 2–3.5cm long or bipinnate with 8–14 pinnae. Pods 30–40cm long; seeds embedded in pulp. Several varieties and cultivars.

> 'Butjoti' Slender pendulous branches.
> 'Nana' Compact and shrub-like.
> forma *inermis* Slender habit and no spines (includes 'Moraine').
> 'Elegantissima' Bushy habit and no spines.
> 'Sunburst' Golden yellow leaves in spring and no spines.

G. japonica Japan. Tree 20–25m. Trunk armed with branched spines 5–10cm long; young branches purplish. Leaves 25–30cm long, pinnate with 16–20 oblong pinnae 2–4(–6)cm long, or bipinnate with 2–12 pinnae. Pods twisted, 25–30cm long.

G. ferox Tree closely related to *G. japonica*. Trunk armed with very stout compressed spines. Leaves often bipinnate with 16–30

ovate pinnae. Of doubtful status; cultivated specimens may be *G. caspica*.

G. caspica Caspian Locust. N Iran. Tree to 12m. Trunk armed with many spines 15cm or more long; young branches bright green and glabrous. Leaves shiny, 15–24cm long, pinnate with 12–20 ovate-elliptic pinnae or bipinnate with 6–8 pinnae. Pods about 20cm long.

G. delavayi SW China. Tree to about 10m. Trunk armed with spines up to 25cm long; young branches downy. Leaves pinnate with 8–16 ovate pinnae 3–6cm long, the lower pinnae smaller (young plants often have bipinnate leaves). Pods 15–35(50)cm long, walls leathery.

Group II: Pods many-seeded, not twisted, but with minute dots. Spines terete.

G. macracantha C China. Tree to 15m. Trunk armed with long, very stiff branched spines and the branches are ribbed and warted. Leaves 5–7cm long, glabrous, pinnate with 6–12 ovate-oblong pinnae 5–7cm long, the lower pinnae smaller. Pods 15–30cm long.

G. sinensis E China. Tree to 15m. Trunk armed with stout conical spines which are often branched. Leaves pinnate, 12–18cm long, rather dull yellowish-green, with 8–14(18) ovate pinnae 3–8cm long. Pods 12–25cm long, dark purplish-brown.

Laburnums are normally small trees, but they can also be trained over arches to form a shady walk, as seen here at the Royal Botanic Gardens, Kew, London, England.

chaeta (*Ceratophorum*) *setosa* being uncommon and not serious. The leaf-miner pest *Leucoptera laburnella* is more troublesome and unsightly.

Laburnum seeds (and those of their hybrid *L.* × *watereri*) are freely formed and can be fatally poisonous to humans and cattle. Amongst domestic animals, horses are more susceptible than cattle and goats. Sheep and rodents have eaten leaves and bark without harm. The hybrid, although with equally poisonous seeds, forms far fewer seed-pods (one to three per raceme) and is therefore the most widely planted laburnum. Where poisoning is suspected, hospital aid should be sought immediately. The poisonous principles are the alkaloids cytisine and laburnine.

Laburnum heartwood is used in cabinet-work and inlay.

A third species, first described under the binomial *Podocytisus caramanicum*, from the southern Balkans and Asia Minor is sometimes transferred to *Laburnum*, but some recent authorities retain it in its original genus. It is a shrub to about 1m (3.3ft), with terminal racemes of golden-yellow laburnum-like flowers but the inflorescence is erect and not pendulous.

Laburnum anagyroides forms an interesting graft-hybrid with *Cytisus purpureus*. It is designated (*Cytisus* + *Laburnum*) and referred to as + *Laburnocytisus adami*. It is not a normal intergeneric hybrid as the tissues of the 'parents' remain separate, those of *Cytisus* forming the outer layers which surround inner tissues derived solely from *Laburnum*. At points *Laburnum* tissues break through the *Cytisus* covering, while some of the branches are pure *Cytisus*. Seeds are occasionally formed, and being derived from inner layers, produce only *Laburnum* plants.

This type of hybrid is also distinguished as a chimaera. It can be propagated vegetatively. The habit resembles the normal laburnums, but the leaflets are smaller and almost glabrous; the racemes are nodding rather than pendulous and smaller, and the flowers a rather dirty purplish. Very interesting botanically but otherwise its ornamental value is that of a botanical curiosity of little visual appeal.

F. B. H.

The Species of *Laburnum*

L. anagyroides (*L. vulgare*) Common Laburnum, Golden Chain, Golden Rain. Mountain woods of C Europe, the Alps, Italy and Yugoslavia. Large shrub or small tree, 7–9(10)m. Leaflets more or less elliptic, 3–8m long, gray-green above, silky-glaucous beneath from the adpressed pubescence. Flowers in pubescent racemes 15–25cm long, appearing late spring and early summer, the bright yellow flowers about 2cm long on usually shorter pedicels. Fruiting pods rounded in cross-section, the upper suture thickened and keeled, but not obviously winged, averaging 5cm, long, dark brown; seeds black. Numerous cultivars.

One of the best-known chimeras is + *Laburnocytisus adami*, a graft-hybrid in which the shoots have a core of *Laburnum anagyroides* surrounded by a skin of broom (*Cytisus purpureus*), resulting in a plant with intermediate characteristics. Occasionally, as in the photograph, the tissues in some parts of the plant segregate and grow a true laburnum or true broom.

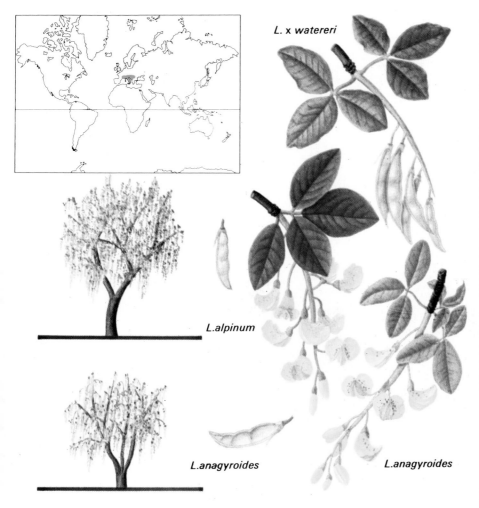

L. x watereri

L.alpinum

L.anagyroides

L.anagyroides

L. alpinum Scotch or Alpine Laburnum. Mountainous woods of Austria, Albania, Switzerland, Czechoslovakia, Italy, Yugoslavia. Shrub or tree to 12m. Leaflets mostly elliptic-oblong, 4–7cm long, ciliate on edge but glabrous or virtually so on lower side. Flowers in slightly pubescent racemes 25–40cm long, appearing 2–3 weeks later than previous species, averaging less than 2cm long on pedicels of about same length. Fruiting pods almost flat in cross-section, glabrous, the upper suture clearly winged; seeds about 5, brown. There are a number of cultivars and this species is a better ornamental choice than the previous one.

L. anagyroides × alpinum = L. × watereri (L. × vossii of horticulturalists). This hybrid has the long racemes of L. alpinum and the more striking flowers of L. anagyroides. Lower surface of leaves and pods also intermediate in pubescence, that is sparingly adpressed pubescent; fruiting pod about 4cm long, less winged than L. alpinum and seeds on average fewer. Pods are rarely developed and for this reason the hybrid is the most commonly planted to reduce chance consumption of the seeds which are just as poisonous. There are a number of cultivars, 'Vossii' being the finest.

False Acacias, Locust Trees
(genus *Robinia*)

Robinia is a genus of about 20 species native to North America and Mexico. They are deciduous shrubs or trees with alternate pinnate leaves that have an odd terminal leaflet (imparipinnate); the stipules are often spinose. The leaflets are opposite, entire and stipelate (with small stipules = stipels). The flowers are typically pea-like, borne mostly in axillary pendulous racemes and flowering in late spring or early summer. The calyx is bell-like, weakly two-lipped while the corolla has short-clawed petals with a large round standard and the keel petals united below. There are 10 stamens, the upper one free

or almost so from the remaining nine which are united into a tube. The pod is linear to oblong, flat, two-valved, containing 3–10 seeds.

False acacias or locusts are hardy in temperate regions and commonly planted for their showy and often scented white or pink to purplish flowers. The wood is somewhat brittle and branches are liable to be broken by strong winds. They are accordingly more useful for planting in poorish soils which reduces lush growth. Propagation is by seed or by grafting with *Robinia pseudacacia* (False Acacia, Black Locust) as a stock.

Probably the most widely planted is the False Acacia, a tree which may reach 26m (85ft) and bears pendulous racemes of fragrant, white, sometimes pinkish, flowers. Other very attractive species are *R. kelseyi* with deep rose-colored flowers and glandular hispid (with rough bristly hairs) pods, and *R. hispida* with rose to pale purplish flowers, also with glandular hispid pods, which are however rarely formed. There are a few hybrids with *R. pseudacacia* as one parent.

F. B. H.

The Main Species of *Robinia*

Group I: Shoots glabrous or at most downy, but not glandular-hispid.

R. pseudacacia False Acacia, Locust, Black Locust. N America, naturalized in many parts of Europe. Tree to 26m, with coarsely fissured bark. Shoots glabrous, stipules usually thorny (spinose). Leaflets 11–23. Flowers in dense, 10–20cm long, racemes, fragrant and white (pink in var *decaisneana*). Pod smooth linear-oblong, 5–10cm long with 3–10 seeds. Much planted as an ornamental. Stipules are not thorny in varieties *umbraculifera* and *bessoniana*.

R. boyntonii SE USA. Shrub to 3m, without thorny stipules. Leaflets 7–13. Flowers in 6–10cm long, loose racemes, pink to rosy-purplish. Pod glandular-hispid (with rough bristly hairs).

R. kelseyi SE USA. Shrub or small tree to 3m. Shoots with thorny stipules. Flowers deep rosy-pink, 5–8 in each raceme. Pod 3.5–5cm long, densely purple and glandular-hairy.

R. elliottii SE USA. Shrub to 1.5m. Shoots hairy to tomentose at first, stipular spines small. Flowers pinkish-purple or purple and white. Pod hispid.

Group II: Shoots and peduncles glandular-hispid. Pod hispid.

R. hispida Rose Acacia, Bristly Locust. SE USA. Shrub to 2m. Shoots and peduncles glandular-bristly. Leaflets 7–13. Flowers pink or pinkish-purple in 3–5 flowered hispid racemes. Pod rarely developed,

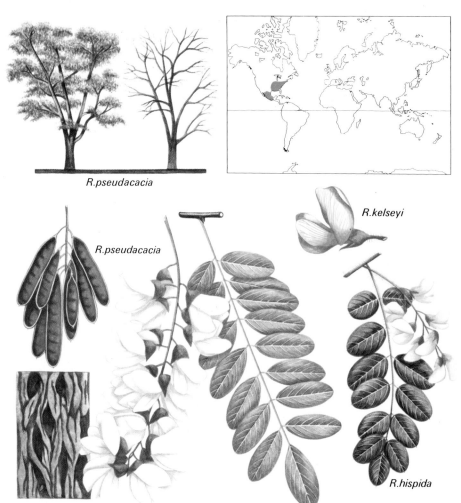

R.pseudacacia

R.pseudacacia

R.kelseyi

R.hispida

Opposite View of the canopy of the Kentucky Coffee Tree (*Gymnocladus dioica*) showing the roughened bark and large bipinnate leaves whch turn a bright yellow in the fall. The popular name derives from the use of the seeds as a coffee substitute by early settlers of North America.

petals and are borne on long stalks on separate trees, the females in panicles 10–20cm (4–8in) or more long, the males about one-third as long. The pod is oblong, 15cm (6in) long and 4–5cm (1.6–2in) across. It is hardy in temperate regions where it is grown for its foliage but it is often reluctant to flower. As winter approaches, the leaflets drop off leaving behind the yellow leaf and leaflet stalks, with the result that the whole tree assumes a rather severe but distinctive appearance. Settlers in its native area ground the seeds to make a drink bearing some resemblance to coffee. The tree also yields useful timber.

Gymnocladus chinensis from China is a tree growing to 13m, with leaves about as long as the previous species but with 20–24 oblong leaflets. The flowers are lilac-purple with bisexual and unisexual flowers on the same tree. The pods are 7–10cm (2.8–4in) long and 4cm (1.6in) across. It is not hardy in temperate regions.

The bark and pods of both plants yield saponins, which have lather-producing properties.

B. M.

5–8cm long, glandular-hispid. Often grown as a graft on *R. pseudacacia*.
R. luxurians SW USA. Shrub or tree to 10(12)m. Shoots and peduncles glandular-hairy or downy, not hispid. Stipules thorny; leaflets 13–25; rachis of leaf pubescent, virtually glandless. Flowers pale pink or almost white. Pod (6)7–10cm long with

gland-tipped bristles.
R. viscosa Clammy Locust. SE USA. Tree 10–12m. Shoots and peduncles glandular-hairy. Stipular spines small or absent; leaflets 13–25; rachis of leaf glandular or clammy. Flowers pink with yellow patch on standard. Pod 5–8cm long, with gland-tipped bristles.

Pagoda Tree
(genus *Sophora*)

Kentucky Coffee Tree
(genus *Gymnocladus*)

Gymnocladus is a genus of two species (possibly four) native to central and eastern North America and eastern China. This distribution, which is also found in other genera, is thought to indicate the remains of a vast geologically Tertiary (65–50 million years ago) forest flora which once occupied the Northern Hemisphere up to the present Arctic regions. They are

deciduous trees with large bipinnate leaves. The flowers are inconspicuous, regular (therefore not pea-like), and the sexes may be on the same or different plants. Each flower has a tubular calyx comprising five sepals, with five petals and 10 stamens. The fruit is a large, thick pod containing large, flat seeds.

The Kentucky Coffee Tree, Chicot or Knicker Tree (*Gymnocladus dioica* = *G. canadensis*) from the eastern central United States grows to about 30m (100ft) high. Its bipinnate leaves may reach 115cm (45in) long and 60cm (24in) wide, the lowest two leaflets are simple, and there are three to seven pinnae, each with 6–14 leaflets (rarely four) and one terminal leaflet. The flowers have greenish-white

Sophora is a genus of about 50–60 species of evergreen or deciduous trees or shrubs, and sometimes spiny, or rarely stout herbaceous perennials. They are native to warm and temperate regions of North and South America, Asia and Australasia. *Sophora tetraptera* has a disjunct distribution between New Zealand, Tristan da Cunha and southern Chile and, since its pods can float on sea water and retain viable seed for up to three years, it was probably dispersed by the ocean currents. One species, *Sophora toromiro*, from Easter Island, was until very recently considered extinct. Indeed no specimens remain in its native habitat, the population having been destroyed by sheep introduced to this island in the 18th century. However, it has been recently reported from Göteborg

A Japanese Pagoda Tree (*Sophora japonica*) in winter dress. Sophoras are much admired for their elegant pinnate leaves and large panicles of small flowers, which often fall to the ground in great numbers.

Botanic Garden, Sweden, that a number of seedlings have been raised from seeds collected by the famous explorer Thor Heyerdahl.

The leaves of sophoras are alternate, odd pinnate, with either numerous (7–80) small or few large opposite leaflets; the stipules are membranous and deciduous. The flowers, which are up to about 2.5cm (1in) long, are white, yellow or rarely bluish-violet and are born in terminal panicles or leafy racemes up to 50cm (20in) long. The calyx comprises five short teeth and the corolla is either typically pea-like or more or less tube-like, the petals pointing forward. The pod is cylindrical or slightly flattened, sometimes winged, up to 25cm (10in) long and is constricted between the seeds to appear rather like a bead necklace; in some cases it is indehiscent.

A few species are more or less hardy in temperate regions and are grown as ornamentals, the clusters of flowers being particularly attractive. They are distinctly sun-loving plants and some, for example the Kowhai, New Zealand Laburnum or Fourwing Sophora (*S. tetraptera*), do best against a wall. Best known in cultivation is the Japanese Pagoda Tree or Scholar's Tree (*S. japonica*) which is native to China and Korea but not Japan. Other species cultivated in temperate regions include

S. macrocarpa (Chile), *S. affinis* (southwest United States) and *S. davidii* (China). Propagation is by seed, green wood cuttings, grafting or by layering. The timber is very hard, that of *S. tetraptera* being used for cabinet-making, as shafts and for turnery work. Fruits of *S. japonica* have purgative properties, whilst its leaf and fruit extracts are used to adulterate opium in China. The fruits of the Mescal Bean or Frijolito (*S. secundifolia*) are used as intoxicants by various American Indian tribes, whilst the red seeds are used for making necklaces.   D. M. M.

Pink Siris, Albizzia
(genus *Albizia*)

Albizia comprises upward of 100 species (perhaps 150), all, except *Albizia occidentalis* from Mexico, native to the tropical and subtropical regions of Asia, Africa, Indonesia and Australia. They are unarmed shrubs or trees growing to 15–25m (50–80ft) high and are usually deciduous but exceptionally more or less evergreen. The leaves are bipinnate with many pairs of small leaflets or few pairs of large leaflets, bearing conspicuous glands on the stalks. The flowers are often showy, pink, yellow-

The Persian Acacia, Pink Siris, Nemu or Silk Tree (*Albizia julibrissin*) has large bipinnate leaves and the flowers, with long protruding stamens, are typical of this genus. This species is the hardiest.

ish or white, born in axillary globose heads or clustered at the ends of branches. The calyx is tubular, five-toothed, and the numerous stamens (more than 10), which protrude and give a tassel-like appearance to the flowers, are united below in a tube. The fruit is a strap-shaped, nonseptate pod (legume) maturing orbicular, compressed seeds. *Albizia* is related to and often confused with *Acacia* which, however, has the stamens quite free to the base, not united.

Few species of *Albizia* are hardy in temperate regions, the best known being the Pink Siris or Persian Acacia (*A. julibrissin*), a native of Iran that is wild or cultivated in countries of Asia extending to China, and is grown in southern Europe as a shade and roadside tree and naturalized in the southeastern United States.

Several species yield a wood that is hard, dense, close-grained, easily workable and rose-red or dark in color, including the East Indian Walnut (*A. lebbeck*), *A. procera*, *A. toona* (Red Siris) and *A. welwitschii*. Other soft-wooded species are used to make matches. Several species are a source of gum or resin and one species, *A. saponaria*, is used in the Philippines for washing, the bark being soapy from the presence of saponins and the fresh wood readily forming a lather with water. Other species such as *A. chinensis*, *A. falcata* (*A. moluccana*), *A. odoratissima* (Ceylon Rosewood, so called because of the fragrant wood) and the previously mentioned *A. lebbeck* are used for shading tea or coffee shrubs in plantations, either by retaining indigenous trees or by planting them from seeds or cuttings.   V. H. H.

Indian Laburnum
(genus *Cassia*)

Cassia is a genus of more than 400 species (perhaps 500–600) found throughout the tropical and subtropical regions of the Old and the New World but absent from the temperate and colder parts of Europe. A few species are cultivated as ornamentals but the genus is mostly known as the source of senna, a purgative which is used in most parts of the world.

The species of *Cassia* are mostly deciduous trees or shrubs but a few are herbaceous plants. The leaves are alternate and paripinnate (pinnate without the terminal leaflet) and the petioles often have glands. The flowers, which are not pea-like but almost regular, are usually yellow, sometimes red or pink, and mostly in clusters. The calyx is tubular with teeth shorter than the tube and the petals are five-clawed. There are commonly 10 stamens but three or five may be absent or modified; the anthers open by apical pores. The fruit is a round or flat pod (legume), winged or four-angled, with numerous seeds sometimes embedded in a pulp.

The North American species are more or less hardy in temperate regions and *Cassia corymbosa* and *C. marylandica* (Wild Senna) can survive an average winter in northern Europe. Other species require glasshouse protection. They favor a sandy loam soil. Propagation is by seed or cuttings.

Common preparations of senna are a hot water infusion of leaves (*Sennae Folium*) and an extract of the pulp surrounding the seeds (*Sennae Fructus*). In the pharmaceutical industry the two main forms are Alexandrian or Khartoum senna from *Cassia acutifolia* (= ? *C. senna* of Linnaeus), a perennial shrub of Egypt and the Sahara and of the Sudan where it is extensively grown on poor sandy soils of the Northern Province, and Tinnevelly senna from *C. angustifolia*, a native of Arabia and Somaliland (and known there as Arabia or Mecca senna) but also cultivated in southern India. A number of other species are also sources. The purgative principles of senna are widely distributed in the plant kingdom and are derivatives of anthraquinone, an organic compound of the greatest importance in

The name Candle Bush aptly describes the upright spikes of flowers of *Cassia alata*.

the dye industry. The principles occur in combination with glucose as glucosides and in *Cassia* there are two principal glucosides, sennosides A and B. Pharmaceutical preparations contain about 2.5 percent of the sennosides and are often mixed with Coriander (*Coriandrum sativum*) to prevent griping.

Several species of *Cassia* are used locally to treat skin diseases. *Cassia alata*, found throughout the tropics, is the Ringworm Senna, so-called because the leaves are used in the treatment of ringworm, and its seeds as a vermifuge. The Sickle Senna (*C. tora*) is similarly used in India. In Central America, leaves of *C. emarginata* are used to treat insect stings and leaves of *C. sericea* are used as wound dressings. Seeds of *C. absus* are used in South Africa to treat eye complaints. Root extracts of *C. sericea* and *C. occidentalis* are used to treat dropsy.

The Indian Laburnum or Golden Shower (*C. fistula*), the most ornamental of all *Cassia* species, is a tree to 10m (33ft) grown in gardens throughout the tropics for its racemes of yellow flowers up to 5cm (2in) in diameter. The Coffee Senna (*C. occidentalis*) is also grown for ornament, and in Africa the seeds are harvested to give mogdad or negro coffee. Smooth Senna (*C. laevigata*) and *C. sericea* are also used as coffee substitutes in Guatemala and Brazil respectively. In Malaysia roots of *C. nodosa* are used for soap.

Cassia wood is hard and dark and is often used locally for tool handles and posts. *Cassia siamea* from India and Indonesia is cultivated for timber used in construction work and the timber of *C. sieberiana* is much valued in tropical Africa for its resistance to termites. *Cassia javanica* has beautifully grained wood and in Indonesia the bark is used in tanning. The bark of the Avaram or Tanner's Cassia (*C. auriculata*) yields 18 percent tannin and is cultivated in its native India.

M. C. D.

Yellow Woods
(genus *Cladrastis*)

Cladrastis is a genus of four species of medium-sized, round-headed, deciduous trees from North America, China and Japan. They somewhat resemble the locusts (*Robinia* spp) but have longer clusters of larger flowers. Their leaves are usually large, up to 33cm (13in) long, alternate and pinnate with 7–15 entire-margined leaflets, the odd one terminal. The flowers are pea-like, white or pinkish and borne in panicles. Each flower has 10 almost free stamens. The fruit is a dehiscent flattened pod containing three to six seeds. The most characteristic feature of yellow woods is the petiole which has a hollow, swollen base that encloses the following year's three buds, the latter later appearing by the horseshoe-shaped leaf scar.

Yellow woods are hardy in temperate regions and are often planted as ornamentals, preferring a reasonable loam soil and sunny position. Propagation is best by seed, otherwise by root cuttings. The Chinese species can be grafted onto *Cladrastis lutea*.

The Yellow Wood (*C. lutea*), from the southern United States, is the most frequently grown ornamental species, notably for its young bright green foliage which turns a brilliant yellow in the fall. This species can reach 20m (66ft) but usually only grows to 12m (40ft) in cultivation. The leaves are 20–30cm (8–12in) long and bear (5)7–9(11) leaflets that lack stipels. The flowers are white and fragrant and borne in pendulous panicles up to 36cm (14in) long. The pod is 7–10cm

The leaflets of the pinnate leaves of the Yellow Wood (*Cladrastis lutea*) are arranged in an alternate manner and the leaf stalk has a swollen base which encloses the following year's buds.

(3–4in) long and wingless. *Cladrastis sinensis* from China is often planted on account of its relatively late summer flowering. It reaches 25m (82ft) in the wild, but otherwise grows to about 15m (50ft). Each leaf bears (9)11–13(17) leaflets which lack stipels. The flowers are white or suffused pinkish and borne in erect panicles 12–30cm (5–12in) long, and the pod is 5–7.5cm (2–3in) long and wingless. The Japanese Yellow Wood (*C. platycarpa*) from Japan is rather like species of *Sophora*, in which genus it was once placed. It is distinguished from the other species of *Cladrastis* by its winged pod and the presence of stipels to the leaflets.

The final species, *C. wilsoni* from China, is closely related to *C. sinensis* but does not flower in cultivation where it is not often seen.

The heartwood of *C. lutea* yields a yellow dye and the wood is used for making gunstocks.

F. B. H.

MYRTACEAE

Eucalypts
(genus *Eucalyptus*)

The eucalypts are a genus of some 500 species of evergreen trees and shrubs, found chiefly in Australia, with a few extending to New Guinea, eastern Indonesia and Mindanao. None is native in New Zealand. They range in height from less than 1m (3.3ft) to over 100m (330ft) in *Eucalyptus regnans*, known in Victoria as the Mountain Ash (the tallest of flowering plants, although surpassed by the coniferous *Sequoia sempervirens*, the Californian Redwood).

Large or small, in forests, scrubs or heaths, eucalypts belong to the dominant stratum, virtually never to the undergrowth. By far the greatest part of natural forest and woodland in the nonarid regions of Australia from the tropics to cool-temperate southern Tasmania is dominated by species of *Eucalyptus*, usually unaccompanied by any other genus in the upper storey. Such dominance of a single genus has no parallel in other continents.

Adaptation to fire is a vital determinant in the distribution of eucalypt-dominated communities. Some species are limited to regeneration from seed after destruc-

tive fires, but most survive fire by new growth of epicormic shoots from resting buds in the bark. Many smaller species are mallees (having several trunks arising from a massive lignotuber beneath or partly above the soil surface). Small lignotubers also characterize young stages of those single-stemmed species which can regenerate from epicormic shoots.

Eucalyptus is traditionally distinguished by the presence in the flower-buds of a floral operculum; the flowers open by shedding these lid-like coverings to expose the style and the numerous stamens. The latter are the conspicuous organs of the flower, attracting various insects (often honeybees) and birds in search of the usually copious nectar. The opercular structures vary considerably in morphological equivalence in the nine subgenera recognized (on these and other grounds) in the most recent classification, and must have arisen independently in several parallel evolutionary lines.

In *Angophora*, previously treated as a separate genus but bound by a complex of morphological and chemical characters to two eucalypt subgenera, the flowers have separate sepals and petals. In some of the other subgenera the sepals are free but the petals are united into an operculum; in others the two whorls form an outer and an inner operculum, whilst in subgenus *Monocalyptus* the single operculum is apparently derived from sepals alone.

Each subgenus or, especially in the case of the largest (*Symphyomyrtus*, with about 300 species), each of the sections into which they may be subdivided has a characteristic range of habitats. For instance, subgenus *Monocalyptus* is almost entirely restricted to acid soils particularly poor in phosphates and other nutrients in regions of favorable rainfall – especially winter rainfall.

Popular classification of eucalypts is based on the more obvious features of bark and timber. Such names as Stringybark, Ironbark, Peppermint, Box, Bloodwood, Blackbutt, Red Gum and Blue Gum are widely and often inconsistently applied – similar names being used in different regions of Australia for quite unrelated species – nevertheless there is some degree of correspondence with the natural affinities expressed in the botanical classification.

Identification is rendered difficult for the nonspecialist by the nature of some of the fundamental criteria (for example opercular structure, anther shapes, leaf venation patterns) and by the number of species in some areas: over 100 are found within a radius of 150km from Sydney. Further complication is caused by intra-specific variation, especially geographic and altitudinal clines (gradients in the absolute or statistical expression of characters). Moreover, there are many species which, although distinct over much of their areas, in certain contact zones produce hybrids or hybrid swarms intergrading to the parent species. This phenomenon was certainly widespread before European

These two pictures clearly demonstrate the extremes of tolerance to water availability that the genus *Eucalyptus* as a whole exhibits. *Right Eucalyptus* seedlings planted on the northern edge of the Sahara Desert, Tunisia, as part of an afforestation scheme and enclosed by palm leaves to protect them from dessication. *Below* The seeds of these River Red Gums (*Eucalyptus camaldulensis*) in Wyperfeld National Park, Victoria, Australia, can only germinate after floods. The picture was taken on only the third occasion this century that River Red Gum regeneration has been possible at Wyperfeld.

Spotted gums. Smooth, pinkish and often mottled bark. Leaves with fine, close lateral veins. Umbels 3-flowered. Fruits urceolate; valves deeply enclosed.

E. citriodora Lemon-scented Gum. NE Australia. Slender tree to 40m. Leaves contain citronellal. Fruit about 12 × 9mm.**

E. maculata Spotted Gum. E Australia. Usually fairly robust tree 35–40m. Leaves slightly discolorous without citronellal. Fruit about 15 × 12mm.**

Subgenus *Eudesmia*
Section *Quadraria* series *Tetrodontae*
E. tetrodonta Darwin Stringybark. N Australia. Tree usually 15–24m. Bark fibrous, persistent. Leaves concolorous, grayish pendulous. Umbels 3-flowered. Fruit somewhat campanulate, about 15 × 9mm, with 4 prominent external teeth (not to be confused with the small valves about rim level).**

Subgenus *Symphyomyrtus*
Section *Transversaria* Mainly large trees. Bark persistent or gum type. Leaves mainly discolorous, lateral veins fine, usually at large angles (50–75°) to midrib. Fruit with valves slightly or strongly exserted.
Series *Diversicolores*
E. diversicolor Karri. W Australia. Tree 45–65(75)m. Gum bark. Umbels 7-flowered. Fruit pyriform to globose, about 11 × 11mm; valves deeply enclosed.***
Series *Salignae*
E. grandis Flooded Gum. E Australia. Tree 35–45(50)m. Gum bark. Umbels 7-flowered. Fruit pyriform, about 8 × 6mm. often sessile; valves thin, slightly exserted, ~incurved.

E. saligna Sydney Blue Gum. E Australia. Tree 35–45(50)m. Gum bark, but often with basal stocking. Umbels 7–11-flowered. Fruit like that of *E. grandis* but usually smaller and valves straight or spreading outward **

E. propinqua Small-fruited Grey Gum. E Australia. Tree 30–35m. Gum bark.

Leaves concolorous. Flowers solitary in typical form, buds warty. Fruit top-shaped, about 15 × 25mm, sessile.*

E. viminalis Manna Gum. S and SE Australia. Tree 20–35(50)m. Gum bark. Leaves concolorous. Umbels usually 3-flowered. Fruit subglobular, about 7 × 5mm (2 lateral ones sessile); valves prominent, exserted.*

Section *Adnataria*, series *Oliganthae*
E. microtheca Coolabah. Inland and N Australia. Tree 12–20m. Bark subfibrous, usually persistent on stem and large branches. Leaves bluish-green. Moderately large inflorescences of 7-flowered umbels. Fruit hemispherical, 3 × 4mm, with large, exserted valves.
Series *Largiflorentes*
E. populnea Bimble Box. E Australia. Tree 10–22m. Bark subfibrous, persistent. Leaves shining green. Inflorescences of 7-flowered umbels. Fruit about 3mm, valves small, enclosed or at rim level.
Series *Paniculatae*
E. paniculata Gray Ironbark. SE Australia. Tree 25–30(40)m. Bark ironbark, persistent. Leaves moderately discolorous. Panicles with mostly 7-flowered umbels. Fruit pyriform to ovoid, about 9 × 7mm; valves small, usually enclosed.**
Series *Melliodorae*
E. melliodora Yellow Box. SE Australia. Tree 15–30m. Bark subfibrous, variably persistent. Leaves concolorous. Umbels 7-flowered. Fruit subpyriform, about 7 × 5mm; valves enclosed.
Section *Sebaria*, series *Microcorythes*
E. microcorys Tallowwood. E Australia. Tree 30–45(50)m. Bark subfibrous, soft, persistent. Leaves discolorous. Umbels 7-flowered, mostly in small terminal inflorescences. Fruit elongated obconic, about 8 × 5mm; valves very small, slightly protruding.

Subgenus *Telocalyptus*
Section *Equatoria*, series *Degluptae*
E. deglupta Kamerere. Philippines, Sulawesi (Celebes). New Guinea and New Britain.

Subgenus *Monocalyptus*
Section *Renantheria*, series *Marginatae*
E. marginata Jarrah SW Australia. Tree 25–35m. Bark fibrous persistent. Leaves discolorous. Umbels 7-flowered. Fruit spherical-ovoid, woody, about 18 × 15mm; valves enclosed.***
Series *Capitellatae* Stringybarks. Bark fibrous, persistent. Leaves usually concolorous. Umbels 7—more than 20—flowered. Fruit hemispherical to globular, typically with exserted valves.
E. baxteri Brown Stringybark. SE Australia. Tree 25–35m. Umbels 7-flowered. Fruit about 11 × 9mm, almost sessile.*

E. eugenioides Thin-leaved Stringybark. E Australia. Tree 20–25m. Umbels 7–11-flowered. Fruit about 6 × 7mm, with very short pedicels.*
Series *Pilulares*
E. pilularis Blackbutt. E Australia. Tree 35–60m. Bark finely fibrous, persistent on lower half of trunk. Leaves discolorous. Umbels 7–11-flowered. Fruit pilular, about 11 × 12mm; valves small, enclosed or to rim level ***
Series *Obliquae* Height varies from the tallest hardwood in the world (*E. regnans*) to mallees. Bark fibrous, persistent or gum type. Leaves typically concolorous, often with oblique base and lateral veins at small angle (15–25°) to the midrib. Fruit ovoid to pyriform, mainly with sunken valves.
E. obliqua Messmate. SE Australia. Tree 10–60m. Bark persistent. Leaves green. The first eucalypt named as such, though some species had been described under other genera. Fruit about 9 × 8mm.***

E. delegatensis Alpine Ash. SE Australia. Tree 35–50(70)m. Bark persistent on lower half of trunk. Leaves bluish. Umbels 7–15-flowered. Fruit about 15 × 12mm.***

E. regnans Mountain Ash. SE Australia. Tree 50–75(100)m. Bark persistent on lower part of trunk. Leaves green, small. Umbels 7–11-flowered, often in pairs. Fruit about 8 × 6mm.***

E. pauciflora Snow Gum. SE Australia. Tree, sometimes crooked, 15–18m. Gum Bark. Leaf venation conspicuous, major lateral veins almost parallel to midrib. Umbels 7–15-flowered. Fruit about 9 × 8mm.
Series *Piperitae* (Peppermints and scribbly gums). Small to moderate-sized trees. Bark fibrous or smooth. Leaves concolorous, often with lateral veins at small angle to midrib. Fruit typically small, with inconspicuous valves often about rim level.
E. radiata Narrow-leaved Peppermint. SE Australia. Tree 12–24m. Bark subfibrous, persistent. Fruit subglobular to subpyriform, about 4 × 4mm.*

Commercial importance
*** significant contributor to commercial pulpwood and timber production
** important, but sometimes restricted to a limited geographical area
* limited importance, due to log form, gum pockets (eg *E. gummifera)* etc

E.tetragona

E.dalrympleana

E. pauciflora ssp
niphophila

(juvenile)

E.glaucescens

(adult)

E.dalrympleana

E.grossa

E.eugenioides *E.glaucescens* *E.parvifolia*

E.kruseana

E.parvifolia

E.ovata

E.pileata

E.callophylla

(juvenile)

E.gunni

(adult)

E.perriniana

(adult)   (juvenile)

E.macrocarpa

settlement but has increased as habitat distinctions have become blurred by clearing, drainage, altered fire regimes etc, over the past 100–200 years.

Apart from differences in flowering period, there seem to be few intrinsic barriers to effective interbreeding between species within any one section (and few if any absolute barriers within any one subgenus). In contrast, no natural or manipulated hybrids are known between species of different subgenera. Thus many species remain distinct only through geographic isolation or by selective survival of progeny in ecologically different though adjacent sites. Consequently, in any one site associated species usually belong to different breeding groups, that is subgenera or sections. In areas of complex physiography or fine mosaics of soil types, this phenomenon is often evident only by careful inspection of the distribution patterns of the species and the environmental determinants.

Eucalypts constitute the major hardwood timber resource of Australia: among the particularly valuable species for sawlog and pole production are the Jarrah (*E. marginata*), Blackbutt (*E. pilularis*) and Messmate (*E. obliqua*). Recently, emphasis has swung to pulp for paper and similar products and especially to chipwood for hardboard production. Massive clearing of timbered land for woodchip production and the subsequent export of the product have met with opposition from Australian environmentalists. Forestry authorities claim that by rotation of such exploitation the eucalypts can be managed as a renewable resource. Nevertheless, general considerations point to widespread adverse affects on wildlife and the aesthetic values of the countryside. Many eucalypt species are important food plants for the indigenous Koala (*Phascolarctos cinereus*), whose metabolism and anatomy have become especially adapted to digest this plant material.

Among minor products derived from the genus the best known are eucalyptus oils, essential oils that have been used medicinally and in flavoring. A frequent constituent is cineole (or eucalyptol).

Several species yield kinos, astringent tannin-containing exudates used in medicine and tanning. The bark of the Brown Mallet (*E. astringens*) contains 40–50 percent tannin and was formerly much used in tanning processes.

Eucalypts are widely planted (eg in Brazil, North Africa, the Middle East, southern and tropical Africa, California,

India and on the Black Sea coast of the USSR) for timber, pulpwood, firewood, shelter (shade trees and windbreaks), erosion control, essential-oil production and ornament. In suitable climates, many species make much better growth in exotic situations than in their native habitat, thanks to higher nutrient status of soils and to absence of destructive insects. The most important species grown outside Australia number only 30 or 40 and are often different from those of greatest importance for timber in Australia.

Cultivation outside their native regions is beset with difficulties. Economic and reliable methods of vegetative propagation have not been developed, so that seed is the only means available. This brings many difficulties, not least that seed from sources outside Australia is likely to be unreliably identified. Even from wild-growing trees seed samples may be wrongly named, be mixtures of more than one species or often include hybrid seed from outcrossings. If one is fortunate enough to have reliably named seed, it is equally important to have appropriate instructions as to germination procedure, potting-off and final transplanting to the permanent position.

Many eucalypts are fast-growing; seedlings can reach 1.5m (5ft) in a year and 10m (33ft) in 10 years or more in some tropical and subtropical species. Because of high rates of transpiration some species were planted extensively last century in swampy areas in Italy and westward and also in similar areas in North Africa. It was claimed that they helped to dry out the land, with consequent antimalarial benefits. One swamp-tolerant species is the Swamp Mahogany (*E. robusta*), a medium-sized tree with rough, brownish bark. The most widely planted species in the Mediterranean area and California is probably Tasmanian Blue Gum (*E. globulus*) a tree reaching 35–45m (115–150ft) with grayish inner bark annually exposed by stripping away of the outer bark. Many other species are cultivated outside Australia, particularly in warm temperate regions such as California, which has the richest introduced eucalypt flora in the United States. The following is a sample of eucalypts grown outside Australia in warm temperate regions: *E. calophylla* (Marri, Red Gum), *E. camaldulensis* (Murray Red Gum), *E. citriodora* (Lemon-scented Gum), *E. dalrympleana* (Mountain Gum), *E. glaucescens*, *E. gomphocephala*, *E. grandis* (Rose Gum), *E. grossa* (Coarse-leaved Mallee), *E. kruseana* (Kruse's

Mallee), *E. macrocarpa* (Mottlecah), *E. microtheca* (Flooded Box), *E. occidentalis* (Flat-topped Yate), *E. ovata* (Swamp Gum), *E. parvifolia* (Small-leaved Gum), *E. perriniana* (Round-leaved Snow Gum), *E. pileata*, *E. saligna* (Sydney Blue Gum), *E. sideroxylon*, *E. tereticornis* (Forest Red Gum), *E. tetragona* (White-leaved Marlock). Noticeably absent are members of the subgenus *Monocalyptus*, mentioned above as important in Australia. This group appears to be particularly dependent on mycorrhizal associations.

In cooler regions, eucalypts are mostly grown for ornament or curiosity. Amongst these is the Cider Gum (*E. gunnii*), a tree reaching 30m (100ft) with strips of pinkish bark peeling to expose a more or less smooth gray underbark. Another hardy species is the Alpine Snow Gum (*E. pauciflora* ssp *niphophila*), a small tree, belonging to the subgenus *Monocalyptus*, growing to about 6m (20ft), with smooth gray or white-streaked bark, peeling every second or third year. Also hardy, except for the coldest areas of temperate regions, is the Tasmanian Snow Gum (*E. coccifera*), a small tree often pruned to keep it shrubby, with strikingly spiraled bark. A vigorous and hardy species less often seen in cultivation is the Urn-fruited Gum (*E. urnigera*), a tree reaching 30–35m (100–115ft), the fruit of which is constricted like an urn.

L. A. S. J.

NYSSACEAE

Dove Trees (genus *Davidia*)

Davidia is a genus of only one species, *Davidia involucrata* (the Dove Tree, Ghost Tree or Handkerchief Tree) from central and western China where it reaches 20m (66ft) in height. It is a deciduous tree, somewhat resembling a lime tree (*Tilia* spp), bearing alternate, broadly ovate leaves with a heart-shaped base and long-pointed tip. The outstanding feature of this species is the conspicuous enormous white or creamy-white bracts, two of which surround each of the small globose flower heads. The flowers lack petals, each head comprising a mass of male flowers with purple anthers and a single bisexual flower. In early summer the sight of a mature tree clothed in the white bracts is quite spectacular. However, trees under

Above Top Flower of the Dove or Handkerchief Tree (*Davidia involucrata*) showing the white involucral bracts that have given the tree its popular name. *Above* The equally distinctive fruits of the same species hang from leafless shoots in the fall.

20 years of age flower sparsely. Later in the season the deep green ovoid fruits, 3×2.5cm (1.2×1in), form a distinctive feature, dangling on long stalks below the leaves and later the leafless shoots.

Dove Trees can be propagated from seeds or by cuttings or layering and only grow well on fertile soil. The type most frequently seen in cultivation is var *vilmoriniana* which lacks the white hairs on the under surface of the leaves that occur on the type variety.

T. W. W.

Tupelos
(genus *Nyssa*)

Outstanding for their fall colors, tupelos comprise a genus of about 10 Asian and North American deciduous trees and shrubs. The best known is the Black Gum or Tupelo (*Nyssa sylvatica*) which is renowned both in its native eastern United States and in cultivation through-

out temperate regions for its striking scarlet and gold colors produced early in the fall. Another notable species is the Water Tupelo, Cotton Gum or Large Tupelo (*N. aquatica*) which grows in the swamps of the eastern and southern coasts of the United States frequently in standing water for much of the year.

Tupelos have simple, alternate leaves, without stipules and minute unisexual flowers, with the sexes on the same or different plants or polygamous. Each flower has five minute sepals and five greenish petals; the females are either solitary or occur in small clusters while the males are clustered in globular heads. The males have 5–10(12) stamens and the females a single style plus a one- or two-chambered ovary. The fruit is a plum-like drupe, often red or purple, containing a single seed (stone).

In cultivation the Black Gum is particularly valuable for wet or acid soils but can survive in drier areas, particularly coastal regions when protected from winds. Propagation is from seeds or by layering, but

Few species can rival the brilliant scarlet and gold colors produced by the Black Gum, Tupelo or Pepperidge (*Nyssa sylvatica*) during the early fall, which makes it a valued ornamental.

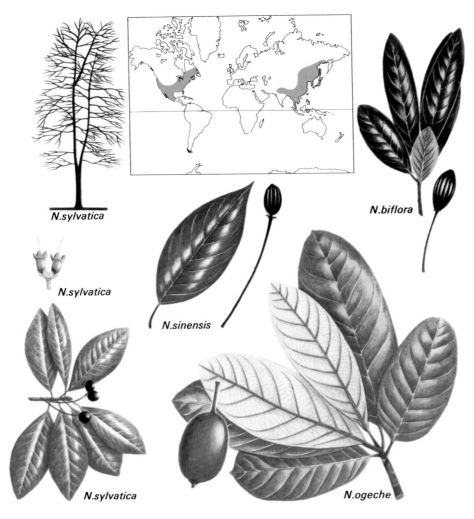

N.sylvatica

N.sylvatica

N.sinensis

N.biflora

N.sylvatica

N.ogeche

midrib; petiole flattened. Flowers axillary, aggregated; stalk slender with silky brown hairs. Young growth red-brown pubescent.
N. javanica Tree to 15m. Branches gray-brown with dense silky pubescence, spotted with prominent lenticels. Leaves as long but broader than *N. sinensis*, green above but silky brown below; peduncle short.

CORNACEAE

Cornels, Dogwoods (genus *Cornus*)

Cornus is a genus of over 40 species of mostly deciduous trees or shrubs that are scattered over temperate regions of the Northern Hemisphere, especially the United States and Asia. The leaves are mostly opposite and the flowers usually small, white, less often greenish or yellowish, their parts in fours. They are clustered in terminal heads or cymes, sometimes surrounded by more or less conspicuous involucral bracts. The fruit is a drupe and the seed a two-celled stone.

They are primarily ornamental plants cultivated for the beauty of their flowers, particularly the bracts, and stem color (often red), and some for the fall color of their leaves. For flowers may be mentioned: the Cornelian Cherry (*Cornus mas*), the Flowering Dogwood (*C. florida*), the Pacific Dogwood (*C. nuttallii*) and *C. kousa*. All these tree-like species grow best in sheltered, semi-woodland or particularly shaded sites, preferring moist, lime-free organic soils. The colored-stem dogwoods are shrubby thicket-forming species and it is the current season's growth that may have vivid winter colors. 'Stooling' or removal of older wood in the spring is carried out to maintain stems of the young wood for maximum effect. This group grows well in moist waterside habitats and includes the Red Osier Dogwood (*C. stolonifera*), including 'Flaviramea' with golden-green stems, and *C. alba* 'Sibirica' with vivid dark red stems. In the European Common Dogwood (*C. sanguinea*), the specific name refers to the fall red color of the leaves rather than the stems which may be a patchy red on one side.

A few species have some value other

seedlings should be planted out as soon as manageable since older saplings do not transplant well.

The soft tough wood of tupelos is valued in commerce for making furniture, boxes and shoes. The Water Tupelo and Sour Tupelo (*N. ogeche*) are valued as bee plants and the fruits of the latter (ogeche limes) are eaten locally.

S. A. H.

The Main Species of *Nyssa*

Group I: Native to the United States

A *Female flowers borne 2 or more together. Fruit small and black; stone smooth or bluntly ridged.*

N. sylvatica (*N. villosa*) Tupelo, Black Gum, Pepperidge. Hillsides or swampy sites. Calcifuge. Oak-like tree to 30m, with broadly conic crown, branches level but curved upward at the tip. Bark angular with checkered pattern. Leaves ovate to obovate, 5–12cm long, entire, glossy dark or yellow-green above, whitish-green below. Female flowers usually 2, sometimes 3, on a single peduncle. Stone almost ribless.
N. biflora Tupelo, Water Gum, Twin Flowered Nyssa. Peaty and swampy habitats. Tree to

15m. Bark with long ridges. Sometimes considered a variety of *N. sylvatica* but distinguished by its spathulate, elliptic leaves. Stone ribbed.
N. ursina A much branched shrub. Leaves smaller than *N. sylvatica*. Flowers conspicuous in clusters. Drupe (fruit) globular.

AA *Female flowers borne singly. Fruit large, purple-red; stone ridged and winged.*

N. acuminata Pine swamps. Shrub to 5m with underground stems. Branches with narrow leaves. Female flower short-stalked. Drupe (fruit) red; stone winged.
N. ogeche (*N. candicans*, *N. capitata*) Sour Tupelo, Ogeche Lime, Ogeche Plum. Riverbanks. Spreading tree to 9m. Stem often crooked. Leaves broad. Drupe (fruit) oblong, longer than stalk, red-purple; stone winged.
N. aquatica (*N. uniflora*) Cotton Gum, Water Tupelo. Tree to 30m. Leaves ovate, 10–16cm long, downy beneath. Female flower long-stalked. Drupe (fruit) purple-blue, shorter than stalk; stone sharply ridged.

Group II: Native to Eastern Asia.
N. sinensis Shrub or tree to 18m. Bark gray, finely fissured. Leaves oblong-ovate up to 15cm long, deep shiny green above, pale green below, pubescent on veins and

than aesthetic. Thus, fruits of the Common Dogwood yield an oil which can be used for illumination as well as for making soap; the twigs are also flexible enough for basket-making. The wood of the Cornelian Cherry is very durable and suitable for small articles such as skewers, handles and the like; its fruit can be made into a preserve.

The genus is commonly divided into four sections which some authorities would raise to generic rank. In the following selection of species, the wider concept of the genus is maintained, the four sections being referred to as four Groups, each Group being given a name which would be the generic name used by those authorities who favor segregation. Relevant here is the common exclusion of two species from *Cornus*, essentially because they are herbaceous. These are the Dwarf Cornel (*C. suecica*), a beautiful arctic-alpine herb growing to 20cm (8in), the flower clusters surrounded by four spreading white involucral bracts – each individual flower purplish-black and fruits red; and the Bunch-berry (*C. canadensis*), which grows to about 25cm (10in) and is slightly woody at the base and has a creeping rootstock; individual flowers are greenish and the flower clusters are surrounded by four to six white involucral bracts; the fruit is scarlet. The new genus created for them is *Chamaepericlimenum* – an unnecessary creation in the present writer's opinion.

F. B. H.

Cornus kousa is a large elegant shrub which every year, in early summer, is covered by tiers of flowers, each enclosed in their conspicuous white bracts.

The Main Species of *Cornus*

Group I: (*Swida = Thelycrania*). Flowers white in clusters without involucral bracts or bracteoles.

A *Leaves opposite. Fruit purplish-black or green.*

C. sanguinea Common Dogwood. Europe including S England. Shrub to 3.5(4)m. Leaves ovate, 4–8cm long, with 3–5 pairs of veins; petiole 4–13mm long. Fruit globose, 6–7mm across, purplish-black. Leaves red in the fall, stems patchy red.
  viridissima has the young stems and also the fruit green.

AA *Leaves opposite. Fruit white or blue.*

C. alba Tatarian Dogwood. China, Siberia. Shrub producing a dense thicket, to 3m, young shoots turning a fine red in the fall. Leaves more or less ovate, 5–11cm long, dark green above, whitish to glaucous beneath, both sides with minute (lens) adpressed hairs, veins 5–6 pairs; petiole 8–25mm long. There are a number of variegated cultivars; also 'Sibirica' with brilliant crimson-red winter shoots ('Westonbirt,' 'Westonbirt Dogwood' and 'Atrosanguinea' are considered to be identical with 'Sibirica').
C. amomum Silky Dogwood. Mainly E USA. Shrub to 3m, winter stems reddish-purple. Leaves more or less elliptic, 5–10cm, brownish woolly-hairy beneath at least on veins; petiole 8–15mm long. Fruit blue or partly white, 6mm across.
C. baileyi E N America. Shrub to 3m, not stoloniferous, branches reddish-brown. Leaves ovate to lanceolate, 5–13cm, woolly beneath when young; petiole 12–18mm long. Fruit white, 8–9mm across. (Cf: *C. stolonifera*.)
C. stolonifera Red Osier Dogwood. N America. Vigorous suckering shrub to 2.5m; young shoots red-purple. Leaves ovate to lanceolate, 5–10cm long, dark green above, glaucous beneath, both surfaces with adpressed hairs; petiole 12–25mm long. Fruit white, 5–6mm across. Not unlike *C. alba* and *C. baileyi*, but is stoloniferous.
  'Flaviramea' is unusual in its greenish-yellow winter stems.

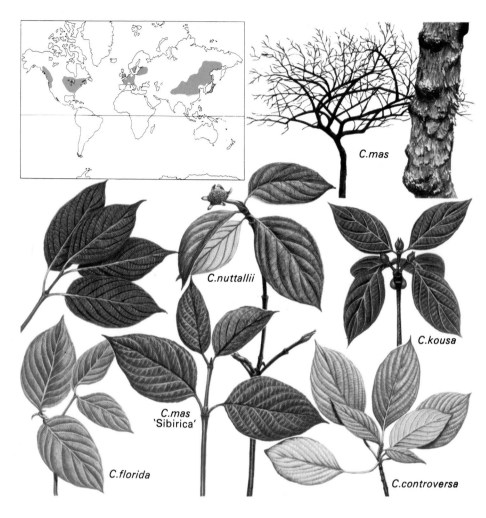

C.mas

C.nuttallii

C.kousa

C.mas 'Sibirica'

C.florida

C.controversa

AAA *Leaves alternate. Fruit black or bluish-black.*

C. alternifolia E N America. Shrub or small tree to 6m. Leaves oval to ovate, 5–12.5cm long, lower surface adpressed pubescent, base tapering into 2.5–5.0cm long petiole. Flower clusters 4–6cm across. Fruit 6–7mm across.

C. controversa Table Dogwood. Japan, China, the Himalaya. Tree 10–16m, branches horizontally tiered. Leaves ovate to oval, 7.5–15cm long, lower surface with adpressed hairs centrally attached; veins 6–8(9) pairs; petiole 2.5–5.0cm; fall colors sometimes purplish. Flower clusters 6–12(17)cm across. Fruit 6–7mm in diameter.

Group II: (*Cornus*). Clusters of flowers with a yellowish involucre (bracts) which is not longer than the flowers and falls off as these open.

C. mas Cornelian Cherry. C and S Europe, W Asia. Shrub or small tree to 8m. Leaves ovate, 4–10cm long, both sides with adpressed, centrally attached hairs; veins 3–5 pairs; petiole 6mm long. Flowers yellow, open before the leaves in early spring, in umbels 18–20mm across, enclosed in 4 short involucral bracts which drop off as the umbel expands. Fruit scarlet, ellipsoidal, (12)15–16mm long. A splendid sight in flower and fruit. Too seldom seen.

Group III: (*Benthamidia*). Clusters of flowers with the involucral bracts white or pink and conspicuously longer than the flowers and persisting after they open. Fruits clustered but distinct from each other.

C. florida Flowering Dogwood. E USA. Shrub or tree 3–6(7)m. Leaves oval to ovate, 7–14cm long. Flowers inconspicuous in a small cluster 12–13mm across, but surrounded by 4 obovate white very conspicuous involucral bracts, notched at the apex and 4–5cm long. Fruit 1cm long. Flowers liable to succumb to frost in temperate regions.

rubra has the bracts pinkish-red.

C. nuttallii Nuttall's Dogwood, Pacific Dogwood. W N America. Tree mostly to 16m, but may reach to 30m in the wild. Leaves oval to obovate, 7.5–12.5cm long. Flowers small in a cluster, 18–20mm across, but surrounded by (4)6(8) large, 4–8cm long more or less broadly oval involucral bracts, pointed or somewhat blunt but not notched at the apex. A magnificent plant, but not succeeding in the north temperate regions except in the warmer parts. The leaves and 'flower' (flower cluster plus bracts) sometimes much exceed above measurements.

Group IV: (*Dendrobenthamia*). Involucral bracts as in Group III, but fruits united into a compound structure or syncarp. (The following flower spring, summer.)

C. capitata Bentham's Cornel. The Himalaya,

China. Half-evergreen tree to 14m in cultivation. Leaves more or less obovate, (2)3–6cm long, densely pubescent on both sides, light green above, glaucous beneath. Flowers with 4–6 yellowish obovate bracts, 4–5cm long. Fruit strawberry-like, 1.5–2.5cm across. Not really hardy in temperate regions.

C. kousa C China, Japan, Korea. Shrub or tree to 6m. Leaves ovate, 4.5–8(9)cm long, margin wavy, veins with tufts of brown hair in their axils; petiole 4–6mm. Flowers in a small dense cluster surrounded by 4 lanceolate ivory-colored involucral bracts, 2.5–5cm long. Fruit like a strawberry, 1.5–2.5cm across. Hardy in temperate regions and a fine ornamental plant.

chinensis Leaves usually larger and more profusely flowering, involucral bracts a little longer. Doubtfully distinct from type.

PROTEACEAE

Silk Oaks
(genus *Grevillea*)

The genus *Grevillea* comprises some 230–250 species predominantly from Australia and Tasmania, with a few in New Guinea, the New Hebrides and New Caledonia. They are evergreen shrubs or trees with alternate leaves that may be simple or compound. The flowers are bisexual, mostly pink to red but some orange or yellow, and are borne in long spike-like inflorescences which are often paired. The perianth consists of one whorl ('calyx') and is usually tubular with four-valvate lobes to which are affixed the almost sessile stamens. The style is elongated, crook-like at first, protruding through the calyx. Pollen is shed on the style (male stage) before the stigma straightens out and becomes receptive (female stage). The fruit is a leathery, often quite woody, follicle with one or two variously winged or wingless seeds.

There are many attractive species, a notable feature being the showy flowers which usually appear in the spring and retain their color for long periods. Silk oaks are not hardy in temperate regions (where they are essentially glasshouse plants), except in the mildest areas, such as south-western Europe. They are frequently grown successfully in more subtropical regions such as California, South Africa and the Mediterranean Riviera. They are intolerant of lime, preferring a more or less peaty soil. Propagation is from young shoots taken about midsummer and kept in a frame, preferably with some bottom heat. If such cuttings fail, grafting on *Grevillea robusta* seedlings (of which seeds are readily available) is generally successful. Plants may also be raised from seeds sown in spring (glasshouse), pricked off and finally repotted for indoor use. Roughly equal parts of loam, peat and sand make a suitable mixture. In winter, such indoor plants, especially near a window, may succumb in an unheated room.

The best known and most commonly cultivated species in tropical and subtropical regions is the Silk Oak or Golden Pine (*G. robusta*). This may reach 50m (165ft) in its native habitat (but hardly 2m (6.5ft) under glasshouse cultivation) and is highly prized for its fern-like foliage, attractive rusty-colored young stems, and almost golden flowers in one-sided clusters. In Kenya, tea planters use it as a shade tree for young tea plants and the timber is valuable for interior furnishings. It is also grown as an indoor foliage plant under the name 'Grevillea.'

The hardiest species are *G. rosmarinifolia*, from New South Wales, a shrub growing to almost 2m (6.5ft) with deep rose-red flowers in dense terminal clusters, and *G. thyrsoides* from Western Australia,

a shrub growing to about 1.5m (5ft) with rose-pink flowers in an extended inflorescence to about 25cm (10in), the flowers clustered toward the top. Other cultivated species (all from Australia) include *G. acanthifolia*, a shrub to about 2m (6.5ft) with dull pinkish flowers; *G. alpina*, a bushy shrub to about 1m (3.3ft) with yellow or dull red flowers in terminal clusters of five; *G. asplenifolia*, a shrub or small tree to 4m (13ft) with attractive foliage and deep rose-pink flowers in dense spikes; *G. banksii*, a shrub or tree to 6m (20ft) with bright red flowers in dense one-sided clusters; *G. glabrata*, a shrub to 2m (6.5ft) with flowers clustered in large pyramid-like panicles, the conspicuous styles white with pink stigmas; and *G. sulphurea*, a bushy shrub to about 2m (6.5ft) with pale yellow flowers in more or less loose clusters, looking like a full pincushion.   D. B.

Banksias
(genus *Banksia*)

Banksia comprises about 50 species endemic to Australia and Tasmania (mostly Western Australia), with one species (*Banksia dentata*) native to New Guinea and the islands of the Gulf of Carpentaria. They are evergreen trees and shrubs, rarely prostrate, with drought-resistant (xeromorphic) characters. The stems are often softly woolly. The leaves are alternate, needle-like or linear, or often of unusual appearance with deeply cut lobes (dissected), usually dark green above and white or reddish-brown with indumentum (hairs) beneath; the margin is variously toothed or spiny, less often entire. The flowers are clustered in dense terminal globose or cylindrical heads of sometimes 1 000, with conspicuous styles and abundant nectar (whence the once popular name, Native Honeysuckle). Relatively few flowers set seed and the final fruit is a hard woody follicle enclosed by bracts and bracteoles which also become woody; the seeds are winged. The mature fruiting head has a cone-like appearance, studded with the protruding, gaping 'mouths' of the woody follicles.

The Bull Banksia (*Banksia grandis*) seldom exceeds 8m (26ft) tall and has golden flower spikes to 30cm (12in) long and ornamental saw-tooth leaves. *Banksia ericifolia* from New South Wales and

Banksia ericifolia from New South Wales, Australia. The brightly colored bottle-brush-like inflorescences are typical of the genus.

Queensland has orange flowers and small linear pale green leaves, while *B. serrata* has dark green serrate leaves, grayish-yellow flowers, and purplish wood that is used for decorative furniture.

Banksias are not really hardy in cool temperate regions except in the very mildest areas; exceptions are: *B. grandis* and *B. serrata*, already mentioned, the Swamp Banksia (*B. littoralis*) and Coast Banksia (*B. integrifolia*).

B. M.

Proteas
(genus *Protea*)

Protea is a genus of about 130 species almost confined to South Africa, a few extending to tropical Africa and as far north as Ethiopia. Linnaeus named the genus after the Greek god Proteus, an old man of the sea who undertook to foretell the future to anyone wanting to know it, but to avoid having to do so, assumed innumerable changes of shape so as to avoid recognition. The name is thus synonymous with changeableness and presumably refers to the diversity of form in the genus.

They are predominantly evergreen shrubs, rarely small trees, with variable

The strangely attractive flower of *Grevillea chrysophaea*, with a yellow, hairy, kidney-shaped perianth from which protrudes the single stout, hairy style, crowned by the yellow, hairless stigma.

Isles of Scilly, off the extreme southwest of Britain.

It would seem worthwhile trying to extend the areas of outdoor planting of these splendid plants where the growing conditions appear favorable. Propagation is usually by seed (which may be hard to come by).

Species that have been successfully cultivated in temperate regions include *P. cynaroides* and *P. repens* already mentioned, and the Oleander-leaved Protea (*P. neriifolia*), the Peach Protea (*P. grandiceps*), *P. susannae*, *P. eximia* (*P. latifolia*), *P. compacta* and *P. scolymocephala*.

B. M.

Oleaster
(genus *Elaeagnus*)

Elaeagnus is a genus of some 45 species native to North America, southern Europe and Asia. They are evergreen or deciduous trees or shrubs with alternate leaves, the undersurfaces of which are often covered with fringed, silvery scales. The flowers are mostly fragrant, bisexual (sometimes unisexual) with a perianth comprising one

Above The highly distinctive inflorescence of a *Protea* species. The cluster of flowers is in the center, surrounded by whorls of tufted bracts.
Right In the foreground, the striking gold-splashed leaves of *Elaeagnus pungens* 'Maculata' with some 'plain' green shoots, and behind a species of *Cotinus* in full fall glory.

alternate and entire leaves that may be with or without stalks and either hairy or glabrous. The flowers, often of great and unusual beauty, are borne in dense cup-shaped heads surrounded by involucres of often strikingly colored bracts which may be smooth or conspicuously hairy; they are usually bisexual with a long, slender, tubular perianth, four stamens, and a superior ovary. The fruit is a bearded nut.

The Giant Protea (*Protea cynaroides*) has the largest heads, sometimes exceeding 30cm (12in) across, with pale red outer bracts having a velvet sheen, and a boss of numerous, woolly, lilac flowers, yellow at their base. This shrub grows to about 2m (6ft) in the wild, or less in cultivation. The Sugar Bush or Honey Protea (*P. repens* = *P. mellifera*) is so called because early settlers to South Africa made a sweet syrup from the flowers for the treatment of coughs and colds. It is much visited by bees, yields an excellent honey and is the national flower of South Africa.

In temperate regions proteas are grown mainly as cool greenhouse plants, the general experience being that they are not hardy enough outside. This view may need to be modified now it is realized that they require a well-drained, rather peaty soil, boisterously windy summers and ample winter rainfall. With such conditions, many species can withstand mildly freezing temperatures during winter. Successful outdoor plantings have now been made in temperate regions such as coastal areas of California (USA), Australia and in the

whorl (calyx) with four petaloid lobes that are more or less at right-angles to the inverted, bell-like tube. The fruit is a one-seeded drupe.

They are mostly quite hardy species, often cultivated for their attractive foliage and fragrant flowers. They grow best on a light, sandy loam, a poor soil enhancing the silvery appearance of the leaves. Propagation is by cuttings for the evergreen species and by seed for the deciduous ones. The accompanying table of species includes the widely grown ornamentals.

The fruits of some species are consumed as preserves or as jellies, for example those of *Elaeagnus multiflora* (Japan) which are tart, but have a good flavor, and *E. philippinensis* (Philippines). The fruit of *E. angustifolia* (southern Europe, western and central Asia, the Himalaya) is made into a sherbet-like drink.

F. B. H.

The Main Species of *Elaeagnus*

Group I: Spring flowering; leaves deciduous.
E. angustifolia Oleaster, Russian Olive. W Europe, naturalized in S Europe. Shrub or small tree mostly 5–7m, sometimes to 12m, shoots and leaves (both sides) with only silvery scales (no brown ones). Leaves more or less lanceolate, 4–8cm long. Flowers with perianth yellow inside, silvery scaly outside. Fruit oval, 12–13mm, silvery scaly, yellow, edible. Much prized for its white shoots and silvery undersides of leaves.
E. commutata Silver Berry. N America, the only native species there. Shrub to 4m, shoots and often leaves (lower side) with brownish scales in addition to silvery ones. Leaves more or less lanceolate, (3.5)4–9cm long. Flowers pendulous, freely produced, very fragrant, yellow within, the calyx-tube much longer than its lobes. Fruit ovoid, silvery, 8–9mm long. One of the most attractive shrubs with its silvery foliage and yellow, and very fragrant flowers.
E. multiflora Japan. Shrub 2–3m. Shoots and lower side of leaves with brownish scales as well as more numerous silvery scales. Leaves elliptic to obovate, 3.5–6cm long. Flowers fragrant, yellowish-white within, silver and brown scales on outside. Fruit oblong, 12–13mm long, a fine orange color. Grown for its abundant, orange-colored fruits. Differs from *E. commutator* and *E. umbellata* by its longer fruit-stalk (18–26mm) and the calyx-tube and its lobes about the same length.
E. umbellata The Himalaya, China, Japan. Wide-spreading shrub often wider than its 4–6m height, shoots and leaves with brown and silvery scales. Leaves lanceolate to oval, 5–10cm long. Flowers on stalks, 6–8mm, pale primrose within, silvery scaly outside, the calyx-tube much longer than

its lobes. Fruit round, 6–8mm across, silvery, finally red. Grown for its flowers and fruits.

Group II: Fall flowering; leaves evergreen.
E. pungens Japan. Shrub to 5m, shoots mostly spiny and with the leaves (underside) brown scaly. Leaves toughish, more or less oval, (4)5–10cm long. Flowers fragrant, pendulous, silvery-white, the calyx-tube longer than its lobes and contracted above ovary. Fruit 12–19mm long, at first brown, finally red. Popular for its fragrant flowers. There are a number of cultivars with more or less variegated leaves, of which, perhaps, 'Maculata' is outstanding.
E. macrophylla Korea, Japan and perhaps China. Spreading shrub 3–4m, brown scales absent, the shoots silvery-white, usually spiny. Leaves more or less oval, 5–11cm long, the upper surface silvery scaly at first, less so when adult, lower surface strikingly and persistently silvery scaly. Flowers very fragrant, more or less pendulous. Fruit oval, 15–16mm long, scaly, with persistent calyx, red.
E. glabra China, Japan. A rambling or climbing shrub to about 6m, often confused with and sold as *E. pungens*, but the shoots are without spines and the lower surfaces of the leaves are dull brownish from the yellow and brown scales, whereas in *E. pungens* the color is whitish. Not uncommonly grown, possibly in mistake for *E. pungens*.

CELASTRACEAE

Spindle Tree
(genus *Euonymus*)

Euonymus is a genus of at least 175 species from Europe, Asia, North and Central America and Australia but centered on the Himalaya and eastern Asia. They are deciduous or evergreen trees and shrubs, rarely creeping or climbing by rootlets, with the young shoots often four-angled. The leaves are typically opposite and sometimes toothed. The flowers, which appear in the spring, are small, white, greenish or yellowish (rarely purple), bisexual, and are borne in three- to seven- (sometimes 15-) flowered cymose inflorescences. The calyx, corolla and subsessile stamens are in fours or fives and the disk is flat, four- or five-lobed, adherent to the three- to five-chambered ovary. The style is short or absent. The fruit is a fleshy capsule which splits into three to five valves, each with one to four white, red or black seeds partially enclosed by a brilliant orange or red aril. The seeds

The brilliant carmine-red capsules of *Euonymus oxyphyllacus*; they have split open to reveal the red seeds which remain attached by a thread to the fruit case.

(believed to be poisonous in all species) are dispersed by birds, which are attracted by the colorful fruits.

The species of *Euonymus* are mainly cultivated for the colors of the fruits and leaves in the fall. They are hardy and require a well-drained loamy soil. Propagation of the deciduous species is by seed, cuttings or by layering; for the evergreen species, cuttings can be taken at almost any time if bottom heat is available.

The Common Spindle Tree (*Euonymus europaeus*) favors calcareous soils and grows to 9m (30ft) in cultivation. An evergreen species with golden and variegated leaf cultivars, *E. japonicus*, is a popular hedging plant often seen in towns and by the seaside. *Euonymus alatus* is one of the most valuable fall coloring shrubs and, like several other species, it has curious growths of cork on its branches. Several species have particularly unusual fruits for which they are cultivated. *Euonymus wilsonii*, an evergreen species, has conspicuous awl-shaped spines on its four-lobed fruits, and *E. americanus* has red spiny warty fruits like those of the Strawberry Tree (*Arbutus unedo*). *Euonymus nana*, a dwarf species from the northern Caucasus, is grown in rockeries.

The wood of some species has been used to make spindles, clothes pegs and skewers; it also makes excellent artists' charcoal. The fruit of *E. europaeus* kills sheep and goats and when powdered has been used to delouse children's hair. This species is also one of the plants on which the Black Bean Aphid (*Aphis fabae*) lays its eggs, and suggestions for its eradication in commercial broad-bean growing areas have been made. Several species (*E. europaeus*, *E. japonicus* and others) are attacked by caterpillars of the genus *Yponomeuta* (small ermines). *Euonymus japonicus* is subject to attacks by the mildew *Cidium eunymi-japonicae* (Erysiphales).

S. A. H.

AQUIFOLIACEAE

Hollies
(genus *Ilex*)

There are about 400 species of hollies, the only temperate or tropical regions lacking them being western North America and southern Australasia. They are sometimes deciduous, more usually evergreen trees or shrubs, with shoots often angled, leaves alternate, and the white unisexual flowers axillary and usually borne on separate male and female plants. The red or black 'berries' are technically drupes containing two to eight seeds. The white wood is tough. The evergreen species are exceptionally hardy attractive trees and shrubs for temperate climates, the European and Asiatic species being adaptable to most soils and sites, while the North American species generally prefer a neutral or acid soil.

Holly folklore is diverse and international. It was held by Celtic druids to symbolize the sun, sprays of it being taken into dwellings during winter months. It is still used as a decoration during the Christmas season, as it was by the Romans during their Saturnalia. Holly was used in divination in Europe, and as a martial emblem by North American Indian tribes, their Black Drink ceremony being based on the emetic leaves of the Yaupon or Carolina Tea Holly (*Ilex vomitoria*). Chimney sweeps once used holly branches in their trade, birdlime is partly made from holly bark, and *I. paraguensis* leaves are the source of maté, a kind of tea made from a boiling water infusion.

European Holly (*I. aquifolium*) from Europe, North Africa and western Asia, is a dense pyramidal tree growing to about

25m (82ft) tall. Its dark green glossy spiny foliage and red winter berries have made it one of the best known and most popular of ornamental plants. About 120 different cultivated varieties have been selected over several hundred years, some being variegated, others with spineless, crisped or puckered leaves of diverse shape. American Holly (*I. opaca*) is the best-known evergreen American species, growing to about 15m (50ft) and containing some 115 cultivars, some providing commercial crops at Christmas. The Black Alder or Winterberry (*I. verticillata*) is a large deciduous eastern North American shrub which bears copious bright red fruit in winter; its purple leaves turn yellow in the fall. There are two cultivars.

Asian evergreen hollies include the Horned Holly (*I. cornuta*) with three- to five-spined leaves, the Japanese Holly (*I. crenata*) a shrub with often tiny obovate leaves and black berries that is sometimes clipped into fantastic shapes or used as a dwarf hedge and *I. pernyi* with stalkless three-spined leaves; all are attractive natives of China. The large serrate leaves, to more than 15cm (6in) long, and orange-red fruits distinguish the Tarajo Holly

The genus *Ilex* (the hollies) contains about 400 species and the best-known – the European Holly (*I. aquifolium*) – itself contains over 100 varieties, such as this compact variegated-leaved form.

(*I. latifolia*) a species from Japan, and a noble holly when well grown. *Ilex insignis* (*I. kingiana*) from the eastern Himalaya is another large-leaved species grown in gardens. The name *Ilex* derives, paradoxically, from the Latin name for the Holm Oak (*Quercus ilex*).

B. M.

The Main Species of *Ilex*

Group I: Evergreen.

I. aquifolium Common or European Holly. Europe, N Africa and W Asia. Bushy tree to 25m, of a much-branched habit, forming a dense pyramidal mass. Leaves glossy dark green, 2.5–7.5cm long, with wavy margins and large triangular spine-tipped teeth; size, outline and toothing of leaves variable within the species and with position on the tree (lower branches tend to carry more spined leaves, possibly a protection against browsing animals). Flowers small, dull white and axillary; plants male, female or bisexual. Fruits round, red and persistent in the winter, containing 2–4 nutlets. About 120 cultivated varieties, many noted for brilliant gold and silver variegation (often on leaf margins) and variety in shape and size of leaves and habit.

I. cornuta Horned Holly. China. Dense shrub 2–3m high. Leaves bat-shaped, rectangular with few (3–5) spines. Fruits red.

I. crenata Japanese Holly. China and Japan. Dense shrub, usually 1.5–3m high with small, often tiny, obovate, shallowly toothed leaves. Fruits tiny, black. Long cultivated; several varieties.

I. dipyrena Himalayan Holly. E Himalaya. Tree to 15m.

I. glabra Inkberry. E USA. Small to medium-sized shrub 1–2m high. Leaves small, dark shining green. Fruits black.

I. insignis E Himalaya. Remarkable large-leaved species.

I. latifolia Tarajo Holly. Japan. Magnificent large-leaved species. Dark, glossy green serrate leaves up to 80cm long, resembling those of *Magnolia grandiflora*. Fruits orange-red.

I. opaca American Holly. E and C USA. Best-known American species. Large shrub or small tree to 15m. Spiny leaves, pale olive-green. Red, stalked fruits. About 115 cultivars.

I. paraguensis Yerba Maté. S America. Small tree with oval leaves to 12cm. Cultivated and wild.

I. perado Azorean or Madeira Holly. Madeira. Small tree with flattish leaves with few spines.

I. pernyi C and W China. Densely branched tree to 9m, with distinctive diamond-shaped triangular-spined leaves. Fruits red.

I. platyphylla Canary Island Holly. Canary Islands. Similar to *I. perado* and regarded by some as a variety of that species.

I. vomitoria Carolina Tea, Cassena, Yaupon, Emetic Holly. SE USA. To 8m. Fruits red.

Group II: Deciduous.

I. decidua Possumhan Holly. SE USA. Medium-sized shrub 2–3m high, occasionally a small tree up to 10m. Stems slender, leaves obovate, crenately toothed. Fruits bright orange or red, lasting well into winter.

I. macrocarpa C China. Small to medium tree. Large fruits resembling black cherries.

I. serrata Japan. Shrub to 5m, with spreading branches, downy ovate leaves and many tiny red fruits.

I. verticillata Black Alder, Winterberry. E USA. Shrub, 2–3m. Purple-tinged leaves, especially in spring, turning yellow in the fall. Fruits bright red and persistent.
  'Xmas Cheer' A selected American clone bearing masses of bright red fruits normally persistent throughout winter.

BUXACEAE

Boxes
(genus *Buxus*)

Best known as shrubs used for hedges and in topiary, the genus *Buxus* contains about 30 species of evergreen shrubs and small trees native to Western Europe, the Mediterranean region, temperate and eastern Asia, the West Indies and Central America. The leaves are entire, opposite, oval, mostly leathery, dark green, shining above, often with inrolled edges and an apical notch. The flowers are unisexual and lack petals; they occur in clusters with a single terminal female flower surrounded by several male flowers below. The male flowers have four sepals and four protruding stamens, the females four to six sepals and a three-celled ovary with three styles. The fruit is a capsule, which splits into three horned valves each containing two shining black seeds.

About six species are commonly cultivated and hardy (except *B. harlandii*) in temperate regions. They do well on any average soil and are lime and shade tolerant. Propagation is by suckers, layering or from cuttings taken in late summer. The most widely cultivated species is the Common Box (*B. sempervirens*) and it is extensively used for hedges especially in towns. Its great tolerance of pruning and shearing makes it a favorite for topiary work. It is a densely bushy shrub or tree growing to 6m (20ft), rarely 9m (30ft). The young shoots are four-angled, slightly winged and minutely hairy with the leaves subsessile, ovate to oblong, widest at or below the middle, 1.5–3(4)cm (0.6–1.2 (1.6)in) long, with somewhat inrolled margins. The horns on the fruit are about half the length of the capsule. It is native to Europe (and probably the British Isles), North Africa and western Asia. There are numerous cultivars including: 'Argentea' (*aureo-variegata*), a very bushy form with leaves more or less bordered white; 'Longifolia' with leaves to 3.8cm (1.5in); and 'Suffruticosa' (Edging Box) a long established edging plant which will grow to about 1.5m (5ft) but is normally kept to 10–12cm (4–5in) high by regular clipping. In the latter the leaves are oval to obovate, 1–2cm (0.4–0.8in) long. 'Arborescens' is an excellent cultivar for screening purposes, 'Gold Tip' has its upper leaves of

I. opaca

I. crenata

I. aquifolium

I. aquifolium

The great tolerance of the Common Box (*Buxus sempervirens*) to clipping has made it a favorite for generations in topiary work. This superb example of the art of garden design using dwarf box hedges, with a trim in progress, can be seen at the Cathedral Garden, Albi, southern France.

the terminal shoots tipped with yellow and 'Pendula' has pendulous shoots.

Another cultivated species is *Buxus microphylla* from China, Korea and Japan. This is a small shrub growing to about 1m (3.3ft) with square, glabrous shoots and leaves that are rather papery, oblong to obovate, 12–20 × 4–8mm (0.48–0.8 × 0.16–0.32in), sometimes notched at the apex and generally wider above the middle. It is a variable species with regional varieties, for instance the variety *japonica* (Japanese Box) has more rounded leaves, *koreana* (Korean Box) has obovate to elliptic oblong leaves 6–15mm (0.24–0.6in) long, while *sinica* from China is a shrub growing to 5.5m (18ft) with downy shoots and ovate to obovate leaves 8–35mm (0.32–1.4in) long. Variety *koreana* is very hardy and much prized in the United States. The Balearic Box (*B. balearica*)

from the Balearic Islands, Sardinia and southwest Spain has larger and duller leaves than *B. sempervirens* which it replaces as a cultivated plant in southern Europe. It is a shrub or tree growing to 9m (30ft) with square shoots that are downy at first. Its leaves are more or less elliptic to oblong, 2.5–4cm (1–1.6in) long and hardly glossy, and the fruits have recurved styles about as long as the capsule.

The most serious disease of the Common Box is the rust fungus *Puccinia buxi*. It is not uncommon, causing brownish spots on the leaves, whose removal is the best remedy. The most serious pest is the Box Sucker Insect (*Psylla buxi*). It causes the so-called 'Box Cabbage Gall.' Buds are infected and the resulting deformities resemble a tiny cabbage about 2cm (0.8in) across. Currently approved pesticides may be used as a cure.

The wood of boxes is hard and often described as of 'bony' texture. It was once used for engravings and is still in demand for decorative work, sculpture, and for making musical instruments, rulers and furniture.   S. R. C.

SAPINDACEAE

Golden Rain Tree
(genus *Koelreuteria*)

Koelreuteria is one of the very few genera of the tropical family Sapindaceae whose species are to be found cultivated in temperate regions. *Koelreuteria* has four species native of eastern Asia (China, Taiwan and Fiji). The best known is the Golden Rain Tree or Pride of India (*Koelreuteria paniculata*) which is a wide-spreading, medium-sized tree reaching 14m (45ft) and is a native of central China but long cultivated in Japan. It bears alternate, odd-pinnate leaves, 15–40cm (6–16in) long, with 11–13(15) leaflets which are coarsely and irregularly toothed. The small bright yellow flowers are produced in late summer in large erect terminal panicles up to

40cm (16in) high. The flowers are followed by yellow-brown papery fruits containing small black seeds.

The Golden Rain Tree is a sun-loving species which thrives on well-drained soil. It is normally propagated from seeds or by taking root cuttings. An erect columnar cultivar, 'Fastigata,' is sometimes found in cultivation as well as a late-flowering form, 'September.' Of the other three members of the genus *K. pinnata* (southwest China) and *K. elegans* (Taiwan and Fiji) are found cultivated in warmer regions; *K. bipinnata* (China) is exceptional in its bipinnate leaves; it grows to 6m (20ft) but is not hardy in temperate regions.

Necklaces are made from the seeds of the Golden Rain Tree and the flowers are reputed by the Chinese to have medicinal properties.

F. B. H.

HIPPOCASTANACEAE

Horse Chestnuts, Buckeyes
(genus *Aesculus*)

Aesculus is a genus of about 25 north temperate species native mainly to North America, the others from southern Europe, India (the Himalaya), China and Japan. They are deciduous trees (one or two more or less shrubby) with a large spreading habit. The leaves are opposite and palmate, each leaf with five to seven (rarely as few as three or as many as nine) leaflets radiating from the end of a long stalk. The flowers are polygamous, irregular, borne in terminal panicles, with four or five sepals, sometimes forming a tube, and four or five petals. There are five to nine stamens on an annular disk, with the filaments free, and the ovary is three-celled with two ovules per cell and a single style. The fruit is a smooth or spiny, firm capsule commonly maturing a single, large shining seed ('conker' or 'buckeye'). There are a number of hybrids. Species with four petals and a smooth capsule are transferred by some to a distinct genus *Pavia* but intermediates do not justify this separation.

Almost all the species and many varieties of them have become well-known ornamentals in parks in temperate regions.

Two of the main features of the Golden Rain Tree (*Koelreuteria paniculata*) can be seen in this picture – the pinnate leaves with coarsely toothed leaflets and the large erect panicles of yellow flowers.

The Horse Chestnut (*Aesculus hippocastanum*), a native of mountainous regions of Greece and eastward to Iran and northern India, was introduced into Britain in the middle of the 16th century. It is the largest chestnut, growing to over 40m (130ft) tall. The flowers are white with a pattern of crimson and yellow spots toward the center. Another fine ornamental is the Red Buckeye (*A. pavia*), a small tree from the southern United States with crimson flowers and smooth spineless fruits. There is a popular hybrid between these two species, *A.* × *carnea*, with pink flowers and smoothish fruits. A number of cultivars and varieties are found in cultivation. Floral forms of the Horse Chestnut include 'Alba' with pure white flowers, 'Baumannii' with double white flowers, 'Rosea' with pink flowers and 'Rubricunda' with red flowers, while 'Pumila' is a dwarf form with deeply cut leaves and 'Pyramidalis' has a broad pyramidal habit.

Most species are hardy in temperate regions except in the more extreme areas and require only a good, deep well-drained soil. Propagation is best from seed for the species, otherwise budding must be resorted to. Stock for the larger species is commonly *A. hippocastanum*; for the smaller ones, *A. flava* or *A. glabra*.

Diseases of horse chestnuts are few. The Coral Spot Fungus (*Nectria cinnabarina*), whilst commonest on dead branches etc, does sometimes attack living trees. The parasite does not infect healthy tissues but gains entrances via wounds. At the first sign of fruiting bodies, the infected branch should be removed and the wound disinfected and sealed.

There are various possible explanations for the derivation of the common name. The bitter fruits may have been used in the treatment of coughs and other ailments of horses. Another explanation is that it

Below The many erect panicles of flowers of the Indian Horse Chestnut (*Aesculus indica*) appear in early summer and like the tree's shape are more delicately graceful than in the Common Horse Chestnut (*A. hippocastanum*). The leaflets also are different: stalked, slender, darker green and often wavy. *Below Bottom* Horseshoe-shaped leaf-scar and bud on Common Horse Chestnut. The small raised areas within the scar are the sealed vascular bundles.

refers to the leaf-scar resembling a horse-shoe. It is much more likely, however, that in popular English botany 'horse' simply means 'coarse' or 'unpleasant,' thus distinguishing the Horse Chestnut (inedible by humans) from the Sweet Chestnut (much esteemed).

Experiments have shown that mashed horse chestnuts could be useful and palatable for cattle. The timber is soft and not durable, but has been used for flooring, cabinet-making, boxes and charcoal. Esculoside, a coumarin glycoside, present in the bark, leaves and seeds of *A. hippocastanum* is used as a sunscreen agent and in the treatment of hemorrhoids and conditions associated with capillary blood vessel fragility. The bark and fruit of some species are used locally to stupefy fish.

In some countries in the spring, the sticky shiny buds are a favorite in floral decoration, while in the fall the usually spherical, often spiny fruits split open to reveal the beautiful red-brown, polished chestnuts which are used by children in the game of conkers.   I. B. K. R.

The Main Species of *Aesculus*

Group I: Corolla with 4 petals, their claws usually longer than the sepals. Winter buds usually not resinous. Fruits smooth or at least not spiny.

A. splendens SE USA. Shrub 3–4m. Corolla scarlet, leaves downy beneath; fruits smoothish.

A. pavia Red Buckeye. S USA. Shrub 3–4m. Leaves slightly downy beneath, especially near the veins. Corolla red but not opening; petals with glands along the margins. Fruits smooth.

A. flava (*A. octandra*) Sweet or Yellow Buckeye. USA. Tree to 30m. Leaves often reddish downy beneath. Corolla yellow; margins of petals with nonglandular hairs. Fruits smooth.

A. chinensis Chinese Horse Chestnut. N China. Tree to 28m. Corolla white. Fruits rough. Winter buds resinous.

A. indica Indian Horse Chestnut. NW Himalaya. Tree to 30m or more. Corolla white with yellow or red blotches at the base of the petals. Fruits rough. Winter buds resinous.

A. californica California (USA). Tree to 12m. Corolla white or pink. Fruits rough. Winter buds resinous.

A. glabra Ohio Buckeye. SE and C USA. Smallish tree to 8m, rarely more. Leaflets usually 5, 3–4cm wide. Corolla yellow-green. Fruits rough. Closely related is *A. arguta* from E Texas, which is similar but has 7–9 leaflets, 2–3cm wide.

A. parviflora SE USA. Shrub 2–4m. Corolla white, occasionally with 5 petals. Fruits smooth.

Group II: Corolla with 5 petals, their claws shorter than the sepals. Winter buds resinous. Fruits spiny.

A. hippocastanum Horse Chestnut or Conker Tree. N Greece, Albania. Tree to 35m. Corolla whitish with red spots. There are a number of cultivars. For example 'Baumannii' has double flowers and does not form fruits.

A. × carnea Red Horse Chestnut. A polyploid hybrid probably with *A. pavia* and *A. hippocastanum* as parents. Tree 10–25m. Corolla red.

A. turbinata Japanese Horse Chestnut. Japan. Tree to 30m. Leaflets 5–7, sessile, obovate, 20–30(40)cm long. Flowers 1.5cm across, creamy colored with red spot, in panicles 25 × 6cm. Fruit pyriform, warty. 5cm maximum across; seed brown.

A. × hybrida (*A. flava × A. pavia*) A hybrid often mistaken for *A. pavia*. Flowers mixed pink or red, the margins of the petals with glands as well as hairs.

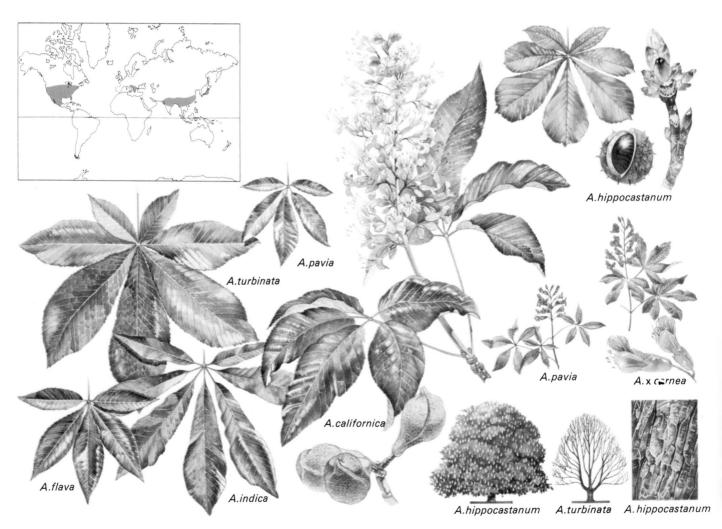

A.hippocastanum

A.turbinata

A.pavia

A.flava

A.indica

A.californica

A.pavia

A. × carnea

A.hippocastanum   A.turbinata   A.hippocastanum

ACERACEAE

Maples
(genus *Acer*)

Acer is a large genus of perhaps 200 species, commonly called maples, ranging over almost all the northern temperate region and extending into the tropics. The great majority are Asian, and many are extremely rare. They are predominantly deciduous trees, rarely evergreen or shrubby, with scaly or smooth bark which in the small 'Snakebark' group is beautifully striped vertically, bright white on a smooth green or gray background. The inflorescence is variable, being in the form of long, pendent catkin-like racemes, as in the Sycamore (*Acer pseudoplatanus*) and Oregon Maple (*A. macrophyllum*), in tight bunches against the shoot as in Red (*A. rubrum*) and Silver (*A. saccharinum*) Maples, small spreading panicles, as in the Norway Maple (*A. platanoides*) or open, erect panicles as in Van Volxem's (*A. velutinum* var *vanvolxemii*) and Trautvetter's (*A. trautvetteri*) Maples. There are five petals (when present), usually yellow, bright yellow in the Norway Maple and pale in the Italian Maple (*A. opalus*), green in the Hornbeam

Many maples are grown as ornamentals. Shown here is a young Norway Maple (*Acer platanoides*) cultivar 'Drummondii', which is prized for its variegated foliage and compact form.

Maple (*A. carpinifolium*) and red in the Japanese (*A. palmatum*) and Red Maples. There are usually eight stamens (sometimes 4–10) on a prominent disc. Each inflorescence usually bears flowers of both sexes, the females toward the base, but a few maples, like Père David's (*A. davidii*), have each inflorescence entirely of one sex whilst a few more, eg *A. argutum*, *A. negundo* and *A. tetramerum*, have sexes on separate plants. Leaves vary in size from the 3cm (1in), entire, elliptic evergreen kind on *A. sempervirens* to those 25cm × 35cm (10in × 14in) and deeply lobed on *A. macrophyllum*, and through an eastern Asian group of five with trifoliolate leaves to the American *A. negundo* with compound leaves of five and seven leaflets. Stature in maples varies from the often shrubby species like *A. tschonoskii*, *A. ginnala* and *A. tataricum*, seldom above 6m (20ft) tall, to large trees, the Sycamore growing as high as 37m (121ft) and *A. macrophyllum* and *A. platanoides* growing to 30m (100ft).

There is a maple for every soil and situation, for winter color, spring flowers, summer foliage and above all for fall color. The Sycamore is among the most resistant of all trees to polluted air and severe maritime exposure, although its native range scarcely includes any seaboard. *Acer ginnala* is at home in city air and in severe cold and is planted in tubs in the streets of Montreal. *Acer rubrum*, *A. saccharum* and *A. saccharinum* thrive in city squares in their native eastern United States of America, alongside the European *A. platanoides*. The Japanese *A. palmatum* in

Many maples produce spectacular displays of color in the fall. Shown here is the Gray-budded Snakebark Maple (*Acer rufinerve*) cultivar 'Albolimbatum' photographed during early fall.

a plethora of fancy-leafed and colored forms decorates town parks and gardens everywhere. Where a site needs slender, spire-like crowns, there are *A. lobelii* and, narrower still, *A. saccharum* 'Temple's Upright' and, the most extreme, *A. saccharum* 'Newton Sentry.' *Acer rubrum* is at home on wet, sometimes swampy sites, and several southern European species, like *A. opalus*, *A. sempervirens*, *A. hyrcanum* and *A. monspessulanum* withstand dry positions. Very alkaline, chalky soils suit *A. platanoides*, *A. cappadocicum*, *A. campestre* and *A. nikoense* but the same species, except *A. campestre*, will grow well on acid sandy soils along with most other maples.

Winter color is nowhere better displayed than by the brilliant coral and scarlet shoots of *A. palmatum* 'Sen-kaki' and the deeper red of *A. pennsylvanicum* 'Erythrocladum', while the shoots of *A. giraldii* are bloomed violet and the trunks of the several snake-bark maples and of *A. griseum* add much to the winter prospect. In March before the trees are in leaf, the bright red flowers clustering along the shoots of *A. rubrum* are decorative although far less spectacular than the bright acid-yellow larger bunches of flowers on big crowns of *A. platanoides* and the pale but larger flowers hanging from *A. opalus*. As the leaves unfold in late April, the purplish-red flowers of *A. diabolicum* 'Purpurascens' hang beneath the leaves as on a parachute.

For summer foliage, the best are *A. buergeranum*, the snake-barks *A. capillipes*, *A. forrestii* and *A. maximowiczii* for attractive small leaves, *A. acuminatum*, *A. argutum* and *A. pectinatum* for decorative lobing, and for handsome substantial foliage *A. macrophyllum* and *A. velutinum vanvolxemii*. For fall color almost any maple earns a place. In New England *A. saccharum* is supreme for the intensity of its orange-scarlet and *A. rubrum* runs the gamut from lemon-yellow to deep purple, but in Europe the best colors are on *A. palmatum* 'Osakazuki,' *A. capillipes*, *A. hersii* and *A. japonicum* 'Vitifolium.'

Propagation for the species is best from seed. For the numerous varieties graftings will be necessary and should be made on stocks of the same species.

Maples are subject to a number of fungal attacks but, in general, few are serious. One serious one is the sac fungus *Ceratocystis virescens* (Sphaeriales) which spreads extensively in the sapwood and usually kills a tree within four years. Less serious is browning of leaf veins by another sac fungus, *Gnomonia platani* (Sphaeriales) or Plane (*Platanus*) Scorch, the commonest conidial stage being known as *Gloeosporium nervisequum*. Undoubtedly, the most conspicuous fungus attack is the well-known and common Maple Tar Spot caused by the sac fungus *Rhytisma* (Phaci-

The Paper-bark Maple (*Acer griseum*) from China is outstanding for its attractive bark which peels in papery rolls laterally, as well as for the crimson and scarlet fall colors of its foliage.

diales). *Rhytisma acerinum* is widespread in northern Europe on Sycamore, less so on the Common Maple (*A. campestre*) and the Norway Maple. In North America other species are attacked by *R. punctatum*. The name Maple Tar Spot is very apt, the leaves appearing as if dabbed with a tar brush leaving numerous 'spots' up to about 1cm across. The trees suffer no serious effect. To avoid the disease fallen leaves should be collected and burnt otherwise they will reinfect trees in the spring.

Pest attacks are more serious, some maple species being badly damaged in spring and summer by leaf-eating insects and weevils. Amongst the former are caterpillars of the Buff-tip Moth (*Phalera bucephola*) and of the Vapourer Moth (*Orgyia antiqua*). Weevil pests are species of the genus *Phyllobius*. Both pests can be controlled by currently approved insecticides.

The timber of a number of species is used commercially. The light-colored, close-grained and soft wood of *A. campestre*, *A. macrophyllum* and *A. negundo* is particularly used for tool handles, turnery and cheap furniture. The harder, heavier, tougher and closer-grained wood of *A. platanoides*, *A. pseudoplatanus* and *A. saccharum* is more extensively used for furniture, flooring and interior finishing of buildings. The Sugar Maple (*A. saccharum*) is the source of maple syrup which is tapped from the trees. The syrup is used as a sweetener for foods, in the manufacture of sugar and as an essential accompaniment to waffles. Kitchen-ware is also made from Sycamore as it scrubs clean easily and does not taint food.

A. M.

The Main Species of *Acer*

Group I: Leaves simple.

A Unlobed leaves only.

A. carpinifolium Hornbeam Maple. Japan. Bushy tree to 10m. Shoots brown. Leaves slender, lanceolate, to 17cm, sharply toothed with 20 or more parallel pairs of veins, turning a good gold in the fall.

A. distylum Lime-leafed Maple. Japan. Tree to 12m with ascending arched branches. Leaves thick, ovate, cordate, 13cm. Flowers on upper half of 5cm erect spike. Fruit pink-brown.

A. davidii Père David's Maple. China. Two forms of this variable species, one a small domed tree to 10m with small, 6cm lanceolate leaves, the other a spreading

tree to 14m with large 15cm oblong-lanceolate leaves turning orange in the fall.

AA Unlobed mixed with 3-lobed leaves.

A. davidii cv 'George Forrest' Most frequent form of the previous species. Snake-barked tree to 16m. Leaves broad, dark leathery, oblong-ovate to 15cm, unevenly toothed, petiole scarlet. Flowers prolific on arched stalks.

A. hersii Hers's Maple. China. Snake-barked tree to 16m with long arching spreading branches, few minor shoots. Leaves rich green, leathery, broad, petiole yellow; crimson and orange in the fall. Fruit big-winged, 6cm across on arching hanging 12cm stalk.

A. sempervirens (*A. creticum*, *A. orientale*) Cretan Maple. E Mediterranean. Low domed tree or bush. Leaves dark, 3–5cm, entire, wavy-edged with variable lobules or lobes. Fruit small in bunches finally red.

AAA Leaves predominantly 3-lobed.

A. buergeranum (incorrectly *A. buergerianum*) Trident Maple. China, Japan. Tree to 15m with brown flaking bark. Leaves in dense masses, narrowed base, with 3 veins, nearly entire, bluish beneath, crimson in the fall. Occasional unlobed leaf. Flowers yellow in domed heads.

A. capillipes Japan. Snake-barked tree to 16m. Leaves glossy rich green turning orange and red, with 10 parallel veins and small lobe each side. Fruit prolific, small, finally pink.

A. crataegifolium Hawthorn-leafed Maple. Japan. Slender tree to 10m with level branches. Leaves and fruit small, red-winged.

A. forrestii Forrest's Maple. China. Snake-barked tree to 11m. Leaves finely toothed, deep green but pale around veins; petiole scarlet.

A. ginnala Amur Maple. NE Asia. Bush or small gray-barked tree to 10m. Leaves deeply toothed, tapered to 7cm, turning deep red early in the fall. Flowers white, small, in erect domed heads.

A. maximowiczii W China. Slender snake-barked tree to 13m. Leaves deeply lobed with white tufts in vein-axils beneath, margin incised and twice serrate.

A. monspessulanum Montpellier Maple. S Europe, N Africa. Densely domed tree to 15m. Leaves at first fresh green but soon dark as if evergreen, 4 × 7cm, lobes widely spread, margins entire.

A. pectinatum E Himalaya. Rare handsome snake-barked tree to 15m. Leaves large, the central and side lobes drawn out into long, sharply toothed tails.

A. pennsylvanicum Moosewood, Snake-bark Maple. NE USA. Small tree with bright green or gray snake-bark. Leaves large, to 20 × 20cm, turning bright gold in early fall.

A. rubrum Red Maple. E N America in all low-lying woods. Slender-twigged, rather shapeless tree to 23m. Flowers bright red along shoots before leaves out. Leaves silvered beneath, petiole red. In the wild,

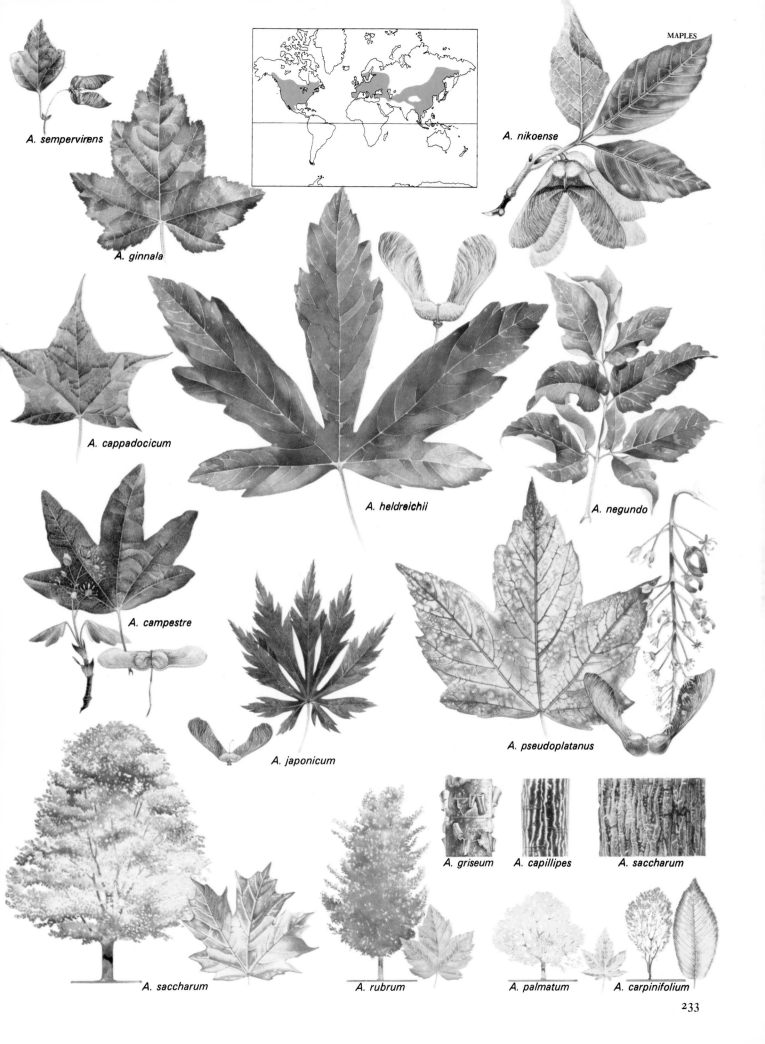

A. sempervirens

A. nikoense

MAPLES

A. ginnala

A. cappadocicum

A. heldreichii

A. negundo

A. campestre

A. japonicum

A. pseudoplatanus

A. griseum   A. capillipes   A. saccharum

A. saccharum

A. rubrum

A. palmatum   A. carpinifolium

233

fall colors every shade from bright yellow through reds and crimson to deep purple, side by side.

A. rufinerve Gray-budded Snake-bark Maple. Japan. Spreading tree opening out to 13m. Leaves often broader than long; rusty hairs or stain on basal veins beneath; rich reds in early fall.

'Albolimbatum' Grayish-green leaves variably speckled and narrowly margined white.

AAAA Leaves predominantly 5-lobed.

A. argutum Japan. Small tree, usually many-stemmed. Leaves deep green with deeply sunk veins and slender serrated tails to lobes.

A. campestre Field Maple, Common Maple. Europe, Africa, W Asia. Domed tree to 25m, shoots often ridged with cork. Leaves small, dark, deeply lobed, with few large, round-tipped teeth, turning a good yellow, sometimes purple in the fall. Fruit 6cm across, wings horizontal, stained pink.

A. cappadocicum Cappadocian Maple. Caucasus to China. Domed crown on smooth gray bole amongst a mass of suckers. Leaves bright green with wire-tipped entire lobes, butter-yellow in the fall.

'Aureum' New leaves (spring and midsummer) bright gold. An elegant and attractive tree.

A. heldreichii Heldreich's Maple. Balkan Mts. Tall domed tree with open crown to 20m. Leaves lobed almost to base, with few triangular teeth; petiole pink, 15cm long. Flowers in erect panicle, yellow.

A. lobelii Lobel's Maple. Italy. Vigorous erect tree with few branches all nearly vertical. Leaves with almost entire lobes twisted at tips.

A. macrophyllum Oregon Maple. Alaska to California. Tree with high dome to 30m; bark fissured, orange-brown. Leaves to 25 × 30cm, deeply lobed; petiole 30cm. Flowers in catkins to 25cm. Fruit with white bristles.

A. opalus Italian Maple. Domed tree to 20m; bark shaggy brown. Leaves with shallow lobes, rounded, irregularly toothed, yellow and orange in the fall. Flowers pale yellow in pendulous clusters.

A. platanoides Norway Maple. Europe and Caucasus. Tree with densely leafed crown to 27m on pale gray finely ridged bole. Leaves with lobes and the few big teeth wire-tipped, bright gold then orange in the fall. Flowers bright yellow in bunches open before leaves.

'Cucullatum' Erect crowned tree to 24m. Leaves semicircular, hooded and crinkled.
'Drummondii' Dense domed crown of generously white-splashed and margined small leaves.
'Faassen's Black' Big, deep muddy purple leaves.
'Goldsworth Purple' Dark purple-leaved form seen in gardens in the USA from coast to coast S to Denver and Atlanta, and in NW Europe.
'Schwedleri' Flowers open 2 weeks later

than in the species type, with dark red calyx and stalk amid red-brown unfolding leaves. Leaf purple-tinged until the fall, when orange and crimson.

A. pseudoplatanus Sycamore, Great Maple. S and C Europe to Caucasus. Tree with dense, domed crown to 25m. Leaves dark green, petiole red or yellow. Flowers on 20cm catkin, appearing with the leaves, petals inconspicuous.

'Brilliantissimum' Dense low crown. Leaves bright pink, then orange to yellow for 2 weeks, then white until dull green.
'Prinz Handjery' Differs from the previous cultivar in purple underside to leaf. Flowers freely.
'Purpureum' A group variably stained purple on underside of leaf.
'Variegatum' Dense trees to 25m. Leaves with bold angular patches and fine speckles of cream or white.
'Leopoldii' Has brightest leaves with some patches stained pinkish or purple.
'Worlei' Leaves bright yellow with red petiole.

A. saccharinum Silver Maple. E N America. Tree with open crown to 30m and ascending arched branches. Leaves deeply lobed and sharply toothed, whitish beneath. Flowers greenish-red to red before leaves, petals absent.

A. saccharum Sugar Maple. E N America. Tree to 25m. Leaves pale green at first, brilliant orange-scarlet in the fall. Flowers bunched, small on very slender stalks, petals absent.

'Newton Sentry' Vertical stem clothed in leaves; few short branches. Bizarre form in some American parks and streets.
'Temple's Upright' Erect but broader than 'Newton Sentry'; branches erect. Frequent in cities of N USA.

A. trautvetteri Trautvetter's Maple. Caucasus Mts. Tree to 20m. Like A. pseudoplatanus except acute brown buds, erect heads of flowers, deeply lobed leaves and big broad wings on fruit bright pink in summer.

A. velutinum var vanvolxemii Van Volxem's Maple. Caucasus Mts. Tree to 25m. Like A. pseudoplatanus with huge pale green leaf to 18 × 15cm, petiole 27cm, brown buds acute and domed flowerhead erect.

AAAAA Leaves with more than 5 lobes.

A. circinatum Vine Maple. N America, British Columbia to California. Slender, usually leaning small tree to 12m. Shoot smooth bright green. Leaves circular with 7 neat doubly toothed lobes turning scarlet early in the fall.

A. japonicum Downy Japanese Maple. Bush, but in cultivar 'Vitifolium' tree to 15m. Leaves to 15cm with 7–11 triangular irregularly toothed lobes, scarlet gold and lilac in the fall. Flowers purple.

A. palmatum Smooth Japanese Maple. Broad tree to 16m with 7(5) narrow finely toothed tapered lobes, varied red in the fall.

'Sen-kaki' Coral-bark Maple. Shoots in winter bright pinkish-scarlet. Leaves small, much toothed, yellowish.

Group II: Leaves compound.

B Leaves trifoliolate.

A. cissifolium Vine-leafed Maple. Japan. Wide, low, mushroom-like tree to 10m tall but 20m across with pale brown and white bark. Leaflets on very slender stalks, ovate, acute, coarsely toothed. Flowers prolific and fruit spreading stiffly on 12cm spikes.

A. griseum Paper-bark Maple. China. Tree to 14m with open, rather upright crown; bark orange to mahogany-red, peeling in papery rolls laterally. Leaflets paired, without stalks, but central leaflet shortly stalked, few teeth, dark green, silvery beneath, crimson and scarlet in the fall; petiole dark pink, hairy. Flowers bell-like, yellow, with leaves, in 3's.

A. nikoense Nikko Maple. C China, Japan. Sturdy conical tree to 14m with smooth dark gray bark. Leaflets broad elliptic, densely white-hairy beneath, scarlet and crimson in the fall; petiole dark pink, densely hairy. Flowers yellow in 3's.

A. triflorum Korea, Manchuria. Similar to Nikko Maple but smaller in all parts and with rough, shredding, peeling bark. Bright scarlet and crimson briefly in the fall.

BB Pinnate leaves; 5–7 leaflets.

A. negundo Ash-leafed Maple, Box Elder. E Canada to California. Low bushy, sprouty tree to 15m. In the wild, the foliage is rich shining bright green; in cultivation, less bright and the colored cultivars are usually planted instead. Flowers before leaves in dense clusters hanging on slender stalks, male and female on separate trees.

'Variegatum' Leaf mostly white in splashes and broad margins, some wholly white. Female only.
'Auratum' Splendid rich gold foliage, greening a little by late summer.

ANACARDIACEAE

Sumacs
(genus Rhus)

The genus *Rhus*, commonly known as sumacs or sumachs, comprises about 150 species from the subtropics and temperate regions of the Old and the New World. Some dozen species are grown as ornamentals in temperate regions for their shape, vivid fall coloring and attractive dense fruiting heads like dark red pyramids at the branch ends.

Sumacs are predominantly small deciduous or evergreen shrubs, rarely climbers or trees, with a characteristic antler-like branching pattern. The leaves are alternate, odd-pinnate, with entire or serrate-margined leaflets. The flowers are borne in conspicuous panicles with male, female and bisexual flowers occurring together on the same plant or separated on different plants. There are usually five sepals and petals (sometimes four or six) and the ovary is superior, maturing to a single-seeded dry globose drupe with a resinous mesocarp. They are not difficult to grow and can be readily propagated by cuttings or layers.

The genus is characterized by a resinous juice and in such species as Poison Ivy (*Rhus radicans*), Oakleaf Poison Ivy (*R. toxicodendron*) and Poison Sumac (*R. vernix*) this juice is a powerful skin irritant and on contact all parts of the body may become inflamed, swollen, ulcerated and very painful. As in similar cases, for example the Giant Hogweed (*Heracleum mantegazzianum*), not all people are affected. Others claim to be affected by merely being near a plant but this is more likely to result, in very susceptible people, from contact with the pollen (especially where the eyes are involved) or from the smoke of burning wood. A first-aid treatment is to wash affected parts as quickly as possible

The Main Species of *Rhus*

Group I: *Rhus* in strict sense. N America, Europe, Asia. Leaves usually pinnate. Flowers short-pediceled, in dense terminal spikes. Fruits reddish. Plants not poisonous.

R. javanica (*R. chinensis*, *R. semialata*) Widespread in Asia from the Himalaya to Vietnam, Korea, China and Japan. Tree to 6m, with antler-like branching. Attacked by a tree louse (*Schlechtendalia* sp) which causes the growth of gall-apples. These have a high concentration of tannin, and are an important source of this substance for the leather industry.

R. copallina Shining Sumac. N America. Deciduous shrub or small tree, unusual in having entire leaflets. Yields tannin.

R. coriaria Tanners' or Elm-leaved Sumac. The only native *Rhus* of mainland Europe; widespread from the Canaries to Afghanistan. A small semievergreen shrub characteristic of Mediterranean 'maquis.' The Arabic name 'sumac' belonged originally to this species. Source of tannins (known commercially as 'sumac' or 'sumach') used in the production of Cordoba and Morocco leathers.

R. glabra N America. Closely allied to *R. typhina*, differing in its shrubby habit and in having glabrous leaves and branches. The cultivar 'Laciniata' has leaflets deeply cut.

R. typhina Stag's-horn Sumac. N America.

Small gauntly-branched deciduous tree to 8m or more with thick pithy branches, often grown in European gardens. Male and female flowers on separate trees, the male tree sometimes known as *R. viridiflora*. The cultivar 'Dissecta' has leaflets deeply cut. *R. typhina* forma *laciniata* is a monstrous form, quite common in the wild, with leaves and bracts deeply cut and the inflorescence partly transformed into twisted bracts.

Group II: *Toxicodendron*. N America, N S America, C and SE Asia. Leaves ternate (trifoliolate) or pinnate. Flowers long-pediceled, in lax lateral panicles. Fruits whitish or yellowish. Plants with poisonous exudates.

R. diversiloba Poison Oak. W N America. Shrub with ternate leaves.

R. ambigua (*R. orientalis*) Japan and China. Closely related to *R. radicans*, differing only in having coarsely hairy rather than smooth or downy fruits.

R. radicans Poison Ivy. Cow-itch. N America. Deciduous shrub with ternate leaves, found in two forms: the climbing form attaches itself to rocks, tree trunks etc by aerial roots and can grow to a considerable height; the bushy form is a loosely spreading shrub up to 3m. The sap is highly poisonous, causing severe blisters to the skin, and even the pollen is irritating to the eyes.

R. succedanea Wax Tree. India to Japan, Malaysia. Deciduous tree to 12m. Leaves pinnate, the leaflets glossy, glabrous, purplish, entire, with numerous parallel lateral veins almost at right angles to the midrib. Was formerly much cultivated in Japan for the fruit, which supplied wax for candles, and for the resin, used as lacquer.

R. toxicodendron Oakleaf Poison Ivy, Poison Oak. SE N America. A sparsely-branched shrub with ternate leaves.

R. verniciflua Varnish or Japanese Lacquer Tree. The Himalaya to China, possibly also native in Malaysia. Deciduous tree to 20m. Leaves pinnate, velvety. Tapped for the resin, which turns black on exposure to air and is used in the lacquer industry (Japanese lacquer). The fruit is a source of wax for candles.

R. vernix Poison Sumac. E N America. Deciduous tree to 6m, often with 2 or 3 main stems. Leaves pinnate, glabrous. Renowned both for its outstandingly fine fall coloration and in being perhaps the most poisonous North American tree.

Group III: Africa and Asia. Leaves 3(5–7)-foliolate. Flowers long-pediceled, in lax terminal or lateral panicles. Fruits green, white, red or brown. Plants not poisonous.

R. chirindensis Red Currant. S Africa, Zimbabwe-Rhodesia. Tree to 25m. Young plants spiny. Leaves not woolly-tomentose beneath. Fruit edible.

R. tomentosa S Africa. Shrub or small tree to 4.5m. Leaves trifoliolate, terminal leaflet the largest, 5–8.5 × 2–3(4)cm, sometimes smaller; all leaflets elliptic to obovate, glaucous, gray to dull green, densely whitish to reddish tomentose below, almost glabrescent above, entire or with 1–2(3) teeth beyond middle; midrib and veins prominent beneath; petiole often red, 1.5–4cm. Flowers minute in dense, terminal, very pilose panicles. Fruit a subglobose drupe. 5–6 × 3–4mm, densely tomentose.

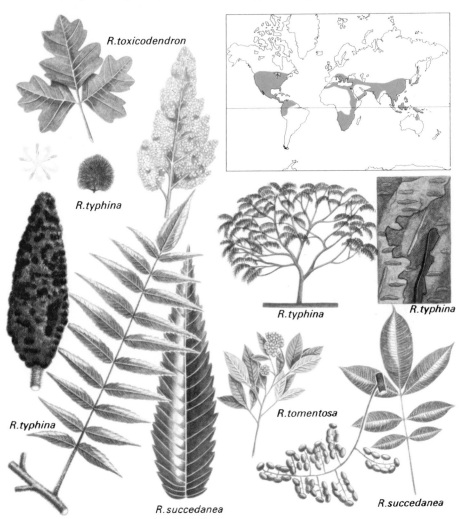

R.toxicodendron

R.typhina

R.typhina

R.succedanea

R.typhina

R.typhina

R.tomentosa

R.succedanea

with a 1 percent solution of potassium permanganate. The same resinous juice is, however, outstanding as an indelible ink for marking linen, being virtually ineradicable. The poisonous principle is urushiol, a derivative of the polyhydric phenol, catechol.

The only sumac native to Europe, *R. coriaria*, now known as the Tanner's or Elm-leaved Sumac, was used by the ancient Greeks as a source of spice, medicine and tannin. Nowadays several species of *Rhus* are commercially important in this latter respect. Thus, tannins from the North American species *R. copallina* (Shining Sumac) and *R. typhina* (Stag's-horn Sumac) produce a dark colored leather, whilst Eurasian species such as *R. coriaria* and *R. javanica* (*R. chinensis*, *R. semialata*) yield a paler leather. In the case of *R. javanica* the tannin is extracted from galls ('nut galls' or 'gall apples') caused by a louse of the genus *Schlechtendalia*, the tannin content being high.

Resin from the bark of the Varnish or Japanese Lacquer Tree (*R. verniciflua*) produces the well-known Japanese lacquer and varnish. The crushed fruits of the Wax Tree (*R. succedanea*) give a wax or tallow which was once the main source of artificial light in Japan.   F. K. K.

RUTACEAE

Citrus Fruits
(genus *Citrus*)

The citrus fruits are a well-known and distinctive group of commercially important tropical and subtropical fruits. The most important genus is *Citrus* which includes Sweet Oranges, Seville Oranges, Mandarins, Grapefruits, Shaddocks, Lemons, Limes and Citrons.

Citrus is a taxonomically difficult genus of perhaps 12–30 'good' species, but varying from 8 to 145 depending on the species concept of competent authorities. The center of origin is China where written references go back to 2000 BC.

The closely related genus *Fortunella* yields the Kumquat (or Cumquat), and the genus *Poncirus* is used as a cold-resistant rootstock and for breeding purposes.

Citrus trees, although originating from warm, wet areas of southeast Asia, grow well over a belt extending from 35° South to 35° North (occasionally as far as 42° North in well-protected Mediterranean

The Stag's-horn Sumac (*Rhus typhina*) is a popular ornamental in many gardens. It is a wide-spreading, sparsely-branched small tree or shrub with leaves that turn brilliant colors in the fall.

areas). Orange-gold types apparently come from cooler climates, where intense color is attained when temperatures drop toward winter, while lemon-yellow types are probably more tropical in origin and growth habits. For the fresh fruit market the best quality is obtained in a narrower subtropical belt (23° to 35° both sides of the equator) where seasonal alternation of temperatures and precipitation occurs. In uniformly wet and warm tropical climates, vegetation tends to be continuous and fruiting irregularly recurrent. The fruit is juicy and sweet, but the rind has a yellowish-green tinge and shipping characteristics are poor, so that the fruit is best suited to processing. Low temperatures are the main obstacle to expansion outside the citrus belt, for citrus fruits are highly sensitive to frost.

The citrus fruits are borne on evergreen trees or shrubs bearing alternate leaves that are dotted with glands which are apparent when held against the light. Leaf-like wings occur on the stalk (petiole). The buds sometimes have a single accompanying spine. The flowers, which occur mostly in clusters (occasionally solitary), are white or purplish-tinged, bisexual, with typically five sepals and petals. The stamens are numerous (15 plus), united into bundles, and the ovary has 8–15(18) cells and a solitary style. The fruit is a large, rather unusual kind of berry known as a hesperidium, with the compartments (orange segments) containing up to eight seeds (sometimes none) embedded in a pulpy flesh. The fruit has a thick skin (peel) comprising an outer thin, colored and fragrant exocarp (flavedo), a whitish spongy mesocarp or pith (albedo) and an inner endocarp, the latter forming the lining of the segments. From the endocarp multicellular juice vesicles grow centripetally to fill the segments, which may also contain seeds. The relative amounts of peel and pulp, the size, juiciness, acidity and flavor vary widely according to species.

Total world cultivated area is about 2.2 million hectares (5.5 million acres), 0.6 million hectares (1.5 million acres) being in the Mediterranean area. Total production in 1975 was about 49 million metric tons (82 percent oranges and mandarins, 10 percent lemons and limes, 8 percent grapefruits). More than 14 percent of the citrus world crop is exported as fresh fruit. This high export percentage is due to the exotic flavor, fragrance and appearance and also to the high vitamin C content and very good shipping properties of the fruit. Competition on European markets is keen

between Mediterranean producing countries, but production from the Southern and Northern Hemispheres is complementary because of opposite seasonal rhythms.

S. P. M.

The Main Species of *Citrus*

Group I: Mature fruits predominantly yellow with or without a greenish tinge. Lemons and Grapefruits.

A *Fruits broadly elliptic oblong (limoniform), less than 10cm across equatorial diameter.*

C. aurantifolia Lime. NE India and Malaysia. Produces small, very acid fruits resembling the lemons, except for the greenish-yellow flesh. Juice is high in vitamin C and is used in drinks, confectionery and other foods. Oil expressed from the fruit is used in confectionery and perfumery. *C. latifolia* (Persian Lime) is sometimes considered a hybrid of the lime and citron; the fruit is larger than the lime and the tree is less susceptible to frost. *C. limettioides* is the Sweet Lime, the fruits of which are used fresh and the roots as rootstocks for other *Citrus* species.

C. limetta Sweet Lemon. Tropical Asia. Produces fruits similar to the Lemon, but

with sweeter, more insipid flavor.

C. limon Lemon. Probably Himalayan region. Produces juicy, acid, yellow fruits on evergreen, thorny, bushy trees that are normally grafted onto a rootstock. The most important acid citrus fruit, ranking second to oranges in overall importance. The juice is widely used in fruit drinks, confectionery and flavoring and is a commercial source of citric acid. Oil of lemon, extracted from the peel, is used in perfumery, for flavoring and as an aid to digestion. Lemon pip oil is used in the manufacture of soap.

C. medica Citron. NE India or S Arabia. Large yellow fruits, with thick fragrant peel and small pulp, produced on small shrubby trees. The peel is used for making candied peel and the fruits used in the Jewish ceremony of the Feast of Tabernacles.

AA *Fruits subglobose, 10cm or more across equatorial diameter.*

C. grandis Shaddock, Pomelo, Pummelo, Forbidden Fruit. Malaya. Produces large yellow fruits with yellow or pink flesh. Similar to grapefruit, but lacks bitterness and has thicker peel and firmer flesh. Little commercial value, but is eaten raw in India and has limited use in candying and for marmalade.

Clusters of loose-skinned mandarin oranges (*Citrus reticulata*) ripening on a tree in Tunisia.

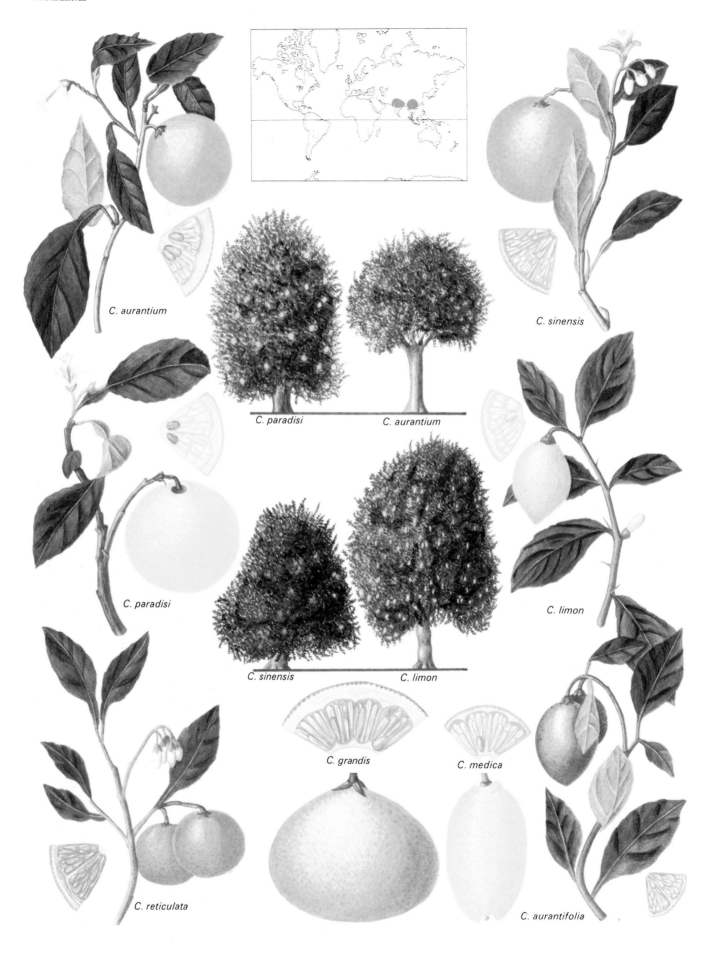

C. aurantium

C. sinensis

C. paradisi

C. aurantium

C. paradisi

C. sinensis

C. limon

C. limon

C. grandis

C. medica

C. reticulata

C. aurantifolia

C. paradisi Grapefruit, Forbidden Fruit. Probably originated in West Indies as a chance seedling of the Shaddock. Large yellow fruits with juicy, bitter-flavored pulp produced in clusters on dense, dome-shaped evergreen trees. Third most important citrus fruit, large quantities being eaten raw, canned or as juice. Grapefruit seed oil is used in soap manufacture.

Group II: Mature fruits predominantly orange color. Oranges.

B *Fruits globose or the polar diameter a little larger than the equatorial diameter. Skin adherent, not easily peeled off.*

C. aurantium Seville, Bitter or Sour Orange, Bigarade. SE Asia. Produces bitter fruits resembling the Sweet Orange. The bulk of the crop is used to make marmalade and the peel is used to relieve digestive complaints, in the distilling of orange liqueurs and to produce oil of bitter orange, an ingredient of some perfumes. Neroli oil derived from the flowers is also used in perfumery. The rootstocks are used for grafting other *Citrus* species.
C. bergamia (*C. aurantium* var *bergamia*) Bergamot. Tropical Asia. Similar to Seville Orange. Bergamot oil extracted from the peel is used in perfumery, especially in the manufacture of eau de Cologne.
C. sinensis Sweet Orange. NE India and adjoining regions of China. Produces round, orange-colored fruits with sweet-flavored pulp. The most important citrus fruit, large quantities being eaten raw, canned or as juice. Also used for flavoring, in marmalades, and oil of sweet orange extracted from the peel is used in perfumery, and as a flavoring agent. Orange seed oil is used in the manufacture of soap.

BB *Fruits slightly flattened (oblate). The polar diameter less than the equatorial diameter. Skin loose, peels easily.*

C. reticulata Mandarin Orange. Cochin China (S Vietnam). Produces loose-skinned, tender, sweet, orange-colored fruits which are increasing in commercial importance as dessert fruits because of their easy peeling character. Several important varieties are cultivated, including the Satsuma (var *unshiu*) and Tangerine (var *deliciosa*).
C. mitis Calamodin, Musk Lime. Malaysia. Produces small orange-colored fruits which have an acid flavor and musty smell. Has limited use in marmalade manufacture, jellies and drinks.

Numerous hybrids between *Citrus* species occur and have been given popular names. Some are listed below. Those with an asterisk (*) are economically and horticulturally important.
  Bitter Sweet Orange *C. aurantium* × *C. sinensis*
  Chironja see Orangelo
  Citrange *C. sinensis* × *Poncirus trifoliata**

Limequat *C. aurantifolia* × *Fortunella margarita*
Orangelo *C. paradisi* × *C. sinensis*
Satsumelo *C. paradisi* × *C. reticulata* var *unshiu*
Siamelo *C. paradisi* × *C. reticulata*
Siamor *C. sinensis* × Tangelo
Sopomaldin *C. paradisi* × *C. mitis*
Tangelo *C. paradisi* × *C. reticulata* var *deliciosa**
Tangelo *C. paradisi* × Tangelo
Tangor Temple Orange *C. sinensis* × *C. reticulata**
Ugli see Tangelo

Note: The distribution map also shows major areas of fruit cultivation (yellow) outside the native regions (brown).

Euodias
(genus *Euodia*)

The genus *Euodia* comprises about 50 species native to south and east Asia, Madagascar, Australasia and Polynesia. They are medium-sized, deciduous or evergreen trees, often aromatic, with naked exposed buds (hidden in the leaf-stalk base in the closely related genus *Phellodendron*). The leaves are opposite and pinnate, and the flowers, which are often unisexual, are small, in flat-topped clusters; there are four or five sepals, petals, stamens and carpels. The fruits are capsular and split open when ripe. Some species are hardy in temperate regions, but these attractive and unusual trees are uncommon in temperate cultivation. The leaves of some species are used for poultices and medicinal teas.

The following hardy species are all deciduous and succeed in all types of soil. *Euodia daniellii* from northern China and Korea is a handsome species in flower and

Flowers of members of the genus *Euodia* are arranged in flat-topped clusters; those of *E. daniellii* shown here open in late summer when they can attract a large number of bees and other insects.

fruit. It grows to 16m (52ft) and has odd-pinnate leaves 22–38cm (9–15in) long with 5–11 more or less lanceolate to ovate leaflets 5–12cm (2–5in) long. The flowers are small, white, and the fruits purplish.

Euodia hupehensis from China is a useful fall-flowering species growing to about 19m (62ft) in cultivation, with smooth, streaked or speckled bark. The leaves are odd-pinnate, 20–25cm (8–10in) long, with five to nine leaflets. The flowers are unisexual on the same tree and similar to those of *E. daniellii*. *Euodia velutina* from Szechwan, China is recognized by the shoots, leaves and fruit being variably downy to hairy. It grows to about 13m (43ft) and has leaves 25cm (10in) long with 7–11 leaflets. It flowers abundantly in late summer followed by purplish-brown fruits.

B. M.

Hop Tree
(genus *Ptelea*)

Ptelea is a genus of about 10 species of shrubs and small trees that are native to North America and Mexico. They are well-known for their strong smelling (aromatic) foliage, each leaf usually tri-foliolate and dotted with translucent glands which are visible when held against light. The flowers are mostly unisexual and densely clustered, each with four or five minute sepals but larger petals and either four or five stamens (abortive in female flowers) or a single ovary that is typically two-celled. The latter develops into a two-seeded, somewhat disc-like, circular samara with a distinct surrounding wing.

The best known species is the Hop Tree, Wafer Ash or Stinking Ash (*Ptelea trifoliolata*) which grows to a height of 8m (26ft) and has bitter bark and fragrant, greenish-white flowers that appear in the early summer, each with four sepals and petals and four stamens in the males. The distinctive winged fruit is greenish-yellow when ripe and the wing is reticulated. The Hop Tree is native to southern Canada and the eastern United States and is not uncommonly cultivated elsewhere, indeed it has become naturalized in several places such as central Europe. Hop trees grow best in slightly shaded conditions on well drained soils. Propagation is by seed sown in the fall or by layering in the spring. The

The Hop Tree or Stinking Ash (*Ptelea trifoliolata*) has distinctive greenish-yellow fruit with reticulate wings and trifoliolate leaves. The fruits were once used to produce home-brewed beer.

latter is important as cultivated plants in some areas rarely set fertile seeds. A number of cultivars exist, such as 'Aurea' with bright yellow leaves. In variety *mollis* the inflorescence and underside of the leaflets are densely hairy. The only other species found in cultivation is *P. crenulata*.

The name Hop Tree recalls the practise in America of using the fruits for making home-brewed beer, the flavor of the fruits (and bitter tasting bark) resembling that of hops.

F. B. H.

Amur Cork Tree
(genus *Phellodendron*)

Phellodendron comprises about 10 species native to northeast Asia. They are deciduous, aromatic trees, the inner bark of which is bright yellow. The young buds are enclosed in the petiole base and the leaves are opposite and pinnate, with odd terminal leaflets. The flowers are inconspicuous, greenish, with the sexes on separate trees. There are five to eight sepals and petals and five to six stamens (sterile in the female flowers). The fruit is a black drupe with five chambers, each with one stone-like seed. Phellodendrons are fairly hardy in temperate regions where they are grown for their attractive yellow leaves in the fall. Propagation is by seed or by cuttings of short shoots with a heel.

The Amur Cork Tree (*Phellodendron amurense*), from northern China and Manchuria, grows to about 15m (50ft) with fissured, corky bark when mature and yellowish shoots. The leaves are 25–38cm (10–15in) long with 5–11 (rarely 13) ciliate leaflets that are hairless beneath (midrib slightly hairy) and more or less glaucous. The fruit, 1cm (0.4in) across, emits a turpentine odor when bruised. The seeds yield an insecticide and extracts of the bark have been used in a preparation

An Amur Cork Tree (*Phellodendron amurense*), so named for its corky bark. Each leaf is compound and bears up to 11 leaflets; they turn a brilliant yellow color in the fall, as can be seen here.

for treating various skin diseases.

Phellodendron chinense from Hupeh in central China grows to about 10m (33ft) with a thin, reticulately ridged bark and purple-brown branches. The leaves are up to 38cm (15in) long with 7–13 (rarely 14) leaflets that are broadly cuneate at the base and more or less hairy beneath, especially on the midrib. The flowers are borne in loose clusters about as broad as they are deep and the fruit is globose, 1cm (0.4in) across. As with *P. amurense* the bark is used medicinally, being known to the Chinese as 'huang-peh.' *Phellodendron japonicum* from central Japan is similar to the previous species but the leaflets are truncate to subcordate at the base and the flower clusters are deeper than they are broad.

B. M.

SIMAROUBACEAE

Tree of Heaven
(genus *Ailanthus*)

Ailanthus is a genus of 8–10 tall deciduous trees, from southeast Asia and northern Australia. The alternate, pinnate leaves resemble those of ashes (*Fraxinus* spp) but have large glandular teeth near the base of the leaflets. They are unusual in that abscission layers form at the base of the leaflets, which often fall before the leaf. The flowers are small, greenish-yellow, borne in long panicles, with male and female flowers often on separate trees; the ovary is deeply divided. The fruit is a one-seeded samara.

The bark of several species is tapped for resin which is used for incense and locally to treat dysentery and other abdominal complaints. The hard yellowish wood is light and, despite its coarse grain, takes a fine polish; it is used for furniture, fishing boats and wooden shoes.

The Tree of Heaven (*Ailanthus altissima = A. glandulosa*) is a suckering tree growing up to 20m (66ft) high. It is often grown as a street tree in Europe and is easily propagated by root cuttings, grafts or suckers. The female tree is preferred as the flowers of the male have an unpleasant odor. The bark is marked with numerous gray fissures and the handsome pinnate leaves grow to 60cm (24in) long with 13–30 leaflets. The fruits are russet in color and

The abundant russet-colored, winged fruits and handsome pinnate leaves of the Tree of Heaven (*Ailanthus altissima*).

sinensis) is quite hardy in temperate regions but requires a good loam soil. It is propagated from seed, less satisfactorily from root cuttings. The Chinese Cedar is sometimes mistaken for the Tree of Heaven (*Ailanthus altissima*) but lacks the glandular teeth at the base of the leaflets. The crushed leaves have a fetid garlic/onion smell, but in China, the young shoots are eaten as a vegetable. As an ornamental, it is increasingly planted along avenues.

The West Indian or Spanish Cedar (*C. odorata*) is a fine tree growing to 33m (108ft) with a smooth bark. It yields an aromatic wood that is well-known as the traditional material for cigar boxes. The tough timber is also used for fence posts and furniture. Its other popular name, Bow Wood, recalls its use by American Indians for making bows and it is still valued as such by present-day archers.

Other cultivated species include *C. dugesii* and *C. fissilis*.

F. B. H.

The timber of West Indian or Spanish Cedar (*Cedrela odorata*) is aromatic and has been traditionally used for making cigar boxes. It also repels insects and has been much used for making closets.

are twisted at each end so that they revolve as they fall, thus traveling further.

In China the silkworm *Attacus cynthia* feeds on *A. altissima* and produces a silk that is cheaper and more durable than mulberry silk, though it is inferior in fineness and gloss. *Ailanthus malabarica* is cultivated in North Vietnam for the leaves which yield a black dye for silk and satin.

M. C. D.

MELIACEAE

Chinese Cedars
(genus *Cedrela*)

Cedrela is a genus of about 20 species of deciduous and evergreen trees and shrubs, about half native to tropical America, including the West Indies, the remainder to southeast Asia and Australia. Their leaves are pinnate with widely spaced leaflets but lacking a terminal one. The flowers are produced in terminal or axillary panicles which are often large and pendulous. Individual flowers are white and yellow and have a four- or five-lobed calyx and four or five petals. There are four to six stamens and a single, protruding style with a capitate stigma. The fruit is a woody or leathery capsule containing numerous winged seeds.

The Chinese Toon or Cedar (*Cedrela*

Pride of India
(genus *Melia*)

Melia is a genus of 8–10 species (but varying from 2–15 owing to the difficulty of delimiting species) native to southern Asia, Indonesia and Australasia, but widely introduced elsewhere for timber and ornament. They are deciduous or half-evergreen trees or shrubs with alternate leaves that are one to three times pinnate. The flowers are bisexual, about 2cm (0.8in) across, white to purplish and borne in panicles. The calyx has five to six lobes and there are five to six free petals which much exceed the sepals. The fruit is a berry. *Melia* is closely related to *Cedrela*, which has once-pinnate leaves, smaller, white flowers and a capsular fruit.

The most noteworthy species is *Melia azedarach*, variously known as Chinatree, Chinaberry Tree, Indian Lilac Tree, Pride of India, as well as Bead Tree – from the seeds that are used for necklaces and rosaries, this last giving the name Arbor Sancta. It is a tree to 15m (50ft) with bipinnate leaves 25–80cm (10–32in) long, flowers in 10–20cm (4–8in) long panicles and roundish, yellow fruits 1.5cm (0.6in) across. It is native to the Himalaya, but is now naturalized in all tropical and subtropical countries where it is a hand-

some sight and often used for street planting. It is marginally hardy in temperate regions and has been grown against south-facing walls in Britain. The fruit has been used in the preparation of an insecticide, and, in the American Civil War, as a source of alcohol. It also yields a good timber. The variety *umbraculiformis*, (Texas Umbrella Tree) which originated in cultivation in Texas, has a flattened crown from the upright and spreading, crowded branches. *Melia dubium* (*M.*

The Pride of India, Indian Lilac or Bead Tree (*Melia azedarach*) has feathery pinnate foliage and orange globular fruits arranged in dense clusters.

composita) is a large Indonesian species with bipinnate leaves 22–60cm (9–24in) long, cultivated in Africa and Australia where it is known as the White Cedar or Ceylon Mahogany. The Neem or Nim Tree from Indonesia is sometimes placed in this genus as *M. indica*, but is now generally restored to its original genus as *Azadirachta indica* (*Antelaea indica*). This is an important tree in India, where it is considered sacred. It yields Margosa, Neem or Nim Oil, extracted from the seeds, which has been used to treat skin diseases and as a hair tonic. An extract from the bark, Cortex Margosae, is used in preparations that reduce dental caries and inflammation of the mouth and the timber is also valuable.

D. M. M.

JUGLANDACEAE

Walnuts
(genus *Juglans*)

Juglans is a genus of some 15 species distributed from the Mediterranean to eastern Asia, and in Indochina, North and Central America and the Andes. They are deciduous trees (rarely shrubs) with pinnate leaves which are aromatic when crushed. Male flowers are in unbranched catkins while the female flowers are few in number, on the same tree. The fruit is a drupe with a fleshy outer layer and an inner 'nut' containing the single seed which contains abundant oil. The closely related genus *Carya* (hickories) differs in having three-branched catkins.

The Common Persian, or English Walnut (*Juglans regia*), from southeast Europe to China, is perhaps the most distinct species, because it is the only one where the nut splits into two halves. The other species are distinguished on vegetative characters and sometimes on details of the fruit; they all further differ from *J. regia* in having serrate, not entire margins to the leaflets.

The species of *Juglans* have many uses. Several are used as timber trees, having beautifully marked and often hard and durable wood which is used in furniture-making, for veneers, and for turning and especially gunstocks; best-known for this are *J. honorei* from Ecuador, *J. mollis* from Mexico, the Black Walnut (*J. nigra*) from North America, the Common Walnut and

A Common, English or Persian Walnut (*Juglans regia*) growing in a field in Drôme, France.

J. sieboldiana from China and Japan. Most of these provide edible nuts but the species most widely exploited for food is the Common Walnut, which is cultivated commercially in the United States of America (especially California), France, Italy, China and India. The nuts also yield oil used for food, soaps and paints. Also exploited for their nuts are the Black Walnut and the Butternut (*J. cinerea*) from North America. The latter, along with *J. mollis*, also provides a dye from the fruit pericarp. Several species of walnut, particularly the Common Walnut, make magnificent ornamental trees in parks and large gardens.

I. B. K. R.

The Main Species of *Juglans*

Group I: Leaflets more or less entire. Nuts with a thin partition, splitting when mature.
J. regia Common, English or Persian Walnut. SE Europe to the Himalaya and China. Tree 20–30m. Leaflets usually 7–9, hairless. Fruits smooth about 3.7–5cm long. Nuts variously sculptured.

Group II: Leaf-scars without a row of hairs on upper edge. Leaflets 9–25, serrate. Fruits hairless or finely hairy. Nuts with a thick partition, not splitting, 4-celled at base.
J. californica S California (USA). Large shrub or small tree. Leaflets 11–15, hairless; nuts deeply grooved. Fruits globose, 1–2cm across.
J. hindsii California (USA). Tree 12–20m. Leaflets 15–19, downy on the veins beneath. Nuts shallowly grooved. Fruits nearly globose, 2.5–3.5cm across. Commonly planted in Californian streets.
J. microcarpa (*J. rupestris*) Texas Walnut. SW USA to Mexico. Small tree to 10m. (The related *J. major* grows to 15m). Leaflets hairless except on the veins

beneath. Fruits globose, 1.5–2.5cm across. Nuts deeply grooved.
J. nigra Black Walnut. E and C USA. Tree 25–35m. Leaflets downy beneath. Fruits compressed-globose, 2.5–3.5cm wide. Nuts irregularly ridged.

Group III: Leaf-scars with a row of hairs on the upper edge. Leaflets 7–19, toothed. Fruits with sticky hairs. Nuts with a thick partition, not splitting, 2-celled at base.
J. ailantifolia (*J. sieboldiana*) Japanese Walnut. Japan. Tree about 20m. Leaflets downy on both surfaces. Fruits in long pendulous racemes, ovoid, about 5cm long, sticky from down. Nuts not ridged or angled.
J. cinerea Butternut. E N America. Tree 15–20m or more. Leaflets downy, with spreading teeth. Mature bracts red or purplish. Fruits 3–5 in pendulous racemes, each more or less ovoid, 4–6.5cm, sticky. Nuts strongly ridged.
J. cathayensis China. Tree to 20m. Leaflets remaining downy, with serrate margins. Fruits ovoid in pendulous racemes, each 3–4.5cm long. Nuts with 6–8 spiny toothed angles.
J. mandshurica E USSR and N China. Tree 15–20m. Leaflets becoming hairless above, with serrate margins. Mature bracts gray or yellow-brown. Fruits in a short raceme. Nut grooved, deeply pitted.

Wing Nuts
(genus *Pterocarya*)

Pterocarya is a genus of eight species of which six are from China, one from Japan and one from western Asia (the Caucasus, Iran). They are deciduous trees growing to 25–30m (82–100ft) with laminated pith and large alternate, pinnate leaves. The flowers are unisexual, borne in pendulous catkins on the same plant, with one to four sepals and the petals absent. The male flowers have 6–18 stamens and the female

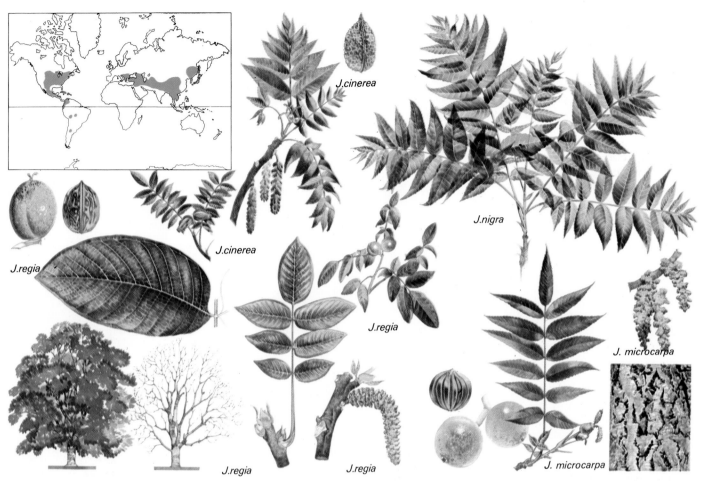

J.cinerea

J.cinerea

J.nigra

J.regia

J. microcarpa

J.regia

J.regia

J.regia

J. microcarpa

The fruits of wing nuts (*Pterocarya* spp) are distinctly winged and hang in long clusters below the shoots. Shown here are those of the hybrid *P. × rehderana*.

a one-celled ovary with a short style and a two-lobed bright pink stigma. The fruit is a small one-seeded nut with two leafy wings, borne in abundance on catkins 20–50cm (8–20in) long. *Juglans* (walnuts) also has laminated pith but is distinguished by the large tough-fleshed drupe with its wrinkled, unwinged stone. In *Carya* (hickories) the pith is continuous and the calyx absent or nearly so.

Several species are grown in temperate regions as ornamentals, for the striking large pinnate leaves and long pendulous fruiting catkins. They are moisture-loving trees and are at their best when planted in a deep loam beside lakes and rivers. Propagation is best from seed, from suckers where these are produced, or from cuttings.

The most commonly cultivated species is the Caucasian Wing Nut (*Pterocarya fraxinifolia*), from the Caucasus and northern Iran, a tree with several superposed naked buds. The leaves, which have 11–25 leaflets and a leaf rachis (central stalk) round in cross section, turn an attractive bright yellow in the fall. The fruit is distinctly winged. It is liable to sucker in moist habitats and produce a thicket. The Japanese Wing Nut (*P. rhoifolia*) from Japan has buds at first with two or three

dark brown scales, and 11–21 leaflets. The winged fruits hang in catkins 20–30cm (8–12in) long. In Japan the timber is used for making sandals and matches. The Chinese Wing Nut (*P. stenoptera*) from China has naked buds and five to nine leaflets. The fruiting catkins are 20–30cm (8–12in) long. The hybrid *P. × rehderana* (*P. fraxinifolia × P. stenoptera*) is hardier and more vigorous than its parents and produces root suckers. The leaves have about 21 leaflets and the rachis is flanged or grooved. The fruiting catkins grow to 45cm (18in) long.

F. B. H.

Hickories
(genus *Carya*)

Carya is a genus of large, fast-growing, deciduous, stately trees chiefly confined to the eastern part of North America, where upwards of 20 species are known, and also represented by two species in Tonkin and China. They grow to over 30m (100ft) and may be elegantly conical as in *Carya cordiformis* or broadly conical as in *C. glabra* and *C. ovata*. The bark is generally gray and smooth but in *C. ovata* it rapidly becomes rugged and shaggy, hence the common name of that species – Shagbark Hickory. The pith of the shoots is solid. The leaves are opposite, characteristically large and compound, yellowish-green and often oily, thick and sweet-smelling, with 3–17 leaflets per leaf, the leaflet size, shape and number varying from species to species. The flowers are unisexual, borne on the same tree, the males in terminal three-pronged catkins and the females in terminal spikes, with two stigmas. The corolla is absent and the calyx absent or nearly so. The fruit is a round to pear-shaped nut surrounded by a husk.

Hickories are cultivated for their wood, ornamental value and edible fruits. The timber produced is very tough and elastic and is used in the manufacture of tool handles. Nurserymen do not favor hickories because they are hard to establish, but once settled they produce excellent fall coloration. Of the edible fruits, the most important is the Pecan nut from *C. illinoensis* (*C. pecan*), a native of the southeastern United States of America, Mexico and parts of South America. The wild trees produce edible fatty nuts (dry

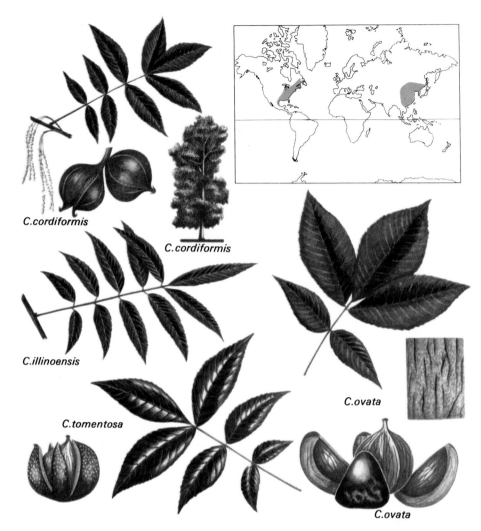

C.cordiformis

C.cordiformis

C.illinoensis

C.tomentosa

C.ovata

C.ovata

The Mockernut Hickory (*Carya tomentosa*) in fall foliage at Kew Gardens, London. The tree is native to the northeastern United States.

drupes), which were eaten by the Indian tribes in these areas, and the use of the Pecan is thought to have made an important contribution to civilization in the New World.

Carya illinoensis trees were planted in Washington, and called Mississippi nuts, as early as 1775, but not until the early 20th century were the nuts planted in large numbers for commercial cropping. The Pecan industry in America is now of considerable importance. Large plantations of trees, usually grown as seedlings and later budded or grafted, or produced from root cuttings, are grown in the southern United States. They require fertile, well-drained soils in an area of adequate rainfall. Individual trees can live as long as 1 000 years, but the life of a commercial orchard is considered to be 100 years.

More than 300 varieties of Pecan are now grown, mainly selections from wild seedlings, which can show a great diversity in the quality of the nuts. Some of the nuts are sold in the shell after a period of drying, although most of the harvest is shelled mechanically and used for confectionery,

sweets, ice cream and the fresh and salted nut trade. The food value of Pecans is high, and the nuts contain a higher fat content than any other vegetable product – over 70 percent. Oil from rejected and mouldy nuts is used for cooking and cosmetic production. New thin-shelled varieties are now being grown, so-called 'paper-shelled pecans' which can be broken with the fingers.

Apart from the Pecan the best edible hickory nuts are produced by the Shagbark Hickory (*C. ovata*), but the tree is not generally cultivated specifically for their production.　　　　S. A. H./W. W. S.

The Main Species of *Carya*

Group I: Leaflets 5–17. Scales of overwintering buds paired, scales valvate, 4–6, broad.

C. illinoensis Pecan. Mississippi Basin (USA). Fast-growing tree to 45m. Trunk buttressed; bark thick-furrowed. Leaflets 9–17. Scales of overwintering buds with bright yellow hairs. Kernel sweet.

C. aquatica Water Hickory, Bitter Pecan. Swamps and rice fields of N America. Tree to 15m. Leaflets 7–13, narrow to broadly lanceolate. Scales without yellow hairs but buds red-brown with yellow glands. Kernel bitter.

C. cordiformis (*C. amara*) Swamp Hickory, Pignut, Bitternut. Woodland and mountains of N America. Tree to 27m. Leaflets 5–9. Scales of overwintering buds without yellow scales but with permanent yellow scurf and curving shape.

Group II: Leaflets 3–9. Scales of overwintering buds imbricate, 6–12, very narrow.

C. ovata (*C. alba*) Shagbark Hickory. N America. Tree to 36m. Bark exfoliating in narrow strips; young branches scurfy, red-brown, becoming gray. Leaflets 5–7, serrate, strongly ciliate, with tufts of hairs at apex of teeth of leaves. Nuts white; kernel sweet.

C. laciniosa Kingnut, Big Shellbark. N America. Similar to *C. ovata* but stouter and buds less pointed. Young branches orange, scurfy. Leaflets ciliate when young but not tufted. Nuts yellow-brown.

C. tomentosa (*C. alba*) Mockernut Hickory. N America. Tree to 18m. Bark dark and deeply furrowed; petioles, branches etc permanently tomentose with curly dense hairs. Velvet gray terminal bud twice as thick as stem behind it. Leaflets usually 7, very large, rarely 5–9, drooping and sweet-smelling, on yellow-pink rachis; largest leaflet in terminal position. Fruits with very thick hard shell and almost empty inside.

C. glabra (*C. porcina*) Pignut, Smoothbark Hickory. Borders of swamps in N America. Tree to 24m. Bark gray-purple, smooth but becoming wrinkled with rust and black folds. Buds, leaves etc unusually small. Nuts smooth, pale brown.

C. ovalis Sweet Pignut, False Shagbark. N America. Similar to *C. glabra* but old bark becoming more shaggy. Branches, leaves etc scurfy. Kernel sweet.

C. pallida Pale Hickory. N America. Bark very pale gray and furrowed.

C. texana Black Hickory. N America. Nuts coarsely ridged and reticulate veined.

C. cathayensis Chinese Hickory. E China. Tree to 25m. Leaflets 5–7, green above, rusty-brown below. Fruits with 4-ridged nuts.

OLEACEAE

Olives
(genus *Olea*)

Olea is a genus of some 35–40 species native to warm temperate or tropical regions from southern Europe (Mediterranean area) to Africa (the main center), southern Asia, eastern Australia, New Caledonia and New Zealand. They are small to medium-sized trees or shrubs with opposite, simple leaves. The flowers

Right Ripe and unripe fruits of the Common Olive (*Olea europaea*). Olives are inedible as gathered from the trees and are subjected to various treatments before storage in brine.

are white, mostly bisexual, borne in axillary panicles or fascicles. The calyx and the tube of the corolla are four-lobed, the corolla lobes valvate or absent, and there are two stamens. The fruit is a more or less ovoid drupe, dark blue to black when ripe.

The best-known species is the Common Olive (*Olea europaea*), very widely grown since ancient times in areas of Mediterranean climate for its edible fruits and the oil expressed from them. The silvery-green foliage and gnarled trunks of olive trees form one of the most characteristic aspects of the vegetation of the Mediterranean basin. Indeed the olive is often regarded as an indicator of the Mediterranean climate and of the limits of Mediterranean vegetation. The Cultivated Olive is known as subspecies *europaea* to distinguish it from the wild form, subspecies *sylvestris*, which has wider leaves, thorny branches and smaller fruits.

Olives have been cultivated since prehistoric times, and constitute a crop of fundamental importance in the daily life, economics and sociology of the peoples of the Mediterranean countries, providing them with their main source of edible oil. In earlier times olive oil was also used for

Olive harvesting in an Olive (*Olea europaea*) orchard, in Tunisia. Much of the harvesting is still undertaken by hand, the only alternatives being by mechanical or hand shaking.

lighting as well as cooking and in anointing the body in religious ceremonies. There are frequent references to the olive in the bible and in Greek and Roman writings and the olive branch is still an emblem of peace. The olive provided much of the wealth of many Mediterraneen communities and still plays a major role in the economy, although the crop is in decline today and the acreages under cultivation have been diminishing for some time. Not only is the crop an ancient one but it has changed little over the millennia and its present decline is largely due not only to changed patterns of agriculture and eating habits but to the fact that the methods of cultivation, propagation and oil production are not properly adapted to modern conditions. Until changes are introduced the decrease in the importance of the olive as a crop will not be arrested.

A factor that has had a major influence on the history and evolution of the olive is its longevity. Trees may survive for 1 500 years or more and are amongst the oldest trees known in Europe. They regenerate from suckers.

Olives are exacting in their climatic requirements – they cannot survive temperatures of −9°C (16°F) or an average temperature of 3°C (37°F) during the coldest winter months although they require some degree of winter chilling to ensure the induction of flowering. Olives are generally grown in groves or orchards, sometimes interplanted with catch crops although preferably not. They may be grown on dry soils without artificial irrigation but heavier and more reliable crops are obtained with irrigation.

There are hundreds of olive cultivars, comprising mixtures of clones, often occupying extensive areas. They are budded onto seedlings or are propagated by cuttings, often by layering. Propagation by these means has been a slow process until recently when mist propagation techniques have been introduced for the rooting of cuttings. Often cuttings are grafted onto the stumps of old trees. Growth is very slow and the olive requires several decades to reach maturity and full productivity. Different styles of cultivation are employed in the various Mediterranean countries: in Spain, for example, three main stems are allowed to develop, either by planting or by splitting the crown, giving a low-growing tree, while in other countries, such as Greece, the trees are allowed to develop a single tall straight trunk.

The olive is not reliable in its cropping,

and a heavy crop one year is liable to exhaust the plant and be followed by a light crop the next year. It is also highly susceptible to wind and heavy rain which can beat down the young fruits and leaves and to spring frosts which can kill the flowers. Harvesting of the crop is by hand or by mechanical shakers. They are hand-picked when straw-colored for green table olives and when black and ripe for table use, cooking or more usually for oil. Olives are inedible as gathered from the trees, and are subjected to various treatments such as steeping in a potash or salt solution which gives rise to a lactic acid fermentation; they are then preserved in brine. Black olives may be stored direct in a brine solution but the best-quality table ones are preserved in a marinade of olive oil, often with various herbs such as species of thyme, rosemary, etc. Green olives are often sold stoned and stuffed with sweet red pepper, anchovy or almonds.

Besides its major use as a cooking and salad oil, olive oil is widely used for medicinal purposes, for canning sardines and other preserves, in dressing wool and in soap manufacture and cosmetics.

Other cultivated species include the Indian Olive (*O. ferruginea = O. cuspidata*) and the Wild Olive (*O. africana*). The wood from several species is decorative and can be finely worked, especially that of the Black Iron Wood (*O. laurifolia*).

V. H. H.

Ashes
(genus *Fraxinus*)

Fraxinus is a genus of some 70 species from the Northern Hemisphere, particularly east Asia, North America and the Mediterranean region. They are deciduous trees, with opposite and mostly pinnate leaves. The flowers, often without petals, are bisexual or unisexual, the sexes variously distributed, and there are usually two stamens. The fruit is winged (samara).

Nordic myths tell that Man was created from ash wood: the Norse word 'aska' means man. The best-known species is the European or Common Ash (*Fraxinus excelsior*), a tree growing to 40m (130ft) with light gray bark and black winter buds. The European Ash is well-known for its appearance, the handsome 'keys' (bunches of winged fruits) hanging from the shoots

being a characteristic sight in the fall.

Diseases of ashes include the mildew *Phyllactinia corylea* (Erysiphales) which may cause defoliation of the European Ash whilst canker due to *Nectria galligena* is not uncommon on the stem and branches of the same species. The bracket fungus *Inonotus hispidus = Polyporus hispidus* (Aphyllophorales) is probably a wound parasite of the European Ash and causes weakening of any subsequent timber. Ash is also one of the hosts of the toadstool *Pholiota squarrosa* (Agaricales), a rather weak parasite.

A common pest of European Ash is the Ash Bark Beetle, whose 'galleries' reduce the tree's vigor and can result in gall-like formations. There are also a number of unsightly galls, for example by the mite *Eriophyes fraxinivorus* (on inflorescences), the homopteran *Psyllopsis fraxini* (leaflets) and the dipteron gall-midge *Dasyneura fraxini* (lower surface of leaf near midrib).

Medicinally, decoctions of the bark of the European Ash were once used to cure jaundice and other complaints of the liver, and a strong extract made from ashes of the wood was used for scabby heads; other extracts were supposed to counteract snake-bites. The Flowering or Manna Ash (*F. ornus*), when the bark is cut, yields a pale yellow juice which acts as a mild laxative and has long been given to children, particularly in Italy and Sicily. The principal use of ash, however, has been for its timber, especially that of the European Ash which is hard but elastic, scarcely warps, is not very susceptible to attack by insects and is thus durable. In the past it was used for making spears and staffs, then for carriage- and wagon-building, as well as for such uses as hop-poles

The open crown, upsweeping branches and pinnate foliage of one of the most graceful of trees, the Common Ash (*Fraxinus excelsior*).

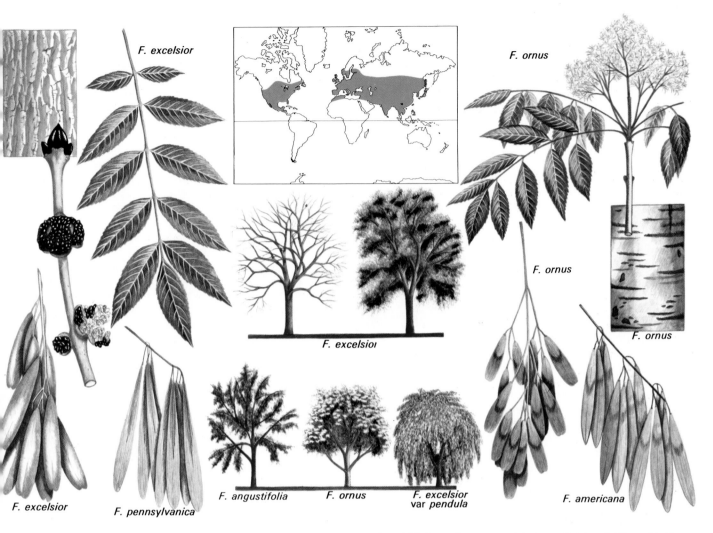

F. excelsior

F. ornus

F. excelsior

F. ornus

F. ornus

F. excelsior

F. pennsylvanica

F. angustifolia

F. ornus

F. excelsior var pendula

F. americana

and tool handles. The timber burns very well and was the original Yule log.

The genus is also valuable as a source of ornamental street and park trees. Some of these have the calyx remaining when in fruit, the best-known being the Arizona Ash (*F. velutina*), the White Ash (*F. americana*) and the Red Ash (*F. pennsylvanica*). Others, in which the calyx is absent or falls early, include the Blue Ash (*F. quadrangulata*), the Black Ash (*F. nigra*) and the European Ash. The Flowering Ash (*F. ornus*) is also frequently seen as a handsome ornamental tree.

I. B. K. R.

The Main Species of *Fraxinus*

Section *Ornus*
Flowers appearing with or after leaves in terminal and lateral clusters on leafy branches. Filaments of stamens usually longer than their anthers. 'Flowering' or 'Manna' Ashes.

A Corolla present.

F. ornus Flowering or Manna Ash. S Europe, Asia Minor. Tree 15–20m. Leaflets usually 7, hairless except along the midrib beneath.
F. floribunda Himalayan Manna Ash. The Himalaya. Tree to 40m. Leaflets usually 7 or 9, hairless above but hairy on the veins beneath.

AA Corolla absent.

F. chinensis China. Tree to 15m. Closely related to *F. ornus*.
F. bungeana China. Shrub or small tree to 5m. Closely related to *F. ornus*.

Section *Fraxinaster*
Flowers appearing before leaves from leafless, lateral buds of previous year's growth. Filaments of stamens mostly shorter than their anthers.

B Flowers with calyx.

F. dipetala California and adjacent areas (USA). Shrub to 4m. Leaflets usually 5, hairless. Petals 2.
F. americana White Ash. N America. Tree to 40m. Leaflets 7–9, usually hairless, occasionally downy beneath. Calyx small, persistent; corolla absent. Wing of fruit terminal.
F. velutina Arizona Ash. SW USA. Tree 8–12m. Leaflets 3–5, usually hairy on both surfaces. Calyx present at fruiting; corolla absent.
F. pennsylvanica Red Ash. E N America. Tree 12–20m. Leaflets usually 7–9, downy at least beneath. Calyx persistent; corolla absent. Wing of fruit decurrent.

BB Flowers lacking calyx and corolla.

F. excelsior Common or European Ash. Europe. Tree to 45m. Leaflets 7–11, hairless except for the midrib beneath.
F. angustifolia Narrow-leaved Ash. W Mediterranean, N Africa. Tree 20–25m. Leaflets 7–13, hairless.
    ssp *oxycarpa* (*F. oxycarpa*) E Mediterranean to Turkestan. Similar but with fewer leaflets, each with a row of hairs near the midrib beneath.
F. nigra Black Ash. E N America. Tree 25–30m. Leaflets 7–11, hairless except along the veins beneath. Calyx present, small, deciduous.
F. quadrangulata Blue Ash. N America. Tree to about 20m. Leaflets 5–11, hairless above, downy beneath. Calyx present, minute, soon falling.

Privets
(genus *Ligustrum*)

Ligustrum is a genus of 40–50 species native to China, Japan, the Himalaya, Indomalaysia and Australia with one species, the European or Common Privet (*Ligustrum vulgare*), in Europe and North Africa. They are mainly deciduous or evergreen shrubs, rarely trees, with simple, opposite and entire leaves. The flowers are bisexual, small, whitish, often heavily perfumed, and borne in terminal panicles. The calyx is four-toothed and the corolla funnel-shaped with four spreading lobes; there are two stamens. The fruit is a berry-like drupe with oily flesh, usually black, and sometimes with a purplish bloom.

Some 16 species, natives of China and Japan, are hardy in temperate regions, being grown mainly as hedging plants or for their flower odor – too heavy and penetrating to be called fragrant. They are not particular as to soil (except the poorest) and are easily propagated from cuttings.

The most popular species for hedging are the Common Privet and its cultivars, although they have the disadvantage of being poisonous. The Common Privet is a deciduous to semi-evergreen shrub growing to 3m (10ft), more rarely to 5m (16ft). The leaves are narrowly oval, 2.5–6cm

Since the 17th century clipped hedges have been a feature of European gardens. Here Common Privet (*Ligustrum vulgare*) provides a formal hedge, set off by a wrought ironwork gate.

(1–2.4in) long. All parts of *L. vulgare* contain a poisonous glycoside (ligustrin) and children have died from eating the berries. It should not be used as a hedge plant for fencing in browsing animals. Horses seem to have a liking for it and fatalities are well-known. Curiously, goats can eat 'considerable quantities' with impunity. The cultivar 'Aurea Marginatum' (Golden Privet) has midgreen leaves with a wide irregular yellow border and 'Variegatum' has leaves edged with creamy-white or yellow. The Japanese Privet (*L. japonicum*), with glossy blackish-green leaves, and *L. ovalifolium*, a semi-evergreen species with leaves shining dark green on both sides, are both widely used for hedging.

The Glossy or Chinese Privet (*L. lucidum*) forms an attractive evergreen tree growing to 15m (50ft), with a hemispherical crown and ovate to somewhat lanceolate leaves, shining dark green above, up to 15cm (6in) long.

The wood of the Common Privet is hard and has been used for making tools; it also makes good charcoal. The seeds of some species are roasted as a coffee substitute, for example those of *L. ibota* from China and Japan, *L. japonicum*, also Japanese, and *L. indicum* (*L. nepalense*) from the Himalaya and Indochina. Insect damage to the stem of *L. ibota* and *L. lucidum* induces the formation of a wax which is used industrially in China.

I. B. K. R.

There are many varieties of the Common Lilac, (*Syringa vulgaris*), a familiar garden shrub or small tree grown for its sweet-scented white, mauve or purple flowers borne in upright clusters.

Lilacs
(genus *Syringa*)

Syringa is a genus of 25–30 species from Asia and southeast Europe, cultivated for their showy flowers in spring and early summer. They are deciduous shrubs or small trees with opposite leaves that are usually entire, rarely lobed or pinnate. The flowers, which are borne in panicles, are bisexual, fragrant and waxy, ranging in color from white to deep purple. The calyx is four-toothed and the corolla tubular with four valvate lobes. There are two stamens, either included or exserted and the ovary has two cells. The fruit is a leathery capsule maturing winged seeds, two to each chamber.

The Common Lilac (*Syringa vulgaris*) from southeast Europe is a very popular species with over 500 named cultivars, many originating in France. It grows to 7m (23ft) and is given to suckering and the formation of epicormic shoots. Such suckers and shoots should be removed.

Lilacs flourish in a good moist loam and are distinctly sun-loving. Propagation is best by layers, but seeds and cuttings can be used. In some instances, grafting on Common Lilac stocks is required.

There are a number of excellent species of *Syringa* from China and central Europe such as *S. reflexa*, *S. villosa* and *S. josikaea* (Hungarian Lilac) which have been used as parents for a great many hybrids such as the 'Canadian hybrids' raised at Ottawa in the 1920's.

Lilacs are subject to a number of micro-fungus diseases but these are not particu-

larly serious. A serious bacterial disease is caused by *Pseudomonas syringae* which can kill practically any part of the plant. Flowers and shoots are blackened and adult leaves become contorted. The only treatment is removal of infected parts as soon as symptoms appear. The blight, *Phytophthora syringae* (Peronosporales) is troublesome, especially on lilacs which have been 'forced' for early flowers. It kills buds and shoot tips. Removal of affected parts and spraying with the current anti-blight mixture is usually effective. Common Lilac and its numerous cultivars seem to be increasingly attacked at the roots by the well-known gill fungus *Armillaria mellea* (Honey Fungus). There is little that can be done about this.

Pests on lilac include the leaf-cutting bee *Megachile centuncularis* and leaf-miner caterpillars of the moth *Gracilaria syringella*. Handpicking followed by burning of affected leaves is helpful and currently available insecticide washes for these particular pests may be tried.

T. W. W.

SCROPHULARIACEAE

Empress Tree
(genus *Paulownia*)

The genus *Paulownia* contains 6–10 species of fast-growing deciduous trees native to China. Best-known is the Empress Tree (*P. tomentosa* = *P. imperialis*) also called the Foxglove Tree for its erect panicles of fragrant, pale violet or rich purple fox-glove-like flowers that are borne in tall erect panicles during May, before the leaves emerge. The latter are long-stalked opposite, ovate, large – normally 12–30cm (5–12in), but up to 1m (3.3ft) on suckering shoots – hairy on the upper surface and distinctly downy on the lower. Leaves of young trees may be lobed and bear one to three points. The fruit is a woody, ovoid capsule containing winged seeds.

The Empress Tree is widely grown in temperate regions but due to its habit of producing flower buds during the late summer and fall, which are then susceptible to winter frosts, flowering the following spring can be unpredictable in northern regions. Other species found in cultivation include *P. fortunei* (flowers with a pale yellow blotch) and *P. kawakamii* (flowers purple-white with purple lines). Paulownias thrive in a well-drained, deep loam in a sheltered sunny position. They can be propagated from seeds or by root, shoot and leaf cuttings. The Empress Tree yields top-quality wood much used in cabinet-making in the Orient.

T. W. W.

BIGNONIACEAE

Bean Trees
(genus *Catalpa*)

Catalpa is a genus of about 13 species of hardy deciduous, rarely evergreen trees, sometimes shrubs, native to America, the West Indies and east Asia, some of which are popular ornamentals. Their leaves are opposite or in whorls of threes, borne on long stalks, and large with an entire or broadly lobed margin. The flowers occur in terminal clusters, each flower with a tubular mostly two-lipped calyx and a tubular corolla with five spreading lobes – two above and three below. There are five stamens but typically only two are fertile. The fruit is a narrow, flattish capsule, 30–60cm (12–24in) long which splits into two valves. The seeds are numerous, compressed and tufted at each end with white hairs.

Catalpas are vigorous and hardy in temperate regions. The persistent long fruits recall Runner Beans (*Phaseolus coccineus*) and this is reflected in their popular name. They are favorite ornamentals, prized for their large leaves, showy clusters of large tubular flowers and the long and persistent pendent fruits, the latter having a compelling appeal. Any reasonably good, moist soil is suitable and they are seen to best advantage as isolated specimens on lawns or as avenue trees. Propagation can be from seed or by cuttings of mature wood. Named varieties are propagated by grafting on seedlings.

The best-known species is the Indian Bean, Common or Southern Catalpa (*Catalpa bignonioides* = *C. catalpa*) which, under favorable conditions, can reach 18–20m (60–66ft) and has a round, spreading head. The crushed leaves, however, do have an unpleasant odor. Cultivar 'Aurea' is attractively conspicuous by its more yellowish leaves. The coarse-grained durable timber of this species and also that of the Western Catalpa, Catawba or Cigar Tree (*C. speciosa*) is used for fence posts and railway sleepers. The bark of *C. longissima* is used for tanning in the West Indies.

S. R. C.

Opposite Lobed leaf of the Empress Tree (*Paulownia imperialis*); these can reach 1m (3.3ft) across on young trees. *Right* The impressive display of upright inflorescences of the Hybrid Catalpa (*Catalpa × hybrida*) make it, and other catalpas, valued ornamentals.

The Main Species of *Catalpa*

In the following selection, the petal background color is white or pinkish, except *C. ovata* where it is yellowish.

Group I: Leaves pubescent with typically unbranched hairs on the lower surfaces – at least on the veins.

C. ovata (*C. kaempferi*) Chinese or Yellow Catalpa. China. Tree 6–10(15)m with spreading head. Leaves opposite, broadly cordate-ovate, 13–25cm long, simple, but with 3–5 pointed lobes. Flowers fragrant, in many-flowered panicles, 10–25cm long, the corollas less than 2.5cm long, yellowish-white, with striped orange and violet-purple spotted markings on the inside of the tube. Fruit (capsule) up to 30cm long. Long cultivated in Japan.

C. bignonioides (*C. catalpa*) Common Catalpa, Indian Bean, Southern Catalpa. N America. Tree 6–20m, with rounded shape. Leaves often in whorls of 3, broadly cordate-ovate, 12–20cm long, simple, but sometimes with 2 small lobes, giving pungent unpleasant odor when crushed or bruised. Flowers in many-flowered panicles, 13–25cm long, the corollas 4–5cm long, white, with striped yellow and purple spotted markings on the inside of the tube which is frilled at the mouth. Fruit 15–40cm long. Cultivar 'Aurea' has more or less yellow leaves. The cultivar 'Nana' is a dwarf form to 2m, possibly covering more than one clone.

C. × hybrida (*C. teasii* = *C. ovata* × *C. bignonioides*) Hybrid Catalpa. Large tree to 30m. Leaves opposite, broadly cordate-ovate, 15–40cm long, similar to those of *C. ovata* but bluish-purple before they are fully expanded. Flowers in many-flowered panicles, 15–40cm long and similar to those of *C. bignonioides*, but rather smaller. Fruit to 40cm long, but does not contain seeds. Cultivar 'J. C. Teas' has purplish unfolding leaves.

C. speciosa Western Catalpa, Catawba, Cigar Tree. N America. Large tree to 30m. Leaves cordate-ovate, 15–30cm long. Flowers in relatively few-flowered panicles, 15–18cm long, the corollas large, 5–6cm in diameter and 4–5cm long, white with a few purplish spots on the inside of the tube, the mouth of which is frilled. Fruit 22–45cm long.

Group II: Leaves quite glabrous on the lower surface.

C. bungei China. Small tree, 6–10m with pyramidal shape. Leaves opposite, triangular-ovate, 8–16cm long, sometimes toothed or angled near the base. Flowers in 3–12-flowered racemes 10–20cm long, the corollas 3–4cm long, white with purple spots on the inside of the tube. Fruit 25–35cm long.

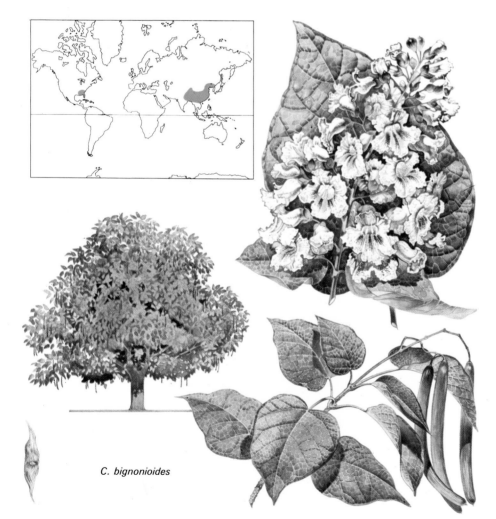

C. bignonioides

CAPRIFOLIACEAE

Elders
(genus *Sambucus*)

Sambucus comprises about 20 species from the temperate and subtropical regions of the Old and the New World. They are mostly deciduous shrubs or small trees (occasionally herbaceous) with opposite, odd-pinnate leaves. The abundant flowers are bisexual, white and small, in flat or more or less pyramidal clusters. There are usually five sepals (minute) and petals (rarely three or four) and five stamens; the ovary is three- to five-chambered. The fruit is a small berry with three to five one-seeded nutlets.

Some half dozen species are either native or hardy in temperate regions, being grown as ornamentals. They are mostly vigorous, invasive, sun-loving shrubs thriving in many soils and habitats, especially where there is a good moisture supply. Propagation is mainly by cuttings.

One species in Britain, the Common Elder (*Sambucus nigra*), has for long been the basis for excellent wines made both from the flowers and the berries ('the English-man's grape'). In past times, in Britain, elderberry wine was used to adulterate red wine made from grapes and thus fell somewhat into disrepute. In recent years the home manufacture of wines both from flowers and especially berries has greatly increased. Elderberry wine if kept for at least six months is a very fine red alcoholic drink. Infusions of roots of this same species are said to have purgative properties.

Elders are host to the ear-like fungus *Hirneola* (*Auricularia*) *auricula-judae*, commonly known as Judas' Ear (incorrectly the Jew's Ear), a reference to the legend that Judas hanged himself on an elder tree, (another candidate for this dubious distinction is the Judas Tree, *Cercis siliquastrum*).

Among the species cultivated as ornamentals are *S. canadensis* (the American Elder) and its cultivars 'Maxima' with huge flower heads, 'Aurea' with greenish-yellow foliage, and *S. racemosa*, an attractive bright red-berried elder with masses of flowers in a distinctly pyramidal cluster. The Common Elder exists in several cultivars including 'Aurea' with leaves golden yellow and 'Purpurea' with leaves flushed purple. T. W. W.

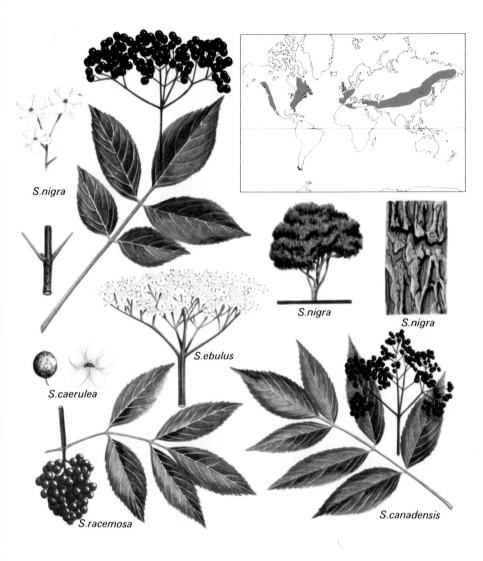

S.nigra

S.nigra

S.nigra

S.ebulus

S.caerulea

S.racemosa

S.canadensis

The Main Species of *Sambucus*

Group I: Flower clusters flat. Pith white. Fruit dark purple or black.

S. caerulea Blue Elderberry. W N America, especially California. Shrub or small tree, 3–15m. Leaves 15–25cm long, compound with 5–7 leaflets. Flowers yellowish-white in early summer in flat umbels. Berries black but covered with an intensely glaucous blue bloom. In California this species is more tree-like, the trunk being up to 40cm in diameter. The berries are used as a food, when cooked. It was also introduced to France and cultivated in Paris in the last century.

S. canadensis American Elder. E N America. Deciduous shrub to 4m with soft pithy stems and branches. Leaves pinnate with 5–11 leaflets, 12cm long. Flowers in convex umbels up to 20cm across, white, produced soon after midsummer. Berries purple-black. Closely related to *S. nigra*.
'Maxima' An extremely robust variety with large leaves and enormous flat flower heads 30cm across.

S. nigra Common Elder. Europe. A very common and widespread deciduous shrub or small tree, 4–8m. Branches and young wood pithy, with rugged fissured bark on older trees. Leaflets 5–7, 10–30cm long. Flowers yellowish-cream or dull white with characteristic scent, in flat umbels 12–20cm across, beginning early summer. Berries prolific, shining black, ripening in September. The juice of the berries has many pharmaceutical properties. It is also used for domestic wine-making and as a syrup for colds and chills. *S. nigra* 'Aurea is the Golden Elder. *S. nigra* 'Albo-variegata' is an attractive variegated form.

S. ebulus Dane's Elder or Danewort. Europe and N Africa, naturalized in British Isles. An unusual herbaceous species producing stout, grooved stems 1–1.2m high each year. Leaves with 9–13 leaflets. Flowers white, tinged pink in flat umbels, 7.5–10cm across. Fruit black. Formerly an important medicinal plant, it was recommended for the healing of all manner of ailments from jaundice to gout.

Group II: Flower clusters more or less pyramidal (not flat). Pith mostly brown. Fruit red, yellow or white (brownish to black in *S. melanocarpa*).

S. racemosa Red-berried Elder. Europe, Asia Minor, Siberia and W Asia. A medium-sized deciduous shrub, 3–5m with coarsely toothed compound leaves. Flowers are produced in April as terminal white pyramidal panicles, followed by the brilliant red fruits in July. Two outstanding cultivars are 'Laciniata,' a decorative cut-leaved variety, and 'Plumosa Aurea,' a fine, golden, cut-leaved shrub.

S. pubens North American species closely related to *S. racemosa*.

S. melanocarpa Shrub to 4m. Leaflets 5–7. Flower clusters about as deep as wide. Fruits black but reddish-brown in some.

Viburnums
(genus *Viburnum*)

Viburnum is a genus of more than 120 species, about half from eastern Asia extending south to Java and the rest divided between India, Europe, North Africa, North and Central America and the Andes of South America. They are predominantly deciduous, sometimes evergreen shrubs or small trees with simple and opposite leaves. The flowers are small, mostly white or pinkish, borne in terminal panicles or flat compound clusters; the marginal flowers are sometimes sterile, larger and more showy. The calyx comprises five small petals, the corolla is lobed with five spreading petals, and there are five stamens. The ovary is single-celled. The fruit is a blue, black or red, berry-like drupe with one stony seed.

The Guelder Rose (*Viburnum opulus*) from Europe grows to about 4m (13ft), with leaves palmately three- to five-lobed, striking red 'berries' and fine leaf colors in the fall. Its cultivar 'Sterile' has large globes of pure white, quite sterile flowers. The Wayfaring Tree or Mealy Guelder Rose (*V. lantana*), a common species of chalk and limestone in Europe, is a deciduous shrub growing to about 4m (13ft) with dense stellate hairs on all parts.

Viburnum is a popular genus in cultivation; about half the species are hardy in temperate regions and they are easy to grow, requiring a good, moist loamy soil. Propagation is mainly from cuttings taken in summer, less frequently by layers; seed is sometimes used. *Viburnum lantana*, a particularly vigorous species, is also used as a stock for grafting. *Viburnum farreri* (*V. fragrans*) has delicately fragrant flowers virtually throughout winter months. Other winter flowerers are *B.* × *bodnantense* and the commonly grown dark evergreen *V. tinus* 'Laurustinus' which has white and pink flowers and is remarkably tolerant of the smoke and grime of towns. Flowering

251

in spring is *V. carlesii*, with sweet-scented flowers that are pink in the bud and pure white when open. Other hybrids include *V. × burkwoodii*, *V. × carlcephalum* and *V. × juddii*. A number of species have popular group names, for example Snowball viburnums with globose clusters of white or whitish flowers such as the Chinese Snowball (*V. macrocephalum* 'Sterile') and the Japanese Snowball (*V. plicatum* 'Sterile'). Particularly useful for their tolerance of shade are the Hobble Bush (*V. alnifolium*) from America and the closely related *V. furcatum* from Japan. The Lacecap viburnums are spring flowering and have large flat stratified clusters of flowers as in *V. plicatum* var *tomentosum*.

The translucent fruits of the Guelder Rose contain valeric acid, an unpleasant smelling fatty acid which was once used medicinally in the treatment of hysteria, although the main source was Valerian (*Valeriana officinalis*). The fruits of *V. opulus* are consumed in Norway and Sweden mixed with flower and honey. The wood of *V. lantana* has an unpleasant smell but it is hard and is used for turnery work. Other species with unpleasant smelling wood are appropriately named *V. foetidum* and *V. foetens*.   F. B. H.

The Main Species of *Viburnum*

Group I: Leaves typically lobed with 3–5 basal veins palmately arranged. Deciduous species.

A *Flowers of inflorescence all similar (no enlarged sterile marginal flowers). Fruit finally red or purple-black. Petiole not glandular.*

V. acerifolium Dockmackie. USA. Shrub to 2m. Leaves more or less ovate, 3-lobed, 5–10(12)cm with coarse teeth. Inflorescence 5–8cm across. Fruit ovoid, 6–8mm, reddish, finally purple-black.
V. pauciflorum Mooseberry. USA, NE Asia. Shrub to 1.5m. Leaves broadly elliptic, lobes shallow or unlobed, 5–8cm. Inflorescence unusually small to 2.5cm across. Fruit nearly round, 7–9mm long, red.

AA *Marginal flowers of inflorescence enlarged and sterile. Fruit finally red, rarely yellow. Petiole glandular in upper part.*

V. trilobum Cranberry Bush. USA. Shrub to 4m. Leaves broadly ovate, 5–12cm, mostly glabrous beneath, toothed to almost entire; petiole glands small, not disc-like. Flowers with yellow anthers. Fruit broadly ovoid, 8–10mm, red.
V. opulus Rose Elder, European Cranberry Bush. Europe, N Africa, N Asia. Shrub to 4m. Leaves 3-lobed, round in outline, 5–10cm; petiole glands disc-like, large. Inflorescence more or less flat; flowers with yellow anthers. Fruit roundish, 8mm across, red. The wild form.
    var *roseum* Guelder Rose. A common horticultural form in which the flowers are all sterile in a globose inflorescence.
V. sargentii NE Asia. Shrub to 4m. Leaves broadly ovate, 7–15cm with 3 toothed lobes; petiole glands disc-like, large. Flowers with purple anthers. Fruit globose, about 8(10)mm across, dark red. Variety *flavum* has yellow fruits.

Group II: Leaves not lobed. Inflorescence either globose ('snowballs') or more or less flat-topped and then with enlarged sterile marginal flowers. Deciduous or partly evergreen.
V. macrocephalum 'Sterile' Chinese Snowball. China. Deciduous to partly evergreen shrub to 4m, winter buds without scales. Leaves elliptic to ovate-oblong, 5–10cm, stellate-pubescent beneath, the veins curving and uniting before reaching the margin. Inflorescence globose, 8–15cm, the flowers all sterile, each about 3cm across. The commonly cultivated form is *V. macrocephalum keteleerii* with flat inflorescence and only the marginal flowers sterile and enlarged.
V. plicatum 'Sterile' Japanese Snowball. China and Japan. Shrub to 3m, winter buds scaly. Leaves broadly ovate, 4–10cm, the margins sharply toothed, the veins straight

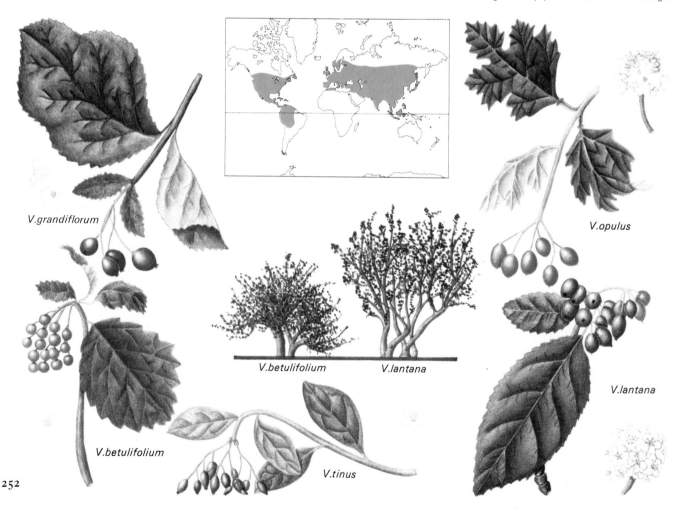

V.grandiflorum

V.betulifolium

V.betulifolium   *V.lantana*

V.tinus

V.opulus

V.lantana

and ending in a tooth. Inflorescence globose, 6–8cm, all flowers sterile. The commonly cultivated form. The wild form is *V. plicatum* var *tomentosum* (*V. tomentosum*) with flat inflorescence and only the marginal flowers sterile and enlarged. Fruit narrowly ovoid, red, finally bluish-black.

Group III: Leaves not lobed. Winter buds with 1–2 pairs of scales. Inflorescence more or less flat-topped and umbel-like with all flowers similar. Deciduous and evergreen species.

B *Evergreen species. Leaf veins curving and uniting before reaching margin except* V. japonicum.

V. tinus 'Laurustinus' SE Europe (Mediterranean region). Shrub to 5m. Leaves entire, ovate to oblong, 5–8cm, dark shining green above, 3-nerved at base. Inflorescence slightly rounded, 5–8(9)cm across; flowers sometimes pinkish, corolla lobes longer than their tube. Fruit ovoid, 6–7mm, dark blue to black. Much cultivated for its winter to spring flowering.
V. davidii W China. Shrub to 1.5m. Leaves elliptic to obovate, 7–13cm, faintly toothed about middle, 3-nerved at base. Inflorescence 5–7.5cm across; corolla lobes spreading, longer than their tube. Fruit ovoid, 6–7mm, blue.
V. cylindricum The Himalaya, W China. Shrub or tree to 13m. Leaves oval to oblong, 8–19cm, not 3-nerved at base. Inflorescence 8–12cm across; corolla lobes erect, shorter than their 4–5mm long tube.
V. japonicum Japan. Shrub to 2m. Leaves glabrous, broadly ovate to almost roundish, 7.5–15cm, dark shining green above, black dotted beneath, the veins extending straight into margin teeth. Inflorescence 7–10cm across; flowers fragrant, corolla lobes spreading or longer than their tube. Fruit broadly ovoid, 8mm, red.

BB *Deciduous species. Leaf veins extending straight into margin teeth, except* V. nudum *and* V. rufidulum.

V. nudum Smooth Withe Rod. USA. Shrub to 5m. Leaves elliptic, 5–12cm, the veins curving and uniting before reaching the almost entire margin. Inflorescence 5–12cm across, pedunculate. Fruit roundish, 8–10mm, bluish-black.
V. rufidulum Southern Black Haw. USA. Shrub or small tree to 10m, shoots with rusty down. Leaves shining dark green, elliptic-obovate, 5–10cm, rusty hairy below. Inflorescence sessile, 7–13cm across. Fruit ovoid, 12–15mm, dark blue. Attractive red fall foliage.
V. dilatatum China, Japan. Shrub to 3m; winter buds scaly. Leaves broadly ovate to obovate, 5–12cm, not 3-nerved at base, margin coarsely dentate, hairy above and below; petiole without stipules. Inflorescence to 12cm across on short peduncle with pubescent axes. Fruit roundish ovoid, 8–9mm, red. Attractive in flower, fruit and fall colors.
V. wrightii Japan. Shrub to 3m; winter buds scaly. Leaves broadly ovate to obovate,

Shoot tip of the Japanese Snowball (*Viburnum plicatum* 'Sterile') showing the sharp-toothed leaves and upright, flat-topped inflorescences with enlarged marginal flowers.

7–13(14)cm, not 3-nerved at base, margin coarsely dentate, pubescent only on veins beneath; petiole without stipules. Inflorescence 5–10cm across, peduncle short, axes virtually glabrous. Fruit roundish ovoid, 8–9mm, red. Handsome in fruit and striking fall colors.
V. betulifolium China. Shrub to 4m; winter buds scaly. Leaves elliptic-oblong to ovate, 3–8cm; petiole stipulate, 1–3cm. Inflorescence to 10cm across, on short peduncle. Fruit more or less globose, 6mm long, red.
V. erosum China, Japan. Shrub to 2.5m; winter buds scaly. Leaves ovate to obovate, 4–8cm, margin with sharp teeth; petiole less than 1cm, stipulate. Inflorescence to 8cm across on short peduncle. Fruit ovoid, 6–7mm long, red.
V. dentatum USA. Arrow-wood. Bushy shrub to 5m; winter buds scaly. Leaves broadly ovate, 3–7.5cm, coarsely dentate. Inflorescence to 8cm across on short peduncle, axes glabrous. Fruit broadly ovoid, 6–7mm long, bluish-black.
V. pubescens USA. Shrub to 3.5m; winter buds scaly. Leaves broadly ovate, 5–10cm, margin coarsely dentate; petiole without stipules. Inflorescence to 10cm across, more or less pubescent. Fruit broadly ovoid, 6–7mm long, bluish-black.
V. molle USA. Bushy shrub to 4m with flaky bark; winter buds scaly. Leaves broadly ovate, 5–12cm, margin coarsely dentate; petiole with stipules. Inflorescence 5–8cm across on long peduncle, the axes more or less pubescent. Fruit ovoid, 10–12mm long, bluish-black.

Group IV: As Group III but winter buds naked (no scales) and all deciduous species with stellate hairs and fine or coarsely serrate leaves (except *V. utile*), the veins straight ending in teeth.
V. lantana Wayfaring Tree. Europe, W Asia. Shrub to 5m. Leaves broadly ovate to oblong, 5–13cm, wrinkled above, densely tomentose beneath, margin with closely set teeth. Inflorescence 6–10cm across, corolla lobes longer than their tubes. Fruit ovoid to oblong, 8mm long, red, finally black.

Attractive for its flowers, fruits and fall colors.
V. veitchii C China, replacing *V. lantana*. Shrub to 2m. Leaves ovate-cordate, 7–12.5cm. Inflorescence 5–12mm across; corolla lobes longer than their tubes. Fruit ovoid, 8–9mm, red, finally black.
V. cotinifolium The Himalaya, replacing *V. lantana*. Shrub to 4m. Leaves ovate to rounded, 5–12.5cm. Inflorescence 5–8cm across; corolla lobes shorter than their tubes. Fruit ovoid, 8–9mm, red, finally black. Pleasing fall colors.
V. utile C China. Evergreen shrub to 2m. Leaves virtually entire, elliptic-ovate to oblong, 2.5–7cm, margin virtually entire. Inflorescence 5-rayed, 5–8cm across. Fruit ovoid, 8–9mm, bluish-black.

Group V: Leaves not lobed. Inflorescence not flat-topped but subglobose to more or less elongated, paniculate (cymose in the fragrant *V. carlesii*). Flowers all similar (no enlarged, sterile marginal flowers).
V. henryi C China. Evergreen (sometimes half-evergreen) shrub or small tree to 3m. Leaves elliptic to ovate or obovate, 5–12.5cm. Inflorescence broadly pyramidal to 10(12)cm long. Fruit ovoid, 6–8mm, red, finally black.
V. farreri (*V. fragrans*) N China. Deciduous shrub to 3.5m. Leaves elliptic to oval, 4–7cm. Inflorescence (2)3–5cm long, the very fragrant flowers appearing before the leaves, the tubular corolla 8mm long. Fruit red. Flowering may begin in late fall making a most welcome winter shrub.
V. grandiflorum The Himalaya. Shrub to 2m but sometimes a tree. Leaves elliptic oblong, 6–9(10)cm, apex acuminate, pubescent beneath on the 7–8 pairs of veins and in their axils. Panicle dense, pubescent, 5–7.5cm across; flowers white, tinged pinkish, 12–18mm across; corolla tube narrow, 12–13mm long. Fruit oval 12–13mm across, purplish black.
V. sieboldii Japan. Deciduous shrub or small tree to 3.5m. Leaves obovate, 6–12cm. Inflorescence 7–10cm long; flowers appearing with leaves, not fragrant, the corolla tube almost obsolete. Fruit ovoid, 10–12mm, pink, finally bluish-black.

Group VI: Hybrids.
V. × burkwoodii (*V. carlesii* × *V. utile*) Evergreen shrub to 2m. Leaves ovate, 3–10cm, glabrous above, densely hairy beneath. Flowers fragrant, at first pinkish, then white, 10mm across, the corolla lobes as long as their tube. Early spring flowering.
V. × carlcephalum (*V. carlesii* × *V. macrocephalum*) Deciduous shrub much like *V. carlesii*, but with larger globular inflorescence to 13cm across, the flowers fragrant, hardly tinged pink, the corolla tube only about 2.5mm long with exserted anthers. Spring flowering.
V. bodnantense (*V. farreri* × *V. grandiflorum*) Bushy deciduous shrub to 3.5m. Leaves narrowly elliptic to obovate, 3–10cm, glabrous beneath except for axillary tufts. Inflorescence more or less elongated, flowers fragrant, deep pink in bud, finally white, 10mm across, tube 7–10mm long Much favored for flowering late fall onward. F. B. H.

TREE CACTI

Many members of the cactus family, Cactaceae, attain tree-like proportions, and their massive candelabra or organ-like appearance adds a unique feature to landscapes of much of Mexico and the southwestern United States. Closest to a conventional woody tree is *Pereskia*, a genus regarded by botanists as the most primitive in the family, and characteristic of tropical forest regions rather than desert or semi-desert. The shoots, although bearing the felted areoles (pits) and spine clusters typical of all cacti, are only slightly succulent and there are large, flat, semi-deciduous leaves. The largest reach 20m (66ft) in height and are hence the tallest of all cacti.

The remaining tree cacti are almost or quite leafless, with much thickened stems that are initially green and have girder-like ribs bordered with areoles bearing spines and, later, flowers. The main trunk may be solitary or with a few erect side branches

Cereus cacti, such as the one shown here in a shrub habitat of northwestern Mexico, can reach over 6m (20ft) in height and have much-branched, column-like stems and a broad crown.

(*Carnegiea*) or much branched to form a broad crown (*Cereus, Pachycereus, Dendrocereus, Cephalocereus* and certain species of *Lemaireocereus* and *Echinopsis* (= *Trichocereus*), to name but a few). Because of the large development of water-storing tissue, mature specimens may weigh many tons, and mechanical strength comes from a hollow cylinder of wood in the form of a close network. The main trunk eventually replaces all its succulent tissue by wood, and may lose its spines and a secondary bark develops, so that its external appearance would be hard to tell from that of a 'normal' tree.

The large genus *Opuntia* also includes some species of prickly pear with a sturdy main trunk that qualify as small trees. Here the crown is composed of chain-like branches of flattened, disc-like joints. Some of the best-known of these tree-like opuntias occur on the Galapagos Islands in the Pacific Ocean, where small groves of these unusual plants still occur.

Cacti form relatively short taproots, even in the largest trees, and support comes from the long, shallow lateral roots that radiate in all directions from the base of the trunk. With the feeding roots mostly within a few inches of the surface, full use can be made of sudden heavy rains, flash floods and condensation from night dews.

Opposite The giant of all tree cacti is the Giant Sahuaro (*Carnegiea gigantea*) shown here in the Arizona Desert. They are slow-growing plants and have a single main trunk that may be branched to give the typical candelabra-like form.

The fluted ribs enable the stems to expand and contract like a concertina in response to variations in water content, without splitting.

Best-known of all tree cacti is *Carnegiea gigantea*, the Giant Sahuaro of southern Arizona, southeastern California and North Mexico. It is strictly localized to areas at altitudes of 200–1 000m (650–3 300ft) which have rocky or gravelly soil in which the surface roots can find adequate anchorage. It is slow growing and subject to so many natural and man-made hazards that at one time its survival seemed unlikely. However, in the areas now set aside as national parks it can still be seen by the thousand, a truly unique type of forest with associated flora and fauna all its own.

Cactus wood is light, fibrous and porous, very strong in relation to its mass. That of *Opuntia* is hard and contains so much silicon that it blunts tools used to cut it. Because of the attractive appearance of the network of perforations, it is mainly in demand for making trinkets and rustic ornaments. Wood of the larger columnar

Below Unusual tree-like cacti, *Opuntia echios* var *echios*, growing in a grove at Conway Bay, Santa Cruz, Galapagos islands.

cacti is slow to decay and finds local use for fencing and rafters. Gila woodpeckers build their nests inside the flesh of the Sahuaro, which reacts by sealing the cavity with a tough layer of cork. When the trunk dies and decays, the flesh rots leaving these boot-shaped nest linings which are used by the Pima Indians as water bottles.

At least nine genera of tree cacti produce edible fleshy fruits which are harvested and eaten raw, dried, made into syrup, jam or candy, or fermented to make wine. Most familiar are the prickly pears although the best come from shrubs rather than the tree-like species. Fruits of the Sahuaro are borne right at the top of the stems and are egg-shaped, 5–7cm (2–2.8in) long, and eventually split open to reveal numerous black seeds in a red pulp. To harvest them, Papago Indians use bamboo-like rods split

from the woody skeleton of dead sahuaros. *Pereskia* fruits are the 'Barbados Gooseberries' of the West Indies.

There are numerous minor uses of tree cacti reported. The small seeds of some are collected, ground up and made into meal. The expressed sap of the Sahuaro is said to make river water drinkable if added to it, by precipitation of the sediment. *Pachycereus pectenaboriginum* owes its name to the very spiny fruit and ribs which are said to be used as a comb. Excellent boundary hedges, impenetrable to man or beast, are possible with arborescent cacti. One way to make a hedge is to cut metre-long stems and plant them in a close row when they will root and grow. Finally, since cactus country is littered with the skeletons of long-dead plants, these form a ready source of wood for camp fires.

G. D. R.

MONO-COTYLEDON TREES

Monocotyledon trees are a kind of plant quite beyond the experience of persons brought up in temperate countries and contribute strongly to the overwhelming impression of strangeness and luxuriance of the vegetation felt on entering the tropics for the first time. All monocotyledonous trees have a certain similarity of appearance which reflects their underlying common characteristics and sets them apart from dicotyledonous (broadleaved) trees. They occur in several different Orders, mainly the Arecales, Pandanales, Zingiberales and Liliales. The stem structure with numerous scattered closed vascular bundles (that is without cambium) is fundamentally different from that of dicotyledons (see chapter What is a Tree?). With few exceptions they lack a secondary cambium. This means that no extra conducting

The fruits of the Coco de Mer Palm (*Lodoicea maldivica*) growing on the island of Mahé in the Seychelles. They are huge, weighing up to 23kg (50lb), and although not the largest fruit they contain the largest seed known in the world.

tissue is formed as the stem ages, and so the size of the crown and number of leaves it can bear is restricted. Moreover, stem thickness does not increase. Leaves usually have sheathing bases and are formed one at a time; this secures them an ample vascular supply. Roots cannot increase in size so increase in water and nutrient supply to the stem depends on an increase in their number; thus monocotyledonous trees characteristically have numerous, often fibrous, roots. Each node bears but one bud. The trunks of many monocotyledonous trees are unbranched, although some are sparsely branched and then the branching is usually dichotomous or apparently so. Most have big leaves, rather few in number.

A minority of monocotyledonous trees of the Liliales (for example *Cordyline*, *Dracaena*, some *Aloe*, *Yucca*, some *Vellozia* species) and *Nivenia* species (Iridaceae) have a special kind of secondary thickening. A cylindrical cambium forms around the inner cortex and this develops closed vascular bundles and secondary cortex. These trees have the same limitations to the development of an extensive root system and vascular supply to the leaves and they resemble in appearance other monocotyledonous trees.

The Palms

The palms (family Palmae or Arecaceae) are one of nature's greatest gifts to tropical Man, with a myriad uses. They form the biggest single group of monocotyledonous trees, with over 200 genera and nearly 3 000 species. Their occurrence is strongly centered in the tropics with some subtropical and a few temperate outliers. As a group they are easy to recognize from all other monocotyledonous trees although they share the same basic characteristics. They produce a few large leaves that are borne one at a time and clustered at the stem tip; they are erect and sword-like in the crown center when young. Leaf construction is more complex than in other monocotyledons. The blade is folded and usually split at the folds which are either displayed along an extended axis, as in the feather palms, or else arise crowded from a short central rib, as in the fan palms. A few species have no splits, and these entire-leaved palms are spectacular ornamentals. Aerial branching of the stem is rare; clump forming is common.

The biggest genus of palms, *Calamus*, some of its allies and a few unrelated palms are climbers, adapted to scrambling through forest by spines borne on leaves, leaf sheaths and the inflorescence. The stem of many commonly reaches 30m (100ft); the longest ever recorded was 169m (556ft) and it is claimed that another which was considerably longer was torn up by elephants before it could be measured.

There is great diversity in inflorescence from the huge terminal panicle of the Talipot (*Corypha umbraculifera*), reaching 6m (20ft) tall by 9–12m (30–40ft) across and containing several hundred thousand flowers, to tiny spikes (for example *Pinanga* spp). Most palms have the inflorescences borne laterally but in a few they are terminal: in these the stem accumulates starch which is expended in a single giant reproductive burst of flowering and fruiting, after which the tree dies. The flowers are small and basically have parts in threes but with much variation. Pollination is by insects or in a few cases (*Cocos*, *Elaeis*, *Phoenix* spp) by wind. Fruits are one or few-seeded and also vary greatly in size, from the Double Coconut (*Lodoicea maldivica*), biggest seed in the world, 45cm (18in) long and weighing 14–23kg (30–50lb), down to pea-sized. They are nearly all indehiscent and many are fleshy.

The greatest number of palms occur in the Asian tropics; Singapore, an island the size of the Isle of Wight, has more kinds than the whole of Africa. Latin America is the region with the second greatest number, including the highest concentration of primitive palms. Colombia probably has the richest palm flora of any single country. In Europe there are only two native palms, both Mediterranean, a species of Date Palm (*Phoenix theophrastii*) on Crete and the Dwarf Fan Palm (*Chamaerops humilis*), very familiar as an ornamental. In Asia the windmill palms (*Trachycarpus*) reach as far north as the southern Himalaya. The Chusan or Windmill Palm (*T. fortunei*) is unusual in withstanding frost and snow and is often cultivated in temperate areas. At the southern limit New Zealand has a single species of palm. Few palms occur wild on more than one continent; exceptions include raffia and the oil palms (*Raphia*, *Elaeis* spp) which span the Atlantic and four genera common to Africa and Asia (*Borassus*,

Opposite The Coconut Palm (*Cocos nucifera*) is probably the most familiar of all palms and to the temperate reader is a symbol of tropical beaches and holidays in the sun. To the local inhabitants it is a vital source of income, food and shelter. A trained monkey is seen here harvesting ripe fruits.

Calamus, Hyphaene and *Phoenix*) and both the Coconut (*Cocos nucifera*) and date palms (*Phoenix* spp).

Palms reach their greatest diversity and abundance in the humid tropics; for example Malaya has about 34 genera and 220 species. They are found from sea level to high in the mountains in all sorts of forest. Species of wax palm (*Ceroxylon*) reach over 4000m (13000ft) elevation in the Andes, above the tree line, and *Ceroxylon alpinum*, found to 3000m (10000ft) in Colombia, is one of the world's tallest trees, attaining 60m (200ft) – a splendid, eerie sight, towering over the dwarf mountain scrub. Palms occur in swamps, for example *Raphia* species in Africa, and a few in mangrove forests, namely *Nypa fruticans* and the Mangrove Date Palm (*Phoenix paludosa*) of Asia and *P. reclinata* of West Africa. Some palms are restricted to semi-deserts, most famous amongst these being the true Date Palm (*Phoenix dactylifera*).

Palms are a well-defined group of plants and are commonly classified as a single family, but this conceals the great diversity of the group, and in fact five separate natural lines can now be recognized, which have each evolved separate distinctive characteristics. The first group contains nearly all the fan palms (Coryphoid line) and many splendid ornamentals, for ex-

Nypa Palms (*Nypa fruticans*) growing among mangroves along the Santabong river, northwestern Borneo. This palm is one of the oldest flowering plants.

The Windmill Palm (*Trachycarpus fortunei*), from eastern Asia, is one of the hardiest of all palms and can be found in many temperate gardens, where, in a sheltered location, it can tolerate a certain amount of frost. It is seen here in a village high in the Cévennes Mountains, France.

ample *Acoelorraphe, Borassus, Corypha, Latania, Sabal, Washingtonia*. The second group has scaly fruits (Lepidocaryoid line) and contains most of the climbers (the rattans), raffia and the sago palms. The third group contains the single species *Nypa fruticans*. This is a very remarkable plant. It is one of the seven earliest flowering plants in the fossil record (dating back 100–110 million years to the Cenomanian) yet has extremely advanced characters of flower and inflorescence. It is now found only from the Bay of Bengal to the Solomon Islands but once grew along the shores of the Tethys sea and to West Africa and America; it is common in the Eocene London Clay flora. The fourth line contains the bipinnate fishtail palms *Caryota* and *Arenga* – the sugar palm genus. Finally, the fifth and most advanced line are the arecoid palms, a huge alliance of nine separate groups including the cocosoid group (Coconut, oil palms, Cohune Nut and a few climbing palms), the vegetable ivory palms (*Phytelephas* spp) of Latin America and the betel nut group (*Areca* spp). Many arecoid palms have the trunk topped by a crown shaft, formed of the erect sheathing bases of the leaves and several are as a consequence of this superbly ornamental, witness the Sealing Wax

Palm (*Cyrtostachys lakka*) in which the crown shaft is scarlet and the stately royal palms (the genus *Roystonea*) which grace many a tropical avenue. Several groups of the arecoid line have evolved diminutive palms of the forest undergrowth and some of which make fine house plants; familiar amongst them are members of the small genus *Howeia* of Lord Howe Island and species of the very big Amazonian genus *Chamaedorea*.

Many towns of the tropics and subtropics are graced by ornamental palms but relatively few species are widely grown and the full diversity remains to be exploited. There is great interest in the warmer parts of North America where the flourishing Palm Society is based; their journal *Principes*, devoted entirely to this one plant family, is a continuous source of information on all aspects of palms.

The uses of palms by Man stretches back into antiquity and is closely woven into the folklore of the countries where they occur. They provide many of the necessities of life, as well as the refinements of leisure – poles, planks, fruits, oils, fats, waxes, starch, sugar, wine, charcoal, medicines, magic, ritual and totem objects, perfumes,

poisons, alcohol, fiber, rattan canes, vegetable ivory, drinking vessels, dragon's blood, beads – the list is endless. Temperate Man has long imported palm products, for example the trade between the Malay archipelago and China is of great age, and during the last century or so has also stimulated the development of great plantations of a few species, mainly Coconut and oil palms; also the Carnauba Wax Palm (*Copernicia prunifera*) is cultivated in Brazil as a source of wax mainly for use in floor polish. Several other palms have potential for large-scale commerce and are likely to become economic as the price of energy from fossil-fuels increases in the future. The production of sugar and alcohol will probably be the first to become economically viable. Fibers are another possibility.

Palms are the pre-eminent source of thatch for tropical Man, and thatch from some species, for example sago palms (*Metroxylon* spp) and *Nypa fruticans* though not of Coconut, is durable for approaching 10 years. Palms also provide poles and planks and the cord to tie them together so that a completely palm-built house is commonplace. Palms are an important tropical source of sugar, prepared by bruising and cutting the young inflorescence then tapping the exuded fluid which continues to flow for many weeks and can be boiled to yield many pounds of sugar, or fermented to produce palm wine or toddy, which by distillation gives a truly potent spirit. The Sugar Palm (*Arenga pinnata*) is a principal source; like so many economic plants its native area

Royal Palms (*Roystonea regiq*) growing in a public park in New Delhi, India.

has never been located and it is only known in cultivation. Lontar or Tal (*Borassus flabellifer*), Coconut and *Nypa fruticans* are also extensively tapped.

The palms which flower just once accumulate starch in their trunks, and from many species this is extracted for human or animal food. The best-known is the Sago Palm (*Metroxylon sagu*) which is native to the Moluccas and New Guinea but now cultivated throughout the eastern tropics. Nowadays palm starch is for most peoples a famine food but in Borneo nomadic jungle dwellers still subsist on the sago of *Eugeissona utilis*. In South America some Indian tribes fell such palms, and return to them some months later to harvest insect grubs which develop in the decaying trunk – several pounds per tree. Millionaires' cabbage, palmito or heart of palm, are names applied to the edible apex of some palms; it is a crunchy, green-white vegetable reminiscent of celery. Harvesting destroys the stem, hence its name. This vegetable is especially eaten in South America where species of *Euterpe* are the main source. In a few palms this 'cabbage' is poisonous, for example *Orania* species, or irritant, for example *Caryota* species, but many can provide food for benighted jungle travelers. Oils and fats can be obtained from the fruits of some palms, pre-eminently Oil Palm and Coconut. Many palms have edible fruits though rather few are widely cultivated for this product, amongst them Salac (*Salacca edulis*) of southeast Asia; the Peach Palm (*Bactris gasipaes*) of tropical America, which is excellent when boiled (this is another palm which has never been found wild), and the Doum Palm (*Hyphaene thebaica*) of Africa and west Asia, which is unusual in its truly dichotomizing trunks and whose fruits taste of gingerbread.

Rattans, the climbing palms of the alliance of *Calamus*, are immensely important throughout the eastern tropics for a host of purposes – rope, furniture, baskets, mats, hammocks, cradles, blow pipes and dragon's blood resin (used in lacquer and medicine). They enter world trade and there is a steady market at high prices; commercial cultivation is only now commencing, as the source diminishes with continuing conversion of their rain forest habitat to agriculture. Palm fibers important in world trade are piassaba (*Attalea funifera* and *Leopoldinia piassaba*) of South America and raffia (*Raphia* spp) from Africa. The latter has the distinction of possessing the world's longest leaf, 23m (75ft) long. Walking sticks are pro-

A Date Palm (*Phoenix dactylifera*) in full fruit against a Mediterranean sky. The date is an important staple food in North Africa and the Middle East.

vided by Malacca Cane (*Calamus scipionum*), the ornamental small lady palms of the genus *Rhapis*, for example the China or Partridge Cane (*Rhapis excelsa*), and Penang lawyers, comprising the larger Malayan species of the genus *Licuala*. Vegetable ivory, once important for button manufacture, is produced from the hard endosperm of palm seeds, important sources being the South American genus *Phytelephas* and Asian *Metroxylon* (the Melanesian pidgin name Hebe Nut is a corruption of Ivory Nut). All these items of international commerce are produced from palms cultivated by villagers or gathered from wild jungle palms. Organized large-scale agriculture is based mainly on the Coconut which provides from its endosperm copra, which is a source of hard vegetable oil and cattle food, from the hard endocarp a very high-grade charcoal used in medicine and the food industries, and from the fibrous mesocarp, coir fiber for rope and matting. More recently Oil Palm has come to be very extensively cultivated, and in Malaya palm oil now vies with rubber in value as an export commodity. The earlier cultivation and breeding work was in West Africa, mainly in small village plantations.

The palms as a group truly then deserve their scientific group name, *Principes* – the princes of the plant kingdom – or in another idiom appealing to the adventurous plantsman 'palms are the big game amongst plants.'

Other Mono-cotyledonous Trees

As we have seen the palms are the largest group of monocotyledonous trees, but there are in addition dendroid groups in several other Orders of monocotyledons. These and the palms have certain important basic features of construction in common which is reflected in a general similarity of appearance, based on their simple stems or crowns with only one or a few orders of branching and rather few large leaves with sheathing bases.

The pandans or screwpines are an entirely tropical genus (*Pandanus*) with 600 species found throughout the Old World tropics. The scientific name comes from the Malay vernacular, and the English name refers both to the compound fruit, reminiscent of a pineapple, and the conspicuously spirally inserted leaves, stiff, leathery, pointed straps with toothed margins borne tightly at the branch tips. Several species have edible fruits and in the New Guinea highlands and some Micronesian islands have until recently been staple food items; there has been

The Joshua Tree (*Yucca brevifolia*) is a distinctive member of the vegetation of the deserts of the southwestern United States. It is seen here in the Mojave Desert, California.

The fan-like arrangement of the leaves and the ribbed stems makes the Traveller's Palm (*Ravenala madagascariensis*) an attractive ornamental which decorates many tropical parks and large gardens.

massive selection and very many different clones (forms) exist. Pandans are also important as a source of fibers for weaving and basketry and one (*Pandanus odorus*) has delicately fragrant leaves used extensively in Malay and Indonesian cooking. *Sararanga* is a related genus, with leaves in four ranks and small, simple fruits in big panicles.

The joshua trees (*Yucca* spp) and dragon trees (*Dracaena* spp) are probably the most familiar monocotyledon trees to inhabit temperate countries because they are cultivated outdoors in Mediterranean and other warm temperate climates, where winter frosts are slight or unknown. Their trunks reach large girth and the crown is formed of a dense mass of clusters of strap-like simple leaves on a few, rather stout dichotomizing branches. Yuccas are native to the southern United States, Central America and the West Indies and have developed a complex symbiosis with a moth which pollinates them and hatches its caterpillars within the ovary. Not all the species are trees. Dracaenas come from northern Africa and the Mascarenes. The famous specimen of the Dragon Tree of Tenerife (*Dracaena draco*) was blown down in 1868 when it was 21m (70ft) tall and 14m (45ft) in girth and supposedly 6000 years old. Dragon's blood, a red resin from the trunk, was known to the Greeks and Romans, and for long believed to come from an animal. These two genera have secondary thickened stems as do

Cordyline and the few tree species of *Aloe*. Some *Cordyline* have purplish or striped leaves and are familiar as ornamentals and house plants; in New Guinea they are totem plants. Most aloes are rosette plants and a few are trees; the genus is confined to the drier parts of southern Africa. The leaves are very fleshy and contain a bitter substance.

The grass trees of Australia (*Xanthorrhoea* spp) have numerous grass-like leaves arising from a trunk which is made up of the fibrous leaf-bases gummed together with a yellow resin which dries hard. They occur in fire-swept scrub and are sometimes called 'black boys' in allusion to the charred, blackened stem. The inflorescences are long terminal spikes. A few species of *Vellozia* reach tree size while others are low barely dendroid shrubs or herbs. The flowers are lily-like, on pendulous racemes.

The great Order of the gingers (Zingiberales) which includes the canna lilies and bananas, has a few tree members. The Traveller's Palm (*Ravenala madagascariensis*) is the most spectacular. Its leaves are banana-like and are displayed like a gigantic fan which is set apically on a stout trunk. The inflorescences are pendulous and few in number but large in size and borne in the leaf-axils. The name comes from the water trapped in the ensheathing leaf-bases – solace for the thirsty traveler. *Ravenala* is effective as a large-sized foil for a public building but planted in groups has the snag that as the tree grows and new

leaves form the plane of the fan slowly rotates, so that an initial effect of formality eventually becomes disarrayed as individual trees develop at differing rates. *Ravenala* comes from Madagascar where it forms huge thickets after felling of moist tropical forest. A very similar genus of two species, *Phenakospermum*, occurs in northern South America. A few species of *Strelitzia* develop trunks. This is a big African genus of mainly herbaceous species, also with banana-like leaves, whose showy flowers are subtended by equally showy bracts, and have copious watery nectar. The yellow, orange and blue colors are typical of bird-pollinated flowers. They are much grown as ornamentals in the tropics. Most strelitzias are herbs, as are the true bananas (*Musa* spp). The apparent stem of a banana plant is in fact the tightly enwrapped leaf-bases, held erect solely by turgor pressure. Eventually a flower stalk pushes its way up the center and produces the familiar terminal inflorescence that develops into a bunch of bananas.

One member of the pineapple family (Bromeliaceae) reaches tree-dimensions. This is *Puya raimondii* of the high equatorial Andes which develops the pineapple-like tuft of leaves apically on a stout stem and ultimately throws up a huge vertical inflorescence spike taller than a man. Also in South America occurs the only dendroid member of the great arum lily family Araceae. This is a swamp plant, *Montrichardia*, and grows in dense thickets at least 3m (10ft) tall, fringing water courses in the Amazon basin rain forests.

Finally we should mention the bamboos which have hard, woody, hollow stems and one of which reaches 18m (60ft) tall and 1m (3ft) girth. They are vitally important in the economy of the seasonally dry tropical countries where they are most abundant. Traditionally they provide building materials, conduits and food vessels, although nowadays there is a growing utilization of bamboos as a source of fibers and cellulose for modern industry including paper manufacture.

T. C. W.

Screw pines, *Pandanus kirkii*, growing along the coast of Kenya, East Africa. Note the prominent aerial roots at the trunk bases.

Left Xanthorrhoea species, 'grass trees,' growing in burned *Eucalyptus* woodland on Cape York Peninsula, Queensland, Australia. Bananas (*Musa* spp) are not in fact true trees since their 'stems' are not made of wood but tightly-packed leaf-bases. However, they reach the stature of small trees although are botanically classed as herbs. *Right Center* A plantation of banana 'trees' with young plants in the foreground and mature plants behind. *Right Bottom* In new plantations, bases of old banana 'trees' are planted from which suckers develop. Only one sucker is allowed to grow and fruits are formed in 12–15 months.

Trees of the Tropics

The tropics have a far richer diversity of trees than anywhere else on earth. Tropical trees have for centuries provided many fine cabinet woods and today provide most of the world's hardwood timber. They also provide many spices, gums, resins, latexes, fruits and medicines whose importance will increase in the future as fossil fuels become scarcer. Numerous tropical trees have spectacular flowers and are widely cultivated for ornament, many of them pantropically. No botanist can consider his education complete without acquaintance with the tropics. Violets and milkweeds grow on trees. The spurges are represented by hundreds of species and dozens of genera. Malaya has over 80 oaks, and whole families occur which are totally absent from the colder parts of the globe.

In the following sections we discuss the important economic and ornamental species from tropical Asia, Africa and America. Important species that are now grown pantropically will be mentioned in the context of their area of origin. The majority of species included are broadleaves; the other main group of monocotyledon trees, including the palms, has been covered earlier.

Opposite The Sal Tree (*Shorea robusta*) is an important source of timber in the Indian subcontinent. *Below* The flavouring mace is obtained from the dried red net-like aril surrounding the seed (nutmeg) of the Nutmeg Tree (*Myristica fragrans*).

TREES OF TROPICAL ASIA

Teak (*Tectona grandis*) one of the most famous and valuable of world timbers, grows wild in the monsoon forests of India, Burma, Thailand and Indochina and has for centuries been exploited, so much so that the more accessible forests have been exhausted. It is also planted there as well as in Java, to which island it was introduced over a millennium ago. Teak needs a climate with an annual dry season and will not grow in rain forests. These in Asia are currently one of the world's main sources of hardwood timbers, meranti or Philippine mahogony (*Parashorea* spp, *Shorea* spp), keruing or opitong (*Dipterocarpus* spp) and kapur (*Dryobalanops* spp) being prominent. These are all members of the single family Dipterocarpaceae, which is dominant in the western Malay archipelago. Export is largely to Korea and Japan for processing to plywood, which is then re-exported to the industrialized West. The monsoon forest tree Sal (*Shorea robusta*) of India, Pakistan and Bangladesh, is second to teak as an important timber in southern Asia. The rain forests too provide many other timbers, including one of the world's lightest ($47–77\mathrm{kg/m^3}$ – $3–5\mathrm{lb/ft^3}$) which comes from *Alstonia spathulata*, and was once used in the manufacture of 'pith' helmets, and fine cabinet woods, for example ebonies (*Diospyros* spp) and rosewood (*Dalbergia* spp) as well as many general purpose light hardwoods. From the peat swamp forests of Borneo comes ramin (*Gonystylus bancanus*) which is used

for mouldings. Nowadays, large areas of rain forest are being cut down and there is an increasing interest in plantations of trees to replace the natural source in the future as this becomes inadequate. Relatively few species are used for this purpose. Some are unfamiliar to the layman, although widely utilized in the tropics, for example *Gmelina arborea*. Others have familiar relatives, for example there are several species of pine tree in monsoon tropical Asia (*Pinus kesiya*, *P. merkusii*, *P. roxburghii*, *P. wallichiana*), and these are well-suited to be grown in infertile, seasonally dry places in the tropics and subtropics. From the rain forests have been selected two relatives of the Monkey Puzzle, the Hoop Pine (*Araucaria cunninghamii*) and Klinki Pine (*A. hunsteinii*) in the New Guinea forests, and another conifer genus, *Agathis*, a relative of New Zealand's famous Kauri Pine. In plantation all of these grow fast into well-formed tall trees and produce valuable pale, close-grained, knot-free timber.

Many of the world's spices come from Asia and mostly from trees. Indeed, outside interest in the Malay archipelago began with the spice trade, and led eventually to the Colonial era as European nations attempted to secure and monopolize the source of supply. Cloves (*Eugenia caryophyllus*) originate here, but are now mainly grown in East Africa, especially Zanzibar (though Indonesia is the principal market, for flavoring the distinctive local cigarettes). Nutmegs (*Myristica fragrans*) came from the Moluccas and the Dutch, having achieved a monopoly there, forbade export of live material only to find the fruits were transported elsewhere by the group of pigeons which are specialist feeders on the family. The wall of the nutmeg fruit provides the spice known as mace. Cinnamon is the peeled, dried and rolled bark of a few species of lauraceous trees of genus *Cinnamomum*, marketed as small cylinders known as quills. Production is greatest in Sri Lanka, from whence the highest grades come. The Seychelles is an important subsidiary center.

Western medicine has never exploited the full range of native Asian drug plants and few feature widely in trade but reserpine, from *Rauvolfia serpentina* is important in treating high blood pressure, producing very few side effects. Derris

comes from the roots of climbers and trees of the leguminous genus *Derris*, its use as an insecticide being first discovered by a surgeon in Singapore. Strychnine is obtained from several species of *Strychnos*, a genus of trees and woody forest climbers; *Strychnos nux vomica* is the main source. There has been more extensive exploitation of resins, gums, waxes and latex for the industrial world, currently at a low ebb with the advent of plastics based on petrochemicals, but with signs of renewed interest. Jelutong, a latex from the giant trees of the genus *Dyera*, is tapped in Malaysia and Indonesia, and is the principal component of bubblegum. Gutta percha is produced from latex, mainly of members of the family Sapotaceae. *Palaquium gutta* is the best source and the latex is extracted either from the leaves with hot water or from the bark. The only remaining use of gutta percha is for temporary dental fillings. Until recently it was used in submarine telegraph cables. It is a better insulant of heat and electricity than rubber. Resin from members of the Dipterocarpaceae and Burseraceae (Damar) and *Agathis* species (Manila copal) still has a small market for a few special-purpose varnishes and paints. In Indonesia pine plantations are used to produce turpentine. The dye gamboge yellow comes from resin produced by trees of the genus *Garcinia* and gives its name to the country Cambodia.

Asia abounds in fruit trees. Some are now cultivated throughout the tropics, for

example the Mango (*Mangifera indica*) of India to Thailand. Others are well-known throughout the region, for example the Rambutan and Pulasan (*Nephelium lappaceum*), Mangosteen (*Garcinia mangostana*) and Durian (*Durio zibethinus*). The last has achieved notoriety from its very strong flavor, likened by some to onion-flavored custard, and from its nauseating smell reminiscent of a malfunctioning sewerage works, but many would agree with A. R. Wallace that 'it is worth a trip to the East to sample a durian.' These fleshy fruits of the western end of the Malay archipelago are replaced eastward in New Guinea and the islands of the western Pacific by a group of nut-trees which are little-known outside their homelands, species of *Barringtonia* and *Terminalia* and of *Canarium* for oil as well as whole kernels. Kenari (*Canarium commune*) is also cultivated for its edible fruit wall in western Indonesia and traded to China.

Breadfruit (*Artocarpus altilis*) is indigenous to the eastern Malay archipelago, and Bligh was in the process of introducing

Tropical fruits that originated in Asia. *Left* The handsome foliage and dangling unripe fruit of the Mango Tree (*Mangifera indica*), now cultivated throughout the tropics. *Below Left* 'Worth a trip to the East,' said A. R. Wallace of the Durian (*Durio zibethinus*), whose strongly smelling spiny fruits each weighing over 1kg (2.2lb) are seasonally offered for sale by itinerant vendors throughout southeast Asia. *Below Right* The fruit of the Breadfruit Tree (*Artocarpus altilis*) contains 30–40 percent carbohydrate and is a staple food of many people of the Pacific islands.

TREES OF TROPICAL AFRICA

The edible fruits of the Indomalaysian Jackfruit (*Artocarpus scortechinii*) form on old wood, and are among the largest in the plant kingdom.

it to the New World at the time of the *Bounty* mutiny. A later attempt was successful. Its edible relatives are several and include the giant Jackfruit (*A. scortechinii*) of which an individual can weigh 25kg (55lb); these latter species are all fleshy and eaten fresh for their flavor rather than as a source of storable starch. Other tree fruits of the Asian rain forests are less well-known elsewhere, they include, to name only a few, Mata Kuching ('Cats' Eyes') (another *Nephelium*, *N. malaiense*), Rambai and Tampoi (*Baccaurea griffithii*, *B. motleyana*), Langsat and Duku (*Lansium domesticum*), Sentol (*Sandoricum koetjape*) and Petai (*Parkia speciosa*).

Ornamental tree species from Asia include a few grown nowadays as houseplants, such as the India Rubber (*Ficus elastica*) and *F. benjamina*, which in the wild is a banyan, and the crotons (*Codiaeum* spp).

Some of the loveliest tropical flowering trees originate in Asia. Pride of Burma (*Amherstia nobilis*) is often claimed the most beautiful of all. It was discovered in a Burmese temple garden in 1826 and soon became world famous. It has proved difficult to propagate and cultivate so remains rare. The flowers hang in racemes 0.6–0.9m (2–3ft) long; each is vermilion and yellow, and averages 20cm (8in) long by 10cm (4in) across. The tree has handsome pinnate leaves 0.9m (3ft) long, and the young leaves hang in brownish-pink tassels. Shower of Gold (*Cassia fistula*) is another beautiful leguminous tree of tropical Asian origin. This is easily grown

from seed and is now very commonly cultivated. It bears its big panicles of golden yellow flowers once or twice a year. The Apple Blossom Cassia (*C. javanica*) is equally lovely with a foaming mass of big pink-white flowers. Yet another legume, deservedly widely cultivated, is the Yellow Flame (*Peltophorum pterocarpum*) with rusty twigs and flower buds and erect yellow panicles later bearing purple-brown pods. This species is native on the coasts. Finally, *Lagerstroemia speciosa*, a tree member of Lythraceae, must receive mention for its lovely copiously-flowered mauve to pinkish panicles; the timber of this genus is highly prized for boat-building.

The most famous curiosities amongst Asian trees are the Upas or Ipoh (*Antiaris toxicaria*) and the strangling and banyan figs (see entry Figs). The former is, with strychnine, the main constituent of arrow poisons and knowledge of it was long withheld from Europeans; to forestall enquiry the myth was propagated that it killed all that came near it, a fantasy which gained extensive currency in Europe. It has a wide range throughout tropical Asia and in many forests is rare, but it is never found in the forest without tapping scars.

The dangling, colorful racemes of the Pride of Burma (*Amherstia nobilis*); it is a rare native of Burma but is commonly cultivated in tropical gardens.

African hardwoods have been the most important of tropical timbers imported into Britain and much of Europe in the last quarter century. Most buildings built since the Second World War have some on show as doors, paneling or stairs. Important kinds are African mahogany (*Khaya* spp), sapele and utile (*Entandophragma* spp) and *Guarea* species. These are all members of the mahogany family (Meliaceae) and come from the rain forests of West Africa. Other rain forest timbers important in international trade are obeche (*Triplochiton scleroxylon*, family Sterculiaceae), gaboon (*Aucoumea klainiana*, family Burseraceae) and *Afzelia* species (family Leguminosae). In addition afrormosia, the timber of *Pericopsis* (formerly *Afrormosia*) *elata*, another legume, has proved a fine substitute for teak for such purposes as laboratory benches, and iroko (*Chlorophora excelsa*, family Moraceae) is also used instead of teak, for example for garden furniture. Many of these timbers are used as facing veneers for plywood in which form their attractive grain and color is well-displayed. Some countries have already passed the peak of their supply, for example Ivory Coast, and in Nigeria the internal market now absorbs a high proportion of production. As the natural rain forests have rapidly become depleted, plantations are being established or alternatively young trees are being planted in lines in logged out forest. Species which need full light and grow fast are used for these purposes and these include several indigenous African species amongst which several *Terminalia* species (idigbo, afara, limba) and *Nauclea diderrichii* (opepe) are important as well, recently, as obeche. In the future these names will become increasingly familiar in the European timber trade. Tropical Africa has no indigenous species of pine tree and species from subtropical Asia and America are extensively planted as well as teak and the Asian *Gmelina arborea*. Tropical Africa also entirely lacks another important family of trees, the Fagaceae, which contains the oaks, beeches and sweet chestnuts.

The African equivalent of South American Balsa is the Umbrella Tree (*Musanga cecropioides*), a fast grower which comes up gregariously in big forest clearings and produces pale light timber. Like Balsa the timber is used for rafts and many village purposes, but it does not enter commerce.

Africa is a useful source of ebony, from some of the many species of the pantropical genus *Diospyros* which occur there (see separate entry).

Flame of the Forest or Flamboyant (*Delonix regia*), rivals the Asian tree *Amherstia nobilis* as the tropic's most glorious flowering tree. Both are members of the Leguminosae. *Delonix* originates in Madagascar and is reputed to have entered cultivation from a single village tree discovered by a missionary. It is now common everywhere in the tropics and subtropics. The flowers are produced once a year. They are vivid scarlet and borne copiously all over the shallow, domed crown. The foliage is finely feathery and briefly deciduous in seasonal climates. The pods are huge, flat and woody, 1m (3.3ft) or more long, borne in pendulous clusters and contain numerous seeds. The African Tulip Tree

Perhaps the strangest of tree floras of Africa can be found in the alpine belt of Kenya. Shown here are 'tree senecios or groundsels' Senecio johnstonii ssp barbatipes on Mt. Elgon.

(*Spathodea campanulata*, family Bignoniaceae) is the other big African ornamental species which is now a common sight throughout the tropics. The flowers are also bright red, but are tubular and with copious watery nectar. They are borne on the outside of the dark green crown and pollination is by bats. The leaves are large, pinnate and opposite. *Spathodea* flowers more or less continuously and this redeems the rather ungainly appearance of its ill-shaped, dense crown. The common red garden Hibiscus (*Hibiscus rosa-sinensis*), a small bushy tree found now in all tropical countries, is believed to have originated in east tropical Africa, but like many cultivated plants it has never been found truly wild.

The most important world tree crop of African origin is coffee. Both *Coffea arabica* and *C. liberica* are indigenous, to the mountain forests of Ethiopia and lowland forests of West Africa respectively; there are also several other species. Coffee is a small tree or shrub, found wild as a component of the forest undergrowth. The Horseradish Tree (*Moringa oleifera*), native from northeast Africa to India, is now widely grown as a village tree throughout the tropics. The roots, like true Horseradish, are a stimulant to digestion. The

Coffee (*Coffea* spp) is the most important world tree crop originating from Africa. *Above* Unripe coffee fruits. Each fruit is a drupe containing two seeds, which are the 'beans' of commerce. *Opposite Top* Coffee flowers. Coffee bushes only flower after rain, which has to be preceded by a drought.

seeds contain a saponin as well as up to 38 percent of an oil (Ben Oil) extracted locally for culinary purposes and once used for oiling clocks and watches. It is scentless, does not go rancid, is an excellent salad oil and makes a good soap. A common small tree of open savanna woodland is the Shea Butter Tree (*Butyrospermum parkii*, family Sapotaceae). The kernels are collected and from them an edible oil extracted which is widely used for cooking. It is a good substitute for lard and can be used for candle- and soap-making. The oil occurs at 45–55 percent by weight of the seeds. The bark of *Butyrospermum* yields a reddish gum, gutta shea. The Miraculous Berry (*Synsepalum dulcificum*) is another small tree or shrub of the Sapotaceae, native to West Africa where it is also commonly planted on farms and around villages. The sweet-acid pulp surrounding the seeds has a curious, powerful, lingering after-effect of sweetness. It has greater effect in sweetening acidity, such as sour fruits than in countering bitterness. Nevertheless even substances so bitter as quinine taste sweet if taken as much as an hour or two after it, hence the common name. *Synsepalum* has been investigated by Western chemists, although interest in sugar substitutes is now directed elsewhere, for example to the monocotyledon herb *Thaumatococcus daniellii* (Marantaceae) which is also from West Africa. The Sausage Tree (*Kigelia africana*, family Bignoniaceae) has a wide range in tropical Africa and is now sometimes cultivated elsewhere in the tropics. The big, hanging, sausage-like fruits and other parts have

various medicinal uses. The Kapok Tree (*Ceiba pentandra*, family Bombacaceae) is very common in tropical Africa and has many uses. It is in fact one of the largest trees of the continent, reaching 49m (160ft) tall and 2m (6.5ft) or more in diameter. It now grows wild as well as being cultivated, but was in fact introduced from America, probably by the Portuguese.

Finally, Africa, like the other tropical continents, has its contingent of curious and fantastic trees. In the Dark Continent many are weird by virtue of possessing huge, grossly swollen trunks. The most famous is undoubtedly the Baobab (*Adansonia digitata*) native to seasonally dry Africa and famous for four things. Firstly, Baobabs live to an enormous age; over 1 000 years has been measured by radio-

Another unusual tree of Africa – the Candelabra Tree (*Euphorbia candelabrum*) grows on the East African savannas and is allied to temperate spurges.

carbon dating and much greater ages by less precise methods. Secondly, the diameter of the trunk, which often reaches 9m (30ft) is out of all proportion to the height of only about 12m (40ft). Thirdly, Baobabs do not continue to grow in size year by year, and big trees may even shrink. This is attributed to periodic droughts. Finally, all parts of the plant are extremely useful, providing timber, fibers, leaves as a vegetable and acid seeds as an important source of vitamin C. The Cucumber Tree of Socotra (*Dendrosicyos socotrana*, only tree member of the cucumber family, Cucurbitaceae) is another weird and little-known 'bottle tree.' A species of *Adenium*, related to the Frangipani of America, also occurs on Socotra and it produces similar beautiful and fragrant flowers and poisonous white sap. There are about 10 species of *Adenium* in total, all African and all have swollen trunks.

In the savanna woodlands of central Africa a number of groups of trees have evolved with their trunks below ground and the leafy crown arising only a little above ground level. This example of convergent evolution in unrelated species is presumably an adaptation to periodic fires; the effect is of an underground forest. The drier parts of Africa also house big dendroid species of the spurge genus *Euphorbia*, with swollen, fleshy, sparsely branched stems, sometimes candelabroid in appearance. This is another example of convergent evolution, in this case the resemblance is to the New World cacti and is a response to aridity of the habitat. But euphorbias have white sap and thorns in pairs rather than clusters.

Finally, the African mountains are famous for two kinds of extraordinary trees, the tree heaths (*Philippia* spp and *Erica arborea*), which form a belt above the rain forests, high on the slopes of the big East African mountains, and which have no equivalent anywhere in the world. These mountains also have the giant groundsels and lobelias (*Senecio* spp and *Lobelia* spp) found above the level of continuous forest and which do have an equivalent in the Andes. Massive stems, big, terminally tufted leaves and lack of branching give these dicotyledonous trees belonging to highly advanced families a resemblance to the dendroid monocotyledons. Some aspects of their form can probably be regarded as a response to the extremely harsh climate they inhabit, although they have sometimes been reckoned primitive relics – hulks of the past history of flowering plant evolution.

TREES OF TROPICAL AMERICA

The true or South American Mahogany (*Swietenia macrophylla*) comes from the rain forests of tropical Central and South America where it is of widespread but usually scattered occurrence. Undoubtedly the most famous timber of the region, it has been sought out ever since the discovery of the New World. The logs are dragged down to a water course and then floated down river for export. Due to nearly five centuries of exploitation *Swietenia* is nowadays a rare tree in much of its range and its cultivation in plantations is seriously hampered by a shoot boring insect *Hypsipyla*. A second genus of the same family, Meliaceae, is of almost equal fame; this is *Cedrela* or the South American cedars, used amongst other things for cigar boxes (see also separate entry). A few other fine tropical American timbers enter world trade. Lignum vitae (*Guaiacum* species mainly *G. officinale*) provides the heaviest of all commercial woods (1 250kg/m^3 – 80lb/ft^3) and is also extremely strong and tough. It is used for bowling balls, pestles, mortars, pulleys and mallet heads. It is resinous and one of its most important uses is for the bushing of the stern tubes of ships' propellor shafts, as it combines the requisite strength with self-lubrication. Lignum vitae was once considered an important medicine. Rosewood comes from species of the legume genus *Dalbergia*. The very light wood balsa (*Ochroma lagopus*), weighing only 150kg/m^3 (10lb/ft^3) is the most important of all pale, light tropical timbers, finding a use in model making and formerly also in airplane construction.

There has not yet been such widescale felling of the forests of Latin America for the world timber trade as has taken place in Africa and Asia and this is because many of the tree species have dense, siliceous timbers and rather short, fluted or twisted trunks. It is still the case that only about 25 species out of the many hundreds which occur make up the bulk of the lumber coming from the whole Amazon rain forest, and of these about half comes from a nutmeg-relative *Virola*. Another fairly important Amazonian timber is jacareuba, from *Calophyllum brasiliense*, which is

The Silk Cotton Tree (*Ceiba pentandra*), whose seed pods (visible in the picture) yield kapok. This specimen, with its characteristically massive trunk, was photographed near Mombasa, Kenya, but the species is native to both Old and New World tropics.

also exploited in Central America, under the name of santa maria. Wallaba (*Eperua falcata*) and greenheart (*Ocotea rodiaei*) are other very heavy timbers which enter world trade. Trees which are beginning to become important for timber plantations are jequitiba (*Cariniana*), *Cordia* and *Leucaena* species (especially *Cordia alliodora* and *Leucaena leucocephala*) and probably much will be heard of them in the near future. But it is the Central American and West Indian pines, mainly *Pinus caribaea* and *P. oocarpa*, which have stolen the scene so far. These species of periodically burned savanna forests are now planted on a huge scale throughout the tropics and subtropics to provide fibers and cellulose, mainly for paper, and on a short rotation of less than 20 years. Central America is the headquarters of the world's oaks (*Quercus* spp) but although many species occur and there are extensive mountain forests they are unimportant in world trade.

Several world famous fruit trees come from tropical America. The Brazil Nut (*Bertholletia excelsa*) is a common, widespread tree of the Amazonian rain forest, regenerating after disturbance of the forest canopy. The individual nuts are borne in clusters inside a hard, woody case like a cannon ball. This species has the curious property of concentrating strontium in the endosperm storage tissues of the nuts, and for a time during the sixties the fruits were perceptibly radioactive due to the accumulation of part of the fallout from aerial atomic explosions. The nuts are collected wild from jungle trees for both local use and export. Avocado Pear (*Persea americana*) is another South American tree now widely grown and highly esteemed. *Theobroma* is a small genus of undergrowth trees

Jacaranda mimosifolia, from Argentina, is widely cultivated in the tropics and subtropics where it grows into gracefully branched trees up to 15m (50ft) tall which become covered by a mass of lilac flowers.

of the western Amazon rain forests and one species, Cacao (*Theobroma cacao*) is now extensively cultivated, mainly in West Africa. Others are grown locally in South America either for cocoa or for their comestible fruits. The range of *T. cacoa* was extended in pre-Colombian times, for it was an important crop for the Central American civilizations, and chocolate, from *chocolatl*, is one of the few Aztec derived words in the English language.

Papaya or Pawpaw is the rather bland fruit of *Carica papaya*, a sparsely-branched treelet with a terminal tuft of large palmately-divided leaves. Like so many crops its exact place of origin is unknown but all its wild relatives are tropical American. All parts have a white latex which contains the proteolytic enzyme papain, an important article of commerce, able to digest 35 times its own weight of lean meat. The Cashew Nut, fruit of *Anacardium occidentale*, originates from the West Indies and is also now cultivated pantropically. The kidney shaped nut is borne on a swollen fleshy receptacle, the Cashew Apple, which is red or yellow and juicy when ripe. The shell contains a highly irritant oil and the nuts are heated before extraction of the kernel to render this less caustic.

Para Rubber (*Hevea brasiliensis*) is of Brazilian origin. The story has been told many times how, in the mid 19th century, Wickham sent seeds to Kew where they were germinated and a few seedlings sent out to Malaya. Of the second consignment a few survived and on them the great rubber plantation industry of the Far East was founded. Recently, new introductions have been made to increase the genetic diversity for crop breeding and other species of the small genus *Hevea* have been studied, although none so far has such promise. Rubber cannot be grown as a pure crop in plantations in the New World because of a devastating leaf blight fungus. A huge prewar plantation company, which involved foundation of the town Fordlandia, failed; but very recently resistant races of tree have been bred. In the late 19th century a major industry grew up within the Amazon based on collecting rubber latex from wild trees, great fortunes were made and the wealthy merchants built elaborate mansions and a great baroque opera house in Manaus, the city of the central Amazon, to which leading European musical companies came on tour. The rubber boom collapsed once the Asian industry got started. Its traces can still be seen in the old part of Manaus and other Amazonian settlements.

The palm-like crown of a Pawpaw or Papaya Tree (*Carica papaya*), showing a cluster of developing fruits. Its precise area of origin is not known but its wild relatives are tropical American.

Minor forest products from tropical America include the dye haemotoxylin from the wood of a leguminous tree, *Haemotoxylon campechianum*; curare, a powerful nerve poison, from the indigenous *Strychnos* species; and chewing gum from the resinous latex (chicle gum) of *Manilkara* (*Achras*) *zapota*. This last is a tree of disturbed forest and is particularly common in Central America on the sites of Mayan and Aztec ruins, having established itself after these habitations were abandoned. *Manilkara zapota* produces an edible fruit, known as the Sapodilla Plum,

Flowers of the White Frangipani Tree (*Plumeria alba*), a beautiful tropical American tree now grown as an ornamental throughout the tropics. The flowers have an exquisite, heavy fragrance.

and is nowadays cultivated throughout the tropics. Fruits of local importance within the region include two palms, the Babassu (*Orbignya speciosa*) and Peach Palm (*Gulielma gassipaes*). Allspice, native to and cultivated in the West Indies, is the rapidly dried unripe fruit of the small tree *Pimenta officinalis*.

Tropical America vies with Asia in the number of superb ornamental flowering trees which originate there. It is the home of some 50 species of the genus *Jacaranda* which have lilac flowers and feathery foliage, of several coral trees (*Erythrina* spp) with their big robust, red or yellow bird-pollinated flowers and of the lovely leguminous tree 'Rose of Venezuela' (*Brownea grandiceps*) with its spectacular heads of deep pink to red blossoms, tightly packed as in a *Rhododendron*, and showy hanging tassels of young pink leaves. The Sandbox Tree (*Hura crepitans*) a relative of the Brazil Nut, is a curiosity of many tropical botanic gardens, with its massive, fleshy, asymmetric flowers crowded on trunk-borne racemes. Napoleon's Button (*Napoleona heudottii*) is another lesser-known relative, as is the Cannon Ball Tree (*Couroupita guianensis*). The Brazil Nut family (Lecythidaceae) is in fact concentrated in the New World tropics. The Buttercup Tree (*Cochlospermum vitifolium*) is aptly named, its brilliant yellow flowers, borne on the bare crown, are each 10–11.5cm (4–4.5in) across. The leaves are deeply palmately lobed and covered below with stellate hairs and the capsule contains numerous small seeds covered with a long white cotton-like floss. But perhaps the most lovely of all tropical American ornamental trees are the frangipani trees (*Plumieria alba* and *P. rubra*). These are small open-crowned trees bearing masses of white or red blossoms of an exquisite, heavy fragrance and are now found planted everywhere in the tropics. In the East they have become associated with temples and burial grounds. Broken parts of the plant exude a copious white latex to which medicinal properties have been attributed.

Other useful trees now planted throughout the tropics are *Gliricidia sepium*, a small, short-boled leguminous species with pale lilac flowers, valuable as a shade tree and for enriching the soil by nitrogen fixation, and the Rain Tree (*Samanea saman*), one of the most useful of tropical shade trees and one which also produces a dark, heavy, stable wood in great demand for turnery. The dried leaves have the heavy, new mown hay scent of coumarin. The name derives from 'to kill a dormouse'

and alludes to the use of scented hay to mask the flavor of rodent poison.

The Kapok Tree (*Ceiba pentandra*) is native to the Amazon region, and is indeed the tallest tree of the hylaean forest, often seen from the rivers as a giant emergent standing head and shoulders above the main forest canopy. It has now become wild in tropical Africa and is widely planted in Asia. The big leathery capsules contain kapok as a covering to the seeds.

To South America goes the distinction of having the tree that grows at the highest altitude – *Polylepis* forms low forests close to the snowline in the equatorial Andes, though these have now been largely removed for firewood and replaced by paramo steppe. In the paramo occurs the giant *Puya raimondii* (see Other Monocotyledonous Trees). Elsewhere in the high Andean paramo occur *Espeletia*, sparsely branching tree composites, the New World counterpart of the African giant groundsels. Weird trees of the mountain and lowland forests are *Clusia*, many of whose species are stranglers like the figs of Asia. Perhaps the most curious tree of all, however, is the Cow Tree of Venezuela (*Brosimum galactodendron*) which is a member of the fig family (Moraceae) and exudes a milky latex in considerable quantity from the cut bark, which has the taste of ordinary milk and is used for just the same purposes.

T. C. W.

'Fruiting' body of the Cashew Tree (*Anacardium occidentale*). Both the red, fleshy receptacle – cashew apple – and the kidney-shaped protruding nut – cashew nut – are edible, the latter after roasting.

Identification of Trees

The following tables are keys to the families and genera of conifers and broadleaves covered in this book. For both groups identification of the family is required before moving on to the keys to genera. Most couplets are dichotomous (eg **3, 3** or **A, AA**) but in cases where there are three or more statements to each couplet a vertical arrow is used to indicate that there is an extra statement to consider (eg **4, 4↓, 4** or **B, BB↓, BBB**). Page numbers following genus diagnosis indicate the first page of the main entry within the book and from there, in many cases, species identification can be made where tables are provided.

Key to Conifer Families

1 Female inflorescence a typical cone comprising a few to many ultimately woody cone-scales and maturing numerous seeds. An important exception is *Juniperus* (junipers) in which the 3–8 cone-scales unite, become fleshy and form the well-known juniper berry-like fruit with one or more seeds: **2**

1 Female inflorescence, or 'cone,' of relatively few scales (about 10 or fewer) which ultimately are fleshy and mature usually 1, sometimes 2 seeds which may be more or less surrounded by whitish or colored aril or epimatium. Sometimes the seed is borne on a receptacle composed of a number of fused sterile bracts: **4**

2 Mostly dioecious species; leaves mostly lanceolate to ovate with many veins but without midrib; pollen sacs often long (to 20cm), more than 10; pollen wingless; each cone-scale a single structure, not comprising a more or less distinct bract- and ovuliferous-scale; only a single ovule per cone-scale; seeds winged or not: ARAUCARIACEAE

2 Not this combination of characters; pollen sacs fewer than 10: **3**

3 Typically monoecious species; leaves linear, single, in fascicles of 2–5(8) or clusters of more than 10, spirally attached as are the cone-scales; pollen winged; bract-scales and ovuliferous-scales clearly distinct, each of the latter with 2 inverted ovules; seeds usually winged: PINACEAE

3↓ Typically monoecious species; leaves linear or awl-shaped, spirally arranged but pairs of connate leaves in whorls of 10–30(40) in *Sciadopitys* and opposite in *Metasequoia*; bract- and cone-scales more or less fused together, spirally arranged, each fused structure with 2–8(9) erect or inverted ovules; pollen wingless: TAXODIACEAE

3 Monoecious or dioecious species; leaves typically scale-like and adpressed in decussate pairs, rarely in whorls of 3 or in 3 ranks, rarely linear, but not uncommonly linear in juvenile forms; cone-scales uniform without distinction between bract- and ovuliferous-scales; ovules one or more on each scale; pollen wingless: CUPRESSACEAE

4 Monoecious or dioecious species; leaves typically spirally arranged, variable: scale-like, linear, more or less lanceolate, oblong, functionally replaced by phylloclades in *Phyllocladus*; 'cones' with 1 or more sterile fleshy bracts, a few upper fertile scales, each with an inverted ovule more or less enclosed by an epimatium (except *Microstrobos*); 'cone' often borne on a much swollen fleshy receptacle (*Podocarpus, Acmopyle*); seed often with basal cup-like aril; pollen sacs 2; pollen with 2–4 wings: PODOCARPACEAE

4↓ Dioecious species with opposite or whorled branches; leaves spirally arranged on vertical shoots, 2-ranked on laterals, linear lanceolate, lower surface with numerous stomatic lines grouped into 2 whitish bands on either side of the midrib; 'cone' of a few decussate pairs of scales each scale with 2 ovules; typically each 'cone' matures a single seed rather like a green olive; pollen sacs 3; pollen wingless: CEPHALOTAXACEAE

4 Dioecious species; leaves more or less linear, spirally attached (more or less opposite in *Torreya, Amentotaxus*), generally appearing 2-ranked in the same plane; 'cone' (very un-cone-like) of several sterile bracts and a single terminal erect ovule; seed partially or almost wholly enclosed by a whitish, orange or scarlet aril; pollen sacs 2–8(9); pollen wingless: TAXACEAE

Key to Conifer Genera by Families

PINACEAE

1 Leaves needle-like, arranged at least on short shoots, in clusters, but not in whorls: **2**

1 Leaves solitary and not in whorls: **5**

2 Needles on short shoots in fascicles of 2–5(8) – a single needle occurs in *Pinus monophylla* – and typically more than 2.5cm long: *Pinus* (p 65)

2 Needles on short shoots in clusters of 10–30(40): **3**

3 Needles dark green and evergreen mostly less than 2.5(3)cm; cones barrel-shaped 5–12cm long, the scales falling away at maturity (after 2–3 years): *Cedrus* (p 79)

3 Needles pale (yellowish) green and deciduous; cones smaller: **4**

4 Bud-scales shortly tapering to a point; male cones in clusters, female cones maturing in one year, the scales then falling away: *Pseudolarix* (p 79)

4 Bud-scales blunt at the apex; male cones solitary; female cones maturing in one year but the scales not then falling away: *Larix* (p 76)

5 Cone with prominently exserted bract-scale, trifid at apex; crushed foliage with characteristic pineapple or citronella smell (not typically resinous); leaves virtually sessile, the leaf bases not obviously decurrent, the bare shoot more or less smooth; winter buds characteristically pointed rather like beech (*Fagus* spp) buds: *Pseudotsuga* (p 75)

5 Not this combination of characters; bract-scales neither exserted nor trifid: **6**

6 Shoots more or less smooth, the circular leaf-scars not in relief; leaves mostly flat; cones always erect: **7**

6 Shoots rough with inclined leaf-scars or from the persistent more or less decurrent and woody leaf bases of fallen needles; cones always pendulous or at least reflexed: **8**

7 Needles grooved on upper surface, the lower surface typically with whitish stomatal bands; cone-scales falling away from axis at maturity: *Abies* (p 71)

7 Needles keeled on upper surface, the lower surface pale (yellowish) green; cone-scales not falling away at maturity: *Keteleeria* (p 81)

8 Needles flat with one resin canal, their short (1–2mm) petioles more or less closely adpressed against the shoot and leaving a more or less semicircular scar; main branches more or less alternating: *Tsuga* (p 74)

8 Needles mostly quadrangular with 2–4 resin canals, sessile on raised decurrent leaf bases and falling to leave a more or less diamond-shaped scar; main branches commonly in (false) whorls: *Picea* (p 68)

TAXODIACEAE

1 Needles 5–10–15cm long, fused in pairs back to back for the whole of their length and with a longitudinal furrow, there being 10–30(40) such pairs arranged in whorls on the shoots: *Sciadopitys* (p 85)

1 Leaves single, not fused in pairs or arranged in whorls: 2

2 Foliage evergreen, bark fibrous spongy, brown to reddish-brown, ultimately shredding, the leaves dark green: 5

2 Foliage deciduous, but semievergreen in *Taxodium mucronatum* which is rare in cultivation; bark different from above, the leaves typically pale (yellowish) green: 3

3 Leaves and branchlets opposite, the leaves linear and branchlets of one kind only: *Metasequoia* (p 82)

3 Leaves and branchlets not opposite: 4

4 Branchlets of 2 kinds: the upper ones persisting, with axillary buds and more or less radially arranged subulate leaves, the lower branchlets deciduous, lacking axillary buds, the leaves 2-ranked in one plane; cone globose to ovoid, stalk short, about 3mm long: *Taxodium* (p 83)

4 Leaves on upper nonfruiting branches 8–13mm long in 3 ranks; those on lower or fruiting branches scale-like; cone obovate, stalk 10–18mm long: *Glyptostrobus* (p 87)

5 Leaves alternate of two kinds: spirally arranged, scale-like, adpressed to slightly spreading, or linear-lanceolate and 2-ranked in one plane, with petiole; cone-scales peltate, nor more than 20: *Sequoia* (p 82)

5 Leaves uniform of one kind only: 6

6 Leaves scale-like, spirally arranged, adpressed or slightly spreading; cone-scales peltate, more than 25: *Sequoiadendron* (p 82)

6 Not this combination of characters; cone-scales flattened-imbricate, each scale with 2–5 seeds: 7

7 Leaves awl-shaped, curved toward shoot, 1–3cm long, apex not spiny, spirally arranged in 5 ranks; bark fibrous spongy; cones globose 1.5–2.5cm across with 20–30 scales, each scale with a recurved mucro and a 3–5–spined crest on upper margin; ovules erect: *Cryptomeria* (p 86)

7 Not this combination of characters: 8

8 Leaves *either* scale-like 1–2(3)mm long, more or less adpressed to shoot and very crowded, *or* up to 10mm(12) and more or less spreading and less crowded; leaf apex sharp-pointed enough to puncture skin; cone globose with 10–16 scales, each scale with 3–6 inverted ovules: *Athrotaxis* (p 86)

8 Leaves more or less distant, margin serrulate, 1.5–6.0(7)cm long, more or less curved linear-lanceolate, base broad, decurrent, spirally arranged but appearing more or less 2-ranked in one plane; cones more or less globose, the scales each with an eroded margin and bearing 3 inverted ovules on the upper surface below a toothed ridge: *Cunninghamia* (p 84)

8 General habit of *Cunninghamia*; leaves densely crowded and more or less awl-shaped, margin entire, curved toward shoot, 3-sided, 5–6(7)mm long when adult with stomatal bands on all sides; cones oblong or subglobose, 12–20mm long with numerous scales, each scale with 2 erect ovules on upper surface: *Taiwania* (p 87)

ARAUCARIACEAE

1 Leaves with parallel venation and without conspicuous midrib, spirally arranged, sometimes imbricate, small and scale-like or awl-shaped and then mostly less than 2cm long, or flat and broad and then up to 5cm long (to 10cm in 3 species from New Guinea); terminal bud inconspicuous, male cones up to 20cm long; female cones large, of numerous woody scales each with apical point and united with it, mostly wingless; seed solitary on each scale and united with it, mostly wingless; generally monoecious: *Araucaria* (p 87)

1 Leaves opposite or alternate, but often appearing 2-ranked, flat, lanceolate-elliptic to ovate with numerous more or less obsolete veins without conspicuous midrib; male cones less than 5cm long; female cones large with numerous woody scales but no apical point; seed solitary on each scale but not united with it, with a single wing but sometimes a rudimentary second; monoecious or dioecious: *Agathis* (p 89)

CUPRESSACEAE

1 Fruit indehiscent and berry-like of 3–6(8) finally fleshy united scales enclosing 1–12 wingless seeds; leaves either scale-like, crowded, closely adpressed and opposite or needle-like or awl-shaped and spreading in whorls of 3 (always this type on young plants): *Juniperus* (p 97)

1 Fruit a woody more or less typical cone, the scales finally separating to release the seeds: 2

2 Cone more or less globose of 3–8 pairs of woody, valvate, peltate scales: 3

2 Cone more or less elongated, ovoid to oblong, the scales flat, not peltate: 5

3 Scale leaves in whorls of 4 arising at same level, about 2mm long: facial leaves narrowly oblanceolate with pointed apex, lateral leaves ovate and somewhat compressed; cones almost globose, 25 × 20mm, with 12–16 scales; fertile scales with 2 seeds having very unequal wings: *Fokiena* (p 100)

3 Not this combination; leaves scale-like, opposite and decussate; seeds more or less winged: 4

4 Cones of 6–12 peltate scales and ripening in the second year; each scale with 6–20 ovules: *Cupressus* (p 89)

4ᴵ Cones typically of (4)6–12 peltate scales and ripening within the year except *Ch. nootkatensis* which mature in the second year; each scale with 2–5 ovules; wings of seed more conspicuous than in *Cupressus*: *Chamaecyparis* (p 92)

4 A much cultivated quick-growing inter-generic hybrid with the foliage of *Chamaecyparis nootkatensis* and the cones of *Cupressus macrocarpa*. Foliage often in flattened sprays, but not always: × *Cupressocyparis* (p 91)

5 Leaves in whorls of 3, scale-like to 3mm long, incurved with pointed tip and borne on shoots more or less round or square in cross section; cone globose 8(10)mm across, of 3 whorls of more or less alternating scales, each whorl having 3 slightly overlapping scales, the upper whorl always fertile, the lower sterile, the middle whorl sometimes fertile; fertile scales with umbo, each scale with 2–6 seeds, each seed with 2–3 wings: *Fitzroya* (p 99)

5 Not this combination of characters; leaves and cone-scales opposite: 6

6 Scales leaves minute (1mm long) and adpressed, mostly decussate, sometimes in whorls, more or less keeled and with blunt point; shoots more or less round or square in cross section; sexes on different plants; cone small of 2 pairs of scales on a stout central axis, only the upper pair fertile, each scale with 2 3-winged seeds: *Diselma* (p 100)

6 Not this combination of characters: 7

7 Cone-scales clearly imbricate; scales not in whorls of 3 or 4: 8

7 Cone-scales not imbricate, laterally adpressed and separating from above downward as valves; scales in pairs or whorls of 3 or 4: 11

8 Cone reflexed of 3–5 pairs of scales, each scale with 3–5(6) winged seeds on its lower surface; branchlets much flattened; leaves broadly elliptical, 5–6mm long: *Thujopsis* (p 94)

8 Each cone-scale with not more than 2 unequally winged seeds beneath each scale, wingless in *Thuja orientalis*: 9

9 Cone pendulous of (3)4–10 pairs of scales, 2–3 middle pairs fertile: *Thuja* (p 93)

9 Cones composed of 2–3 pairs of scales: 10

10 All the leaves of equal length and long decurrent; cones erect, each of 3 pairs of scales with subapical recurved spine, the lowest pair small, recurved, middle pair alone fertile, the upper fused together: *Calocedrus* (p 95)

* For most species commonly in cultivation, the branchlet foliage of *Chamaecyparis* is arranged in more or less flattened sprays (phyllomorphs) and the cones do not exceed 10mm across; in *Cupressus*, the branchlet foliage is in more than one plane and the cones are 2–3cm across. Exceptions are *Cupressus torulosa, C. funebris* and *C. lusitanica* var *benthami* – all with flattened sprays of foliage and cones 8–16mm across.

10 Facial leaves bluntly diamond-shaped, smaller than laterals, scarcely 1mm long; laterals incurved awl-shaped 1.5–4.5mm long: *Austrocedrus* (p 96)

11 Cones with 6–8 scales arranged in whorls of 3 or 4: 12

11¹ Cones with 4 scales in 2 pairs: 13

11 Cones with 3 whorls each of 3 scales: *Fitzroya* (see 5 for further details) (p 99)

12 Scale leaves in ranks of 3; cones with 2 whorls, each of 3 scales; seeds 2–9 on each scale, each with 1–3 broad wings: *Callitris* (p 97)

12 Scale leaves arranged in 8 vertical rows; cones with 2 whorls, each of 4 scales; seeds virtually unwinged: *Neocallitropsis* (p 100)

13 Lateral and facial (especially juvenile) leaves different (dimorphic): 14

13 Adult leaves at least not dimorphic: 16

14 Branchlets flattened (phyllomorphs); the shoots appearing jointed owing to the scale leaves barely overlapping, the lateral leaves the larger and long decurrant; cone terminal and globose, 8–12mm across, outer surface of scales deeply grooved; seeds with 2 broad wings, widening upward: *Tetraclinis* (p 100)

14¹ Cone leathery, the upper pair of scales 2–3 times longer than lower pair and all with a triangular basal appendage (below middle); lateral leaves 4–5mm, the facial shorter: *Papuacedrus* (p 96)

14 Not the respective characters of the above two genera, but foliage in more or less flattened sprays (phyllomorphs): 15

15 Cone-scales with curved dorsal mucro; only 1 seed per fertile scale; stomata on both sides of leaf: *Libocedrus* (p 95)

15 Cone-scales with minute dorsal boss; 1 or 2 seeds per fertile scale; facial leaves about one-quarter length of the laterals, the latter to 4.5mm with longitudinal groove on both sides; stomata virtually confined to lower leaf surface: *Austrocedrus* (p 96)

16 Fertile scales of cone similar, each with 5 or more ovules; seeds 12 or more per cone, each seed 2-winged: *Widdringtonia* (p 100)

16 Ovules and seeds 1 or 2 per cone-scale: 17

17 Leaves about 1mm long, more or less keeled; cone with conspicuous central axis; each upper fertile cone-scale with 2 ovules; seed 2mm long, a little longer than its scale and with typically 3 wings: *Diselma* (p 100)

17 Leaves about 2mm long, with white stomatal bands and more or less keeled; cone with inconspicuous central axis, 1 ovule per fertile cone-scale with 2 very unequal wings: *Pilgerodendron* (p 96)

PODOCARPACEAE

1 True leaves scale-like, found only on seedlings; replaced by expanded branchlets (phylloclades) which may be simple and leaf-like and spirally arranged or lobed or pinnate and arranged in whorls, both types up to about 5 × 0.75cm; cones irregularly more or less globose about 6–13mm across, of one or more fleshy scales, each scale with a protruding arillate ovule; seeds more or less ellipsoidal, small, about twice as long as its scale; 'cone' often colored green or red: *Phyllocladus* (p 105)

1 Branchlets not expanded; leaves not replaced by phylloclades: 2

2 Tree with branchlets opposite or in whorls of 3 or 4; leaves linear, spirally arranged but characteristically twisted and curled 12–18mm long, tapering to sharp, horny point, and lower surface with a broad, whitish stomatic band on each side of the midrib; 'cone' irregularly globose finally fleshy, 8–13mm across, of a few pyramidal furrowed scales, the upper scales each with 2 inverted ovules; seeds flattish, ovoid, 3–4mm long, brown and shiny: *Saxegothea* (p 104) (cultivated specimens in the absence of fruit are often mistaken for *Podocarpus andinus* and *vice versa*.)

2 Not this combination of characters: 3

3 Bushes or shrubs with overlapping scale-like leaves up to 2.5mm long; scales of 'cone' fleshy either of 4–8 scales with erect ovule (epimatium absent), seed without aril or more than 8 scales and inverted ovule, the seed with scarlet aril (epimatium present): 4

3 Other character combinations; mostly trees: 5

4 'Cone' 6–9mm long, of more than 8 scales, each scale finally with an inverted arillate seed (epimatium present): *Microcachrys* (p 105)

4 'Cone' 2–3mm long, of 4–8 scales; ovule erect, seed not arillate (epimatium absent): *Microstrobos* (p 104)

5 Epimatium free from the integument of the ovule; ovule at first inverted, finally more or less erect; 'cone' of 1–8 scales, each scale with a solitary ovule; seed shed with attached short basal cup-like aril: *Dacrydium* (p 102)

5 Epimatium joined with the integument of the ovule; seed often borne on a fleshy receptacle: 6

6 Foliage like *Taxus* (yews) of sessile linear leaves about 0.5–2cm × 2–3mm, appearing 2-ranked in one plane; ovule erect, borne on a fleshy receptacle of 7–9 fused scales, only the upper scale fertile and maturing a single seed; epimatium shorter than seed: *Acmopyle* (p104)

6 Leaves very variable in shape and texture, size from small and scale-like up to 30 × 5cm; 'cone'-scales mostly 2–4, but may be more, only 1 or 2 fertile and bearing a single inverted ovule of which only one matures to a seed; remaining sterile scales often, but not in all species, fused together to form a fleshy, edible, colored receptacle; the epimatium is well developed and surrounds the whole seed and falls with it: *Podocarpus* (p 101)

CEPHALOTAXACEAE
Only one genus: *Cephalotaxus* (see family diagnosis) (p 105)

TAXACEAE

1 Leaves opposite, linear-lanceolate, 3–13.5cm long, with raised midrib on both surfaces, that on lower surface flanked by whitish stomatic band; seed surrounded by more or less orange aril open at the top; male inflorescence pendulous: *Amentotaxus* (p 109)

1 Not this combination of characters; leaves inserted spirally: 2

2 Leaves linear, 7–15cm long and up to 3.5mm wide, spirally arranged; male cones in dense axillary spikes 12–16mm long; seed 12–16mm long, ovoid to ellipsoidal, enclosed, except at extreme tip, by a fleshy aril: *Austrotaxus* (p 109)

2 Not this combination of characters; male inflorescence never in spikes: 3

3 Stalk of male inflorescence with 8 decussate, sterile, more or less ovate scales 2–3mm long; the ovule-bearing stalk similar but with 16–18 scales, the uppermost 4–5mm long and surrounding the ovule; aril cup-shaped, white; leaves twisted at base and appearing 2-ranked in same plane, linear 12–25mm long: *Pseudotaxus* (p 109)

3 Not this combination of characters: 4

4 Leaves linear, yellowish-green beneath without stomatic bands or lines, rarely exceeding 25mm long, spirally inserted but often, though not always, appearing 2-ranked; seed surrounded to just above the middle by scarlet aril: *Taxus* (p 107)

4 Leaves 12–80mm long, linear to linear-lanceolate, sharply pointed, lower surface with one longitudinal stomatal band in a sunken furrow on either side of a raised midrib; seed mostly broadly ellipsoidal, 25–45mm long, surrounded by a thin, fleshy aril – whitish, green, reddish-brown, sometimes purple-streaked: *Torreya* (p 108)

Key to Broadleaved Families and Aberrant Genera

1 Plants with white latex or milky resin (cut petiole, pedicel or branchlet): 2

1 Not so: any juice watery: 4

2 Leaves opposite, lobed; stipules absent: ACERACEAE (*Acer*) (part)

2 Leaves alternate, rarely opposite (*Broussonetia*) and then with (deciduous) stipules: 3

3 Leaves odd-pinnate (terminal leaflet present) or with just 3 leaflets; flowers with petals: ANACARDIACEAE (*Rhus*)

3 Leaves simple, sometimes lobed, the lobes more or less constricted toward the base; petals absent, the perianth a single whorl, its parts and the stamens typically 4, the latter opposite the perianth lobes: MORACEAE

4 Flowers with modified calyx and corolla, the sepals and petals being united in the bud stage to form a 'lid' (operculum) which falls off as the flower opens; stamens numerous, exceeding petals, free or united in bundles opposite the petals; ovary with 2–5 chambers. Trees or shrubs (not climbers) with alternate leaves (opposite in very young plants), aromatic when crushed: MYRTACEAE (*Eucalyptus*)

4 Not this combination of characters: 5

5 Horsetail (*Equisetum*)-like woody plants lacking ordinary leaf-like foliage, with striate jointed stems and branches bearing whorls of small teeth-like scales; perianth absent in female flowers which are clustered in a head; male flowers with a single stamen accompanied by 2 small scales and up to 2 inconspicuous perianth scales; fruiting heads forming woody, more or less globose cone-like structures, the winged nutlets protruding between hard persistent bractlets: CASUARINACEAE (*Casuarina*)

5¹ Flowers typically with a single distinct perianth whorl or none: petals absent or reduced to inconspicuous scales or glands, the perianth whorl rarely petaloid: 6

5 Flowers typically with two perianth whorls, the calyx mostly green(ish), the corolla colored; calyx sometimes absent: 23

6 At least the male flowers arranged in catkins: 7

6 No flowers arranged in catkins: 10

7 Male and female flowers in catkins, perianth absent; ovary superior; leaves alternate, simple, lobed or not: 8

7 Typically only flowers of one sex in catkins; at least one sex with perianth: 9

8 Fruit a capsule with many woolly seeds; dioecious plants, the male catkins *either* erect with the exserted stamens subtended by a gland *or* pendulous and the stamens subtended by a fimbriate bract: SALICACEAE

8 Fruit a 1-seeded nut or samara; female flowers 2–3 in the axil of a scale, styles 2; catkins mostly pendulous: BETULACEAE

9 Ovary inferior, styles 2; leaves pinnate: JUGLANDACEAE

9 Ovary inferior, styles 3–6; leaves simple; fruit a nut: FAGACEAE

10 Ovaries 2 or more, the carpels free from one another: 11

10 Ovary solitary of 1 carpel or more than 1 carpel fused together: 13

11 Perianth absent, flowers not in heads; leaves opposite and palmately veined: CERCIDIPHYLLACEAE (*Cercidiphyllum*)

11 Perianth present: 12

12 Hypogynous flowers, the perianth of 6 or more petaloid lobes; carpels numerous, spirally arranged on an elongated receptacle; leaves simple, the stipules falling to leave a circular scar; fruit 1-seeded: MAGNOLIACEAE

12¹ Similar to above but stipules absent and ovaries not on an elongated receptacle: WINTERACEAE (*Drimys*)

12 Perigynous flowers; leaves alternate: ROSACEAE

13 Perianth absent; flowers in globose heads; ovary inferior, 6–10 celled: NYSSACEAE (*Davidia*)

13 Perianth present: 14

14 At least the female flowers in globular heads or dense spikes or lining the inside of a hollow receptacle: 15

14 Not so: 16

15 Nodes sheathed by stipules; leaves palmately lobed; fruit a nutlet: PLATANACEAE (*Platanus*)

15¹ Nodes not so sheathed; leaves palmately lobed; fruit a capsule: HAMAMELIDACEAE (*Liquidambar*)

15¹ Leaves pinnate or absent and then replaced by flattened petioles; fruit a legume: LEGUMINOSAE (*Acacia*)

15 Fruit neither a nutlet nor a legume but a fleshy syncarp, the individual fruitlets borne externally or within a hollow receptacle: MORACEAE

16 Trees or shrubs with superior ovary: 17

16 Trees or shrubs, the ovary inferior or virtually so; leaves alternate, fruit drupe-like: 22

17 Leaves opposite: 18

17 Leaves alternate: 20

18 Fruit dehiscent; leaves simple, entire, unlobed: BUXACEAE (*Buxus*)

18 Fruit an indehiscent samara; leaves mostly compound or lobed: 19

19 Samara single with one wing; leaves typically pinnate: OLEACEAE (*Fraxinus*)

19 Samara double with 2 wings; leaves simple, palmately lobed or 3–7 foliolate: ACERACEAE

20 Anthers opening by hinged flaps; *either* leaves unlobed, evergreen and pleasant or unpleasant smelling when crushed *or* leaves deciduous and the adult leaves at least more or less 3-lobed: LAURACEAE

20 Not this combination of characters: 21

21 Ovary of 1 chamber, styles 2; flowers bisexual or unisexual; fruit *either* a nutlet surrounded by a more or less broad membranous wing *or* a more or less oblique drupe: ULMACEAE

21 Ovary of 1 chamber, style 1; perianth petaloid, more or less tubular, often narrowly so and splitting as flower opens; stamens 4, more or less sessile on upper part of tube or one on each perianth lobe; flowers solitary, in racemes or large heads: PROTEACEAE

22 Shoots and alternate leaves more or less scurfy with peltate or star-shaped scales; ovary of 1 chamber: ELAEAGNACEAE (*Elaeagnus*)

22 Plants not scaly; *either* ovary with 1(2) chambers and inflorescence without conspicuous bracts *or* ovary with 6–10 chambers and inflorescence with 2 conspicuous white bracts: NYSSACEAE

23 Petals free to the base, falling off singly (polypetalous): 24

23 Petals more or less united at least toward the base and forming a longer or shorter tube, the corolla falling as a whole (gamopetalous): 46

24 Ovaries 2 or more, the individual carpels free to the base: 25

24 Ovary *either* of one carpel *or* of several united carpels: 30

25 Stamens numerous (more than 10): 26

25 Stamens 10 or fewer: 32

26 Ovary superior and flower *either* hypogynous *or* perigynous: 27

26 Ovary inferior, perianth and numerous stamens arising above it; a free calyx tube absent: 29

27 Hypogynous flower: 28

27 Perigynous flower with differentiated sepals and petals; leaves typically alternate and serrate: ROSACEAE

28 Sepals and petals imbricate, the latter large (more than 3.5cm across), typically more than 5, often in whorls of 3, spirally arranged on an elongated axis; stipules conspicuous and falling to leave a circular scar; fruit a pod or achene: MAGNOLIACEAE

28 Not this combination; sepals valvate or shortly united below, 2–4(6), distinct from the small (less than 3.5cm across) corolla; ovaries not on an elongated axis; stipules absent or minute, not leaving a circular scar; fruit a berry: WINTERACEAE (*Drimys*)

29 Woody not fleshy plants; leaves typically alternate and toothed, stipules typically present: ROSACEAE

29 Woody not fleshy plants; leaves without stipules, usually evergreen and entire, often gland-dotted (hold against light) and aromatic when bruised: MYRTACEAE (*Eucalyptus*)

30 Leaves alternate and bipinnate, fruit a 1-chambered legume: LEGUMINOSAE (*Albizia*)

30 Not this combination: 31

31 Leaves alternate; sepals valvate; ovary of 2 or more chambers; fruit indehiscent: TILIACEAE (*Tilia*)

31 Not this combination; leaves opposite, at most only simply pinnate; sepals and petals typically 4; evergreen plants: EUCRYPHIACEAE

32 Ovary superior: 33

32 Ovary inferior: 45

33 Perigynous flowers with 2 or more free carpels; leaves not pellucid punctate, typically alternate and toothed with stipules: ROSACEAE

33↓ Hypogynous flowers with 2 or more free carpels, the stamens inserted below the ovary: 34

33 Hypogynous flowers as before, but 2 more carpels united to form a 1 to many-chambered ovary: 35

34 Leaves gland-dotted (hold against light); *either* pinnate or 3-foliolate and fruit a samara; *or* apparently simple and the fruit a lemon: RUTACEAE

34 Leaves not gland-dotted; leaves pinnate with 13–41 leaflets; fruit a samara: SIMAROUBACEAE (*Ailanthus*)

35 Ovary of 1 chamber with more than 1 ovule attached to the wall; leaves alternate, typically compound; fruit a legume: LEGUMINOSAE

35 Not this combination: 36

36 Leaves alternate, odd-pinnate or of 3 leaflets; stamens 5; styles 2–5; fruit a drupe with 1 seed: ANACARDIACEAE (*Rhus*)

36 Style solitary; ovary of 2 or more chambers: 37

37 Flowers clearly irregular: 38

37 Flowers virtually regular: 40

38 Leaves simple; anthers opening by pores: ERICACEAE (*Rhododendron*)

38 Not so: 39

39 Leaves opposite, digitate: HIPPOCASTANACEAE

39 Leaves alternate, bipinnate: SAPINDACEAE (*Koelreuteria*)

40 Leaves opposite or in whorls – if alternate, then fruit a lobed capsule: 41

40 Leaves alternate: 42

41 Leaves typically pinnate; fruit always a single samara: OLEACEAE (*Fraxinus*)

41↓ Leaves typically simple, often lobed, rarely 3–7-foliolate; fruit always a double samara: ACERACEAE (*Acer*)

41 Fruit a dehiscent lobed capsule of 4–5 chambers: CELASTRACEAE (*Euonymus*)

42 Leaves compound: 43

42 Leaves simple, often spiny; flower parts in 4's or 5's; fruit a berry-like drupe: AQUIFOLIACEAE (*Ilex*)

43 Leaves 3-foliolate; fruit dry: RUTACEAE (*Ptelea*)

43 Leaves pinnate or bipinnate: 44

44 At least some of the leaves bipinnate; flowers in conspicuous panicles before the leaves; stamens 8 or less, free below: SAPINDACEAE (*Koelreuteria*)

44 Leaves pinnate or bipinnate; stamens 5 or 10, united below: MELIACEAE

45 Leaves alternate, more or less serrate, stipules present; stamens more than twice petal number; fruit a pome: ROSACEAE

45 Not this combination. Plants with no prickles but with star-shaped hairs; styles 2, free to the base; fruit a woody capsule: HAMAMELIDACEAE

46 Ovary superior (hypogynous flower): 47

46 Ovary inferior (half inferior in Styracaceae) (epigynous flower): 53

47 Number of stamens equal to at least twice number of petal lobes: 48

47 Number of stamens not more than the number of petal lobes and alternating with them: 50

48 Stamens arising free from corolla; style solitary; fruit a 5-chambered capsule: ERICACEAE

48 Stamens united to corolla tube; styles and chambers of ovary 2 or more: 49

49 Stamen filaments more or less united into bundles; fruit a capsule: THEACEAE

49 Stamen filaments free, not united into bundles; styles 4; fruit a berry: EBENACEAE

50 Deciduous trees with opposite large broad leaves (at least 10 × 10cm); flowers irregular, conspicuous and trumpet shaped with 4 fertile stamens; fruit a capsule opening along midribs of carpels, with numerous ovules on a central axis: SCROPHULARIACEAE (*Paulownia*)

50 Corolla regular, stamens up to 5; ovary solitary: 51

51 Leaves opposite; stamens less than 5, mostly joined to corolla, but alternating with lobes: OLEACEAE

51 Leaves typically alternate, sometimes appearing whorled (*Pittosporum*); stamens 5, free from corolla; ovary solitary: 52

52 Anthers opening by apical pores (slightly elongated in *Oxydendrum*), style present; fruit a capsule: ERICACEAE

52↓ Anthers opening by longitudinal slits; style present; fruit capsular; seeds resinous: PITTOSPORACEAE (*Pittosporum*)

52 Anthers opening by longitudinal slits, but style absent, the stigma virtually sessile; fruit a drupe; seeds not resinous: AQUIFOLIACEAE (*Ilex*)

53 Anthers not laterally cohering to form a tube round the style; leaves alternate; stamens twice as many as corolla lobes: 54

53 Anthers as above, but stamens 4–5; leaves opposite: CAPRIFOLIACEAE

54 Stamens united at base; anthers opening by slits; fruit a dry, winged drupe: STYRACACEAE

54 Stamens free; anthers opening by apical pores; fruit a berry: ERICACEAE

Key to Broadleaved Genera by Families

Where only one genus occurs in a family, this is accompanied by a short diagnosis to distinguish it from other related genera not dealt with and the plant under examination must comply with the short diagnosis.

MAGNOLIACEAE
A Leaves entire, acute or tapering at apex; fruit a dehiscent follicle: *Magnolia* (p 112)
AA Leaves lobed, more or less truncate at apex; fruit a samara (indehiscent): *Liriodendron* (p 114)

WINTERACEAE
Sometimes included in Magnoliaceae, but stipules absent and floral axis short: *Drimys* (p 116)

LAURACEAE
A Leaves entire, not lobed, evergreen, faintly pungent but pleasant when crushed; flowers bisexual, typically with 12(8–14) stamens: *Laurus* (p 116)
AA↓ Leaves entire, not lobed, evergreen, painfully pungent when crushed and sniffed; flowers bisexual; stamens 9: *Umbellularia* (p 117)
AAA Leaves deciduous, at least some (mainly adult ones) lobed; flowers unisexual: *Sassafras* (p 118)

CERCIDIPHYLLACEAE
Deciduous trees with mostly opposite, broadly ovate leaves; flowers dioecious; stamens numerous; carpels 3–4(5): *Cercidiphyllum* (p 118)

PLATANACEAE
Trees with scaling bark; leaves alternate, palmately lobed and veined; petiole base enlarged and enclosing axillary bud: *Platanus* (p 119)

HAMAMELIDACEAE
A Trees; leaves palmately lobed and veined; flowers unisexual monoecious, in dense clusters; petals absent: *Liquidambar* (p 122)
AA↓ Trees; leaves with stellate pubescence, sinuate-dentate; flowers bisexual; petals absent: *Parrotia* (p 123)
AAA Shrubs; leaves penninerved, more or less sinuate-dentate; flowers bisexual; petals conspicuous, strap-like (linear): *Hamamelis* (p 121)

FAGACEAE
A Male flowers solitary or in threes; leaves usually less than

8cm long, evergreen or deciduous; involucre 2–4 lobed; fruit a 3-angled nut: *Nothofagus* (p 130)

AA[↓] Male flowers numerous in pendulous globose heads; female flowers in 2's; leaves deciduous, usually more than 8cm long when adult; involucre (cupule) distinctly prickly; fruit a 3-angled nut: *Fagus* (p 128)

AAA[↓] Male flowers numerous in pendulous catkins; female flowers solitary or in 2 to numerous flowered spikes; fruit a subglobose or more or less elongated nut (acorn) without angles, the involucre (cupule) basal or almost enclosing the fruit, its surface rugose or variously scaly to prickly: *Quercus* (p 123)

AAAA[↓] Male flowers in upright spikes and leaves deciduous, dentate; ovary 6-chambered involucre prickly (burr); terminal bud absent: *Castanea* (p 133)

AAAAA Male flowers in upright spikes; leaves entire or dentate, evergreen: B

  B Involucre (cupule) of fruit more or less cup-shaped, virtually smooth; nut ovoid, solitary: *Lithocarpus* (p 136)

  BB Involucre covered with branched spines (burr); nuts 3 in each burr and triangular in cross section: *Chrysolepis* (p 136)

BETULACEAE

  A Perianth present in female flowers, absent in male; nut enclosed in more or less leafy involucre formed from united bracteoles: B

  AA Perianth present in male flowers, absent in female; nut more or less flat, often winged or with margin; involucre absent: C

  B Female flowers few, more or less bud-like; acorn-like (hazel) nut enclosed by leafy involucre: *Corylus* (p 143)

  BB[↓] Female flowers numerous in short, erect spikes; male flowers appear in the fall; involucre tubular or bladder-like: *Ostrya* (p 144)

  BBB Female flowers in long pendulous catkins; male flowers appear in spring; involucre flat, 3-lobed: *Carpinus* (p 141)

  C Stamens 2, the filaments divided; fruiting catkins with 3-lobed deciduous scales: *Betula* (p 136)

  CC Stamens 4, the filaments not divided; fruits forming a black, woody cone-like structure composed of 5-lobed persistent scales: *Alnus* (p 139)

CASUARINACEAE

Horsetail (*Equisetum*)-like plants, the foliage leaves replaced by whorls of minute scales: *Casuarina* (p 143)

THEACEAE

  A Leaves evergreen; flowers erect with deciduous sepals; fruit a subglobose capsule with 1–3 large (2cm) seeds: *Camellia* (p 145)

  AA Leaves deciduous; flowers with evident stalk; seeds numerous, smaller, more or less flat: *Stewartia* (p 148)

TILIACEAE

Trees with star-shaped hairs; leaves alternate, simple; peduncle with large, oblong, partly adnate bract: *Tilia* (p 148)

ULMACEAE

  A Leaves with 3 more or less prominent basal veins; remaining veins less than 7, virtually pinnate; bark usually smooth without fissures; perianth free to the base; fruit a drupe: *Celtis* (p 154)

  AA Not this combination of characters; pinnate veins of leaves 7 or more: B

  B Bark typically fissured; leaves typically oblique and twice serrate; fruit a broadly-winged nut (samara): *Ulmus* (p 150)

  BB Bark typically smooth; leaves simply serrate; perianth joined below; style excentric; fruit an oblique drupe without wing: *Zelkova* (p 153)

MORACEAE

  A Leaves entire but may be lobed; stipules large, completely clasping the stem, soon falling to leave circular scar; flowers borne on the inside of a fleshy receptacle (syncarp) which becomes the edible fig: *Ficus* (p 155)

  AA Not this combination; stipules small: B

  B Leaves entire, not lobed; branches spiny; 'fruit' cluster a globose syncarp 10–14cm across, the individual drupelet fruits borne externally each on a short stalk: *Maclura* (p 159)

  BB Leaves crenate-serrate, possibly lobed; branches not spiny: C

  C Flowers borne in small similar catkin-like spikes; ripe fruit red, like a loganberry: *Morus* (p 158)

  CC Male flowers in pendulous catkins; female flowers borne externally in globose heads; 'fruit' cluster a globose syncarp, the individual ripe fruits protruding on a fleshy stalk: *Broussonetia* (p 160)

SALICACEAE

  A Catkins pendulous, the scales typically laciniate; leaves mostly broad with long stalk; flowers with basal cup-shaped disk: *Populus* (p 164)

  AA Scales of catkins entire, the male catkins at least typically erect; leaves mostly more or less lanceolate with short stalk; flowers with one or more basal glands: *Salix* (p 160)

ERICACEAE

  A Flowers urn-shaped in large terminal panicles; anthers with 2 long reflexed awns; ovary superior; fruit a more or less warty berry; leaves evergreen: *Arbutus* (p 173)

  AA Not so; anthers without awns; fruit a capsule: B

  B Fruit a septicidal capsule; corolla more or less funnel-shaped, more than 1cm long, weakly irregular, the 5–20 stamens typically upturned; leaves typically entire, evergreen or deciduous: *Rhododendron* (incl. *Azalea*) (p 168)

  BB Fruit a loculicidal capsule; leaves deciduous, serrulate; flowers urn-shaped, less than 1cm long: *Oxydendrum* (p 174)

EBENACEAE

Deciduous or evergreen trees or shrubs; leaves alternate, simple, entire; flowers dioecious; ovary superior: *Diospyros* (p 175)

STYRACACEAE

  A Flowers solitary or in racemes; ovary superior or virtually so; fruit neither ribbed nor winged; corolla 5(8)-lobed: *Styrax* (p 176)

  AA Some flowers in axillary clusters; ovary inferior; fruit with 2–4 wings; corolla 4-lobed: *Halesia* (p 177)

PITTOSPORACEAE

Evergreen trees or shrubs; leaves alternate but sometimes appearing whorled, mostly entire without stipules; flowers not blue, petals less than 15mm long; fruit a capsule: *Pittosporum* (p 177)

EUCRYPHIACEAE

Evergreen trees or shrubs; leaves opposite, simple or pinnate, and stipulate; sepals 4, petals 4(5); stamens numerous; fruit a capsule: *Eucryphia* (p 178)

ROSACEAE

  A Flowers perigynous with superior ovary; leaves serrate, simple; fruit a drupe typically of 1 carpel; sepals 5, petals conspicuous: *Prunus* (*sensu lato*) (p 196)

  AA Flowers epigynous with an inferior ovary; leaves simple or compound, entire in *Cydonia* and *Mespilus*; fruit a pome of 2–5 more or less united carpels: B

  B Leaves pinnate with odd, terminal leaflet: *Sorbus* (part) (p 184)

  BB Leaves simple, unlobed, lobed or variously dissected: C

  C Leaves entire or almost so and flowers 2–5cm across, solitary: D

  CC Leaf margins variously toothed, lobed or dissected: E

  D Fruit globose, 2–3cm across, brownish with persistent leafy calyx lobes, open above and with 5 'stones' (endocarp stony): *Mespilus* (p 183)

  DD Fruit 5–7cm across, more or less pear-shaped, yellowish, without leafy calyx lobes, closed above with many 'pips,' the endocarp being papery and not stony: *Cydonia* (p 183)

  E Deciduous trees or shrubs, typically with leafless spines (rarely spines absent); leaves variously toothed or lobed; flowers 12mm or more across in cymes or panicles; fruit with 1–5 bony nutlets: *Crataegus* (p 179)

EE Not this combination of characters; fruits with 'pip' seeds only (papery endocarp): F

F Inflorescence corymbose or paniculate; flowers less than 10mm across; the 5 chambers of the fruit each with 1–2 seeds: *Sorbus* (part) (p 184)

FF Inflorescence of umbels or racemes or flowers solitary; flowers more than 15mm across: G

G Each chamber of fruit with numerous 'pips' (more than 4): *Chaenomeles* (p 184)

GG Each chamber of the fruit with not more than 2 seeds: H

H Ovary and fruit incompletely divided into 6–10 chambers; flowers typically in terminal racemes and styles 5: *Amelanchier* (p 186)

HH Ovary and fruit with 2–5 chambers, each chamber with 2 seeds; deciduous trees and shrubs with umbel-like inflorescence: J

J Flowers with petals some shade of pink; styles joined below; fruit an 'apple' without grit cells or very few such cells: *Malus* (p 187)

JJ Flowers typically with pure white petals; styles free below; fruit a 'pear,' the grit cells numerous and evident: *Pyrus* (p 192)

LEGUMINOSAE (*Fabaceae*)

A Flowers regular – not pea-like – petals, valvate, sometimes absent: B

AA Flowers irregular, typically pea-like: G

B Leaves replaced by flattened petioles functioning as leaves; flowers typically yellow in close globose or cylindric spike-like clusters; stamens numerous (more than 10) long exserted, the filament not, or scarcely joined below: *Acacia* (part) (p 201)

B Leaves 1–2 pinnate: C

C Stamens numerous (more than 10) long exserted; petals 4–5, valvate: D

CC Stamens 10 or fewer; petals imbricate; flowers not in close clusters: E

D Flowers as in B above, the stamens not or scarcely joined at the base; fruit mostly opening by 2 valves: *Acacia* (part) (p 201)

DD Flowers as in B above but stamen filaments more or less united to form a tube below; pod indehiscent: *Albizia* (p 212)

E Flowers mostly yellow; leaves 1-pinnate; stamens 5–10, but some often infertile: *Cassia* (p 213)

EE Flowers greenish to more or less white, not conspicuous; leaves 1- or 2-pinnate: F

F Trees lacking spines; leaves 2-pinnate with entire leaflets; flowers in loose terminal panicles: *Gymnocladus* (p 210)

FF Trees typically with spines; leaves 1–2-pinnate with more or less toothed leaflets; flowers in spike-like racemes: *Gleditsia* (p 206)

G Leaves typically simple, with palmate venation, more or less kidney-shaped, 6–12cm long; flowers light or deep pink, borne on trunk or branches before the leaves: *Cercis* (p 205)

GG↓ Leaves compound, 3-foliolate; flowers in pendulous racemes, the 10 staminal filaments united below in a tube; calyx 2-lipped; flowers yellow in *Laburnum* (p 207); more or less purplish in *Laburnocytisus* (p 207)

GGG Leaves odd-pinnate with 5 or more leaflets: H

H Trees with white or yellow(ish) flowers, inflorescence pendulous; stamens 10; pod flat, not jointed: I

HH As above, but flowers in upright panicles; pod terete, jointed: *Sophora* (p 210)

I Inflorescence paniculate; leaflets alternate: *Cladrastis* (p 214)

II Inflorescence a raceme; leaflets opposite: *Robinia* (p 209)

MYRTACEAE

Evergreen trees, rarely shrubs; leaves alternate in *Eucalyptus* (often opposite in young plants of that genus); calyx lobes and petals unite in a 'lid' (operculum) which falls off as flower opens; stamens numerous; fruit a capsule opening above by 3–6 valves: *Eucalyptus* (p 214)

NYSSACEAE

A Leaves tapering to more or less rounded at base, margin entire or with a few scattered teeth; inflorescence with 2(3) conspicuous, ovate white bracts to 16cm long: *Davidia* (p 218)

AA Leaves cordate at base, margin toothed; inflorescence without bracts: *Nyssa* (p 219)

CORNACEAE

Inflorescence axillary or terminal; leaves typically deciduous, entire, opposite (alternate in *C. alternifolia*, and *C. controversa*); flowers white, bisexual in corymbs or umbels: *Cornus* (p 220)

PROTEACEAE

A Flowers bisexual, one in the axil of numerous conspicuous, elongated bracts forming a head; upper and lateral lobes of elongated, narrow perianth fused laterally to form a spoon-like structure with 3 more or less sessile stamens with laterally cohering anthers, occupying the 'bowl' of the 'spoon'; leaves alternate, the margins entire; fruit a nut with one seed: *Protea* (p 223)

AA Flowers bisexual, but two in the axil of each bract; perianth lobes not fused, the surface of each flat and bearing a more or less sessile stamen; leaves entire or variously toothed and dissected; fruit a follicle with (2)4 seeds: B

B Flowers in racemes or axillary clusters; style disc- or cone-like above; follicles thin-walled: *Grevillea* (p 222)

BB Flowers crowded in large (10–50 × 5–20cm) cone-like heads; style not obviously enlarged above; follicles hard, woody, enclosed by bracts and bracteoles: *Banksia* (p 223)

ELAEAGNACEAE

Deciduous or evergreen trees or shrubs with peltate to star-shaped grayish to brownish scales, especially on lower leaf surface; leaves entire, alternate, without stipules; sepals and petals 4, the corolla tube much exceeding the ovary; fruit drupe-like: *Elaeagnus* (p 224)

CELASTRACEAE

Deciduous or evergreen trees or shrubs; leaves mostly opposite; fruit a 4–5-chambered capsule mostly lobed or winged: *Euonymus* (p 225)

AQUIFOLIACEAE

Evergreen or deciduous trees or shrubs; leaves typically alternate, entire, toothed or spiny; petals oblong to obovate, united below; sepals persistent: *Ilex* (p 226)

BUXACEAE

Evergreen trees or shrubs; leaves opposite, entire; fruit a capsule: *Buxus* (p 227)

SAPINDACEAE

Deciduous trees; leaves alternate, odd-pinnate or bipinnate, leaflets serrate; flowers yellow, irregular, in large terminal panicles; fruit a bladder-like capsule; seeds black: *Koelreuteria* (p 228)

HIPPOCASTANACEAE

Trees or shrubs; leaves opposite, digitately 3–9-foliolate; stipules absent: *Aesculus* (p 229)

ACERACEAE

Predominantly deciduous trees, rarely shrubs; leaves opposite 3–5(7)-foliolate or simple and then typically palmately lobed: *Acer* (p 231)

ANACARDIACEAE

Deciduous or evergreen trees or shrubs, rarely climbers; leaves alternate, 3-foliolate or odd pinnate; flowers with petals; inflorescence a panicle without sterile branches: *Rhus* (p 234)

RUTACEAE

A Leaves apparently simple comprising 1 'leaflet,' but petiole mostly with leaflet-like wings or margins; fruit of an orange, lemon, grapefruit or tangerine type etc: *Citrus* (p 236)

AA Leaves compound: B

B Leaves trifoliolate, alternate, deciduous; branches without spines: *Ptelea* (p 239)

BB Leaves pinnate and opposite: C

C Winter buds hidden within petiole base; fruit a drupe: *Phellodendron* (p 240)

CC Winter buds exposed in leaf axils; fruit a follicle: *Euodia* (p 239)

SIMAROUBACEAE
Deciduous trees; leaves alternate, odd-pinnate; leaflets 13–41 with 1 or more glandular teeth near the base; inflorescence terminal; fruit separating into 2–5(6) compressed samaras: *Ailanthus* (p 240)

MELIACEAE

A Leaves typically bipinnate; flowers to 2cm across, tinged purple; fruit a drupe: *Melia* (p 241)

AA Leaves once-pinnate; flowers smaller; fruit a septicidal capsule: *Cedrela* (p 241)

JUGLANDACEAE

A Branches with solid continuous pith; perianth absent or inconspicuous; fruit a dehiscent drupe with almost smooth stone: *Carya* (p 243)

AA Branches with septate-laminate pith; perianth clearly visible: B

B Fruit indehiscent, stone wrinkled, wing absent: *Juglans* (242)

BB Fruit a pendulous catkin of winged nuts: *Pterocarya* (p 242)

OLEACEAE

A Leaves deciduous, typically pinnate, rarely 3-foliolate or simple; fruit a winged achene (samara): *Fraxinus* (p 246)

AA↓ Leaves deciduous, simple, rarely pinnate (*Syringa*), fruit a drupe or berry: B

AAA Leaves evergreen, simple; corolla-lobes valvate; fruit a drupe or berry: C

B Corolla 4-lobed, never yellow, its tube at least as long as the lobes; fruit a capsule: *Syringa* (p 248)

BB As B, but flowers white or creamy and fruit a berry-like drupe: *Ligustrum* (p 248)

C Flowers in axillary clusters; leaves often silvery scaly beneath; fruit a drupe: *Olea* (p 245)

CC Flowers in terminal panicles; leaves smooth beneath; fruit a berry: *Ligustrum* (p 248)

SCROPHULARIACEAE
Trees with large broad opposite leaves 12–25–50cm long; stamens 4; fruit a loculicidal capsule: *Paulownia* (p 249)

BIGNONIACEAE
Mostly deciduous trees, leaves opposite or whorled, margin entire, toothed or lobed, ovate; stamens 2; fruit a long, pendulous, pod-like capsule, the seeds tufted at each end: *Catalpa* (p 249)

CAPRIFOLIACEAE

A Corolla typically rotate; leaves pinnate, style very short, 3–5-lobed; no capitate stigmas; fruit berry-like with 3–5 seeds: *Sambucus* (p 250)

AA Corolla rotate, leaves simple, lobed or not; style very short 3–5-lobed; no capitate stigmas; fruit a drupe with 1 seed: *Viburnum* (p 251)   F. B. H.

Bibliography

The publishers acknowledge the following reference sources:

Bailey, L. H. (revised 1949). *Manual of Cultivated Plants.* The Macmillan Company, New York.

Bailey, L. H. & Bailey, E. Z. et al. (1977). *Hortus Third.* Macmillan Publishing Co Inc, New York; Collier Macmillan, London.

Bean, W. J. (8th edn 1970–1976). *Trees and Shrubs Hardy in the British Isles* (vols. 1–3). John Murray, London.

Blackall, W. E. (revised & edited, R. J. Grieve, 1954, 1956). *How to know Western Australian Wild Flowers.* The University of Western Australia Press, Nedlands, Western Australia.

Carr, J. D. (1976). *The South African Acacias.* Conservation Press (Pty) Ltd, Johannesburg, London, Manzini.

Chittenden, F. J. (ed) (2nd edn 1956–1969). *Dictionary of Gardening.* Clarendon Press, Oxford.

Dallimore, W. & Jackson, A. B. (4th edn revised Harrison, R. G.) (1966). *A Handbook of Coniferae & Ginkgoaceae.* Edward Arnold, London.

Davis, P. H. & Cullen, J. (2nd edn 1979). *The Identification of Flowering Plant Families.* Cambridge University Press, London, New York, Melbourne.

Dyer, R. A. (1975). *The Genera of South African Plants.* Praetoria. (A new edn of E. P. Phillips' work of the same title.)

Engler, A. & Prantl, K. (eds) (2nd edn 1926, vol 13). *Die Natürlichen Pflanzenfamilien.* Wilhem Engelmann, Leipzig.

Engler, A. & Melchior et al. (12th edn 1954, 1964). *Syllabus der Pflanzenfamilien.* Bros Borntraeger, Berlin.

Exell, A. W. et al (1960–1978). *Flora Zambesiaca.* Crown Agents for Overseas Governments & Administration, London.

Gaussen, H. (1943–1968). *Les Gymnosperms, Actuelles et Fossiles.* Toulouse.

Heywood, V. H. (ed) (1978). *Flowering Plants of the World.* Oxford University Press, Oxford, London, Melbourne.

Hillier's Manual of Trees & Shrubs (4th edn 1977). David & Charles, Newton Abbot.

Komarov, V. L. (ed) *Flora of the USSR* (vol IX, 1939, vol X, 1941). Moskua-Leningrad. English translation by Israel Program for Scientific Translation.

Krüssman, G. (2nd edn 1960). *Die Nadelgehölze.* Paul Parey, Berlin & Hamburg.

Mitchell, A. F. (1972). *Conifers in the British Isles.* HMSO, London.

Mitchell, A. F. (1974). *A Field Guide to the Trees of Britain & Northern Europe.* Collins, London.

Ohuri, J. (1965). *Flora of Japan.* Smithsonian Institute, Washington, D.C.

Perry, F. (1972). *Flowers of the World.* Hamlyn, London, New York, Sydney, Toronto.

Polunin, O. & Everard, B. (1976). *Trees & Bushes of Europe.* Oxford University Press, London, New York, Toronto.

Rehder, A. (2nd edn 1940). *Manual of Cultivated Trees & Shrubs Hardy in North America.* Macmillan Publishing Co Inc, New York.

Schneider, C. K. (1904–12). *Illustriertes Handbuch der laubholzkunde.* Gustav Fischer, Jena.

Tutin, T. G. & Heywood, V. H. (eds) (1964–1980). *Flora Europea.* Cambridge University Press, Cambridge, New York, Melbourne.

Willis, J. C. (8th edn by H. K. Airy Shaw 1973). *A Dictionary of Flowering Plants.* Cambridge University Press, Cambridge, New York, Melbourne.

Glossary

Abaxial On the side facing away from the stem or axis.

Achene A small, dry, single-seeded fruit that does not split open to release its seeds.

Acicular (of leaves) Needle-like (Plate II).

Acuminate (of leaves) Narrowing gradually by somewhat concave edges to a point (Plate IV).

Acute (of leaves) Tapering by straight or slightly convex edges to a point (Plate IV).

Adnate Joined or attached to; said of dissimilar organs joined together, eg stamens to petals.

Addressed = Appressed Pressed closely to the axis and pointing to the shoot tip.

Aecidial A stage in the life cycle of a rust fungus when aeciospores are produced within a fruit body (aecium) which then bursts through the epidermis of infected plants to release the spores.

Albedo The whitish, spongy layer lying between the outer skin (flavedo) and juicy segments of *Citrus* fruits such as oranges and lemons.

Alternate (of leaves) Arranged with one leaf at each node of the stem (Plate VI).

Amplexicaul (of leaves) With leaf bases clasping the stem (Plate VI).

Anastomosis Joining by cross connections to form a network.

Androecium All the male reproductive organs of a flower; the stamens; cf gynoecium.

Angiosperm A flowering plant – a plant that produces seeds enclosed in an ovary; broadleaves, palms and palm-like species are angiosperms. (See also Flower, Ovule, Seed.)

Anther The terminal part of a stamen, usually borne on a stalk (filament) and developing to contain pollen within the pollen sacs (Plate III).

Apiculate (of leaves) With a short, sharp, often flexible point (Plate IV).

Apophysis (of cones) The exposed outer surface of the ovuliferous-scale.

Appressed See Addressed.

Arborescent Tree-like in size and appearance.

Aril (adj arillate) A fleshy outgrowth either from the hilum or funicle of a seed or from the stem, as in the yews.

Aristate (of leaves) Tapering to a sharp point (Plate IV).

Auricle (adj auriculate) (of leaves) Small ear-like projection at the base (Plate II).

Awl-shaped (of leaves) Narrow, triangular, flat, stiff, sharp-pointed and usually less than 13mm (0.5in) long.

Awn A stiff, bristle-like extension of an organ.

Berry A fleshy fruit without a stony layer and usually containing many seeds.

Bipinnate (of leaves) A pinnate leaf with the primary leaflets themselves divided in a pinnate manner; cf pinnate (Plate II).

Bisexual Bearing both male and female reproductive organs in a single flower.

Bract A modified leaf, often scale-like.

Bract-scale (of cones) A modified leaf which subtends the ovuliferous-scale to which it may be fused to form a single scale (Plate I).

Broadleaved tree Any tree that belongs to the subclass Dicotyledonae of the class Angiospermae (flowering plants).

Bullate Blistered or puckered.

Caducous Falling off easily or prematurely.

Calyx Collective term for all the sepals of a flower (Plate III).

Cambium A layer of cells which occurs within stem and roots and divides to produce either secondary vascular tissues (vascular cambium) or cork (cork cambium).

Capitate Head-like.

Capitulum An inflorescence consisting of a head of closely-packed stalkless flowers.

Capsule A dry fruit which normally splits open to release its seeds.

Carpel One of the flower's female reproductive organs, comprising an ovary and a stigma, and containing one or more ovules (Plate III).

Catkin A hanging cluster of unisexual flowers.

Chromosomes The thread-like strands of DNA which occur in the nucleus of living cells and carry the units of heredity – the genes. Normal cells contain two sets of chromosomes, one derived from each parent.

Ciliate (of leaves) With hairs protruding from the margin (Plate V).

Cladode A flattened stem which has assumed the form and function of a leaf.

Clavate Club-shaped.

Clone A group of plants that have arisen by vegetative reproduction from a single parent, and which therefore all have identical genetic composition.

Compound (of leaves) With the leaf blade divided into separate segments (leaflets).

Concolorous Of uniform color.

Conduplicate Folded longitudinally upward or downward along the axis so that the ventral or dorsal sides face each other.

Cone-scale (of conifers) A general term applied to the elements that make up a female cone and subsequently the fruiting cone, that is the bract-scale, ovuliferous-scale or the product of the fusion of these two. In the mature cone the term cone-scale is applied to the main contributor to the structure of the cone (Plate I).

Cone = Strobilus The reproductive structures of conifers and their allies. Female cones are formed of *either* alternating ovuliferous-scales in the axils of bract-scales *or* these scale-pairs are fused to form a series of cone-scales. The ovuliferous- or cone-scales bear naked on their surfaces ovules which contain the eggs. After pollination and fertilization the scales become woody, less often fleshy, the whole structure forming the characteristic fruiting or mature cone which bears the seeds on the surface of the scales. The term cone-scale is often generally applied to the component that contributes most to the final fruiting cone. Male cones consist of clusters of pollen sacs and are short-lived after pollen dispersal (Plate I).

Conidial A stage in the life cycle of certain fungi in which sexual spores (conidia) are produced.

Conifer A cone-bearing tree.

Connate Joined or attached to; said of similar organs fused during formation, such as petals.

Convolute Rolled together.

Coralloid Much-branched.

Cordate (of leaves) Heart-shaped (Plate II).

Corolla All the petals of a flower (Plate III).

Corymb (adj corymbose) A rounded or flat-topped inflorescence like a raceme but the flower stalks are longer on the outside so that the flowers are at about the same level.

Cotyledon The first leaf, or pair of leaves, of an embryo within the seed. In conifers there are more than two cotyledons for each embryo.

Crenate (of leaf margins) Shallowly round-toothed with indentations no further than $\frac{1}{8}$ of the distance to the midrib (Plate V).

Crenulate Very shallowly round-toothed with indentations no further than $\frac{1}{16}$ of the distance to the midrib.

Cryptogam A general term applied to plants that do not produce seeds.

Cultivar (abbreviation cv) Cultivated variety. A taxonomic rank used to denote a variety that is known only in horticultural cultivation. Cultivar names are nonlatinized and in living languages; typographically they are distinguished in a nonitalic typeface, with a capital initial letter and enclosed in single quotation marks, for example *Betula pendula* 'Fastigiata.'

Cuneate (of leaves) With the base gradually tapering (Plate II).

Cupule A cup-like structure surrounding some fruits.

Cuspidate (of leaves) With an abrupt, rigid, apical point (Plate IV).

cv Abbreviation for cultivar.

Cyme (adj cymose) An inflorescence in which each terminal growing point produces a flower, with subsequent flowers produced from a lateral growing point, so that the oldest flowers are at the apex, or center if flat.

Deciduous Shedding leaves seasonally.

Decurrent (of leaves) With the leaf base continuing down along the stem. (Plate VI).

Decussate (of leaves) Arranged in opposite pairs on the stem, with each pair at 90° to the preceding pair.

Dehiscent Opening to shed pollen or seeds.

Deltoid (of leaves) Triangular (Plate II).

Dentate (of leaf margins) Toothed, with the teeth pointing at right angles to the midrib (Plate V).

Denticulate (of leaf margins) Minutely toothed (dentate).

Dicotyledon One of two subclasses of angiosperms which contains the broadleaved trees; a plant whose embryo has two cotyledons; cf monocotyledon.

Plate I Cone structure. Details of the structure of the cone-scales of mature or fruiting cones of conifers, showing the position of the bract-scale (1), ovuliferous-scale (2) and seeds (3), the latter having developed from the fertilized ovules. (a), (b) Douglas Fir (*Pseudotsuga* sp) showing that the scales are distinct from each other. (c), (d) Arbor-vitae (*Thuja* sp) showing that the bract- and ovuliferous-scales are fused to form a single cone-scale (4). (a), (c) sectional view from side; (b), (d) view from above. The term cone-scale is often loosely applied to the scale that contributes most to the fruiting cone irrespective of origin.

Digitate (of leaves) With leaflets arranged as the fingers of a hand; palmate (Plate II).

Dimorphic Having two different shapes and/or sizes within the same species.

Dioecious Having male and female flowers or cones borne on separate plants; cf monoecious.

Diploid Having in the nucleus of its cells two sets of chromosomes, one from each parent.

Discoid Orbicular with convex faces; disc-like.

Discolorous Not the same color throughout.

Dissected (of leaves) Irregularly cut into segments.

Distichous (of leaves) Arranged in two vertical rows.

Dorsal Upper.

Drupe A fleshy fruit containing one or more seeds, each surrounded by a stony layer.

Ecotone The band of vegetation which forms a boundary between two major vegetation types, as between forest and grassland.

Elliptic (of leaves) Oval-shaped with the widest axis at the midpoint (Plate II).

Emarginate (of leaves) With a shallow notch at the apex (Plate IV).

Endemic A species or population which is either restricted to a special habitat and/or a very limited geographical range.

Endocarp The innermost layer of the fruit immediately surrounding the seed.

Endodermis A cylinder of cells surrounding the vascular bundle of a root. All substances passing in or out of the vascular cylinder must pass through the center of these cells, not between them.

Ensiform (of leaves) Sword-shaped (Plate II).

Entire (of leaf margins) Without incisions or indentations (Plate V).

Epicalyx A ring of bracts below an inflorescence.

Epicormic (of shoots) Developing from dormant lateral buds on the trunk which have become active, for example due to damage.

Epidermis The outer protective, usually single-celled, layer of many plant organs, particularly leaves and herbaceous stems.

Epigynous (of flowers) With the sepals, petals and stamens inserted near the top of the ovary.

Epimatium (of conifers) The fleshy covering of some seeds, as in *Podocarpus*.

Epiphyte Living upon another plant but not dependent on it for nutrition.

Excurrent (of veins) Projecting beyond the lamina of a leaf.

Exfoliating Cracked or splitting off in flakes or scales.

Exserted Protruding.

Falcate (of leaves) Sickle-shaped (Plate II).

Fascicle A cluster or bundle.

Fastigiate (fastigate) Erect with many branches parallel to the main stem.

Female cone (of conifers) A cone on the scales of which the female sex organs (the ovules) are borne (Plate I).

Female flower A flower containing functional carpels but no fertile stamens.

Filament The stalk of an anther (Plate III).

Filiform Thread-like.

Fimbriate (of margins) Fringed, usually with hairs.

Flavedo The outer, thin, colored and fragrant skin of *Citrus* fruits, such as oranges and lemons.

Flower The structure concerned with sexual reproduction in angiosperms including broadleaves and monocotyledonous trees. Essentially it consists of the male organs (androecium) comprising the stamens, and female organs (gynoecium) comprising the ovary, style(s) and stigma(s), usually surrounded by a whorl of petals (the corolla) and a whorl of sepals (the calyx) (Plate III).

Follicle A dry fruit which splits open along one side only.

Forma or **form** A taxonomic division ranking below variety and used to distinguish plants with trivial differences.

Fruit Strictly the ripened ovary of a seed plant and its contents. Loosely the whole structure containing ripe seeds.

Funicle The stalk of an ovule.

Genus A taxonomic rank grouping together more or less closely related plants. The genus title is the first word of the species binomial. A genus may be divided into subgenera, sections and series, in descending order of hierarchy.

Geophyte A plant that survives from growing season to growing season by means of dormant underground buds, as in bulbs.

Glabrescent Becoming devoid of hairs.

Glabrous Without hairs or projections.

Glaucous With a waxy, grayish-blue bloom.

Globose Spherical; rounded.

Gymnosperm A seed plant in which the seeds are not enclosed in an ovary; conifers are the most familiar example.

Gynoecium All the female reproductive organs of a

Plate II Leaf shapes.

flower, comprising one or more free or fused carpels.

Haploid Having within the nucleus of its cells only one complete set of chromosomes, as in the gametes or sex cells.

Hardy Able to withstand extreme conditions, usually of cold.

Hastate (of leaves) Shaped like an arrowhead with the basal lobes outturned (Plate II).

Head A cluster of sessile or short-stalked flowers.

Hilum The scar left behind on a seed after separation from the stalk.

Hispid Covered with very long stiff hairs.

Hybrid The offspring of two plants of different taxa, most often species.

Hydathode A gland which exudes water.

Hypanthium A cup-shaped enlargement of the floral receptacle or the bases of the floral parts, which often enlarges and surrounds the fruits, eg the fleshy tissue in rose-hips.

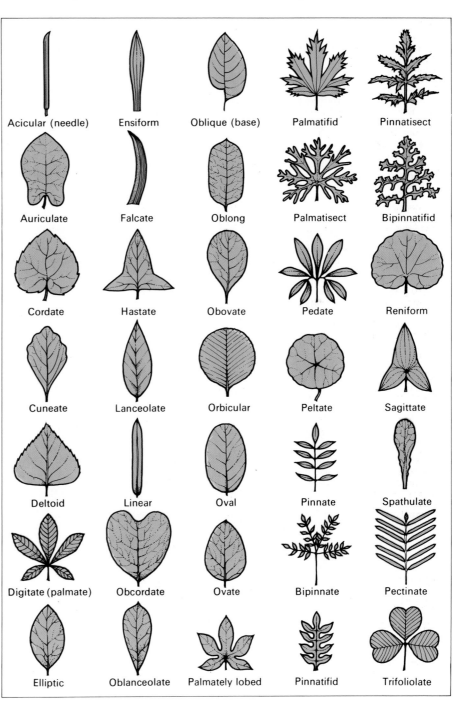

Hypoderm(is) A layer of thickened cells which lies immediately below the epidermis.

Hypogynous (of flowers) With sepals, petals and stamens attached to the receptacle or axis, below and free from the ovary.

Imbricate (of sepals and petals) Overlapping, as in a tiled roof; cf valvate.

Imparipinnate (of pinnate leaves) With an odd terminal leaflet; cf paripinnate.

Incised (of leaves) With margins deeply and sharply cut (Plate V).

Indefinite (of flower parts) Of a number large enough to make a precise count difficult.

Inflorescence Any arrangement of more than one flower.

Inserted Growing from another organ.

Introgression The transfer of genetic material from one population to another by hybridization followed by backcrossing.

Introrse Directed and opening inward toward the center of the flower, as in the opening of anthers to shed pollen.

Involucre A whorl of bracts below an inflorescence.

Irregular (of flowers) Not regular (Plate III).

Lacerate (of leaf margins) Irregularly cut.

Laciniate (of leaves) Deeply cut into narrow ribbon-like projections which may be lobed (Plate V).

Lamina The thin flat blade of a leaf.

Lanceolate Narrow with tapering ends, as a lance (Plate II).

Leaflet Separate segment of a compound leaf.

Lenticel A pore through the bark which allows gaseous exchange.

Liane (liana or vine) A climbing annual or perennial plant with an elongated twining stem.

Lignotuber A woody tuber (swollen underground root or stem).

Linear (of leaves) Elongated, with parallel sides (Plate II).

Lobe (of flowers) A rounded segment of the corolla and/or calyx.

Lobed (of leaf margins) With large round-toothed incisions.

Locule The chamber or cavity of an ovary or anther.

Plate III Representations of half flowers of angiosperms showing the main structural features. *Left* An irregular flower. *Right* A regular flower.

Loculicidal (of fruits) Splitting open longitudinally along the midrib of each segment of the wall.

Long shoot (of conifers) An elongated shoot produced by rapid annual growth.

Male cone The male reproductive structure of conifers. Each male cone comprises a series of modified leaves (microsporophylls) on the under surface of which are pollen sacs (microsporangia) within which the pollen grains develop. Male cones are often clustered together into groups.

Male flower A flower containing functional stamens, but no carpels.

Mallee Common name for some species of *Eucalyptus* which have a dwarf or shrubby habit. In a wider sense the term describes the vegetation zone which these plants dominate.

Mature cone A woody or fleshy cone containing mature seeds; fruiting cone.

Megasporophyll (of conifers) The modified leaf which bears the ovules.

Mesic With adequate or high moisture availability or needs.

Mesophyll The internal tissues of a leaf which are concerned with photosynthesis; also, a term used to describe leaves of size between $2025mm^2$ and $18222mm^2$ – the size range for most leaves from broadleaved trees living in temperate climates.

Microphyllous (of leaves) Small, up to $2025mm^2$, often found on xerophytic plants; cf. nanophyll.

Microsporangia A structure in which microspores (pollen grains) develop.

Microsporophyll (of conifers) The modified leaf on the surface of which the pollen sacs (microsporangia) develop.

Midrib The central supporting strand of a leaf.

Monocotyledon (adj monocotyledonous) One of two subclasses of angiosperms, which contains the palms amongst others; a plant whose embryo has one cotyledon; cf dicotyledon.

Monoecious Having separate male and female flowers on the same plant; cf dioecious.

Monopodial With a single main axis from which laterals arise.

Montane The zone of mountain vegetation primarily occupied by forests, above which occurs alpine vegetation.

Mucro A short sharp point formed by the extension of the midrib.

Mucronate (of leaves) Terminated by an abrupt

short, sharp point (Plate IV).

Naked Not enclosed by scales or other coverings such as petals.

Nanophyll Very small leaves with an area not exceeding $225mm^2$.

Needle (of leaves) An elongated slender, needle-like leaf usually over 5cm (2in) long.

Numerous Usually meaning more than 10; cf indefinite.

Nut A dry, single-seeded and indehiscent fruit with a woody wall.

Obconic Inversely conical.

Obcordate (of leaves) Inversely heart-shaped with the notch at the apex (Plate II).

Oblanceolate (of leaves) Lanceolate with the apex broader than the base (Plate II).

Oblate Globose, but wider than long.

Obligate Only able to live in one way, as with obligate parasites, ie plants that can only survive as parasites.

Oblique (of leaves) With unequal bases (Plate II).

Oblong (of leaves) Longer than broad, with the sides more or less parallel for most of their length (Plate II).

Obovate (of leaves) Having the shape of an egg with the narrow end below the middle; inversely ovate (Plate II).

Obtuse (of leaves) With the tip bluntly rounded (Plate IV).

Operculum A lid.

Opposite (of leaves) Occurring in pairs on opposite sides of the stem (Plate VI).

Ovary The hollow basal region of a carpel, containing one or more ovules and surmounted by the style(s) and stigma(s). It is made up of one or more carpels which may fuse together to form one or more chambers (Plate III).

Ovate (of leaves) Having the shape of an egg with the narrow end above the middle (Plate II).

Ovoid Egg-shaped.

Ovule The female reproductive structure that contains the egg cell. The ovule develops into the seed after fertilization. In gymnosperms the ovules lie naked on the ovuliferous-scale while in angiosperms they are enclosed in an ovary (Plate III).

Ovuliferous-scales (of cones) Highly modified lateral branches of the female cone which arise in the axils of bract-scales and bear the naked ovules. They

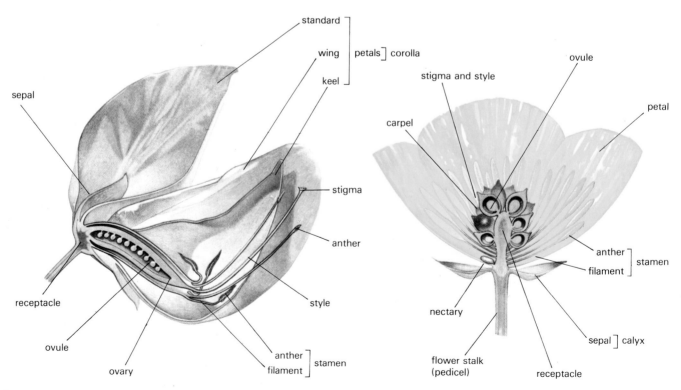

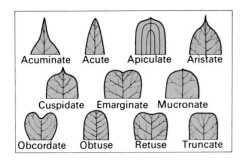

Plate IV Leaf tips.

may be woody or fleshy and in some cases fuse with the bract-scales to form a single scale (Plate I).

Palmate (of leaves) With more than three segments or leaflets arising from a single point (Plate II).

Palmatifid (of leaves) Cut in a palmate fashion, about half-way to the base (Plate II).

Palmatisect (of leaves) Cut in a palmate fashion, usually more than halfway to the base (Plate II).

Panicle A branched inflorescence of stalked flowers.

Paripinnate (of pinnate leaves) Without a terminal leaflet.

Pectinate (of leaves) Arranged like the teeth of a comb (Plate II).

Pedate (of leaves) Palmately-lobed with the outer leaflets or lobes again divided or cleft (Plate II).

Pedicel The stalk of a single flower (Plate III).

Peduncle The stalk of an inflorescence.

Peg (of conifers) A short lateral stem-projection on which a leaf is produced and which persists after leaf fall.

Peltate (of leaves and scales) More or less circular and flat with the stalk inserted in the middle (Plate II).

Pendulous Hanging loosely or freely.

Penninerved With veins extending parallel to each other from the midrib to the edge.

Perfoliate (of leaves) Stalkless with the leaf bases enclosing the stem so that the latter appears to pass through the leaf center (Plate VI).

Perianth The floral envelope whose segments are usually divisible into an outer whorl (calyx) of sepals, and an inner whorl (corolla) of petals. The segments of either or both whorls may fuse to form a tube.

Pericycle A cylinder of tissue lying immediately inside the endodermis of a root.

Periderm The outer protective layer of woody organs; it includes the cork, cork cambium and phelloderm.

Perigynous (of flowers) Having the stamens, corolla and calyx inserted around the ovary, their bases often forming a disk.

Perules Scales enclosing a bud; bud-scales.

Petal A sterile often highly colored segment of the flower; one of the units of the corolla (Plate III).

Petaloid Petal-like.

Petiolate With a leaf stalk (petiole) (Plate VI).

Petiole Leaf stalk.

Phylloclade A flattened stem resembling and functioning as a leaf.

Phyllomorphs Young shoots that are spray-like and flattened in one plane.

Physiognomy The general appearance of a community by which it is recognized.

Pinna The primary division of a fern leaf.

Pinnate (of leaves) Compound, with the leaflets in pairs on opposite sides of the midrib; cf imparipinnate, paripinnate (Plate II).

Pinnatifid (of leaves) Cut pinnately to about half-way to the midrib (Plate II)

Pinnatisect (of leaves) Pinnately divided, but not quite as far as the midrib (Plate II).

Plicate Folded as a fan.

Podzol A soil profile that has a distinct layer of humus overlying a zone of pale-colored leached soil with below that a zone containing the leached particles. Typically developed on well-drained soil with cool climate and high rainfall.

Pollen Collective name for the pollen grains.

Pollen sac The male reproductive body within which pollen is produced.

Polygamous Having separate male, female and bisexual flowers on the same plant.

Pome A fleshy false fruit the main flesh comprising the swollen receptacle, as in the apple.

Puberulent Covered in fine hairs.

Pubescent Covered in soft, short hairs.

Pulvinus A swelling at the base of a leaflet or leaf stalk, concerned with movement in response to a stimulus.

Punctate Shallowly dotted or pitted, often with glands.

Pyriform Pear-shaped.

Raceme An inflorescence consisting of a main axis bearing single flowers alternately or spirally on stalks of about equal length. The apical growing point continues to be active so there is usually no terminal flower and the youngest branches or flowers are nearest the apex.

Racemose Arranged like a raceme; in general any inflorescence capable of indefinite growth.

Receptacle The tip of the pedicel or cone stalk to which the organs of the flower or cone are attached (Plate III).

Regular (of flowers) Radially symmetrical (Plate III).

Reniform (of leaves) Kidney-shaped (Plate II).

Resin canal A space or channel within an organ that is lined with secreting cells and filled with resinous material.

Resinous Covered with or having a sticky yellowish secretion.

Reticulate With the surface marked with a system of ridges.

Retuse (of leaves) With the leaf-tip very slightly notched (Plate IV).

Revolute With margins rolled under.

Rhomboid Diamond-shaped with the widest axis at the midpoint.

Rotate Wheel-shaped.

Rugose Covered with coarse, netted lines.

Runcinate (of leaves) Coarsely toothed or incised, with the teeth pointing toward the base (Plate V).

Sagittate (of leaves) Shaped like an arrowhead (Plate II).

Samara A dry fruit in which the wall is extended to form a flattened membrane or wing.

Saprophyte A plant that obtains its nutrients from organic remains of plants and animals.

Savanna Grassland with scattered patches of woodland or individual trees.

Scale A small, membranous or sometimes stiff, reduced leaf.

Scale leaf (of conifers) A small, adpressed leaf with overlapping margins.

Scion (of grafts) The part inserted into the stock.

Section A subdivision of a genus ranking between subgenus and series.

Seed The unit of sexual reproduction developed from a fertilized ovule, which either lies naked on the ovuliferous-scale as in gymnosperms (including conifers) or is enclosed in fruit as in angiosperms (including broadleaves and palms).

'Sensu lato' In a broad sense.

Plate V Leaf margins.

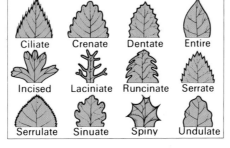

'Sensu restricto' (*sensu stricto*) In a narrow or strict sense.

Sepal A floral leaf or individual segment of the calyx of a flower, usually green (Plate III).

Septate Divided into chambers by walls.

Septicidal (of fruits) Splitting open longitudinally along the chamber walls so that the carpels are separated.

Septum A wall between chambers.

Seral One stage in the succession toward a climax vegetation.

Seriate Arranged in a row.

Series A subdivision of genus ranking below section.

Serrate (of leaves) Saw-toothed, with sharp, ascending teeth (Plate V).

Serrulate (of leaves) Minutely serrate (Plate V).

Sessile Without a stalk (Plate VI).

Sheathing (of leaves) With a sheath that encases the stem (Plate VI).

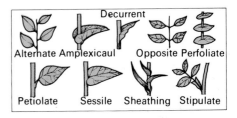

Plate VI Leaf arrangement and attachment.

Short shoot (of conifers) A very short lateral shoot which grows slowly if at all and bears the leaves.

Shrub A perennial woody plant with well-developed side-branches that appear near the base, so that there is no trunk. They are less than 10m (30ft) high.

Simple (of leaves) Not divided into leaflets.

Sinuate (of leaf margins) With shallow and smooth indentations (Plate V).

Somatic All parts of the plant except the gametes or gamete mother cells.

sp Abbreviation for species (singular).

Spathulate Spoon-shaped (Plate II).

Species The basic unit of classification. Species are grouped into genera and variations may be broken down into subspecies, variety and forma (form) in descending order of hierarchy. A species' name consists of two units (binomial): the genus title and specific epithet, both italicized and only the initial letter of the genus part capitalized, for example *Betula pendula*.

Spinose Spiny.

Spiny (of leaves) With spine-tipped lobes (Plate V).

Sporophyll A modified leaf which bears reproductive organs.

spp Abbreviation for species (plural).

ssp Abbreviation for subspecies.

Stamen The male reproductive organ of a flower. It consists of a bilobed anther, usually borne on a stalk (filament) (Plate III).

Staminode A sterile, or reduced, stamen.

Sterile Not involved in reproduction; not bearing sex organs.

Stigma The receptive part of the female reproductive organs on which the pollen grains germinate; the apex of a carpel. (Plate III).

Stipel (adj stipelate) A leafy or scale-appendage like at the base of a leaflet stalk.

Stipule (adj stipulate) A leafy appendage, often paired, and usually at the base of the leaf stalk (Plate VI).

Stoloniferous Producing stolons – shoots that root at the tip and produce new plants.

Stomata Pores that occur in large numbers in the epidermis of plants, particularly leaves, and through which gaseous exchange takes place.

Stomatal bands Areas of leaves that have a high density of stomata (pores) and thus appear paler or a yellowish color.

Striate With longitudinal lines.

Style The elongated part of a carpel or ovary bearing the stigma at its apex (Plate III).

Subgenus A subdivision of a genus ranking between genus and section.

Subglobose Almost globose (round or spherical).

Subspecies A taxonomic division ranking between species and variety. It is often used to denote a geographical variation of a species.

Subulate Very narrowly triangular.

Sulcate With longitudinal grooves.

Sympodial Without a main stem or axis but with a number of more or less equal laterals.

Syncarp A multiple fleshy fruit.

Synonym Said of a name once applied but now rejected in favor of the correct one.

Taxon Any taxonomic group, as a species, genus, family etc.

Teleutospore A thick-walled, overwintering spore produced by rust fungi.

Terete Cylindrical.

Tomentose Covered in dense, interwoven hairs (trichomes).

Transfusion tissue (of conifer leaves) A zone of tissue lying on either side of the vascular bundle.

Trichome A hair.

Trifid Divided into three parts or lobes.

Trifoliolate (of leaves) With three leaflets (Plate II).

Triquetrous Three-angled with the sides usually concave.

Truncate (of leaves) With the tip cut straight across.

Tube The cylindrical part of a corolla and/or calyx.

Tubercle (adj tuberculate) A rounded often warty swelling or protuberance.

Turbinate Top-shaped.

Umbel A flat-topped inflorescence with the flower stalks arising from a common point.

Umbo (of cones) A projection on the apophysis of the cone-scale; it may bear a spine or prickle.

Undulate (of leaf margins) With shallow indentations and wavy in the vertical plane (Plate V).

Unifoliolate (of leaves) With a single leaflet that has a stalk distinct from the entire leaf stalk.

Unisexual Of one sex.

Urceolate Urn-shaped.

Valvate Touching at the edges but not overlapping.

Variety A taxonomic division ranking between subspecies and forma, although in the past often used as the major subdivision of a species. Such taxa are named by adding the italicized variety name, preceded by var, to the parent species name, for example *Pinus ponderosa* var *arizonica*. It was once used to designate variants of horticultural origin or importance, but the rank of cultivar should now be used for this category, although many names of horticultural origin still reflect the historical use of the variety rank.

Vascular strands The bundles of tissue which conduct water and nutrients around the plant; veins of a leaf.

Ventral Anterior or in front; uppermost; nearest to the axis.

Vernal (of flowers) Opening in the spring.

Villous Covered by long, soft, interwoven hairs.

Viscid Sticky or glutinous.

Viviporous (of seeds) Germinating before becoming detached from the parent.

Xeromorphic Having characteristics which are adaptations to conserve water and so withstand extreme dry conditions.

Index of Common Names

Index of Latin Names

285